JEWS, CHRISTIANS, MUSLIMS

A Comparative Introduction to Monotheistic Religions

JOHN CORRIGAN
Arizona State University

FREDERICK M. DENNY
University of Colorado, Boulder

CARLOS M.N. EIRE
Yale University

MARTIN S. JAFFEE
University of Washington

Prentice Hall, Upper Saddle River, New Jersey 07458

Library of Congress Cataloging-in-Publication Data

Jews, Christians, Muslims : a comparative introduction to
   monotheistic religions / John Corrigan . . . [et al.].
      p.   cm.
   Includes bibliographical references and index.
   ISBN 0-02-325092-5
   1. Judaism.   2. Christianity.   3. Islam.   I. Corrigan, John,
(date)
BM561.J49   1998
291.1'4—dc21   96-51045
                                                             CIP

Editorial Director: Charlyce Jones Owen
Acquisition Editor: Angela Stone
Editorial Assistant: Elizabeth Del Colliano
Director of Production and Manufacturing: Barbara Kittle
Managing Editor: Jan Stephan
Project Manager: Linda B. Pawelchak
Manufacturing Manager: Nick Sklitsis
Prepress and Manufacturing Buyer: Lynn Pearlman
Cover Director: Jayne Conte
Cover Art: The Dome of the Rock, Temple Mount, Israel/Leo de Wys, Inc.
Director, Image Resource Center: Lori Morris-Nantz
Photo Research Supervisor: Melinda Lee Reo
Image Permission Supervisor: Kay Dellosa
Photo Researcher: Francelle Carapetyan
Electronic Art Creation: Asterisk Group
Marketing Manager: Jennifer Weinberg

This book was set in 10/12 Palatino by Americomp
and was printed and bound by RR Donnelley & Sons Company.
The cover was printed by Phoenix Color Corp.

 © 1998 by Prentice-Hall, Inc.
Simon & Schuster/A Viacom Company
Upper Saddle River, New Jersey 07458

Printed in the United States of America
10 9 8 7 6 5 4 3 2 1

ISBN 0-02-325092-5

Prentice-Hall International (UK) Limited, *London*
Prentice-Hall of Australia Pty. Limited, *Sydney*
Prentice-Hall Canada Inc., *Toronto*
Prentice-Hall Hispanoamericana, S.A., *Mexico*
Prentice-Hall of India Private Limited, *New Delhi*
Prentice-Hall of Japan, Inc., *Tokyo*
Simon & Schuster Asia Pte. Ltd., *Singapore*
Editora Prentice-Hall do Brasil, Ltda., *Rio de Janeiro*

TO OUR STUDENTS

CONTENTS

Part III
Authority   155

Part IV
Worship and Ritual   213

Part V
Ethics   277

Part VI
Material Culture   341

Part VII
Religion and the Political Order   419

PREFACE

Late in the sixteenth century, an Italian miller, prompted by his Roman Catholic inquisitors, penned the following lines:

> I Domenego Scandella, called Menocchio of Montereale, am a baptized Christian and have always lived in a Christian way and have always performed Christian works, and I have always been obedient to my superiors and to my spiritual fathers to the best of my power, and always, morning and night, I crossed myself with the sign of the holy cross, saying, "in the name of the Father and of the Son, and of the Holy Spirit."

The town priest later added to the church records that "if the internal can be judged by the external" Menocchio was "Christian and orthodox." Menocchio was curious and thoughtful, however, and had come to his own conclusions about certain aspects of the faith. Reasoning against the grain of church dogma, he refused to believe that God had created the world, he rejected the divinity of Jesus Christ, and he dismissed the Gospels as mere stories invented by bored clergy. Moreover, he knew the Koran to be "a most beautiful book," and he compared his difficulties at the hands of his inquisitors to those of Joseph, a Jew sold by his brothers into bondage in Egypt.[1]

The faith of Mennochio was complex. He mingled allegiance to official church teachings with trust in his own theological probings. And he balanced devotion to the visible marks of religious belief—the "externals"—with wariness of certain features of the Christianity practiced by his townsfolk. His religious faith was well informed in some ways, poorly informed in others, sometimes grounded in standard doctrine and at other times unfocused and searching. His belief afforded him both comfort and uneasiness. His religious life appeared orthodox, and yet he departed from orthodoxy. He was aware of the existence of other religious faiths and of differences of emphasis among the various branches of his own. To remark that his faith was not simple seems a truism.

As we begin the study of Judaism, Christianity, and Islam, we ought to bear in mind that the intricacies of religious faith manifest in the life of Menocchio are represented in all three of these religions. Complexity, not simplicity, is the hallmark of religious belief among Jews, Christians, and Muslims and the consequence of centuries of the accumulated sediments of traditions. And although we should not view the life of a sixteenth-century Italian Catholic male as a typical case of belief, we nevertheless should recognize that adherents of each of these Western religious traditions share in some measure the predicament of Menocchio. That predicament is best understood as the experience of the capability of religion to supply answers to questions about cosmic order, destiny, truth, and good and evil, while at the same time actively questioning its own legitimacy and adequacy. Religion, in a sense, is a question about the sufficiency of tradition to give meaning to life, as much as it is a lived assent to that tradition.

Judaism, Christianity, and Islam, when viewed in this way, are seen to be elaborate, highly textured, and dynamic systems of belief and practice. We cannot comprehend them merely as statements of doctrine or ritual codes. Inasmuch as we can understand these religions, we do so by recognizing an element of ourselves, the human element, within them. That means that we must be willing to explore the ways in which the ambiguities, alterations, and contradictions of human experience are present in religion as much as in any other aspect of culture. Only in so doing can we appreciate the genius of Judaism, Christianity, and Islam in fashioning worldviews that respond to that experience.

The study of religion, as we shall see, is not focused on a narrow spectrum of culture. Rather, it is an exploration of enduring ways of constructing and representing meaning in human life. As such, it is an essential part of an education in the humanities, and it requires the same careful and methodical approach as do all the fields upon which it draws, including history, literature, philosophy, and language. To study religion is to dip into a rich cultural soup, tasting not merely the broth or the meat or the vegetables or the grains of rice and barley, but savoring as well the concoction of flavors, the convergence of individual ingredients in the whole. Religion, in short, is not a discrete component of human life, separate from other aspects of culture. It is found in the very bones of a culture, in the manifold ways that communities and individuals think and act and feel. Accordingly, learning about religion means discovering the webs of influences, the practical activity, and the aspirations that make us human.

Centuries ago, Rabbi Eleazar ben Pedat, echoing the scriptural book of Genesis, observed that a person "eats and drinks, procreates, performs natural functions, and dies like an animal" and at the same time "stands erect, speaks, thinks, and has vision like an angel." This is not a unitary depiction of humankind, nor is it meant to be. It tenders an image of human life as both fragmented and whole. And it suggests the way in which we should view religion, namely, as a phenomenon characterized at once by coherency and diversity in its vision and expression. Religion, as we shall see, resists explanation and can be identified only approximately. Accordingly, it is essential that we keep in mind that no definition of religion is sufficient, that religion can be modeled, or represented, in certain ways for the purpose of gaining understanding about it; but it cannot be reduced to that model. We should expect to encounter prayers, myths, places of worship, rituals, and codes of behavior when we study religion; but we should expect to encounter much more as well.

In the parlance of the late twentieth century, Rabbi Eleazar ben Pedat "knew Judaism." But his knowledge did not come merely from his lifelong study of Jewish law. It was as much, or even more so, a product of his faith. He knew Judaism as a believer. This introduction to Western religious traditions will not furnish anyone with an insider's understanding, a believer's experience of Judaism, Christianity, or Islam. The purpose of this introduction is not to foster belief (that is, to make one an "insider"), nor to arm readers with arguments with which they might seek to undermine the claims of these religions. Rather, like any undertaking in the humanities, its objective is to provoke and inform reflection about the production and transmission of culture, about differences and similarities among various groups of people, and about our simultaneously fragile and durable conceptualizations of the meanings of life.

Judaism, Christianity, and Islam are three separate religions. But let us not overplay difference. We must recognize the distinctness of religious traditions, the distance between one's own worldview (religious or not) and the worldviews of others. But we should keep in mind as well that all three of these traditions took shape within the network of cultures we call the "West." As Western religious traditions, they share an ample background of influences ranging from Greco-Roman civilization in the Mediterranean to the Zoroastrian traditions of Mesopotamia. Judaism, Christianity, and Islam all are monotheistic religions. They embody characteristically Western views of the individual. They share a linear view of history, a belief that God created the world from nothing and that creation is progressing toward its fulfillment. And their common background includes their influences upon one another: Christianity emerged out of Judaism, and Islam is deeply indebted to both Judaism and Christianity. As we undertake the study of these traditions, we should bear in mind that our sensitivity to similarities will amplify our capability to see differences. That is, the more fully we appreciate the various historical convergences among Judaism, Christianity, and Islam, the better equipped we will be to identify divergences, or the truly distinctive features of each religion.

This introductory text, then, orders its subject in seven parts, ranging from scripture and tradition to religion and the political order. In each part, three chapters describe the ways in which Judaism, Christianity, and Islam have constructed their distinctive systems of meanings. The writing balances the historical perspective with the comparative. In other words, it addresses historical sets of questions such as "When did this religion begin?" or "How did its expansions and contractions affect its organization over time?" or "What have been the means by which members are initiated?" Alongside this concern for historical particularities within each tradition, the text explores religion at a comparative, or more general, level. That is, it explores the frameworks of religious meaning that organize specific beliefs and practices into a coherent whole. In the case of each religion, it asks open-ended questions such as, "What is worship? community? authority?" In describing the nature of religious life, it recognizes the role of expectations and motivations that inform specific articles of belief and practice. This approach, we might say, is akin to the enterprise of the geologist who investigates the ongoing and often barely perceptible shifting of tectonic plates deep in the earth in order to better understand the visible features of the earth's crust. Like the geologist, we will concern ourselves with what is immediately apparent—doctrines, rituals, art, and so forth—as well as with what is less obvious.

In this introduction to Western religions, we see that religious traditions do not enter the world complete or intact but, rather, are always in the process of shifting and reversing, consolidating and expanding. In short, each generation finds new meanings to tradition, just as the Muslim writer Al-Jahiz observed in the ninth century:

> God has assigned to each generation the natural duty of instructing the next and has made each succeeding generation the criterion of the truth of the information handed down to it. For hearing many unusual traditions and strange ideas makes the mind more acute, enriches the soul, and gives food for thought and incentive to look ahead.[2]

In Part I, we explore the manner in which ideas that emerged in oral and written forms found expression as Scripture, as the core of tradition. As participants in the print culture of the late twentieth century, we assume that a standard process of invention and inscription governs the production of books: an author gets ideas, writes them down on paper, and sells the resulting manuscript to a publisher who prints and markets it as a "book." This process, however, has virtually nothing in common with the production of the ancient literatures that we know as the Hebrew Bible, the New Testament, and the Qur'an. As we shall see, the "books" of Judaism, Christianity, and Islam began as stories transmitted by word of mouth and took authoritative written form through long and complicated operations involving a great many communities scattered across space and time. So complex was the process of their creation that our contemporary notions of author, of precise time and place of origin, and of a book as a finished product impede rather than speed our understanding of these literatures. Nevertheless, the holy writings of these religions have proven astonishingly durable, as each succeeding generation—in the words of Al-Jahiz—has applied its own criterion of truth to its investigation of the meaning and worth of these stories. In our own study of scripture and tradition, we explore the manner in which certain stories came to be valued above others, how authoritative collections were formed, and how subsequent interpretations of those collections have confirmed previous meanings and formulated new ones.

Part II presents the monotheistic theologies of Judaism, Christianity, and Islam. Monotheism, the shared theological orientation of these Western religious traditions, views reality as a sacred totality, as a sacred whole created by a personal God. That God enforces order and sustains life but is transcendent, not limited or controlled or conditioned in any way by the created world. Accordingly, the burden of monotheism has been to explain how God is present in the world, cognizant of and attentive to the needs of women and men, and at the same time beyond the world, ethereal, distant, or simply "other." As we see, monotheistic doctrines in all three of these religions are constantly being refashioned as groups of believers in various contexts seek to articulate the meanings of God's simultaneous transcendence of and investment in the world. How is God different from the world? What does it mean to know God? How does one discern the will of God? In what manner is God present among humanity? Such questions, which form the bedrock of monotheistic worldviews, are never fully answered in Judaism, Christianity, and Islam. But the act of questioning is itself a form of devotion, an expression of faith, because it is grounded in trust that the questions can be answered, that the approximate and imperfect explanations articulated in monotheistic doctrines do point toward eternal truths. We see how the actual practice of theology varies significantly from one tradition to another. And we should bear in mind that each of these three traditions professes a distinctive form of monotheism. In Judaism, we find monotheism closely interwoven with messianism. Among Christians, the Trinity—three persons in one God—is the distinguishing feature. And in Islam, emphasis on the unity of God is paramount.

Religious authority, especially in its relation to community, is the subject of Part III. We should recognize at the outset that authority is not some potent, free-floating commodity that certain persons or groups manage to capture and then exercise. Rather, authority is always grounded in a certain collective understanding of community life, in a sense of group identity that includes both the history of that group as well as its vision of its future. Authority, in short, arises out of community consensus about the meanings of life. Images of authority—certain individuals, activities, writings, and so forth—convey that consensus of meaning. Such images are part of a community's presentation, or performance, of its self-understanding, as it confirms and reconfirms itself for the benefit of new and old members as well as for outsiders. In Judaism, Christianity, and Islam, religious scholars or clergy are obvious figures of authority: rabbis, priests, ministers, members of the ulama, and other religious professionals are easily distinguishable as symbols of community traditions and conventions. But authority is represented in other ways as well: in all three of these religious traditions, we find that certain places, writings, spoken words, and so forth, forcefully represent the authority of the community. And we should not overlook the fact that historically men and women lacking any formal training as religious professionals have emerged from obscurity to represent the community in dramatic ways. As we investigate the communities of Judaism, Christianity, and Islam, then, we see how authority exists not as an item of merchandise passed along from one hand to another, but as the product of the ongoing efforts of communities to define themselves.

In Part IV, we turn our attention to worship and ritual. For Jews, Christians, and Muslims, worship is not an activity limited to certain places or certain times. In all three Western religious traditions, worship is a way of life, a perspective on all of the details, large and small, of a person's life. Worship is the recognition of the interwovenness of God, the community, and the individual. It is private and public, personal and communal, highly structured and relatively unstructured. There are, however, certain times and spaces that carry special meaning for worship for Jews, Christians, and Muslims. There are specific places—the synagogue, the church, the mosque—where persons gather to worship collectively. And there are certain times of years—Passover, Christmas, Ramadan—that call for worship of a special order. Moreover, in the life of each individual, there are moments when worshipful acknowledgment of God and the community are of exceptional importance. Such occasions include birth, puberty, marriage, and death. Worship at such times, and at many other times as well, is precisely ordered in ritual forms, or styles of religious practice, that encode for the community the religious meanings of the event. In expressing those meanings, ritual reminds the community of its history and importance and its vision of its future, and in so doing reinforces personal and group identity and sense of purpose. Ritual accomplishes this because it is fluid and multidimensional, capable of adapting to the changing circumstances of community life and capable of deploying meanings on several planes: for the individual, for the local community, for the universal membership, and so forth. Ritual accordingly both conserves tradition and enlarges it as it orders the practical activity of worship.

Judaism, Christianity, and Islam all are known as models of "ethical monotheism." In Part V, we investigate the meaning of the term "ethics" with regard to each of these traditions and distinguish the ways in which Jews, Christians, and Muslims conceive of proper action, the pursuit of good in one's everyday life. In each case, scripture provides a framework for personal decisions about conduct and attitude in everyday matters. And it is essential that we recognize that Jews, Christians, and Muslims vary in their view of that scriptural base as "law." But there is agreement among all three traditions that scripture alone is insufficient as a guide to decisions about one's actions. Alongside scripture, large and detailed bodies of literature are recognized as authoritative in their observations about human motives and their determinations of just courses of action. From scripture and these other authoritative writings come composite understandings of justice, virtue, responsibility, and holiness. By the same token, images of evil take shape from these sources and with them depictions of the consequences of wrongdoing. As we study this aspect of religion in the West, we see that the locus of ethics, the crux of issues of right and wrong, is the ground on which individual and society are related. And it is this notion of the individual, as separate from and yet embedded in society, that gives these traditions a markedly Western stamp. It is common background appropriated in different ways for three distinct systems of ethics.

Part VI describes the material culture of Judaism, Christianity, and Islam. Material products such as architecture, art, dress, print items, and so forth are kinds of texts that communicate the worldviews of various Jewish, Christian, and

Muslim communities. In the curve of a dome, the lines of an icon, or the style of a head covering, we can "read" something about the history and aspirations of the community that has fashioned these products. The "language" of material culture, in fact, is as effective in representing religious identity as the spoken words of prayers or sacred stories, or the disputations of religious scholars. In some cases, material culture speaks more loudly than any of these. Our study of material culture is a particularly valuable part of learning about Western religious traditions. We literally can see in the constant borrowing of forms among Jews, Christians, and Muslims the extent to which these religions drew on common backgrounds, as well as the degree to which they directly influenced one another at various times in their histories. We can also observe how religious communities came to embrace styles that differed from those of their neighbors as part of a process of distinguishing themselves from other traditions. Material culture, moreover, offers a way into understanding routine in the lives of Jews, Christians, and Muslims. In the clothes people wear, the food they prepare, the buildings they construct for worship and work, and other such products, we glimpse religious life at the street level, as it unfolds in its everyday detail.

Religious community is not the only kind of community. There are communities of language, ethnicity, and gender, among others. In Part VII, we turn our attention to political communities, to relations between religious institutions and those of the political order. Several patterns of relations are detectable in the encounters of Jews, Christians, and Muslims with the state. In general, however, those relations are ongoing experiments that test the limits of the authority of both religious communities and political entities. Should the state be administered according to policies that are grounded in a religious worldview? Can the state override the authority of the religious community if the latter promotes a way of life repugnant to the state? Will the state comprehend a multiplicity of religious communities? Will one religion be favored over another? The consequences of such questioning are long histories of reconceptualizing the nature of both religious community and political community in places where Western religious traditions have flourished. And that process of rethinking religious community embraces every aspect of religion from ritual to ethics to material culture. In fact, the relation of religion to the political order frequently is the context for the most dramatic developments within a religious community, whether that be wholesale retrenchment in tradition or a flowering of new visions. This is especially obvious at the end of the twentieth century, at the end of the Cold War, as we witness a host of civil wars, revolutions, and "cleansings" in which religion plays a leading role.

The approach of this book—which is by now perceptible—is to explore Judaism, Christianity, and Islam in their breadth and depth and to avoid treating them as isolated cultural phenomena. This means first of all viewing each tradition in its linkages with other aspects of culture, ranging from intellectual life to art to political organization. It also means investigating, as would a geologist, aspects of religion that are not immediately visible in the myths, worship practices, and social organization of each tradition. And it means recognizing that these three traditions are related to one another because of certain overlapping features of their backgrounds as well as a centuries-long process of influence of one tradition upon another. There are, of course, distinctive elements in each of these traditions that have been sharpened by centuries of religious practice and are usually recognized as characteristic aspects of each tradition. We should recognize that the grounds on which these religions intersect are equally important, however, if we are to appreciate Western religious traditions in their richness and complexity.

Religion, finally, is about the manner in which men and women live. It is about decisions that persons make and the activities in which they engage, about whom they talk to and what they say in the course of a day. Religion cannot be abstracted from the everyday lives of those who embrace it. The study of religion accordingly is more than merely exposing oneself to creeds, statements of doctrines, manners of theological argument, devotional practices, and pictures of houses of worship. It requires of us an effort to understand how standard belief and practice, the controlling ideas and images of a religious tradition, could have coalesced from the life experiences of millions of people. And it requires as well that we appreciate how Jews, Christians, and Muslims routinely depart from standard or formal religion in their personal lives as they act individually to graft new ideas and behaviors onto the vine of their religious faith. There are inside each of these traditions lively religions of the people, of the *populus*. At times, expressions of popular religion have come into conflict with formal religion. At other times, popular religion has existed comfortably alongside the core of tradition. In either case, the cultural vitality and creativity of Judaism, Christianity, and Islam are grounded in the fluidity and the dynamism of these traditions, as they are appropriated, interpreted, and challenged by the people who live them.

NOTES

1. Carlo Ginzburg, *The Cheese and the Worms: The Cosmos of a Sixteenth-Century Miller,* tr., John Tedeschi and Anne Tedeschi (New York: Penguin, 1983), pp. 87, 109, 101.
2. Al-Jahiz, *The Proofs of Prophecy,* in F. E. Peters, *Judaism, Christianity and Islam: The Classical Texts and Their Interpretation* (Princeton: Princeton University Press, 1990), p. 594.

JEWS, CHRISTIANS, MUSLIMS

The Prophet Muhammad, on the Eve of His Ascent into Heaven, Praying with Abraham, Moses, and Jesus at the Aqsâ Mosque in Jerusalem. A Muslim artist, in what is now Afghanistan, produced this illustration in the fifteenth century. Representations of the Prophet were not uncommon at that time; but in general, Muslims have not permitted graphic representation of the Prophet Muhammad or any holy personage from the Islamic, Christian, and Jewish traditions.

PART I

SCRIPTURE AND TRADITION

Western religious traditions are just that: traditions. They are not traditional in quite the same way in which we speak of persons who favor wing-tip shoes, or curtsy, or bring gelatin molds on picnics, or like to do things "the way Grandma and Grandpa do them." Rather, Judaism, Christianity, and Islam are traditional in a more complex and encompassing way. They do indeed preserve centuries of accumulated judgments about the value of certain beliefs and behaviors. But, additionally, they are hardwired to challenge traditional meanings, promote interpretation, and adapt to changing historical circumstances. In short, Judaism, Christianity, and Islam are dynamic traditions, poised between their embrace of the past and the articulation of new meanings.

There is an additional, more specific meaning of tradition of which we must be aware as we begin this part. Each of the religious traditions of Judaism, Christianity, and Islam is, in fact, the product of many distinctive, competing traditions. These many traditions, which frequently overlap in certain aspects but nevertheless retain unique elements, coalesce to form the larger tradition. In this part, we explore this process, observing how various traditions are consolidated within Judaism, Christianity, and Islam. We see as well how that process of consolidation is never complete, how these three religions are constantly interpreting and judging the strands of traditions that shaped them, sometimes in the process creating the stuff of new traditions.

All these strands of traditions characteristically are kept alive orally or in writing. In the latter case, we may speak of a specific book, one that is highly valued by a community of believers and passed from generation to generation, as one

1

strand of tradition in the makeup of a religion. Historically, certain of these books, these traditions, acquired such authority that they became "scripture" and are preserved unchanged from century to century. Scripture, however, must be interpreted and applied. It must be mined for meanings that respond to the questions and concerns of each new generation. Accordingly, scripture itself becomes the source for a wide range of traditions of interpretation, of books that are considered valuable by the community because they articulate the meanings in scripture.

Western religious traditions are "traditional," then, in several related ways: each is itself the product of the intertwining of many strands of traditions. Those various strands in most cases survive as books, and some of them eventually were recognized as scripture. The commentaries on scripture that arose with Judaism, Christianity, and Islam themselves became traditions of interpretation, so that Judaism, Christianity, and Islam preserve tradition in scripture while they at the same time generate new traditions that are grounded in that scripture.

This part on scripture and tradition is, in short, not merely about the names and dates and authors of certain holy books. It is about the processes by which those books came to be judged as authoritative by religious communities. And it describes the ways in which communities have acted to confirm the authority of scripture through the practice of interpretation.

CHAPTER 1

SCRIPTURE AND TRADITION
IN JUDAISM

THE BIBLE'S HISTORY AND THE HISTORY OF JUDAISM

According to the stories recorded in Genesis, the first book of the Hebrew Bible, Judaism has its historical origins in an act of obedience. One day long ago, for reasons never clearly explained, the Creator of Heaven and Earth announced to an obscure Mesopotamian peasant named Abram a stunning proposal:

> Go forth from your native land and from your father's house to the land that I will show you. I will make of you a great nation, and I will bless you; I will make your name great, and you shall be a blessing. I will bless those who bless you and curse him that curses you; and all the families of the earth shall bless themselves by you. Abram went forth as the Lord had commanded him. (Gen. 12:1–3)

Abram, the Bible relates, went forth as he was told, neither questioning nor resisting the divine command. God soon changed his name to Abraham, "the father of a multitude of nations" (Gen. 17:5). And the rest, as they say, is history.

The pages that follow trace the impact of the Hebrew Bible's image of Abraham's obedience as well as that of many other biblical heroes, upon the history of Judaism. But in order to do so, it is important to keep a basic postulate in mind: the history of Judaism portrayed in the Hebrew Bible, as a history beginning with Abraham's act of obedience, is a vividly imagined *interpretation* of the Judaic past that has a profound impact upon later Jewish generations. But, for all that, it is not an actual *record* of an event from the past.

3

Before beginning our discussion of the history of Judaism, we must explore for a moment the meaning of this observation and its implications. As comparative historians of religion, our task is not merely to repeat the biblical story of the origins of Judaism. Rather, our task is, first, to offer a theory of how that story came into focus at a particular moment in the history of the Jews. Second, we attempt to show how that story was understood through centuries of interpretation. We ask: how did the story of Abraham's obedience come to define a model of piety in ancient Judaism? How was it transformed, as successive generations of Jews found in it the meaning of their own obedience to God?

The Interaction of Scripture and Tradition

In order to begin historical thinking about the Hebrew Bible's depiction of the origins and history of Judaism, it is important to keep in mind two terms of special significance for historians of religions. These terms are "scripture" and "tradition." By scripture, we mean a writing or a collection of writings preserved by religious communities as authoritative sources of teaching or worship. Scriptures are commonly read aloud as the basis for inspirational teaching, may be quoted in the course of a community's prayer services, and commonly serve as the basis of elaborate interpretive reflection by members of religious communities.

The main point to remember about scriptures is that they are historical objects crafted in human cultures. The texts are preserved by human memory and recorded in human languages, even if they are believed to have originally been delivered to the writers, complete and perfect, by a god or heavenly messenger. They enjoy special prestige as "holy" or "sacred" texts only because human communities have at some point agreed to treat them in certain ways. Any text regarded as scripture came to be so because a community, formally or informally, so decided. This decision is often a source of conflict, as different segments of a larger community might dispute whether this or that writing is truly authoritative for all members. Thus it often happens that a text that is scripture in one community is simply a book in another. The disputes within the early Christian communities over the extent of Christian scripture—about which you will read elsewhere in this part— are a case in point.

The decision to regard a text as scripture often brings into play the second term we have introduced, tradition. Most simply, tradition means "that which has been handed down from the past." It is tradition that sustains a writing in the life of a religious community long enough for it to acquire the exalted status of scripture. There are relatively few examples of writings penned by a single known author, that have attained scriptural authority in that author's own lifetime; even the Qur'an, as you will learn in your study of Islam, is an ambiguous case. Usually, a writing has been transmitted for some generations—or even centuries—before achieving its scriptural place in a community's life. That is, a particular writing was a tradition, *a book handed on as valuable,* before it became a scripture, *a book authoritative because it is holy.*

Once a traditional literary work becomes scripture, it is usually preserved in a fixed text that cannot be changed or emended. Copies are made, but great effort is invested in ensuring that the text is reproduced word for word and letter for letter, for nothing in the holy writing can be lost or altered. This leads to yet another way in which tradition is important in understanding the life of scriptures. As scriptures are handed on from generation to generation, they must be *interpreted* so that the unchangeable text continues to remain meaningful to those who revere it.

Unfamiliar words cannot be replaced with more up-to-date terms; rather, they must be defined. Obscure concepts or morally troubling events cannot be revised to suit contemporary tastes; rather, they must be explained. In many cases, translations must be made for those who are unfamiliar with the original language of the scriptural texts. All of this work of transmitting the meaning of scriptures without altering the original texts is also tradition—*the tradition of interpretation.* Commonly, religious communities sharing identical scriptures—think of Judaism and Christianity in relation to the Hebrew Bible—will differ dramatically in their interpretive traditions. Such differences of interpretive tradition have nourished religious controversy, given birth to competing religious communities, and even inspired religiously motivated persecutions of communities stigmatized as "nonbelievers" or "heretics."

Scripture and tradition, to summarize, are intertwined realities, two sides of a coin. Scripture is the collective term for literary traditions that enjoy the veneration of a specific community. A "canon," or closed collection of scripture, is also a tradition, passed on as a unique and unchangeable record of communal memory, belief, and discipline. Finally, there are continuously evolving traditions of scriptural interpretation, which transmit to new generations the rich meanings latent in the unchanging scripture. We can perhaps capture the interpretation of scripture and tradition in a single phrase: *fluid literary traditions solidify into unchangeable scripture; scripture in turn generates new forms of fluid literary tradition through interpretation.*[1]

Abraham and the Origins of Judaism

Perhaps this excursion into the nature of scripture and tradition will help us clarify the problem with which we began—the relation of the biblical picture of the Israelite past, such as the story of Abraham's obedience, to actual records of historical events. The Hebrew Bible, which sketches the core images of Judaic origins as remembered by all forms of Judaism, did not come into being all at once as a collection of writings between sober black covers. Rather, it began life as an amorphous body of diverse traditions, many preserved in oral form in virtually complete independence of one another. These traditions were formulated at a time well before Jews could point to a Bible as the official collection of revealed writings.

This means that nearly all of the literature of the Bible reached written form many centuries after the events it describes. That is, most biblical writings were composed by people who did not personally witness the history they recorded. Rather, they relied upon stories received from tradition for their knowledge of the

ABRAHAM, ISAAC, JACOB, AND THE KINGDOMS OF JUDAH AND ISRAEL

The biblical books of 1 Samuel, 2 Samuel, 1 Kings, and 2 Kings describe the history of the two kingdoms that divided Israelite political and religious life from the tenth through the sixth centuries BCE. The Kingdom of Judah was, according to the biblical texts, founded by David (ca. 1000 BCE). A dynastic battle ensued after the death of his son Solomon (ca. 961–922 BCE). This resulted in the formation of two kingdoms, that of Judah in the southern part of the Land of Israel, and that of Israel in the north. Israel fell to the Assyrians in 722 BCE, and Judah was conquered by Babylonia in 587 BCE.

Many historians claim that the competition of these kingdoms for religious and political legitimacy is part of the background of the Genesis stories describing Abraham, Isaac, and Jacob. Judean traditions, for example, claim that King David's first capital, Hebron, was purchased by Abraham (Gen. 23). Similarly, northern traditions portray Jacob as having purchased Shechem, the capital city of the Kingdom of Israel (Gen. 33:19). Both southern (Gen. 28: 10–19) and northern traditions (Gen. 35:1–7) locate Abraham's grandson Jacob at the shrine at Beth El, which lies in a territory over which each kingdom claimed control.

It is impossible to *prove* that such stories first originated in the context of political and religious rivalry between the two kingdoms. But the coincidences are suggestive.

past. Moreover, they often revised or combined traditional stories in order to make points of contemporary relevance. As you might imagine, this has important implications for our interpretation of the Abraham story.

On the basis of the lifestyle ascribed to him in the book of Genesis, that of a herder sometimes forced to migrate with his flocks in search of food, Abraham seems to have lived a life typical of the Middle East in the early second millennium BCE. The problem with claiming that stories about him come from that era is simple: the same kind of life was not unusual throughout all subsequent centuries and, in fact, continues to be lived by some Middle Eastern peoples even in modern times. More important, stories *about* Abraham do not seem to have been known until the eighth or ninth centuries BCE. These were the early centuries of the ancient Israelite kingdoms of Judah and Israel. In these kingdoms, stories of Abraham's migrations in the land were closely associated with religious or political centers important to each kingdom. Finally, the present version of the Abraham story is recorded in a written text, the book of Genesis, which most contemporary historians believe could have been composed in its present form no earlier than the fifth through the fourth centuries BCE.

So, although the image of the absolute obedience of Abraham makes a powerful statement of what it means to follow the God of Israel, it is not a statement that originates in the eighteenth century BCE. Rather, as we know it from the book of Genesis, it seems to be a product of a more recent period. It tells us that Jews of that (as yet unspecified) period *believed* in their ancient origins, and it tells us how they proposed to act in light of those beliefs. But we learn nothing from it about the actual religion of Abraham or even whether he ever existed as a human of flesh and blood. The Bible's story of the first Jew, Abraham, is best read as a picture of what later Jews sought to become.

This sobering thought applies equally to all of the Bible's most famous depictions of the early history of Israel—including God's rescue of his people from Egyptian oppression, God's revelation of covenantal teachings to Moses and all Israel at Mt. Sinai, and God's exile of his people from their land as a punishment for disobedience. The Bible provides eyewitness accounts of *none* of these events, except, perhaps, for the last. Nearly all of these images have their origins in literary traditions that, only gradually, were compiled into the collection of writings we call the Hebrew Bible.

When historians of religion speak of "the origins of Judaism," therefore, we must mean something different from what the Hebrew Bible or Jewish tradition means. We cannot begin our historical account with Abraham's act of profound and silent obedience, or even with the Bible's vivid depiction of God's thunderous revelation of his eternal will at Mt. Sinai and Israel's submission to it. These biblical images of Judaism's origins are not windows revealing ancient events, but murals that obscure whatever might lie beneath the surface. In order to identify the painters of this mural, we begin by trying to identify a time and a place in which such traditions about obedience and other similarly heroic actions began to be gathered together into a coherent collection of authoritative writings. We search, in other words, for those recorders of Israelite tradition who found in the recitation of the acts of such heroes as Abraham compelling images upon which to model their own lives.

Our search begins, therefore, not in ancient Mesopotamia or even in Egypt, but at a somewhat more recent moment, practically "modern" by comparison. Judaism most probably has its traceable origins in the post-Exilic Persian province of Yehud, part of a larger territory known to ancient Jews as "the Land of Israel" and to their later Roman conquerors as "Palestine."

Judaism has its origins, to be sure, in profound acts of human obedience. But these are not the obedient acts of Abraham. The obedience, rather, is that of other Jews who, it must frankly be said, described an Abraham they sought to emulate. Judaism has its source, therefore, in a remarkable act of historical imagination, one that created an image of the Israelite past so powerful that, through it, a future was secured as well. How did this act of imagination come about, and who is responsible?[2]

The Torah in the Canon of the Hebrew Bible

An answer emerges from an examination of the present version of the Hebrew Bible itself and the way it unfolds the story of Israel's past. In the form preserved in Jewish tradition, the Hebrew Bible is divided into three smaller canons called the Torah ("Teaching"), the Nevi'im ("Prophets"), and the Ketuvim ("Writings"). Each of these canons is a kind of peg upon which hang the narrative strands of the biblical story.

The Torah describes the origins of the world and the history of the Israelite

The Land of Israel in the Persian Empire

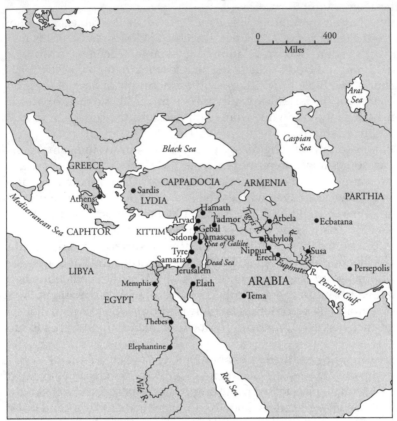

(*Source:* W. Lee Humphreys, *Crisis and Story: An Introduction to the Old Testament*, 2nd ed. Mountain View, CA: Mayfield Publishing Company. Reproduced with permission.)

nation from its beginnings with Abraham to the death of its great leader, Moses. The central focus of the Torah is the description of a series of covenants, or promises, sealed between God and Israel. Abraham, his son Isaac, and his grandson Jacob receive the first covenants. The earliest covenantal promises assure God's human partner of numerous offspring and a homeland (e.g., Gen. 15:4–7; 28:13–15). Upon Jacob's reception of the covenant promise, his name is changed to Israel to indicate a transformed relationship to God (Gen. 32:23–33; 35:9–12). These family-centered covenants are later broadened into a national covenant agreement between God and all of Jacob/Israel's descendants at Sinai (Exod. 20–25). In return for the people Israel's obedience, God promises to grant it a rich land and protection from its enemies. The narrative continues in Nevi'im, which describes the history of Israel's life in the land chosen for it by God, the rise and fall of the kingdoms of Israel and Judah, and the events surrounding the loss of the land at the hands of Assyrian and Babylonian invaders. The major thesis of Nevi'im is that the

THE CANON OF THE HEBREW SCRIPTURES AS PRESERVED IN RABBINIC JUDAISM

Torah (Teaching)	*Nevi'im (Prophets)*	*Ketuvim (Writings)*
Bereshit (Genesis)	Yehoshua (Joshua)	Tehilim (Psalms)
Shemot (Exodus)	Shofetim (Judges)	Mishlei (Proverbs)
Vayiqra (Leviticus)	Shemuel 1–2 (Samuel)	Iyyov (Job)
Bamidbar (Numbers)	Melakhim 1–2 (Kings)	Shir Hashirim (Song of Songs)
Devarim (Deuteronomy)	Yeshayahu (Isaiah)	Root (Ruth)
	Yirmiyahu (Jeremiah)	Ekhah (Lamentations)
	Yekhezkel (Ezekiel)	Kohelet (Ecclesiastes)
	Hoshea (Hosea)	Ester (Esther)
	Yoel (Joel)	Daniel (Daniel)
	Ahmos (Amos)	Ezra (Ezra)
	Ovadyah (Obadiah)	Nekhemyah (Nehemiah)
	Yonah (Jonah)	Divrei Hayamin 1–2 (Chronicles)
	Meekah (Micah)	
	Nakhum (Nahum)	
	Khabakuk (Habakkuk)	
	Tzefanyah (Zepheniah)	
	Khaggai (Haggai)	
	Zekharyah (Zechariah)	
	Melakhee (Malachi)	

land was lost because of Israel's repeated violations of its covenant agreement of obedience to God. The story concludes in the last books of Ketuvim, which depict the eventual resettlement of the land by a remnant of the original people. That return, as the Bible interprets it, was made possible only by Israel's sincere repentance of its earlier disobedience and its commitment to comply with all aspects of the original covenant.

The basic plot of the Hebrew Bible, then, is simple: it narrates the history of a covenant. That covenant is made in the Torah, broken by Israel in Nevi'im, and restored by God in Ketuvim. In addition to this basic narrative line, the Bible contains as well a wide variety of writings that, in one way or another, supplement or amplify the plot. They are distributed throughout the canons of Nevi'im and Ketuvim in particular. The former canon supplements the sad history of Israel's loss of its land with a series of books of poetic condemnations of the faithlessness of Israel and celebrations of the covenantal loyalty of God. These are ascribed to ancient seers known as "prophets." The Hebrew word for "prophet," *navi* (plural: *nevi'im*), means "spokesperson." Their message—alternately of despair and great hope—dominates this canon and explains why it acquired the name Nevi'im. The

Ketuvim, for its part, introduces its optimistic image of Israel's return to its land with a diverse collection of writings. These include, among others, prayer texts (the book of Psalms); philosophical reflections on the meaning of suffering and happiness (the books of Job and Ecclesiastes); and stories about ancient sages and pious, courageous women (the books of Daniel, Ruth, and Esther).

The canonical version of the Hebrew Bible, then, is essentially a drama in three acts that contains its own commentary—a sophisticated piece of literary work. The Torah sets the fundamental theme, which is then amplified in exquisite detail in Nevi'im and Ketuvim. In order to discern the elements of this drama prior to their canonical presentation, we must first ask when its basic plot might have originated. We begin by pointing out a simple fact: the Bible ends its story—in the books of Ezra and Nehemiah—with the return of small groups of Jews to the Land of Israel from a captivity in Babylonia. If, like all stories, the Bible begins with the end already in mind, we may conclude that much of the Bible's depiction of early Israelite history is told from the perspective of those who are seeing the story whole from the vantage point of their own day. Accordingly, the core narrative of the Hebrew Bible was probably not conceived until sometime after the return of Judean exiles to their ancestral territory. Such a return began no earlier than 539 BCE, when Cyrus, the Persian conqueror of Babylonia, granted to the exiles of his domain the right of repatriation.

The plot of the Hebrew Bible, therefore, raises and answers questions that were fundamental to descendants of those Jews who had resettled the Land of Israel and wished now to abide safely in it. The story they told was essentially a confession of guilt. It explained how God's special people were descended from a great hero of absolute obedience. But it also showed that through persistent violation of Abraham's example, Israel came to suffer the loss of its political independence and homeland. What would it mean in such a setting to begin the history of Israel with the now-famous story of Abraham's obedience? The image of Abraham's wordless obedience in leaving his native Babylonia for an unknown land proclaims that the restoration of Jews from Babylonian captivity was more than an arbitrary action governed by the Persian emperor. Rather, it was under the control of the very God whom Abraham obeyed. The descendants of the exiles, most of whom had known no other home than Babylonia, modeled their own repopulation of the land of Israel after that of Abraham and saw in Abraham's obedience to the divine call a way of expressing their own. The present generation sought to secure the promise to Abraham—of progeny, land, and blessing—by reenacting his obedience and perfecting the life of obedience once and for all.

The origins of the biblical narrative and those of Judaism are, therefore, closely bound together. The Judaism we find in the Hebrew Bible emerged as a distinct communal identity after 539, among a small group of Judean exiles who resolved to secure their life in their ancient homeland. There they built a center of sacrificial worship and civic administration, a Temple. On the one hand, this Second Temple represented a religious commitment—the community's intention to serve the Creator of Heaven and Earth. On the other, it served an important political purpose, for it proclaimed the divine guidance of the priestly leaders who, by

Persian decree, administered the law of the society. So the Temple symbolized the claim of the priestly political leadership to embody the ancient covenant community of Israel. It authorized them to shape all of Israel by their covenantal traditions. We suppose, therefore, that the priestly administrators of this Second Temple played a central role in drawing together what remained of the ancient historical traditions of pre-Exilic Israel into the beginnings of a coherent national history, a history of ancient covenants with the same God now worshiped in the restored Temple. Indeed, the centrality given in the Hebrew Bible to the priestly scribe Ezra in teaching the Torah of Moses to the restored community (see, for example, Neh. 8–9) points toward the primacy of priestly groups and scribal intellectuals in the formation of the new covenantal society and its literary tradition.

But here we are only supposing, for the centuries between the mid-sixth and the late-fourth centuries BCE—what historians call the "Persian Period"—are the most obscure in the entire history of Judaism. Nevertheless, it is clear that the Persian Period provided the context for a crucial transition in early Judaism. The cultural remnants of the vanished Israelite kingdoms of antiquity were reconstructed by Babylonian Jews intent on governing the ancient homeland of Israel as they believed it always ought to have been governed—by the revelation given to Moses at Sinai. Thus they organized the diverse narrative and legal traditions of the restored community of Israel into a carefully plotted epic of Israelite history and a program for national survival. In later Jewish writings, the first part of this epic was called the Torah of Moses. In the canonical version found in synagogue scrolls and printed Bibles until the present day, it is, as we have said, a history of the universe from the moment of its creation by the God of Israel down to the death of the people's greatest prophet and leader, Moses. Organized into five scrolls or books, it makes a single simple case: that everything Israel needs to serve God in perfect obedience was long ago displayed in the loyalty of patriarchs such as Abraham and revealed once and for all in the revelation of God's covenant law at Sinai through Moses. The main concerns of early Judaism can be surmised from the single-mindedness of the Torah's retelling of the past. No matter what sort of ancient Israelite traditions it gathers together, it makes sure to structure the narration around a single theme: God's overpowering love for this creation is constantly rebuffed by the rebellious desires of humanity.

Legends, for example, about pre-Israelite human history are told in such a way as to foreshadow the later rebellious behavior of Israel under its covenant with God. The well-known story of the first man and woman in the Garden of Eden is a case in point (Gen. 2:4–3:24). Given by God everything they could possibly require by way of material comforts, Adam (whose name means "earth-creature") and Eve ("fecundity") are commanded only to refrain from certain forbidden fruits in the center of the Garden. This they prove unable to do, and neither do they show any genuine remorse when God discovers their act. As punishment, God expels the humans from his Garden, making it impossible for them ever to return. As the story tells it, this is the moment that pain, suffering, and death enter the world. At the very origin of human history, then, the Torah finds a spirit of human rebellion that incurs the divine punishment of exile.

The Torah, moreover, sees Israel's history as a re-enactment of human history within the confines of a single people. The covenant-making event at Mt. Sinai is described in the book of Exodus (18–25) as a moment of close bonding between God and Israel, with Israel eagerly entering into agreement to observe all the laws of God. Yet 40 days after entering into that agreement of its own free will, with Moses still on the mountain communing with God, Israel begins to pine for a substitute deity and creates for itself a golden calf to worship (Exod. 32:1–35).

As the Torah describes it, only Moses' active intervention on behalf of his people prevents God from destroying them in punishment. Then God permits the Israelites to build a wilderness Tent of Meeting in which God promises to make his presence available among the people (Exod. 35–40). From that Tent he reveals all of the laws by which he is to be worshiped and through which Israel will express its love of him (the book of Leviticus). Yet what is Israel's response? Much of the fourth book of the Torah, called Numbers, is concerned with stories in which Israel complains against the rigors of its desert wanderings, yearns longingly for its period of Egyptian servitude, and in other ways forgets or evades its responsibility to God (e.g., Num. 11:1–34; 12:1–16; 14:1–36).

The Torah ends, in Deuteronomy, with a long speech of Moses in which he predicts that if this spirit of disobedience continues after Israel is brought into its land, the promise of the land will indeed be revoked. The chilling choice offered by Moses in the following passage is only one of many examples (Deut. 30:15–20):

> See, I set before you this day life and prosperity, death and adversity. For I command you this day, to love the Lord your God, to walk in his ways, and to keep his commandments, his laws and his rules, that you may thrive and increase, and that the Lord your God may bless you in the land that you are about to enter and possess. But if your heart turns away and you give no heed, and are lured into the worship and service of other gods, I declare to you this day that you shall certainly perish; you shall not long endure on the soil that you are crossing the Jordan to enter and possess. I call heaven and earth to witness against you this day: I have put before you life and death, blessing and curse. Choose life—if you and your offspring would live—by loving the Lord your God, heeding his commands, and holding fast to him. For thereby you shall have life and shall long endure upon the soil that the Lord your God swore to your ancestors, Abraham, Isaac, and Jacob, to give to them.

The Torah ends with this choice ringing in the ears of its audience: obedience or rebellion? life or death? the Garden or Exile?[3]

Toward a Uniform Collection of Scripture

Although the basic scriptural story extending from the creation of the world until Israel's return from Babylonia seems certainly to have existed by the fourth century BCE, the present literary division of that story into the canons of Torah,

Nevi'im, and Ketuvim and the inclusion of various supplementary writings took many centuries. Certainly the Torah and the historical narrative of Nevi'im were revered as uniquely authoritative very early on. But the process by which the entire present collection of writings came to constitute scripture—like so much else in early Judaism—is difficult to reconstruct with certainty.

Indeed, it is remarkable that any uniform collection of Jewish scriptures emerged at all. In the first place, the Jewish world after the fourth century BCE was anything but homogeneous. In addition to a small community centered around Jerusalem and other locations in the ancient homeland, most Jews of this period were scattered in lands as far apart as Egypt and Babylonia. Despite the superficial uniformity of a shared Hellenistic culture, which we discuss in Chapter 4, Jews lived under competing and often warring political empires and spoke a variety of languages from Greek to Aramaic. The restored Temple in Jerusalem and its priesthood enjoyed high prestige among most of the dispersed Jewish world, but no authoritative religious or political institutions extended from Jerusalem to legislate on such crucial matters as the nature and content of scripture.

By the third century BCE, Jews of Egypt became so comfortable with the Greek culture of Hellenized Egypt that they began to translate the Torah and other Hebrew writings into that language. This collection, which came to be called the Septuagint, gathered together many works not found in later versions of the Hebrew Bible. Aramaic- and Hebrew-speaking Jewish communities of Palestine preserved as well a wide variety of writings that seem to have enjoyed scriptural status for a time, even though they are not found in the present collection of the Hebrew Bible. Some of these writings were also translated into Greek and preserved in later versions of the Septuagint. One of these versions serves as the foundation of what Christians call the "Old Testament." But, however much they might have been valued by some Jewish groups of this period or to emerging Christianity, these other writings ultimately had little impact upon later Judaic tradition. The primary reason is that they did not find their way into the main collections of scripture transmitted by most Jews after the rise of Christianity.

To conclude: the process by which certain books attained scriptural status whereas others enjoyed it for a time and then ultimately lost it is difficult to trace. It does seem likely, however, that major responsibility for the preservation and transmission of the present canon of the Hebrew Bible can be placed in the hands of a group of first- and second-century CE teachers who called each other by a distinctive honorific term, Rabbi, "My Master." Rabbinic writings from the third century and onward, which discuss the names and even arrangement of scriptural books, correspond closely to the present Hebrew Bible. So there seems to be some important connection between the rabbis and the current canon of scriptures. Since the religious vision of the rabbis is, in any event, crucial to the development of Judaism from the second century until well into the sixth and seventh, it is important to focus on the nature of this group, its own understanding of its origins and teaching, and the ways its grasp of the Torah shaped later Jewish interpretative tradition.[4]

TRADITION AND THE SHAPING OF JUDAISM'S SCRIPTURE

The Hebrew Bible did not happen all at once. The chart that follows attempts to isolate key stages in the transformation of pre-scriptural traditions of ancient Israel into the canonical collection accepted by rabbinic Judaism.

Principle Sources of Ancient Israelite Tradition, ca. 1000–587 BCE

Primarily Oral Traditions

1. Heroic epics
2. Priestly ritual practices
3. Public oratory

Primarily Written Traditions

1. Civil and ritual law codes of royal scribes
2. Civil and ritual law codes of priestly scribes
3. Royal archives
4. Chronicles of royal deeds

Persian Period, ca. 539–323 BCE

1. 450–400: Selected oral and written traditions composed into the "Torah of Moses"
2. 450–400: Completion of written histories of pre-Exilic monarchies (Joshua-Kings)
3. 450–350: Systematic compilation of prophetic oracles
4. 450–350: Early collections of psalms and proverbs
5. 400–350: Completion of written history of post-Exilic restoration community (Chronicles and Ezra-Nehemiah)

Hellenistic Period, ca. 323–63 BCE

1. 350–160: Composition of Esther, Ruth, Job, Ecclesiastes, Song of Songs, Daniel
2. 250–200: The Torah and other Hebrew writings are translated into Greek by Egyptian Jews
3. 200: Canon of Nevi'im circulates with Torah as a scriptural collection
4. 200–100 CE: Jubilees and other works compete with Torah and Nevi'im as authentic scriptures

Roman Period, ca. 63 BCE–320 CE

1. 100 CE: Rabbinic tradition defines the present boundaries of Jewish Canon
2. 200 CE: Rabbinic tradition begins to claim exclusive legitimacy as the true meaning of scriptures
3. 300 CE: Septuagint is abandoned by Jews and becomes basis of Christian Old Testament by 300 CE
4. 300 CE: Surviving nonrabbinic traditions of scriptural interpretation are absorbed into the interpretive traditions of rabbinic Judaism and Christianity

SCRIPTURE AND INTERPRETIVE TRADITION IN RABBINIC JUDAISM

The Origins of Rabbinic Judaism

The early rabbinic movement reflects one aspect of a general attempt by Palestinian Jewry to recover from a devastating political defeat, the 70 CE sacking of the Second Temple in Jerusalem by Roman armies. The Temple's destruction, the death blow to an anti-Roman Jewish revolt begun in 66, was catastrophic for a variety of reasons. It destroyed the symbol of Jewish political independence and obliterated a major center of financial and cultural wealth. Most important of all for the history of Judaism, the principal site of Jewish sacrificial worship was razed.

Let us focus on this last issue. For centuries, Jews in Palestine and throughout the Mediterranean and Middle Eastern worlds had viewed the Jerusalem Temple as the tangible symbol of God's covenantal protection. Within it was housed the earthly manifestation of God's presence. The sacrificial offering of animals to God in the Temple was a principal means of drawing divine blessing into the Land of Israel and its people. In response to priestly sacrifice, it was believed, God brought the rains and made the land, herds, and the Israelites themselves fertile. The sacrificial service, moreover, made atonement for inadvertent violations of the Torah covenant and thus cleansed the people and individuals who felt polluted by sin and, therefore, bereft of divine blessing. Without the Temple, how would Jews maintain the atoning practices that erased the effects of sin and brought healing to the world? How would the covenantal relationship be enacted and where?

The founders of rabbinic Judaism seem to have emerged within a half century after 70 with at least the outline of an answer. But we can reconstruct that answer only on the basis of sayings preserved in later rabbinic writings of the third to sixth centuries. With the Temple in ruins, they are said to have taught, the effects of the abandoned sacrificial system could now be secured by alternative media: prayerful self-scrutiny before God, on the one hand, and the diligent study of God's revealed will, on the other. With the means of sacrificial atonement annihilated, total obedience to God's will, as expressed in detailed loyalty to his commandments, served in their stead.

It is not easy from our present standpoint to identify the social origins of these rabbis. But there are clues. Some teachers who were recalled by later rabbis as being important transmitters of early tradition—men with names such as Shemaiah, Avtalion, and Gamaliel—are also mentioned in nonrabbinic writings of the first century. There they are identified with a group known as the Pharisees, by all accounts rather important participants in the political and religious life of Jerusalem prior to the destruction of the Temple. Although rabbinic Judaism cannot be equated with the Judaism of the Pharisees, it is likely that at least some Pharisees were instrumental in the formation of what later came to be rabbinic Judaism.

One can perhaps think about this with the help of a model drawn from

Herod's Temple Compound in the First Century CE

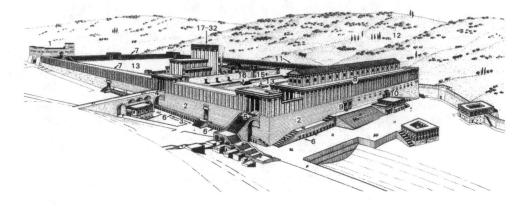

KEY: 1. Tha Antonian Fortress
      2. Retaining Wall
      3. West Wall Street
      4. Wilson's Arch
      5. Robinson's Arch
      6. Shops
      7. Porticoes
      8. The Royal Portico
      9. The Exit Gate
      10. The Entrance Gate
      11. Solomon's Portico
      12. The Mount of Olives
      13. The Court of Gentiles
      14. The Entrance to the Platform
      15. The Exit from the Platform
      16. Steps and Balustrade Prohibiting Gentiles
      17–32. The Temple and Inner Sanctum

(*Source:* Reproduced by permission of the artist, Leen Ritmeyer.)

American history. Although the founders of the American polity were deeply influenced by a European political philosophy named the Enlightenment and the Enlightenment's ideas played a key role in the American Constitution, the American polity and its constitution continued to grow and develop long after the Enlightenment vanished as a coherent political and philosophical movement. So, too, with rabbinic Judaism. Pharisees contributed, along with other Jews of the post-Destruction era, to what became rabbinic Judaism. But Pharisaic Judaism, which vanished by the second century CE, did not define what rabbinic Judaism would ultimately become.

Just who these Pharisees were is not an easy question to answer. Readers of the Christian Gospels meet the Pharisees as religious hypocrites who challenged Jesus' authority and who may have had a hand in his crucifixion. Fanatically loyal to what the Gospel of Mark calls "traditions of the elders" (e.g., Mark 7:1 ff.), the Pharisees are said to have been more concerned with having clean hands and tithed food than with true love of God and humanity. Other first-century CE writings, particularly those of a Jewish historian named Josephus, portray the Pharisees as a popular political party concerned with fostering deep loyalty to the Torah among the masses as well as teaching certain ancestral traditions not included in the Torah itself (e.g., Jewish Antiquities, 13:11–17, 288 ff.). The later rabbis, we have seen, recall at least some Pharisees as being important transmitters of ancient tradition.

Whether the Pharisees were hypocrites, as the Gospels claim, or religious democrats as Josephus holds, is not for us to determine, for we have no evidence other than these partisan depictions. But what does seem certain, because it is the only thing that our otherwise irreconcilable sources agree upon, is that the Pharisees placed a great premium on something called "ancestral tradition," which was not written in the Mosaic Torah, but somehow governed its application to life. Historians know very little of what this pharisaic tradition might have contained. But what we do have is the testimony of later rabbinic Judaism, in which the term "Torah" figures prominently as something far richer than the physical scroll of Mosaic teachings read in synagogues, richer even than the entire collection of scripture itself. Torah comes to stand for the entire body of Jewish religious tradition, both what is *written* in the Torah of Moses as well as the *interpretations* needed to embody the Torah of Moses in life.

In the aftermath of the loss of the Jerusalem Temple as the principal means of atonement before God, it is likely that the rabbinic focus on prayer and study as rituals of atonement was grounded by these sages in their distinctive understanding of ancestral tradition as Torah. If God required absolute obedience, and if the destruction of the Temple made many of his commandments impossible to fulfill, then it was only through interpretive traditions preserved outside scripture that Jews could begin to reconstruct their covenantal relationship with the God of Abraham, Isaac, and Jacob.[5]

The Rabbinic Written and Oral Torah

An important insight into the nature of rabbinic interpretive tradition and its relation to scripture is recorded in a third-century CE rabbinic writing, the title of which is probably best translated as "The Founders" (Hebrew: *avot*):

> Moses received Torah on Sinai, and passed it on to Joshua, Joshua to elders, and elders to prophets. And prophets handed it on to the men of the great assembly. They said three things: (1) Be prudent in judgment. (2) Raise up many disciples. (3) Make a fence around the Torah.

The passage continues with a lengthy list of later sages, living well after the return from Babylonian exile, each of whom receives Torah from his predecessor and passes it on to disciples. This list of teachers, which includes pharisaic figures and rabbinic sages known to have lived as late as the early third century CE, makes the claim that the tradition passed on as Torah by the rabbis begins with Moses and remains intact for well over a thousand years.

One of the interesting things about this list of teachers—apart from the extraordinary claim for continuity of teaching itself—is the way in which Torah, received by Moses and passed on to his disciples, is distinguished from *the* Torah, the actual document recording the Mosaic legislation. One builds a "fence" around the *documentary* Torah of Moses with the *interpretive tradition* of Torah preserved by the rabbis. Indeed, in rabbinic perspective it is precisely tradition that constitutes the fence around *the* Torah (Avot 3:13).

From Avot's perspective, *traditional* Torah passed on in rabbinic teaching constitutes a systematic safeguard against the violation of the *scriptural* Torah of Moses. Rabbinic Torah, as ancient interpretive tradition, enables Jews to properly embody laws, values, and norms of the scriptural Torah in their own pattern of life. That pattern of traditional belief and behavior, transmitted in rabbinic teaching and practice, is nothing less than Torah itself, the embodiment in public and private life of what God wanted for Israel when he revealed its basic outline, *the* Torah, to the entire community on Sinai. Thus, according to rabbinic Judaism, *rabbinic tradition and scripture together constitute Torah*; indeed, each requires the existence of the other in order for genuine covenantal obedience to exist.

This perception of the inseparability of rabbinic tradition and the Mosaic scripture is expressed in rabbinic writings of the fourth and fifth centuries in a remarkably apt image. These writings, which we discuss more extensively later, speak of *two* Torahs having been revealed on Sinai. One of these, called the Written Torah, is the actual scroll of Mosaic teachings preserved in the scriptures and read in the synagogues. In a derivative sense, it includes as well the entire canon of the Hebrew Bible. The second, called the Oral Torah, is claimed to have been transmitted by God to Moses by word of mouth alone. This memorized, orally recited Torah has accompanied the Written Torah since the beginning and, indeed, constitutes the authentic interpretation of the Written Torah's many commandments. Most important, the only way this Oral Torah can be learned is by long and diligent discipleship to a rabbinic sage who has committed the essentials of the Oral Torah to memory.

It is small exaggeration to say that the crucial human relationship of early rabbinic Judaism occurred between the rabbinic sage and his disciple. The disciple, a kind of apprentice rabbi, served the sage in a variety of capacities, from butler to death-bed consoler, much like other young men in the Hellenistic world

Mishnah Avot's Chain of Transmission Linking Mishnaic-Rabbinic Tradition to Sinai

The Prophetic Chain of Transmission

Moses

Joshua

the Elders

the Prophets

> This chain carries the tradition of Torah through the period from Moses to the destruction of the First Temple.

Transmitters of the Early Second-Temple Period

Men of the Great Assembly

Shimon the Righteous

Antigonus of Sokho

> This chain carries the tradition of Torah from roughly the time of Ezra up to the early second century BCE. The Men of the Great Assembly and Antigonus of Sokho are known only from rabbinic texts.

The Age of the Pairs (Late Second-Temple Period)

Yose b. Yoezer and Yose b. Yokanan of Jerusalem

Joshua b. Perakhyah and Nittai the Arbelite

Judah b. Tabbai and Shimon b. Shetakh

Shemaiah and Avtalion

Hillel and Shammai

> Rabbinic tradition views "The Pairs" as holding the offices of Patriarch and Supreme Court Justice respectively throughout the Hasmonean and early Roman Period in the Land of Israel. They are known primarily from rabbinic texts.

The Age of the Mishnaic Sages (Late Second Temple–Post Temple)

Rabban Gamaliel I

Rabban Yokanan b. Zakkai

Rabban Shimon b. Gamaliel I

Rabban Gamaliel II

Rabban Shimon b. Gamaliel II

Rabbi Judah b. Shimon b. Gamaliel

> The title Rabban (Our Master) is a form of Rabbi (My Master) and appears first with these figures. All but Rabban Yokanan b. Zakkai are recalled in rabbinic tradition as having served as Patriarch. Rabban Yokanan is recalled as reconstituting the study of Torah in a coastal town called Yavneh after the Destruction of the Temple in 70 CE.

might serve a teacher of philosophy or rhetoric. In return, the disciple had the opportunity to study his master's every word and gesture as an exemplification of what it means to fully master Torah. Although some sages or their disciples might have recorded some teachings in writing, the essence of the sage's teaching were his words of Torah and the way his behavior embodied Torah.

Rabbinic tradition, then, worked in two ways. As a pattern of behavior learned by imitation, it was tradition transmitted by example. By imitating the sage, a disciple incorporated Torah into his very being. As an interpretive tradition for the transmission of the meaning of scripture, rabbinic tradition was an intellectual commodity learned by studying and mastering the rabbi's oral teachings. To the degree that many sages argued that their patterns of behavior were themselves based upon interpretation of the Torah, these two types of tradition were often fused into one. It is for this reason that the actual literature of rabbinic Judaism, when it came to be written down, consisted almost entirely of words of Torah ascribed to specific rabbis and depictions of how these words were exemplified by their actions in specific contexts.

The Literature of the Oral Torah

The earliest document recording rabbinic tradition, compiled roughly around 200–225 CE, is called the Mishnah (i.e., "Repeated Tradition"). Later rabbinic historical memory unanimously ascribes the Mishnah's compilation to Rabbi Judah the Patriarch, a rabbinic sage who also served as Rome's governor of the Palestinian Jewish community (see Chapter 19). The work called Avot, from which we quoted earlier, is included in the Mishnah along with more than 60 other treatises on various aspects of Jewish law. Each treatise, in whole or in part, is devoted to a specific legal topic and presents diverse rabbinic discussions about how best to implement the divine commandments contained in the Torah of Moses regarding that topic. The basic assumptions governing the compilation of the Mishnah are clear: God spoke once in the Torah of Moses and revealed his commandments; he continues to speak through the traditional Torah of the rabbis. This latter Torah explains how to perform his commandments so that they can have their healing impact upon the covenantal relationship. The sum of rabbinic explanations are called *halakhah* or "procedure," that is, procedure for implementing the commandments. To follow the rabbis' halakhic procedures is to do God's will, as transmitted to Moses on Sinai.

The interpretive tradition of Oral Torah did not stop with the Mishnah, but it continued to grow in subsequent centuries as the Mishnah spawned later schools of technical interpretation. Gradually, the interests of rabbinic students of the Written and Oral Torah ranged far beyond strictly halakhic matters and soon included extended reflection upon other concerns central to the interpretation of the Bible: ethical issues, historical recollections, and theological speculation. These fell under the category of *aggadah*, "teachings" designed to foster a desire to serve God in obedience to the rules of halakhah.

Eventually, these two types of interpretive tradition were gathered together

TERMINOLOGY AND CHRONOLOGY OF RABBINIC LITERATURE

In rabbinic literature, it is convenient to distinguish between *types* of tradition in which knowledge was transmitted, *forms* of their transmission prior to their editing into finished compilations, and, finally, the *works* into which these traditions are compiled.

Types of Tradition

1. *Halakhah*—tradition about legal or ritual practice
2. *Aggadah*—tradition about history or theology

Forms of Transmission

1. *Midrash*—halakhic or aggadic tradition transmitted as an explanation of a biblical verse
2. *Mishnah*—halakhic or aggadic tradition transmitted without reference to a biblical verse
3. *Talmud*—analysis of a halakhic tradition

Major Compilations of Rabbinic Tradition

1. *Mishnah*—The halakhic collection supervised by Rabbi Judah the Patriarch in the Galilean city, Sepphoris, ca. 200–225. "Mishnah" means "repeated/memorized tradition."
2. *Tosefta*—A halakhic collection similar to, but larger than, the Mishnah, edited anonymously by 300 CE in Palestine. Tosefta means "supplement," i.e., to the Mishnah.
3. *Mekhilta of Rabbi Ishmael*—A third- to fourth-century Palestinian midrashic compilation in which the legal portions of the Book of Exodus are provided with both halakhic and aggadic comment. All rabbinic authorities mentioned in this compilation are from the first to early third centuries.
4. *Sifra*—An almost exclusively halakhic midrash on Leviticus. It is probably from third- to fourth-century Palestine. All rabbinic authorities mentioned are from the first to early third centuries.
5. *Sifre*—A pair of midrashic works on Numbers and Deuteronomy, mixing both halakhic and aggadic types of tradition. Most authorities are identical to those of Sifra and Mekhilta.
6. *Bereshit Rabba*—An enormous compilation of aggadic traditions that comment on every verse of Genesis. It is rich in traditions in the names of third- and fourth-century sages and is probably edited in Palestine by the fifth century.
7. *Vayiqra Rabba*—This aggadic midrash focuses on Leviticus, using the first verses of the scriptural chapters as occasions for long homiletic discourses. Like Bereshit Rabba, it is probably from fifth-century Palestine.
8. *Talmud Yerushalmi*—The "Palestinian Talmud," a mostly halakhic commentary on the Mishnah (Palestine, ca. 425). "Talmud" means "curriculum."
9. *Talmud Bavli*—The "Babylonian Talmud," compiling halakhic and aggadic materials into an encyclopedic commentary on the Mishnah (Mesopotamia, ca. 525).

into immense, encyclopedic compilations of rabbinic teaching. The most famous and important of these compilations are called the Talmud (Hebrew: "curriculum") of Palestine (ca. 425) and the Talmud of Babylonia (ca. 525). Both Talmuds are Mishnah commentaries that, in the course of exploring halakhic applications of the Mishnah, include as well vast amounts of aggadic commentary on the Hebrew Bible. The Babylonian Talmud remains today the most revered classic of rabbinic teaching among observant Jews. Other rabbinic teachings, of biblical interpretation in particular, were gathered together from the third to the sixth centuries in yet other large collections of lore called *midrash*, "interpretation" or "commentary." Unlike the Talmud, which is organized as a Mishnah commentary, works of midrash are normally organized around books of the Bible as explicit Bible commentaries. Although such midrash can be of an halakhic or an aggadic character, most of the surviving midrashic literature is dominated by aggadic themes.

In all, within five or six centuries after the catastrophe of 70 CE, Judaism had undergone a monumental transformation under the guidance of the rabbis. Halakhic inquiry had constructed a system of Jewish ritual observances that served as a whole to replace the ancient Temple's sacrificial media of atonement. Theological and historical midrash had constructed powerful links between the biblical images of Israel and contemporary Jewish self-understanding. Reading the Written Torah through the spectacles of the Oral, rabbis and the Jews they influenced experienced an intimate sense of continuity between past and present, a self-evident trust that their pattern of life and belief now conformed to the sacred patterns and beliefs represented by tradition. Their halakhah was nothing but the Torah of Moses, whom the rabbis knew as "Moses, Our Master," the source of all halakhah tradition. Their obedience was nothing but the obedience exemplified at the very beginning of Israel's history by the wandering herder known as "Abraham, Our Father," who, as the Babylonian Talmud claims (Yoma, 28b), "fulfilled the Torah even before it was revealed."[6]

SCRIPTURE AND TRADITION IN THE HISTORY OF JUDAISM

Many centuries were to pass before rabbinic Judaism became the Judaism of most Jews. In the Middle East and Europe, the victory of rabbinic Judaism was not complete until roughly the tenth century. Even after rabbinic Judaism became the dominant form of Judaism, it underwent a number of important transformations in medieval times. In modern times, the transformations have been especially profound, as we shall see in some subsequent chapters. But whether we consider antirabbinic forms of Judaism, forms that were developed by rabbinic communities themselves, or even some postrabbinic contemporary forms of Judaism, we find that nearly all take the rabbinic distinction between Written and Oral Torah— Scripture and tradition—as a fundamental point of departure. In this conclusion of our study of scripture and tradition in Judaism, it is useful to briefly consider two of the various forms of Judaism that coexisted with that fostered by the talmudic rabbis.

The Karaites

The first, Karaism, began as an explicit rejection of the rabbinic concept of Jewish tradition. Historians know little about how Middle Eastern Jews responded to the rabbinic interpretation of Torah. The Talmuds, it is true, acknowledge the existence of Jews who showed disrespect to rabbis or tried to evade their laws. Archeologists have dug from the earth synagogue remains and other artifacts that suggest that many Jews of the third through seventh centuries practiced their Judaism in relative disregard of rabbinic norms (see Chapter 16). Nevertheless, it is not until the eighth century and thereafter that we are able to trace a fully developed anti-rabbinic Judaism with its own legal traditions, theology, and institutions. Originating in Baghdad, the capital of the Islamic Abbasid Empire, it came to bear the name of Karaism, "Scripturalism."

Both Karaite and rabbinic historians link the origins of Karaism to a talmudic scholar, Anan b. David, who became convinced that the rabbinic Oral Torah was a human construct serving the interests of rabbinic authority. Anan's teachings about the human origins of rabbinic Oral Torah were highly controversial. Moreover, they were taken up and amplified by other like-minded individuals who, for a variety of reasons, challenged rabbinic authority to govern the religious and political lives of Jews in the Islamic lands. In response, generations of rabbinic religious leaders used both intellectual polemics and political attacks to try to suppress the diverse antirabbinic communities. It is unlikely that Karaism was ever a single centralized movement. But by the tenth century, it had clearly fragmented into a number of distinct Judaic communities that existed mostly in Islamic countries and the Balkans until the twentieth century. There remain Karaite communities in the United States and in Israel to this day.

The controversial nature of Karaite teaching is not hard to appreciate. Karaite polemicists, such as the tenth-century Jacob al-Kirkisanai, adduced biblical and even rabbinic texts to prove that Oral Torah stemmed not from Moses, but from the rabbis themselves. It had, therefore, no binding authority over the practices of Jews. But the core of Karaite polemics concerned the centrality of the scriptural text for defining Jewish covenantal life. Various Karaite biblical scholars, using the most advanced means of linguistic analysis available in the Islamic world, claimed to recover the original meaning of biblical rules. They showed, moreover, how these rules conformed to Karaite, rather than to rabbinic, customs. Under their influence, Karaite communities developed their own practices, which were often quite distinct from and stricter than those preserved in rabbinic halakhah.

Since halakhic tradition determines, among other things, the texts of prayers, the dietary practices, the calendar of religious festivals, and the procedures of marriage and divorce, it soon became clear that rabbinic and Karaite Jews could not pray together, eat at the same table, celebrate holidays at the same time, or even intermarry. Although Karaism did not replace rabbinic Judaism, it nevertheless remained powerful enough to pursue its own life for centuries. What is important about Karaism in the present context is the way its intellectual leaders came to formulate their understanding of the relation of scripture and tradition.

As did rabbinic Judaism, Karaism accepted the Written Torah as the binding revelation to Israel. There was no attempt, for example, to broaden or diminish the scriptural canon accepted by the rabbis or to use versions of texts other than those accepted by rabbinic tradition as Written Torah. Of interest is the way Karaism solved the question of tradition's relation to scripture. Rejecting the Oral Torah of the rabbis, Karaism nevertheless was compelled to substitute the results of its own biblical interpretation as another form of binding tradition. This is called by such terms as the "yoke of inheritance" (*sevel hayerushah*) or, simply, "tradition" (*ha'atakah*). Even though Karaite communities were permitted in principle to formulate their own rules based upon "individual" interpretations of the Torah, as a matter of fact the results of such interpretations often defined communal discipline as surely as any rabbinic halakhah. So, apart from its ideology, the Karaite rejection of rabbinic tradition was not a rejection of the *necessity* of tradition in order to live a life of covenantal obedience to God. Rather, it was a rejection of the *rabbis* as guardians of tradition. Its antitraditionalism, quite simply, created an alternative tradition, also regarded as intimately linked to the Torah of Moses.[7]

The Kabbalists

In contrast to Karaism, other forms of rabbinic Judaism enriched Jews' appreciation of the Written Torah not by rejecting the Oral Torah but by filling it with vastly new meanings. The emergence in the eleventh through the thirteenth centuries of Kabbalah is a case in point. Kabbalah, which we discuss in greater detail in Chapter 4, seems to have emerged in Northern Spain and Southern France as a kind of speculative philosophy about the inner life of God. Kabbalist, however, did more than think about the divine life. They believed they could, through certain meditative practices associated with the performance of commandments, *experience* that life in an intimate way. Kabbalah, in other words, was a crucial supplement to the life of halakhah as a means of securing complete atonement and thus encouraging the continued flow of divine blessing into the world.

Unlike Karaism, Kabbalah is not an antirabbinic movement, but a profoundly rabbinic one. All the early Kabbalists we know about were fully obedient rabbinic Jews, and many were, in fact, famous halakhic authorities and students of the talmudic writings. The great thirteenth-century French talmudist Moses b. Nahman (Nahmanides) is only the most illustrious example. The Kabbalists' commitment to rabbinic tradition is evident particularly in the way in which they imagined the relation of their own theories about the inner life of God to the quite different images of God assumed in the Written and the Oral Torah. It is summed up in the term "Kabbalah" itself, an old Hebrew word that means "tradition." For the Kabbalists, however, Kabbalah refers to a hidden tradition of scriptural interpretation known to a few, a tradition of the secret meaning of the Written Torah. They often refer to this Kabbalah as containing the "secrets of the Torah," the "esoteric Wisdom," or the "path of Truth." Borrowing images from Spanish romantic poetry of the day, they refer to the Kabbalist as the "lover" of the Torah who courts the lovely Lady and adores her beautiful soul, obscured as it is under the "garments" of laws and stories that cover her.

Now who, in the Kabbalistic view, transmits these truths regarding the esoteric meaning of the Torah's laws and stories? From whom does the Kabbalist draw his mysterious knowledge? If you have understood rabbinic Judaism, you will already have guessed the answer. The Kabbalah is claimed to be Mosaic teaching transmitted in highly secret form to the early Mishnaic teachers and from them to the Kabbalists themselves. The Kabbalah's complex theories of the divine life are, in other words, nothing more or less than the innermost form of the Oral Torah revealed on Sinai. For Kabbalists, the true meaning of the Written Torah is, as it is for all rabbinic Jews, found in the Oral Torah. But, as we see in Chapter 4, the Kabbalistic version of the ultimate knowledge contained in the Oral Torah is unimagined by the Oral Torah known to the talmudic rabbis of Late Antiquity.[8]

The examples of Karaism and Kabbalism, although sketchy, should illustrate the immense power of the rabbinic concept of Oral and Written Torah over Judaic thought regarding the Hebrew Bible. No Judaism emerging in the wake of rabbinic Judaism could imagine the Torah without at the same time imagining a supplementary tradition of interpretation that spelled out the covenantal implications for contemporary Jews. In rabbinic and antirabbinic communities alike, there was no covenantal relationship between God and Israel without the aid of an authoritative tradition linking a Jewish community's practices to the primal revelation in scripture.

Chapter 2

Scripture and Tradition in Christianity

Imagine creating a new religion that could be defined and understood only according to the beliefs of another faith. Imagine also claiming that this new religion fulfilled all the promises of the other and at the same time nullified it. Imagine that, in order to make yourself understood, you would have to employ the terms and symbols of the older faith and yet deny their legitimacy. The earliest Christians had to do just this. This paradoxical situation might be more clearly understood through example: one piece of twentieth-century American fiction serves us well.

In her novel *Wise Blood*, Flannery O'Connor creates the character of Hazel Motes, a tortured young preacher who despises Christianity yet feels compelled to be religious about his lack of faith. Hazel sets out to establish his own new church, proclaiming:

> I preach the Church Without Christ. I'm member and preacher to that church where the blind don't see, the lame don't walk, and what's dead stays that way. Ask me about that Church and I'll tell you it's the Church that the blood of Jesus don't [sic] foul with redemption.

Through this negative image of the nature and function of Christ, Hazel's pronouncement sheds light on the essence of the Christian faith and of the process of its own self-definition. Christianity is a religion that promises redemption from sin and death through belief in the person and work of one Jewish man, Jesus of

Nazareth, who is proclaimed to be the "Christ," or the "Anointed One," the "Messiah," the savior expected by Yahweh's chosen people. Reduced to its barest elements, the history of Christianity is the history of how this Jewish savior has been made the focal point of religious life by individuals and societies. Hazel's preaching is, in fact, a negation of the central claim of the Christian faith, as announced by Jesus himself when he was asked by the disciples of John the Baptist if he was the Messiah:

> Go tell John what you have seen and heard: how the blind recover their sight, the lame walk . . . the dead are raised up, and the poor have the good news preached to them. And blessed is he who takes no offense at me. (Luke 7:22–23)

Hazel's seemingly irrational proposal is not much different from the radical news preached by Jesus' earliest disciples, for as Hazel preached a church without Christ, the earliest Christians promoted a Judaism without Jews, that is, a Jewish religion that was not to be limited to the direct descendants of Abraham, or to those who followed the Law of Moses. Much like Hazel, these believers in Jesus paradoxically juxtaposed the "old" and the "new" and retained many of the outward structures of the old faith while stripping them of their traditional meaning.

Jesus as Universal Savior

All that is known about this man Jesus comes from Christian documents that portray him as the Messiah. The barest facts of his life, as told in these documents, are as follows: Jesus was a Jew, born in Palestine while Augustus Caesar was Roman emperor; at some point in his adult life, he became an itinerant teacher and healer who was credited with miraculous powers by an ardent group of followers; he also alienated the elites of his day to such an extent that he was crucified alongside two criminals by the Roman authorities; shortly after this humiliating execution, his disciples began to claim that he had risen from the dead and ascended to heaven and that he would soon return to establish justice and to exercise rulership of the whole earth.

An offshoot of Judaism, Christianity shares much with its parent religion, particularly in regard to its conception of the divine, its understanding of the divinity's revelations to particular human beings, its sense of election, its hope for redemption from the evils of this world, and its inclination toward a communal (rather than individualistic) definition of the truths contained in that revelation. Nonetheless, Christianity differs substantially from Judaism, for at the core of its central story stands the rejection of Jesus' Messiahship by his people. Though Jesus' disciples were also Jewish, their community could not remain a Jewish sect for very long after the death of Jesus. Since their belief in his Messiahship was considered a heresy, or false belief, by the majority of the Palestinian and Diaspora Jews, Jesus' followers had no choice but to redefine their self-identity. Moreover, they soon embarked on a missionary enterprise that extended the promises of election and salvation to Gentiles, or non-Jews. In redefining their self-identity, then, Jesus' earliest disciples also reinterpreted the meaning of revelation, of election, and of salvation: they extended the boundaries of membership in the people of God far beyond the confines of the Jewish community. Jesus was the Savior promised by God to the Jews, they claimed, and he had come to redeem not just the descendants of Abraham, but all who would believe in him, regardless of their ancestry. The oldest surviving Christian document puts it this way:

> For as many of you as were baptized into Christ have put on Christ: there is neither Jew nor Greek, there is neither slave nor free, there is neither male nor female; for you are all one in Christ Jesus; and if you are Christ's, then you are Abraham's offspring, heirs according to promise (Galatians 3:27–29)

Within that first generation after the death of Jesus, then, his followers had become something other than a Jewish heresy. They had become a new, distinct religion.

SCRIPTURE AND INTERPRETIVE TRADITION IN CHRISTIANITY

Scripture and Revelation

No matter how much early Christians sought to distance themselves from Judaism, however, they remained inextricably bound to it and to its notion of revelation. Claims of Christian truth rested squarely on the Hebrew sacred texts: Jesus was the Messiah "promised beforehand through his prophets in the holy scriptures" (Rom. 1:2). Jesus and the earliest Christians shared with other Jews a faith in the revelatory power of sacred texts. They believed that God had predicted the future Messiah to come in various ways, veiled as well as plain, in all the books of the holy Jewish scriptures. Jesus himself was believed to have pointed to specific passages that proved his Messiahship, and the gospel narratives of the life of Jesus are filled with references to the fulfillment of scripture. This tendency is dramatically summed up in one of the accounts of Jesus' resurrection. (Luke 24:13–35), when he appears to two grieving and bewildered disciples who do not know what to make of the crucifixion and of rumors that his corpse had vanished from its tomb. Jesus reproves them: "O foolish men, and slow of heart to believe all that the prophets have spoken." Then, "Beginning with Moses and all the prophets, he interpreted to them in all the scriptures the things concerning himself." These disciples finally realize that Jesus' tragic death had been part of the divine redemptive plan all along. "And their eyes were opened," continues this narrative, "and they said to one another, 'Did not our hearts burn within us while he talked to us on the road while he opened to us the scriptures?' " It was precisely this procedure—this "opening" of sacred texts—that firmly bound Christians to the Jewish scriptures and at the same time drove them away from the Jewish community.

Moreover, from that moment when they embarked on this kind of scriptural exegesis, it appears that Jesus' followers also began to perceive that he was divine and that his self was thus a direct revelation of God. By the end of the first century

CE, the Christian community could boldly proclaim that the Word of God itself was embodied in Jesus: "In the beginning was the Word, and the Word was with God, and the Word was God . . . And the Word became flesh and dwelt among us." (John 1:1, 14). This meant, of course, that for these earliest Christians who have left us surviving documents, the person of Jesus Christ became the literal embodiment of God's revelation. The faith of these Christian communities was thus centered on a complex notion of revelation: the Word of God was not simply contained in a set of texts or in interpretations of those texts, it was also incarnate in Christ himself; and it had been made most fully manifest in the agony on the cross and in the glory of the empty tomb. His every action, his ever utterance, his every drop of blood not only fulfilled the scriptures but also embodied and transcended them.

The Christian Scriptures

It stands to reason that a faith so firmly anchored in the sacred texts of its parent religion would develop holy scriptures of its own. Christians did develop their own scriptures, but not overnight. The first generation broadcast its message almost exclusively by word of mouth and saw no pressing need to assemble its own sacred scriptures, especially because it expected Christ to return at any moment. This oral tradition was closely linked to personal contacts with Jesus' disciples and their immediate followers and was inseparable from their claims to authority. It was a message embodied in its messengers, accessible not only in the stories they told and the lessons they taught, but also in the symbols they used and in the rituals they instituted in the name of Jesus. Even as late as the early second century CE, we can find Christian leaders exclaiming that these personal connections that stretched back to Jesus and his apostles were superior to texts. Papias, bishop of Hierapolis, is reported to have said:

> If ever any man came who had been a follower of the elders, I would inquire about the sayings of the elders: what Andrew had said, or Peter, or Philip, or Thomas, or James, or John, or Matthew, or any other of the Lord's disciples. . . . For I did not consider I got so much profit from the contents of books as from the utterances of a living and abiding voice.[1]

As the expected return of Christ was delayed, and the years passed, and the number of believers continued to expand, the need for written documents gradually became manifest; with the passing away of that first generation of Christians, having an exclusively oral tradition became ever more impractical. Continuity and order were at stake. Christians had to preserve those crucial stories and lessons that had given shape to their community.

When Christians of the late first and early second centuries CE developed their own sacred texts, they had no intention of replacing the sacred Jewish scriptures; they simply added their own books to them, creating a "New" testament as distinguished from the "Old." The formation of this New Testament was gradual, complex, and somewhat haphazard. Jesus had left behind no writings of his own. Furthermore, his disciples made no attempt for quite some time to write down an account of his life or a summary of his teachings. In fact, the oldest Christian documents are not the gospels, which tell the Jesus story, but the letters of Paul of Tarsus, a Jewish convert to Christianity who had not known Jesus in the flesh and who had for some time even persecuted Jesus' followers. These letters date from roughly the mid-fifties to mid-sixties CE, about twenty to thirty years after the crucifixion. Paul's epistles speak of the risen Christ and of the salvation offered to those who believe in him. They are not historical accounts, but letters written by a missionary in which he instructs, advises, and admonishes some of the Christian communities he had helped establish. These letters were reverently saved and later shared with Christians in other places. By the end of the first century CE, Paul's letters had begun to assume the authority of scripture among many Christians. In fact, Paul's authority had become so significant that even some documents written by others were ascribed to him.[2]

But by the time that the Pauline writings had begun to assume the status of holy writ, other documents had joined them. Chief among these were four separate accounts of Jesus' story, the gospels. The English word "gospel" means "good news" (from the Old English "godspel"). This is the same meaning of the original Greek word given to these documents, "evangelion." Though scholars remain uncertain about the authorship of these narratives, they do not generally doubt the claims to apostolic origin made by all four of them. Whether the evangelists Matthew, Mark, Luke, and John actually penned these documents matters less than the fact that four different early Christian communities saw fit to tell the same story from four distinct perspectives.

The four gospels are not detailed historical narratives of the life of Jesus; they are accounts of salvation history, and they are testimonies of faith. Though they tell the story of Jesus' public ministry and of his death, they also tell of his resurrection and his imminent return, and of the ways in which he fulfilled the prophecies of the Hebrew scriptures. The gospels were written to bolster the faith of those who already believed that Jesus was the Messiah and to win converts to their new religion.

What had been a largely oral tradition, handed down piecemeal and in no particular order, gradually became a set of texts. It is quite likely that some earlier written versions, now lost, provided the basic structure and content for Mark, the earliest of the four gospels. Written sometime between the mid-sixties and late seventies CE, the gospel of Mark, in turn, provided the framework for two other accounts, Matthew and Luke, which contain much of the material from Mark and add to it from their own oral tradition. Matthew was most likely written for a Jewish Christian community in the eighties, Luke for Gentiles in the late eighties or early nineties. These three gospels, known as *synoptic* (Greek, *syn*: together; *opsis*: view) because they are similar in structure and content, differ substantially from the fourth, John, which was written at the end of the first century. Except for the narrative of Jesus' passion, this fourth gospel shares little material with the other three. Moreover, it approaches Jesus from a different perspective. As Clement of Alexandria put it, ca. 200 CE, "Aware that the physical facts about Jesus had been presented in the other gospels . . . John wrote a spiritual gospel."[3]

But why *four* gospels, and not just one? Given the vast distances separating

The Four Evangelists,
from the *Treasury Gospels*

Many medieval manuscripts of the gospels contain illustrations of the four evangelists, or gospel writers, Matthew, Mark, Luke, and John. Christians believed each of these men to have been divinely inspired. The texts of their gospels (or the "good news" of Jesus Christ's saving work) were sacred scripture, the Word of God himself. The person of the writer was not believed to have intruded into God's telling of the story. (*Source:* D.Y./Art Resource, NY)

the early Christian communities and the great variety in cultural and ethnic traditions encompassed by them, what is truly surprising is that *only* four gospels came to be regarded as scripture. The author of Luke's gospel openly admits that "many writers" had preceded him in the attempt to "draw up an account of the things that have happened among us" (Luke 1:1). The truth is that at least nineteen gospels have survived, which means that more than twenty were probably in circulation by the third century. Among the more notable of these are the ones that claimed apostolic derivation, such as the Gospel of Thomas (parts of which could be older than Mark's gospel), and the Infancy Gospel of Thomas (which focuses on the childhood years of Jesus), the Gospel of Peter, the Gospel of Philip, the Gospel of James, the Gospel of Mary, and the Gospel of Nicodemus. Others claimed a particular geographic or ethnic identity, such as the Gospel of the Egyptians, the Gospel of the Hebrews, the Gospel of the Nazoreans, and the Gospel of the Ebionites.

This abundance of gospels was due mostly to the growth of "gnostic" sects within Christianity, especially in the second century CE. "Gnosticism" (Greek *gnosis:* "knowledge") is a term used to describe a certain approach to religion that was prevalent in the early Christian era. The vast majority of gnostics were "dualists," that is, they believed that human beings were spiritual entities trapped in an evil material world and that they could be freed, or saved, only through secret knowledge. The content of this knowledge and the means by which it was dispensed varied tremendously among gnostics, but they shared in common a tendency to produce texts that claimed to distill some new revelation.

The four gospels now found in the New Testament were not only among the earliest to be written, but were also produced by those communities that eventually gained control of the Christian religion. This alone reveals much about the process of scriptural formation in early Christianity, and about the development of the concept of a sacred scripture among Christians. For a text to be considered holy writ, it had to meet certain criteria. First, it had to be considered authentic, that is, as derived from the initial community of Jesus and his disciples. Second, it had to be valued as inspired and revelatory, that is, as derived directly from God. Third, it had to be accepted by consensus, that is, it had to belong to a wide range of communities, and especially to communities that spoke with commanding authority.

An assortment of other texts that fit these criteria would eventually find their way into the Christian scriptures. Chief among these are The Acts of the Apostles, which is really the second part of Luke's gospel and continues the history of the early Christians, particularly of Paul's missionary journeys, into the sixties CE; and the Book of Revelation or Apocalypse of John, a collection of symbolically encoded prophecies that detail the "eschaton," that is, the end of the world and the coming rulership of Christ, written by and for a suffering, persecuted community. A few other brief epistles round out the list of Christian scripture: James, I and II Peter, and Jude.

The Christian Canon

Arriving at a definitive "canon," or list of scriptures, involved judging the authenticity, doctrinal soundness, and communal acceptance of texts. (The Greek *kanon* is derived from *kanna*, a measuring device made from reeds.) This was a lengthy and complex process. Inasmuch as the selection of texts was inextricably bound to certain theological or ecclesiastical viewpoints, the history of the development of the canon of the New Testament is also the history of the struggle for the definition of orthodoxy in the first four centuries CE.

In the second and third centuries CE, various rival forms of Christianity, each of which claimed to be the one true faith, competed for supremacy. The differences among some of these Christian communities were immense. Some preferred to remain closely attached to Judaism. Others went to the other extreme, seeking to divorce Christianity as much as possible from Judaism. Others were inclined toward syncretism, gleefully blending their interpretation of Christ with Greek philosophy and oriental mystery religions. Each of these traditions had its own sacred texts. The twenty-seven books now known as the New Testament were the texts ratified by the Christians who conquered and prevailed in this heated contest. These Christians described themselves as orthodox and catholic, and their ascendancy over all rival claimants to the truth and to universal dominion is reflected in these two self-imposed names. "Orthodox" means "correct belief" (Greek, *ortho:* straight; *doxa:* opinion or judgment). "Catholic" means "universal" (Greek, *katholikos*).

Among these orthodox and catholic Christians, the development of a definitive canon of sacred texts took nearly four centuries. The earliest surviving list to include all of the books now known as the New Testament is from the year 367 CE. Older lists exist, of course, but they do not match exactly. For instance, the so-called Muratorian Canon, which has been dated circa 190 CE, omits some books (Hebrews, James, I and II Pet.), wavers on one (Revelation), and includes others that were later excluded (Revelation of Peter and the Wisdom of Solomon). Other early lists include the First Letter of Clement and The Shepherd of Hermas.

Oddly enough, it was someone outside the orthodox community who spurred the elementary formation of the New Testament canon. In the mid-second century CE, a Christian named Marcion was the first to draw up a list of "authentic" sacred texts. But since these scriptures did not at all square with the versions in use by many Christians, he called attention to the question of authenticity and forced the orthodox to come to terms with the concept of a canon. Marcion was eager to sever the ties between Christianity and Judaism and taught that the Hebrew scriptures were not compatible with the new revelation offered by Jesus Christ. Undoubtedly influenced by gnostic dualism, Marcion proposed the existence of two deities: one good and spiritual, revealed by Jesus; the other harsh, materially inclined, and sometimes malevolent, revealed in the Hebrew scriptures. Jesus was indeed the savior of the human race, but he was not the Messiah prophesied in the Hebrew scriptures. Those promises, made by the untrustworthy creator God of the material world, had not been kept. Instead, the good God of the realm of spirit had intervened, finally revealing himself in human history through the person of Jesus. The message of salvation was dramatically simple: the material world created by the Jewish God was evil, and Christ could help one overcome it.

Since, according to Marcion, the Hebrew scriptures had revealed a seriously flawed God, Marcion supported his claims with new scriptures. His "New Testament" consisted of portions of the Gospel of Luke and of some of Paul's letters, carefully purged of any passages that might have contradicted a dualistic theology. But what about the other gospels that were already in wide circulation? As Marcion saw it, Jesus' disciples had misunderstood him and his mission on earth. Only Paul, who did not know Jesus in the flesh, had correctly received this new revelation, and it was only in his "genuine" letters and in the "authentic" gospel

The Jewish Matrix of Christianity

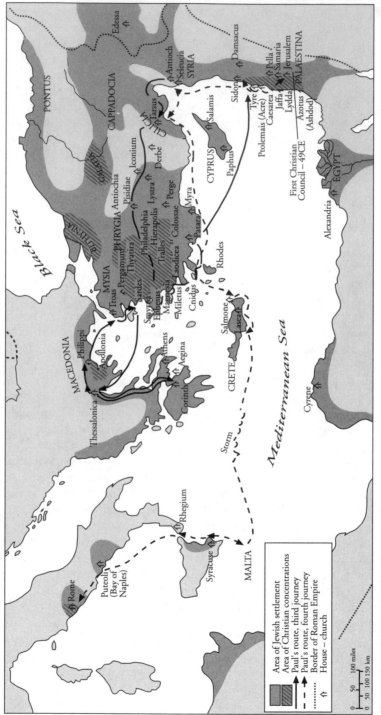

Area of Jewish settlement
Area of Christian concentrations
Paul's route, third journey
Paul's route, fourth journey
Border of Roman Empire
House – church

0   50   100 miles
0 50 100 150 km

(*Source:* Copyright © Carta Ltd., Jerusalem)

written by his disciple Luke (not in the "adulterated" versions of those texts in use by others) that the "wrong" interpretation of the Jesus story found in those other gospels was finally set right.

Marcion was rejected outright by the orthodox, but obtained a substantial following and created a rival church that survived into the fourth and fifth centuries CE. Alongside Marcion, other dualistic gnostic sects began to develop their own sets of scriptures, which they claimed were the authentic record of an oral tradition that others had misinterpreted. In addition to the gnostic gospels previously mentioned, other documents proliferated, with seemingly apostolic titles such as Paul's Letter to the Laodiceans, Paul's Letter to the Alexandrians, the Acts of John, the Acts of Peter, the Acts of Andrew, the Book of Thomas the Contender, the Apocalypse of Paul, the Apocalypse of James I and II, and the Apocalypse of Mary.

The "canonization" of texts was related to the appearance of strong rival claims to authenticity and authority. It is no mere coincidence, then, that the first lists of scripture begin to appear among the orthodox shortly after the emergence of Marcion and the gnostic sects.

The Interpretation of Scripture

Lawyers, journalists, and police officers have long known that witnesses to the same event will each have their own version of what happened, and that no two accounts will match exactly. The more complex the event and the more significant it seems, the more likely it is that rival interpretations will arise. As the proliferation of Christian sects and scriptures made clear, the meaning of Jesus' new revelation could be understood in various ways. Different individuals and communities arrived at their own interpretations of Christ's salvific work from divergent vantage points. This is a universal religious phenomenon. Religion interprets reality through myth, symbol, and ritual. These means of cognition are not one dimensional, or arranged in terms of simple linear logic. On the contrary, since they aim to reconcile the paradoxes and mysteries of human existence, they are multidimensional, nonrational expressions that thrive on the coincidence of opposites. This means that each and every truth claim is fraught with *meaning* and open to interpretation. When meaning is sought, it is always sought through some cognitive structure, through some hermeneutic (Greek, *hermeneus:* interpreter). In other words, when people try to make sense out of something, they can do so only through those ideas, symbols, and thought processes that are already familiar to them.

In the case of Jesus and Christianity, the process of interpretation centers on the meaning of a man, his words, and his actions. One scene in the irreverent film *Monty Python's Life of Brian* has captured the essence of this process. The character of Brian, who has been mistaken for Jesus, is being pursued by a mob of would-be followers who are eager to invest his every move with meaning. In his haste, Brian loses a sandal; the mob stops in its tracks to ponder what this might mean and immediately divides into two conflicting interpretive camps. One group sees this from a communal perspective, as a ritual gesture; half the mob decides that Brian has generously left the sandal for the community as a relic to be worshiped, and they immediately begin to venerate it. The others, in contrast, view it from a more individualistic perspective, as a practical lesson; perceiving this as a gesture of humility worthy of imitation, these followers each cast away one sandal. Such is the nature of hermeneutics.

To further complicate matters, the process of interpretation is inseparable from the oral and textural traditions that relayed the Jesus story, for the central figure himself died young and left behind no definitive writings of his own. This means that for Christians the revelation of Jesus is not only inextricably bound to each community's consensus of interpretation—its hermeneutic—but also to the authority structure that determines and certifies that hermeneutic. Jesus left behind his disciples, and it was they who began the task of interpretation. One theme sounded in all early Christian literature, whether orthodox or heretical, is the need for interpretative authorities whose pedigree can be traced in some way back to Jesus and his inner circle of disciples. Consequently, no oral or written tradition could be divorced from the social organization that transmitted it and interpreted it.

The earliest Christians had no "Bible" apart from their immediate social organization. It was the assembly of the faithful as a whole, the church (Greek, *ekklesía*), and more specifically, the leaders of that community that interpreted the scriptures. This was so not only because it had been the church and its leaders that defined which texts were "scriptural," but also because the texts themselves were not intended as much for private reading as for public sharing within a ritual context. The so-called Muratorian canon of ca. 190 CE determined the scriptural quality of texts according to their suitability for liturgical use. If a document was not considered revelatory, it was not to be read in church. This means that early Christians could not conceive of scripture as some independent source of authority. On the contrary, since most Christians were illiterate and copies of the scriptures were not abundant, the bulk of the faithful could only *hear* scripture read to them in church a little at a time, almost always as part of the ritual celebration of the sacred meal, the eucharist. It was principally through the mediation of the clergy—of those authorized by the community to lead and interpret—and in the context of a restricted social setting that early Christians could approach scripture.

From their earliest days, Christians developed a clearly defined authority structure. By the early second century CE, the orthodox communities were being led by bishops (Greek, *episkopos:* overseer), and their subordinates, the presbyters (Greek, *presbyteros:* elder). These church officials claimed their authority to be derived directly from Christ and the apostles. The First Letter of Clement, ca. 96 CE, a text that was considered part of scripture by some Christian communities, made this abundantly clear:

> The apostles received the gospel for us from the Lord Jesus Christ; Jesus, the Christ, was sent from God. Thus Christ is from God and the apostles from Christ. In both instances the orderly procedure depends on God's will. And so the apostles, after

receiving their orders . . . preached in country and city, and appointed their first converts, after testing them by the Spirit, to be the bishops . . . of future believers.[4]

Ignatius of Antioch, writing just a few years after Clement, put it more bluntly:

> For Jesus Christ . . . is the Father's mind, as the bishops, too, appointed the world over, reflect the mind of Christ. . . . It is clear, then, that we should regard the bishop as the Lord himself.[5]

Of course, both Clement and Ignatius were arguing so strenuously for epis-copal authority because it was being questioned and challenged. But the dis-senters, for the most part, challenged specific authorities rather than the concept of an authority structure. Most of those who refused to go along with the orthodox developed an authoritative interpretive elite of their own. This was certainly true in the case of Marcion and of most gnostic sects.

These elite interpreters seem to have been keenly aware of their own hermeneutics, and it did not take long for them to formulate theories of interpre-tation. By the early third century, clearly defined interpretive theories were al-ready widely accepted by Christian leaders. We know from the work of Origen (ca. 185–254), a scholar from Alexandria, in Egypt, that orthodox Christians accepted a triple sense of meaning in scripture. In his enormously influential work, *On First Principles,* Origen outlined these three layers of meaning. Every text of scripture, he argued, was divinely inspired and revelatory on three different levels. First came the literal level: each text could be read for its simplest meaning. "Jesus wept" (John 11:35), for instance, narrated the fact that Jesus actually shed tears as he approached the tomb of Lazarus. To understand this plainest meaning, one did not need divine inspiration. At a second and deeper level, which could be per-ceived only with divine assistance by those who were spiritually advanced, each passage also revealed moral lessons that could be applied to daily living. "Jesus wept" could thus also teach Christians about compassion. At the third and deep-est level, which could be understood only by a small core of spiritually gifted elites, scripture passages revealed hidden spiritual truths. To these few Christians, "Jesus wept" could disclose the most profound mysteries of the universe, such as the very essence of God, or the relation between God the Father and God the Son, or the nature of God's incarnation in Jesus.

This allegorical interpretive approach rested on the assumption that the whole universe is permeated with symbols and "types" of a higher, invisible real-ity. According to this world view, all things have a double aspect, one material and sensible, the other spiritual and mystical. Revelation, as Origen and his fellow in-terpretive elites saw it, was the mystical unfolding of spiritual realities that lay hidden in the letters of scripture. Unaided by God, the mind of a human could not penetrate the meaning of these sacred texts:

> This is because the treasure of divine wisdom is hidden in the baser and rude vessel of words . . . because the weakness of our understanding is not strong enough to dis-cover in each different verse the obscure and hidden meanings . . . [because] divine

The interpretation of scripture was not a task open to all Christians but was restricted to church elites. Pope Gregory the Great, also known as "the last of the fathers" (sixth century) because of the richness of scriptural citations in his writings, is here depicted as directly inspired by the Holy Spirit. The dove whispering in his ear is none other than God himself, telling Gregory how to teach Christians the scriptures correctly. Gregory writes what he hears, and this in turn is copied by monks below him. In this manner did the medieval Catholic church conceive of the dissemination of truth through the proper authorities. In this case, Gregory's inspiration derives from three sources: one, his office as a pope; two, his personal holiness and charisma; and three, his position as a teacher of all Christians, much like all the revered Fathers. (*Source:* Foto Marburg/Art Resource, NY)

matters are brought down to men somewhat secretly and are all the more secret in proportion to anyone's disbelief or unworthiness.[6]

Origen's search for scriptural meanings took him into interpretive dimensions far beyond the "rude" letter: so far, in fact, that many of his teachings ended up being condemned by the orthodox. (Among other things, Origen believed in reincarnation and denied the existence of hell.) Nonetheless, his influence on orthodox Christian exegesis was immense. By the fourth century CE, the art of interpreting scripture allegorically had matured considerably among Christian intellectuals. In the Greek-speaking Christian world, orthodox theologians such as Athanasius, Basil, and Gregory of Nyssa sealed its acceptance; in the Latin-speaking world, much of the credit goes to Augustine of Hippo.

From the third century on, Christians approached scripture as an inexhaustible, multilayered universe of meaning, and allegorical interpretation at the hands of the intellectual elite became normative. Origen's three levels of meaning were further refined and eventually expanded. In addition to the literal, moral, and spiritual levels, Christians sought an "anagogical" meaning in scripture texts, that is, a reference to secrets concerning the afterlife and Christ's future kingdom. A Latin rhyme that remained popular in Christian schools for nearly twelve hundred years (from the fifth to the sixteenth century) summarized this hermeneutical tradition for many generations of students:

> *Littera gesta docet,*
> *Quid credas allegoria,*
> *Moralis quid agas,*
> *Quod tendas anagogia.*

In a very loose English, the rhyme means:

> The letter shows us what God and our fathers did,
> The allegory shows us where our faith is hid,
> The moral meaning gives us rules of daily life,
> The anagogy shows us where we end our strife.[7]

SCRIPTURE AND TRADITION IN THE HISTORY OF CHRISTIANITY

The Place of Scripture Among Christians, ca. 450–1600

Since Christian truths were ostensibly revealed in scripture, all sound thinking was expected to be firmly anchored in it. The citation of biblical texts, therefore, gave structure to all religious discourse, not just in form, but also in content. Ultimately, every church teaching and each theological utterance had to be anchored in scripture. Yet, the use of allegory allowed Christian interpreters greater freedom

The Graeco-Roman World

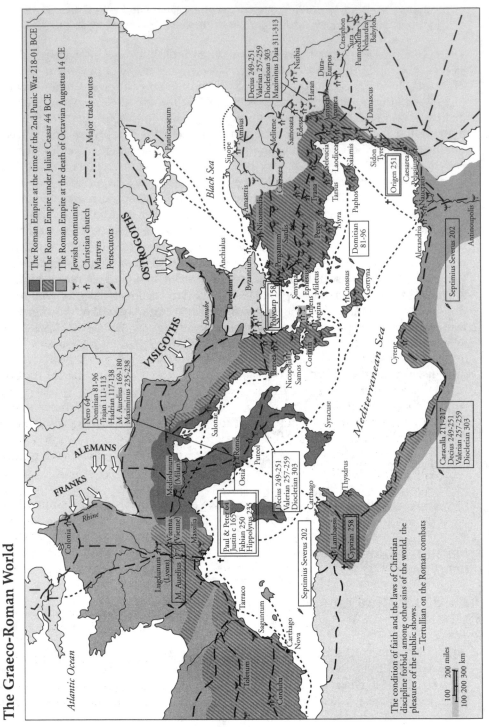

The condition of faith and the laws of Christian discipline forbid, among other sins of the world, the pleasures of the public shows.
— Tertullian on the Roman combats

(*Source:* Copyright © Carta Ltd., Jerusalem)

of movement within the sacred precincts of scripture; it also provided Christian theology with flexibility, giving it the capacity to intertwine written and oral traditions, and to continually adapt to ever-changing circumstances.

In the fifth through sixteenth centuries, scripture remained firmly in the hands of the church elites who had mastered the accepted exegetical methods. Through a complex system of checks and balances, church authorities monitored the interpreters, but the process of defining "orthodoxy" was seldom smooth or painless. Differences of opinion and controversies could turn ugly. Rival parties could condemn one another to hell for "false teaching" while citing the same texts. Excommunications could lead to schisms—the creation of separate churches—and schisms could lead to permanent alienation. In some extreme cases, such as those of the Monophysite heresy and the Donatist schism in North Africa, these estrangements could lead to even the dissipation and disappearance of Christianity in some regions. Major controversies were most often dealt with through meetings of bishops, known as synods or councils. The pronouncements of these assemblies would always be anchored in scripture, but the ultimate claims to authority made by them would be that they were directly inspired by the Holy Spirit and that they held firm to the apostolic tradition; they continued to speak in that "living and abiding voice" that Papias and other early Christians had understood as parallel to scripture. For more than a thousand years, Christians understood revelation as something safeguarded by the church and its leaders. Scripture was at the heart of all theology and ritual, but it was commonly agreed that the sacred texts themselves were embedded in an ongoing process of interpretation. This process was clearly in the hands of the clergy, and among them the chain of authority led in an upward direction. The question of where the ultimate authority resided, however, proved divisive. After the Roman Empire collapsed in the fifth century, the Christian communities in its eastern and western halves gradually drifted apart. In the areas that had once been the western Empire, where the preferred name for the church was "Catholic," the bishops of Rome continually increased their claims to be the ultimate authority. In the eastern regions that became the Byzantine Empire and in the Slavic nations missionized by the Byzantines, where the church favored the name "Orthodox," a more collegial understanding of authority prevented the Roman claims from being accepted. Although these two major branches of the Christian faith separated in 1054, principally over the issue of Rome's claims to supremacy, both the Catholic and the Orthodox churches approached scripture similarly and developed their theology through common interpretive structures. Within both churches, the Bible was read in a matrix of interpretive traditions and could not be appropriately decoded apart from the writings of the early Church Fathers, the pronouncements of councils and synods, and the commentaries of saintly clerical scholars.

Their role as guardians and interpreters of scripture gave the Christian clergy a privileged place in society and intensified the distinction between them and the rest of the Christian community, the laity (Greek, *laikos,* from *laos:* the people). Three other factors contributed to this differentiation. First, relatively few laypeople could read, though literacy rates varied from place to place and from time to time. Second, since all texts had to be copied by hand—a laborious and time-consuming task—the Bible could not be easily reproduced. Third, a language barrier prevented many laypeople in the West from understanding the Bible. In the Orthodox East, where Greek was spoken, literate Christians could at least read the New Testament in the original Greek text and the Old Testament in the Greek Septuagint translation; where Slavic was spoken, a translation was made available. In the Catholic West, where knowledge of Greek practically vanished between the fifth and the fifteenth centuries, the Bible existed only in the Latin translation of Jerome, known as the "Vulgate." Latin, the tongue of ancient Rome, was not spoken by most of the western laity, even though it continued to be used for all church ritual. It was a language that had to be learned and was thus restricted to the educated elite. The peoples of western Europe, then, did not have a Bible in their own languages.

Among the Orthodox, no substantial challenge has ever been made against this highly institutionalized, multilayered, traditionalist view of revelation. In the West, however, it is a different story, for Catholic Christianity was eventually rent asunder over the interpretation of Scripture. Some dissenters in the West who denied the interpretive monopoly of the church elites—the popes, councils, bishops, clerics, and theologians—began to argue that the Bible alone was the ultimate authority and even translated it into languages spoken by the laity. In fourteenth-century England, John Wycliffe and his followers, known as Lollards, were declared heretics for promoting such a teaching and for translating the scriptures into English. In the early fifteenth century, John Hus spread Wycliffe's ideas to Bohemia in central Europe. After gaining a large following, his teachings, too, were condemned. Hus was burnt to death at the Council of Constance in 1415, but his adherents, the Hussites, could not be easily eradicated.

Wycliffe and Hus were forerunners of a greater challenge that arose a century later: the Protestant Reformation. Whereas they had failed at overturning a thousand years' worth of tradition, others succeeded. Almost simultaneously, from 1517 to 1525, the German monk Martin Luther in Saxony and the Swiss priest Ulrich Zwingli in Zurich began a revolt against established church authority that gathered momentum and could not be stopped. At the heart of their theology stood the concept that had guided Wycliffe and Hus: *sola scriptura* (scripture alone). As they and their followers saw it, the church had become corrupt because it had buried the divine, revelatory truths of scripture under too many layers of humanly devised traditions. In other words, Luther and Zwingli attacked the interpretive authority claimed by popes, councils, bishops, and theologians. Measuring the authenticity of every rite and doctrine according to scripture, Luther and Zwingli made many changes in theology, worship, and social organization.

Though they both claimed to base their reforms on scripture, Luther and Zwingli could not agree fully with each other. Their strongest disagreement concerned the *eucharist*. What did Jesus really mean when he changed the ritual of the Jewish passover meal? How was one to understand the eating of bread and drinking of wine that Jesus commanded of his disciples? Was this a communion with the body of Christ, or a memorial celebration of his spiritual presence? When they finally met to resolve the issue in 1529, their divergent hermeneutics prevented them from reaching an accord. The key text consisted of a mere four words, but it was by no means insignificant: "this is my body" (Matt. 26:26; Mark 14:22; Luke 22:19). Luther read "is" literally, Zwingli allegorically; Luther insisted that the bread and wine changed somehow into Christ's body and blood; Zwingli could not accept this as possible and offered instead a metaphorical interpretation. So, despite their agreement on many teachings, including that which gave to scripture the highest authority, these two branches of the Reformation went their separate ways, one to become known as "Lutheran," the other as "Reformed."

Luther and Zwingli also disagreed with others in their midst who—as they saw it—appealed incorrectly to scripture. In Saxony, Luther contended with Andrew Karlstadt, one of his colleagues at the University of Wittenberg. Interpreting scripture more literally than Luther, Karlstadt pressed for the abolition of religious images and for greater changes in worship. Luther also opposed Thomas Müntzer, an apocalyptically minded extremist who sought to hasten the return of Christ through an armed insurrection against all established powers. In Zurich, Zwingli thwarted the efforts of some of his flock to restructure the church according to a more literal understanding of the New Testament: eventually, he would end up persecuting those who taught that "true" church should consist only of adult believers who shun all forms of violence and refuse to take part in civil government.

These persecuted radicals, who called themselves "Christian brethren" but would come to be known as "Anabaptists" because they rejected infant baptism (that is, they refused to initiate children into church membership) would eventually disagree among themselves and divide into various distinct communities. One branch of these Anabaptists would abandon pacifism and turn to violence instead. Although most tried to pattern themselves after the church described in the New Testament, some sought models in the Old Testament. Some identified so strongly with scripture that they went so far as to believe that certain individuals or communities fulfilled specific prophecies, or even literally embodied scriptural figures through reincarnation.

The unraveling of Christian unity in the sixteenth century was not brought about so much by lone individuals, however, as by different rival communities, each of which claimed to be the "true" church that remained faithful to Jesus and his apostles. Though the Protestant Reformers cried "sola scriptura!" and even encouraged Bible reading among the laity in vernacular translations, none (except a handful of individuals) sought to do away with a church and an interpretive elite. Luther despised the name Lutheran, which came to be applied to the churches established in parts of Germany, central Europe, and all of Scandinavia, but he remained convinced this institution was essential for salvation and that the Bible could not be approached in any way that diverged from the interpretation of its clerical elite. During Luther's lifetime, of course, he remained the principal interpreter; after his death in 1546, a struggle for leadership ensued among rival factions that was not settled until 1588 in the Formula of Concord, a document that

Western Religion at the End of the 16th Century: Majority Populations (Minority Populations not Represented)

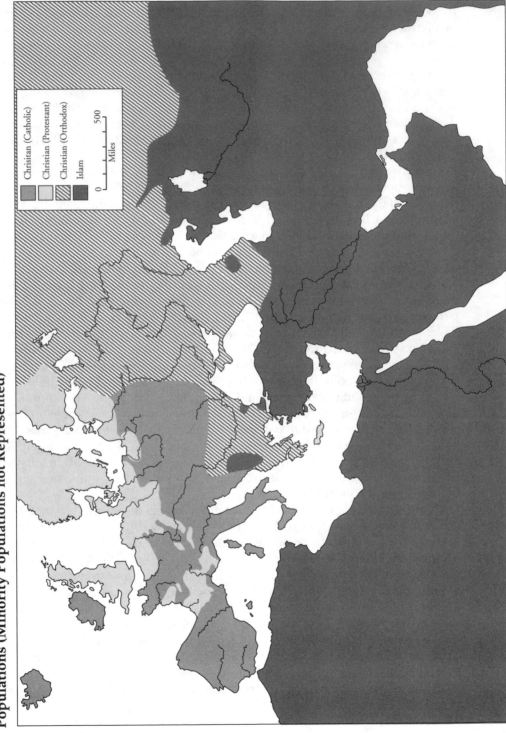

THE CHRISTIAN ART OF BIBLICAL INTERPRETATION

Following guidelines established in Judaism, Christians have long believed that every biblical texts has four simultaneous inexhaustible levels of meaning: the literal (historical), the allegorical (spiritual), the moral (tropological), and the eschatological (anagogical). The following is an example of the ways in which one seemingly simple text can be interpreted on all four levels.

"Jesus Wept" (John 11:35)

1. *Literal/Historical:* On this level, scripture provides a narrative of events, and there is not much room for interpretation. In John's gospel, we are told that Jesus broke into tears when he came to the tomb of his recently dead friend, Lazarus. This, the shortest sentence in the gospels, reveals a simple fact.

2. *Allegorical/Spiritual:* The spiritual lessons to be drawn from any passage are endless, and here there is plenty of room for interpretation. The fact that Jesus wept can be plumbed for meaning. Most frequently, this passage has been interpreted as revealing the compassion of God for the human race and the full humanity of Jesus.

3. *Moral/Tropological:* Here, too, multiple lessons may be drawn. The most obvious ethical message is that of imitation: all Christians should try to emulate Christ. In this case, imitation requires compassion, as well as a desire to alleviate the suffering of others. If Jesus wept, then so should all Christians.

4. *Eschatological/Anagogical:* In weeping for Lazarus and his family, Jesus showed the fullness of sorrow to be associated with death, but these tears could also indicate joy over the resurrection. In fact, right after he weeps, Jesus goes on to raise Lazarus from the dead. As death brings sorrow, so does it bring joy and the promise of a better life to come.

ensured the supremacy of those who called themselves "True Lutherans" (Gnesio-Lutherans) and were opposed to the moderate approach of Luther's successor, Philip Melanchton.

Zwingli and the Reformed, too, thought of the Bible as an ecclesiastical revelation; that is, they believed that the Bible spoke only in the context of a "true" church. After the death of Zwingli in 1531, command of this branch passed to other hands; from 1536 to 1564 leadership was gradually assumed by the Frenchman John Calvin, reformer of the church at Geneva, author of the single most influential summation of Reformed biblical theology, *The Institutes of the Christian Religion.* From his base in Geneva, on the border between France and Switzerland, Calvin successfully exported Reformed ideology to other nations and helped to lay the foundation for "Calvinist" churches throughout Europe, most notably in his native France and in the Netherlands, England, Scotland, Germany, Hungary, and Poland. Calvinism, as his biblically centered theology came to be known, would have a profound influence among religious dissenters in England who opposed the state-sponsored reforms of the Anglican church. These "Puritans," who sought to cleanse the Church of England from all traces of what they perceived as "idolatry," "Romishness," and "popery," would eventually gain the upper hand for some time in the seventeenth century and would also establish English colonies in North America.

Though these divisions still persist, the current peaceful coexistence of many Christian denominations was not painlessly achieved. Doctrinal disagreements led to bloodshed. From the 1520s to the 1640s, more than five generations of Western Christians were led into nearly continuous religious warfare. Catholics and Protestants fought on city streets and battlefields; Anabaptists and other dissenters were executed or exiled. Religion and politics became indistinguishable, and at the center, at least ideologically, stood basic disagreements over the interpretation of scripture. By the end of the Thirty Years' War (1618–1648), a conflict that killed thousands and ravaged much of central Europe, western Christendom had reached an impasse.

Scripture and the Heart

Exhausted by the Thirty Years' War, Christians after 1650 gradually began to divest themselves of the ideal of an all-encompassing Christian society. Even the compromise policy of *cuius regio, eius religio,* which made the religion of the ruler the religion of the domain, proved in practice to be unworkable and so gave way in the seventeenth century to experiments with religious toleration. The subsequent proliferation of distinct groups in early modern Christianity challenged the faith of Christians whose experience of tradition was grounded in trust in its universality. At the same time, the proven successes of Christians in propagating and sustaining variant forms of Christianity represented a broad ongoing commitment to comprehending Scripture as instituted in practice and history. Accordingly, the flowering of new traditions and communities hastened the demise of hopes for a comprehensive Christianity at the same time that it drove a process of renewal. And at the center of that renewal was the emphasis on the individual that had emerged during the Reformation.

Who were the interpreters of Scripture who framed and reframed Christian traditions after 1650? And how did they interpret? Protestants negotiating the turbulent religious waters of the time employed different strategies in reconceiving tradition and grounding it in fresh interpretations of Scripture. Some groups came to believe that "older is better." They read the Bible literally—one form of interpretation—searching for clues to the religion of the earliest Christians. Frustrated by the theological disputes and organizational problems that hounded Lutheran and Calvinist churches, the radical wing of the Reformation already had professed the ideal of simple communal life governed by a literal reading of the Bible. After 1650, this fondness for older or "primitive," Christianity was intensified by lay disenchantment with formalism in worship and church organization. Simplicity, in biblical interpretation and in church life, proved increasingly attractive as Christians sought clear-cut and unambiguous guidelines for spiritual development.

One way in which simplicity was cultivated was through "religion of the heart," a style of religion that valued above all direct emotional experience of the divine. This "pietism" was formed in a number of different ways and from various strands of traditions. In some instances, such as the case of the Quaker philosopher Lady Anne Conway, kabbalistic ideas were influential. In all cases, pietism was characterized by a rigorous moral legalism rooted in a strict biblicism. Nourished by English Puritan Lewis Bayley's *The Practice of Piety* and Lutheran pastor Philip Spener's *Pia Desideria*, pietistic emphasis on the Bible, prayer, and the moral life bore various kinds of fruit in the seventeenth and eighteenth centuries. English Puritans, the Moravian Brethren under the leadership of Count von Zinzendorf in Saxony, and numerous other groups appeared in Europe as dissenting congregations or as circles of laity who met regularly for Bible reading and prayer. Many of these groups devoted themselves to the production of vernacular editions of the Bible.

Pietists claimed to interpret the Bible with the heart. Or, as they might say, to simply believe the truth of the Bible. Disdaining doctrinal polemics, they shifted the focus of religion to the heartfelt embrace of the Word of God, in agreement with Spener's dictum: "It is not enough that we hear the Word of God with our outward ear, but we must let it penetrate to our heart."[8] Moreover, pietists cultivated a style of preaching that was plain in its references to scripture and aimed at coaxing an awakening of emotion rather than on proving doctrine. Methodism, which began as a prayer society at Oxford organized by John and Charles Wesley in 1729, marked the ripening of pietism into faith that Scripture, preached plainly from the pulpit, kindled the "new birth" of conversion.

Revelation and Science

The focus on the experience of the individual—the "hearing Scripture with the heart"—that underlay pietism surfaced in a radically different way during and after the Enlightenment. Fundamental to the eighteenth-century Age of Reason was the notion that the universe was governed by physical and moral laws that were detectable by the individual who cultivated the faculty of reason. From that trust in the faculty of reason arose the scientific method, concisely stated in Isaac Newton's *Opticks* (1704) as "making Experiments and Observations, and in drawing general Conclusions from them by Induction." Grounding their analyses in that method, scientists of various sorts by degrees discovered a history of the world—including its inhabitants—that was inconsistent with the account of the Old Testament. The new picture of the world appeared initially in the theories of astronomers and geologists and was given shape most dramatically by the naturalist Charles Darwin, whose findings about evolution were published as *The Origin of Species* (1859).

Discoveries about the earth's past, vigorously supported by claims for the truth of science, were accepted by some people as compatible with Christian faith. More often, Christians (especially those inclined to biblical literalism) either outrightly rejected the claims of science or lost their bearings trying to reconcile the emerging scientific view of the world with traditional Christian understandings of creation.

More important, science immediately and directly affected biblical criticism. The groundwork for modern biblical criticism had already been laid by Baruch Spinoza, who was born into a Jewish family in Amsterdam but later was excommunicated by a rabbinic court because of his beliefs. Spinoza had argued in *Tractatus Theologico-Politicus* (1670) that since God was revealed in nature, scripture was not essential to religion. During the course of the Enlightenment, other critics made similar pronouncements. At the same time, however, scholars concentrated in unprecedented fashion on philology and archeology as tools in the service of historical analysis of the Bible. In short, the Enlightenment undermined the authority of Scripture while simultaneously unleashing a monumental critical effort to ascertain truth in Scripture.

Searching for the truth in Scripture, biblical scholars to an increasing extent detected instead the human hands of the authors who wrote the documents that, taken together, constituted the Bible. Accordingly, as Johann Gottfried von Herder argued in the late eighteenth century, the Bible was a religious literature, a composite of fact and fiction that was to be sorted and analyzed just as one would study any ancient literature.

Biblical scholarship that developed against this background of criticism coalesced in Germany in the nineteenth century. Ferdinand Christian Baur, the central figure of the influential Tubingen school, exemplified in his work the determination of historical criticism to view every part of the New Testament against the circumstances of its origin. The consequences of such a view of Scripture were far-reaching. Baur's student David Friedrich Strauss, for example, set out in his *Life of Jesus* (1835) to distinguish myth from fact in the gospel narratives; and although Strauss faithfully affirmed that the birth, miracles, and resurrection of Jesus were eternal truths, the book nevertheless cast doubt upon the factual accuracy of the New Testament. As the decades passed, other writers catalogued contradictions and inconsistencies in both the Old and the New Testaments, called into question the authorship of many books, and argued that narratives had been laid down in strata rather than fashioned out of whole cloth. "Higher criticism," as this type of scholarship was called, challenged traditional understandings of the Bible that were grounded in belief in supernaturalism and scriptural inerrancy.

Responses to Enlightenment Criticism of Tradition

At the same time that biblical criticism was discovering the hidden world of Scripture to stand in glaring opposition to the beliefs of biblical literalists, even more sweeping criticisms of religion per se were voiced in Europe and America. Such criticism came from the frequently overlapping areas of the emergent social sciences, from political concerns, and from the perspective of gender. Karl Marx and Friedrich Engels articulated a comprehensive criticism of religion based on class considerations. In America, many Christians were bewildered and disheartened by ambiguities in Scripture that allowed for its appropriation alternately to defend and condemn the institution of slavery. And as the nineteenth century wore on, some people began to question the truth of the biblical portrayal of women. One of these was the American women's rights activist Elizabeth Cady Stanton, who complained in 1895 that "the Bible teaches that woman brought sin and death into the world, that she precipitated the fall of the race, that she was arraigned before the judgment seat of heaven, tried, condemned and sentenced. . . . Here is the Bible position of women briefly summed up."[9]

Beginning in the nineteenth century, there were three patterns of responses to these criticisms, suspicions, and social protests about the Bible. One response, which has remained a part of Christianity through the twentieth century, was to embrace belief in a simpler world, a mental world less complicated by modernity. It was manifested most visibly in the resurgence of the pietistic view of the encounter with Scripture as a matter of the heart. The Protestant revival of the first half of the nineteenth century accordingly harnessed Romanticism to the cause of biblical religion. It attracted to its ranks a host of people frustrated with the Enlightenment, ranging from Isaac de Costa, a Jew who abandoned Deism to become an outspoken defender of Calvinist orthodoxy in the Netherlands, to Madame de Krudener, a Baltic noblewoman who experienced a sudden conversion at Riga and became an itinerant evangelist to the upper classes. The evangelical revival, which waxed and waned throughout the nineteenth century led to Protestant fundamentalism in the early twentieth century. *The Fundamentals: A Testimony to the Truth,* which was published serially between 1910 and 1915 by a group of American theologians, forcefully rejected "higher criticism" and reiterated supernaturalism and the inerrancy of scripture. Fundamentalism remained an influence upon Christianity throughout the twentieth century. It was joined by Pentacostalism, a related movement that emerged from evangelical Protestantism and likewise embraced a conservative biblicism.

The second response to the discoveries of higher criticism and politically driven calls for religious reform was the replacing of literalism in some quarters by liberalism. By no means an unqualified endorsement of Enlightenment rationalism, liberalism nevertheless resonated with the eighteenth-century interest in portraying Jesus as a moral teacher rather than as a redeemer. It grew from the same soil as Thomas Jefferson's "The Life and Morals of Jesus of Nazareth," a composite document that Jefferson had created by pasting together snippets of philosophy and moral lessons literally cut from the New Testament (and about which a satisfied Jefferson wrote in 1816: "A more beautiful or precious morsel of ethics I have never seen"[10]). Liberals in the nineteenth and early twentieth centuries stressed morality above all in religion and gave precedence to reason over supernaturalism. For Protestant liberals such as Albrecht Ritschl and Adolf von Harnack in Germany, as much as for their counterparts in England and America, the Bible remained authoritative, but only because science, history, and experience—that is, reason—showed it to be so. Liberalism, then, attempted to redefine tradition in such a way as to engage modernity directly.

In Roman Catholic circles, a third response to post-Enlightenment biblical criticism was underway by the late nineteenth century as well. Since the Reformation, the Roman Catholic Church had sought for fresh ways in which to articulate its interpretation of Scripture in such a manner as to reassert its claim to power over Christendom. That effort reached its peak when representatives to the First Vatican Council, which was convened in 1869, forcefully reiterated a conservative agenda. On the heels of that meeting, Rome turned its attention to the rise of historical-critical investigations of the Bible and identified such endeavors as "modernist," that is, as counter to Catholic orthodoxy.

The crisis of Modernism in Roman Catholicism was represented most dramatically by Roman condemnation of the scholarship of the French priest Alfred Loisy. Loisy had drunk deeply of Protestant biblical criticism and in the 1890s began to question the doctrine of the inerrancy of the Bible. But at the same time, he grew increasingly more determined to show that the Roman Catholic Church was the true church. Accordingly, his writings were an attempt to reconcile his Catholic faith with scientific currents in philosophy and history. Unlike the case of Protestantism, in which the principle of sola scriptura was deeply embedded, Roman Catholics believed that the tradition of the church—the doctrines, practices, and styles that came to be part of the church as a historical institution—was important alongside Scripture as a guide to belief. Loisy argued that even though biblical criticism was a legitimate enterprise (Loisy rejected supernaturalism and biblical literalism), the Roman Catholic Church nevertheless evidenced in its historical development proof that it was of divine institution. In *The Gospel and the Church* (1902), Loisy adopted the approach of liberal biblical criticism, extending it so far as even to question the liberal Protestant notion of a "pure" primitive Christianity. Loisy affirmed instead the truths of the Christian Church as products of history.

The citadel mentality of Rome that characterized nineteenth-century Catholicism gave way in the mid-twentieth century to a spirit of ecumenism. The Second Vatican Council (1962–1965) accepted religious pluralism and enacted numerous liturgical and pastoral reforms. It also produced the Dogmatic Constitution on Divine Revelation, a theological document that accepted modern biblical criticism and downplayed the notion that the historical development of the church was a revelation equal to scripture. Instead, it affirmed that revelation was "contained" in scripture and that it was interpreted by the church, throughout history, with the help of the Holy Spirit. Accordingly, the Council strongly encouraged Catholic laity to engage scripture directly and even approved a Protestant translation (Revised Standard Version) as suitable for Catholic use.

New Revelations

In the centuries since the Reformation, the coalescence of new strands of Christianity has in most cases been rooted in fresh interpretations of the biblical record of revelation. In some cases, however, new revelations and new scriptures have been adopted alongside the Bible as guides to Christian belief. Such was the case of the New Jerusalem church founded in 1788 by English followers of the Swedish mystic Emanuel Swedenborg. Believing that God had called him to deliver the last in a progression of five revelations (the third and fourth being the Old and the New Testaments), Swedenborg wrote extensive biblical commentaries and numerous theological treatises, some of which came to be understood by his followers as scripture. Swedenborgian societies (one appeared in Baltimore in 1792) dramatically enlarged their membership in the nineteenth century. In America, Johnny Chapman ("Johnny Appleseed") planted the seeds of Swedenborgianism throughout the American Midwest, and those seeds continued to bear fruit throughout the century in religions such as Spiritualism, Theosophy, and New Thought. It was during this time as well that another Christian religion was born of a revelation received by Joseph Smith and reported by him in *The Book of Mormon* in 1830. Mormonism reopened the issue of canon by adding new material that extended stories from both the Old and the New Testaments and as a religious movement has been enormously successful in persuading persons of the authenticity of this new composite of scriptures.

Since the sixteenth century, Westerners increasingly have come to value not only literacy—reading and writing—but the book, written literature itself, as well. The Bible, as the most widely published and circulated book, initially contributed to the prestige of the book and later benefited from the fact that it is a book. Indeed, so closely have the book and the Bible ("the Book") been linked that, in some places and some times, to read even nonbiblical writings has been to be religious. The authority of new revelations and the popular religions that have emerged from them—Swedenborgianism, Mormonism, and Christian Science, among others—have been directly related to the increasingly easy and speedy circulation of Christian scriptures (new and old). Conversely, among the most difficult challenges that have faced Christian missionaries have been encounters with oral cultures in which neither literacy nor respect for the book is present.

In the modern period, each of the many streams of Christianity continues to marshal support from scripture for its beliefs. There is by no means agreement on the meaning of the record of Christian revelation recorded in the Bible. And new revelations still appear. Popular religions continually emerge as products of new interpretations of the Bible, or through the supplementation of the Bible with other revelations, or in the combining of biblical revelation with beliefs drawn from other scriptures. As Christianity has become increasingly global in its reach during the twentieth century, tradition frequently has exhibited its fluidity and adaptability. But in the global religious marketplace, ideas about inerrancy of scripture and biblical literalism continue to be fundamental to the debate about the meaning of revelation.

CHAPTER 3

SCRIPTURE AND TRADITION IN ISLAM

THE QUR'AN AND THE PROPHET

Muhammad and the Qur'an cannot be separated; they are intimately related in the process of scriptural revelation. The remarkable circumstances and events, centering on the prophetic career of Muhammad, led to the founding of Islam as the third of the great monotheistic world religions. Arabia, in the period of the magnificence of the Eastern Roman Empire of Constantinople and the Persian Empire of the Sassanids, was a cultural and religious backwater of feuding tribes and polytheistic cults. No one would have expected a world-historical religious revolution to arise from such a setting. But the combination of Muhammad's spiritual and moral perceptions and the particular social, political, commercial, and cultural conditions of Mecca ignited a religious movement that soon changed forever the commitments and boundaries of the world from Spain to India.

Islam, the religion of "submission" to God, may be seen both as a particular historical venture that got under way in the seventh century CE and as a virtually perennial attitude of serious people, regardless of which "brand name" religion they follow. Like its older siblings, Judaism and Christianity, Islam looks back in time to the patriarchs and matriarchs Abraham, Sarah, Hagar, Ishmael, Isaac, Rebecca, Jacob, Rachel, and Joseph, as well as the tribes and sees in them mighty stirrings of spiritual consciousness and moral awareness.

Pre-Islamic Arabia

The pre-Islamic Arabians of Hijaz, the western sector of the Arabian Peninsula— stretching from Mecca in the south to the Gulf of Sinai in the north—worshiped many deities, both male and female. Tribes and clans honored their ancestors at local sanctuaries. The Ka'aba sanctuary in Mecca housed some 360 idols on the eve of Islam. Among the most important deities were Hubal, a male in human form connected with divination, rain making, and victory in battle; Allāh, the supreme creator deity; and Allāh's daughters, Allāt, Manāt, and 'Uzza. Allāh was revered as the greatest of all gods, but his cult was not properly speaking a monotheistic religion. Jews worshiped their traditional God, who was called Al-Rahmān, "The Merciful," in Arabic. Christians called their God "the Lord," or Al-Rabb in Arabic. The Ka'aba is thought to have had, in addition to the numerous idols, pictures on its interior walls of biblical subjects, including Abraham, Jesus, and Mary.

The Arabs of Hijaz were tribal peoples without codified laws or a common government. Although their past was dominated by pastoral nomadic ways of life, by Muhammad's time there were towns as well as the two substantial urban enclaves of Mecca and Medina. The former was an ancient sanctuary and pilgrimage site that prospered greatly from trade, especially the long-distance caravan commerce that extended south to Yemen (the biblical Sheba), east to the Persian Gulf, and north to Palestine, Syria, and Egypt. Medina was an agricultural oasis with a large Jewish population. The classical Arabic language of poetry united all Arabs into a common cultural-linguistic family, even though regional dialects and fiercely independent clan and tribal patterns of life had prevented political unification until the coming of Islam, which as a combination of religion and ideology was able by Muhammad's death to unify the Arabs into a kind of supertribe. Islam united people through a common faith and value system, whereas the old Arabian society was united by kinship. The kinship bonds of Arabs continue to this day to be potent factors in social life, but Islam early modified their political aspects, in the process providing Arabs with a means to form community bonds with peoples throughout the Afro-Eurasian land mass.

Literacy was spotty, but inspired speech was quite common in the world in which the religion of submission as a specific, historical movement arose. Poets and seers exercised great influence through verse and rhymed prose, entertaining friends, excoriating enemies, inspiring the fainthearted and finding lost valuables. Although Jews and Christians were known in ancient Arabia, they were neither numerous nor influential outside a few localities. Nevertheless the Arabs were proud of their heritage, which could be traced in part to Abraham, Hagar, and Ishmael, as well as to Joktan, the grandson of Shem, and to Ketura, another of Abraham's wives.

Poetry, the principal artistic medium of the ancient Arabs, was composed in a highly stylized form of Arabic, which was difficult to speak extemporaneously, but virtually everyone could understand it. The ability to compose poetry in

Christianity and Islam

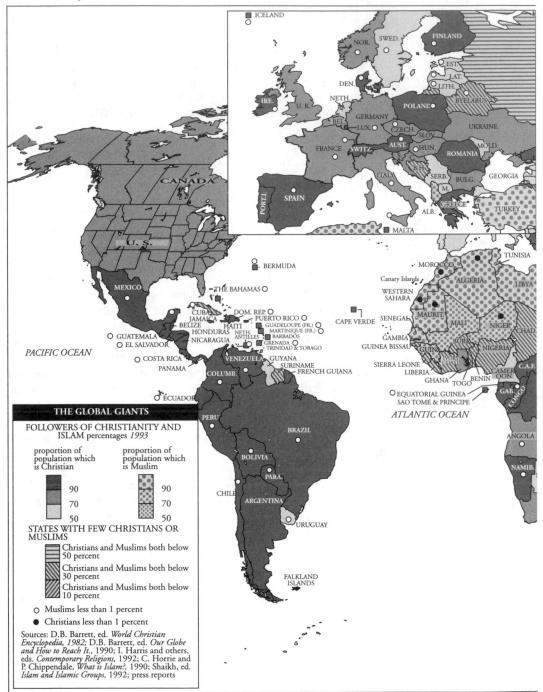

THE GLOBAL GIANTS

FOLLOWERS OF CHRISTIANITY AND
ISLAM percentages 1993

proportion of
population which
is Christian

proportion of
population which
is Muslim

90
70
50

90
70
50

STATES WITH FEW CHRISTIANS OR
MUSLIMS

Christians and Muslims both below
50 percent

Christians and Muslims both below
30 percent

Christians and Muslims both below
10 percent

○ Muslims less than 1 percent

● Christians less than 1 percent

Sources: D.B. Barrett, ed. *World Christian
Encyclopedia, 1982;* D.B. Barrett, ed. *Our Globe
and How to Reach It.*, 1990; I. Harris and others,
eds. *Contemporary Religions,* 1992; C. Horrie and
P. Chippendale, *What is Islam?*, 1990; Shaikh, ed.
Islam and Islamic Groups, 1992; press reports

(*Source:* Copyright © Myriad Editions Limited, London)

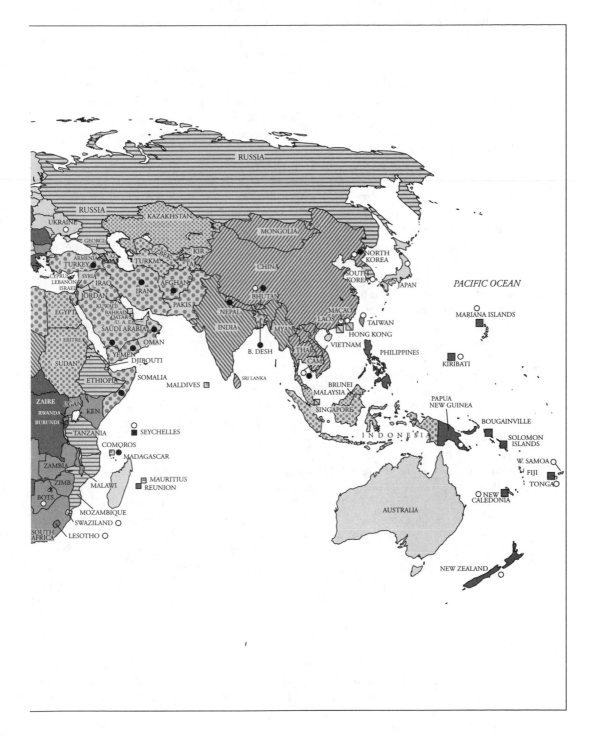

RUSSIA

RUSSIA

UKRAINE

KAZAKHSTAN

MONGOLIA

GEORGIA

ARMENIA
TURKEY

UZBEK
TURKM

KIR
TAJ

CHINA

NORTH
KOREA

SYRIA
CYPRUS
LEBANON
ISRAEL
JORDAN

IRAQ

AFGHAN

IRAN

SOUTH
KOREA

JAPAN

PACIFIC OCEAN

EGYPT

KUWAIT
QATAR
BAHRAIN
U. A. E.

PAKIS.

BHUTAN

NEPAL

MACAO
LAOS

MARIANA ISLANDS

SAUDI ARABIA

OMAN

INDIA

MYANMAR

TAIWAN

HONG KONG

ERITREA

YEMEN

DJIBOUTI

B. DESH

VIETNAM

THAI.

PHILIPPINES

KIRIBATI

SUDAN

CAMB.

ETHIOPIA

SOMALIA

MALDIVES

SRI LANKA

BRUNEI
MALAYSIA

ZAIRE

UGAN

KEN

SINGAPORE

INDONESIA

PAPUA
NEW GUINEA

BOUGAINVILLE

RWANDA
BURUNDI

TANZANIA

SEYCHELLES

SOLOMON
ISLANDS

COMOROS

MADAGASCAR

W. SAMOA

FIJI

ZAMBIA

ZIMB

MALAWI

MAURITIUS
REUNION

TONGA

NEW
CALEDONIA

BOTS.

MOZAMBIQUE

SWAZILAND

SOUTH
AFRICA

LESOTHO

AUSTRALIA

NEW ZEALAND

classical Arabic was evidence of being inspired by a sort of muse known as a *jinnī* ("genie"). The ability to excite, thrill, enchant, insult, threaten, or terrify by means of rhymed speech was as potent a possession as were horses and arms. In some ways, it was more powerful, because a single poetic characterization of an individual—whether praising or damning—lives as long as the language endures. Hijaz had periodic bardic contests that drew large audiences. Powerful and wealthy persons patronized poets, who sang their masters' praises and lampooned their enemies. Poetry also contained much genealogical and historical information about the Arabs, a sort of national archive of the past, containing especially accounts of battles and great events.

The Arabic language, which is closely related to the neighboring Semitic languages Hebrew, Aramaic, and Syriac, was in pre-Islamic times incompletely developed in written form. The coming into being of the Qur'an ("recitation") as Islam's revealed scripture, especially after it had been written down, led to the further development of written Arabic as the sacred text was collected into a standard form and promulgated throughout the Islamic empire. In fact, the large numbers of peoples in the Fertile Crescent, outside Arabia, who continued to speak Aramaic into Islamic times made for a culturally and linguistically receptive audience for the new revelation carried by the cognate Arabic language. When the Qur'an was spread throughout Aramaic-speaking regions of Iraq, Palestine, and Syria, it immediately had a somewhat familiar feel: linguistically, because of its cognate language; conceptually, because of its ethical monotheism, which we discuss in Chapter 6.

The Arabs, as far back as we have records, had been profoundly affected by their language's ability to stir both the intellect and the emotions. Poets were thought to possess a kind of occult power. And throughout the ancient Semitic world was a strong association between the bestowing of the craft of writing and the revelation of divine laws for humankind's guidance and edification. Verbal contracts and oaths had long provided a sort of moral and social glue in commercial and political relations in Arabia and the Near East. God, or a god, was often witness to promise making so as to foster promise keeping. The famous "Mizpah benediction" of Genesis 31:49–50—whose first verse is still recited by Jews and Christians—ably expresses this matter. A heap of stones had been piled to mark a quite worldly covenant that was made between Jacob and Laban:

> The Lord watch between you and me, when we are absent one from the other. If you ill treat my daughters, or if you take wives in addition to my daughters, though no one else is with us, remember that God is witness between you and me. (NRSV)

Just as the Torah, Israel's law, was received from heaven in written as well as in oral form, so also Muslims believe that their authoritative guide, their "Criterion of truth," was sent down as the earthly revelation of a heavenly prototype, known as the "Mother of the Book," preserved on a "guarded tablet." The idea of a scripture descending from a heavenly prototype may be traced back long before

Islam in the Semitic world of the ancient Near East. In the case of the Qur'an, the coming down was only in oral form, although later it was written by scribes. But in its first appearance, the Message was made public in a "clear Arabic speech" directed at what was essentially an oral society whose minds and hearts were calibrated by poetic imagination. Biblical religion—particularly Christian missions—had never made much headway in pagan Arabia. But the inimitable oral Qur'an, which was cast in the Classical Arabic tongue of the poets and their people, conquered all. In fact, the Qur'an came to be regarded as the criterion of pure Arabic, thus increasing the prestige of all Arabic poetry while spreading Arabic through religion.

That God's final message for humankind would be revealed in the language of the angels is a matter of providence. When a Muslim recites and prays by means of the Qur'an, she or he participates in a heavenly discourse even while struggling with the challenges and tragedies of earthly life. Even as Muhammad was often comforted and empowered by the coming down of Qur'anic revelations, so also are Muslims who live with their precious book.

Muhammad the Prophet of Islam and the Descent of the Qur'an

The intimate relationship between Muhammad and the Qur'an has been effectively characterized by Seyyed Hossein Nasr, a leading contemporary Muslim thinker:

> Once it was asked of the Prophet how he could be remembered and the nature of his soul known to the generations after him. He answered, "By reading the Qur'an." And it is in studying the life, teachings and significance of the Prophet that the full meaning of the message of Islam as contained in the Qur'an can be understood.[1]

The revelation of the Qur'an and the manner in which it came to be accepted and used as scripture in Islam is quite unlike the situation in Judaism or Christianity, although there are some parallels with the revelation of the Torah to Moses on Mt. Sinai and the inspiration of the prophets of ancient Israel. By Muhammad's time—he was born ca. 570 CE—the tradition of prophecy and revealed scripture was an old idea in the Semitic Near East, and it was generally believed that God appointed or sent prophets to people and entrusted them with holy books for specific nations. Jews and Judaism were well known in parts of Arabia, and there were also Christians here and there, as well as travelers and merchants from the two biblical monotheisms and Zoroastrianism, the scriptural religion of the Persians of the time, some of whose ethical and theological doctrines paralleled biblical religion.

Muhammad was born into the clan of Banū Hāshim, a respectable branch of the powerful Quraysh tribe of Mecca, an important caravan city as well as cultic center for traditional polytheistic Arabian religious practices. Although the ancient

TIMELINE OF THE EARLY HISTORY OF ISLAM IN ARABIA

ca. 570	Birth of Muhammad
595	Marriage of Muhammad and Khadija
610	Muhammad's Call to prophecy by the Archangel Gabriel at Mt. Hira
610–622	Prefoundations of the umma in the Meccan Phase of the Prophet Muhammad's career: attracting a following, teaching the Qur'anic message, developing political and leadership skills, growing persecution of Muhammad and the Muslims by the Meccan oligarchy, seeking a secure base for the Muslims
622	The hijra—"emigration"—to Yathrib, which comes to be known as Medina (lit. *Madīnat al-Nabī*, "The City of the Prophet"). Founding of the umma, the Muslim "community"
624	The Muslims' victory in the Battle of Badr against the invading Meccan punitive force. Although subsequent battles would go against the Muslims, Badr established a triumphant attitude and provided a firm conviction that would sustain the Muslims thenceforth. Change of *qibla* (prayer direction) from Jerusalem to Mecca.
630	Muhammad and the Muslims' conquest of Mecca and destruction of the idols at the Ka'aba, rededicating the sanctuary to monotheistic worship. Islam triumphant throughout Arabia.
632	Death of Muhammad. Selection of Abu Bakr to be the first caliph ("deputy") and founding of the institution. The following years would see the spread of an Islamic empire, with conquests extending from the Atlantic to India and Central Asia.

Arabs did not have a scripture that guided their religious practices, their poetry was regarded in almost a sacred way. They greatly honored their ancestors and offered sacrifices of various kinds to their deities, which were venerated not only in the form of idols but also at sanctuaries marked by stones, trees, or springs. Tribal burial sites had a sacred quality and served as safe places for people seeking asylum. Many traditional Arabian sacred stories were known, of course, but stories featuring biblical figures were also recounted. The Qur'an contains many references to such biblical figures as Abraham, Moses, David, Solomon, Mary, and Jesus. Although they were neither Jews nor Christians, it is safe to assume that the first hearers of the prophetic message in the form of recitation could understand the references to earlier scriptural persons and events from those traditions because they were part of the general cultural literacy of Arabia. The Sura of Joseph, for example, which is number 12 in the Qur'anic canon, is in general like the account in the Bible (Gen. 37–50), but briefer and lacking many biblical details. It seems plausible that the story was well enough known, whether in its biblical form or in some popular retelling, that the version transmitted by Muhammad, with its distinctive point of view, did not need rehearsing of its details.

Western, non-Muslim scholars have often assumed that Muhammad gained his knowledge of biblical religion from Jews and Christians residing in Arabia. The lack of precise agreement between biblical and Qur'anic accounts and details, however, has suggested to some that borrowing was from oral tradition. Muhammad's illiteracy would have prevented him from studying the Bible himself, although there were literate people living in Mecca and Medina, the city where Muhammad established the Islamic state after the *hijra,* or "emigration" in 622.

The Islamic position on the sources of the Qur'an emphatically denies either borrowing from the Jewish and Christian Bibles or Muhammad's own composing of it. Muslims hold as a bedrock article of their faith that the Qur'an, in its entirety, is the revealed word of God delivered to Muhammad by the archangel Gabriel in an ongoing series of revelatory encounters between 610, when Muhammad's "call" to prophecy occurred, until 632, the year of his death.

Muhammad was orphaned early in life and brought up, first, by his grandfather, then by his uncle. The future prophet gained a reputation for honesty and reliability as a youth. As a young man, he was employed by an independent businesswoman named Khadija. Khadija, a widow, owned a caravan company, which Muhammad came to manage, accompanying it on trips, probably as far as Syria. As a boy, Muhammad had traveled in that direction also, when, according to a famous account, a Christian monk met him and predicted that Muhammad would someday be a prophet. Although several interesting stories about Muhammad's youth have been preserved, it is not until his public career as religious and political leader that we find substantial amounts of historical information about his life and work.

Khadija admired her employee for his business acumen and his high moral values and proposed marriage to him. The union, consummated in 595, produced several children (two sons, who died early, and four daughters, who survived) and lasted until Khadija's death in 619, before the hijra to Medina. Muhammad had a secure livelihood as Khadija's husband, and the two lived happily together in a monogamous marriage. The relative leisure that married life afforded enabled Muhammad to pursue meditative activities that his sensitive nature sought. He came to practice solitary retreats during the hot months. Once, when engaged in such a vigil in a cave on Mt. Hira, outside Mecca, he experienced a profound vision.

Muhammad felt a mysterious and frightening presence in the cave. He was pressed down hard by some creature and commanded to "Read!" He replied, "I cannot read!" The voice persisted, with Muhammad experiencing great pressure and discomfort. The voice then announced, "Recite!: In the Name of your Lord who created, created humankind from a blood-clot. Proclaim! And your Lord is most bountiful—He who taught by the Pen—Taught humankind what they did not know."

The Arabic word translated as "recite" and "proclaim" is *"iqra',"* which also means "read." Because Muhammad was illiterate, it is probable that the meaning in the passage is "recite," or "proclaim." In any case, the passage quoted is generally believed by Muslims to constitute the first stage in the revelation of the Qur'an, Islam's scripture, and is found in Sura ("chapter") 96, verses 1–5, of the canonical copies of the entire Qur'an. It is interesting to note that the first revealed word, "*iqra'*," is composed of the same Arabic root (*q-r-'*) as "qur'ān," which means "recitation." As there is much convergence and mutual resonating of roots in Arabic poetry, belles lettres, and, especially, in the Qur'an, translation is most difficult and elusive.

The presence in the cave is held to have been the archangel Gabriel, who would accompany Muhammad throughout his prophetic career as the agency of revelation from God. Muhammad reported his dramatic experience to Khadija, who believed that her husband had indeed been in the presence of something wonderful. A Christian cousin, Waraqa ibn Naufal, upon being consulted about the event, suggested that it was comparable to Moses receiving the Torah at Sinai. As the revelations continued to descend over the ensuing years, Waraqa's prescient observation was borne out by parallels between Moses and Muhammad that are striking: both were given divine commandments for their people; both led their communities to a new existence in distant locations; both were judges and military leaders, as well as prophets and religious guides; both experienced the full range of life's possibilities, including marriage and parenthood; and both struggled tirelessly to teach and apply God's laws in the common life.

Just as in Judaism and Christianity, so also in Islam is God's will discovered in the historical processes of the communities devoted to revering and living by his commands. The Qur'an tells of prophets and nations of previous times, including several biblical traditions. It relates God's mighty acts of the past with his present purposes of providing both warning and good news to the hearers of the Qur'anic message.

The progressive revelations of the Qur'an were in a dynamic interrelationship with the unfolding events in the Meccan and, later, Medinan environments. The process of revelation is known in Arabic as *wahy*, a sort of idea-word inspiration that came upon Muhammad's "heart," as the Qur'an itself declares:

> And lo! it is a revelation of the Lord of the Worlds,
> Which the True Spirit hath brought down
> Upon thy heart, that you may be among the warners,
> in plain Arabic speech. (26:192–195)

In the passage just quoted, the word translated as revelation is *tanzīl*, which means "sent down." That which is sent down from on high is considered to be divinely revealed. The spatial metaphor is in keeping with a premodern cosmology, but the notion of wahy is not itself physical and spatial, but it is ideational, emotional, and aural, a form of verbal inspiration believed to be from God. Another term for inspiration is *ilhām*, but that does not have its origin in a transcendent, divine source; rather, it is inspiration from within, as from dreams and imagination.

A Muslim Man Reading the Qur'an after Afternoon Prayer

(*Source:* F. M. Denny)

Ilham is thought to be a spiritual awareness, but it does not have the status of revelation.

A precise description of wahy as process is difficult to provide. The traditional view is of a literal verbal inspiration that came to Muhammad, as well as to prophets before him, from Gabriel, who would visit Muhammad. According to one *ḥadīth* (a report on something Muhammad said or did):

> The Messenger of Allah (peace and blessings of Allah be on him), used to exert himself hard in receiving Divine revelation and would on this account move his lips. . . . So Allah revealed: "Move not thy tongue with it to make haste with it. Surely on Us devolves the collecting of it and the reciting of it." (Qur'an 75:16, 17) . . . So after this when Gabriel came to him the Messenger of Allah (peace and blessings of Allah be on him), would listen attentively, and when Gabriel departed, the Prophet (peace and blessings of Allah be on him), recited as he (Gabriel) recited it.[2]

Muhammad told of experiencing discomfort when the revelations came upon him; sometimes the feeling was like the ringing of a bell in his ears, and he would sweat even on a cold day. The presence of Gabriel was sometimes expressed by a sense of heavy weight on the Prophet.

Muhammad's prophetic inspiration may be compared with the biblical prophets, whose religio-moral sensibilities were grounded in the push and pull of historical conflict and the challenge of upholding the covenant with God. Muhammad rarely had an easy life, neither as a child and youth nor as a religious and political leader in Mecca and Medina. He sustained a continuous discipline of meditation and prayer, often spending the late night hours receiving and memorizing the Qur'anic revelations. Although many of the revelations relate to the times and breaking events of Muhammad's life as prophet and leader, they are not thought by Muslims to have been caused by historical events. Rather, may we think of the Prophet's career as being at the meeting point of historical process and his own evaluative response to that process. His response had deep moral and spiritual sources, and Muhammad was acutely aware that he was called to be a major factor in the unfolding fortunes of his people.

In some ways, the life of Muhammad is more important for his followers than the life of Jesus is for Christians. Jesus' life and ministry led to a redemptive conclusion in his death on the cross and the subsequent resurrection faith that proclaimed that the sacrifice constituted, in its fullest sense, victory over death. The ministry of Jesus must always be viewed from the perspective of the crucifixion and resurrection. Muhammad, on the other hand, was only a human being whose death was like that of other human beings. But in the details of Muhammad's life—so far as they can be known—Muslims find instruction, inspiration, and guidance for their lives. Muhammad's great character, faith, and courage led in the forging of a moral and religious rebirth in Arabia. His tireless labors in spreading the message of Islam throughout the Arabian Peninsula led to the establishment of a new world religion.

According to Muslim belief, Muhammad is not the mysterious force behind the success of the Islamic venture; rather, God was at work in the prophetic career of Muhammad. And the Qur'an, Muhammad's only miracle, as he claimed, is entirely the word of God. But because it was entrusted to Muhammad, Muslims realize that their Prophet was an indispensable element in the definition as well as the development of the Islamic belief and behavioral system. We consider in Chapter 9 the beliefs about Muhammad as a perfect pattern for human life that developed in later Islamic history. It can be generalized at this point that the Qur'an provides the central doctrines of Islam: its theology, salvation doctrine, cosmology, and anthropology—or doctrine of the nature of human existence. Muhammad's teaching, on the other hand, not only reinforces the Qur'anic doctrines but also adds much in the way of specific precepts and examples concerning the conservation, cultivation, and application of the Qur'anic message.

Muhammad gained a modest following during the years of his activities in Mecca, from 610 to 622. Most of the new Muslims were of the humbler classes. Only one, Uthman, who had married one of Muhammad's daughters, was from the Meccan oligarchy. It became clear that this group of Muslims would need to have a safe place to develop their community, because Mecca was becoming increasingly hostile toward the monotheists, who were perceived as a threat to traditional values and to the lucrative pilgrimage activities at the Ka'aba sanctuary complex.

Indeed, the little Muslim community experienced persecution and abuse.

Some of its members were harshly treated, including the black slave Bilal, whose owner tried to force him to renounce Islam by placing a heavy rock on his chest and tying him down in the midday sun. But Bilal persisted in calling upon God and was finally purchased and then set free by Abu Bakr, one of the leading followers of Muhammad from Meccan times and later the first caliph of the umma after Muhammad's death. Bilal long served as Muhammad's *mu'adhdhin* (muezzin, caller to prayer), and his ringing voice is legendary in the memory of Islam.

An attempt to secure a safe haven for at least the most vulnerable of Muslims in Ethiopia failed. An official Meccan expedition journeyed to bring the Muslims back in chains in a manner reminiscent of Paul the Pharisee's mission to Damascus to bring back the apostate Jews—now Christians—for punishment in Jerusalem. Later, Muhammad sought a refuge for his followers in the nearby mountain town of Ta'if, but the inhabitants threw stones at him, driving him away. In Mecca, danger and persecution increased. Muhammad and his Muslim followers had to endure insults and actual physical abuse, for example, when they wanted to worship at the Ka'aba sanctuary, which they honored as a holy temple of monotheism.

SCRIPTURE AND INTERPRETIVE TRADITION IN ISLAM

The Ka'aba was believed to have been originally built by the Patriarch Abraham and his son Ishmael as the first sanctuary dedicated to the worship of the one, true God. The Ka'aba cult had degenerated over the centuries into a polytheistic sanctuary. As Muhammad's prophetic career developed, it would focus on the restoration of the Meccan sanctuary to its Abrahamic status as the center of monotheism. In the eventual process of accomplishing this, many pre-Islamic practices of the polytheists were retained with what was believed to be their original meaning from Abraham's time. The Qur'an itself declares that its message is not new:

> Say ye: "We believe in Allah, and the revelation given to us, and to Abraham, Isaac, Jacob, and the Tribes, and that given to Moses and Jesus, and that given to (all) Prophets from their Lord: We make no difference between one and another of them: and we are submissive [i.e., are Muslims] to Him." (2:136)

Even if the old message has been brought once again in the Qur'an, however, that message is also held by the Qur'an to have been distorted by both the Jews and the Christians. Both the Torah and the Gospel are held by the Qur'an to have been divinely revealed to Moses and to Jesus, respectively. But the originals have been lost and, instead, distortions and accretions of the two religions are held to have supplanted them. The disagreements between the Qur'an and the Bible, therefore, stem from the corruptions that long ago entered into the beliefs and practices of the two older religions. The Qur'an has come in the latter days, then, as a mercy, not only to the unscriptured and barbaric Arabs, but to all humankind as a setting straight of the record, as it were. Nevertheless, the Qur'an teaches respect for and peaceful relations with the "People of the Book"—meaning the Jews and Christians, who have, in some sense at least, revealed scriptures—and commands the Muslims to invite them to Islam as the fulfillment of Abrahamic monotheism:

> They say: "Become Jews or Christians if ye would be rightly guided." Say thou: "Nay! (I would rather) the Religion of Abraham, the True (way), and he joined not gods with Allah." (2:135)

Eventually, after extended negotiations, Muhammad concluded an agreement with representatives from the far-off agricultural city of Yathrib, which came later to be known as Medina (the "City" of the Prophet). Yathrib was experiencing serious intercommunal conflicts. Its leaders saw in Muhammad, who now had a wide reputation as an honorable and wise man, a potential impartial arbitrator for the situation. The Prophet stipulated certain conditions for his and the Muslims' migration, including the acceptance of his prophetic authority and conversion to Islam, which the Medinan emissaries accepted on behalf of their city.

Muhammad and his Muslim followers accomplished the emigration from Mecca to Medina in late summer 622. This great event, the hijra (emigration), marked the beginning of the Islamic lunar calendar and the founding of the umma. The Muslim community would henceforth be a religious state, governed by God through the Qur'anic revelation and by God's Prophet.

Muhammad's charismatic authority continued to grow during the exciting Medinan years during which all of Arabia would eventually profess Islam. In fact, the charisma of the Prophet Muhammad would gradually be transferred to the community that he founded. And the increasing respect for and imitation of Muhammad's manner of believing, worshiping, leading, and living engrained the ways of the Prophet—his *sunna*, as it is called—in the umma. In this sense, we may speak of the Muslim community as a "Muhammadan" community, although to do so should not be interpreted as meaning that the Muslims consider Muhammad to be divine. That is why "Muhammadanism" is unacceptable as the name of the religion of Islam, because it is God alone who is worshiped and obeyed. And when obedience is given to the Prophet, or to his teachings and example, that is because God commanded it in the Qur'an when he said: "Ye have indeed in the Messenger of Allah an excellent model for anyone whose hope is in Allah and the Last Day" (33:21). Furthermore, Muhammad's worth in the eyes of the Muslims is declared in the revelation itself:

> Allah and His Angels send blessings on the prophet: O ye that believe! Send ye blessings on him, and salute him with all respect. Those who wrong Allah and his Messenger—Allah has cursed them in this world and in the hereafter and has prepared for them a humiliating punishment. (33:56–57)

The Qur'an served, in the Medinan years, both as prayerbook for daily worship and as lawbook. Thus, its contents after the hijra show clearly the manifold aspects of a complete human community, with its own religious laws, social regulations, economic principles, military requirements, and political procedures. This final aspect was not fully or clearly spelled out in the Qur'an, or by Muhammad, so that after the Prophet's death the umma experienced a crisis of succession. Although the situation was rescued by the coming forth of Muhammad's oldest companions—Abu Bakr and Umar figured centrally—subsequent Islamic history would know many political difficulties with respect to basing itself on clearly defined and universally accepted principles. No one has doubted that Islamic political order should be combined with right worship and just government, but the problem has been how to systematize the process satisfactorily. It is one thing to declare that a people will live by the Qur'an as its constitution; it is quite another to pursue that ideal in practical terms. In the present day, Iran and Saudi Arabia are examples of nations striving to live under the governance of the Qur'an and Muhammad's teachings, known as the Sunna.

The Qur'an as Canonical Scripture: Its Collection and Standardization

Muhammad realized the need to collect the Qur'anic contents into a coherent whole before his death. He and his secretary, Zayd ibn Thabit, apparently did much of the planning for this task, but it was not completed until after Muhammad's death. We are not sure how or when or by whom the divisions into *suras* (chapters) and verses were made, and by whom the names of the suras were decided, but it seems that those are not matters of revelation. Although there were somewhat differing codices (manuscript volumes) of the Qur'an in existence during the caliphates of Abu Bakr and Umar, the third caliph, Uthman, saw to it that a standard written text was completed by appointing a commission under the leadership of Zayd in the 650s.

The spreading Arab-Muslim empire and the mounting deaths of people who know the Qur'anic text by heart (known as *qurrā'*) are said to have motivated a sense of urgency to promulgate a single edition. By Uthman's time, the far-flung Muslim armies had several varying texts of the Qur'an in different regions of the expanding empire. Quarrels broke out when troops brought together from different theaters disagreed over the correct pronunciation of the text during their massed congregational prayer services. Under Zayd's commission, all known Qur'anic materials, gathered from writing media such as wood, skin, bones, stone, and "the hearts of men" were reviewed and compared for their authenticity by trusted persons who had known Muhammad and had heard many of the passages in their original contexts.

The origin of the Qur'an and its acceptance as the canon of Islamic scripture are coterminous with the life and prophetic career of Muhammad. There never was much of a controversy about what constituted the revealed text, although somewhat varying collections of the contents were in circulation during the first generation after the Prophet's death. Uthman's collection, however, although it was preserved in a primitive Arabic script (more on this follows), has been standard until today. A somewhat technical subfield of Qur'anic studies is the variant "readings" of the standard Uthmanic text, but they have to do with dialectal variants and not with the actual contents. Specialists in recitation have always memorized all the variants and transmitted them to the present in chains between teachers and students. For all practical purposes, only one of the famous "Seven Readings" of the Qur'an is in use today, that called Hafs.

Note that whereas the Jews have preserved until the present their Torah mostly on parchment scrolls, so that the form persists as a virtually sacred object in synagogues, Muslims have always held the paged volume to be the proper form of preserving the written text of their revealed message. The Arabic word *muṣḥaf* (pronounced moos-huff) means "book," in the sense of a physical volume of sheets bound or otherwise gathered in some manner. In a worship or study context, Muslims will often say "Where is the Mushaf?" or "Please hand me that Mushaf," meaning the copy of the Qur'an. Some years ago in Egypt, a project to record the recited Qur'an in its entirety was discussed. The planners and religious officials worried that selling sound recordings of the Holy Qur'an in stores where popular music was sold might be blasphemous. But they solved the problem by employing the phrase "The Recited Mushaf" on the album covers, instead of "The Recited Qur'an." Everyone knew what the title meant, but it was thought to be a sort of necessary taboo word in place of the sacred word that is the name of the revelation. Interestingly, the phrase "recited Qur'an" is somewhat redundant, because Qur'an itself means "recitation." What is meant, of course, is not the written text, the reading, but the actual performance of reciting out loud. The orality of Islamic scriptural piety comes from the orality of the "text" itself.

Achieving a Standardized Written Text of the Qur'an—Parallels with the Hebrew Text of the Jewish Bible

Although the Uthmanic edition has always been the common standard text, much was done in later centuries to improve the orthography of its written text. The problem was that when the Qur'an was collected and written down, the written consonantal Arabic text was without a fully articulated alphabetic script, without standard voweling, and with variations in spelling. The situation was similar in Judaism, with its unvoweled consonantal Hebrew text of the Bible. The following example will give a sense of the situation, which you should try to read, although there are no vowels provided:

frscrndsvnyrsgrfthrsbrghtfrthnthscntntnwntncncvdnlbrtnd
ddctdtthprpstnthtllmnrcrtdqul

In case you are wondering what this unvoweled passage is, it is the opening sentence of Abraham Lincoln's Gettysburg Address: "Four score and seven years ago our fathers brought forth on this continent, a new nation, conceived in liberty, and dedicated to the proposition that all men are created equal." See what a difference vowelization makes?

In both Arabic and Hebrew, the script was a sort of shorthand that required a fair knowledge of the language and its idiom in order to use with facility. Muslim textual scholars gradually perfected a full voweling of the written text of the Qur'an, in Iraq, around the tenth century CE. Of the greatest interest is the achievement of the parallel task of voweling of the Hebrew Bible at approximately the same time and also in Iraq, or Babylonia, as Judaism traditionally refers to Mesopotamia. The voweled and otherwise fully articulated Hebrew text of the Bible is called the Masoretic text, from Masorah, "tradition." Both the Qur'anic textual scholars—known as *muqri'ūn*—and the Jewish Bible scholars—known as Masoretes—performed great services for their communities in standardizing their respective Scriptures' written texts, for voweling regulates many differences in meaning. In addition to voweling, aids were added to correct cantillation of the two texts, for both Muslims and Jews love to chant their scriptures in worship and meditation (eastern Christians have long practiced this, too). The standard exemplars that were created—of both the Hebrew Bible and the Qur'an—enabled copyists thenceforth to reach a high degree of accuracy in transmitting the written text.

Although revealed as an oral message, the written Qur'an has been of incalculable importance in the spread of Arabic literacy and Islamic communal identity throughout vastly dispersed Muslim populations in Europe, Africa, and Asia. What is more, the beautiful Arabic script has had the profoundest influence on Islamic aesthetics, which feature Qur'anic calligraphy as well as a wide range of arabesque shapes executed in a rich variety of media, including textiles, wood, metal, stone, ceramics, and leather.

The Organization of the Qur'an's Contents

The Qur'an is about the length of the New Testament of Christianity, divided into 114 chapterlike suras of uneven length, with a general arrangement of longer ones followed by shorter ones. This ordering we may call the canonical arrangement. It has nothing to do with the chronological sequence of revelations. Muslims also have a chronological ordering of the suras and even of passages within suras. The basic chronology is between the contents revealed in Mecca and in Medina. The Meccan suras are often short, with a dramatic, even urgent quality in the communication of God's warning of a coming judgment and admonition to surrender and obey. References to earlier people's spiritual successes and failures are frequently made, for example, biblical precedents. The passages treating biblical figures and events are similar to Jewish midrash in many ways. And to a person used to the Bible versions, they often seem to have a curious point of view, although they are recognizably within the same extended family of related traditions.

The Medinan suras are longer and, as has been mentioned, contain much material of a legislative and practical sort for the governing of the Islamic state, as

**The Ninety-Nine "Most
Beautiful Names" of
Allah Inscribed in a
Poster**

(*Source:* F. M. Denny)

well as more explicit instructions concerning ritual. Muslims make no distinction
as to the religious merits of the Meccan as compared with the Medinan suras, for
both categories are divine revelation, but for different times and circumstances.
And although it is possible to relate the contents to historical events, the Qur'an
transcends them by addressing enduring issues of religious and moral importance

for people who strive to follow Islam's "Straight Path," the synonym for the religion that is mentioned in the opening sura, a prayer for all Muslims known as "Al-Fātiḥa" (The Opening):

> In the Name of Allah the Merciful, the Benevolent.
> Praise belongs to Allah, the Lord of the worlds,
> The Merciful, the Benevolent, Master of the Day of
> Judgment. You do we worship and your aid do we seek.
> Guide us along the straight path, the path of those
> You have blessed, not those whose portion is wrath,
> Nor who are straying.[3]

The Qur'an is also divided into equal sections for purposes of regular reading and recitation over the period of a month or a week. Marginal notations mark these divisions in the text; it is common for an individual or small group to recite one-thirtieth—one day's worth on a monthly circuit—at a sitting. Depending on the style of recitation selected—slow and embellished or at a moderate tempo and plain—the period may be two or three hours or only an hour and a half.

Qur'anic Exegesis

The exegesis, or interpretation, of the Qur'an is a highly technical field of religious scholarship. Some of the Prophet's Companions began the practice by providing commentaries using their knowledge of the Prophet's own life and teachings, as well as many oral and written sources from the Jewish and other traditions in Arabia. By the third Islamic century—about 900 CE—a mature level of Qur'anic exegesis, known as *tafsīr* (lit., explanation), had been reached in the great commentary of the renowned Persian historian al-Tabari (d. 923) Al-Tabari's conservative approach collected all relevant traditions about a passage and judiciously weighed them, usually concluding with the author's own position but often leaving the matter open to the reader. This "traditional" tafsir represents the most common type, to the present. Another kind of tafsir is "rationalist," moving beyond the mere literal meaning and seeking to reconcile and harmonize difficulties and inconsistencies by means of critical discourse. This type of tafsir, although sometimes impressive, has not dominated the field; it is considered too independent and liberal. A third type of tafsir features symbolic and allegorical interpretations of the Qur'an, often far from the plain meaning; this type has been favored by Sufi mystics.

The science of tafsir requires advanced mastery of linguistic, philological, rhetorical, legal, historical, and theological discourses and is thus reserved for relatively few scholars in any generation. Popular, accessible commentary is widely available for the general Muslim public, who chiefly want practical guidance for

THE EXEGETE AL-BAIDAWI ON SURA 18:83/82 (d. 1291 CE)

> They will question thee concerning Dhū l-Qarnain. Say: "I will recite to you some of his story."

Reference here is to the Greek (*rūmī*) Alexander, king of Persia and Greece (*rūm*). He is also designated as king of the East and the West, and for this reason has been given the name "the one with the two horns (*dhū l-qarnain.*)" Or (he is so called), because he roamed all over the two horns of the earth, namely the East and the West; or, because two generations (*qarnān*) of men passed away during his lifetime; or, because he had two "horns," that is, two braids of hair; or, because his crown had two horns. Since one who is brave is called a "ram," it is (also) possible that this nickname was given to Alexander on account of his bravery, because he battered his enemies like a ram. There is disagreement as to whether Alexander was a prophet; it is, however, agreed that he was believing and just.

Those who raise the question (in this verse) are either the Jews, who advance this question in order to put Muhammad to a test, or the unbelievers of Mecca. . . .

Source: From Helmut Gätje, *The Qur'ān and Its Exegesis: Selected Texts with Classical and Modern Muslim Interpretations,* tr. and ed., Alford T. Welch (London: Routledge and Kegan Paul, 1976), p. 120.

their lives rather than specialist discussions of such things as grammar and lexicography. Qur'an commentaries for readers who do not know Arabic are available in countries such as Pakistan, India, Malaysia, and Indonesia, and works of tafsir are increasingly available in English. Even in vernacular languages, however, interpretation has to address issues pertaining to the original Arabic text.

The Qur'an in the Life of the Muslims

The Qur'an is used as the fundamental source of guidance on all matters of life and is the major authority for Islamic law and theology. But the Qur'an is also a comfort and joy to Muslims through its aural and visual splendors. Calligraphy has already been mentioned. Even more important is recitation of the Qur'an following the correct rules of performance and using appropriate melodies and modes. The science of Qur'anic recitation is known as *'ilm al-tajwīd.* Although the conceptual level of the Qur'an—its informative dimension—is central for Islamic faith and order and is the preserve most especially of tafsīr, its performative dimension is equally meaningful at the emotional level and in worship and other contexts. Many public, civic, educational, social, cultural, and even commercial events in Muslim societies are opened by recitation of the Qur'an. Qur'an recitation can daily be heard on the radio and television in Muslim countries, and often it is accompanied by instruction on the scripture's meaning for daily life. In Malaysia, for example, a popular Qur'an program is broadcast over television in the early evening every day, featuring well-known scholars from centers of Islamic education such as Egypt and Saudi Arabia.

In every generation since the beginning of Islam, many of the faithful have undertaken the considerable task of memorizing the entire text of the Qur'an. One who achieves this is called a *ḥāfiz,* literally one who is a "guardian" or "caretaker" of the Qur'an. In special institutes, Muslims learn effective techniques in memorization of the Qur'an. Some who learn the text by heart go on to earn their livings as professional reciters. It is always interesting to attend a Muslim academic conference and witness a display of Qur'anic knowledge whenever a dispute over a matter arises, when a Qur'anic proof text or clarification is immediately needed. Inevitably, one or more participants is a hafiz and provides the precise passage or correlation needed at the moment.

In today's computer age, Qur'anic software is available in a wide variety of formats. One program has the Arabic text of the Qur'an, together with a vernacular translation in one of several languages, plus lexical and exegetical as well as historical aides, making it a simple matter to do word searches and to generate all kinds of data printouts on an endless variety of subjects. Some programs even have full sound capability, so that the operator can hear any portion of the text recited, a great boon for persons trying to learn the correct pronunciation, melodic modes, and rhythm of recitation.

The Qur'anically empowered personality makes no essential distinction between comprehending God's message and experiencing God's presence, for the two are simultaneously present in mind and heart. Muslims believe that when the Qur'an is recited aloud, God's "tranquility," called *sakīna* (cf. Hebrew *shekhina*), descends as a guiding and comforting presence. So the orality of Qur'anic piety continues today as before as an essential dimension of being Muslim.

In this chapter, we have considered the pre-Islamic background of Islam and some of the elements within it that figured in the transition to the Islamic period of Arabian and then world history. We have considered how the Qur'an and the Prophet Muhammad appeared on the scene, and, in an inseparable charismatic relationship in a specific historical context, proceeded to form a new religious consciousness and reform Arabian society along monotheistic lines, with a self-conscious connection with the ethical monotheisms of Judaism and Christianity. Allah and his Prophet achieved this and in the process brought forth a new scripture for humanity, the Qur'an. The Qur'an, as live recitation, fit well into the oral-aural world of Arabic poetry and oracular locution. There was something providential about God's speaking through an unlettered servant in a manner that made even the superbly ear-trained Arabs take notice. The Qur'an is considered by Muslims to be the central miracle of the religion, and Muhammad said so, as well, claiming no special powers for himself.

But Islam has another kind of scripture, based on reports of the Prophet's teachings and acts during his career in Mecca and Medina. The Prophet's own behavior came to be regarded as exemplary and is known as the Sunna, remembered, even embodied, through human imitation of Muhammad in the form of habits, procedures, sayings, and the like. It is also known in a literary form called the *ḥadīth*, a report of a specific saying or action of the Prophet. Many thousands of hadith reports have been preserved in authoritative collections. Together they compose the Sunna in literary form. This Sunna became for the umma an authoritative guide for faith and order second only to the Qur'an, which it often interprets and contextualizes. We look at the Prophet's Sunna, his "custom," in Chapter 9 and show how it complements the Qur'an in providing a comprehensive law for the Muslims. In Chapter 6 we review the basic doctrine of Qur'anic monotheism and learn how the belief in the Divine Unity is understood by Muslims.

SCRIPTURE AND TRADITION
QUESTIONS FOR DISCUSSION AND REVIEW

1. Jews, Christians, and Muslims believe that the will of God has been communicated to them in various ways and that scripture records those communications. In what ways has divine revelation come to Jews, Christians, and Muslims? What personages have served as mouthpieces for divine revelation? What sorts of things are "revealed" by a revelation?

2. Judaism, Christianity, and Islam are called religious traditions, and each emerged through a process that included the inventing, reinterpreting, combining, and rejecting of many original traditions. These original traditions, as we have seen, took the form of "oral traditions" that circulated among communities of believers, and some eventually became scripture. What is oral tradition? What manner of things are contained in oral tradition? Who promotes and guards oral tradition? What are some examples of competing and overlapping oral traditions?

3. Over time, oral traditions are inscribed as the sacred books or writings of scripture. In the case of each of the three traditions—Judaism, Christianity and Islam—when and how did the transition from oral tradition to scripture begin? What persons or groups were involved in the process?

4. The process of the formation of scripture is influenced by the social and political settings, the historical circumstances, and the times in which holy writings emerged. How did historical contexts help to shape the content of the Old Testament, the New Testament, and the Qur'an? What local religious

ideas that predated the formation of Jewish, Christian, and Islamic oral tradition and scriptures influence those traditions? In what ways do the scriptures of these three religions evidence the influence of one religion on the other?

5. At some point in the development of scripture, a set collection of writings becomes canonical. How is canon formed? Who decides which writings should be included and which should not? When did the writings of Jews, Christians, and Muslims take the form in which they exist today as canon? What are the canonical writings of each of these three religious traditions?

6. In the long process of the formation of a canon, persons continually seek to interpret the various writings that are candidates for inclusion in a canon. This act of interpretation leads to the acceptance of some writings and the rejection of others. This process of interpretation continues after there has been general agreement on what writings constitute scripture. What is interpretation? Who are the "interpreters" and how do the interpreters "interpret"? Can anyone interpret scripture? Can the writings of some interpreters come to occupy a place of importance alongside scripture? How are such interpretations understood to be related to scripture?

7. The process of interpretation is ongoing, with traditions of interpretation developing in various places at various times. Describe some traditions of interpretation in Judaism, Christianity, and Islam.

PART II

MONOTHEISM

Judaism, Christianity, and Islam are monotheistic religions. Each professes belief in one God, but each differs in certain ways in conceiving that God. In this part, we see how each of these three religious traditions has detailed the meanings of monotheism. We see how the experiences of religious communities influence their reflections on the meanings of monotheism and, conversely, how their embrace of monotheism has conditioned their lived experience of religious community.

Jews, Christians, and Muslims acknowledge scripture as the foundation of their monotheistic worldview. Followers of each tradition, however, read scripture through a variety of lenses. Diverse philosophical, political, ethnic, language, and gender contexts historically have furnished those different lenses, so that even within a single tradition, significant shades of meaning exist. By remaining aware of this fact of diversity, we are able to better understand that monotheism is not an abstract concept, a somehow pure idea that floats in the air over the everyday affairs of human life, and that was at some point in the past simply appropriated by Judaism, Christianity, and Islam for their various purposes. Early Jews, Christians, and Muslims did not select monotheism as a creed in the way one would select a flavor of ice cream. Monotheism grew out of the experiences of a great many communities, taking shape in oral traditions, in writings, in scripture, and through the ongoing process of the interpretation of scripture. What this means, again, is that monotheistic doctrines are reflections of the experience of religious communities in the world.

The constitutive elements of monotheism in each of these three traditions were fashioned through debate, and they continue to undergo refinement, expansion, and alteration by the same process. This should not surprise us, given the difficulty of the questions monotheism provokes, such as, for example, How is God present in the world and yet infinitely distant from it? What is the relation of God to other communities? How is the world of matter related to the God who created it? Debate, as we see, contributes directly to the vitality of monotheism in the West, both within the three major religious traditions and across them.

Our study of monotheism in the West should provoke a wide range of questions for us as well. Some of those questions may intersect with the probings of theologians—scholars who actively represent particular traditions. Other questions will be of a more general nature, about why certain ideas seem to appeal to certain communities, or why communities sometimes undergo revolutions in their thinking about God, or, perhaps, how religion is intertwined with culture. Debate about issues such as these is as important to the vitality of communities of learning as specifically theological debate is to the life of a religious tradition.

CHAPTER 4

MONOTHEISM
IN JUDAISM

STRUCTURING ELEMENTS OF JUDAIC THEOLOGY

The Hebrew Bible was not written in a cultural vacuum. Indeed, its characteristic religious vocabulary draws richly upon the symbols and idiom of the Canaanite and Mesopotamian cultural traditions within which Judaism emerged. For example, biblical images of God appearing amidst thunderous noise (e.g., Exod. 19, Psalm 29) are indebted to ancient Canaanite religious poetry about Baal, the god of the storm. So, too, portrayals of Israel's God presiding over a council of subordinate divine beings (e.g., Psalm 82) retain images associated with El, the chief god of the Canaanite pantheon. Finally, images of God in combat with primordial monsters (e.g., Job 40–41) have much in common with ancient Mesopotamian stories about the creation of the world after a battle among the gods.[1]

Such appropriations of surrounding religious images to express Jewish conceptions did not end with the writing of the Bible. Rather, the long history of Judaism and the worldwide dispersion of the Jews have required Judaism to continuously reinterpret biblical images in terms of cultural traditions that the Jews themselves did not create. In this chapter, we attend to a variety of ways in which Judaic cultures have accomplished this feat of continual theological reinterpretation, in which distinctly Judaic images and ideas are distilled from larger cultural traditions shared by Jews with their neighbors. Of particular interest are two abiding theological preoccupations of Judaism, the uniqueness of God as Creator—monotheism—and the persistent question of how God's biblical promises regarding the redemption of Creation will come to pass—the concept of the Messiah.

God, Torah, Israel, and Messiah

Before moving directly to our analysis, it is important to focus on some of the symbols that inspire such persistent interpretive activity—the structuring theological elements of Judaism or the basic concepts defining its view of the world.

With the exception of the term "Messiah," Judaism's basic symbolic vocabulary received its fundamental definition in the biblical story itself. As we have seen, that story is about a unique and sovereign God, the Creator of Heaven and Earth, who calls into being a special people, Israel, to serve as his means of bestowing blessing upon all humanity. The means of communication between God and Israel is, of course, the Torah, the divine word revealed on Mt. Sinai. Israel's acceptance of the Torah seals the covenantal relation of God and his people. By virtue of it, Israel is empowered to call upon God for protection and sustenance. This triad, God-Torah-Israel, is assumed throughout the Hebrew Bible, in which God is understood simultaneously as the Creator of the World, the Revealer of the Torah, and the Redeemer of Israel.

The fourth key term is a bit more difficult to account for. Etymologically, Messiah means "one who is anointed with oil" to fulfill a divinely appointed purpose. In the Torah, particularly in the book of Leviticus, this term refers frequently to the officiating priest who conducts the sacrificial service in the Tent of Meeting. In the ceremony consecrating him to his task, olive oil was poured on his head (Lev. 8:12). Although the Torah's use of the term had some resonance in certain Jewish writings of the Second Temple period, the meaning that Messiah has had for most of the history of Judaism derives from its usage in the historical and visionary writing collected in Nevi'im, the second section of the scriptural canon.

Here Messiah refers to one anointed to serve as King over the Israelite people in its Land. At least one biblical author, whose work is preserved in the book of Isaiah, conferred this title on the Persian Emperor, Cyrus, whose decree enabled Jews in his realm to resettle the Land of Israel (Isa. 45:1). More often, however, the title of Messiah is ascribed to King David. He is remembered in the historical writings of Nevi'im (I Sam.–II Kings) as the greatest and most loyal of Israel's kings, and in Psalms he is referred to explicitly as the "Anointed" (Ps. 18:51). By extension, the term also refers to all descendents of David's line who sat on his throne. All were Messiahs, sanctified by the oil poured upon them to the sacred task of governing Israel in loyalty to God's Torah. All enjoyed and benefited from the vow that God is said to have made to David: "Your line on the throne of Israel shall never end, if only your descendants will look to their way and walk before me as you have walked before me" (I Kings 8:25).

Now, as the biblical story of Israel's kings develops, it becomes clear that most of them did not "look to their way and walk before" God as David is said to have done. All but a few are depicted as morally unworthy of the sacred task invested in them. One after the other, recalls the Bible, they sinned against God, introduced idolatrous worship into his Temple, and caused (or permitted) Israel to go astray. Indeed, under the guidance of such Messiahs, Israel became so estranged from God that he raised the Babylonian Empire to destroy the kingdom begun by David. The exile to Babylonia is the tragic result.

THE NAMES OF THE GOD OF ISRAEL

Jewish tradition, from the Bible through rabbinic literature, is rich in terms that designate the Creator of Heaven and Earth. In these traditions, the Creator is always imagined as a male, although he may exhibit some feminine traits.

Often, he is referred to in the Bible by his proper name. This is spelled with the Hebrew letters corresponding to Y-H-W-H. How these letters may have been pronounced in ancient Judaism is unclear, for since Second Temple times Jews have routinely avoided its use. Since rabbinic times, Jews reading the biblical text will use the term *Adonai* (Lord) when coming to this name. When you read an English translation of the Bible and come upon the word Lord in reference to God, the underlying Hebrew is probably Y-H-W-H.

Y-H-W-H is referred to in a variety of ways in the Bible. Among the most common is *Elohim* (God). Sometimes this appears in shortened form as *El* as in *El Elyon* (The Supreme God), or *El Shaddai,* an obscure term that probably means "The All-Powerful God."

In rabbinic literature, the most common names for God are *Hakadosh Barukh Hu* (The Blessed Holy One) and *Harakhaman* (The Merciful). Especially in the prayer literature of rabbinic culture, he is invoked by such terms as *Adon Olam* (Eternal Lord), *Goel Yisrael* (Redeemer of Israel), and *Noten Hatorah* (Giver of the Torah). In these names alone, one can find a rich evocation of rabbinic Judaism's conception of *Elohei Yisrael* (The God of Israel). The kabbalistic literature has bequeathed to Judaism the evocative term *En Sof* (The Infinite).

In most forms of Modernist Judaism, the traditional rabbinic terms survive, although most Jews are comfortable with the English "God" or its equivalents in other European languages. Orthodox and Traditionalist Jews in particular tend to prefer the Hebrew circumlocution *HaShem* (The Holy Name), derived from biblical and rabbinic tradition.

Aside from a shadowy figure named Zerubavel, who appears to have led the early post-Exilic community in the Land of Israel in reconstructing the Temple (Hag. 1–2, Zech. 4), the biblical text knows of no Davidic heir who could take up permanent reigns of leadership. For the most part, the Jews of the Second Temple period were governed by priests and scribal deputies who served as officials of the reigning Empire. Even the small Hasmonean Kingdom, which enjoyed independence for less than a century (152–63 BCE), was never led by a Davidic descendant. As centuries passed, glowing prophesies, such as this one from Ezekiel, seemed increasingly difficult to understand:

> My servant David shall be king over them; there shall be one shepherd for all of them. They shall follow my rules and faithfully obey my laws. . . . I will be their God and they shall be my people. And when my sanctuary abides among them forever, the nations shall know that I the Lord do sanctify Israel. (Ezek. 37:24–28)

In place of fulfillment of such prophesies came their interpretation. During the centuries prior to the destruction of the Second Temple in 70, hopes such as Ezekiel's came to be projected against a cosmic, rather than a merely historical and political, screen. Messianic redemption became, for many groups of Jews, much more than restoration of national autonomy in this-worldly historical time. Rather, as the culmination of God's original plan for Creation, it would be presided over by a divinely appointed figure who would be sent to the world by God to signal the end of history, restore all Israel to its Land, preside over the resurrection of the dead, and inaugurate the final Kingdom of God.

Early Christian interpretations of the career of Jesus of Nazareth represent one version of Jewish messianic belief, and historically the most successful. But the thought of a crucified Messiah ultimately had little resonance in hearts that longed for the return of Israel's dominion and kingship. Especially during the post-Christian centuries, in which rabbinic culture gained increasing influence over the Jewish theological imagination, all claimants to the title of Messiah were tested by rather simple criteria. Is the so-called Messiah truly of David's family? Are signs of the Kingdom of God apparent? And, most important, is he a master of Written and Oral Torah? Naturally, the answers to all such questions are matters of interpretation. What can be said is that for most of the history of Judaism, most rabbinic Jews have answered them all in the negative. Whereas the Messiah is believed to be coming, he is never quite here. The promise of God is received in perfect trust, but a sceptical eye is cast upon anyone who would claim to be the fulfillment of the promise. The attitude is well summarized in a piece of rabbinic advice: "If you are about to plant a sapling and you hear the Messiah has come, plant the sapling and then go to greet him" (Avot d'Rabbi Natan B, 31). The Messiah may not be the Messiah, so why waste the tree that will one day bear fruit?

We now review the basic symbolic vocabulary of Judaic theological reflection. God, Torah, and Israel constitute, as it were, the *vertical axis* of Judaic thought. Israel on earth is linked to God in Heaven through the medium of Torah, divine self-disclosure through speech. This stable relationship is dependent upon Israel's loyalty to God, expressed through diligent study and performance of the Torah's commandments. In rabbinic formulations, the commandments must be performed in accord with halakhic norms. The main questions for Jews, from this perspective, are, What has intervened to disrupt this stable relationship? Why is Israel in distress rather than enjoying the blessings of closeness to God on its ancient soil?

At this point, the static, vertical image is supplemented with a *horizontal or historical dimension*—the fact of Israel's rebelliousness and sin. Israel is responsible for its historical situation of exile. But it also has in its hands the means of redemption—the Torah, for the Torah can heal Israel's relationship to God and can thereby hasten the redemptive miracles associated with the Messiah. Through Torah, Israel becomes worthy of God's love, and it is God's love—and pity—that will, in time, bring the Messiah.[2]

Nearly all Judaic theologies have existed since the end of the Second Temple period within this basic structure. Some types of Judaism will stress one element of this structure over others; some will introduce into this structure novel elements or arrange them in distinctive patterns. But the basic elements remain surprisingly stable across the cultural and historical spectrum of Judaism. They are the substance of what any theology must talk about if it is to gain a hearing among Jews. Let's turn, then, to some illustrative cases.

The Structure of Judaism's Basic Symbolic Vocabulary

Vertical Axis of Revelation

God

|

|

|

|

Torah

|

|

|

Israel ———————————— **Mitzvot** ———————————— **Messiah**

Horizontal Axis of Time

In the vertical dimension of Revelation, God's will, expressed as Torah, is disclosed to Israel. In the horizontal plane of time and history, Israel's obedience to the Torah's commandments (*mitzvot*) brings reality to its perfection, with the coming of the Messiah.

Judaic Theology in Diverse Cultural Settings

Monotheism in the Hellenistic Idiom

Steeped as the Hebrew Bible is in Canaanite and Mesopotamian images, the religious culture of early Judaism was equally immersed in an emerging Mediterranean world culture. From the late fourth century BCE and onward, nearly all Jews, wherever they lived, shared in various degrees a larger cultural tradition called *Hellenism*. A form of classical Greek culture that proved infinitely adaptable in many different lands, Hellenism spread throughout the ancient Middle East through the conquests of Alexander the Great, whose empire at the time of his death (323 BCE) stretched from Italy to India.

We cannot here describe the immense diversity of Hellenistic culture, for in each conquered territory the culture of the Greek soldiers and traders who stabilized the territory merged with the dominated cultures to produce a series of local variations on a common Hellenistic theme. Thus, distinctively Greek forms of political association—the independent city or *polis* composed of free citizens—spread throughout the territories under Alexander's domain and took distinctively North African, Syrian, or Mesopotamian forms. Similarly, Greek scientific, philosophical, and literary traditions spread widely and developed in a variety of countries. Most

The Jewish Diaspora of the Greco-Roman Period

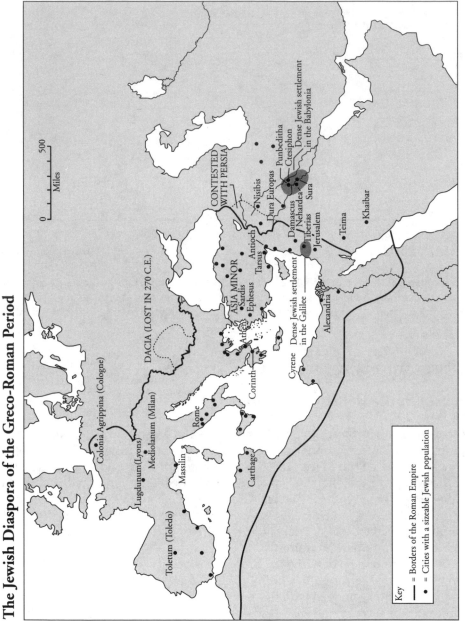

(*Source:* Robert M. Seltzer, *Jewish People, Jewish Thought*, p. 246. Reprinted by permission of Prentice Hall, Upper Saddle River, NJ.)

important from our present perspective, the gods of Greece were included in the religious systems of native populations to produce diverse local syntheses.

Judaism, the provincial culture of one such native population, proved remarkably resistant to Greek polytheism. But Jews began early on to express themselves in terms made available by the larger Hellenistic environments in which they lived. For example, Jews living in Alexandria, a major Egyptian port city and the center of learning in Hellenistic Egypt, developed a rich tradition of reinterpreting Jewish customs and ideas in Greek aesthetic and intellectual terms. Indeed, the most famous Jewish figure of Alexandria—the first-century CE philosopher, Philo—wrote commentaries on the Torah in which he explained and defended Judaism as a system of revealed truth that comprehended and anticipated the purely rational truths known to Greek philosophy. Jews remaining in the Palestinian homeland were equally absorbed into the larger stream of Hellenistic culture. As has been frequently observed, midrashic interpretation of the Bible—which, we recall, the rabbis regard as Mosaic tradition transmitted from Sinai—employs methods and technical terms that are similar to those used by Hellenistic scholars to interpret Greek classics such as the epics of Homer.

Hellenistic cultural traditions, indeed, penetrated beyond the forms of Jewish thought to the core of the Jewish theological vocabulary, seen most clearly in the way Hellenistic Jews imagined and spoke of the God of Israel. Although the Hellenistic world was polytheistic in religion, acknowledging the honor due to a variety of gods, it tended to be monotheistic in philosophy. Hellenistic philosophers—whose interests extended to topics that today might be called physics, psychology, and ethics, as well as metaphysics—grasped a profound unity at the source of all existing things. This unity constituted the universal God or encompassing Mind behind all the diverse gods whose stories were recounted in local mythological traditions. For this reason, when Greek travelers discovered the Jews and learned of their religion, many of them saw in Judaism's monotheism a kindred spirit and concluded that the Jews were a race of philosophers. The Jews had to discover, by a variety of experiments, the degree to which their own conceptions of the God of Israel might or might not fit into Hellenistic models.

For some Jews—Alexandria's Philo is a prime example—the fit was almost complete. Philo interpreted the Bible's Creator of Heaven and Earth as nothing but the Greek Source of All Being; he saw in God's creation of the world through speech a parabolic expression of the philosophical idea that the world was grounded in Mind (*nous*). The world, in turn, was externalized from Mind as the Word (*logos*), which Philo identified with the Torah of Sinai. What the Bible held to be a covenantal contract between Israel and God became, in Philo's system, a metaphysical power through which all reality came into being.

The most difficult element of Jewish thought to articulate in terms of Greek philosophy was the particular connection between the universal God and a particular ethnic group, Israel. Greek philosophy had no need of a deity who, like the God of Israel, chose certain nations for specific revelations denied to others. As noted, Philo addressed this problem with great ingenuity, for example, by viewing the particular covenantal Torah as a principle of universal being. Continuing in this vein, Philo saw Israel as the bearer of philosophical truths that lay at the basis of the power of all rational beings to know God. But even for him, the creative and revealing God was intimately bound up with God, the Redeemer of Israel. The uniqueness of God's relation to Israel could not be so easily glossed over.[3]

Rabbinic literature, because of its vast range, provides the richest source of examples of how certain groups of Hellenistic Jews—those within the influence of the rabbis—used a variety of popular Hellenistic images to imagine the Universal Creator as, at the same time, the particular God of Abraham, Isaac, and Jacob. A common image, which has deep roots as well in the Bible's royal imagery of God, is drawn from the visible trappings of Hellenistic government—the image of God as a heavenly version of the Roman emperor, dwelling in his palace, surrounded by angelic courtiers and bureaucrats. The image is developed in many rabbinic parables in which a biblical verse imputing an attribute to God is followed by the phrase: "What is this like? It is like a king of flesh and blood."[4]

A helpful example is the following fourth-century rabbinic Bible commentary (Sifre Deut. 306):

> Rabbi Judah used to say: It is like a king of flesh and blood who had administrators in his province. He made an agreement with them and handed over his son to them, saying: Whenever my son does my will, be nice, refresh him, indulge and feed him, and let him drink. But when he does not do my will, do not let him touch anything of mine. Similarly, when Israel does the will of God, what is said concerning them?— "The Lord will open for you his bounteous store, the heavens." (Deut. 28:12) And when Israel does not do the will of God, what is said concerning them?—"For the Lord's anger will flare up against you, and he will shut up the skies so that there will be no rain." (Deut. 11:17)

In this parable, God's relationship to Israel is modeled upon that of an earthly king who must delegate his child rearing to deputies. The text even uses the Greek term *epitropoi* to describe these administrators, who constantly enact the king's will regarding the son's rearing. This serves as the model for understanding the biblical image of Heaven offering or withholding rain in response to Israel's loyalty to the Torah. Natural forces, universally available to all humanity, are the "deputies" of the Master of the World, doing his particular will in response to Israel's merits. The universality of God, imagined through the political images of Rome's world empire, is defined as perfectly compatible with his specific relationship to Israel.

The degree to which Jews shared Hellenistic conceptions of the world is particularly evident in certain forms of religious contemplation. Some ancient texts portray rabbis as having cultivated a kind of heavenly travel in which, at the end, they glimpsed a vision of the Creator of the World sitting on his throne surrounded by ministering angels. These visionary writers imagine the cosmos in terms common to the rest of the Hellenistic world, that is, the present world is a domain of coarse materiality, above which stretches a series of seven planetary spheres beginning with the moon and ending with Saturn, each more rarified and ethereal than that beneath it. At the top, beyond Saturn, lies the sphere of the fixed stars, the signs of the Zodiac, which govern the destinies of all beings, including

The Ptolemaic Cosmos of Greco-Roman Antiquity

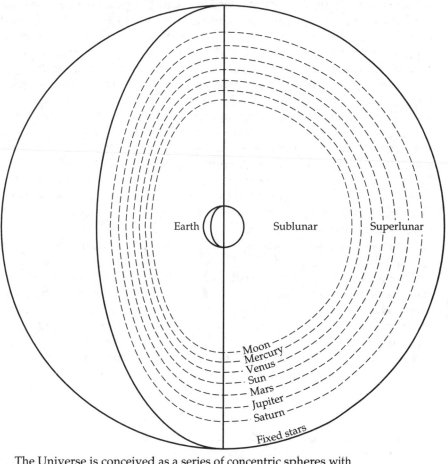

Earth   Sublunar   Superlunar

Moon
Mercury
Venus
Sun
Mars
Jupiter
Saturn
Fixed stars

The Universe is conceived as a series of concentric spheres with the Earth at the core and the ethereal sphere of the fixed stars at the periphery. In many religious systems of the Hellenistic world, the spatial movement from the core to the periphery corresponds to a progressive refinement of being, from coarsest materiality to the most rarified spirituality. (*Source:* Luther H. Martin, *Hellenistic Religions: An Introduction.* Used by permission of Oxford University Press.)

the gods. Many seekers in the Hellenistic world sought to travel in contemplation beyond the stars, to experience the final freedom from death in this life.

This general conception of the geography of religious experience shapes the imagination of the rabbinic heavenly traveler as well, even as he defines a distinctly Judaic version of the Hellenistic heavens. Hellenistic travelers, of course, must pass through the seven planetary spheres known to Hellenistic astronomy. Their rabbinic counterpart must ascend through a series of seven heavenly *hekhalot*. The term *hekhal* ("chamber" or "hall") is borrowed from the great chamber of the Temple that contained the Ark of the Covenant, above which hovered the Divine Glory. But in the rabbinic conception, each such chamber is arranged in a cosmic ladder, each rung guarded by an angelic keeper who attempts to bar him entrance. Upon reciting a series of secret charms, or answering certain riddles, the visionary ascends still higher until, entering the seventh hall, he passes beyond the stars and the signs of the Zodiac toward the actual "Chariot" (*merkavah*) of God.

The Chamber of the Chariot Room corresponds to the inner sanctuary of the Temple, where God's presence once engulfed the officiating priest. Now it is a heavenly realm beyond the power of destiny and death in which the traveler, like his priestly predecessor, enters eternity. And whom does he encounter? Not an abstract Cosmic Mind, but the Holy One of Israel and his angels. There the traveler prays with them as they praise and sanctify God in the liturgy Israel uses on earth: "Holy, holy, holy is the Lord of hosts, the whole world is full of his glory." Upon his descent to earth, a careful retracing of the method of ascent itself, the traveler then shares with his disciples the outlines of his vision and teaches them to achieve it themselves.[5]

Here, as in the case of the parables of the king of flesh and blood, rabbinic Judaism draws upon commonly available images of the world—images shared by all members of society—to articulate in particular its own distinctive conception of the universal God as the Holy One of Israel. The cultural idiom shows the similarity of Jewish religious aspirations to those of their neighbors: to escape mortality for immortality. Yet the symbols are distinctive to Judaism, expressing its fundamental conviction of the Jews' special place in the cosmic scheme, however that scheme may be imagined.

Messianism in Islamic and Christian Settings

Rabbinic Judaism, then, richly mined the political and cosmological images of polytheistic Hellenism in order to express its own monotheistic theology. Yet most of the history of Judaism has, in fact, proceeded under Christianity and Islam, great monotheistic civilizations that regarded themselves as inheritors and masters of Hellenistic culture. The former dominated the territory of the Roman Empire from the early fourth century onward. The latter, from the seventh century, constituted the primary religious culture of the Middle Eastern centers of Jewish population. Our present concern will be the interaction, within these cultures, of rabbinic and popular Jewish thought regarding the crucial historical concept of Judaism—the connection between God's governance of the world and messianic redemption from Exile.

From the eighth through the fourteenth centuries, Jews experienced Islam and Christianity in diverse geographical and cultural settings. Ancient Jewish communities in Palestine (Israel), Babylonia (Iraq), and Persia (Iran) predated and witnessed the Islamic transformation of these territories; likewise, Jews followed

Islam into the Iberian peninsula (Spain and Portugal) in the eighth century and remained until both Jews and Muslims alike were expelled by Catholic conquerors in the thirteenth through fifteenth centuries. European Jews, for their part, had begun settling in trade centers of Germany and France even prior to the Christianization of the Roman Emperor. They formed the foundation of a western and central European Jewish culture that, from the tenth century onward, would call itself Ashkenaz, after an obscure biblical place. Ashkenazic Jews understood themselves to constitute a Jewish community with linguistic, cultural, and ritual traditions distinct from the Jews of Spain (Sephardic Jews) and other Islamic lands.

Details about the culture of Ashkenazic and Sephardic Jewries occupy us in Chapter 16 and the diverse character of their social and political experience is explored in Chapter 19. For now we must be satisfied with a few general traits shared by most Jewish communities of the medieval period. First, the legal conditions under which Jews lived encouraged them to form close-knit communities, normally under the authority of rabbinic experts in talmudic law. Although rabbinic applications of halakhah were by no means identical in all locales, enough of a shared tradition of rabbinic learning existed to ensure much continuity across diverse geographical and cultural areas. A second constant of great importance in understanding the Judaism of this period is that wherever Jews lived, they were dominated politically and socially by monotheistic peoples claiming to have the authoritative versions of the revelation originally offered to Israel.

In Christian lands, Jews were regarded as remnants of those "scribes and Pharisees" of the New Testament who, out of blindness to the plain meaning of their scriptures, had persecuted the Son of God. As a cursed community, Jews were permitted only limited privileges regarding where they could live and how they could pursue their livelihoods. In Islamic lands, Jews shared with Christians and some other communities the status of a "protected population" (Arabic: *ahl al-dhimma*). As monotheists, they could be permitted to live among Muslims, but they were subjected to taxation and other disabilities that ensured their second-class social status. Insofar as Jews in particular are recalled in the Qur'an to have rejected Mohammad's claim to prophecy, they often bore the opprobrium of those regarded as persecutors of God's final Messenger.

Whereas the political and social domination of the Jews made excellent practical and theological sense from Christian or Islamic perspectives, it was, of course, both a practical burden and a theological puzzle for Judaism. Scripture had indeed predicted that a rebellious Israel would one day be subjugated to nations that did not know the God of Israel. But why had God chosen to punish his people at the hands of others who claimed to inherit the revelation originally given to Israel? Throughout this period, an old rabbinic model of biblical interpretation was routinely applied and amplified. The dominating Islamic and Christian empires were personified as descendants of Ishmael and Esau, the elder brothers of Isaac and Jacob, respectively (Gen. 21, 27–28). Because of its sins, Israel had been placed under the heel of brothers who had originally been rejected from covenantal closeness to God. But how long would he wait to reveal to the world that his *original* chosen community remained the *only* such community? It is not surprising, then, that throughout the period under discussion, many Jews became preoccupied with the question of messianic redemption.

In the Middle East, Islam's sudden conquest of a seemingly universal Christian empire seems to have quickened messianic expectations among both rabbinic scholars and the masses. Shortly after the establishment of Islamic rule, rabbinic authors began to produce elaborate theoretical works about the signs of the advent of the Messiah. For the most part, however, rabbinic messianic concerns remained confined to literary speculation. Genuine messianic uprisings, to the contrary, in which masses of Jews acknowledged a living person as the Messiah, seem almost exclusively to be the product of spontaneous, popular sentiment rather than the result of rabbinic instigation.

In Persia in particular, from the seventh century onward, Muslim and Karaite historians documented a series of Jewish messianic movements under inspired leaders innocent of disciplined rabbinic training. One of the first, led by Abu Isa of Isfahan, involved an armed revolt against Muslim rule and had to be crushed by the army of the Abbasid Caliph Abd al-Malik. Abu Isa died in the fighting, yet his followers—perhaps influenced by Persian-Islamic traditions regarding the hidden Imam (Arabic: "leader")—maintained for generations the belief that his death was illusory. He lived yet and was expected to return at some future moment to lead them back to the Land of Israel, where he would establish his kingship.

Another well-known movement thrived in the twelfth century around Daud al-Ruhi (David of the Spirit) of Azerbaijan. Like his predecessor, al-Ruhi also incited local Jews to violent and anti-Islamic resistance; and like Abu Isa, the latter, too, was killed. Nevertheless, in the name of al-Ruhi, Jews are reported to have taken to the roofs of their houses at midnight, expecting to sprout wings with which they would fly to Jerusalem, there to greet the Messiah and help him rebuild the Temple. Similar events continued to be reported well into the twelfth century in Baghdad and elsewhere.[6]

All we know of these messianic movements, unfortunately, is recorded by observers—Muslim, Karaite, and rabbinic—who regarded them as preposterous fantasies of unlettered fools. It is difficult, therefore, to infer what the messianists thought about matters such as God's will and the meaning of messianic redemption. Their theology is lost to us in the works that preserve memory of their deeds. Therefore, for the richest information on how Jews thought of God's role in the process of messianic deliverance, we must turn to rabbinic theological writings, which record the beliefs of a small but influential elite within Jewry.

From the thirteenth century and onward, Jewish theological thought was expressed in a new idiom that began to have great appeal among many rabbinic scholars. Called Kabbalah, we met it briefly at the end of Chapter 1. Originating in eleventh-century Christian Provence (Southern France), spreading rapidly to areas of Spain recently recovered from Muslim control, and from there to Islamic North Africa and the Middle East, Kabbalah quickly became an international theological idiom among rabbinic scholars and their chosen disciples.[7]

The primary vehicle of the Kabbalah's spread was a book, the Zohar (Book of

Splendor). For the most part, it was probably the work of the late-thirteenth-century rabbinic kabbalist Moses b. Shemtov de Leon of Guadalajara. Composed, however, in the style and languages of ancient rabbinic midrashic and talmudic literature, the Zohar represents itself as the teachings of the famous mishnaic sage and martyr Rabbi Simeon b. Yohai. After some controversy attending its "discovery" by de Leon, the Zohar was taken by many to constitute an authentic mystical midrash from mishnaic times. Moses de Leon surely viewed his own role in its production not as a forger, but as a prophetic vehicle of ancient tradition. At any rate, kabbalists came to regard the Zohar as a key without which the true meaning of the Torah was all but inaccessible. This key enabled the holder to identify and even participate in hidden moments in the internal life of the divine Mind. Many kabbalists held, in fact, that halakhically prescribed ritual and meditative practices could have a profound impact upon God's life, an impact so powerful that the coming of the Messiah would be an inevitable result. Thus, the Zohar reaffirmed in its own way the intimate connection between God, the Torah, and messianic redemption.

How did kabbalists imagine that they could attain such intimate and influential knowledge of the divine Mind? The central assumption of the Zohar is that the Torah, as divine Speech, reveals the psychology of the divine Speaker, just as human speech reveals that of the human speaker. This conception, of course, bears some similarity to Philo's conception of God as Mind, who externalizes the world in Speech. The kabbalistic tradition found in the Zohar, however, seems to have reached this idea independently of Philo and certainly took it in directions Philo would never have imagined. The letters, words, and stories of the Torah, in the Zohar's view, are but the most external expressions of a divine inner life that undergirds all existence. And that inner life is indeed something to behold.

Drawing upon traditions of thought deeply embedded in Christian and Islamic interpretations of Hellenistic philosophy, the Kabbalists imagined God as an infinite, unknowable source of vitality. Beyond form, beyond gender, beyond all concepts of any kind, God nevertheless stands at the foundation of all existing things. In this unknowable form, God is identified as *En Sof*, the "Infinite." What we can know about God are the aspects of divine being that link the known world to the unknown divine foundation of being. These knowable aspects of divine being are hinted at in the Torah; the Kabbalah calls them *Sefirot* ("spheres of being"). These Sefirot, ten in number, are nothing less than the creative powers of God. Understood as pairs of gendered opposites—male and female, compassion and judgment, right and left—they proceed out of the infinite divine Nothingness, combining and interacting in various ways to produce all dimensions of natural and supernatural reality. The task of the kabbalist is to know the various relations of these sefirotic powers and, surprising as it may seem, to use his own powers of thought, word, and deed to trace and even alter their interaction.

How is it possible for humans to alter divine powers, and why should they need to? The Zohar's answer brings us to the heart of the Kabbalah's concerns. The Torah's stories of repeated human disobedience to God are hidden references to the fact that since creation, human rebelliousness has upset the proper balance of

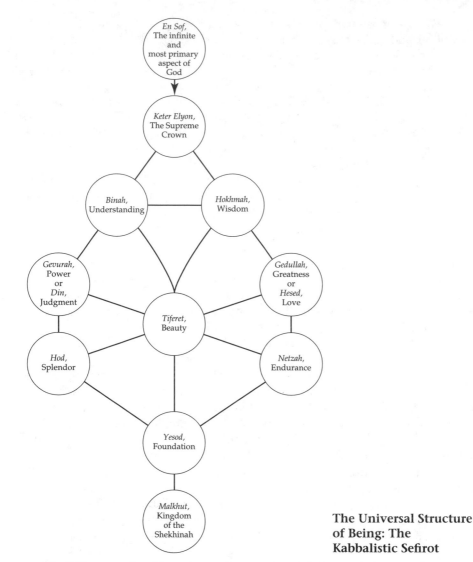

The Universal Structure of Being: The Kabbalistic Sefirot

The Sefirot are often likened to a "Cosmic Tree" or "Primordial Man," the form of which is taken to underlie all existing things, the way DNA encodes the potential of biological organisms. The primordial expression of the Sefirot is in the unfolding of Divine Consciousness from the Nothingness of En Sof. This is called the "World of Emanation" (*olam ha-atzilut*). Once unfolded, this Divine Consciousness expresses itself in creative activity that produces three "Lower Worlds," those of "Formation" (*yetzirah*), "Creation" (*beriah*), and "Action" (*asiyah*). The latter is the empirical world of human experience. Insofar as all worlds share the identical sefirotic structure, it is possible for events in the world of Emanation to impact upon lower worlds, just as it is possible for events in the world of Action to alter the structure of the upper worlds. (*Source:* Robert M. Seltzer, *Jewish People, Jewish Thought,* p. 431. Reprinted by permission of Prentice Hall, Upper Saddle River, NJ.)

divine powers in the world of the Sefirot. The original creation, at the time of the Garden of Eden, was perfect and harmonious because all the sefirotic powers were in their proper order and relation, enabling the vitality of the divine life to perfectly infuse all aspects of reality. Human sin, however, disrupted this harmony. All of history, as the Torah describes it, is an attempt to restore that original harmony. This, indeed, is why the Torah was given to Israel—to enable God's special nation to use the Torah as a medium for restoring the proper balance of divine powers. Properly restored, the sefirotic channels will enable the vitality of divine blessing to reinfuse the world as at the moment of creation.

You will have by now guessed that the restoration of proper order in God's inner life has a crucial outward manifestation in nature and history—the fulfillment of the messianic promise. The restoration of the world to its primordial perfection is at the same time the moment at which Israel is restored to its Land. At that moment, with humanity streaming to Jerusalem to join Israel in sacrificial service in the Temple, all the world reenacts the original situation of Eden, all life combines to stand in perfect love and obedience to God. "The unity of the upper and lower worlds," in the Zohar's idiom, is complete. The immediate awareness of God, impossible in historical time because of the disruptive power of sin, will be unhindered at the end of time, available to all.

The central role in the restoration of the harmony of the divine inner life is, of course, played by Israel. It does so by following the commandments of the Torah in total and wholehearted devotion. Each commandment, when performed in accord with the requirements established by the halakhah, and in Kabbalistic awareness of their cosmic impact, has the power to cause a small modification in the divine life in the direction of unification and harmonization. Each failure to perform a commandment, similarly, introduces yet another small note of discord into the divine life. The intention of the Kabbalah is to encourage Jews to comply totally with halakhic norms so that the collective power of obedience will overwhelm the forces of discord and reestablish the original state of sefirotic harmony. In a genuine sense, then, the precursor of messianic redemption is Israel itself. Its loyal obedience alone sets the stage for an almost reflexive act of God that brings the promised Messiah into history as a necessary consequence.

In comparison to the popular messianic activism we have already observed, the Zohar's scholarly messianic theory is largely pacifist. The key to redemption has nothing to do with organized political action, nor is redemption conceived in political terms. Rather, redemption is essentially a metaphysical concept that is made concrete in history by Jews who are following the basic principles of halakhah under the guidance of rabbinic authorities. Some talmudic traditions had long ago asserted that the Messiah would come if all Israel kept the Sabbath or offered proper prayers three times a day. The Zohar is an immensely complex expression of this view in the images of Spanish metaphysical parable.

Despite this contemplative focus on ritual life as the means for stimulating redemptive developments, traditions that developed on the basis of zoharic thought eventually produced a variety of more activist postures. One of them, in the mid-seventeenth century, occasioned the most disruptive messianic movement in the history of Judaism, encompassing Jews of Islamic and Christian lands alike. This most recent Messiah, a Turkish Jew named Shabbatai Zvi, drew to himself an avid following. Handsome in appearance and gifted with a charismatic personality, Shabbatai Zvi was also driven at times to exhibitionistic violations of major and minor aspects of halakhah. For example, he at times would eat foods, such as certain types of animal fat, that were forbidden by the biblical dietary code. On one occasion, he is said to have celebrated all the major festivals of the Jewish calendar in a single week.

These "strange practices," as they were called, normally drew reactions from ridicule to pity. Nevertheless, some were convinced, on the basis of little-known traditions in the Talmud, the Zohar, and later kabbalistic writings, that such behavior indicated that the messianic age—when the restrictions of the Torah would be lifted—was dawning. The dawn came, on September 16, 1666, in a totally unexpected way. After some months of confinement in a Turkish prison on charges of political agitation, the Messiah was granted an interview in the court of the Ottoman Sultan. Instead of demanding the prerogatives of his messianic office, however, Shabbatai Zvi denied any knowledge of his messianic mission. Moreover, clearly in fear for his life, he displayed his sincerity by converting to Islam. Changing his name to Aziz Mehmed Effendi, he was rewarded with a royal pension.

The conversion of the Messiah did not kill the hopes of his followers any more than a crucified Messiah had disappointed the disciples of Jesus fifteen hundred years earlier. To the contrary, it inflamed them. Interpreted in kabbalistic terms, the conversion of Shabbatai Zvi was trumpeted by some as the proof of his messianic calling. He had merely descended into the depths of cosmic evil in order to redeem from imprisonment all the sparks of divine life that, since creation, had awaited their restoration to the fullness of the Sefirot. As Messiah, Shabbatai Zvi had redeemed God; God would now act to inaugurate the final messianic drama.

That drama, of course, never received its staging. Nevertheless, Jewries throughout Europe and the Middle East were torn in controversy over the status of Shabbatai Zvi's messianic claims. Some believers followed their Messiah into Islam. Others, in Europe, converted to Catholicism. Thousands remained within Judaism but continued to await the outer signs of the inner redemption he had made available. Not even the death of the Messiah in 1676 killed belief in his mission. The Shabbatean movement survived "underground" for centuries in Islamic and Christian lands despite severe political antagonism from governments and furious religious repression by rabbinic leaders. Even into the nineteenth and twentieth centuries, the epithet "Shabbatean!" threatened many Jews who attempted to radically alter Jewish social, political, or religious life in response to the dawning modern age.[8]

JUDAIC THOUGHT IN MODERN EUROPEAN CULTURE

Throughout centuries of life in Christian and Islamic lands, Jews lived among people for whom the reality of God was unquestioned. Christians, Muslims, and Jews could all agree on the basic fact that a universal God had created the world and

Waare afbeeldinge van Sabetha Sebi *den genaemden herſteller des Joodtſchen Rijcks.*

ij pourtrait de Sabbathai Sevi *qui ſe dict Restaura teur du Roïaume de Juda & Iſrael.*

Shabbatai Zvi, the Seventeenth-Century Messiah

This portrait of Shabbatai Zvi is said to have been made by an eyewitness to his activity in Smyrna, Turkey. It was published in Amsterdam in 1669 by Thomas Coenen, a Protestant minister. Chaplain to the Dutch merchant community in Smyrna, Coenen took great interest in documenting the excitement surrounding Shabbatai Zvi's career as a Messiah. (*Source:* Robert M. Seltzer, *Jewish People, Jewish Thought*, p. 471. Reproduced by permission of Prentice Hall, Upper Saddle River, NJ.)

continued to guide its destiny. Disagreements concerned details—whether God's revelation was most clearly manifest in the Torah, in Christ, or in the Qur'an; or whether his love was most uniquely available within Israel, the Church, or the Umma. By the seventeenth century, however, the situation had begun to change, especially in Christian Europe.

The theological foundations of European Christendom had begun to crack under the pressure of the sixteenth-century Reformation, and with them the social and political arrangements of medieval Europe. Such powerful forces as the emergence of empirical natural and historical sciences, the development of international capitalist economies, and the disintegration of political absolutism had, by the middle of the eighteenth century, raised in the European trading classes hopes for radical transformations of traditional social patterns. Among these was the displacement of the Church from the center of intellectual and political life and the creation of societies in which religious traditions and institutions would play a private rather than a public role.

With the entry of many western and central European Jews into the life of modern states in the eighteenth and nineteenth centuries, the Judaism of European Jewry began to undergo massive changes as well. In Chapters 10 and 19, we describe the social changes in greater detail. For our present purposes, however, it is helpful to point to changes in the European intellectual world, in particular, the various rationalist or secularist programs for perfecting human society known collectively as the "Enlightenment." This movement, and others in its wake, had a profound impact upon Jewish conceptions of God and the question of messianic redemption. A schematic model of Judaic theological discussion in modern times will help to sort out some of the details.[9]

Recall for a moment what we identified at the beginning of this chapter as the basic elements of Jewish theology. The vertical axis of ideas connects God to Israel through the Torah; the horizontal plane links Israel to messianic deliverance at the end of history, again through the Torah. This basic structure is the framework of modern Jewish thought as well, although each term undergoes dramatic reinterpretation. We may detect three basic interpretive patterns within which most of the modern and contemporary forms of Jewish thought can be organized. For convenience's sake, we'll call them the "Secularist," the "Modernist," and the "Traditionalist" patterns. All of them, in one way or another, responded in very basic ways to the general currents of modern European social and political thought.

Let us turn first to the Secularist pattern. Some of the most influential forms of Secularist Jewish thought, especially those associated with Socialism or Zionism, were inspired by European efforts to usher in a new epoch of world history through a radical transformation of medieval society and politics. Socialism and nationalism were among the most important of these European ideologies, and many Jews attempted to transform Jewish society as well according to socialist or nationalist theories. Naturally, the attempt to think about the Jews in wholly secular categories had important effects on the way the theological elements of Judaism were conceived.

Following the tendency of secularist revolutionary movements to ground

MAIN JEWISH IDEOLOGICAL/RELIGIOUS RESPONSES TO MODERNITY: THE NINETEENTH-CENTURY MOVEMENTS

Secularist Responses

1. *Zionism:* Emerging in eastern Europe in the 1880s among secularized young intellectuals, the movement identified the Jews as a national group similar in character to other emerging European nations. By 1904, under the leadership of the Viennese Jew Theodore Herzl, Zionism became a vocal advocate for Jewish national rights in Ottoman Palestine.

2. *Bundism (Jewish Socialism):* Like Zionism, a movement of young eastern European intellectuals attracted by ideas of revolutionary social change. Rejecting nationalism on ideological grounds as an expression of Capitalism, Bundists sought to solve the problems of Jewish poverty and exploitation by joining forces with non-Jewish Socialist revolutionaries.

Modernist Responses

1. *Reform:* The German movement for reform of synagogue worship developed from 1810 to 1840 into a comprehensive theory of how Judaism might be freed from halakhic norms so as to survive in modern culture. Led for decades by Abraham Geiger, Reform was particularly powerful in western and central Europe, spreading to North America by the 1850s.

2. *Orthodoxy:* Originally a movement of German Jews wishing to be legally regarded as a Jewish community separate from Reform, Orthodoxy developed by the 1850s into a self-consciously "modern" movement attracting western and central European Jews. Its main ideological leader Samson Raphael Hirsch argued that strict loyalty to the laws of the Torah could coexist with rich participation in the intellectual, cultural, and political life of modern nations.

3. *Positive-Historical (in North America, "Conservative"):* Born of the conflict between Reform and Orthodoxy, Positive-Historical Judaism sought to avoid Reform's antihalakhic bias and Orthodoxy's commitment to a literal theory of revelation. Holding that the Torah was in great measure a historically evolving pattern of Jewish life, leaders such as Zachariah Frankel held that halakhic norms could be carefully changed so as to permit greater Jewish participation in modern life. A minor movement in Europe, it became very popular among North American Jewish immigrants from eastern Europe from the 1880s onward.

   Reconstructionist Judaism established its independence from Conservative Judaism during the 1930s and is today a rapidly growing North American synagogue movement committed to the idea of "Judaism as a civilization" rather than as a formal belief in theological ideas.

Traditionalist Responses

Centered mostly in central and eastern Europe, Traditionalists are usually divided into *Hasidism* and *Mitnagdism,* both of which have their roots in the eighteenth century. The former movement is usually characterized by close circles of devoted followers of a charismatic holy man (*Tzaddik*). The latter movement, rejecting such Tzaddiks as religious charlatans, tend to revere more mainstream rabbinic scholars. By the nineteenth century, both groups saw that they needed to take common cause against the various modernizing movements of central and western Europe. Small, but vigorous, Traditionalist communities thrive today in North America, Israel, and Europe.

Mapping the Modernization of Jewish Thought

In order to keep track of the ways in which European Jews reinterpreted their basic symbols (God-Torah-Israel-Messiah), it is helpful to keep the following in mind.

Modes of Nineteenth- to Twentieth-Century European Thought That Influenced Jews

1. *Nationalism:* Humanity is divided into competing national groups. Each shares a common language, land, history, and political future. The goal of the nation is the creation of an independent state on its own territory.

   > Nationalism undermined traditional religious loyalties by making the national state, not the religious community, the ultimate object of citizen's allegiance.

2. *Historicism:* The past is best known by critical sifting of various sorts of evidence. Historical knowledge is built upon "objective facts" that can be established by historical study.

   > Historicism undermined traditional religious belief by casting doubt upon the historical reliability of religious writings such as the Bible.

3. *Scientific Naturalism:* The natural world is governed by "objective laws" that scientific experiment can discover. Science is the process of discovering these laws.

   > Scientific Naturalism undermined traditional religious belief by showing that biblical stories of creation, for example, contradicted the findings of geology.

Jewish Reactions (Western and Eastern Europe, North America)

1. *Secularism (Socialism/Zionism):* These scientific ideologies viewed the Jews as an oppressed nation that could relieve its oppression through political means.

   > God was replaced by history as the source of moral norms. Israel was no longer the Chosen People, but an oppressed nation yearning to be free. Torah became the national folklore. Messiah was reinterpreted as the people's liberation from persecution.

2. *Modernism (Reform, Positive-Historical, Orthodoxy):* These religious movements embraced the idea of the Jews as a "faith community" politically loyal to the non-Jewish nation in which it lives. God and Torah were stressed as sources of ethical values. Israel was the community of faith destined to share these ethical values with humanity. All awaited the final spread of these values in the coming Messianic Era of human liberation.

The groups differed on the extent to which they regard the Torah as an actual revelation of unchanging laws. They also disagreed on how much of modern scientific and historical thought could be permitted to enter Jewish thought, especially regarding revelation of the Torah.

3. *Traditionalism (Hasidism and Its Eastern European Opponents):* Bitterly divided over the legitimacy of hasidic charismatic leadership, all Traditionalists nevertheless shared an absolute rejection of western European Jewish Secularism and Modernism.

   Traditionalists retained the fully supernatural premodern understandings of God-Torah-Israel-Messiah.

their claims to truth in the prestige of science and empirical observation, Jewish Socialists (in Yiddish: *Bundists*) and Zionists often abandoned belief in God altogether, viewing all religious ideas as tools by which exploitive, elite institutions of the propertied classes maintained social and political control over the masses. Clearly, then, if the Torah had any place in a future Jewish society, it could not be as a revealed source of eternally binding laws! Accordingly, many Bundists and Zionists conceded that the Torah was an indispensable historical document created by Jewish tradition itself. But as a prescientific collection of superstition and fantasy, it could be granted no authority over modern Jews. A kind of national folklore, it could be preserved as a cultural heritage and source of historical identity, but not as a covenantal medium of communication with the God of Israel.

In fact, the only element of the vertical axis to retain its plausibility was Israel, the Jewish people. But here, too, there was a difference. Israel ceased to be the Bible's "kingdom of priests and a holy nation." Instead, it was conceived as a historical community of language and blood-relationship analogous to the emerging national groups of Europe. Because images of Israel as the obedient servant of God were seen as outmoded survivals of the "Age of Religion," the conception of Israel as the sinning, wayward covenant-partner also lost its meaning. The tragic history of Exile was now understood sociologically; no longer punishment for rebellion, it was reinterpreted as oppression under the irrational, prescientific prejudices of Gentile powers.

Such a reconception had necessary reverberations as well along the horizontal, messianic axis of traditional Jewish thought. Instead of awaiting the Messiah by serving God through the Torah, the Jews could and should work to end their history of oppression and contribute to the creation of a new world characterized by justice for all nations. Thus, political revolution, the technological transformation of society, or other visions of profound social change constituted the goal of all history to which the Jews could contribute. For many Jews, belief in a dawning age of political and social justice replaced the miraculous events associated with traditional messianic images. Whereas Bundism was effectively crushed by Stalinist persecutions during the 1930s, Zionism went on to create a Jewish state in the ancient homeland. As a national ideology, it continues to shape the identity of many Jewish Israelis who regard themselves as alien to Judaism as a system of religion.

The Modernist strand of modern Jewish tradition is, in fact, a variety of diverse movements. Much divided them, but all shared a commitment to redefining Jewish religious belief and practice so that these could continue to nourish Jews committed to the emerging European culture of scientific reason and national identity. Mostly German or central European in origin, the Modernist movements still survive as contemporary Reform Judaism, Conservative Judaism, and some types of Orthodoxy. Reconstructionist Judaism, beginning in the 1930s as an offshoot of the Conservative movement, is unique to American Jewry. The original nineteenth-century Modernist groups were no less in touch with progressive European trends of thought than were their Secularist competitors. But they retreated from political revolution. Instead they argued that the Jews could thrive in Europe only through the reinterpretation of Judaism as an apolitical religious faith suitable for citizens of religiously neutral civil societies.

Under the impact of these concerns, the essence of Jewish faith was usually identified with those aspects of the vertical axis of Jewish thought, such as monotheism, regarded as fostering high ethical ideals and universal humanist values. As with the ancient philosopher Philo, Jewish Modernists stressed the universal concern of God for all humanity, expressed especially in the idea of God as Creator. Less emphasized were particularistic biblical images of God as Redeemer of Israel.

Modernists still regarded the Torah as a profound religious text, for it constituted an important cultural link with Europeans, who revered it as part of the Christian Old Testament. But, except within Orthodoxy, the belief in the revelation of an Oral and Written Torah at Sinai was usually reinterpreted more naturalistically. Increasingly, the biblical scriptures and the traditions of the Talmud were seen as human creations representing the moral teachings of brilliant prophets and sages. Though important, they could not stand in the way of further development by contemporary Jews. The importance of halakhic traditions, too, was rethought. Most Modernist circles prized the halakhic tradition as a source of ethical teachings rather than as a code of binding laws that would require Jews to distinguish themselves socially and culturally from non-Jews. In Chapters 10 and 13, we explore some of the implications of this view for the modern shape of Jewish religious practice.

As with our Secularist model, the Modernist reinterpretation of the vertical axis of Jewish thought has reverberations on the historical plane as well. In general, whatever was regarded as unscientific or ethnocentric by European standards came under careful scrutiny. Some Modernist circles, particularly within the Reform communities, abandoned all belief in the Davidic Messiah who would miraculously lead Israel back to its ancient Land, rebuild the Temple, and preside over the resurrection of the dead. They viewed the Modern Age aborning as the hoped-for Messianic Era in which all peoples would dwell in peace.

Others, represented by Positive-Historical or Conservative Judaism, retained a formal commitment to premodern assertions of messianic belief, tacitly assuming all the same that such beliefs were peripheral rather than central to Judaism.

Such Jews took great pains to point out that messianic beliefs had little historical or political relevance in the present age. They were merely hopes that would be realized in some distant future. In the meantime, Jews would be content and honored to participate with their fellow citizens in the betterment of society and the general human march toward progress.

Other Modernists, often grouped under the label Orthodoxy, were as committed to European culture as they were to retaining most of the miraculous elements of premodern monotheistic and messianic theory. They insisted upon the historical factuality of the biblical and rabbinic pictures of revelation and used their university educations to supply historical arguments to support their views. They regarded the halakhic tradition as absolutely authoritative and demonstrated how even the most obscure of halakhic norms contained crucial ethical messages. Citing excellent talmudic precedents, they held fast to rabbinic conceptions of the messianic days, though they discouraged speculation about the precise moment of its dawning. Jews, they insisted, harbored no imminent hopes of national restoration and so could be regarded as loyal citizens and full participants in the destinies of the lands in which they lived.

Modernists of whatever variety dominated the theological discourse of western and central European Jewry. But a third important pattern of modern Jewish thought, the Traditionalist, was embraced by small groups in western and central Europe. Its largest following, however, lay in the huge Jewish populations of the eastern lands of the Austro-Hungarian and Russian Empires. In some ways the Traditionalists are the most difficult to characterize. In the first place, Modernist Orthodoxy had strong sentimental affinities with Traditionalism and often took similar positions on questions of an halakhic character. So both Traditionalists and the Modernist Orthodox share much. But the Modernist Orthodox regarded the Traditionalists, who had no interest in European culture, as "primitive." Traditionalists, for their part, viewed the Orthodox as "assimilationists" who had an unhealthy desire to imitate non-Jewish fashions.

A second difficulty in understanding Traditionalism is that it was often understood by both Modernists and Traditionalists themselves as a direct continuation of premodern Judaism, untouched by modern culture. In some ways, this is so. The more inflexible Traditionalists, for example, categorically rejected all forms of modern social, political, and philosophical thought as "defiled." They refused to accept most of the occupational and social patterns of modern European culture, often closing themselves quite willingly in Jewish enclaves and refusing to send their children to available public schools. Intellectually, they continued to inhabit the thought world of the Talmud and of Kabbalah long after other Jews abandoned them as outdated.

Nevertheless, the need to defend their culture against Jewish Secularism and religious Modernism required the most articulate Traditionalists to know and understand their opponents. Here a few generalizations are appropriate. In Traditionalist circles, the entire premodern structure of Jewish thought remained substantially intact, interpreted within the framework of rabbinic and kabbalistic

Key Terms of Dispute Among the Various Modernist Jewish Movements

Reform

God: The principle of moral conscience that unites humanity.

Torah: Historical record of Israel's discovery of universal morality. "Revelation" is a moral experience rather than a historical event.

Israel: A people blessed with unique moral insight.

Mitzvot: A premodern discipline for preserving moral insight. Only ethical mitzvot are binding on modern Jews.

Messiah: The future unification of humanity under the principles of liberal nationalism.

German Orthodoxy

God: Traditional talmudic conceptions of God coexist with increased stress on God as an ethical being who trains humanity in principles of virtue.

Torah: An unchangeable record of divine revelation. Modern historical research in the Bible is rejected as the result of loss of faith.

Israel: Biblical story of Israel's chosenness is affirmed in all respects. There is, however, a new stress on Israel's mission to share its moral insights with the non-Jewish nations.

Mitzvot: Binding obligations of the covenant relationship. Halakhic tradition can be modified only after very careful deliberation by rabbinic scholars.

Messiah: Retains a miraculous theory of messianic redemption. But holds that beliefs about the end of history do not prevent Jews from being politically loyal to the countries in which they are citizens.

Positive-Historical (Conservative)

God: Takes an evolutionary approach to biblical and talmudic views of God and affirms that Jewish concept of God continues to develop as Jewish moral sophistication increases.

Torah: Torah is the record of Israel's growing awareness of what it means to live in relation to God.

Israel: Israel is a historical civilization that links modern Jews together in a common community of faith.

Mitzvot: The behavioral expressions of evolving religious and moral insights. Halakhic norms must change as these insights develop. The right to change halakhic norms resides in the decision of the community as a whole.

Messiah: The Messianic idea symbolizes the completion of human moral and religious growth. The "miracles" of messianic times are symbolic ways of speaking about the moral transformation of humanity in the coming future.

images. God was still imagined, as biblical and rabbinic thought had imagined him, as a cosmic King announcing decrees, charting covenantal violations, and granting merciful forgiveness in response to repentance. He continued to commune with Israel through his revealed Torah, the meaning of which was explained in terms of talmudic and kabbalistic tradition. And Israel, of course, remained obliged to obey the Torah in hopes of messianic redemption "speedily and in our day."

In what way, then, is it helpful to regard Hasidic or Mitnagdic Traditionalism as a modern form of Judaism? The answer may be found by analyzing a single word: "Yiddishkayt" (Jewishness). In the Judeo-German ("Yiddish") language of Eastern European Jewry, Yiddiskayt referred to much more than the legal, theological, or ritual traditions we have been calling "Judaism." It encompassed as well the folkways, modes of dress, cuisine, language, and personality traits cultivated throughout the European Jewish society of medieval and early modern times. Precisely these aspects of Jewish life were rapidly disappearing among even the most observant Orthodox Jews of western and central Europe as they substituted European national languages and other cultural patterns for those of the premodern European Jewish world. Among Eastern European Traditionalists, by contrast, this entire complex of Jewish folkways was defined as the very essence of what had to be defended and preserved in Modernity.

In other words, despite deep gulfs in conceptions of history and the nature of natural science, Traditionalists were very similar to the Romantic nationalist thinkers of modern Europe in one crucial respect. They viewed the various European peoples as bearers of seamless, organic cultures that ought not be commingled. Yiddishkayt—Jewish culture—was not peripheral to the halakhic structure of Judaism. Rather, Yiddishkayt was of a piece with halakhic tradition and could not be distinguished from it without violating the integrity of both. There was no way for Jews to accommodate modern European lifestyles without fatally damaging the wholeness of Yiddishkayt.

Thus the specific historical culture of Eastern European Jewry was equated with Torah and had to be defended with the vigor required of a defense of Torah. The defense was mounted, of course, most vigorously against the most dangerous of enemies—those Modernist Jews of western and central Europe who insisted that Torah and modern European culture could be organically integrated. In contrast to the example of Reform, Conservative, and Orthodox Jewish groups, Traditionalism defined itself as a culture of absolute resistance to modernity. But by this very choice it entered into a distinctly modern debate about how Judaism would survive the challenges of Modernity.

The Traditionalist pattern, as it has developed over the past century or so, also reveals its modernity in another important way, in its absorption of essential aspects of modern culture, despite itself. Precisely as modern historical and natural science have claimed greater domains of knowledge from religion, Traditionalist Judaism has tended to define Torah as a body of historical and, increasingly, scientific truth. The defenders of Torah find themselves waging a protracted cultural battle against a competing body of historical and scientific errors, the results of modern scientific and historical scholarship. At stake in this battle are the heart and soul of Israel and its covenantal destiny. Accordingly, although European secularist ideas are the general enemy, they are so only because they have infiltrated Israel in distinctively modern forms of Jewish commitment. For much of the nineteenth and twentieth centuries, therefore, the Traditionalist pattern has tended to see all Jewish deviations from its own path—Secularist and Modernist alike—as various forms of hidden Shabbateanism, following the "false Messiah" of modern culture.

This accounts for Traditionalism's usual dismissal of messianic activism in either secular or religious forms. Conformity to the strictest interpretation of the halakhic tradition is regarded as the necessary inoculation against Secularist and Modernist reinterpretations of Judaism, as well as against the dangers of messianic attempts to subvert halakhic discipline, as in the time of Shabbatai Zvi. In recent years, however—perhaps as a result of the tremendous destruction of Jewish life in Europe during World War II and the establishment in 1948 of the State of Israel as a secular democracy (Chapter 19)—there have been renewed expectations of an imminent messianic deliverance of Israel.

This is especially clear within a sector of Traditionalist Judaism called Habad or Lubavitch Hasidism.[10] We discuss the eighteenth-century origins of Hasidism as a whole in Chapter 7. Habad, for its part, is one of the oldest continuous Hasidic communities, founded in the White Russian town of Lyady in the late eighteenth century. After the death of the founder, Rabbi Shneur Zalman, in 1812, the community moved to the nearby town of Lubavitch, where its charismatic leaders ("Rebbes") reigned until the Communist Party persecutions of Jewish and Christian religious leaders in the 1920s. From there, the leadership moved to Vilna, Poland, and, as World War II began to enclose European Jewry in 1941, to Brooklyn, New York. The last of the seven Rebbes of Habad, Rabbi Menachem Mendel Schneerson, assumed his position in 1951 and died in June 1994 after two years of stroke-induced paralysis.

Upon first assuming his position as Rebbe, Rabbi Schneerson began to teach that messianic redemption would certainly come to the current generation. In order to prepare for the Messiah's coming, Jews need only commit their lives to bringing him. They could do so through single-minded devotion to the study of Torah and loyalty to the most Traditionalist of halakhic norms. The link between redemption and Torah is, of course, a common theme of rabbinic Judaism. It was the timing of Rabbi Schneerson's message that was crucial. Six million Jews—many of them extremely pious—had recently died hideously in Europe (Chapter 19). He drew upon venerable rabbinic ideas—quite familiar to all Traditionalists—that held that messianic redemption would be preceded by unprecedented catastrophe. Such "birth pangs of the Messiah," as they were called, corresponded in his view to the events that he himself had only narrowly escaped.

His teaching inspired his followers. Taking up lives as "emissaries (*shlukhim*) of the Rebbe," they established Habad communities in cities and towns throughout North America, Israel, and other centers of Jewish life. There they encouraged Modernist and Secularist Jews in particular to engage in basic acts of halakhic piety. By convincing Jewish women to light Sabbath candles or Jewish men to wear

Rabbi Menachem Schneerson, the Seventh Lubavitcher Rebbe: A Twentieth-Century Messiah

Rabbi Schneerson is here pictured prior to his incapacitating stroke of 1992. The Rebbe's death in 1994 is viewed by some of his followers as a period of testing prior to his imminent return as Messiah. (*Source:* AP/Wide World Photos)

rabbinic prayer amulets (*tefillin*), Habad emissaries hoped to nurture in them the sentiments that might make active messianic longing a reality for all Jews. A fragmented community of a few hundred survivors of European death camps in 1951, the movement claimed tens of thousands of committed members by 1990. But their influence in the Jewish communities of North American and Israel spread far more widely than official membership lists might suggest.

By the early 1990s, however, many influential followers had become convinced that the Rebbe himself was the expected messianic figure. His refusal to refute these convictions or to confirm them increased the passions of both his followers and those who regarded with suspicion the messianic ferment surrounding him. When a massive stroke deprived the Rebbe of speech in 1992, speculation about his messianic career did not diminish. Rather, it increased, with Habad communities around the world using the available print and electronic media to declare what was called "an international campaign to bring *Moshiach* [Messiah]."

Bumper stickers and pamphlets portrayed a portrait of the Rebbe above the slogan "Moshiach Is Coming—Be a Part of It!"

With the Rebbe's death, Habad now faces a crisis in its messianic convictions. Some groups in the movement continue to insist that the Rebbe will imminently return from death to claim his messianic title. Others—aware, perhaps, of the resonance of such ideas with Christian themes—insist that the precise identity of the Messiah remains unclear and that the Rebbe's role was merely to remind Jews and the world of the desperate need for messianic deliverance. It is a debate that will continue over the next generation, as Habad Hasidism sorts out the theological and religious consequences of various interpretations of the Rebbe's failure to rule as Messiah in his own lifetime.

Habad Hasidism constitutes a minority of Traditionalist Jews, Hasidic or Mitnagdic. It has an even smaller following among Modernist Orthodox Jews. Both groups have admired Habad's successful mission to marginally observant Jews and have recognized Rabbi Schneerson as a major religious leader. But the messianic excitement of the 1990s generated heated criticism. During the Rebbe's lifetime, many Traditionalists recounted the sad history of Sabbatean messianism, citing antimessianic proof-texts from the Talmud to refute Habad messianists. After the Rebbe's death, they are even more opposed to those who anticipate his imminent return from death as Messiah.

Among Modernist Orthodox Jews, the controversy was officially addressed in the late spring of 1996 by a major organization of American Orthodox rabbis. At its annual convention, the Rabbinical Council of America alluded to events in Habad with the following resolution: "In light of disturbing developments which [sic] have recently arisen in the Jewish community, the Rabbinical Council of America . . . declares that there is not and never has been a place in Judaism for the belief that Messiah son of David will begin his messianic Mission only to experience death, burial and resurrection before completing it."[11]

Although the messianic debate is fiercest within the various streams of Traditionalism and Orthodoxy, it has drawn wide attention among all groups of Jews. Many committed Secularists, in both Israel and North America, tend to view this latest messianic ferment with amusement or disdain, as did the observers of the supporters of Abu Isa and the like twelve centuries ago. Others, including large numbers of Reform and Conservative Jews, are often pulled in two directions, moved by the vitality of a genuine messianic movement in the midst of secular American and Israeli culture, yet repelled by deeply bred fears of the consequences of messianic disappointment. In any case, that a messianic movement within Hasidism can generate such debate among all Jews in the late twentieth century testifies to the vitality of Jewish theological symbols despite two centuries of immense social upheaval and intellectual ferment.

CHAPTER 5

MONOTHEISM
IN CHRISTIANITY

Imagine, if you can, a square circle. Or boiling ice. Or a man who is his own mother. Or the sound of one hand clapping. Paradoxes such as these point to a peculiar human trait: the ability to conceive of things that are impossible, unimaginable, and self-contradictory. Such thinking is at the heart of the Christian religion. Christianity, in fact, is a religion that thrives on paradox, for it believes in the existence of an infinite, all-powerful God who transcends everything humans can imagine and is beyond contradictions. *The Divine Names* (ca. sixth century), one of the most influential mystical treatises of the Christian tradition, attempts to describe this God as

> that Transcendent Godhead which super-essentially surpasses all things. . . . The mystery beyond all mind and reason. . . . It has no name, nor can It be grasped by the reason; It dwells in a region beyond us, where our feet cannot tread.[1]

Yet, even more paradoxically, Christianity is also a religion centered on the belief that this God revealed himself most fully in Jesus Christ, a human being. Christian theology, ritual, and ethics are derived from core beliefs that affirm the coincidence of opposites: a God who is One and at the same time Three; a savior who is at once divine and human, eternal and mortal; a redemption that simultaneously fulfills and postpones God's promises. Consequently, its symbols, too, are profoundly paradoxical: the cross as the assurance of bliss; bread and wine as the body and blood of the savior; images of the human virgin Mary as Mother of God.

Though the singular God worshiped by Christians is the same one worshiped by Jews and Muslims, the monotheism of Christianity is acutely complex and paradoxical. One ancient Christian legend summed up this insight in narrative form. It is said that Augustine of Hippo (354–430), one of the greatest Christian thinkers, was once walking along the seashore meditating on the nature of God. As he pondered the ineffable mystery of the Trinity, Augustine suddenly came upon a small boy playing near the surf and stopped to watch him. The boy was running to and from the water's edge, repeatedly filling a seashell with water and emptying its contents into a hole in the sand. Augustine asked him, "What are you doing?" The boy explained that he was trying to empty out the whole sea into the small crater he had dug out of the sand. "That's impossible!" declared Augustine. "You think this is impossible?" retorted the boy, who was really an angel sent by God. "It would be far easier for me to drain all the seas into this puny hole," he said, "than for you to ever comprehend the Trinity." Having thus reminded Augustine of the depth of God's mystery through the use of paradox, the child/angel vanished. Though this legend cannot be found in Augustine's works, it is undoubtedly true to his teaching on God. "When will you be able to say: This is God?," he wrote, "Not even when you see him, for what you shall see is ineffable."[2]

Augustine and many other Christians have puzzled over the mystery of God, not so much out of curiosity, perhaps, as out of a desire for uniformity of belief among Christians. And here we encounter yet another paradox, for belief in a God who transcends all thought has historically led Christians to insist that there can be only one way of thinking about him. In brief, Christian monotheism is inseparably linked to the Christian concept of "orthodoxy," or right belief: as there is but one God, so can there be but one truth, one church, and one correct faith. Or, as the apostle Paul summed it up in the first century: "One Lord, one faith, one baptism."

The principal sources for the development of Christian monotheism were, of course, the sacred scriptures of the New Testament. But these texts often spoke of God in ways that defied Jewish monotheistic conventions. What sort of monotheism could be derived, for instance, from Jesus' words at the end of the Gospel of Matthew (28:18–19): "All authority in heaven and on earth has been given to me; go, therefore and make disciples of all nations, baptizing them in the name of the Father and of the Son and of the Holy Spirit"? Distinctions between a "Father," a "Son," and a "Spirit" were an enigma. Since enigmas tend to elicit multiple interpretations, the mystery of the triune God would prove to be especially divisive among Christians, a community that prized uniformity of belief.

The complexity of Christian monotheism stems from its belief in Jesus as the Messiah promised to the Jews. From the very beginning, Christians proclaimed Jesus as the Son of God and as the source of a new revelation. This belief not only separated Jesus' followers from the rest of the Jewish community, as we have seen, but also marked the beginning of a distinct monotheistic tradition. But what, precisely, did it mean to call Jesus "Son of God," to call him "Lord," and to worship him as "Savior"? What did it mean for Jesus to call God his "Father"? Moreover, who was the "Holy Spirit" that Jesus and his disciples invoked and spoke about?

Theology and ritual depended on each other, for God was not simply a topic for theological discourse, but rather a being to be addressed in prayer, the end point of all religious activity. As the Latin formulation put it, the *lex orandi* (rule of prayer) and the *lex credendi* (rule of belief) that defined the Christian community were inseparable. This means that the process of defining and refining those structures of ritual and belief has been as much a social as an intellectual process. The development of worship and theology goes hand in hand with the process of community formation in Christian history, for as Christians have differed on their interpretation of the mystery of God, distinct churches have been created.

It could be said, then, that whereas the mainstream of the Christian tradition has been remarkably consistent in its thinking, this consistency was gained through exclusion, through a painful process in which some Christians were rejected as heretics. Consequently, although it is easy to summarize what the dominant church traditions have said about God, it is difficult to encompass all the possible variations that have arisen in two thousand years and that continue to appear in our own day. For the sake of clarity and simplicity, we limit ourselves here to those traditions that have proved most enduring and influential.

THE GOD OF A NEW REVELATION: FATHER, SON, AND HOLY SPIRIT

The Christian Scriptures abound with references to God as Father and to Jesus as Son, and they also proclaim the divine influence of the Holy Spirit among Jesus' followers. The sheer number of these references is imposing. Take Father, for instance: it is used over 170 times in the four gospels. John's gospel alone refers to "the Son" or "Son of God" about thirty times. "Holy Spirit" appears forty-three times in the *Acts of the Apostles.*

Belief in Jesus as the Messiah carried with it belief in a new revelation. The *Letter to the Hebrews* made this clear in its opening passage:

> In many and various ways God spoke of old to our fathers by the prophets, but in these last days he has spoken to us by a Son, whom he appointed the heir of all things, through whom also he created the world. (Heb. 1:1–2)

As this text implies, the source of the new revelation, the Son, was himself the creator of the world. The God who thus revealed himself was more complex than the God of the prophets. The gospel of John expanded on this theme in its resounding preamble:

> In the beginning was the Word, and the Word was with God, and the Word was God. He was in the beginning with God; all things were made through him . . . and the Word became flesh and dwelt among us, full of grace and truth; we have beheld his glory, glory as of the only Son from the Father . . . And from his fulness have we all received grace upon grace. For the law was given through Moses; grace and truth

Spread of Christianity to the 13th Century

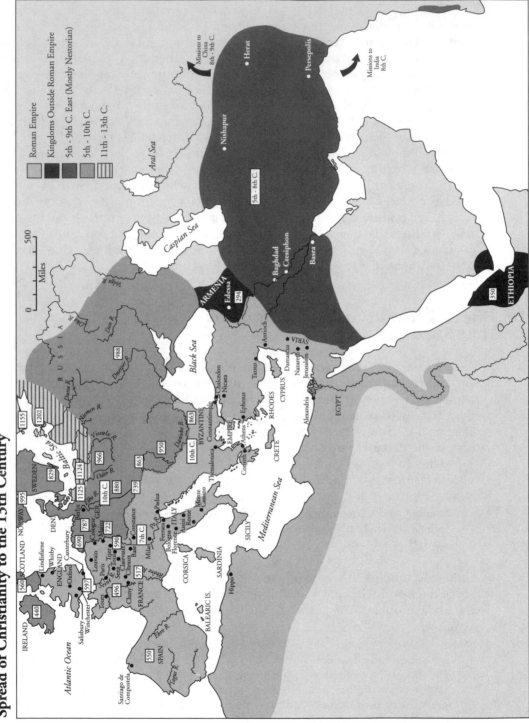

Legend:
- Roman Empire
- Kingdoms Outside Roman Empire
- 5th - 9th C. East (Mostly Nestorian)
- 5th - 10th C.
- 11th - 13th C.

Missions to China 8th - 9th C.

Missions to India 8th C.

Herat

Persepolis

Nishapur

5th - 8th C.

Aral Sea

Caspian Sea

Baghdad

Ctesiphon

Basra

ARMENIA

Edessa 294

ETHIOPIA 350

Volga R.

Don R.

Dnieper R.

988

RUSSIA

Black Sea

Antioch

SYRIA

Damascus

Nazareth

Jerusalem

Chalcedon

Nicaea

Tarsus

Ephesus

CYPRUS

RHODES

Alexandria

EGYPT

Niemen R.

Vistula R.

Oder R.

1155

1202

SWEDEN

Baltic Sea

829

995

1124

1125

966

950

863

10th C.

BYZANTINE

Constantinople

EMPIRE

Thessalonica

Athens

Corinth

CRETE

Mediterranean Sea

NORWAY

SCOTLAND

Lindisfarne

Whitby

ENGLAND

Oxford

Canterbury

Salisbury

Winchester

560

597

440

IRELAND

Atlantic Ocean

Berlin

787

722

690

DEN.

Elbe R.

Cologne

Mainz

10th C.

GER.

880

739

Constance

Basel

7th C.

Milan

Padua

Po R.

Monte Cassino

Ferrara

Bologna

ITALY

Florence

Assisi

Rome

Louvain

Paris

Seine R.

Troyes

Sens

Clairvaux

Cluny

590

517

496

FRANCE

Tours

Rhône R.

CORSICA

SARDINIA

SICILY

BALEARIC IS.

Hippo

Ebro R.

Tagus R.

SPAIN

550

Santiago de Compostela

500

Miles

0

108

came through Jesus Christ. No one has ever seen God; the only Son, who was in the bosom of the Father, he has made him known. (John 1:1–3, 14, 17–18)

This is perhaps the single most important text in the development of Christian thinking on God. The naming of Jesus as Son of God the Father pointed unmistakably to distinctions within the deity. Furthermore, the identification of Jesus as the Word of God not only proclaimed him as the ultimate revelation and fulfillment of the Jewish scriptures, but also placed Christian thinking squarely within the Hellenistic philosophical tradition and the gentile (non-Jewish) community, for the concept of "the Word" could be found in Stoicism, one school of Greek philosophy.

Stoics taught that the world had been brought into existence by a higher intelligence, the *Logos,* the Word, or reason, or ordering principle. The acceptance among early Christians of this Word, or Logos, indicates how pagan Hellenistic thought could intermingle with Judaism; it also points to the evolution of Jewish monotheism into something distinctly new within a different social context.

As much as it was influenced by Hellenism, Christian monotheism was not articulated by philosophers in ivory towers; on the contrary, it was forged by churchmen in the heat of controversy. And it stands to reason that the first great step taken toward some clearer definition involved coming to terms with the difference between the "new" and the "old" revelations, between the God of the Jews and the God of the Christians. Once again, as in the case of the history of the Christian scriptures, it was Marcion who raised the question around 144 CE by asserting that the Christian God was *not* the same one who had revealed himself through Moses and the prophets. Arguing for the existence of two gods—the harsh, vindictive God of the Old Testament and the loving God of the New—Marcion denied monotheism. Marcion and his followers established a church of their own and for several generations became the dominant form of Christianity in some parts of the Roman Empire. Though Marcion's dualist Christianity did not survive past the third century, his challenge proved enduring in one significant way: Marcionite dualism forced orthodox Christians to articulate their monotheistic belief and to affirm that they worshiped the same God as the Jews. By rejecting Marcion, orthodox Christians took a significant step toward determining the identity of the Father, for it now became clear to them that it was God the Father who had revealed himself in the Old Testament.

Having come to terms with Marcion and his two gods, Christians still faced the problem of clarifying how the Father, the Son, and the Holy Spirit related to one another and how they could be a single God. Moreover, Christians still needed to define the role of each of these divine realities in the new covenant of salvation. If God had revealed himself more fully in the Son (Jesus), what was to be made of the work of the Spirit? The Acts of the Apostles and the letters of Paul reveal that the earliest Christians firmly believed in a very active Holy Spirit. Deprived of the earthly presence of Jesus, the apostles received the gift of the Spirit to inspire and enlighten them in their missionary work:

When the day of Pentecost had come, they were all together in one place. And suddenly a sound came from heaven like the rush of a mighty wind, and it filled all the house where they were sitting. And there appeared to them tongues as of fire, distributed and resting on each one of them. And they were all filled with the Holy Spirit and began to speak in other tongues, as the Spirit gave them utterance. (Acts 2:1–4)

This, as the apostle Peter would explain, was the fulfillment of the prophecy uttered by Joel in the Old Testament:

And in the last days it shall be, God declares, that I will pour out my Spirit upon all flesh, and your sons and your daughters shall prophesy, and your young men shall see visions, and your old men shall dream dreams. (Joel 2:28; Acts 2:17)

The apostles and the first generation of Christians frequently appealed to the direct inspiration of the Spirit. Paul's community in Corinth, for instance, had members who prophesied (that is, interpreted the faith of the community and foretold the future) and others who spoke in tongues (that is, who spoke in a mysterious language that could be understood only by others who were similarly inspired). These gifts could prove divisive. Paul advised the Corinthians to measure the authenticity of the Spirit's gifts by their ability to bind the community together:

I thank God that I speak in tongues more than you all; nevertheless, in church I would rather speak five words with my mind, in order to instruct others, than ten thousand words in a tongue. (I Cor. 14:18–19)

To prophesy or to speak in tongues was to claim authority. In a community where the gifts of the Spirit abounded, as in Corinth, such claims to authority could be kept in balance by the presence of someone who claimed a special relationship with the Son, such as Paul or some other apostle.

But what happened when the generation of the apostles passed away, when there were no longer any who had known the Son and his disciples? How would the role of the Spirit then be interpreted or tested? One claim that gained wide acceptance in the mid-second century was that of Montanus, a Christian from Asia Minor who boasted of a special "charisma," or gift, from the Spirit. Convinced that the Spirit spoke directly through him, Montanus prophesied the end of the world and called for stricter and more self-denying behavior among Christians. Other prophets, both male and female, soon made similar claims, giving rise to a movement of charismatic prophecy. The charismatic utterances of Montanus and others were accepted by many as a new revelation from God, for these prophets spoke in the first person as the "Paraclete" or Spirit. Two women in particular, Prisca and Maximilla, gained prominence among these Montanists. The fact that many of their specific prophecies failed to come true did not lessen the popularity of this form of Christianity. It must be kept in mind that Christians at this time were being persecuted throughout the Roman Empire and that the promise of an imminent apocalypse seemed especially attractive to many of them. The Montanists, like the Marcionites, formed a rival Christian church that did not survive past the third century; and they also helped clarify Christian monotheistic thinking. By insisting on the continued presence and influence of the Paraclete, Montanus and his followers called attention to the divine nature of the Holy Spirit—a belief that the orthodox found difficult to deny.

What the orthodox did deny, however, was the notion that the Spirit could continue to reveal *new* truths through charismatic leaders. Montanus and his followers were rejected as false prophets. Against their claim to prophetic Spirit-filled authority, the orthodox bishops raised the claim to *apostolic* authority. Although they did not deny the continuing influence of the Spirit, the orthodox limited revelation strictly to the time of the apostles. God, they claimed, continued to speak through his church on earth, but this voice of the Spirit was limited to those men who could trace their episcopal office directly back to the apostles. Furthermore, the teachings of this church were to be limited strictly to only those teachings that were revealed to the apostles. In effect, the Spirit came to be identified with the church itself. As Irenaeus of Lyons put it in the second century, "where the Church is, there is the Spirit of God, and where the Spirit of God is, there is the Church and every grace."[3]

By the end of the second century, orthodox Christians had thus identified the Father as the God of the Old Testament and the Spirit as the voice of the church. Explaining the Son, and his relation to the Father and Spirit, however, would take about five more centuries.

The notion of a Son of God was not alien to the gentile world. Myths of gods who begat divine offspring by themselves or who mated with each other and even with humans to produce lesser divinities abounded in the polytheistic religions of the ancient world. Neither was the idea of an incarnate deity a strange one, for the gods of the gentiles were believed capable of assuming human—as well as animal—form. It was also widely believed that humans could become gods. Some of the Roman emperors, for instance, proclaimed themselves divine and demanded worship from their subjects.

Analogous thinking could also be found in sophisticated Hellenistic philosophies that had abandoned the polytheistic myths of the ancient world. Two schools of thought in particular had affinities with Christian belief. We have already encountered one of these, Stoicism, which had developed the concept of Logos, or Word, as the agent of creation. The other was Neoplatonism, especially as articulated by Plotinus (208–270 CE), who taught that all reality emanated in a descending order from a triune source: the One, the "Nous" (Mind), and the "Psyche" (Spirit). These affinities were a two-edged sword: one edge helped clear a path for the spread of Christianity, making it easier for non-Jews to accept Jesus as a divine/human savior and the Father, Son, and Spirit as divine entities; the other edge could cut through the bonds of Christian unity, giving rise to vaguely pagan ideas that threatened to compromise Christian monotheism.

DEFINING THE TRIUNE GOD

Orthodox Christians believed their God was the God of the Jews and that he had revealed himself as Father, Son, and Spirit; but if this God was indeed the same as that of the Jews, he had to be One, not Three. Since the Christian Scriptures revealed the mystery without explaining it, how could such a paradox be explained? It was no idle question, for the identity of the Christian community hinged on such distinctions.

Arriving at some consensus was necessary, but immensely difficult. So many different opinions were voiced concerning the Son and his relation to the Father and the Spirit in the first seven centuries that they cannot all be mentioned here. It was a painful process. Quite often, those who thought they were defending orthodoxy found themselves branded as heretics. Conversely, some who were stripped of their bishoprics and exiled for heresy eventually found their position vindicated as orthodox. Rival churches arose; some flourished for a while and then declined and vanished; others survived. Throughout this long and complex struggle for definitions, two constant patterns emerged. First, the process of the definition of orthodoxy was usually set in motion by the appearance of some teaching that sought to give greater clarity to Christian monotheism. Second, those who sought to make the paradoxical more comprehensible tended to be rejected by the orthodox; in contrast, those who most strenuously defended the ultimate mystery of paradox set the tone for orthodoxy.

Concerning the Son and his relation to the Father and the Spirit, the orthodox eventually proclaimed the following: there is but one God who is three distinct persons, Father, Son, and Holy Spirit. Each person of this "trinity" is fully divine, eternal, and distinct, but these are not three gods. The formulation accepted as orthodox at the Council of Nicaea in 325 CE employed Greek philosophical terminology not found in scripture to explain what was believed to have been revealed in the New Testament. The Son was fully divine, proclaimed this council, "one in being with the Father" (Greek: *homoousios*, from *homo* [the same] and *ousia* [essence or nature]). This formulation did not please all Christians, however, for it sought to overturn certain teachings that had arisen and were popular in some places. The history of this controversy is complex, but a brief overview might shed light on the dynamics of the definition of orthodoxy.

Seeking to oppose gnostic and Marcionite dualism, and to avoid falling into tritheism (belief in three gods), some Christians in the second century stressed the unity, or "monarchy," of God. One such teacher, Sabellius, gave prominence to the idea that there was but one God who had different aspects and related to humanity in different ways, sometimes as Father, sometimes as Son, and sometimes as Holy Spirit. In other words, God simply had different modes of dealing with the

Domenico Tintoretto:
*The Trinity Adored by
the Heavenly Choir*

The Trinity is a paradoxical doctrine that, by definition, defies comprehension. This has not deterred Christian artists from trying to depict the mystery of the triune God, especially in the late medieval and early modern Catholic West. Here the Father is depicted as an old man with a flowing white beard, the Son as the crucified Savior Jesus Christ, and the Spirit as the dove at the foot of the cross. (In the gospels, the Spirit is said to descend as a dove on Jesus at his baptism.) (*Source:* Jacopo Robusti, called Tintoretto, Venetian School, 1518–1594. Collection of the Columbia Museum of Arts, gift of the Samuel H. Kress Foundation.)

human race. This teaching, known as "modalism," "modalistic monarchianism," or "Sabellianism," was opposed by some Christian communities, for it stressed the unity of the divine at the expense of distinctions. One Christian who rose to the challenge was Arius (250–336), a presbyter at Alexandria in Egypt. Seeking to overturn Sabellian modalism, Arius moved in the opposite direction and stressed the distinction between the Father and the Son. "Arianism," as Arius's position came to be known, proposed the following explanation to the mystery of the Three-in-One: Father, Son, and Holy Spirit were not equally divine. Only the

Father was eternal. The Son had been brought into existence by the Father; and so had the Spirit, after the Son.

Arianism was logical and rational. Arius and his followers argued that it made no sense to speak of a Son who did not somehow come into being after his Father. But this logical proposition made the Son a lesser deity, or even a creature. The Arian Son was above creation, but below the Father, in a position not unlike that of the Neoplatonic Nous, or Mind. Though this teaching seemed attractive to many, even to some in high places (such as the bishop who baptized Emperor Constantine on his deathbed), it also proved frightening to others who saw it as a threat to monotheism. Chief among those who opposed Arianism was Athanasius of Alexandria (296–373). Against Arius's logic, Athanasius proposed a more mystical understanding that was no less logical:

> In and of himself, he [the Son] is properly the wisdom, reason and power of the Father—light, truth, righteousness, virtue itself, the express image and splendor and likeness of the Father. In a word, he is the consummate fruit of the Father, the sole Son and changeless image of the Father.[4]

Attempts at compromise failed. Proposing, for instance, that the Son was "similar" to the Father did not solve the problem. Since the difference between "similar substance" and "same substance" in Greek boiled down to one letter (*homoiousios* versus *homoousios*), some pagans ridiculed Christians for arguing over an *iota*. But it was not only theologians and bishops who debated such questions. The hymns of Arius were sung by sailors and dockworkers. According to Gregory of Nyssa, it was hard to steer clear of theology in Constantinople around 380:

> If you ask someone to give you change, he philosophizes about the Begotten and the Unbegotten. . . . If you say to the attendant "Is my bath ready?," he tells you that the Son was made out of nothing.[5]

Athanasius eventually prevailed against Arius, for it was Athanasian theology that carried the day at Nicaea and helped give shape to the definitive statement of Christian orthodoxy, the creed (from Latin, *credo*, "I believe"). The creed of Nicaea evolved into a longer prayer recited by the Christian faithful in church during every celebration of the eucharist. Contained in this prayer's opening passage is the summation of orthodox monotheism:

> We believe in one God, the Father almighty, maker of heaven and earth, and of all things visible and invisible; and in one Lord Jesus Christ, only-begotten Son of God, born of the Father before all ages; God from God, light from light, true God from true God; begotten, not made, one in being with the Father; through whom all things were made.[6]

Arianism did not vanish after its condemnation at the Council of Nicaea in 325 and the Council of Constantinople in 381; on the contrary, it gained strength and spread even beyond the borders of the Roman Empire. At times, it seemed to the orthodox as if the Arians had won. "The world groaned to find itself Arian," observed Jerome in the fourth century. But the tide gradually turned against the Arians. Although it was championed by some Germanic tribes who later conquered parts of the Roman Empire, Arianism faded out among them, and all but vanished by the late sixth century.

DEFINING THE INCARNATE GOD

Christian monotheism included yet another paradox beyond the Trinity: that of the Son's manifestation in the person of Jesus. If accepting Jesus as the Messiah involved thinking of him as the Son of God, it also involved thinking of God as human. How could this be? Given the attributes ascribed to God, it seemed logically impossible to claim he could be human. How could the omniscient, omnipotent, and eternal creator and ruler of the universe become a human being? Could God really have had to learn to walk and talk as an infant? Could God have fully experienced all the limitations, humiliations, and frustrations of human experience? Could God have sunk so low as to have bowel movements, bad breath, and a runny nose? Even more shocking, could God really have been tempted to sin as a human being? Could he have suffered pain and died?

The answer consistently given to all these questions by the orthodox would be "Yes!": the Christ, or Savior, was *both* fully divine and fully human. This paradox is as difficult to come to terms with as that of the Trinity. Consequently, the development of "Christology" (the theological term for thinking about Christ) took place much in the same way as that of trinitarian doctrine, through the refutation of "heresies" that seemed to somehow compromise the integrity of some element in the paradoxical nature of the God of the New Testament. In the case of Christ, the paradoxical tension that begged for definition was that between the humanity and the divinity of the incarnate God. What, exactly, did it mean to say that a Jewish man, Jesus, was the Son of God?

Of the many answers given to this question, five played a prominent role in the final formulation of orthodox teaching and in the splintering of the church in the Near East.

1. One of the oldest Christologies was *docetism*. As early as the first century, some Christians with gnostic tendencies avoided the paradox of a God/man altogether by claiming that Jesus had not been fully human: he only *seemed* to have a real human body. Since these Christians viewed material existence as evil, they found the notion of an embodied God inconceivable and offensive. This docetism (Greek, *dokeo*: to seem or to appear) was rejected by the orthodox, who insisted on genuine embodiment. If God had not become fully human, argued the orthodox, how could humanity be saved? In the words of Gregory of Nazienzen, "What is not assumed is not saved."[7]

2. Another early christology was *adoptionism*. Adoptionists solved the paradox of the God/man in a way that resembled polytheistic notions of divinization:

THE SEVEN ECUMENICAL COUNCILS AND THEIR CHRISTOLOGICAL/TRINITARIAN DEFINITIONS

Two major questions dominated early Christian thinking:

1. The relationship between the Son and the Father.
2. The relationship between the divine and the human in Christ.

Arriving at an agreement on a "correct" doctrine was not easy. As answers were proposed and debated, they eventually came to be judged "true" (orthodox) or "false" (heretical) by councils of bishops. Outlined here are the prime concerns of the seven general councils accepted by the Catholic and Orthodox churches.

Council	Doctrine
Nicaea 1 (325)	The Son is one in being with the Father.
Constantinople 1 (381)	The Holy Spirit is fully divine, and Jesus Christ has a real human soul.
Ephesus (431)	Jesus Christ is both human and divine.
Chalcedon (415)	Jesus Christ is one person in two natures.
Constantinople 2 (553)	Two natures of Jesus Christ reaffirmed.
Constantinople 3 (681)	Jesus Christ has two wills, human and divine.
Nicaea 2 (787)	The incarnation makes it possible for Christians to make images and venerate them.

Jesus was not an eternal deity, but rather a man like all others who had been divinized by God. In other words, they taught that the man Jesus turned divine when God "adopted" him as his Son. The orthodox rejected this teaching on two accounts: it denied the full incarnation of God and turned Christ into a lesser deity.

3. A more complex solution was offered by *Apollinarianism* in the late fourth century, ironically, in an effort to combat Arianism. Stressing the full divinity of Christ, Apollinaris of Laodicea proposed the following: though Jesus was human, the Word itself took the place of his human soul or mind. This approach to the paradox, thought Apollinaris, defended both the divinity of Christ and the unity of his personality:

> The Word himself has become flesh without having taken on the human mind, a mind changeable and enslaved to filthy thoughts, but existing as a divine mind, unchangeable and heavenly.[8]

Orthodoxy rejected Apollinaris on the grounds that his teaching compromised the full humanity of Christ.

Alonso Cano, *The Vision of Saint Bernard* (ca. 1658–1660)

Many Christian mystics have claimed extraordinary experiences in which the boundaries between this world and heaven dissolve. Some of these phenomena are intrinsically linked to the central mysteries of the Christian faith. St. Bernard of Clairvaux (twelfth century), rapt in prayer, claimed to have been breast-fed by an image of Mary. As interpreted here by Alonso Cano, a Baroque Spanish painter, the vision of St. Bernard is a graphic testimony of many Catholic Christian beliefs, above all those doctrines that emphasize the reality of the incarnation of God and his love for the human race. (*Source:* Bridgeman/Art Resource, NY)

4. *Nestorianism* was another Christological reaction to heresy that ironically became a heresy itself. Sensing Apollinarian tendencies in the Christian liturgy, Nestorius, a fifth-century bishop of Constantinople, objected to invoking Mary in prayer as the "Mother of God" (Greek, *Theotokos*: God-bearer). Nestorius was accused by the orthodox of having turned Christ into a two-headed monster, for he argued that Christ's humanity and his divinity were joined only by a moral union, rather than by an ontological one. What difference did this teaching make? For Nestorius it meant that what applied to the human in Christ did not apply to the divine, and vice versa. This is why he objected to Mary being called the Mother of God, even though Christians had been using the term since ancient times. The orthodox, in contrast, insisted that God's incarnation in Jesus was so full that one could say that God had experienced human existence in the same way as all humans, except for never having given in to sin. It was possible, therefore, for the orthodox to say of God whatever could be said of Jesus: "God was born of Mary"; "God was an infant and child"; "God wept"; "God spit"; "God suffered"; "God bled"; "God died"; "God rose from the dead."

Nestorius sparked an intense and prolonged controversy. Though he was condemned by the Council of Ephesus in 431, he nonetheless obtained a large and devoted following within the Persian Empire, beyond the jurisdiction of the Christian emperor at Constantinople. Free to reject the Council of Ephesus, these Nestorian Christians in Syria and Mesopotamia broke with the Orthodox Church and continued to thrive as "the Church of the East." In the medieval period, these Nestorian Christians sent missionaries eastward into the Asian continent. Small Nestorian Christian communities actually survived in China until shortly before the arrival there of Western Europeans in the sixteenth century. In the Near East, this church still survives, despite centuries of persecution.

5. The fifth great Christological disagreement arose, once again, through an effort to combat heresy. Attempting to stress the unity of Christ's two natures over and against the Nestorians, some theologians argued that Christ was "*from* two natures" but not "*in* two natures." Such a Christology came to be labeled "Monophysite" (Greek *mono*: = one; *physis*: = nature), for it stressed the supremacy of the divine in Christ, even to the point of saying that his humanity was swallowed up in the divinity, "like the sea receiving a drop of honey."

Monophysitism was condemned at the Council of Chalcedon in 451. In its confession of faith, this council turned the condemnation of this and earlier heresies into an affirmation of the incarnation as the supreme paradox and coincidence of opposites:

> Following therefore the holy Fathers, we confess one and the same our Lord Jesus Christ, and we all teach harmoniously that he is the same perfect in Godhead, the same perfect in manhood, truly God and truly man, the same of a reasonable soul and body, consubstantial with us in manhood, like us in all things except sin . . . one and the same Christ, Son, Lord, unique; acknowledged in two natures without confusion, without change, without division, without separation—the difference of the natures

being by no means taken away because of the union, but rather the distinctive character of each nature being preserved, and each combining in one person and *hypostasis*—and not divided or separated into two persons.[9]

This decision was rejected by many Christians, however, especially in Egypt and Syria. As had been the case with Nestorianism at Ephesus, the unity of the church was diminished by a conciliar definition. Repeated attempts at compromise over the next three centuries proved futile and helped only to generate other questionable Christologies. In 681, those who proposed that Christ was *in* two natures but had only a single divine energy ended up condemned as *Monoenergists*; and others who proposed that Christ was *in* two natures but possessed only a divine will saw themselves condemned as *Monotheletes*. Passing judgment on such complex theological paradoxes was risky but unavoidable for the Christian elites. Even those in the highest places could fall into disgrace. Pope Honorius at Rome, for instance, agreed with Monothelete propositions in a letter. Years later, after Monothelitism had been condemned, his grave was desecrated and his remains thrown into the Tiber River.

Monophysitism not only refused to go away, but splintered into various rival churches, throwing entire regions into institutional and social chaos. By the sixth century, for instance, there were six rival Monophysite leaders claiming to be the legitimate bishop of Alexandria. When Muslim armies conquered Syria and Egypt in 634–639, they helped seal the schism between Chalcedonians and non-Chalcedonians. Now that they were beyond the boundaries of the Christian Empire of Constantinople, these churches could not be coerced into submission and thus endured, despite centuries of Muslim domination. It should be noted that these surviving non-Chalcedonian churches have always seen themselves as "orthodox" and identified themselves as such: the Coptic Orthodox Church, the Ethiopian Orthodox Church, the Armenian Orthodox Church, the Syrian Orthodox Church (also called "Jacobite," after one of its sixth-century leaders, Jacob Baradaeus), and the Syrian Orthodox Church of the Malabar, in South India (whose members are called "St. Thomas Christians" because they claim the Apostle Thomas as their founder).

The Trinitarian and Christological controversies produced clearer definitions of Christian monotheistic belief. Orthodox Christianity incorporated the theology of Nicaea, Ephesus, and Chalcedon into its creed, and these precise definitions thus made their way into the minds and hearts of believers through ritual. Though few could understand the full complexities of their monotheism, as articulated by the councils, all could affirm the same belief in the creed whenever they attended church. Reduced to its barest elements, orthodox Christian monotheism proclaimed the existence of a triune God who had become a human being. The trinity was explained in precise language as three distinct persons (*hypostases*) in one essence (*ousia*); the Christ was defined as one person (*hypostasis*) in two natures (*physis*).

The legacy of these doctrinal disagreements was twofold and not free of paradox itself. Although it is true that debates over the trinity and Christ were the means whereby Christians came to terms with their own complex monotheism, it

Christian Schisms

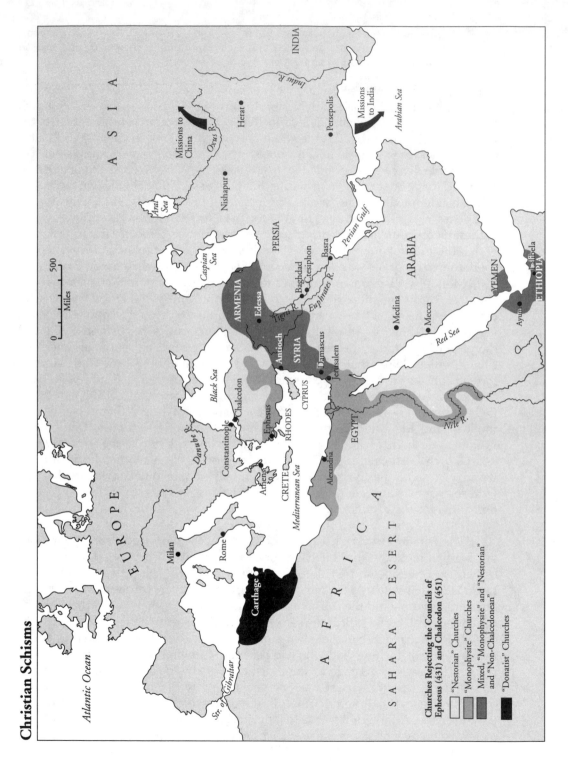

Churches Rejecting the Councils of Ephesus (431) and Chalcedon (451)

- "Nestorian" Churches
- "Monophysite" Churches
- Mixed, "Monophysite" and "Nestorian" and "Non-Chalcedonean"
- "Donatist" Churches

ASIA

EUROPE

AFRICA

INDIA

PERSIA

ARMENIA

SYRIA

CYPRUS

EGYPT

ARABIA

YEMEN

ETHIOPIA

CRETE

RHODES

SAHARA DESERT

Atlantic Ocean

Mediterranean Sea

Black Sea

Caspian Sea

Aral Sea

Red Sea

Persian Gulf

Arabian Sea

Nile R.

Oxus R.

Indus R.

Tigris R.

Euphrates R.

Danube

Str. of Gibraltar

Missions to China

Missions to India

Miles

500

Herat

Nishapur

Persepolis

Edessa

Baghdad

Ctesiphon

Basra

Antioch

Damascus

Jerusalem

Medina

Mecca

Axum

Lalibela

Chalcedon

Constantinople

Ephesus

Athens

Alexandria

Rome

Milan

Carthage

can also be said that the competing interpretations generated by this process of definition led to a loss of unity among Christians. Unanimity of belief was thus purchased through division and exclusion. To differ on the subject of God was to be in error. The heretic, or false believer, was not to be tolerated. A modern observer unfamiliar with terms such as *hypostasis* (person), *ousia* (essence), and *physis* (nature) could easily be inclined to think that these doctrinal quarrels were much ado about nothing. To think this way is to misunderstand the value of such precision in Christian history. Defining orthodoxy and identifying heresy was essential when one affirmed belief in "one Lord, one faith, one baptism" (Eph. 4:5).

God in the Middle Ages

The conciliar definitions of Nicaea, Ephesus, and Chalcedon set the boundaries for all subsequent Christian thinking on God and his incarnation. This is not to say that Christians stopped thinking about their monotheism after the seventh century. Surely, trinitarian and christological discussions abounded in the medieval period, but Christians in this era, for the most part, limited themselves to interpreting what had already been defined. Sometimes, this process of elaboration or clarification could result in controversy, as in the cases of Gottschalk (ninth century) and Peter Abelard (twelfth century) who were accused of Trinitarian errors. But one development stands out over all others in this period: the so-called "filioque" controversy, which contributed to the straining of relations between the Catholic West and the Orthodox East. One Trinitarian question that remained unsettled in the dispute with Arianism was the relation of the Holy Spirit to the Son and the Father. If the Father begot the Son, what about the Spirit? Does the third person proceed from the Father alone, or is the Son somehow involved in the process? In the ninth century, a bitter dispute arose over this point. At issue was the insertion of one Latin suffix into the creed by Western Christians: "*Credo . . . in Spiritum Sanctum, Dominum et vivificantem: qui ex Patre Filioque procedit.*" (The conjunction "and" can be inserted into a sentence in Latin by means of the suffix *que* being added to a word. In this case, the word in question is "Filio*que*": "I believe . . . in the Holy Spirit, the Lord and life-giver, who proceeds from the Father *and* the Son.") The creed in use since 451 had simply stated that the Spirit proceeded from the Father.

This seemingly minor change in the creed, reminiscent of the slight difference between homoousious and homo*i*ousios, was also related to the Arian heresy. As is the case with so many fine points of Christian theology, the distinction in question was far from trivial in the minds of many. This addition to the creed was a defense of the full divinity of the Son *and* the Spirit, against the Arian belief in their subordinate status. The Iberian theologians who added this "clarification" to the creed at the Third Council of Toledo in 589 did not think they were coming up with something novel; on the contrary, this belief had long been prevalent in the West and was considered faithful to conciliar Trinitarian definitions.

This change in the creed was gradually adopted throughout the West, and by

Major Medieval Heresies

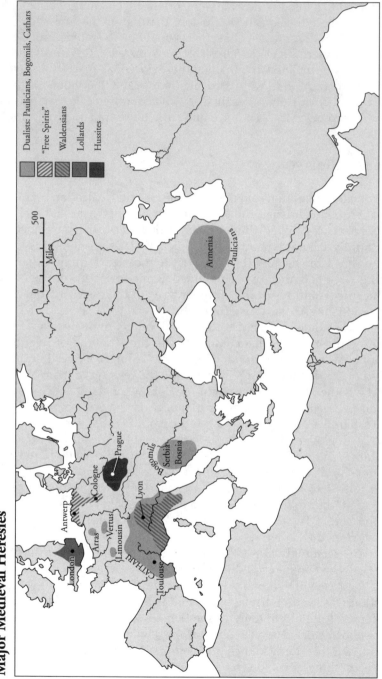

Dualists: Paulicians, Bogomils, Cathars

"Free Spirits"

Waldensians

Lollards

Hussites

Armenia

Paulicians

Prague

Bogomils

Serbia

Bosnia

Lyon

Cologne

Antwerp

Vertus

Arras

Limousin

CATHARS

London

Toulouse

500

Miles

0

the late eighth century, it was in use throughout the Frankish Empire; Eastern Orthodox Christians, however, saw it as heretical. In 867, this "innovation" was condemned by Photius, the Patriarch of Constantinople, and a schism arose with Rome. Though the schism between East and West caused by this condemnation was healed, the matter was not resolved to anyone's satisfaction. The creed recited or sung in the Latin liturgy of the Western Roman Empire continued to include the filioque, and, despite repeated Eastern protests, the change was officially accepted at Rome in 1014. When the churches of Rome and Constantinople broke with each other in 1054, their disagreement over the filioque proved to be one of the chief obstacles to reconciliation. The Orthodox remained adamantly opposed to it, even at a popular level. Though representatives of the Orthodox church accepted the theology of the filioque twice—first at the Council of Lyons (1274) and later at the Council of Florence (1439)—they refused to change their creed. Moreover, these agreements were resoundly rejected by the Orthodox faithful, some of whom chose to die rather than submit to this Western "heresy." To date, this controversy poses an obstacle to the reunion of the Orthodox and Catholic churches.

Medieval Christians might have had some disagreements over the Trinity, but they remained, for the most part, staunchly committed to monotheism. Nonetheless, there were some notable exceptions, for in both the Christian East and the Christian West there were localized resurgences of gnostic dualism. These medieval dualists differed somewhat in their beliefs according to time and place, but they professed a common teaching: that there were two deities in cosmic conflict, one evil—the creator of the material world (sometimes identified as Satan), and the other good—the ruler of the spiritual realm revealed by Christ. Salvation for these Christians meant release of the soul from its material prison, the body. Their Christology, naturally, was docetic.

This should sound familiar. Gnostic dualism had never fully vanished outside the borders of the Roman Empire, and contacts between the Empire and the world beyond, especially Persia, allowed for the infiltration of dualistic religion into the Christian world. The first major resurgence of Christian dualism took place in Asia Minor in the seventh century, among a sect known as the Paulicians (it is uncertain whether they are named after the Apostle Paul or after Paul of Samosata, a third-century monarchian). Though persecuted by the Christian emperors of Constantinople, some of these dualists managed to survive. A significant remnant emigrated to the Balkan Peninsula, where they gave rise to yet another sect, known as the Bogomils (so-called because their founder's name was Bogomil, which is the Bulgarian form of "Theophilus," or "God-lover").

Trading contacts with Western Europe gradually spread dualistic ideas beyond the Balkans. By mid-twelfth century, a wide swath of territory stretching from northeast Spain, across southern France, and into north-central Italy was dominated by an alternative dualistic church. These Western heretics were known as Cathars (from the Greek for "pure"), or Albigensians (after their stronghold of Albi, a town in southern France). Like their predecessors the Paulicians and Bogomils, the Cathars saw the material universe as the creation of the devil, interpreted

TOP TEN OFFICIAL BELIEFS OF MEDIEVAL CHRISTENDOM

1. *God.* There is but one God. This God created the universe, and He rules and sustains it. God is good, omnipotent, omniscient, omnipresent, just, merciful, and loving. He is immanent in his creation, yet also transcends it. He dwells in the highest empyrean Heaven, along with His angels and saints but is also definitely present on earth—albeit normally hidden from the human senses.

2. *The Trinity.* God is a Trinity. One God in three persons, each fully divine, sharing in the divine essence or nature: Father, Son, and Holy Spirit.

3. *The Incarnation.* God the Son became a human being, Jesus of Nazareth, the Messiah or Christ promised to the Jews. Jesus Christ was both fully human and fully divine: one person with two natures.

4. *Sinful Humanity.* Humanity is in dire need of redemption from suffering, death, and moral failure. Though created in the image and likeness of God, humanity had lapsed from its original condition through the sin of the first pair of humans, Adam and Eve. This original sin of disobedience so altered divine/human relations as to make humans susceptible to pain, illness, and death; it also separated humanity from God and made all humans naturally prone to violence, cruelty, and all sorts of vices and depraved behavior.

5. *Redemption.* God became human in Jesus Christ so He could redeem humanity. This redemption was effected principally through the crucifixion, death, and resurrection of Jesus. Yet this redemption was partial in the here and now: suffering, death, and sin will not be fully overcome until Christ returns from Heaven at the end of human history, to rule over a new earth, and to pass judgment on the behavior of every human who ever lived. The date of Christ's return would remain a mystery until the very end (though many would wrongly try to read "signs" of its approach and to pinpoint specific years for it).

6. *Life After Death.* Though mortal after the fall of Adam and Eve, humans were created for eternity and will live forever after their bodily deaths. The condition of their everlasting existence depends on their relation to God and the Church. Salvation hinges on right belief and right behavior. To gain the everlasting bliss promised by Christ, one has to be baptized, and to believe in him and obey God's commandments: those who follow Christ fully will join him in heaven and receive a new everlasting body; those who do not accept Christ or who live immoral lives will be condemned to eternal suffering in hell. Those who believe in Christ, but sin moderately (the majority of Christians) will have a chance to be cleansed immediately after death in purgatory, an intermediate, temporal place of suffering.

7. *Revelation.* There is but *one* truth revealed by God Himself. The full contents of the True Faith were revealed in the Holy Scriptures as interpreted by the elites who run the Church that Christ himself established, and which is constantly guided by the Holy Spirit.

8. *One Holy, Universal, and Apostolic Church.* There can be only *one* true Church directly descended from Christ's apostles, and outside this church there is no salvation. This church is led by the bishop of Rome, who is the successor of the apostle Peter, and who acts as the Vicar of Christ on earth.

9. *Communication with God.* God is approachable. Ritual and prayer are essential for salvation, and for daily existence on earth, because it is through these that Heaven and earth can intersect, and that spiritual and physical healing can take place. Humans can commune directly with God and improve their lives in myriad ways through this contact. Miracles are certainly possible: one can even eat the flesh of the risen Christ in a consecrated wafer.

10. *The Communion of Saints.* The church is composed not only of those alive on earth, but of all Christians who have ever lived. It is not only appropriate, but also advisable to venerate the saints, their images, and their relics, for the dead already in Heaven can be addressed in prayer, to intercede for the living on earth. The Virgin Mary, as Mother of the Incarnate God, is an especially powerful intercessor. Conversely, those on earth can pray for the dead in purgatory, to lessen their suffering and hasten their release.

salvation as release from the flesh, and believed Christ could not have taken a real, "disgusting" human body. Sexual intercourse and procreation were regarded as evil, since it was the means whereby spiritual essence became further entrapped in matter. It was said of the Cathars that they cringed at the sight of crosses and infants.

The fate of both the Bogomils and the Cathars was tragic. In the Balkans, persecution over several centuries reduced the number of Bogomils but failed to wipe them out completely, especially in Bosnia, which remained their stronghold. In the fifteenth century, when the region was conquered by the Ottoman Turks, these remaining Bogomils converted to Islam, giving rise to the existence of a Muslim people inside Christian Europe. (And, sadly, as Yugoslavia dissolved at the end of the twentieth century, their descendants fell prey to another persecution—that of "ethnic cleansing.") The Cathars fared even worse than the Bogomils. After attempts to convert them through preaching failed, Pope Innocent III launched a crusade against them in 1208. For the next twenty years, armies led by northern nobles descended on the Cathar strongholds of the south and wiped them out by means of the sword. The full horror of this war against heresy can best be comprehended, perhaps, through a single incident, the siege of Béziers in the south of France. This city was controlled by the Cathars, who had forced the Catholic bishop to flee, but it still contained many Catholic Christians as well. When asked by the invading soldiers, "How shall we differentiate between the heretics and the true believers when we conquer the city?," the exiled bishop replied: "Kill them all, let God sort them out."

God in the Renaissance and Reformation

Christian conceptions of God underwent some changes during the cultural renewal known as the Renaissance, which held the classical pre-Christian past in high esteem, and also during the religio-political upheaval known as the Reformation, which tore asunder the unity of Catholic Western Europe. Surprisingly, however, the changes were nearly imperceptible. Though the Renaissance fostered a new approach to authority, redefining some of the key paradigms of Christian thinking, it did not give rise to many individuals or movements that sought to re-shape monotheistic beliefs. It did lay the groundwork, however, for the rise of skepticism and modern science, and these developments, in turn, would affect Christian monotheism profoundly.

The Protestant Reformation, for all its defiance of established authority, re-mained profoundly conservative in regard to monotheistic theology. In fact, Chris-tology and Trinitarian theology were two of the few theological subjects that Catholics and Protestants could agree on. This is not to say that there were no dis-senters at all when it came to monotheism. Indeed, there were some in the radical fringes of the Reformation who denied the Trinity and the divinity of Christ, but they were in a minority and were subjected to persecution by both Catholics and Protestants. One such heretic was Miguel Servet, or Servetus, a Spanish physician and amateur theologian, who not only made significant discoveries regarding the human cardiovascular system, but also had published treatises in which he chal-lenged the doctrine of the Trinity. Servetus harkened back in his theology to a form of modalistic monarchianism and was condemned by both Catholics and Protes-tants, especially by the Protestant leader John Calvin. Hunted down and impris-oned by Catholic authorities in France, where he had gone into exile under an as-sumed identity, Servetus managed to escape; incredibly, he fled to Protestant Geneva, John Calvin's city, where he was burned alive for his heresy in 1562. Other anti-Trinitarians managed to survive and thrive, most notably in Poland, under the leadership of two Italian exiles, Fausto and Lelio Sozzini. Their followers, known as Socinians were relatively few in number and never posed much of a challenge to Trinitarian monotheism in this period. Nonetheless, they were har-bingers of things to come in subsequent centuries.

Others also strayed from traditional monotheism in this early modern pe-riod. The archives of the Inquisition give us glimpses of some of these individuals, who could be found both among the elite and at the bottom of society. One of the most celebrated cases was that of Giordano Bruno, a man of learning who was burned in Rome in 1600 for teaching that God and his creation were one and the same thing—in other words, that the visible universe was God (a theological posi-tion known as pantheism). An obscure case recently brought to light was that of a poor miller from northern Italy named Menocchio, who was executed for denying the existence of God and proposing that the universe had come into being on its own. There is no telling how many people in Christian Europe at this time were kindred spirits to Bruno and Menocchio. Though we have documents from church tribunals, both Protestant and Catholic, these archives cannot give a full account-ing of skeptics and freethinkers, for many could have simply chosen not to voice their beliefs. Abundant documentation from church tribunals in this period shows that the faithful did not always fully understand the complexities of orthodox doc-trine. When quizzed about the Trinity, for instance, some could reply that it con-sisted of "God," "Christ," and "the Virgin Mary."

The Nativity, 1140–1143. Mosaic in La Martorana (Church of Santa Maria Dell'Ammiraglio), Palermo

The Virgin Mary and her divine infant son, Jesus. Christians believe in the paradoxical existence of a God-man who was born of a woman like all other humans, but who is the eternal God himself. Mary's exalted place in Orthodox and Catholic piety as mother of God rests upon her willing acceptance of God's plan of salvation, that is, on her agreeing to make possible the incarnation of God. (*Source:* Alinari/Art Resource, NY)

The most serious challenge to traditional monotheism in the early modern age came not from ignorance or any specific heresy concerning God, however, but rather from an attitude or mentality known as spiritualism.

In the sixteenth century, as Christendom was plunged into religious warfare, some so-called spiritualists boldly denied the need for a church or a precise theology. More significantly, they redefined the notion of revelation, claiming that God could reveal himself inwardly to every person. Sebastian Franck, for instance, dismissed the Bible as "the paper pope" and went on to say:

> Consider as thy brothers all Turks and heathen wherever they be, who fear God and work righteousness, instructed by God and inwardly drawn by him, even though they have never heard of baptism, indeed, of Christ himself, neither of his story in scripture, but only of his power through the inner Word perceived within and made fruitful. . . . There are many Christians who have never heard Christ's name.[10]

Though these spiritualists had relatively little impact on their societies, they pointed the way for others who came later and reached more radical conclusions. Take, for instance, the case of Sebastian Castellio, a spiritualist who dared to publicly denounce the execution of Servetus. Castellio argued for an idea that was a greater threat to traditional monotheism than any antitrinitarian theology: he called for toleration and for an end to all religious persecution. By relativizing faith (that is, by saying that each person could find his or her own truth in God), Castellio undercut the foundation of a millennium and a half of Christian theology. Within two generations of Castellio's lifetime, such thinking would become more commonplace in Western Europe, and as a consequence, the God of Christendom would change drastically—at least for those who wanted him to change.

God the Great Governor of the World

On a windless summer day in 1624, Lord Herbert of Cherbury took into his hands a stack of manuscript pages, knelt in his chamber, and prayed: "I am not satisfied whether I shall publish this book, *De veritate*; if it be for thy glory, I beseech thee to give me some sign from heaven; if not, I shall suppress it."[11] Herbert was worried that his book overemphasized the role of reason (and understated the role of faith) in religious belief. Not to worry: Herbert received the sign for which he prayed and with a clear conscience published his book. A century later, it was clear that the book indeed had challenged orthodox belief at its heart and had accelerated the process of debate that eventually led in the West to a sweeping program of reverence for the "faculty of reason."

"Is religious belief rational?" was the most urgent question on the lips of Christians during the eighteenth-century Age of Reason. Religions characteristically require both correct belief ("orthodoxy") as well as correct practice ("orthopraxis"), but the relative weighting of the two can vary from one religious tradition to another. In Christianity, orthodoxy generally has been foregrounded by church officials (but "official" Christianity sometimes has been less appealing to certain populations than "unofficial" forms; and ritual, or practice, sometimes carries meanings more effectively than creeds). In any event, it is fair to say that concerns about the nature of Christian religious belief—for example, its logic or coherence or, in this case, its rationality—historically have been of particular importance for Christians.

Western religious traditions, of course, had for centuries been well acquainted with claims for the role of reason. As we have seen, the Greek intellectual tradition that influenced the development of cultures in the West included a form of reasoning (*logos*) about the divine, or *theologia*. In the tenth century, the Jewish scholar Saadya had distinguished between revelational laws and rational laws in his *Book of Doctrines and Beliefs*. The Muslim theologian al-Ghazali (d. 1111) wrote pointedly about the usefulness of reason in thinking about God. Abelard's twelfth-century *Sic et Non* was a major contribution to the development of rational argument in Christian theology. Renaissance and Reformation writers, the Dutch humanist Erasmus (b. 1466), and René Descartes, the Catholic mathematician and philosopher who was a contemporary of Herbert, all had practiced theology as rational discourse about God. Why, then, did the question "Is religious belief rational?" lead to such overwhelming debate among Christians in the eighteenth century? The answer: reason recently had been firmly linked to human autonomy, and that led to the supposition that if religious belief were rational, then reason alone was sufficient to know God. For a religion that over many centuries had constructed its theology, ritual life, patterns of authority, and moral codes on the bedrock of divine revelation, the notion that humans were capable of discerning by reason the essence of religion was shocking and insurgent and as potentially threatening to orthodoxy as was spiritualism.

Let us look at the Enlightenment context for this development. The Enlightenment began as a joint scientific and philosophical investigation into this manner in which persons come to know things, or epistemology. At the heart of this enterprise was trust in "criticism" as the method by which truth was discovered. Casting a suspicious eye on the received wisdom of scripture and church, Enlightenment thinkers described a physical world governed by immutable laws (for example, Isaac Newton's laws of gravity) that were interconnected in such a way as to form a harmonious whole of creation. And if rational science could discover physical laws, why not moral ones as well? Religion accordingly became less a matter of the supernatural and more a matter of the natural.

Indeed, "natural religion" was the popularized term that indicated the drift of theology. Natural religion had emerged in rudimentary form in Lord Herbert's treatise as an amalgam of several ideas: there was a Supreme Being who must be worshiped through the proper use of human faculties and the cultivation of virtue; sin was a deviation from that course and required repentance so that the immortal soul would be rewarded rather than punished by divine justice in the afterlife. Over the course of the eighteenth century, these ideas served as a platform for various forms of natural religion. In one of its forms, natural religion appeared in Europe and America as "Deism." At its extreme, it led to skepticism of the sort associated with the French freethinker Voltaire (b. 1694) who attacked clerical leadership as exploitive priestcraft and supernatural truth as superstition.

The Enlightenment and its immediate aftermath manifested various levels of conflict between claims for the capabilities of human reason and traditional Christian supernaturalism. The consequences for religion are best understood, however, as part of a process of adaptation in which religion and the new learning struck various bargains. In fact, from the complicated negotiations between Christian orthodoxy and Enlightenment ideas about human autonomy, there emerged sophisticated defenses of Christianity on the grounds of its inherent reasonableness. "Reasonable Christianity" subsequently proved itself the most durable religious product of the Enlightenment, serving as a superstructure for a multiplicity of Christianities over the course of the next two centuries. Reasonable Christianity was represented typically by English latitudinarians such as John Tillotson, the archbishop of Canterbury, who preached religious tolerance (or latitude) and defended the Bible by appealing to reason. By shifting the focus of the debate in such a way as to claim that reason confirmed key points of revelation rather than contradicted them, the churches were in many cases not only successful in dampening the fire of doubt but in fact were able to reinforce their position. Christianity was conceived anew as both supernatural and rational, undergirded by both reason and revelation. Articulating this view was to prove a Herculean task for theologians; but late in the Age of Reason, hope ran high that the fine print of the contract would confirm the spirit of the agreement.

We should view the Enlightenment as a force with which Christianity had to come to terms and that transformed Christianity as had nothing before. Roman Catholicism has found much of the Enlightenment not to its liking, especially during the nineteenth century when Pope Pius IX, in *Syllabus of the Chief Errors of Our Time* (1864), condemned the following belief: "Every individual is free to embrace and profess that religion, which, guided by the light of reason, he or she shall consider true." But to see the Enlightenment as a pitched battle between upstarts who proposed reason as the key to the discovery of truth arrayed against legions of church traditionalists who accepted only revelation is to misapprehend the spirit of the age. Indeed, like Lord Herbert, who published a book that subverted orthodoxy but who prayed first for a sign to proceed, the Enlightenment was conflicted. In the end, it supplied arguments both for demolishing and for shoring up belief.

Against this background, we should understand that the Enlightenment served in general to diminish the distance between God and humanity. That is, to an increasing extent, Christians conceived their God as integrally related to the laws of nature and morality that, as science had discovered, knitted the cosmos together as an organic whole. God became the "great governor of the world," the author of the laws of nature, the divine craftsman. Christians referred to "nature and nature's God" and wrote animatedly about how God was "revealed" in nature. Proponents of the laws of nature challenged orthodox Christian notions of deity grounded in belief in the essential mystery of God. Typical of the former was the French Deist Comte de Volney, who wrote at the end of the eighteenth century that the law of nature

> is the constant and regular order of facts, by which God governs the universe; an order which his wisdom presents to the senses and to the reason of men, as an equal and common rule for their actions, to guide them, without distinction of country or of sect, towards perfection and happiness."[12]

Unlike Giordano Bruno, Volney was not executed for reconceptualizing the relationship between God and creation.

Jesus Christ the Moral Teacher

An assortment of new emphases and reconceptualizations of the Trinity blossomed in the hothouse of Enlightenment thinking. One of these was the emphasis on Jesus Christ as a moral teacher, and it came about as part of a project of theological transformation in which ideas about providence—or help from God—eclipsed older notions of divine judgment.

The God of premodern Christianity often was depicted as a legal God, a chronicler of the sins of humanity, a judge mysterious in his anger. This was the God that frightened Martin Luther beyond toleration and predestined souls to hell in John Calvin's theology. As the Enlightenment brought God more clearly into focus as a rational being who treated humanity according to reason and as the distance between God and humanity consequently was diminished, Christians increasingly looked to Jesus as a moral exemplar. There was nothing new in the tendency to search for manifestations of spiritual excellence in the lives of others: martyrologies and hagiographies (lives of saints) and accounts of the life of Jesus had been available to the faithful in one form or another virtually throughout the history of Christianity. The new emphasis was on the humanity of Christ, on Christ as a teacher who knew his audience because he was one of them. Jesus appeared as a wise, compassionate, and helpful guide, an example of spiritual maturity and teacher of a sublime morality. Thomas Jefferson's "The Life and Morals of Jesus of Nazareth"—a compendium of the "lessons" of Jesus that Jefferson cut from the New Testament and pasted together in series—typifies this turn in thinking about God. Jefferson's "bible" avoided references to the divinity of Jesus (miracles, divine commission, etc.) and foregrounded instead various parables, the virtues identified in the Sermon on the Mount (Luke 6:20–49) and teachings on forgiveness and justice.

The preference for a more human Jesus eventually led to sweeping theological reformulations. Foremost was the rise of Unitarianism. It appeared originally in Poland and Transylvania in the late sixteenth century as an assortment of religious movements—most visible were the Polish Brethren and the Lithuanian Brethren—claiming that Jesus Christ was not really God. The term "Unitarianism" came into use about 1549 in Transylvania in connection with debates about the nature of Jesus Christ. Although Roman Catholic authorities were successful in limiting the growth of the movements, they still survive in Hungary and Romania.

Unitarianism was more successful in England and America. The first English Unitarian Congregation was founded in London in 1774. Influenced by the ideas of Joseph Priestley and Richard Price, Unitarianism took shape in England essentially as a rejection of the doctrine that Jesus Christ was a part of the Godhead. Instead, Jesus was viewed as a human being who served as a kind of emissary, or

mediator, between humanity and God. In America, William Ellery Channing articulated this theological position to an audience in Baltimore in 1819, arguing
Christ's inferiority to God and, like Thomas Jefferson, stressing the responsibility
of humans to live morally. Although the growth of Unitarianism in North America
and England has generated a diversity of views about the meaning of Christianity,
Unitarians in the twentieth century in general affirm the unity of God (as opposed
to a distinction of three parts) and the humanity of Jesus and recognize in Jesus the
ideal model of moral responsibility.

Christian Monotheism and Prophetic Religion

Central to the project of Protestant reformers in the sixteenth century was their affirmation of the authority of the Bible. Acknowledging that authority involved
their acknowledging as well the Holy Spirit, the third member of the Trinity, as the
inspirer of the Bible. Roman Catholicism had for most of its history officially recognized the guidance of the Holy Spirit in the general life and faith of the community of believers. More specifically, Catholics expressed confidence in the gifts of
the Holy Spirit to church leaders. This emphasis on the Holy Spirit—and especially on personal experience of direct revelations from the Holy Spirit—as we
have seen has served to complicate doctrines of God in Christian monotheism.
Historically, it has served as well as a dynamic element in both Protestantism and
Catholicism, as a basis for resistance to perceived corruption of tradition, and as a
stimulus to new directions in religious thinking.

After the Reformation, Christians, and especially Protestants, sharpened
their focus on the Holy Spirit. In many cases, this took place alongside growing
popular perceptions of the corruption of religion and/or the decay of morality and
often led to religious protest movements. Accordingly, flurries of Christian interest
in the Holy Spirit frequently have been linked with millennialism.

Illustrative of growing popular interest in the Holy Spirit were the Cami-
sards, or "French Prophets," who appeared in France late in the seventeenth century. Many in the Camisard movement claimed possession by the Holy Spirit and
experienced ecstatic frenzies and direct revelations. Camisard revelations ranged
from prophecies of the imminent Protestant overthrow of the papacy to the resurrection of religious leaders from the dead. When Camisard influence crossed the
channel, it sparked the religious visions of a group of English Quakers. Under the
leadership of Ann Lee, who claimed a revelation that Jesus was the "male principle" in Christ and that she was the "female principle," these "shaking Quakers,"
or Shakers, eventually found a home in North America, where their number grew
large in spite of their belief that marriage (that is, sexual relations) was the root of
all depravity. At about the same time, the Anglican Joanna Southcott also began
experiencing religious visions that by the early nineteenth century were communicated in sixty-five books of her prophecies and through the activities of her substantial popular following.

Christians have developed various understandings of the role of the Holy

Spirit in religious life in recent centuries. Those understandings have ranged from an enlarged sense of the desirability of a "baptism of the Holy Spirit" to belief in the possibility for personal advance—through the agency of the Holy Spirit—into an elevated condition of "holiness." The growth of Wesleyan and Methodist churches, Holiness movements, and the ongoing appearances of millennial groups in Europe and the Americas have evidenced the appeal of this form of popular piety.

One mark of the growth of the religion of the Holy Spirit is the dramatic twentieth-century rise of Pentecostalism (named for the descent of the Holy Spirit upon the Apostles seven Sundays after Easter, or on "Pentecost"). Pentecostalism describes a religious life that can include conversion experiences, religious healing, millennialism, prophecy, and spiritual ecstasies and charisms (such as glossolalia, or speaking in tongues). Pentecostals until the late twentieth century tended to be drawn largely from the ranks of the dispossessed, recent immigrants, racial and ethnic minorities, and the working class. Characteristically, they have rejected worldly fame and gain and embraced a vision of religion as continuous discovery of the new and unexpected. The prophetic element in Christianity, then, is best understood as a reflection on one's predicament in the world and the possibility for rising above it through the supernatural help of the Holy Spirit. In this sense, the Holy Spirit is for most Christians a Spirit of presence and a Spirit of transformation.

In some contexts, ideas about the Holy Spirit have been strongly influenced by thinking about spirits in general. This is especially visible in the encounter of Christianity with primal religions. In Afro-Christian religions, primal traditions about ancestor worship, spirit possession, and the easy exchange between the natural and the supernatural worlds condition understandings of the nature and function of the Holy Spirit. It is not uncommon for ecstatic ritual in these religions to be driven by experience of the "power" of a "spirit" who may represent ancestors, supernatural forces, and the third member of the Trinity all at the same time. The case of Haitian *vodou* is similarly illustrative. Vodou spirits have both African and Catholic names as a consequence of the religion's genesis in Haiti. French Catholicism merged with the religions of African slaves there, resulting, for example, in an identification of St. James with the warrior Ogou, and Saint Gerard with Gede, who is associated with sex, death, and humor. Such blendings of theologies, although not always directly focused on the Holy Spirit, nevertheless represent something of the way in which the third member of the Christian Trinity has come to play the leading role in some forms of Christianity.

CHAPTER 6

MONOTHEISM
IN ISLAM

DOCTRINES AND PRACTICES

Islam means "surrender," and the person who has surrendered to God is a "Muslim." Those two words share a common root *s-l-m*, which also produces the word *salām*, meaning "peace." Salam is cognate to Hebrew *shalom*. Salam means more than peace as a mere absence of war or conflict. Salam is well-being, wholeness, health, and felicity. When Muslims greet each other with *Al-Salāmu 'alaykum* ("Peace be with you!"), they wish their brothers and sisters all of these, with the greeting being reciprocated as *wa 'alaykum al-salām* ("And with you be peace!").

Islam is the Qur'anically revealed name of the monotheistic religion founded in Arabia under the prophetic leadership of Muhammad. The first obligatory act, or "pillar," of Islam is the bearing witness to God's unity and the messengerhood of Muhammad. *Lā ilāha illā Allāh!—Muhammad rasūl Allāh:* "There is no god but God. Muhammad is the Messenger of God." This formula, known as the *Shahāda*, or "witnessing," is the fundamental confession of Islamic faith. It is sufficient to declare the Shahada with sincerity before a Muslim witness to become a Muslim. The confession of Islamic faith through the Shahada is both a doctrinal statement—something belonging to the realm of theology—and a ritual act that proclaims one's allegiance and values for all to witness. The Shahada expresses the basic doctrines of Islam and is thus a sort of miniature creed. This chapter presents and interprets the basic beliefs of Islam as a monotheistic faith.

Doctrine comes under the category of faith, known in Arabic as *īmān*. One

BASIC DOCTRINES AND PRACTICES PRESCRIBED IN THE QUR'AN

The essential doctrines proclaimed in the Qur'an are (1) the Divine Unity, (2) Belief in Angels, (3) Revealed Scriptures taught by Prophets, (4) a Last Judgment, and (5) Divine Decree and Predestination. As a religious system, the Qur'an also enjoins on the believers several required devotional acts and duties, which are often referred to as the "Five Pillars of Islam": (1) witnessing to the unity of God and the messengership of Muhammad, (2) worshiping five times daily in a prescribed manner, (3) almsgiving, (4) fasting for a whole month during daytime, and (5) making a pilgrimage to Mecca. (These pillars are described in detail in Chapter 12.)

who has faith is known as a *mu'min*, "a believer." The two correlated terms, *islām/muslim* and *īmān/mu'min*, have similar grammatical forms. The Qur'an speaks of īmān as a higher order of religious awareness than islām, although both are essential and complementary.

> The desert Arabs say, "We believe." Say [God is addressing Muhammad], "You have not believed; say only "We have submitted, for faith (īmān) has not yet entered your hearts." (Sura 49:14)

Following is a summary of the basic Qur'anic doctrines that should be categorized under the heading iman, "faith."

The Divine Unity

The first belief is in the absolute unity and sovereignty of God, the doctrine known in Arabic as *tawḥīd*. This word has verbal force and literally means "to acknowledge as one" and "to make one." At the purely conceptual level, it points to the unity of God, but at the action level it is a commitment to reflect that unity in religious allegiance. Put another way, Muslims seek unity of purpose and of their community as a celebration of God's oneness. God is so holy and solitary that he has no comparison or connection with any aspect of creation. His uniqueness is beyond rational comprehension. This radical view has not predominated in the history of Islamic theology, although it is implicit in any expression of radical unity. But Muslim mystics have interpreted God's unity as including in union those who adore him. Such adoring contemplatives experience annihilation of their separate selves through an absorption in God.

The Qur'an expresses the idea of the divine unity frequently, as in the following short Sura:

In the Name of Allah, Most Gracious, Most Merciful.
Say: He is Allah, the One and Only;
Allah, the Eternal, Absolute;
He begets not, nor is He begotten;
And there is none at all like Him. (112)

Tawhid's opposite is association of anything with God, known as *shirk.* Shirk is the one unforgivable sin, because it entails a denial of God's true nature, to which nothing may be added or subtracted. It is, in short, idolatry. According to the Qur'an:

Allah does not forgive associating anything with Him. But He forgives other than that as He wills. But the one who associates (anything) with Allah has indeed strayed far away. (4:116—adapted)

The confirmed *mushrik,* "idolater," is usually thought to be beyond God's forgiveness, but in another Sura we read:

Say: 'O my servants who have transgressed against their souls. Do not despair of the mercy of Allah; for Allah forgives all sins. He is oft-forgiving, most merciful. (39:53)

The confirmed mushrik's repentance may not be received, but one who temporarily lapses and then sincerely repents will find mercy. When God's servants sin, they must show sincere repentance, which includes mending their ways in a positive change of course.

The Qur'anic doctrine of God is similar in most respects to the Jewish and Christian understandings of God. A poignant revelation concerns the abiding quality of God's inner nature:

All that is on the earth will perish:
But the Face of your Lord shall remain—
Full of majesty and honor. (55:26–27)

The Face (*wajh*) of Allah is mentioned several times in the Qur'an and stands as a vital symbol of God's personal nature.

Belief in Angels

The second article of īmān is belief in the reality of God's angels (*mal'ak*, pl. *malā'ikah*), who are his faithful, unquestioning servants. Angels existed before humans and are made of light. The Islamic teachings about angels belong in the general Near Eastern context, with elements traceable to ancient Iran. The angels exist in a hierarchy at the top of which are four archangels: Gabriel, Michael, Israfil (of the trumpet); and Izra'il (the angel of death). Gabriel (Arabic, Jibrīl) has already been introduced as the angel of revelation of the Qur'an to Muhammad.

The belief in angels also extends to acknowledgment of other supernatural beings. In addition to angels are the *jinn*, invisible beings often similar to humans and made of fire (humans are made of clay). The jinn comprise a large class with quite different types included, from upright, morally aware members capable of religious commitment and salvation to frightful and evil devils, at the head of which is Iblis, a fallen angel who refused, when commanded by God, to bow down to Adam.

Revealed Scriptures and Prophets

The third major element of īmān is belief in divinely revealed scriptures entrusted to human prophets chosen by God. Muhammad is the last in a long line of prophets who have been entrusted with divine messages. The Qur'an confirms what was revealed before and corrects errors and corruptions that prior communities have allowed to occur. The Qur'an states that "to every community (*umma*) there is a messenger (*rasūl*)" (10:47).

Prophets are subdivided into two categories. The first is designated by the word *nabī*, "prophet," which means someone to whom God has spoken and who prophesies within a specific community according to an already received message. There are many thousands of nabīs of this type. The second type, also a nabī, is known by the word *rasūl*, meaning "messenger" or "envoy." This type of prophet bears a new revelation to a particular people. The Qur'an teaches that no distinctions should be made among the prophets, for all are God's chosen bearers of revelation. At least twenty-five prophets are named in the Qur'an, including such biblical figures as Moses, Job, Abraham, Jesus, Noah, Jonah, and Joseph.

Muhammad is known as "Seal" of the Prophets, because he is the last messenger before the final judgment. As Seal, Muhammad certifies the true prophecy of old and closes the book, as it were. On numerous occasions the Qur'an declares that its message is not new, but a reiteration and clarification of what had been revealed before to many earlier peoples, as was observed in the Qur'anic quote in Chapter 3 (2:136; page 63).

The Last Judgment

The fourth category of doctrine is belief in a final judgment at the end of time. Among the names of this event are *yawm al-dīn*, "the Day of Religion/Doom." Numerous references to the last judgment appear in the Qur'an, and a vast commentarial tradition developed later. The last judgment will bring an upheaval in nature, with the seas boiling over, the mountains moving from their foundations, the sunny sky folded up and darkened, stars falling, and so forth. The dead will arise from their graves in a general resurrection before each soul is judged alone before God. Heaven and hell will be brought near, and the saved will be rewarded with paradise whereas the damned will be sent down below to undergo terrible sufferings in the fire. One of the terrifying heralds of the final day will be the trumpet blast of the archangel Israfil, which wakes those sleeping in their graves.

Ablution Taps with Canopy at Sultan Hasan Mosque and Madrasa (theological college) in Cairo, Egypt

(*Source:* F. M. Denny)

Although the signs and wonders attending the final judgment are impressive enough, at the core of the event is a moral structure with an outcome in humankind's accountability for their acts and lives. The Qur'an and all other revealed scriptures will, until the resurrection, have served as warnings. If people will not heed the warnings and obey Allah, then they will have no excuse when called to the judgment. Each person will be confronted with a full record of her or his deeds while on earth.

And the Record Book (*al-kitāb*) will be laid open; and you will see the evildoers in great consternation about what is in it. They will say: "Ah! woe unto us! What a Book is this! It leaves out nothing, small or great, but takes account thereof!" They will find all that they did, and your Lord will not treat a single one unjustly. (18:49)

The Divine Decree and Predestination

The final major element of doctrine under īmān is a belief in God's ultimate authority over all that occurs, a difficult doctrine that has led some toward a fatalistic acceptance of whatever happens as God's will. I suggest that the doctrine be looked at as much from a psychological as from a logical point of view. Certainly an almighty and all-knowing and eternal God must logically control all that happens, whether in an active or a passive sense. That is, God may act to effect a happening, or he may withdraw and permit something to find its own outcome within his natural laws and even the working of chance within those laws. But God has willed either event, whether or not he has desired a particular outcome. Even though the Qur'an emphasizes God's power and control throughout, it also holds up human responsibility as the indispensable condition for the moral life. A kind of push and pull occurs between God's will and predestination and humans taking responsibility for their actions. Both, in a sense, are simultaneously real. But such a mystery is better understood at the psychological or spiritual level than at the reductive logical level, at which propositions collide and proofs contend. One traditional saying has it that when confronted with the paradox of divine omnipotence and human responsibility, one should believe in predestination but live and act as if it didn't exist.

ISLAMIC MONOTHEISM: A WIDER PERSPECTIVE

The basic doctrines of the Qur'an contain all the elements that later were to be more fully elaborated in Islamic theological discourses. Qur'anic monotheism has much in common with Jewish and Christian ideas, especially with the former. And like the two older religions, Islam's conviction about the divine unity is not an arid, abstract matter, although it does have a profound intellectual quality born of reflection combined with spiritual insight that finds expression in ethical living. Islamic conviction does not begin and end with the human mind but is based in a mutual relationship with the living God.

> And call not, besides Allah, On another god, There is
> No god but He. Everything (That exists) will perish
> Except His own Face. To Him belongs the Command,
> And to Him will ye (All) be brought back. (28:88)

The expression "Face of God" (*wajh Allāh*) is a good example of the personal quality of God. It does not refer to a literal face but means the essence of God, which is personal. An often remembered "divine saying"—that is, a divine thought expressed in the Prophet Muhammad's words—goes: "I was a hidden treasure and I wanted to be known, therefore I created the universe." This yearning for contact with other persons is at the core of the Qur'anic doctrine of God. The cosmos was created out of the divine mercy and with it was also provided God's attending guidance for the world's stewards, the human race. God's guidance is in the form of rational awareness, which he shares with his human servants, as well as the signs in nature and the messages in sacred scriptures entrusted to prophetic messengers, beginning with Abraham.

The pre-Islamic Arabians were polytheists, by and large, although Jews and Christians were found in some places. Allah was worshiped, alongside many other deities, as the supreme being who had created the universe. But there is a fundamental difference between recognizing a supreme being, one that stands at the top of a hierarchy of deities, and an only god. The preaching of Muhammad insisted that people should desist from worshiping diverse gods as there was no basis for so doing, that there is no god but God, and to behave as if there were is to be lost in denial of what is real. This is *shirk*, "association" of creature with Creator, the greatest sin of which a person is capable, as mentioned earlier in this chapter.

The Arabs before Muhammad were a divided and quarrelsome collection of communities distributed throughout the Arabian Peninsula. They shared a common high language—Classical Arabic—but did not have a need or desire to unify at the political level. Not until a strong monotheistic doctrine was spread throughout the peninsula did political unity become possible. The Arabs of old raided each other constantly and only occasionally concluded temporary alliances for mutual benefits. But political unity did not come about simply as a result of a new religious awareness. Islam and the command to spread it raised the possibility of hitherto unimagined wealth and power, which immediately accrued to the conquering tribes as they ventured beyond the frontiers of the peninsula to the rich, sedentary countries of Egypt, Palestine, Syria, Iraq, and beyond. The unification of Arabia is the first major political consequence of tawhid. If a people, however fractious and bellicose, can find a means of coming together, they will constitute a formidable force for realizing their common goals. The Qur'an speaks of the Muslims as an umma that will succeed, will be saved, even, if its members hold on tightly together to the *ḥabl Allāh*, "lifeline of God."

> O ye who believe! Fear Allah as He should be feared, and die not except in a state of Islam [i.e., submission]. And hold fast, all together, by the lifeline of Allah, and be not divided among yourselves; and remember with gratitude Allah's favor on you; for ye were enemies and He joined your hearts in love, so that by His grace ye became brethren; and ye were on the brink of the Pit of Fire, and He saved you from it. (3:102–103—adapted)

Not only did the Qur'an vigorously oppose Arab polytheism, it also pointedly rejected the Christian Trinity as polytheistic, saying:

O People of the Book! Commit no excesses in your religion: nor say of Allah aught but the truth. Christ Jesus the son of Mary was (no more than) a Messenger of Allah, and His Word, which He bestowed on Mary, and a Spirit proceeding from Him: So believe in Allah and His Messengers. Say not "Trinity": desist. It will be better for you: for Allah is One God: Glory be to him; (Far exalted is He) above Having a son. (2:171)

Many other passages in the Qur'an attest to the absolute oneness of God. The rejection of the Christian notion of the Trinity is a hallmark of Islamic theological apologetics and polemics and a major obstacle in the two religions' otherwise often reassuring attempts at interreligious dialogue. Islamic and Jewish doctrines of the oneness and nature of God are highly compatible. (Indeed, Muhammad in Medina hoped and expected that the Jews would unite with the Muslims, seeing no serious doctrinal or ritual impediments in so doing. That was not to be, because a fateful split occurred based on politics.)

Also in the Hadith—sayings of the Prophet Muhammad—we find abundant testimony to Islamic monotheism. For example, concerning īmān, which includes both belief in the vital, personal sense and in theological doctrine, we have Muhammad's words:

Īmān (faith) has over seventy, or over sixty, branches; the most excellent of these is the saying, There is no god but Allah. . . .
Whoever dies while he knows that there is no god but Allah enters paradise.[1]

Doctrine, Creeds, and Theologies

Muhammad was not a theologian, nor is the Qur'an a treatise on systematic theology. But both the revealed Scripture and the Messenger's teachings are deeply theological in their meanings and directions. They provide inexhaustible sources for systematic theology in a manner that parallels the Bible. Significantly, although Muslims have a general consensus about what the fundamental theological doctrines of Islam are, they never developed an official creedal statement that was required of all Muslims. The uniform structures of Islamic thought and devotion center in acts of worship ('ibādāt) contained in the pillars of Islam: prayer, almsgiving, fasting, and pilgrimage. Thus, Islam is an enacted faith more than it is a theological system. As an enacted faith, it is vitally concerned with matters of ethics and law, with *doing* the truth and not merely comprehending it in an intellectual manner.

The first pillar, the Shahada, is a kind of minimal creed, as was earlier observed, and it is required of all Muslims; but it is so general as to need considerable elaboration to understand fully. Attempts by Muslim scholars to articulate doctrines in concise, creedal forms have been based on the contents of the Qur'an, the teachings of Muhammad (which form a kind of commentary on the Qur'an), and some historical events of the early community. But those statements, however widely accepted, are not required of Muslims in order to be in good standing in the community (unlike the various creeds that have emerged in branches of Christianity, such as the Apostle's Creed, the Nicene Creed, and the Westminster Confession).

The Jews resemble the Muslims in the absence of a universal, required creed. Though attempts at composing creeds have been made by Jews, for example, by the great medieval philosopher-theologian Moses Maimonides in his famous "Thirteen Articles of Faith," even that profound creedal summary has never been made a binding test of Jewish commitment (although it is widely respected and appears in prayer books as part of the great legacy of Jewish doctrine and liturgy). Yet both the Muslim and Jewish communities are clear about their beliefs and ritual requirements and both are strongly legal in orientation. Somehow, belief, however doctrinally articulate and refined, is empty without expression in religious and moral acts based on God's command and done to his glory.

Muslims have a nearly uniform liturgy worldwide, without benefit of clergy or standard creed. The forms and practices of worship are themselves the creed, acted out with the heart and the body within the community. Everything in the acts of worship (described in Chapter 12), can be interpreted as having theological meaning because of the divine imperative to serve God above everything else and to remember him in all thoughts and acts. One of Muhammad's Companions asked the Prophet what true goodness (*iḥsān*) was. Muhammad answered: "That thou worship Allah as if thou seest Him: for if thou see Him not, surely He sees thee."[2]

Theology as a constructive enterprise emerged in connection with unsettled questions about the revelation, Muhammad's teachings, and how they should be applied to the experiences of the community in the early generations. There were also urgent issues concerning the religious claims of Jews and Christians and the traditional religious understandings and practices of the lands to which Islam was carried during the great conquests and migrations from Arabia. Muslim thinkers discussed doctrinal issues through a formal discourse known as *kalām* (lit., "discussion, talk"). Eventually, kalām evolved into dogmatic theology and took on varying forms as *'ilm al-kalam*, "the science of (theological) discourse." A practitioner of this discipline was known as a *mutakallim*. Some significant advances in theological thinking were contributed to monotheism by Muslim theologians as they strove to relate the contents of the revelation to the contexts of common life.

As was true of early Christianity, early attempts at creedal summaries were motivated principally by heresies and the need to refute them. For example, the Apostle's Creed was instituted as a baptismal confession in Rome and was aimed at Gnostic errors, among them the denial of Jesus' actual death and bodily resurrection ("was crucified, dead and buried, and on the third day he rose from the dead"). Theologians also wanted to provide consistent articulations of doctrine, so as to avoid future heresy and straying and to strengthen the community. This is paralleled in the great Jewish scholar Maimonides' drafting of "Thirteen Articles of Faith," mentioned earlier.

Although the Shahada's first, fundamental clause is the witnessing to the oneness of God, a widely circulated early Muslim creed is silent about both the divine unity and Muhammad's messengerhood. Probably it was thought to be superfluous to include them, since the Shahada is essential for all Muslims. Rather do we see, among the ten brief clauses in the creed known as "Greater Understanding" (*fiqh akbar*), matter pertaining to intracommunal differences. For example, the first article states: "We do not consider anyone an infidel on account of sin; nor do we deny his faith." A puritanical element considered the grave sinner to be a threat to the community at large, rather than a free and independent agent. The emerging consensus viewed such a person as someone needing to repent and reform, but not to be banished or executed. Article four states: "We disavow none of the Companions of the Apostle of Allah; nor do we adhere to any of them exclusively," a statement directed toward the Shi'ites, who were loyal to Ali (Muhammad's son-in-law) as the only authentic successor to Muhammad. Article six reads: "Insight in matters of religion is better than insight in matters of knowledge and law," which has been interpreted to mean that "serving Allah is better than gathering knowledge."[3] The following article states: "Difference of opinion in the community is a token of divine mercy." The commentators point out that such difference applies only to difference in legal opinions, not to differences pertaining to the foundational doctrines of Islam, such as monotheism, the divine origin of the Qur'an, and Muhammad's exemplary role as prophet.

A later and more elaborate attempt at a creed contains much more in the way of theological substance. It is popularly known as *Fiqh Akbar II* and is a product of a period—the 900s—when advanced theological disputes had become commonplace. A brief excerpt about the divine nature will give some idea of the creed's high level of discourse.

> Allah the exalted is one, not in the sense of number, but in the sense that He has no partner; He begetteth not and He is not begotten and there is none like unto Him. He resembles none of the created things, nor do any created things resemble Him. He has been from eternity and will be to eternity with His names and qualities, those which belong to His essence and those which belong to His action.[4]

The creed contains a statement about the nature of the Qur'an, whether it was created in time or is eternal as God's Speech. The famous rationalist theological school, the Mu'tazilites, flourishing for a period as the official court school in the capital of Baghdad in the 800s, held that the Qur'an was created in time and could not in any way be regarded as divine, lest the Muslims risk bitheism, belief in two gods. Their point was, in part, that an eternal Qur'an would be parallel to the Christian doctrine of the incarnation of the divine Word in Jesus of Nazareth. We have already seen how the Qur'an rejects the Trinity. A dual god would be conceptually just as blasphemous as a triune god, according to strict Muslim principles, so the Mu'tazilites argued. Nevertheless the Qur'an is, as a modern scholar

Classic-Style Minarets Surrounding Mosque-Tomb Complex of Sufi Saint Sidi Ahmad al-Badawi, Tanta, Egypt

(*Source:* F. M. Denny)

put it, an "inlibration," "Word made Book" in human history, paralleling in important ways the Christian doctrine of the incarnation, or "Word made Flesh," in the person of Jesus of Nazareth.[5]

The eventual consensus was that the Qur'an is indeed eternal, but the manner in which this doctrine was safeguarded and expressed is contained in the creed under examination:

[the Qur'an is] the speech of Allah, written in the copies, preserved in the memories, recited by the tongues, revealed to the Prophet. Our pronouncing, writing and reciting the Kuran is created, whereas the Kuran itself is uncreated.[6]

When the Qur'an is read and recited with belief, there is a wondrous sense of being in the presence of God's eternal Word and being guided, comforted, protected, and refreshed by it. This is parallel to the experience of Holy Communion for Christians, when the bread and cup are shared and Christ's passion and redeeming atonement are recalled and received with thanksgiving through the Eucharistic words of the Lord's Supper. The eventual argument in favor of a doctrine of the eternal, uncreated Qur'an proceeds, it would seem, not from formal theological dialectic but from individual and group experience of the transforming and empowering presence of the recited Qur'an, which renders both Allah and his Messenger present. We are speaking here of a central mystery, not a mere intellectual problem. To be sure, the article in Fiqh Akbar II does contain a sophisticated formal discussion, but it is not sustained for its own sake but for the benefit of the believers. The article moves from faith to intellect and back to faith. Distinguishing between the temporal acts of reciting and writing down the Qur'anic text and the nature of the message itself is a reflective process predicated on a prior surrender to the Word as revealed in the Qur'an. It is, in sum, an exercise in right ordering.

Another concern in monotheistic religion is anthropomorphism, speaking of God in human terms and thus risking loss of the transcendent, mysterious, and finally unknowable nature of the divine essence. The Mu'tazilites, again, were keen on safeguarding Islamic belief from attributing creaturely qualities to God, such as physical members (hands, eyes, etc.), spatiality (occupying a literal throne in heaven), emotions, and so forth. The problem is that the Qur'an often speaks of divine attributes that are shared with the created order. Examples: "So glory to Him in Whose *hands* is the dominion of all things" (36:83); "But construct an ark under Our *eyes*." (11:37); "Allah is He that *heareth* and *seeth* all things" (4:134); "The *wrath* of Allah is on them." (48:6); "Then He established Himself on the *Throne*" (13:2); "Allah is the *friend* (or protector) of the righteous" (45:19). We have already noted the face (wajh) of Allah.

With respect to the rationalist theologians, such anthropomorphisms were interpreted metaphorically, not literally. The Fiqh Akbar II, however, seeks a middle course between radical deanthropomorphism and its literal opposite. Acknowledging the purely intellectual conflict of attributing human qualities to God and at the same time preserving his (the very pronoun is a gender representation, from the created realm) transcendence, the text reads:

It must not be said that His hand is His power or His bounty, for this would lead to the annihilation of the quality [that is, "handedness"]. . . . No, His Hand is His quality, without (asking) how [*bilā kayfa*].[7]

The mysteries of God exceed human abilities to comprehend. It is sufficient that God has revealed guidance for salvation, without imagining that his servants should also know his true nature. God reveals his nature and purposes in his own way, and within the limits of human understanding in the spatial-temporal order of creation. If humans cannot rationally comprehend or reconcile what God has revealed and willed, then they must submit and accept "without (asking) how"— bila kayfa—as the passage just quoted asserts. The Mu'tazilites were not prone to suspending critical judgment, but considered reason as a reliable guide to unraveling the mysteries of being. Their metaphorical interpretation of anthropomorphic passages in the Qur'an enabled their acceptance while still retaining a rational stance in theology. The general Sunni rejection of Mu'tazilism was based on the view that the rationalists had effectively turned God into a rational principle, thus failing to yield to His transcendent and inscrutable sovereignty as "The Most Gracious, Most Merciful, . . . Lord of All the Worlds," as He is characterized in the Sura "The Opening."

Some other issues that occupied the minds of Muslim theologians were whether humans had free will or were predestined, whether there are variations in the excellence of God's names, whether prophets are sinless (they are), whether prayer performed standing behind an unbeliever is valid (it is.) All Muslim theologians in one way or another had eventually to agree that human free will was necessary for there to be authentic religious and ethical behavior, else humans would be puppets of God.

Muslim theology has had both its Sunni and Shi'ite exponents. What has been provided here has been largely a Sunni viewpoint. Shi'ite kalam continued to retain some Mu'tazilite principles and perspectives, combined with that community's prevailing commitment to its religious teachers as possessing supernatural wisdom received from the holy imams of the tradition, beginning with Muhammad, and continuing through Ali, Husayn, and others, all bearers of a "Muhammadan Light" (*nūr muḥammadī*) that preserves from error and guarantees truth.

Sufi Ideas About Monotheism

The Muslim mystics, known as Sufis, arose as a more inward and contemplative expression of Islam during the early centuries when the caliphate was in its glory from India to Spain, roughly from the 700s to the 1200s CE. A characteristic of Sufism has been renunciation of materialism and the seeking of a life of spiritual poverty, known as *faqr*. The word "Sufi" apparently derives from the Arabic word *ṣūf*, "wool," referring to the coarse woolen garments that Muslim mendicants took to wearing as a distinctive marker of their spiritual questing. Dissatisfaction with the official Islam of the mosque and law courts led the Sufis to cultivate a variety of spiritual disciplines intended to bring believers into a more intimate relationship with God in this life and in preparation for the next. "Die before you die!" has been a constant admonition of the Sufis. That is, one should review one's life and prepare for the inevitable death to come by reflecting on one's mortality and seeking guidance toward the satisfaction of God. If one lives for God's pleasure alone, then what happens to the individual matters not a bit. Though simple to state, this thought can be fatuous without a sense of the depths to which Sufi masters probed in the pursuit of union with God through the more esoteric disciplines of meditation and retreat. A great range of Sufi doctrines and practices developed across the Muslim world, from sober reflection and living in close adherence to the Islamic Shari 'a, or Law, to frankly antinomian and countercultural forms of behavior that despised the admiration of humans and sought only the pleasure of Allah, to ecstatic Sufis who became "drunk" with the love of their Lord and lived as "friends" of Allah, who in turn was friend to them in intimate spiritual union. This last type of Sufis contributed some of Islamic civilization's most arresting and sublime poetry, in Arabic, Persian, Turkish, Urdu, and Malay, especially.

A central issue in Sufi understandings of monotheism is whether one can have union with God and what that might mean. In one sense, union with God may be annihilation of the individual, personal self. That is a kind of subtractive union, which leaves God alone at the end. Anther way to think about this is by means of close association with God, not in the sense of shirk as association, of course, but through bonds of intimate friendship and trust. The majority of Sufis have sought something like this. Still another approach has been characterized as pantheistic, because it sees all creation as ultimately identified with God. The "Unity of Being," or *wahdat al-wujūd*, doctrine has had a troubled career, with most Muslim authorities condemning it as nonmonotheistic because it abandons the transcendence of God over all his creation.

An example of radical Sufi monotheism—or, as some have thought, pantheism—is the martyr-mystic al-Hallaj (d. 922). Al-Hallaj was a truth-seeker who traveled far in his life, through the Fertile Crescent and the Indian subcontinent. He learned about Christianity, Hinduism, and Buddhism, among other religions. As a young spiritual seeker in Baghdad, he had offended the more senior Sufis by moving from one master to another without receiving the necessary confirmation from the prior one, a serious breach of ethics as well as a symptom of something other than submission. The Sufi novice has always been required to present her- or himself to the master, or shaykh, as if she or he were a corpse to be washed before burial.

Al-Hallaj came to have a considerable influence over others and founded a school of mysticism. He claimed to have reached such a state of intimate union with God that his own ego was lost, annihilated, and only God's self remained. Al-Hallaj expressed this doctrine in an unsettling phrase: *Anā al-Ḥaqq*, "I am the Truth." Al-Ḥaqq is one of God's many beautiful names, so the mystic was actually claiming identity with God. The advanced Sufis understood what al-Hallaj was trying to express. All Muslims of his time knew that "everything perishes except His face" (28:88). But al-Hallaj's statement could mislead the uninitiated, for whom it would be confusing and thus dangerous. Al-Hallaj was brought before the authorities and required to recant his doctrine and specifically its public expression. Al-Hallaj refused and was subjected to a horrifying execution by crucifixion, dismemberment, and burning. He still did not recant but expired with forgiveness of his persecutors on his lips.

Al-Hallaj claimed to be a strict monotheist, but the opinions of subsequent

**Desert Men in Southern Jordan with Traditional Headdresses
and Robes, Enjoying Tea**

(*Source:* F. M. Denny)

generations of Muslims are divided. The Persian poet and spiritual guide Jalal al-
Din Rumi (d. 1273), a great Sufi of a later era, held that the statement "I am the
Truth" is actually a statement of great humility. Had al-Hallaj declared that "I am
the servant" of God (*anā al-'abd*), he would have affirmed two existences, his own
and God's.

> But he that says "I am God," that is, "I am naught, He is all; there is no being but
> God's." This is the extreme of humility and self-abasement.[8]

We introduced the idea of "oneness of being" earlier. Some scholars have
considered al-Ḥallāj to be saying something other than that the universe is composed of essentially one substance, God. Al-Hallaj seems to have held to the fundamental distinction between God and his creation, between time and eternity,
that has been a fundamental doctrine of Islam and its close monotheistic siblings,
Judaism and Christianity. To be sure, there have been independent spiritual visions and voices in all three of those traditions. The monistic doctrine of "oneness
of being" (*waḥdat al-wujūd*) is often associated with the Andalusian mystic Ibn
Arabi (d. 1240), but even he never seems to have mentioned the concept in his
writings. It is closer to the truth to consider al-Hallaj as an exponent of the "oneness of witnessing" (*waḥdat al-shuhūd*). He devotes himself exclusively to God, and

God rewards and confirms his devotion with an ecstasy of awareness, a rapture in which he is seized by God. The declaring of "I am the Truth," then, is a witnessing to the workings of God within al-Hallaj. Rumi was convinced that this witnessing liberated al-Hallaj from the subjectivism of self-awareness and effected his deliverance to God-awareness.

Some Sufis have emphasized repentance from sin and being aware of the great distance between God and humanity. Others—probably the majority—have felt moved more by God's love than by his justice, without in any way denying the latter. Rabi'a al-'Adawiya of Basra, an influential woman Sufi saint of early times—she died in 801—made love the central truth of Islamic devotion. Rabi'a had been a slave as a girl but was later freed. She was a spiritual adviser to both men and women. A man once approached her and asked whether God would turn toward him if he repented. She answered that he would not, that only if God had already turned toward the man would he be able to repent, that it is always God's anticipatory grace that changes what is in the hearts of humans. Rabi'a was told by a man that he had not sinned in a long time, whereupon she responded: "Your existence is a sin to which no other sin can be compared."[9] Rabi'a's bluntness seemed not to have gained her enemies. Rather, a consensus held that it was part of her authority. She had been slave to a human, then she became slave to God, and that is what Islam is all about: being God's slave instead of a slave to self and all the uncertainties attending thereto. Rabi'a would be remembered if she had shared only the prayer that Muslims have never tired of quoting:

> O God! if I worship Thee in fear of Hell, burn me in Hell; and if I worship Thee in hope of Paradise, exclude me from Paradise; but if I worship Thee for Thine own sake, withhold not Thine Everlasting Beauty![10]

Orthodoxy and Orthopraxy in Islam

Islam is a religion in which *doing* the truth is more important than simply knowing what is required. Law is more important than theology in the sense that obeying God's commandments is open for everyone of even minimal intelligence, whereas understanding the mysteries of doctrine is for only a few. The bias of Islam in favor of law and worship is often called by specialists "orthopraxy," from Greek roots meaning "right practice." Orthodoxy, on the other hand, means "correct doctrine" and is thus biased toward thought and opinion. Both doctrine and practice are of central importance in most if not all religions, but there is usually a spectrum on which one or the other is more heavily weighted. Christianity has often been preoccupied with doctrinal matters, and the existence of widely accepted creeds exhibits a conceptual bias. Judaism and Islam, overall, are much closer to each other as orthopraxic religions than either is to Christianity.

Islam is certainly also concerned with correct doctrine, with orthodoxy. But without an outcome in the behavior and ordering of Muslim individual and common life, the teachings of the Qur'an and the Sunna of the Prophet Muhammad (which is discussed in Chapter 9), plus the considerable body of commentary on them, are unfulfilled.

The Islamic doctrine of tawḥīd, the Divine Unity, contains within it both a conceptual and dynamic dimension. Conceptually, tawhid does indeed mean God's Oneness, which is finally mysterious rather than a matter of simple number. The term tawhid does not entail a notion of a static, perfect monad, untouched and untouchable. Rather, tawhid has a definite active, verbal quality in that it means, properly, "making one." God is one, and God calls the worlds into being to reflect his unity, by which is meant, in part, his integrity, his wholeness, his perfection, his goodness. It is God's nature to reach out in a personal way to share with his creatures the wonders of his power and glory.

Humans cannot muster any power and glory of their own; but they can participate with God as his vicegerents, or deputies, on earth, his "caliphs," as the Qur'an calls them.

> Behold, thy Lord said to the angels: "I will create a vicegerent (*khalīfa*) on earth." (2:30)

> Say: "Praise be to Allah, and Peace on His servants whom He has chosen (For His Message). (Who) is better? Allah or the false gods they associate with Him? . . . Who listens to the (soul) distressed when it calls on Him, and who relieves its suffering, and makes you (Mankind) inheritors [caliphs] of the earth? (27:59, 62)

The Qur'an shows throughout that God not only gives commands to humans; more important, he also calls them to meaningful service as his heirs and agents on earth. Each human being has a set term of life, during which he or she can participate in the calling of vicegerent. The Muslim community, the umma, is "the best nation brought forth from the people, enjoining the good and prohibiting the bad" as the Qur'an states (3:110). It has the special charge to lead the human family in realizing God's intention of caliphhood.

God has shared with his human creatures three essential attributes of his own: intelligence, will, and speech.[11] Humans are the highest order of creation, even higher than angels, who lack the individual free will of humans. Of course, free will can and often does get one into trouble. The angels exclaimed, when God informed them of his intention of making Adam and his progeny caliphs on earth:

> "Wilt Thou place therein one who will make mischief therein and shed blood?— whilst we do celebrate Thy praises and glorify Thy holy (name)?" He said: "I know what ye know not." And He taught Adam the names of all things. (2:30)

God then paraded all things before the angels and bade Adam to tell them their names, including their inward qualities. Thus, humans inherited directly from God the power of physical and spiritual-symbolic discernment. Angels have faith, but they leave understanding to God and, as it turned out, to humankind who have a special relationship to God. God ordered the angels to bow down to Adam. All did except Iblis, who refused. (It is not clear whether Iblis is considered an angel or a *jinnī*, one of the invisible beings of fire who parallels humankind and also possesses intelligence, will, and speech and the capacity to submit to God as Muslims. In any event, Iblis becomes the Devil in Islamic cosmology.)

Tawhid is in the nature of God, but it is also a task of humankind as vicegerents. It entails demonstrating one's belief by behaving in ways conducive to the worship and service of God. One cannot truly understand God's unity without striving toward unity in the Muslim community. This is done in many ways— personal, communal, political, economic, liturgical—and the variety of ways must themselves be harmonious and mutually enhancing. Perhaps the most dramatic exhibition of making God's religion one is the five pillars. The daily Salat-prayer services, for example, are nearly uniform throughout the world. Wherever one may be, one knows exactly what to say, how to perform the postures, and what is required in the way of etiquette before, during, and after the performance. Muslims rejoice in this treasure of a heritage passed down to them, for it reminds them of being one people in service of the One God.

Monotheism in Islam is the doctrine of humankind accompanying Islamic theology. Humans are created essentially good, on a sound constitution, or *fiṭra*, the primordial nature that is in harmony with both God and nature. Humans make mistakes, both intellectual and moral, and they are sometimes prone to unimaginable evil; but their fundamental nature as creatures made in the image of God has not been and cannot be tarnished. The fiṭra, however, can be forgotten, suppressed, or ignored, but that is something quite different from the Christian doctrine of original sin that Islam, as well as Judaism, rejects. In a sense, living as God's caliph in the world is the highest form of fulfilling one's fiṭra. Living in complete submission to Allah empowers the Muslims in the world, for if the only real fear is disobeying God, then the opportunities for managing the moral and spiritual order of the world are boundless.

MONOTHEISM

QUESTIONS FOR DISCUSSION AND REVIEW

1. Judaism, Christianity, and Islam are monotheistic religions and as such have much in common. Each religion nevertheless is distinctive, and that distinctiveness is grounded in the manner in which each articulates specific emphases in its monotheistic theology. What is theology? Who are theologians and how do they go about their jobs?

2. Monotheistic theologies, like all theologies, have been influenced by the cultural settings in which they emerged. Identify some of the features of the settings in which Jewish, Christian, and Islamic versions of monotheism first took shape. What are the distinctive theological emphases in Judaism, Christianity, and Islam, and how can those emphases be understood in relation to the cultural settings? Is the notion of redemption present in these religions? How does the Christian conception of the Trinity compare to the Islamic understanding of Allah? Is a notion of a "people" relevant to all three traditions?

3. Theologies develop and change alongside transformations in the social and political worlds in which they thrive. How have the theologies of these three religions changed in various historical and cultural settings? What has been the influence of Hellenism?

4. Jewish, Christian, and Islamic theologies all feature a powerful, transcendent God. For all three traditions, that God nevertheless is present in the world. How is this belief in evidence in each religion?

5. Jews, Christians, and Muslims place varying emphases on religious creeds. What is a religious creed? To what extent does each religion emphasize "correct belief" and "correct practice"? What is the role of faith in each religion?

6. Creeds often take shape as religious communities seek to limit the influence of competing religious ideas. That competition frequently comes in the form of "heresy." How can this process be observed in the cases of Judaism, Christianity, and Islam?

7. Some theological developments are characterized by an emphasis on mystical union with God, whereas others work within a decidedly rationalistic framework. How are such varying emphases visible in the theologies of Judaism, Christianity, and Islam?

PART III

AUTHORITY

A religious leader speaks with authority, scripture is venerated as authoritative, and certain markings on a large building inspire a sense of the authority of a religious tradition. Leader, scripture, house of worship, all are sources of authority—or are they? In fact, in none of these cases is the actual source of authority apparent. Religious authority is perfectly displayed—and perfectly hidden—in the life of a religious community. Community itself is the ground of authority. Without community, there would be no leader, no scripture, no synagogue, no church, no mosque. Authority is invisible in the sense that the integrative and disintegrative forces that drive community life are too complex and active to be definitively mapped. Authority is visible, however, in the regard of members for their community and in their manifest respect for collective life. Leaders, scriptures, and religious architecture all are important, then, as emblems of that self-understanding and respect, but not as actual sources of authority.

There are many conceptualizations, many styles of religious authority in Judaism, in Christianity, and in Islam. There are, of course, obvious differences among the three traditions, and within each tradition there likewise is a spectrum of ideas about the nature and function of authority. The forms of authority differ because communities differ. Even with a religion, the circumstances of life among members can vary enormously. Rural settings frequently engender experiences of collective life that differ from those of urban dwellers. Ethnic dissimilarities within a tradition likewise shape social life in different ways. Gender, economic status, and even climate are among other variables that bear upon group life and can affect the manner in which persons conceive authority. In view of this, we must keep

155

in mind that communities frequently have plural identities. For example, a single community will identify itself simultaneously as a nation (or part of a nation), as a language group, and as a rural population. And such a community will conceive the exercise of authority in a fashion that responds to the various contexts of its collective life.

The preeminent symbol of authority is the religious leader. Who are religious leaders? Why are they acknowledged as such? How do they exercise authority? What are their relationships to the communities they lead? How is their authority correlated with the authority of religious law or doctrine? In every case, leadership is constructed in such a way as to answer the needs of the community. Those needs, again, may be diverse, grounded as they are in the plural contexts of community life. Thus, we may discover among a single community several different styles of leadership, all of which are keyed to specific aspects of the experiences of the members.

Members of a religious group experience authority in a way that outsiders might initially find difficult to understand. We should remember that authority is not merely law, doctrine, scripture, religious office, ceremony, or other discrete elements of a tradition. Authority originates in the experience of the individual in community, as part of a rich environment of lived ideas and expectations about both the past and the future. The more energetically we explore that environment, the better positioned we will be to understand religious authority.

CHAPTER 7

AUTHORITY
IN JUDAISM

We have seen that the central story of the Hebrew Bible describes the checkered history of a special, covenantal relationship between the Creator of the Universe and the descendants of Abraham. This conviction of God's covenantal love, and the corresponding obligation of Israel to become worthy of that love, extends well beyond the biblical literature. It is the fundamental starting point of all Judaic understandings of what it means to be Israel, the Holy People of God. It should come as no surprise, therefore, that covenantal metaphors play an active role in the actual institutions of Jewish communities. Extending beyond the purely intellectual or imaginative realm of theology and mythic memory, conceptions of covenant have a powerful impact on social relations as well. We see in this chapter that particular ways of interpreting the nature of Israel's covenant translate into specific types of communal structure and organization.

Ideas about the covenant, for example, are built into assumptions regarding the nature of communal boundaries: who is inside Israel and who is outside, and how is the border maintained and sometimes crossed? Similarly, covenantal understandings are explicitly appealed to in defining specific roles within the community: who has the authority to establish communal norms, and who is obliged to follow them? How are established sources of authority challenged, and what happens to those who do so? Every form of Judaism has addressed these questions; and, in all of them, specific conceptions of covenantal existence have been crucial in providing answers.

BIBLICAL METAPHORS OF COVENANT COMMUNITY

You will recall from Chapter 1 that Judaism was formed between the fifth and third centuries BCE, among a community of Judean Israelites living under the domination of Persian and then Egyptian-Hellenistic empires. At the dawn of the Hellenistic period, a small national center had existed for some centuries in the ancient homeland, and long-standing communities were already thriving in Egypt and Mesopotamia in particular. Calling themselves "Israel," a name indicating descent from the biblical patriarch Jacob (e.g., Gen. 35:9–12) or "Yehudim" (Judeans), after their homeland, they were everywhere referred to in Greek as *ioudaios*. Our English word "Jew" stems ultimately from this ancient usage, as do its cognates in all European and Middle Eastern languages (e.g., German: *Jude*; French: *Juif*; Arabic: *Yahud*).

Jews living in their ancient land during the Hellenistic period did so largely under domination of foreign governments. They shared with non-Jews the land that, in the Torah's phrase, "I, the Lord, have given you" (e.g., Exod. 20:12, Num. 15:2, Deut. 3:20). It was theirs and not theirs at once. Many of those living in other lands, correspondingly, did so as "exiles," severed limbs from a national body that remained always disjointed. So wherever one looked in the ancient world, one found Jews, but nowhere did they constitute a majority of the country in which they lived. Not even in their own land could they look around them and see a society governed by their own people in accord with their own traditions. Indeed, as we have seen in our discussion of the formation of the scriptural canon and the tradition of Oral Torah, it took many centuries before great numbers of Jews would reach agreement as to precisely what those national traditions were or how they were to be observed.

The covenantal metaphors found in the early Jewish religious writings gain their coherence when we interpret them in light of this social reality of national dispersion. The scattered nature of Jewish societies is the setting in which the emerging religious literature of the Jews developed such an acute interest in a single, persistent question: who is this people that shared a common collective name—Israel or Judeans—and little else? The idea of covenant is a way of addressing this situation and gaining some control over it. How, then, despite the stubborn facts of social and political experience, did the Jews come to imagine themselves as a single people bound to one another across territories and empires by unbreakable bonds of covenantal obligation?

The canonical literature of the Hebrew Bible, reaching its present form, as we recall, well into the Hellenistic period, and other noncanonical writings of similar antiquity propose many models of covenant and community. We focus briefly on four common models of Israel. These affirm that Israel is in some essential way (1) a nation led by prophets, (2) a liturgical community led by priests, (3) a state led by kings, and (4) a disciple community led by sages. You may notice that in each of these—with the rare exception of certain prophetic figures—communal leadership is imagined as an exclusively male prerogative. One important consequence is that women's exercise of religious leadership in Judaism has been minimal until recent decades. We explore some of the consequences of this fact in Chapter 10, in which we survey modern developments in Jewish ritual life.

At issue in this chapter, however, is how each of these models has played a dual function in certain exemplary Judaic communities. In the first place, a particular conception of Israel and its leadership has usually served as a model for an existing Jewish society, explaining Jews' obligations to one another. Second, the models frame the way in which Jews have then imagined their collective identity as a people related by covenant to the Creator of the World. As we see, these four covenantal models constantly overlap. That is, when Jewish communities reflect on Israel's covenantal existence in terms of one biblical image, they will almost inevitably shape that image to fit coherently with one or more of the others.

A Nation Led by Prophets

The Torah's diverse descriptions of Moses' relationship to Israel are fundamental to all Jewish thinking about covenant and community. Indeed, in biblical memory, it is only through the leadership of Moses that Israel was transformed from a collection of families and clans into a nation (*'am, goy*). Moses does so, according to the biblical stories, primarily by bringing before the people irrefutable testimony to the presence of God, God's power, and God's exclusive love and concern.

Such testimonies include Moses' ability to perform wonders, such as turning the waters of the Nile into blood (Exod. 7:19–24) or causing the waters of the Sea of Reeds to part (Exod. 14:26–29). But more important, Moses' prophetic leadership lies in being chosen by God as the human medium through which to reveal God's will, the Torah, to Israel (Num. 12:1–9). The image of Moses as a mediator of God's will—who brings the good news of God's love and the terrifying portents of his anger (Deut. 28:1–69)—is essential to all biblical descriptions of figures, such as Isaiah, Jeremiah, and others, who are also remembered as prophetic leaders. Thus, when the Bible imagines Israel as a covenant nation, it often places at the center of that nation a prophetic leader who emulates Moses' ability to bring into the midst of the nation the direct confrontation with God's love and will.

A Liturgical Community Led by Priests

When the Torah describes the years of Israel's wandering in the wilderness, it stresses that Moses was not the sole leader of the people. Rather, he shared leadership with his brother Aaron, who served as priest. The idea that Israel is a liturgical community, "a kingdom of priests (*memlekhet kohanim*) and a holy nation (*goy kadosh*)" (Exod. 19:6), is just as important to the Bible and later forms of Judaism as is the model of a nation led by a prophet. But what exactly is a liturgical community?

As described in the books of Exodus through Numbers in particular, Aaron and his descendants played a critical role not only in the social life of Israel, but in

A COMMUNITY OF WOMEN IN EARLY JUDAISM

Although Judaic religious communities have usually been dominated by male leaders, there is one tantalizingly vague reference to a possible exception. The first-century philosopher Philo writes in this his book *On the Contemplative Life* of a monastic society of Jewish philosophers called the Therapeutae ("Healers"). This group, according to Philo, was divided into separate male and female monastic communities. Both lived a sexually celibate life, practiced contemplative disciplines, and studied philosophy. They met communally only in celebration of the Sabbath or other special festivals. According to Philo's description, at such public gatherings the women were sequestered behind partitions from which they listened to men discourse on philosophy. In this way, says Philo, "the modesty becoming to the female sex is preserved, while the women sitting within earshot can easily follow what is said, since there is nothing to obstruct the voice of the speaker" (*Life* 33). Unfortunately, little is known about how these monastic women organized their own communities. A good place to begin a study of the religious lives of these and other Jewish women of antiquity is the recent book by Ross Shepard Kraemer, *Her Share of the Blessings: Women's Religions Among Pagans, Jews, and Christians in the Greco-Roman World* (New York and Oxford: Oxford University Press, 1992), pp. 106–27.

the good order of the universe as well. Their central duty was to offer sacrificed animals on the holy altar that had been built in the wilderness Tent of Meeting. This was a kind of movable shrine within which dwelt the "glory of God," a mysterious presence hovering above the altar, by which the God of Israel communicated to Moses and Aaron (e.g., Exod. 25:22). During the period of the Israelite monarchy, the site of sacrificial service was shifted to the inner shrine of the Jerusalem Temple. Whether offered in the later Temple of the earlier Tent of Meeting, the main function of this service was to cleanse the people of the cumulative effects of their tendency to rebel against God and his designated human leaders. The blood of the innocent sacrificial victim, spilled on the altar, was a substitution for that of the guilty humans who offered it. Israelites, who owed their lives to God, were now cleansed and set free to rededicate themselves to lives of obedience to the covenantal laws revealed to the community by Moses on Sinai.

The centrality of the priests, whose sacrificial procedures brought atonement for Israel, was not limited to the religious life of the people. Of equal importance was the role of the sacrificial service in maintaining the proper functioning of the cosmos. Especially in later centuries, when entire squads of priests served in the enormous complex of the Second Temple, the priestly service was understood to ensure the coming of the rains in their season and the fertility of the land, the herds, and even the people Israel. As we have seen in Chapter 1, it was through the priesthood that the creative and restorative power of God—the basis of all reality—was channeled into the world for the benefit of all creatures. In light of this, you can appreciate why this service was called in Hebrew, *'avodah,* a word that means not only "liturgy," but "work" as well.

What does it mean, then, to imagine Israel as a liturgical community, a "kingdom of priests and a holy nation"? The point is that the world is sustained in its normal course only in and through the covenantal loyalty of Israel (e.g., Lev. 26:1–45). Its obedience to the will of God, as expressed in its performance of his covenant commandments, is itself a kind of sacrificial service on behalf of the universe as a whole. Thus, the Torah revealed by a prophet, Moses, serves at the same time as the standard of covenant loyalty exhibited by a nation of priests, the descendants of Aaron. As long as the Second Temple stood, it represented the visible presence of God's blessing. Not surprisingly, Jews throughout the diaspora made regular donations for its upkeep and, when possible, would make pilgrimages to the Temple to live out the reality of being a priestly people.

A State Led by Kings

By the time the various collections of Hebrew scripture were drawn together, the ancient Davidic dynasty was a distant memory. As recalled in the books gathered in the canon of Nevi'im, it served as the model not for an existing Jewish community, but rather for an ideal community that would exist in the future. As we observed in Chapter 4, biblical ideas of kingship, especially as preserved in the books ascribed to Israel's prophets, inspired visions of the messianic restoration of the people Israel to its former glory as a unified community ruling the Land of Israel according to the laws of the Torah.

A few moments of reflection on the biblical image of David will reveal the complex way in which the image of the righteous king governing a righteous kingdom in accordance with the laws of the Torah (Deut. 17:18–20) resonates with other covenantal models. In the Bible, David is not merely a political functionary, but a vehicle of God's will. He was not elected by the people but was appointed by a prophet, Samuel (I Sam. 17:13). Indeed, he is credited, as reputed author of many Psalms, with having enjoyed the spirit of prophecy himself. His reign, therefore, and that of his heirs, represents for the Bible a visible symbol in this world of the divine kingship to which Israel is ultimately subject. God's special covenant with Israel through the family of David is eternal: "I have found David, my servant; anointed him with my sacred oil . . . I will establish his line forever, his throne, as long as the heavens last" (Ps. 89:21, 30).

By Hellenistic times, however, the Davidic dynasty was ancient history. In the extended present of Israel's exilic existence, to the contrary, biblical models of statehood described little that people found in their own social and political experience. To be sure, in the later rabbinic period, the prestige of Davidic origins would be claimed by important Jewish political leaders of Palestine and Mesopotamia (see Chapter 19), who bore the corresponding titles of Patriarch ("leader of the Homeland") and Exilarch ("leader of the Exiles"). These were officials appointed by non-Jewish emperors. For most of the Jewish history, then, images of Davidic royalty provided a glorious past now departed. In contrast, Jews measured their humble present; and in its terms, they savored anticipations of a wondrous future. The social unity provided by the model of the righteous Davidic state stemmed from its power to create a community of common memory and destiny. Except for periodic episodes of messianic expectation (see Chapter 4), it has had little impact on the actual structure of existing Jewish societies.

A Disciple Community Led by Sages

A final basic metaphor of Jewish covenantal existence, unlike those already discussed, does not dominate the biblical canon. Rather, it surfaces in isolated settings, receiving its richest amplification in other Jewish writings of the Hellenistic period. Images of Israel as a disciple community absorbing the teaching of sages, masters of the Torah's wisdom, are common in such biblical writings as the Book of Proverbs. They appear as well in the Book of Ecclesiastes, ascribed to the sage-king Solomon, and in other works, such as Psalm 119. The noncanonical Wisdom of ben Sirah (known in Christian tradition as Ecclesiasticus) is particularly rich in celebrations of the sage as a source of wisdom and Torah, a proper leader of the people: "It is the duty of those who study the scriptures not only to become expert themselves, but also to use their scholarship for the benefit of the outside world" (Preface to ben Sirah).

The covenant ideal represented by the leadership of the sage is one of study, particularly study of God's wisdom as revealed in the created order, and God's will as revealed in the Torah. The books of Proverbs and ben Sirah regard wisdom (*khokhmah*) as a constituent principle of reality. She is often personified as a woman and appears as an almost divine being, similar to the *sophia* (wisdom) of Greco-Roman philosophy, who lived with God even before creation (e.g., Prov. 8:22; Sirah 24:3–12). Absorbing the wisdom of the sage, the Israelite disciple is transformed into a model of wisdom, exemplifying in every word and deed the wisdom of the Creator as disclosed in the Torah (Prov. 3:1–26; Ps. 119:9–16).

The covenantal model of Israel as a community of disciples in the path of wisdom was particularly attractive to Jewish communities in the Hellenistic diaspora, familiar as they were with the claims of Greek philosophy to chart a life of wisdom and virtue. With the Torah as their philosophical charter and the sage as their philosopher, such Jews would find a rationale for Jewish communal exclusivity that, at the same time, resonated profoundly with the values of the surrounding environment. The writings of Philo of Alexandria, discussed in Chapter 4, offer many examples of how the biblical image of Moses as covenantal prophet is thoroughly reconceived in light of Hellenistic models of the true sage as philosopher.[1]

APPLICATIONS OF BIBLICAL MODELS IN THE DEAD SEA YAKHAD

With such an array of possible models of covenantal community before them, how did ancient Jews apply them in the construction of their own common life? This question is difficult to answer in detail because of the scarcity of reliable evidence about the structure and government of ancient Jewish societies prior to the rise and spread of rabbinic Judaism.[2]

There is, fortunately, one Jewish community of Second Temple times whose surviving writings richly describe the nature of its internal organization. This community seems to have called itself the *Yakhad* (Community). Because it flourished in the Judean Desert south of Jerusalem, in a barren region called Wadi Qumran, contemporary scholars often refer to it as the "Qumran community." Founded in the mid-second century BCE, it persisted for about two centuries prior to its destruction during the Jewish revolt of 66–73 against Rome.[3]

Some of the Qumran community's writings seem to have been preserved in a large library of many other ancient Jewish texts, now widely known as the Dead Sea Scrolls. In these scrolls, we find numerous references to the Yakhad's leadership, initiation procedures, and other illuminating information. A description of how the biblical covenantal models are applied in the Yakhad provides an instructive contrast to other applications of covenant models in later forms of Judaism.

The origins of this community are obscure and scholars remain divided in their theories. A commonly held view is that the Yakhad originated in a group of Jerusalem priestly families. The founders seem to have felt disenfranchised by the political restructuring of the Jerusalem priesthood in the wake of a civil war among Palestinian Jews (168–165 BCE). This war culminated in the creation of an independent Judean kingdom under the priestly Hasmonean family, known in Jewish tradition as the Maccabbees. Whereas later Jewish tradition established the winter Festival of Hanukkah in commemoration of the Hasmonean victory, the members of the Yakhad were not among those who found Hasmonean leadership a cause for celebration. These priestly families, and others whom they were able to attract to themselves, rebelled against the ascendancy of "the Wicked Priest" appointed by the Hasmoneans (Commentary on Habakkuk, column 9) by leaving Jerusalem and creating an alternative priestly community in the caves of Qumran overlooking the Dead Sea.

Claiming descent from Aaron through his own descendant, Zadok, they interpreted their separation from Jerusalem as a self-exile of the pure and holy genuine priests from the impure, illegitimate priests who had gained control of the Temple. They awaited a time in the near future when God would restore the true descendants of Zadok to the Temple in a cosmic battle, between the "Sons of Light" and the "Sons of Darkness," that would usher in the end of time and the direct rule of God.

The Yakhad's communal discipline must be interpreted against this background. Before us is a small, cohesive society viewing itself as the "true" Israel, surrounded by wicked imposters arrogantly claiming to be God's covenantal partner. Although such famous Dead Sea Scrolls as the Damascus Rule and the Community Rule are not in total agreement about all aspects of the Yakhad's structure and government, there is enough agreement to permit some valid generalizations.

It is clear, to begin with, that the model of a liturgical community stands at the center of the Yakhad's covenantal self-understanding. As an example, we

THE DEAD SEA SCROLLS: WHAT'S IN THEM?

The scrolls and other literary fragments found in the Qumran area contain many different kinds of writings. Those which have proved most interesting to scholars are the following.

Copies of Biblical Texts

At least parts of every biblical text except for Esther have been identified. These are interesting because many represent versions earlier than those that came to be canonized in rabbinic tradition. Through these texts, we can learn what biblical books looked like before the rabbinic period.

Copies of Known Extra-Canonical Works

Christian tradition knows of works, such as the Book of Jubilees or the Book of Enoch, that are called "Apocryphal" or "Pseudepigraphal." These are Jewish texts of the Second Temple period that never entered the later rabbinic scriptural canon. Many such texts are among the Dead Sea Scrolls. Whereas formerly they were known only in Amharic or Armenian translations, they can now be studied in their original Hebrew or Aramaic versions.

Works of Biblical Interpretation

Among the scrolls is the Genesis Apocryphon, a retelling of the stories of the Book of Genesis in Aramaic. Other texts represent a type of biblical commentary known only from Qumran, the *pesher* commentary. These are commentaries to biblical books such as Habakkuk and Nahum, which show how the prophetic oracle refers to events in the life of the Qumran community. Finally, the Temple Scroll seems to be a rewriting of Deuteronomy that reflects the writer's (and perhaps the Yakhad's) views about the proper conduct of the sacrificial system.

Behavioral Codes

Both the Community Rule and the last portion of the Damascus Rule concern standards for behavior within the community. These are crucial for understanding the inner life of the Yakhad.

Historical/Eschatological Writings

Most of the Damascus Rule offers a historical summary of the Yakhad's origins, couched in allusions to biblical texts and contemporary references. The War Rule provides details for a final battle, at the end of time, between the Yakhad (the Sons of Light) and its enemies (the Sons of Darkness).

A Selection from the "Scroll of Thanksgiving Hymns," One of the Nonbiblical Scrolls Found in the Qumran Caves

A principal difficulty in interpreting the scrolls is the fragmentary state of their preservation. As in this example, scholars must often speculate about the words that are lost in portions of scrolls that have rotted. (Robert Schlosser/Huntington Library)

quote from the Damascus Rule's interpretation of a verse from the prophetic book of Ezekiel:

> *The Priests, the Levites, and the sons of Zadok who kept the charge of my sanctuary when the children of Israel strayed from me, they shall offer me fat and blood* (Ezek. 44:15). The *Priests* are the converts of Israel who departed from the land of Judah, and (the *Levites*) are those that joined them. The *sons of Zadok* are the elect of Israel, the men called by name who shall stand at the end of days. (Vermes, p. 99, emphasis in original)

This statement contains the Yakhad's self-understanding in a nutshell.

Ezekiel's references to descendants of Zadok are read as a prediction applicable to the Yakhad community—a community of "the elect" who have separated themselves from the rest of Israel in preparation for the end of days. With the Jerusalem Temple polluted, the members of the Yakhad saw their own communal life as a pure sacrificial offering that alone brought atonement and purification from the increasingly heavy weight of Israel's sinfulness. The biblical distinction between "a kingdom of priests" and the nations of the world was now interpreted in a fresh way: the Yakhad alone is Israel, all other Jews outside its boundaries becoming as the nations of the world.

The covenantal metaphor of the liturgical community is not the only one apparent in the Qumran writings. Members also viewed their covenantal loyalty as a matter of discipleship in the path of wisdom, as we learn from the first column of the Community Rule:

> All those who freely devote themselves to [God's] truth shall bring all their knowledge, powers, and possessions into the Community of God, that they may purify their knowledge in the truth of God's precepts and order their powers according to His ways of perfection and all their possessions according to His righteous counsel . . . (Vermes, p. 70)

The model of discipleship in wisdom is so crucial because of the larger cultivation within the Yakhad of an inward turning of conscience that must precede a person's entrance into the covenant community. According to the Damascus Rule (column 8), members of the Yakhad saw themselves as converts who entered a "New Covenant in the land of Damascus" (that is, Qumran). As such, each convert served a period of discipleship at the fringes of the community and learned how to follow its specific interpretations of the rules of the Torah. Both the Damascus Rule and the Community Rule list scores of such rules that govern all areas of personal life, interpersonal relations, hierarchies of communal authority, and ritual matters.

Individuals had to demonstrate over a period of two years (Community Rule, column 6) their suitability to join the community of the wise, "who heed the voice of the Teacher" (Damascus Rule, column 8). During this period, disciples were denied full participation in the community's ritual meals. Finally, after standing an examination before a council composed of communal leaders, the disciples were welcomed into the community, contributing all their material possessions to the collective welfare.

The texts seem to assume that initiates were male. Most probably, their wives and children became part of the community as the male was welcomed within it. There seems to be no evidence that single women might be initiated, or that married women could join on behalf of their husbands and children. Such independence from men was exercised only rarely by women of Greco-Roman antiquity, unless they were exceptionally wealthy.

The borders of the Yakhad, obviously, were not easy to cross. Like those of the liturgical community of the Priests, one was required to become cleansed physically and spiritually so as not to pollute the common life that constituted the Yakhad's sacrificial offering. Similarly, one could move from outside the group to the inside only by becoming a disciple and learning in a period of initiation the distinctive lifestyle that distinguished the wise and pious from the ignorant and wicked.

From whom did one learn at Qumran? The Community Rule describes ritual meals presided over by Priests. These meals also seem to have served as teaching occasions at which "there shall never lack a man among them who shall study the Law continually, day and night, concerning the right conduct of man with his companion" (Community Rule, Vermes, p. 77). At this point, the covenantal models of discipleship and the liturgical community extend imperceptibly into the Bible's favorite metaphor of a nation led in its covenantal life by an inspired prophetic leader.

Some writings of the Yakhad speak of a mysterious Righteous Teacher (*moreh tzedek*), an inspired leader raised by God who disclosed to the original members of the Yakhad important mysteries contained in Scripture (Damascus Rule, column 1; cf. Commentary on Habakkuk, column 2). It is unclear how his authority was preserved and transmitted in later generations. It seems beyond doubt, however, that scriptural study at Qumran, under subsequent Teachers, was regarded as a kind of revelatory experience, a prophetic phenomenon in which the Torah's "hidden things" (Deut. 29:28) became manifest to all. This was especially so, perhaps, in the teaching of new initiates by the inspired interpreter of the Torah: "When they have been confirmed for two years in perfection . . . they shall be set apart as holy. . . . And the Interpreter shall not conceal from them, out of fear of the spirit of apostasy, any of those things hidden from Israel which have been discovered by him" (Community Rule, Vermes, p. 81).

Let us summarize what we have learned about the Yakhad at Qumran. All four covenant models know from the Hebrew Bible are activated at some level of the community's experience. In interpreting its separation from the rest of Israel, priestly models of covenantal purity come to the fore. Images of disciples apprenticed to sages govern the passage of outsiders into the inner life of the Yakhad, and once within, members experience a profound agreement with the secret meanings of the Torah, delivered with the force of prophecy. Finally, the entire purpose of the community's life together is directed toward the future, the imminent end of history when God will once again take his visible place as King over a righteous Israel.

In the Yakhad's structure, we see how the various covenantal models of the Hebrew Bible are embodied by a group for which "covenant" means total separation from other Jews, interpreted as penitential submission to God's will. Versions of its covenantal exclusivism, in rather different communal forms, remained live options in later Judaism, as we have seen in the discussion in Chapter 4 of some of the modern movements of Jewish Traditionalism.

COVENANTAL MODELS AND RABBINIC TRADITION

Fascinating as it may be, the Yakhad is an obscure footnote in the history of Judaism. Until the Dead Sea Scrolls were discovered in 1948, historians knew hardly anything about the Yakhad, and Jewish tradition passed on few memories of this group. If, therefore, we want to know how covenantal models have informed the lives of Jewish communities since the early centuries of the common Era, we must turn our attention to rabbinic Judaism and the types of Judaism it has spawned.

In what follows we look at two developments. The first is the rabbinic model of covenant community as articulated in the talmudic literature of late antiquity, the literature of Oral Torah. The second is Hasidism, an Eastern European movement of Jewish mystical piety that has attracted many Jews from the late eighteenth century until today.

Classical Rabbinic Covenant Community

Like the Qumran Yakhad, classical rabbinic Judaism drew upon the entire range of biblical covenantal models. But there is one crucial difference: whereas the Yakhad used covenantal models to enforce a rigid distinction between itself and other Jews, rabbinic Judaism was for most of its ancient and medieval history a movement seeking to bring the entire Jewish people within the boundaries of the biblical covenant.

Ironically, this universalizing tendency in rabbinic Judaism stems from the same covenantal metaphor that, at Qumran, explained religious separatism and exclusivism. This is the priestly metaphor of the liturgical community. You will recall from Chapter 1 that rabbinic Judaism developed a distinctive penitential system of covenant renewal after the catastrophes of the first and second centuries CE. Central to its vision was the idea that loyalty to the laws of the Torah, as interpreted by the rabbinic sages of Israel, constitute a sacrificial practice capable of brining atonement between God and Israel on behalf of the world.

Thus, in rabbinic thought, to be "a kingdom of priests and a holy nation" meant nothing less than to follow the entire Torah of Moses as contained in the tradition of Oral Torah. In short, scrupulous commitment to the transformation of all public and private life in accord with halakhic norms was the crucial sign of Israel's covenantal loyalty. In this view of matters, the rabbinic sage functioned much like the High Priest of the vanished Temple, whereas Jews in general served as the priestly masses whose actions produced the conditions of the Temple's holiness. Centuries after the Temple was destroyed, the Babylonian Talmud affirmed that "wherever Israel was exiled, the Divine Presence went into Exile with them" (Megillah 29a). The liturgical community is the center of holiness once manifested in the Temple and the ancient Tent of Meeting.

But rabbinic Jews were priests only in metaphor, and this was fully recognized. Unlike the priesthood, inherited as a matter of birth, any male Jew could aspire—*ought* to aspire—to become a sage. And what, after all, is a sage? Preeminently, as you'll recall from our discussion of the first paragraph of Mishnah Avot in Chapter 1, the sage was one who stood in a line of revealed tradition—Oral Torah—that began with Moses on Sinai.

By linking the sage's wisdom to what is revealed in Oral Torah, rabbinic Judaism at a stroke joined two important covenantal models, the community gathered around a wise teacher and the nation drawn into being by a prophet. But the model of the sage takes precedence. As the Babylonian Talmud reports: "From the day that the [First] Temple was destroyed, the gift of prophecy was taken from the prophets and given to the sages" (Baba Batra 12a). Therefore, whereas the rabbinic community saw Israel as the "descendants of prophets" (Palestinian Talmud, Shabbat 19:1), it held out as a behavioral imperative the goal of becoming "disciples of the sages" (*talmidei khakhamim*), students of the sages' Oral Torah.

This model of discipleship—one that ought to include the entire community of Israel, rather than small coteries of the "elect"—was crucial in the spread of rabbinic Judaism throughout the Middle East from 200 CE to 600 CE. Rabbinic sages focused their attention on two social goals. On the one hand, by a period of protracted initiation into the details of rabbinic piety, they sought to draw young Jewish men and their families into the circle of rabbinic tradition. On the other hand, rabbinic sages wanted to govern Jewish society, beyond the circle of immediate disciples, on the basis of rabbinic covenantal life as contained in the Mishnah and the rest of Oral Torah. Thus, as we see in Chapter 19, they sought and readily gained permission from Roman and Mesopotamian authorities to establish themselves as key functionaries in the state bureaucracies that helped to administer Jewish communal affairs.

For the sages, therefore, it was not enough to be a private religious guide; one had to be as well a public servant, responsible for communal order. While seeking, through moral suasion and personal example, to convert Jewish individuals to the halakhic path, they used political power to assert the authority of halakhic tradition as Jewish public law. As a method of personal piety, rabbinic Judaism sought an inner transformation of ethnic Jews into a "holy People," a truly covenantal community. As a social policy, rabbinic Judaism sought to shape the public dimension of Jewish society according to halakhic norms, regardless of the inner feelings of the larger community.

If Jewish farmers could be made to grow their crops in accord with halakhic norms, if Jewish merchants could be required to employ rabbinically regulated weights and measures, if Jewish litigants could be required to accept rabbinic mediation, then the transformation of the inner life of Israel would follow closely upon the transformation of its public life. All of Israel could become a covenant community of disciples inwardly as well as externally.

The Sages of the third to the sixth centuries who created the vast talmudic literature were, in fact, correct in their judgment. By the end of the first Christian millennium, both European and Middle Eastern Jewries submitted as a matter of course to rabbinic legal jurisdiction. They also prayed in accordance with rabbinic liturgical rules; accepted a rabbinically designed calendar; raised their young, married, buried their dead under rabbinic regulations; and engaged in marital relations in accord with the strictures of rabbinic propriety. People calling themselves "disciples of the Sages" studied and practiced halakhah as a form of penitential sacrifice, under the guidance of rabbis whose authority was linked to Moses, Israel's great prophet. Memories of prophetic nationhood served the larger transformation of Israel into a priestly community led by men who combined the roles of priest, sage, and prophet into a single persona.

The only covenantal model awaiting embodiment was that of royal dominion. Although the Patriarchs and Exilarchs described further in Chapter 19 claimed Davidic ancestry, few claimed plausibly or for very long to be the Davidic heir promised in Scripture. That was a matter that awaited the decision of God, who alone could hasten the ingathering of the Exiles. But that day, as we saw in Chapter 4, could come only in response to Israel's fulfillment of its own covenantal responsibilities.[4]

The Hasidic Covenant Community

Wherever the rabbinic sage dominated, so too did the covenantal models sponsored by the sage's vision of Judaism. Our appreciation of the suppleness of Jewish covenantal models will be sharpened, therefore, by asking: what happens when rabbinic authority is successfully challenged within Judaism? How are biblical covenantal models, so successfully appropriated by rabbinic tradition, employed to sponsor new types of Jewish communities? In Chapter 1, we have already met a famous medieval example in the Karaites, the Middle Eastern Jews who rejected the rabbinic Oral Torah. Now we can briefly sketch a further instance, drawn from the Eastern European movement of popular mysticism that came to call itself *Khasidus* (Hasidism, "Piety").

Hasidic legend links the movement's origins to a charismatic teacher, the Ukrainian kabbalist and healer Israel ben Eliezer Baal Shem (1700–1760). In Hasidic lore, he is universally known as the Baal Shem Tov or, for short, the Besht. Little is known about the life of the Besht beyond what is recorded in the rich literature in Hasidic folklore. It is, moreover, difficult to pinpoint the actual origins of the movement that developed after his death. Historians have documented the existence of fervently pious Jewish mystical groups in eastern Europe prior to the Besht. In addition, it has been suggested that key traits of early Hasidism, such as the use of song and dance to achieve intense emotional states and the dominance of charismatic leaders, are the influence of that era's Russian Orthodox "Old Believers," a Christian sect living in the areas in which Hasidism originated.

Be that as it may, a collection of stories concerning the Baal Shem Tov, the *Praises of the Besht* (published in 1814), recalls him as a meek teacher of children, given to seclusion in the forests of Podolia until he began his career as a spiritual guide. On the basis of these legendary images, Hasidism continues to treasure the memory of origins among the simple and unlettered Jews of the impoverished Polish-Ukrainian countryside. Hasidic Jews have tended to view their movement as a kind of revolt against a sterile academicism infecting rabbinic scholarship of that era.

It is difficult to verify this memory. Indeed, one of the earliest followers of the Besht, Rabbi Jacob Joseph of Polnoyye, was a famous scholar who served as a communal rabbi. Nevertheless, there is no doubt that many early Hasidic writings portray Hasidism as an attempt to re-create a covenant community characterized by a passionate life of inner piety. As opposed to the official communal Rabbi, a salaried scholar who resolved halakhic questions or presided over the curriculum of the talmudic academy, the Hasidic Rebbe (Yiddish: "Master") or Tzaddik (Hebrew: "Righteous One") typically had no formal position in the structure of Jewish institutional life. His authority over others depended on their conviction that he had forged a unique spiritual path. He, rather than the Rabbi, had the power to guide his disciples (Hasidim) through the storms of personal spiritual quest to a secure and abiding relationship with God.

Especially in the first half century of Hasidism, till the beginning of the nineteenth century, Hasidic Rebbes were often regarded as dangerous charlatans by established rabbinic leaders. In 1772, for example, the greatest rabbinic scholar of Lithuania, Rabbi Elijah of Vilna, published an official halakhic edict forbidding Lithuanian Jews from having any social or economic relations with Hasidic leaders and their followers. A decade later, the first published book of Hasidic teachings, Rabbi Jacob Joseph of Polnoyye's *Toledot Yaakov Yosef*, was subject to censorship and burning. Nevertheless, Hasidism succeeded within a generation or two in attracting a diverse following in eastern Europe, including many respected masters of classical talmudic learning.[5]

The reason for Hasidism's success in eastern Europe was, no doubt, due to the way Hasidic Rebbes were able to link the innovations of their own distinctive spiritual paths to the accepted values of rabbinic Judaism. For example, the path for seeking sustained daily experience of God was often called *'avodah,* a term deeply resonant with biblical and rabbinic ideas of divine service. And indeed, many Rebbes, like their talmudic ancestors, stressed the liturgical character of the covenantal life.

Their innovation was to extend that liturgical understanding of life beyond prayer and other halakhically regulated activities to include one's entire relationship to the world and others. It was only through *'avodah sh'b'gashmiut* (the service of God through the corporeal body) that the Hasid could reach the highest stages of illumination characteristic of *'avodah sh'b'rukhaniut* (spiritualized service). In this latter service, the Rebbe, of course, was the acknowledged master, guiding his fledgling Hasidim toward a form of divine service that would lead them from bondage to matter and the tempests of physical passions.

Hasidism's bond of the leader to the led reminded talmudically trained Jews of the early rabbinic intimacy between the sage and the disciple. The main difference, however, was that the Rebbe did not commonly ground his authority solely on his scholarship in rabbinic law. Some masters, like the founder of Habad Hasidism, Shneur Zalman of Lyady (1745–1813), were brilliant halakhic scholars whose authoritative legal decisions commanded respect even among opponents of Hasidism. But by and large, early Hasidic Rebbes concerned themselves primarily with the inner lives of those Hasidim who constituted their following. They were particularly adept at applying the complex, esoteric traditions of the medieval Kabbalah to concrete moral and religious concerns.

Moreover, Hasidic Rebbes were often described in royal terms; they were "kings" presiding over "courts." Their "kingdoms," however, were the environs of humble eastern European *shtetlakh* (Yiddish: "hamlets") such as Mezhiritch,

The Lubavitch Movement to Return Jews to Judaism

Since the early 1950s, the Lubavitch Hasidic movement has made a concerted effort to spread its teachings among Jews alienated from the conventional institutions of American Jewish life. Often, outreach centers called Chabad Houses are set up near university campuses or in suburban Jewish areas. In them, religious services, classes, and, often, Sabbath and Festival meals are provided free of charge. In the above photo, a Lubavitch Hasid instructs a college student in the procedure for blessing ritual items associated with the autumn festival of Sukkot. (*Source:* Mal Warshaw)

Lubavitch, Berdichev, or Chernobyl (now remembered primarily for its nuclear disaster), where Rebbes made their homes. Many masters, because of their intimate role in the religious quests of their disciples, were reputed to have prophetic gifts in addition to royal prerogatives. Thus, the prayers of the Rebbe were considered to have special power in Heaven. He could, as well, foretell the future and—like prophets and sages mentioned in the Zohar and other mystical writings—heal the sick of body and spirit.[6]

These aspects of Hasidic leadership teach us about the distinctive character of Hasidic covenantal life. Like the Yakhad, Hasidic communities tended to have a separatist self-understanding, viewing themselves liturgically as special centers of holiness and covenantal life distinct from the rest of Jewish society. But, like early rabbinic communities, they were also committed to expanding the boundaries of Hasidism by repentance, to include as many Jews as possible in the intimacy of covenantal life.

The pressures of the past two centuries have combined to make most contemporary Hasidic communities intensely separatist in their attitudes to the larger Jewish world. In this, they share much with other non-Hasidic Traditionalist Jews discussed in Chapter 4. A key exception is the Habad community. Habad's messianism, noted in Chapter 4, is expressed partially through a high-profile missionary effort among Jews. In this, Habad sees itself as continuing a tradition begun with the Besht. Encountering the Messiah in a dream, the Besht is said to have asked "When will the Master come?" The reply, as recorded in a collection of the Besht's teachings called the *Keter Shem Tov*, constitutes a mandate for the Habad community: "You will know of it in this way: when your teaching becomes famous and revealed to the world, and when that which I have taught you . . . will spread abroad."[7]

Our survey of three types of Jewish covenantal community yields an interesting result. Each draws upon the same body of covenantal models, yet each produces a distinctive type of communal life. Between the rigidly separatist ethos of the Yakhad and the missionary inclusiveness of the early rabbinic sages lies the Hasidic Court, separatist or expansionist in turn as it responds to historical circumstances. In each community, liturgical ideas of covenant define the borders of the common life. Yet, within those borders, a variety of other models drawn from prophetic and wisdom images play significant roles, defining relations between leaders and followers, those who wield authority and those who submit to it out of a sense of covenantal obligation to God.

CHAPTER 8

AUTHORITY
IN CHRISTIANITY

In the film *The Blues Brothers*, two ne'er-do-wells named Jake and Elwood receive a special call from God to prevent the closing of the Orphanage of St. Helena of the Blessed Shroud, where they were reared. Claiming they are on "a mission from God," the brothers manage to raise enough funds to save their orphanage, but in the process they also demolish an entire shopping mall, break every traffic law in the state of Illinois, and end up behind bars singing "Jailhouse Rock." Their call from God, though genuine, is not accepted by the police, and in the end, it does not free them from obedience to the law. Similarly, in the gospels, Jesus' mission as the Son of God is not readily apparent to the established authorities. When Jesus demolishes the stalls of the merchants and money changers in the Temple, his holy zeal brings him into conflict with the powers that be. As the gospel of Mark tells the story, "The chief priests and the scribes and the elders came to him and said: 'By what authority are you doing these things, or who gave you this authority to do them'?" (Mark 11:27–28). A few days later, Jesus is found guilty of blasphemy and is nailed to a cross, his mission from God rejected by the leaders of his community.

CHRISTIAN CONSTRUCTION OF AUTHORITY

The Power of Jesus

To claim authority is not the same as to have authority. Authority is not an abstract quality. Authority always means power: the ability to command others, to lead, to speak definitively, to make decisions, to effect change. A political reality and a necessity for the survival of human societies, authority is inseparable from community. To have authority is to have dominion over others' lives, to shape a community. Authority can evoke adoration, respect, or fear. In Christianity, the authority of Jesus Christ has always been essential to the identity of the community and its message of salvation. At the end of Matthew's gospel (Matt. 28:18–19) the resurrected Jesus gathers his disciples and says to them: "All authority in heaven and on earth has been given to me. Go therefore and make disciples of all nations, baptizing them in the name of the Father and of the Son and of the Holy Spirit, teaching them to observe all that I have commanded you." Three fundamental concepts are proclaimed in this gospel passage. First, Jesus here bases his new religion on his authority, his dominion over Heaven and earth. Second, this authority is delegated to the disciples themselves, who, in turn, are asked to acquire followers of their own and create a new community. Third, the disciples are empowered to carry out a dual task: to perform rituals and to teach.

In the minds of Western Christians who read this passage in the Vulgate Latin translation, authority and power were indistinguishable, for the Latin word *potestas* used here by Jesus can mean both things. The Latin text reflected an ancient tradition. From the earliest times, Christian writers associated the power of God with the power structure of their community. As was pointed out in Chapter 5, this means that Christians tended to believe that the truth of God's revelation was inseparably bound to the church's authority. The Christian community saw itself as constituted and sustained by Christ's divine authority. This authority, in turn, was believed to have been delegated to the apostles and their successors, the clergy. Hence, Ignatius of Antioch could say a mere eight decades after the death of Jesus: "You should all follow the bishop as Jesus Christ followed the Father. Follow too the presbytery as you would the apostles; and respect the deacons as you would God's law. Nobody should do anything that has to do with the Church without the bishop's approval."[1] As Ignatius and other early Christian leaders saw it, when Jesus instructed his disciples to baptize all nations, he gave his authority to them and their successors. In other words, a core elite within the community claimed from early on that Jesus had entrusted them with the truth and the power of redemption. These elites would become the Christian clergy.

Apostolic Office

This clerical claim to authority, however, has not been the only one accepted by the Christian community. Throughout its long history, Christianity has manifested both personal and impersonal forms of authority. At times, individual Christians have been recognized as authoritative religious guides on the basis of their extraordinary character, their personal charisma, or their saintliness. Such was the case of Jesus, of those persecuted for their faith, of ascetics, of saints, of visionaries, and of persons who otherwise exemplified moral good. Though potent at times, this personal form of authority has never prevailed among Christians. More often than not, it has been the clergy who have led the community by virtue of their office: priest, minister, bishop, pope. This impersonal form of authority—impersonal because it is grounded in the rationally established legal norms and regulations of the community rather than in personal qualities—has been predominant in Christianity for most of its history. Since it has been the clergy who have exercised the most authority over the Christian community, let us examine their role first.

By the second century, the axiom of "apostolic succession" had developed into a defining characteristic of the Christian community's identity. To be able to trace the lineage of any community's clergy back to the apostles was to guarantee the authenticity of their authority. In the third century, Tertullian could see truth and salvation as dependent on apostolic succession:

> And so the churches, many and great as they may be, are really the one primitive church issuing from the apostles, which is their source. So all are primitive and apostolic, while all are one. . . . If this is so, it follows straightaway that all doctrine which accords with those apostolic churches, the sources and originals of the Faith, must be reckoned as the truth, since it preserves without doubt what the churches received from the apostles, the apostles from Christ, and Christ from God.[2]

Such a concept of authority stood in sharp contrast to the claims made by some other early Christians, especially the Marcionites, Montanists, and the gnostics. The authenticity and legitimacy of the clergy's authority, for Tertullian and the Orthodox, resided neither in charismatic powers (special gifts of the Spirit or direct revelations from God) nor in secretive oral traditions, but rather in their being able to prove that their appointment to office was derived in an unbroken line of succession from Jesus. Ironically, Tertullian eventually changed his thinking on this point and became a follower of Montanus, that prophet who downplayed apostolic succession and claimed to be directly inspired by the Holy Spirit—which shows us that no single concept of authority could prove dominant among all communities, or even within the mind of a single individual.

Within two generations after the death of Jesus, the apostolic office of the clergy had become an emblem, a representation of the authority embodied in the church. More specifically, the clergy had become the guardians of truth, the chosen few who could interpret scripture correctly and formulate doctrine for the Christian community. Their claim to authority raised the Christian clergy to an exalted position within the community, for it made them intermediaries between God and humanity. Clerical authority, then, became contingent both on the church's trust in the reliability of scripture and doctrine and on the church's need for the services that the clergy provided as teachers and ritual specialists. A simple formula evolved among orthodox Christians: no clergy, no salvation. As Cyprian of Carthage put it in the third century:

> The Church is made up of the people united to their priest and the flock that cleaves to its shepherd. Hence you should know that the bishop is in the Church and the Church is in the bishop, and that if any one be not with the bishop he is not in the Church.[3]

A hierarchy quickly developed among Jesus' disciples. The apostle Paul mentioned a variety of offices (I Cor. 13:28): "God has appointed in the church first apostles, second prophets, third teachers, then workers of miracles, then healers, helpers, administrators, speakers in various kinds of tongues." Christian documents from the second and third generations indicate the existence of three principal offices: at the summit of the clerical hierarchy were the bishops or "overseers" (Greek: *episkopos*); in the middle, below the bishops, there were presbyters or "elders" (Greek: *presbyteros*); at the base, there were deacons or "servants" (Greek: *diakonos*). The title of "priest" (Latin: *sacerdos*) would eventually be assigned in the Christian West to the presbyters or elders.

How was it that a religion that initially professed universal brotherhood and the reversal of the world order so quickly became a rigidly organized power structure? Had not Jesus said (Matt. 23:11–12): "He who is greatest among you shall be your servant; whoever exalts himself shall be humbled, and whoever humbles himself shall be exalted"? There is no simple answer to this question, but it should not seem surprising that the new, persecuted religion that sought to "make disciples of all nations" should have sought survival through greater organizational definition. It also stands to reason that Christians could not so easily step out of their own cultures. In a hierarchical society such as that of late antiquity, the absence of hierarchies would have been unthinkable for most people. In fact, the existence and well-being of a community at that time were believed to depend on hierarchical order: hierarchy was the structure of creation itself. The metaphor of the body was often employed by early Christian writers to explain the necessity of hierarchical order within the community (including Paul in I Cor. 13:12–31): the church as the "body of Christ" could no more function without a head than could any human body. In time, the clerical hierarchy came to be seen as a direct reflection of the organization of Heaven. This kind of thinking reached its fullest expression in the writings of Pseudo-Dionysius the Areopagite (sixth century), *The Celestial Hierarchies* and *The Ecclesiastical Hierarchies*. These two treatises, which came to have a profound influence on Christian thinking, described the offices of the clergy in the visible church on earth as counterparts of the angelic celestial hierarchy. To contemplate the power structure of the church in this manner, then, was to gain a glimpse of Heaven.

The Question of Supremacy

Though early Christian bishops shared a common office and a common authority, some bishops claimed greater dignity and power. The development of this hierarchy within a hierarchy was directly related to the urban structure of the Christian community. Early Christianity was largely an urban phenomenon: its social structure demanded the close proximity of its members and clergy in towns and cities. A close-knit community that gathered regularly for worship could not easily be established or maintained in the countryside, where vast distances and the unrelenting demands of agricultural life made fellowship and communication difficult. No wonder, then, that non-Christians came to be called "pagans" (*paganus* is the Latin word for "country-dweller"). No wonder, too, that the bishops of five important cities came to be regarded as having a stronger voice: Jerusalem, the holy city where it all started; Antioch, where believers were first called "Christians"; Alexandria, the second city of the Empire; Rome, the ancient capital of the empire; and Constantinople, the new capital of the empire. The bishops of these cities shared a greater dignity of office as "first among equals." Their place in the community was signified by their title of "father," for they were addressed as heads of the Christian family through the name of *papa* (English: pope) or *patriarch,* notwithstanding the advice of Jesus to his disciples, "Call no man your father on earth, for you have one Father who is in heaven" (Matt. 23:9).

Two profoundly different views of episcopal authority emerged in the first five centuries of Christian history, and the disagreement only intensified with the passage of time. In the eastern Mediterranean basin, it was generally believed that all bishops shared a common authority: the five patriarchs might hold a more exalted place in the church, but even they had no greater power than the sum total of the episcopate. In the western Mediterranean, however, the bishops of Rome steadily increased their claims for supremacy in the church. This claim was not based on the obvious practical reason that Rome was the political center of the Empire and that its Christian community was more influential and had deeper pockets than all others, but rather on a theological argument. The bishops of Rome claimed a greater authority than all other bishops—even above that of the popes of Jerusalem, Antioch, Alexandria, and Constantinople—because they believed that they were the successors in office of the apostle Peter and were also convinced that Jesus had given Peter supreme authority over the entire Christian community. The key words of Jesus cited in support of this claim would later be carved in colossal golden letters over the main altar of the pope's church, St. Peter's Basilica in Rome.

> You are Peter, and upon this rock I shall build my church, and the powers of death shall not prevail against it. I will give you the keys of the kingdom of heaven, and whatever you bind on earth shall be bound in heaven, and whatever you loose on earth shall be loosed in heaven (Matt. 16:18).

Whereas eastern Christians continued to think of church authority as shared by bishops and to depend on assemblies of bishops (councils and synods) for ultimate governance and conflict resolution, western Christians steadily increased the claims for Roman papal supremacy. In the fifth century, Pope Leo I did much to magnify the influence of the "see" of Peter. (Since bishops ritually presided over their communities while seated in a central place of honor in church, their office came to be known as a "chair" or "see" [Latin: *sedes*], and their church building as a "cathedral" [Latin: *cathedra*].) First, he played a key role in the settlement of Christological disputes at the Council of Constantinople (451) and strengthened the Roman see's teaching authority and its reputation for inerrancy: whereas other sees had fallen into heresy, some repeatedly, Rome had remained constantly orthodox. Second, he began to develop a theology of the papal office that all subsequent Roman bishops expanded upon: Leo distinguished between the office of Peter and the person of the bishop of Rome, referring to himself as the "Vicar of

Peter." Employing Roman law, Leo clarified the position of the pope as successor to Peter: the bishop of Rome, as office holder, continued the legal personality and the power of the first bishop, Peter. Moreover, Leo conceived of Peter's authority as monarchical: Peter and his successors rule the church in the same way a prince rules his state. Though he was the first to employ this title, Leo was no innovator. He was building on an idea already widely accepted in the West. In the fourth century, for instance, Saint Jerome had written to pope Damasus:

> Since the East, rent asunder by feuds of long standing, is tearing to shreds the seam-less robe of the Lord . . . I think it my duty to consult the chair of Peter. . . . As I follow no leader save Christ, so I communicate with none save your Holiness, that is, with the chair of Peter. For this, I know, is the Rock upon which the Church is built. This is Noah's ark, and he who is not found in it shall perish when the flood overwhelms all.[4]

Such thinking did not sit well in the Christian East, where the see of Peter was granted primacy, but not supremacy. The rift between East and West deepened as the Roman bishops built upon Leo's claims. Between the eighth and the twelfth centuries, when the Roman popes began to use the title Vicar of Christ, the gulf became unbridgeable. Papal claims to supremacy were one of the chief causes of the schism between the Catholic and the Orthodox churches in 1054 and still remain a major obstacle to their reunion at the end of the twentieth century.

Conciliarism

Within medieval Catholicism, some events made thinking along Orthodox lines necessary in the fourteenth and fifteenth centuries, when the papacy fell into disarray. Between 1305 and 1377, the papacy came under the domination of the French monarchs and even moved to Avignon in southern France. During this period of papal weakness and corruption, known as the "Babylonian Captivity," some theologians began to argue that supreme authority resided in the councils of the church rather in the papacy alone. This theory, known as "conciliarism," gathered strength as the crisis of the papacy deepened, for in 1378, after the papacy moved back to Rome, the situation worsened. Suddenly, the election of a new Italian pope was challenged by the French bishops who elected a pope of their own at Avignon. Now there were two popes, each supported by an equal number of European monarchs. How was this problem to be solved? Many thought the solution could come only from a council. The crisis lingered for two generations. Both Urban VI (the Roman pope) and Clement VII (the Avignon pope) were succeeded by other "legitimate" claimants to the papacy. In 1409, conciliar theory was put into practice at the Council of Pisa, but the intended solution made the problem only worse. Following conciliar theory, the Council of Pisa convened itself. (After all, how could councils have ultimate authority if they needed to be convened by any other power?) This council deposed both the Avignon and the Roman popes and elected its own new pontiff, Alexander V. Much to everyone's dismay, the Avignon and Roman popes refused to accept the council's authority. Now there were three popes, not just two.

Conciliarists tried once again, with a slight legal twist, to solve the problem through a council. The Council of Constance (1414–1415), convened not by its own authority but rather by that of the Holy Roman Emperor Sigismund, successfully removed all three claimants to the papal office and reinstated a single pope in Rome. How did it succeed where Pisa had failed? It all came down to power and authority. With the backing of the emperor and the support of other Christian monarchs, the Council of Constance could enforce its rulings. Even though the Avignon pope, Clement XIII, refused to abdicate, he had no monarch and no community that would support him. His continued insistence on being the "real" pope became a moot point.

Conciliarism had triumphed, but by renewing the papacy it also dug its own grave. The Roman pope who was asked to step down, Gregory XII, ensured through a legal maneuver the eventual demise of conciliarism. Pope Gregory agreed to abdicate on two conditions: that his legitimacy (and that of his Roman predecessors) be confirmed by the council and that he be allowed to retroactively convene the council. By agreeing to these terms, the Council of Constance affirmed that its authority was grounded on the Roman pope's power to call it into being. The crisis of the Great Schism (1378–1415) had ended with a renewed Roman papacy. Subsequent popes would do their utmost to affirm their supremacy over councils and would ultimately prevail. In 1460, Pope Pius II (ironically, a conciliarist in his youth) condemned all claims to conciliar supremacy as "erroneous and abominable." It would take other challenges to finally overturn papal claims to authority in the West.

Authority Challenged

Though predominant, clerical authority has never been supreme in Christian history. Moreover, the distinction between the two categories "clergy" and "laity," so crucial in the minds of the ruling elite, did not always sit well with the faithful at large. For as long as there have been clerics claiming special powers and privileges, there have also been anticlerical tendencies among Christians.

Anticlericalism comes in many varieties, from the milder forms that aim to reduce clerical privileges or abuses, to the more extreme kinds that call for the abolition of the clergy. Anticlericalism can be found at the apex of society, among Christian monarchs, and also at the bottom, among the poor and dispossessed. Anticlericalism can be passive, a way of thinking; and it can also be aggressive, a way of actually rebelling. At one time or another, all these varieties of anticlericalism have been manifested in Christian history. Let us focus on some of the more significant episodes, leading to the Protestant Reformation.

In late antiquity, a major challenge to clerical authority arose in the wake of persecution, especially in North Africa. The practical question raised was this: does a cleric who denies his faith in the face of persecution still have any legal or moral authority within the Christian community? To many in North Africa, who came to be called *Donatists*, the answer was clear: clergy who deny the faith cease

FAILED COUNCILS

Not all councils have succeeded at resolving crises among Christians or in having their authority accepted. Even some of the most "successful" councils, such as Ephesus (431) and Chalcedon (451), were not universally accepted by all Christians. Listed below are the major councils that have met with significant failures.

Ephesus 449 "The Robber Council"	Convoked by Emperor Theodosius II, and packed with bishops who supported a monophysite Christology, this council deposed Flavian, the Patriarch of Constantinople, and rejected the legates of Pope Leo I. Its decisions were overturned in 451.
Hieria 753	Convoked by Emperor Constantine V, but without representation from Rome, Jerusalem, Antioch, or Alexandria, this council condemned the veneration of images by Christians and called for their destruction. Its pronouncements were reversed by the Second Council of Nicaea in 787.
Lyons 1274	Convoked by Pope Gregory X with the support of the Byzantine Emperor Michael VIII and attended by many delegates from Constantinople, this council achieved the reconciliation of the Catholic and Orthodox churches, at least on paper. Lyon's formula of union was immediately rejected by the vast majority of the Orthodox clergy and laity and would later be formally repudiated. Emperor Michael VIII would be denied Christian burial for his efforts at reunion.
Pisa 1409	Convoked by many Roman Catholic cardinals to heal the Great Schism, this council formally deposed both claimants to the papal throne at Rome and Avignon and elected a new pope to replace them. Because its authority was rejected at Rome and Avignon and at the secular courts that supported the two "deposed" popes, the Council of Pisa intensified rather than healed the schism by creating a third pope.
Basel 1431–1449	Convoked by Pope Martin V according to the provisions set forth at the Council of Constance (1414–1415), which called for regularly scheduled councils, this council refused to accept papal supremacy. It was pronounced schismatic by the pope, but continued to meet anyway, and in 1439 "deposed" Pope Eugenius IV and elected its own antipope.
Florence 1438–1439	Convoked by Pope Eugenius IV as his alternative to the antipapal Council of Basel, this was in effect its legitimate continuation. Once again, as at Pisa in 1409, a formula of union was reached with the delegates of the Orthodox church. Though the union was achieved on paper, it was not embraced by the Orthodox. In fact, many of the Orthodox delegates who had agreed to the union renounced their signatures as soon as they were back in Constantinople.

to be legitimate leaders. This meant, of course, that for the Donatists clerical authority was believed to reside not in some abstract impersonal office, but rather in the person of the cleric who was expected to be nothing less than a good, upstanding Christian. Misbehavior was not to be tolerated on the part of the clergy; an unworthy priest was a contradiction in terms. In other words, those who abused their office, lost it. This meant two things: (1) the leadership of the church was to be composed of saintly men; and (2) the validity of the sacraments depended on the morality of the clergy.

Donatism was opposed by St. Augustine, who argued against its perfectionist tendencies. According to Augustine, whose views eventually prevailed, the personal sins of the clergy could in no way diminish the validity of their office or of the sacraments they administered. For Augustine, the church was not a club for saints, but rather a school for sinners. To make salvation dependent on a holy clergy, he argued, would be foolishness, for all human beings, even the clergy, are prone to sin. Donatism in North Africa was eventually wiped out through persecution by the Roman authorities, but its way of thinking was not easily vanquished.

In the Medieval West, clerical corruption led to the rise of various reformist groups, many of which had Donatist tendencies. One of the first major challenges made to clerical authority came from the Waldensians in the twelfth century. The followers of Peter Valdes (or Waldo), much like the Donatists, challenged the validity of the sacraments administered by unworthy priests. Furthermore, they called upon the clergy to renounce all claims to property and to live in a state of poverty. Waldensians, who were numerous in northern Italy and southern France, focused on the Bible as the ultimate authority and rejected many aspects of medieval Christian ritual, such as prayers for the dead and the veneration of saints and relics. In the later Middle Ages, during the crises of the Avignon papacy and the Great Schism, similar ideas were put forward in England by John Wycliffe (1130–1184) and his followers, the Lollards, and in Bohemia by John Hus (1372–1415) and the Hussites. All three of these movements challenged the notion that the clerical office granted an indisputable authority to the clergy, and all three were declared heretical. Though persecuted for generations, they could not be fully extinguished.

Gender and Authority

There is no getting around the fact that until recently, women were excluded from the power structure of Christian communities because their gender excluded them from the clerical state. This is not to say that women have exercised no authority in Christian history for two millennia, for individual women have at times wielded considerable power over various communities, but rather to point out that the clergy were male and that female authority among Christians before the twentieth century has tended to be one of person rather than of office. Women in Christian history have not necessarily challenged clerical authority but have complemented it in various ways.

The early Christians had deaconesses who probably served alongside male deacons. In the second century, the Montanists had female prophets, such as Prisca and Maximilla, who were central authority figures. Some gnostic groups, too, seem to have had female leaders. But these were all short-lived and, for the most part, were heterodox ministries. By the fourth century, when Christianity became the state religion of the Roman Empire, the clerical state was exclusively male and had been that way for a long time. Surely, there had been many women martyrs. There were also an ever-growing number of female monastics. But there were no female bishops or priests; the sacramental power structure remained closed to women.

Women saints, most of them monastics, often exercised moral authority over the Christian community at large. A good example is Catherine of Siena (1347–1388), who settled many disputes and who also managed to convince Pope Gregory XI to move from Avignon back to Rome. Holy women could influence monarchs as well. Another nun, Maria de Agreda, served as a confidante and adviser to King Philip IV of Spain (1621–1665). Women visionaries could gain renown and eclipse the significance of the male clergy. Hildegard of Bingen (1098–1179) corresponded with the emperor as well as with several kings and bishops; she was even given approval to undertake preaching missions. Teresa of Avila (1513–1582) spearheaded a reform of her Carmelite order that eventually encompassed the male Carmelites as well. Her mystical gifts imbued her with authority and power. Though her male confessors and superiors ostensibly had control of her life, they acknowledged and even encouraged her extraordinary pursuits. St. Teresa wrote several books against her own wishes, simply because she had been ordered to do so by her male superiors, but these writings eventually earned her the title of "doctor" of the Catholic Church, an honor reserved for the likes of male theologians such as Augustine and Aquinas. Visionaries could also get into trouble, however. Joan of Arc (1412–1431), a French peasant girl who claimed to receive heavenly messages, rallied the king of France and his armies to victory over the English in the Hundred Years' War. Clad in armor, her hair cut as short as a man's, Joan of Arc marched into battle with the voice of the Archangel Michael ringing in her ears. The French king and those around him eagerly followed this young woman's lead. The English, however, viewed Joan with suspicion and alarm, and when they captured her, she was burnt as a witch. Centuries later, Joan and the French were vindicated when the Catholic Church condemned her execution as a great injustice and pronounced her a saint. Saint Joan of Arc's case shows clearly how males were willing to accept women in spiritual charismatic offices, but it also shows the dark side of this attitude. It was generally believed that women possessed a more sensitive spiritual nature than did men and were more naturally inclined to mystical experience. But this was not necessarily good; if women could enter into relationships with the divine so easily, they could also be led astray by the devil. In the late Middle Ages, the theologian Jean Gerson argued that women were more "unstable" than men, and were thus more susceptible to demonic temptations and "false" visions. In the Middle Ages there seemed to be little middle ground: spiritual women tended to be viewed either as saints or as witches.

In many ways, the status of women in Christianity before the Reformation is typified by the Virgin Mary, who was a symbolic summation of Christian feminin-ity. Mary was revered as a paradox and a coincidence of opposites: a virgin mother. In a culture that prized virginity and stressed sexual purity, Mary was the most exalted paradigm. At the same time, in a culture that also prized motherhood and the family and stressed the significance of God having become flesh in a woman's womb, Mary was the most venerable archetype of parenthood, in some significant ways even more approachable than God the Father himself. Whereas Mary was seen as a gentle, indulgent mother, God tended to be viewed as a stern judgmental father. Since Christ was God, he, too, could be viewed as fearsome. Martin Luther said that he used to tremble each time he saw a painting of the Last Judgment in his monastery and that he would implore Mary to have mercy on him and calm her son's anger. In times of plagues, which were considered punishment for the sins of a community, Mary would be asked to employ her motherly love to soften God's wrath. A common motif of medieval sacred art is the image of Mary extending a protective shield over the human race, sheltering it from God's wrath-ful arrows.

Popular piety did not always take fine theological distinctions into considera-tion. Trinitarian theology could dissolve among uneducated Christians. Mary and God could be confused by ordinary Christians. Some statues of Mary, for instance, opened up to reveal the entire Trinity in her womb. Many simple lay folk apparently thought of Mary as one of the three persons in the divine triad. We know this from Inquisition documents in which people identified the trinity as The Father, the Son, and the Virgin Mary. Though elite theologians knew better, Mary was divinized in popular culture. In effect, she became the feminine aspect of the deity. The titles used for Mary reveal much to us about the ways in which Catholic and Orthodox Chris-tians conceived of Heaven and of Mary's place before God. As "Mother of God" she could plead with her son Jesus and could even make him change his mind. One of the most popular gospel narratives was John 2:1–12, which told how Mary actually forced Jesus to perform a miracle against his will. As "Queen of Heaven" she had plenty of power to wield in the celestial court, as well as direct access to God's ear. In a faith that conceived of Heaven as a court and of God as approachable only through advocates and intercessors, much as an emperor or king on earth, who would be inaccessible to common folk, Mary was the supreme mediatrix. This partly explains why so many churches, cathedrals, and shrines were dedicated to Mary and why theologians came to refer to the church itself as a mother.

As Mary wielded her power, so did other women. Female saints, mostly mar-tyrs and virgins, also interceded for the human race. They had certainly not exer-cised official clerical power on earth, but once dead they could be approached for all sorts of favors. St. Anne, Mary's mother and the grandmother of Jesus, was an immensely popular saint. Few, if any, bothered to consider that Anne was men-tioned only in some apocryphal gospels and that she had been a good Jewish woman rather than a Christian. Early Christian martyrs such as Lucy, Agatha, and Catherine of Alexandria were also popular. Local women saints were numerous and their veneration intense. When St. Elizabeth of Hungary died in 1231, a mob ripped her clothing to shreds and even took small pieces of her flesh to venerate as relics. Furthermore, it was commonly believed that the corpses of many women saints remained whole for decades, even centuries, and that they exuded miraculous fluids and odors. (The corpses of male saints could do this as well, but this phenomenon was more frequently associated with women.) The oil and blood that flowed from these bodies were believed to effect miraculous cures. St. Teresa of Avila proved herself superior to many of her male contemporaries not only through her mystical experiences and writings, but also through her body, which according to many eyewitnesses did not decompose after her death and could effect many miracles. In sum, the power wielded by women could be immense, even if it was not clerical.

HISTORICAL DEVELOPMENT OF AUTHORITY AFTER 1500

The Reformation

Much of what had been proposed by the Waldensians, Lollards, and Hussites again came to the fore in the sixteenth century. What we now call the Protestant Reformation was in large part a revolt against the authority claims of the clerical hierarchy of the Roman Catholic Church. Armed with the spiritual battle cry *sola scriptura!* (scripture alone), the followers of Martin Luther (1483–1546) and Ulrich Zwingli (1484–1531) denied the authority of the pope and redefined the nature and function of the clergy and the sacraments. Radiating from Saxony and Switzerland, the reform movement set in motion by Luther and Zwingli quickly engulfed much of Western Christendom. But it is not the history of this Reformation per se that concerns us here. What we need to focus on is the change in authority structures that it occasioned.

Luther and Zwingli both rejected the notion of a permanent, indelible clerical office. The Christian clergy, they believed, were to be ministers of the Word, not "priests" who mediated the sacraments to a subservient laity. The office of a cleric was determined strictly by his function as preacher and servant of the community: it was not an independent, permanent status that made the clergy ontologically different from everyone else. In other words, all Christians shared a common office, but some merely took on the job of ministering to others' spiritual needs. In 1520, Luther exclaimed:

> The clergy claim to be superior to the Christian laity, who, nevertheless, have been baptized with the Holy Spirit. The clergy can almost be said also to regard the laity as lower animals, who have been included in the church along with themselves. . . . Now we who have been baptized are all uniformly priests in virtue of that very fact. The only addition received by the priests is the office of preaching, and even this with our consent.[5]

Furthermore, Luther and Zwingli rejected the pope's claims to supremacy and identified him as the Antichrist. In their view, the Roman Catholic clergy were abusive tyrants who had corrupted the church beyond measure. This charge struck a responsive cord at a popular level: even if they could not understand the more abstract concepts of Luther's and Zwingli's theology, the laity could easily comprehend the need for a reform of the clergy.

On a practical level, the Protestant Reformation began as an anticlerical revolution, and the changes it occasioned in the authority structure of church and society were profound. Take one example, the city of Geneva: before the Reformation, this city of ten thousand inhabitants had roughly four hundred clerics; immediately after the Reformation (1536), the city made do with a paltry ten clerics, a 97.5 percent reduction! Moreover, many of the privileges enjoyed by the medieval clergy were taken away. The Protestant clergy were now regarded as common citizens and had no special privileges: unlike Catholic priests, they could be taxed, for instance, or prosecuted in civil courts. But did this mean that the power of the clergy was diminished among Protestants? Did the "priesthood of all believers" actually become a reality? No. Paradoxically, in most places, the Reformation increased the authority of the clergy over their communities. Protestant cities such as Zurich and Geneva became theocracies, that is, communities governed in the name of God by the clergy. The public and private behavior of the laity was closely monitored in Geneva by the Consistory, a tribunal headed by clerics; wearing "lascivious" (sexy) shoes, using "foul" language, or giving one's child an "unchristian" name could earn a layperson a few days in prison. The anticlericalism of the leaders of the Reformation was in essence not anticlerical at all; it was a repudiation of the privileges of the Catholic priests, and a redefinition of authority that actually increased the clergy's influence over society.

Among the so-called "Radicals" of the Reformation, a different conception of the community called for a new understanding of authority as a new paradigm of the relation between church and state. The Radicals believed that the church should be a purely voluntary association. Consequently, they rejected the practice of state-enforced infant baptism. In brief, the Anabaptists rejected the notion of a "Christendom," that is, a society in which all the people are Christians by compulsion and in which church and state are closely intertwined. Though they agreed on this point, they differed widely on their conception of authority. At one extreme, for instance, the Anabaptist community of Münster was ruled despotically by a king/prophet and a court of elders. In contrast, the Hutterites and Moravian Brethren developed a more communal understanding of authority. At the other extreme, spiritualists such as Sebastian Franck argued that there should be no visible church at all, or clergy, or sacraments; between God and each individual soul, no earthly authority should ever intervene.

The Reformation also effected a change in the status of women in the church by doing away with monasticism. Without convents, Protestant societies had no place for women except in the home, as wives and mothers. Female monastics had been able to lead somewhat independent lives and even to exert a measure of leadership and authority in the church: it could be said that nuns had a quasiclerical position. The Reformation did away with this. In addition, by denying the intercession of the saints, Protestantism dethroned Mary and all the other female saints who had been venerated for centuries. Since nearly 50 percent of all church art was

Burning of the Anabaptists at the Stake

The Anabaptists were persecuted throughout Europe in the sixteenth century. They viewed their persecution as a sure sign of their being the true church, following early Christian paradigms. After torture and executions such as this, the corpses were sometimes left out as a public reminder of the consequences of heterodoxy. In Münster, Anabaptist corpses were hung from the churchtower in cages. The cages remain there to this day, a symbol of religion gone wrong. (*Source:* Foto Marburg/Art Resource, NY)

devoted to Mary and the saints before the Reformation, the removal of these feminine representations marked a definite shift away from a gender-balanced feminized piety to a more masculine one.

By the time of the Thirty Years' War (1618–1648), there were many different Christian communities in the world, each claiming to possess the legitimate authority Jesus had entrusted to the One True Church. The Catholics had the pope; the Orthodox had their patriarchs and councils; the Anglicans had bishops and a national church; Lutherans had ministers of the Word and, in some places, also bishops; Anabaptists tended to have elders; most Calvinists had presbyters and consistories, others believed in the independence of each congregation; and the spiritualists did not even have a church. The dissension produced by these conflicting claims was profound, and the warfare that erupted among Christians did little to make them reach an accord on the question of authority. The most profound effect of these disputes was the weakening of the authority of the Christian religion over Western culture and society as a whole.

"Private Judgment"

A new claim to authority, that of "private judgment," emerged with the Enlightenment. The Enlightenment, as we have seen, challenged the reliability of the Bible and the truth of church doctrines. In so doing, it magnified doubts about clerical authority. Enlighteners—like various reformers before them—criticized the professional failures of the clergy (moral laxness, neglect of duty, inordinate pursuit of luxury and pleasure, and so forth); but their criticism was more sweeping than that of their predecessors. They disputed the entire ground of clerical authority from the standpoint of their trust in "reason." Enlighteners, upholding the capability of the individual to cultivate personal understanding of religious truth, argued that the assistance of a religious professional was not essential to spiritual advancement. If persons could by a rational process of private judgment grasp religious truth and discern moral good, then they did not need the clergy as spiritual mentors. In short, these several vines of early modern Christianity—criticism of clerical performance, impeachment of the scriptural and doctrinal sources of clerical authority, and especially the emerging confidence in private judgment—grew together and yielded the mixed fruit of anticlericalism and lay authority.

We have seen how various challenges to authority arose regularly throughout the course of Christian history. Montanism and Donatism rejected clerical hierarchy. In the twelfth century, Arnold of Brescia preached a communal ideology deeply critical of ecclesiastical luxury and led an insurrection that drove the pope from Rome. The fourteenth-century English anticlerical satire *Piers Plowman* rejected clerical authority in favor of "Resoun" and "Conscience." And the Reformation featured several species of anticlericalism. Anticlericalism in its most dramatic form appeared in the late eighteenth and nineteenth centuries, however, and especially during the French Revolution; the early years of the Revolution featured not just the wholesale rejection of the authority of the clergy, but the execution of clergy as well on grounds of conspiracy and treason against the Revolution. So, for

Apparition in the Sky at Hamburg, 1571

Popular beliefs among Christians have not always been entirely "Christian." Many ancient pre-Christian beliefs and practices survived well into the modern era, some to the present day. Church authorities struggled but could not fully eradicate many "superstitions," such as the reading of portents and prophecy in clouds, meteors, thunder, and lightning. (*Source:* The Granger Collection)

---

example, in December 1794 in the otherwise quiet town of Angers, fifty-eight Roman Catholic clerics were tied together in pairs and thrown from boats into the Loire river, in a process described as "de-Christianization by immersion."

Books and pamphlets that described various sorts of clerical treachery fueled popular opposition to "priestcraft" during the nineteenth century. Not the least of these was Tom Paine's *The Age of Reason*. Roman Catholic clergy bore the brunt of the criticism, and Protestants experienced it as well. We should keep in mind, however, that anticlericalism never has been simply a rejection of the authority of the clergy. It has included an appeal to other, new forms of authority. The Enlightenment notion of private judgment accordingly has fueled appeals to lay authority as well as attacks upon the clergy. During the nineteenth century, lay authority coalesced as a more significant aspect of religious community in virtually all

Christian groups. Through their impressive achievements in a host of ambitious missionary undertakings and reform movements, Christian laity asserted themselves as leaders and gained confidence for forays into other aspects of church life (especially liturgical matters). In the United States, a process of "democratizing" Protestant denominations took place as women, African Americans, and the poor began to claim authority previously wielded by white male religious professionals. In France, lay leadership and involvement in the Society of St. Vincent de Paul exceeded that in any Roman Catholic organization up to that time. In Norway, by the end of the nineteenth century, lay men and women had organized their own "prayer houses" within the state church (Lutheran) and had staffed them with lay preachers. In the twentieth century, this process was accelerated, most noticeably in the Roman Catholic church, as the Second Vatican Council (1962–1965) framed invitations to the laity to participate more fully in church life.

We should recognize as well that the centuries-long movement toward enlarged roles for the laity in the leadership of Christian churches has forced churches to broaden their thinking about the nature and function of authority and, especially, to rethink traditional notions about the exclusivity of authority. Witness the ordination of women in the recent past of certain Protestant denominations and the ongoing invention of official roles for Catholic laity in public worship. We find as well an increasingly positive public response to the authority of laity who preside over storefront churches, television ministries, streetcorner mission enterprises, and other religious phenomena that once seemed far removed from Christian orthodoxy.

Modern Encounters with Other Religious Communities

Christianity is a conversionist religion. That is, Christians since the first century have actively and often vigorously sought to convert persons of other faiths to their own. Islam is conversionist in the same sense. Judaism is not.

Persons who belong to a religious community accept the authority of its religious scriptures, doctrines, and religious leaders. In the encounter of one religion with another, however, we frequently witness some measure of competition, some effort on each side to persuade the other of the legitimacy of its authority. At times, the means of that persuasion has been patient and respectful discourse. Historically, it more often has been the case that Christian efforts of persuasion have been intolerant, overbearing, even brutal. The devastating Thirty Years' War (1618–1648) in Europe represents one such encounter of different Christian groups vying for overarching authority. The various Crusades (including "oil Crusades") against Islamic "infidels" since the eleventh century and the long history of Christian antisemitism—punctuated by the expulsion of Jews from the Iberian peninsula in 1492, by Russian pogroms in the nineteenth century, and by the "final solution" of the Third Reich—epitomize the frequently vicious nature of the encounter of Christian groups with non-Christian faiths.

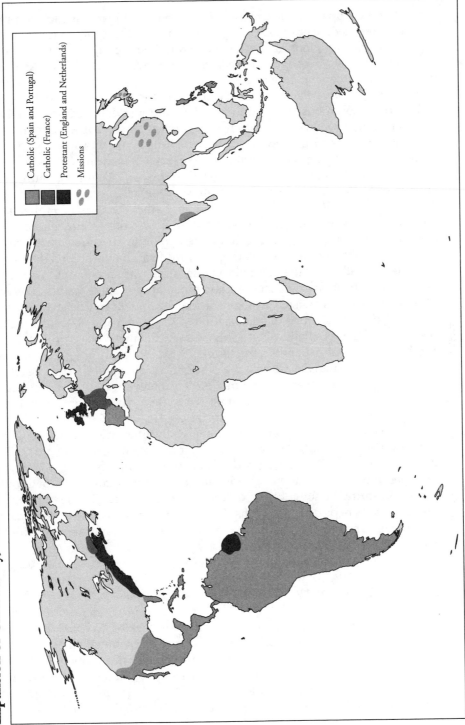

Expansion of Christianity, 1492–1700

When European explorers learned to circumnavigate the globe and brought forth the so-called "Age of Discovery," they opened the door as well to encounters with the primal religions long established on other continents. The tone for those encounters was set in 1493 by the *Padroado* of Pope Alexander VI. The Padroado articulated an agreement between Spain and Portugal to divide between them the world beyond Europe and to work to convert all non-Christians whom they met. Christopher Columbus enlarged this understanding when he interpreted his own work of exploration in explicitly religious terms: "God made me the messenger of the new heaven and the new earth of which he spoke in the Apocalypse of St. John. . . . Let Christ rejoice on earth, as he rejoices in heaven in the prospect of the salvation of the souls of so many nations hitherto lost."[6] Beginning with the second voyage of Columbus, priests were posted on vessels destined for the Americas, Asia, and Africa. Recruits from the Roman Catholic orders of Franciscans, Dominicans, and Jesuits accordingly spread out across the globe seeking to evangelize the native inhabitants who greeted the explorers. By the seventeenth century, Roman Catholic missionaries were joined by Protestants in North America and elsewhere. In all cases, the missionary enterprise was an attempt to assert the authority of Christianity against the claims of natives. Some natives converted to Christianity; others resisted evangelization. But whether Christian missionaries were foiled in their efforts or successful in one sense made no difference to European churches. By the mid-nineteenth century, the missionary project of converting the world to Christianity came to represent, especially among Protestants, the essence of a Christian life. Christian women and men molded in the ideals and ambitions of Euro-American culture made the nineteenth century an extraordinary period of missionizing, of proclaiming the superiority of their religion and, implicitly, of the cultural apparel in which it was dressed.

By the late twentieth century, a somewhat different spirit guided Christians' thinking about the authority of their religion vis-à-vis other religions. The ecumenical movement that developed at mid-century had envisioned relations between religions as grounded in understanding rather than in competition for absolute authority. In some cases, that vision has resulted in greater cooperation among members of different faiths. But Christianity nevertheless still carries the baggage of centuries of confidence in its own authority, in its superiority to other faiths.

Community and Authority

I once taught at a university in a state that was seeking to come to terms with a rapidly growing population of incarcerated men and women. Prison officials periodically would call me, a religious studies professor, asking advice on how to treat prisoners who refused compliance with prison procedures on religious grounds. So, for example, a warden would ask me if there were in fact a religion that required of its adherents very long hair, long fingernails, various accessories to dress, personal ornamentation, or a certain diet. I responded by suggesting that the prison should contact the person's priest, minister, rabbi, shaykh, or other religious authority. Frequently, the official would contact me a second time, reporting that no authority could be found and proposing to me, then, that the person did not belong to a religious community and therefore was not really religious.

Is it possible to be Christian and yet not stand in any relation to religious authority? The answer to this question hinges on how one conceives the relation between religious authority and religious community. Throughout the history of Christianity, to be a Christian has meant to belong to a community. Changes in conceptions of religious authority that have taken place since the late Middle Ages have been accompanied by transformations in thinking about the nature of religious community. Over time, the notion of Christian community as an earthly reflection of a divine essence of Christian community, of a perfect society, has given way to an image of Christian community as just that: a community of flesh and blood humans professing Christian beliefs. At the same time, Christian thinking about authority increasingly has departed from the notion that a person who exercises religious authority is qualitatively different from other persons. Instead, Christians have tended to experiment with models of authority that are based on the conviction that power is to be shared. And it is no accident that this development has taken place alongside the modern movement away from monarchical rule and toward democratic government.

Illustrative of a new understanding of the relation between community and authority is that which originated within the Society of Friends (Quakers). Quakers, as they emerged in the 1650s, articulated a view of community founded on the belief that God could speak through any receptive person. Quakers asserted the equality of women and men, young and old, highborn and lowborn and rejected sacraments, creeds, and priesthood. In place of the usual representations of ecclesiastical authority and status, they affirmed the authority of the Spirit speaking through members of the Meeting, or congregation. Such communications might take the form of songs, prayers, or messages; and the person who delivered them was said to "appear in ministry." But any notion of distinction of spiritual status was rejected by Quakers. Authority for Friends was diffuse. In theory and in practice, it was shared, rather than concentrated in the hands of professionals. Accordingly, the Quaker conception of authority does not fit well with the modeling of authority as either charismatic or impersonal. Instead, it suggests a type of religious order that attempts to uphold the authority of the Spirit-filled individual alongside that of the community.

One of the most significant and potentially transformative challenges to traditional understandings of Christian authority has been feminist theology, which has criticized the patriarchal character of authority. In developing that criticism, feminists have taken a variety of approaches, but in general have endeavored to reconceptualize the nature of community. Rejecting hierarchically structured community, feminist theologians have argued instead for models of community grounded in an ideal of interdependency or partnerships between individuals, and between humanity and nature. The experience of community as diverse but inclusive accordingly grounds the paradigm of "shared authority." Neither Bible, nor religious office, nor tradition is an independent source of authority. Together with the individual believer and the larger Christian community, they form a matrix of sources, the whole of which feminist theology takes to be authoritative and dynamic.

CHAPTER 9

AUTHORITY

IN ISLAM

The Muslim umma is a global fellowship of people who recognize God as sovereign ruler of all humanity. The Muslims are God's "mid-most nation," following him and calling others to submission. Muslims have traditionally held that no separation should exist between religion and state, that Islam is a complete way of life that leaves no independent secular sphere in its midst. In reality, Muslims have been obliged to sustain their existence in a wide variety of arrangements short of a theocratic state governed by the Shari'a, the holy law of Islam.

MUHAMMAD'S SUNNA AS PERFECT PATTERN FOR MUSLIM LIFE

The supreme authority for Muslims is the divinely revealed Qur'an, which was discussed in Chapter 3. But a second major authority, the record of Muhammad's teachings and acts, is contained in literary form in the Hadith. The Qur'an speaks of Muhammad's authoritative role:

> You have indeed in the Messenger of Allah a beautiful pattern (of conduct), for anyone whose hope is in Allah and the Final Day, and who invokes Allah much. (33.21)

> Obey Allah and obey the Messenger, and beware: If you turn back, then know that it is Our Messenger's task to deliver a clear proclamation. (5:92)

These are but two Qur'anic statements about Muhammad's position next to the revelation. The charismatic qualities of the Prophet no doubt did much to lead people to submission as Muslims. But the Qur'an was a major part of that charisma. Both the Qur'an and the Prophet became living legacies of authority and empowerment for the umma in later years. The umma became a charismatic community through its total acceptance of God and Muhammad as guides. As we observed earlier, the Qur'an teaches what the Muslims are to believe and do, whereas the Prophet's Sunna holds out a pattern of conduct that the Muslims are to imitate—not only the what, but also the how of living Islamically.

The development of the Prophet's Sunna as guide for the umma was a gradual process. Included in it was the evolution of a science of "traditions," those traditions that we shall henceforth call by their technical name of *hadīth* (lit., "report, narrative"). During the Prophet's lifetime, the Muslims had immediate access to him. But after his death, memory of his teachings and behavior had to suffice. Many reports were preserved and handed down from generation to generation, sometimes in family circles. As the need for more extensive guidance grew in the expanding umma, specialists in the developing fields of law and theology collected ḥadīths far and wide. This process was sometimes like fieldwork, requiring arduous journeys. Persons who, like Jewish sages, spent their lives in the study of the Qur'an and its interpretation were highly esteemed. But even greater esteem was accorded the scholars who added to their study of written texts (known as *kitāba*) knowledge gained from traveling to distant and often unique oral sources, a process known as *riḥla* (loosely "field trips").

It was not long before hadith specialists realized that the quality of their findings varied greatly. How to assess the authenticity of the hadiths they collected? A scholarly discipline known as the "science of men" was created that brought together as much information as possible about the transmitters of hadith. Were they reputable? Did they live at times and places that would make their positions in a chain of transmitters credible? Did they have good memories? Were they particular about small details? These and other questions were raised in this science that has bequeathed to scholarship vast amounts of biographical data about early Muslims as well as technical knowledge about the hadiths.

The science of hadith culminated in the second and third Islamic centuries in several respected collections. Two of these collections were held over all others, because they contained traditions that had survived the most rigorous tests of authenticity. Both collections are known as *ṣaḥīḥ*, "sound." One is by Muhammad Ismā'īl al-Bukhārī (d. 870), the other by Muslim Ibn al-Ḥajjāj (d. 875). In addition to the two sound collections are four other collections that are also held in high esteem and much used for legal and doctrinal purposes as well as for personal guidance. All six collections have a virtual canonical status among Sunni Muslims. Shī'ites also have hadith collections, which differ in many respects from the Sunni ones and feature Ali, Muhammad's son-in-law and the third Caliph, and his followers, as major transmitters. Shī'ites (Muslims who believe that Muhammad designated Ali as his successor) also recognize Ali's authority alongside

Muhammad's. Ali's sayings are collected in a separate collection, known as "The Way of Eloquence" (*Nahj al-balāgha*).

Following is an example of a sound hadith from the collection of al-Bukhari:

> Maḥmūd ibn Ghaylān reported to us and said: ʿAbd al-Razzāq reported to us and said: Ibn Jurayjīn said: Nāfiʿu told us that Ibn ʿUmar used to say that the Muslims, when they arrived at Medina gathered together so as to set a time for Salat prayer. No call was given for it. So one day they talked about it and some of them said: "Have a bell like the bell of the Christians." Others said: "Rather, have a bugle like the horn of the Jews." ʿUmar said: "Would you not appoint a man who should sound a call for prayer?" The Messenger of Allah said: "O Bilal, get up and give a call to prayer."[1]

This interesting hadith is in two parts. The first is the chain of transmitters, known as the *isnād*. The second is the report itself, known as the *matn*. The "science of men," mentioned earlier, is applied to the isnad. That part of a hadith is of the greatest concern for Muslim scholars, for it is the key to the report's authenticity. It is easy to imagine the Prophet having said all manner of things, but plausibility is no argument for authenticity. Only the isnad provides reliable guidance. If a report is supported by more than one chain of transmitters, for example, from separate geographical regions, all the better. Even a broken or incomplete isnad has value, because it is in the nature of things for something to be lost occasionally in transmission, while the report may be credible otherwise. A perfect isnad, on the other hand, sometimes raised suspicions because of the possibility of forgery. Al-Bukhārī had more than half a million different hadiths to choose from as he went about collecting materials. He settled on about 2,600 as sound examples (after duplicates as well as doubtful reports were taken into account). But hadiths of a lower status than sound are often highly regarded as well as being of the greatest importance in law. For example, there are categories of "acceptable" and "weak" hadiths that have authority. But lower grades, such as forgeries or "unknown" reports have no authority, although they may be of considerable interest to historians because of what they attempt to say. That is, even a phony hadith provides useful information about what people might have been trying to bring under Islamic authority, sometimes for honorable reasons. The result, however, was a pious fraud.

To give some idea of the variety of subjects of hadiths, the following should be of help:

1. *Concerning revelation to Muhammad:*
   The Prophet . . . felt, when the revelation was sent down upon him, like one in grief, and a change came over his face.[2]
2. *Concerning true religion:*
   Religion is faithfulness to Allah and his Messenger and to the leaders of Muslims and Muslims in general.[3]
3. *Concerning ritual purification:*
   Prayer is not accepted without purification, nor charity out of what is acquired by unlawful means.[4]

**Worshippers at Friday
Salat Service, Kuala
Lumpur, Malaysia**

(*Source:* F. M. Denny)

4. *Concerning ending a marriage:*
   With Allah, the most detestable of all things permitted is divorce.[5]

5. *An anecdote about the livelihood of future prophets:*
   The Prophet said: "Allah did not raise a prophet but he pastured goats." His companions said, and thou? He said: "Yes! I used to pasture them for the people of Makkah for some carats [a unit of currency]."[6]

6. *Concerning table manners:*
   'Umar ibn Abū Salāmah said: "I was a boy being brought up in the care of the Messenger of Allah (peace and blessings of Allah be upon him) and my hand was active

in the bowl, taking from every side. So the Messenger of Allah (peace and blessings of Allah be on him) said to me, "Boy! Say *Bismillāh* (in the Name of Allah) and eat with thy right hand and eat from the side nearest to thee." So this was my manner of eating afterwards.[7]

7. *Concerning exertion in the way of Allah:*

The most excellent *jihād* ["exertion," sometimes in the form of armed conflict in defense of Islam] is the uttering of truth in the presence of an unjust ruler.[8]

As can be seen in this brief sampling, hadiths cover a wide range of subjects. In addition to the aforementioned examples, they treat theology, Qur'anic exegesis, the fine points of ritual (prayer, pilgrimage, fasting, almsgiving), business transactions, marriage, clothing and adornment, personal hygiene, wills and inheritance, cultivation of land, and so forth.

The somewhat long hadith (see page 197) about how the Muslims decided on the means of calling the faithful to prayer is an interesting indicator of how the early community distinguished itself from the similar religions of Judaism and Christianity. Muslims have always had some aversion to the sound of bells as a call to prayer, because they are loud and a public announcement of a rival religion. The sound of the human voice chanting the call to prayer was thought to be the ideal medium, because the human voice recites God's word and communicates with him in prayer.

Although written collections of hadiths are indispensable for Islamic law and theology, as well as for many other aspects of guiding the community, it should not be thought that the Prophet's Sunna is known only through a literary record. The way of Muhammad is known definitively through the behavior of Muslims and transmitted by example, as from mother to child in managing the humble personal tasks of the toilet and in simple courtesies; in the social relations of schoolmates who are taught to share and look out for one another's welfare; in conjugal relations wherein spouses are admonished to respect each other's rights to pleasure and dignity; in the behavior of fathers, who are encouraged to kiss their children (in direct rebuke of some bedouin who thought such behavior was soft); in the rights of guests (who are entitled to three days hospitality, no questions asked); and in many other matters.

The imitation of Muhammad is as fully developed in Islam as is the imitation of Christ in Christianity, if not more so. Muslims are utterly respectful of Jesus as one of God's greatest prophets. But Muslims are also aware that Muhammad lived a more complete human life—being businessman, husband, father, spiritual guide, military commander, judge, arbitrator, ruler—and thus can serve as a universal paradigm of the fulfilled human life. As was observed in Chapter 3, Muhammad and Moses are similar in this respect, with the added parallel of being deliverers of their people, Moses through the Exodus and Muhammad through the Hijra, both of which were dramatic separations from oppression.

Although orthodox Muslim opinion insists that Muhammad was no more than a human, over the centuries there developed traditions about Muhammad that viewed him as a supernatural figure who existed before the creation of the world and who exists eternally with God. Poetic odes to this idealized figure have had wide currency in Arabic and vernacular Islamic languages. Many Muslims chant popular odes to Muhammad on his birthday. There is a recitation of the ninety-nine "Most Beautiful Names" of the Prophet that parallels the chanting of the ninety-nine "Most Beautiful Names" of Allah.[9] And so close is the identification of individual Muslims with their beloved Prophet that it should not be surprising that when negative remarks are made about Muhammad, every Muslim feels wounded, for each believer carries in her or his identity a sense of the Sunna in habits of the mind, heart, and body. The controversy over Salman Rushdie's novel *The Satanic Verses*, which Muslims see as blasphemous in its treatment of characters closely resembling Muhammad and his family, should be seen in light of the Prophetic Sunna as guide for the umma alongside the Qur'an.

THE SHARĪʿA AS ISLAM'S SUPREME AUTHORITY

From earliest times, Muslims have trusted in their manifest destiny as a community submissive to God (an *umma muslima* in Sura 2:128), a "justly balanced community" (*umma wasaṭan* in Sura 2:143), "the best community evolved for humankind, enjoining what is honorable and forbidding what is dishonorable" (Sura 3:110). The authenticity of the umma has been as minimally defined as to acknowledge as Muslims those who observe a common direction of prayer (*qibla*) of the Kaʿaba in Mecca, whatever else they might disagree on. To claim that Muslims have always been of one mind concerning their interpretation of what is their ultimate authority is to be persuaded by later models of authentication and orthodoxy.

Several centuries passed before the umma was able fully to identify and analyze the authoritative sources of its faith and order so as to be usable as the bases for a legal system. Early legal experts employed personal opinion (*ra'y*) as well as scriptural and customary precedent. As we saw in Chapter 6, difference of opinion in the umma was acknowledged in one early creedal formulation as "a token of divine mercy."[10] This view applied only to legal difference and not to doctrinal or theological dissension.

Consensus (*ijmāʿ*) has always been a powerful force in establishing authenticity in faith and practice, especially for the majority Sunni community. In a sense, ijmaʿ has been both a boon and a bane, for once it had been reached on a wide range of issues, many thought that further elaboration, interpretation, and application amounted to unlawful innovation, or *bidʿa*, which is heresy. This process of approaching wide communal consensus in legal matters is known as the "closing of the Gate of Ijtihād" and is thought to have been complete by the third century of the Hijra, when the major law schools had been established. Individuals, however, continued to claim the right of "individual legal decision making," or *ijtihād*, most notably the Syrian Ibn Taymiyya (d. 1328) whose influence has been considerable in modern Muslim reform movements of the more puritanical kind, such as the Wahhabis in Arabia. The necessity of ijtihad has been claimed by a wide variety of contemporary Muslim activist movements that are often labeled as "fundamentalist" in the Western media.

The center of Islamic concern in all times and places is the Sharī'a, which is often misleadingly defined simply as the "law" of Islam. Sir Hamilton Gibb, an influential Islam specialist of a generation ago, once provided a definition that goes as follows:

> The science of law is the knowledge of the rights and duties whereby man may fitly conduct his life in this world and prepare himself for the future life. The Sharī'ah . . . was never erected into a formal code, but remained, as it has been well said, "a discussion on the duties of Muslims."[11]

Formal law there is, indeed, in Islam, but it is subsumed under the guiding idea of Shari'a as God's "ordaining of the Way" humankind is to follow.[12] Shari'a, in its widest sense, may be compared to the Jewish idea of Torah in its widest sense. In its narrower sense as jurisprudence, it resembles Jewish halakhah. The Shari'a is both God's teaching and his legislation for humanity. An old meaning of the Arabic term *sharī'a* is the "way to the watering hole."

Thus, the Shari'a ensures life in a mutual relationship of responsibility to and benefits under God. God is not cold to his servants' needs and feelings. As a special kind of hadith, known as a "divine saying" (*ḥadīth qudsī*), puts it,

> I am as My servant thinks I am. I am with him when he makes mention of Me. If he makes mention of Me to himself, I make mention of him to myself; and if he makes mention of Me in an assembly, I make mention of him in an assembly better than it. And if he draws near to Me a hand's span, I draw near to him an arm's length. And if he comes to Me walking, I go to him at speed.[13]

God is believed to be speaking through Muhammad in such divine sayings, which are neither Qur'anic revelation nor the Prophet's personal discourse (as reported in hadiths), but somewhere in between. Sometimes they are characterized as God's thoughts in Muhammad's words. Another divine saying is,

> The Apostle of God said: "When God finished the creation, He wrote in His book, which is there with Him, above the Throne: 'Verily, My mercy overcomes My wrath.'"[14]

The emphasis of Islam on law is an indicator of the religion's concern for what we introduced in Chapter 6 as orthopraxy, "right practice." Orthodoxy, in the sense of "correct doctrine," is of course of fundamental importance, but right conceptualizing alone is not a fulfillment of one's duties as a Muslim. Remember that for Muslims, knowing what is the truth must have an outcome in performing what is true by obeying God's commandments.

A non-Muslim scholar of Islam, such as a religious studies professor in a Western country, typically knows much more about Islamic doctrine than most Muslims do. But what prevents the outsider, however sincerely motivated and carefully trained in the textual tradition, from grasping fully the essence of being Muslim is the absence of participating in that "enjoining the honorable and

Visitors Paying Respect at Shrine of Muslim Saint Sunan Kudus, Kudus, Central Java, Indonesia

(*Source:* F. M. Denny)

forbidding the dishonorable," which the Qur'an so frequently commands. Put another way, only when one has put his or her "life on the line" as a Muslim (or Jew or Christian), can one begin to know what it means to be a committed member of that faith community.

THE SOURCES OF JURISPRUDENCE (*UṢŪL AL-FIQH*)

The development of Islamic law was necessary for administering both religion and state in the vast domains that came under Muslim rule, from the Atlantic coasts of North Africa and Spain to India and Central Asia within a century of the Prophet's death. Much of traditional law and customs of the conquered regions was adopted alongside Islamic teachings and practices. But the most important sources were the Qur'an and the Sunna. But even those treasuries of wisdom and guidance were not sufficiently detailed to cover the myriad issues that arose in the complex societies of Islamic civilization. A third source of law was ijma', "consensus," which has been introduced earlier. A fourth source that was widely, though not universally, accepted was arguing by analogy, known as *qiyās*. The four sources—Qur'an, Sunna (using hadith), consensus, and analogical reasoning—are known as *uṣūl al-fiqh*, "the sources of jurisprudence."

The Arabic word *fiqh* means "understanding" in matters of jurisprudence. Knowledge of the Qur'an and other sources is called *ʿilm* (the word means "knowledge" and is also used to mean "science"). Persons possessing Islamic *ʿilm* at a specialized level and who are also respected for their morals and wisdom are known as *ʿUlama'* (sing. *ʿālim*). These scholars of Islamic law are the supreme authorities in the interpretation and application of the Qur'an and Sunna. In a sense, the *ʿUlama'* constitute a kind of clergy, but there is no priesthood in Islam, nor ordination in a sacramental manner for the purpose of empowering individuals to perform sacramental acts. All Muslims are equally capable of performing prescribed rites that lead to salvation. The *ʿUlama'* more nearly parallel Jewish rabbis, except that they usually have had more political power as members of a governing community. Some of the *ʿUlama'* are appointed as judges (*qāḍī*) by rulers, a position that was both powerful and sometimes subject to strong political pressures and the danger of compromise.

But the majority of *ʿUlama'* live private and professional lives of study, teaching, and providing religious and legal guidance to Muslims in such matters as divorce, inheritance, business transactions, community relations (as with non-Muslims), and so forth. Legal specialists may issue an opinion called a *fatwā*, which may or may not enjoy wide acceptance. As with all legal systems, debate is a way of life. One who issues a fatwa is known as a *muftī*.

POLITICAL AUTHORITY IN ISLAM

The Caliphate

Beginning with the founding of the umma in Medina after the Hijra in 622, Muslims have struggled with the challenge of how to govern. Muhammad served as the charismatic ruler during the crucial years of the umma's formation, and he enjoyed great success as he unified the peoples of the Arabian Peninsula. But when he was gone, a crisis of succession arose. The close Companions of the Prophet succeeded in asserting themselves immediately after his death by proclaiming Abu Bakr as *khalifa*, "successor," "deputy." This Arabic term received a strong religious meaning from its Qur'anic usage, where it refers to Adam as God's "vicegerent" on earth (Surah 2:30). King David is also mentioned as one whom God made a khalifa on earth (Surah 38:26). Adam stands for humankind as a whole. A more specific reference to political authority is in Surah 6:165: "It is He [i.e., Allah] who had made you his agents (*khalā'if*, pl. of khalifa) on earth. He has raised you in ranks, some above others, that He may try you in the gifts He has given you."

The word khalifa is rendered in English as caliph. The related word *khilāfa* means "caliphate," the office and institution that would govern the Muslims, at least in a symbolic sense, for several centuries. The caliphs of Medina, who immediately succeeded Muhammad in all but his prophetic capacity (he was the final prophet to be appointed by God), are known as the "Rightly-Guided Caliphs" (*al-Khulafā' al-Rāshidūn*) and enjoy preeminence in the history of that ruling institution. The caliph was a political and military leader, primarily, but his rule was believed to be legitimate only if he safeguarded the Shari'a and its interpreters, the 'Ulama'. In Medina, the caliph reigned over a growing empire and had to deal with increasingly complex foreign and international relations. Furthermore, the umma was divided about who should be caliph.

The Shi'ites

A faction of Muslims was loyal to Ali, the Prophet's cousin and son-in-law. Ali was a young man when the Islamic movement began, but he was also one of the first converts to the new religion. He was a person of considerable spiritual and moral insight and was also an intrepid warrior. His partisans came to be known as the *shi'at Alī*, the "Party of Ali." They and their leader claimed that Muhammad had selected Ali to be the Prophet's successor upon his death. The other major Companions, such as Abu Bakr and Umar, did not know of this arrangement and disbelieved the claim. They came to control political affairs upon Muhammad's passing, as has been noted. But Ali and his followers continued to press their claim. Finally, after the death of the third caliph, Uthman, by assassination, Ali was elevated to the office. His rule was stormy and ended in his assassination in 661 by a disappointed former partisan. A member of Banu Umayya, Uthman's strong clan, became the fifth caliph, ushering in the Umayyad Caliphate, which ruled from Damascus until its overthrow in 750 by a combination of forces that included Shi'ites.

Ali, who ascended to the caliphate in 656, moved the center of his operations to Kufa, a garrison city near the desert border with Iraq. The immense Arab-Muslim empire by that time required a centralized government closer to the crossroads of civilization represented either by Mesopotamia, in Ali's and the Shi'ites' case, or Damascus, as the Umayyads preferred. The Shi'ites continued to seek what they believed to be their rights as the ruling class. Ali was recognized as the first Imam, "leader," of the movement. Ali and Muhammad's daughter, Fatimah, had two sons who were to become important players in the quest for leadership of the Muslims. Hasan, the older, succeeded Ali, but he was prevented by the superior Umayyad forces from assuming the caliphate. He finally abdicated his right after receiving a monetary settlement from Mu'awiyah, the first Umayyad caliph, upon which he retired to Medina, where he died eight years later. The Shi'ites claim that Hasan was poisoned by the Umayyads, but the evidence is inconclusive. In any event, Shi'ism would increasingly develop a tragic identity as its adherents experienced repeated disappointments and reversals through history.

Hasan had a younger brother, Husayn, who would become Shi'ism's greatest figure after Ali. When Mu'awiyah died, his son Yazid became caliph without an election. Husayn was the next in line as Shi'ite ruler. He accepted an invitation to travel from Mecca to Iraq, where he was promised support for his bid to the caliphate. Husayn and a number of his followers traveled to Iraq but were intercepted by a vastly superior Umayyad force at Karbala'. After several days of being cut off from drinking water, Husayn and his troops fought the Umayyad forces and were annihilated. Ali's severed head was transported to Damascus for public display (lest anyone else get the idea of fomenting a rebellion and to prove that Husayn had, indeed, been eliminated).

The deaths of Husayn and his followers were immediately regarded by the Shi'ites and their sympathizers as martyrdom. It had little political effect at the time but grew into a religious story of mythical proportions in the development of the various Shi'ite branches. Added to the disaster experienced by Husayn was the fact that it was none other than Muhammad's grandson who had been killed by fellow Muslims, so it was an intracommunal tragedy, as well.

The Shi'ite idea of the Imam is that he is an infallible guide who acts as intermediary between God and the Muslims. The Shi'ites see the office as hereditary, having been established by the Holy Prophet himself. Shi'ites believe that a "Muhammadan Light" dwells in each of the Imams and is handed down from one to another in an unbroken lineage. Shi'ite political theory, therefore, sees leadership as a divine right for descendants of the Prophet through Ali and Fatimah, Hasan, Husayn, and succeeding Imams. Shi'ism split into factions over just who and how many Imams there finally were. But the majority of Shi'ites believe that there were a total of twelve Imams, the last one having mysteriously disappeared through a process of occultation. The twelfth Imam lives in a supernatural state, not on earth. He inspires earthly Shi'ite leaders and, according to some, will return at the close of history as a messianic figure. The doctrines of the Shi'ite Imam are complex and varied and cannot be treated in detail here, but it is helpful to add that the Iranian revolution of recent history is very much anchored in the belief that Husayn's martyrdom has salvific meaning and power for today's Shi'ites and that the hidden Imam continues to rule through his earthly representatives, preeminently Iran's Ayatollah Khomeini. The Shi'ite branch that rules Iran is known as the "Twelver" or "Imami" branch.

The Shi'ite branch of Islam appeared very early in Islamic history, although its full development into a religious subcommunity with many distinctive doctrines took centuries. Shi'ites greatly honor their spiritual leaders and tend to obey their instructions and guidance because of the belief that God works his will through such inspired leaders. The people who became Sunnis, however, completely disagree with the Shi'ite doctrine of political leadership belonging in the Prophet's lineage. Although Sunnis venerate the memory of Ali, Fatimah, and the Shi'ite leaders, they do not agree that they should have been caliphs because of their relationship with Muhammad.

The Sunnis

The majority of Muslims came to refer to themselves as *Ahl al-Sunna wa'l-Jamā'a,* "The People of the [Prophet's] Sunna and the Community [in the sense of mainstream]." The Shi'ites also follow the Sunna of the Prophet, although they have their own collections of authentic hadiths, as was noted earlier. But the Sunnis see themselves as the main body of the umma, with leaders who should be selected by a process of consensus. Even so, the Sunni doctrine of the caliphate insisted that a caliph had to be a descendant of the Quraysh tribe, but not necessarily of the Prophet. Once a candidate was brought forth, the Sunnis asked for a pledge of support of his rule. In fact, many Sunni caliphs came to power through dynastic succession, although the form of pledging allegiance was retained. The Umayyad caliphs of Damascus were considered by their successors to be merely Arab "kings," without the sacrality that was associated with the memory of the Rightly Guided Caliphs of Medina. Their successors, the Abbasids, who built Baghdad in Iraq as their capital, took many of the trappings and symbols of ancient Iranian kingship and made the caliphal office an exalted oriental despotism. The caliph came to be cut off from the public and was approached with great trepidation. He had his executioner at his side when holding court, and visitors were required to carry their burial shroud with them. The caliph in Baghdad annually made at least a ritual gesture of going out to conquer the enemy empire of Byzantine Christian Constantinople. He also had his name mentioned in the Friday prayer service (and alert listeners often paid attention in order to see whether a coup d'état had occurred, for the new ruler would insist on having *his* name mentioned).

Titles of Leadership. Already, in Umayyad times, the title of the caliph as "Deputy of the Messenger of Allah" had been shortened to "Deputy of Allah" (*khalīfat Allāh*), a change that did not escape the notice of the pious. Another title, which is traced back to the reign of the second caliph, Umar, is "Commander of the Faithful" (*amīr al-mu'minīn*). Still another title was "Shadow of God on Earth." The term *imām*, which in its simplest and commonest sense refers to the leader of congregational prayer, was also applied to the Sunni caliphs, but with a different meaning from its elaborated Shi'ite sense. Finally, any greatly admired religious scholar or spiritual guide may also be accorded the title imam, for example Imam Ghazali, the theologian and mystic (d. 1111).

Sunni and Shi'ite Law Schools. Following the last example, imam is a title attached to the names of the founders of the four great Sunni schools (Arabic: *madhhab*, pl. *madhāhib*, lit., "way, policy, orientation") of law: Imam Malik (d. 795) of the Maliki madhhab, Imam Abu Hanifa (d. 767) of the Hanafī madhhab, Imam al-Shai'i (d. 819) of the Shafi'i madhhab, and Imam Ahmad ibn Hanbal (d. 855) of the Hanbalī madhhab. The four Sunni madhahib are all considered equally orthodox. For the most part, they hold sway in their own traditional regions, although in large cities representatives of each may be found. The Shafi'i madhhab, which is a moderate school, predominates in Egypt and Southeast Asia. The Hanbali madhhab, very puritanical and conservative, is the official school of Saudi Arabia. The Maliki madhhab, with historical ties to Medina, is prominent in North Africa and the Sudan. The Hanafi madhhab, which originated in Iraq, is the most liberal and flexible, with major followings in Turkey, the Indo-Pakistan subcontinent, and Iraq.

Shi'ite schools operate in their areas of major population, especially Iraq, Lebanon, and Iran. The two leading schools are the Ja'farī, of the Twelve-Imam branch, principally found in Iran, and the Zaydi, found in Yemen. The Ja'fari school is named for the great Shi'ite scholar of early caliphal times, Ja'far al-Sadiq (d. 765), who was a teacher of the two great Sunni legal scholars already mentioned: Malik ibn Anas and Abu Hanifa. All Muslims hold Ja'far al-Sadiq in the highest regard. The Zaydi school is named for Zayd, who was the son of the fourth Shi'ite Imam Zayn al-'Abidin. A sectarian movement arose around Zayd, claiming him as the fifth Imam. The movement came to center in Yemen as the Zaydi school of Shi'ite jurisprudence. Zaydi law is the closest to Sunni jurisprudence of any of the Shi'ite legal schools. Once, when I had the privilege of interviewing the Grand Mufti of Yemen, a great Zaydi judge, I asked about the differences between Shi'ites and Sunnis in that ancient Muslim country. He gently remonstrated that there are no Shi'ites and Sunnis in his country, only Muslims with differing madhhabs.

Sunni-Shi'ite Relations. The Sunni caliphate ended ingloriously with the Mongol sack of Baghdad in 1258. Already, rival caliphs had long since arisen in Spain and Egypt, so that the Abbasid caliphs were little more than figureheads most of the time after the 900s. For a period around 1000 CE, a Shi'ite dynasty ruled in Baghdad, propping up the Sunni caliphate for political reasons, while severely restricting its powers. But the symbol of caliphal leadership continued to be compelling long after the fall of Baghdad, so that attempts at restoring the caliphate were sustained for periods in Egypt and, more recently, by the Ottoman Turkish rulers in Istanbul. The dying gasp of the caliphate occurred after World War I, with the fall of the Ottoman Empire and the rise of the modern Turkish state. Muslim parties interested in restoring the caliphate have continued, but without success.

Both Sunni and Shi'ite Muslims, the former numbering over 80 percent of the umma and the latter about 15 percent, plus some much smaller sects, consider themselves to share one fundamental religious doctrine and set of ritual duties. They acknowledge one Qur'anic revelation, and although Shi'ites and Sunnis differ on aspects of the Sunna, the principle of Muhammad's authority as model for the true Muslim way of life holds for both. Sunnis and Shi'ites worship together, with only minor differences in liturgical detail. When Shi'ites and Sunnis speak of their differences, they normally describe them as political and not religious in the doctrinal and ritual senses. Thus, Muslims of whatever subcommunity enjoy a far greater unity of belief and practice than do either Christians or Jews in the modern period.

Ijtihād. All Muslims invest great commitment in consensus, although Sunnis follow it more in law than do Shi'ites, who trust in their divinely guided leaders. A particularly pointed hadith of Muhammad declares: "Truly, my umma shall never agree together upon an error." The notion of a charismatic community could hardly be more strongly affirmed. When the (Sunni) Muslims, acting through their trusted scholarly representatives, traditionally came to a common agreement, then the whole community was thought to be provided with true guidance. But the

**Boy Playing and Man Praying at Open-Air Mosque near the
Dome of the Rock, on the Temple Mount, Jerusalem**

(*Source:* F. M. Denny)

principle of ijmaʿ, consensus, which was discussed earlier, caused a general rigid-
ifying of Muslim legal and theological discourse. Blind imitation, known as *taqlīd*,
came to take the place of *ijtihād*, independent legal decision making. But new ijtihad can also be approved by consensus, so there is a principle of continuing interpretative activity that enables the Muslims to meet the challenges of changing
times, of which modernity has provided many. One who practices ijtihad is known
as a *mujtahid*. This is one of the most honored roles in Islamic history, although it
could also be hazardous during times of retrenchment and conservatism.

The Qur'an states that "Allah will never change the condition of a people until they change what is in themselves" (13:11). Although this passage may be interpreted in a variety of ways, modern Muslim reformers have often cited it as a call
to rise up and shake off the dated ideas and practices of the past and restore a fresh
Qur'anic consciousness in Muslim affairs. The educational patterns of Muslim
peoples have traditionally looked toward the past and taken pride in a once glorious Islamic civilization. Rote memorization is still found in many Islamic regions,
although it is steadily being replaced by more discursive methods of education.
The Qur'an and Hadith and traditional religious and moralizing texts have served
as the basic curricular materials for the majority of Muslims until this century and
in many places still do. But the spirit of ijtihad, whose root meaning is intellectual

"exertion," has motivated many Muslims to update their methods while preserving their authentic sources of Qur'an and Sunna. Ijtihad has the same Arabic root as jihad, "exertion" in the way of God, including sometimes armed conflict in the sense of a holy war. But Muhammad taught that there are two jihads, a lesser one and a greater one. The former is armed conflict against the enemies of Islam and the Muslims, whereas the latter, the greater, is each Muslim's struggle with her or his own sins and temptations in the venture of living Islamically.

This chapter has surveyed several main ideas, processes, and institutions of religious authority in Islam. The emphasis has been on public Islam and the Muslim community in general, although the individual-personal appropriation of Muhammad's Sunna has also been emphasized as a vital component of Islamic faith and practice. The more or less official class of religio-legal leaders, the 'Ulama', are connected with the mosque and with the political authorities who are traditionally supposed to protect them as guardians of Islam. But there are also religious leadership roles other than the 'Ulama'. There are preachers, spiritual guides of mystical orders of Sufis, saints, and teachers. Some of these roles will be described and analyzed in later chapters.

AUTHORITY

QUESTIONS FOR DISCUSSION AND REVIEW

1. Authority is represented in various ways in Jewish, Christian, and Islamic religious literature. What are some of the models of authority drawn from scripture that are important to each of the religious traditions? What are the similarities and differences among those models? How, in general, do the models compare across the three traditions?

2. For Jews, Christians, and Muslims, religious authority is grounded in certain notions of religious community. What are some forms of religious community in each of the three traditions? How are certain understandings of community related to conceptions of authority?

3. Communities sometimes pattern religious authority in highly ordered and precise ways, and sometimes they incorporate a measure of ambiguity or flexibility into their articulation of the structure of authority. Sometimes, a single tradition will manifest a complex understanding of authority in which these models exist side by side. Is authority defined clearly in all three traditions? Is it highly structured? To what extent is flexibility manifest in the way authority is structured? What are some cases in which flexible and rigid models exist side by side?

4. Religious authority is represented in communities in an assortment of ways, but particularly in the form of specially designated persons. These religious professionals exercise authority in the community by virtue of their status as religious officeholders. What are some of the religious offices in each

tradition? What are the responsibilities and privileges of religious officeholders in each community? To what extent might persons who do not hold office exercise authority in the community? Can the authority of a person who does not hold religious office ever supplant that of an officially recognized authority?

5. Jews, Christians, and Muslims construct new models of authority as the conditions and expectations of community life change. This process of adaptation can occur gradually over time or it can emerge rapidly out of volatile social and political conditions. In what ways has religious authority changed within each tradition as members of the religion respond to new historical forces and social influences? How does each tradition differ from the others in the solutions that it finds to changing circumstances of life? In what ways does each tradition maintain continuity to older forms of authority in the course of adapting?

6. Political authority and religious authority have been closely related within each tradition at various times. What are some examples of the ways in which this has occurred within Judaism, Christianity, and Islam? To what extent is religious community seen as identical to political or civil community in those cases?

7. Religious authority often is closely connected to the administration of religious law. How has this been evidenced in Judaism? In Christianity? In Islam?

PART IV

WORSHIP AND RITUAL

In Judaism, Christianity, and Islam, worship is a matter of everyday life. The prayers, deeds, and religious meditations that make up the piety of a Jew, a Christian, or a Muslim are not limited to certain times of the day or days of the week. They are part of religious practice, which is the ongoing personal translation of faith into forms of devotion suited to the activities and responsibilities of a person's daily life. Religious practice, while grounded in doctrine, is thus commonly open ended and inventive.

Worship is, of course, a group activity as well as a personal endeavor. Public worship is organized around certain seasons of the year, days of the week, and times of day. It is structured in specific events and detailed activities. In some cases, elaborate ceremony forms the context for public worship. But public worship is not separate from everyday piety. In both cases, the aim is to communicate with God.

Jews, Christians, and Muslims structure public worship in ritual. This does not mean, however, that these three traditions are equally reliant on ritualized forms of worship. It is best to view ritual as a spectrum ranging from minimally structured worship at one end to highly structured worship at the other. Judaism, Christianity, and Islam—including the various subdivisions within each—occupy different places along such a spectrum. At certain times these religions appear similar in their promotion of a carefully defined order of worship. As we see, however, there are differences in the way each religion conceives the nature of public ritual and, indeed, the desirability of the ritual form itself.

Religious communities agree on styles and forms of public worship and diligently oversee their enactment. The obvious reason for this is that Jews, Christians, and Muslims regard traditions of public worship, refined over many centuries, as effective means to communicate their thoughts and feelings to God. Less obvious, but no less important a reason, is that public worship represents the community itself. It displays for nonbelievers and confirms for co-religionists deeply held beliefs and attitudes about personal and communal life. It demonstrates the understandings of the past and of the future that ground the identity of the community. In short, worship is a performance, an acting out of meanings that a community embraces as valuable, as well as a context for the cultivation of spirituality.

Worship as an important component of the culture of the Jews, Christians, and Muslims undergoes periodic adaptations, in the same way that other aspects of culture are subject to change. As the circumstances of community life fluctuate, as new visions for the future emerge, and as fresh appraisals of the past are made, worship is altered. In representing the life of the community, worship both sustains tradition and serves as a medium in which evolving self-understandings of community can be expressed.

CHAPTER 10

WORSHIP AND RITUAL
IN JUDAISM

The priests of the Jerusalem Temple offered their last sacrificial service nearly two thousand years ago. Yet to this day, the liturgical worship of Judaism and many aspects of personal piety remain dominated by images and patterns derived from the Temple.[1]

The ways in which Jews have understood the significance of the synagogue as a communal gathering place reveals this impact. The term "synagogue" comes from the Greek language. It originally applied to any communal gathering, without regard to the ethnic identity of the participants. During late Second Temple times and the first two centuries CE, the term commonly bore a specifically Judaic meaning and was often used as a synonym for the "official Jewish community" of a given town or region. Thus, the phrase "the synagogue of Rome" would refer to the Roman Jewish community, not specifically to a piece of real estate. Only later did "synagogue" come to designate the *place* in which the community met. These meetings might involve communal business or education, and the building that housed them might serve as well as a central point for distribution of charitable services or as a hostel. Not until the fifth or sixth centuries does it uniformly and exclusively mean a place of worship.

Most of the rabbinic literature of the third through sixth centuries takes for granted that the synagogue (Hebrew, *bet haknesset*: "meeting place") is a specific building that can include public study activities but serves principally as a place of worship. As such it came to be called as well a *mikdash me'at* ("Temple in miniature"). Reflecting the larger rabbinic conception of prayer as a substitute for the original sacrificial service, the location of the worshipful gathering is described as a kind of temple. In contemporary Jewish communities, houses of worship are known by any of these terms—synagogue, bet haknesset, or Temple. Everywhere there is a common perception among Jews that the activities of the house of worship continue, however tenuously, the most ancient form of Jewish divine service.[2]

In ancient and medieval Judaism, however, worship included much more than what happened in the synagogue. As we have seen, Jews within the halakhic system of the rabbis imagined the entire substance of public and private life as a kind of divine service or avodah. In this chapter, therefore, our first concern is to trace the principal aspects of rabbinic worship and to show how halakhic tradition extended worshipful attitudes and actions well beyond the strict confines of public prayer gatherings.[3] Most of our descriptions apply equally to contemporary Orthodox and Traditionalist Judaism.

Second, we ask how rabbinic conceptions of worship have fared among Modernist Jews beyond the narrow spectrum of Orthodoxy and Traditionalism. How have the vast majority of Modernist Jews responded to the all-embracing halakhic conception of avodah? How have they conceived of the worshipful life within the constraints of societies that define religion as a personal "faith" separate from secular or worldly concerns? By way of illustration, we offer sketches of the transformations of Reform Jewish synagogue life in nineteenth-century Europe and the ritual innovations among Jewish feminists in contemporary North America.

THE HALAKHIC SHAPING OF RELIGIOUS EXPERIENCE

The Content of Worship

When the Temple stood, its priests offered daily sacrifices at dawn and shortly before twilight to the accompaniment of psalms and hymns. With the Temple gone, only the memory of sacrifices at set times of the day; and the songs, remained. Early morning and early evening, each day of the year, rabbinic Jewish communities gathered in their synagogues to offer the "sacrifice of the lips," the standardized prayers of common Jews that replaced the blood, fat, and meat of slaughtered cattle.

Until modern times, these gatherings were largely composed of men, as were the groups of rabbinic masters who designed the halakhic guidelines for public worship. Just as male priests once officiated in the Temple, so, too, male Israelites took up the official duties of the synagogue. Women were welcome to pray in the synagogue but could not constitute the quorum of ten males necessary to constitute an official representation of the entire Israelite community. By early medieval times, rabbinic synagogues eventually came to maintain a separate section for women. Called the "Women's Courtyard" (*ezrat nashim*), after the similarly named quarter in the ancient Temple compound, it has taken the form in some congregations of a balcony above the area in which men pray. At times, it is a thin partition within the same space; elsewhere, it is an adjoining room from which the men's worship can be observed or overheard. In modern times, one finds it only in Orthodox or Traditionalist synagogues.

Even the names of the worship services, *shakharit* (dawn offering) and *minkhah* (evening grain offering) recall the original setting of the Temple. When, in the early rabbinic centuries, yet a third worship service was instituted, it, too, was linked to the Temple liturgy. Offered at nightfall (*maariv* or *aravit*), it was said to correspond to the hours during which the sacrificial meat offered at minkhah continued to burn on the altar. In halakhic custom, minkhah and maariv are normally recited just before sunset and just after the stars appear, separated by a short period of Torah study.

The core of the worship service is an amalgam of what the halakhic tradition regards as two separate obligations incumbent on all Jewish males. The first obligation, to offer public prayer at fixed moments, is satisfied at shakharit and minkhah by the recitation of a fixed prayer containing nineteen separate benedictions. Originally numbering eighteen blessings, it retains the name "The Eighteen" (*shmoneh esreh*), and is also known commonly as the *amidah* or "Standing Prayer." These open with a series of praises of God, continue with petitions for this-worldly communal well-being, reach a climax with prayers for communal redemption from exile, and culminate with thanksgiving and requests for peace. In accordance with its name, the amidah is recited while standing upright, eyes downward, as one would stand before royalty.

The prayer is first recited in a whisper, each worshiper praying alone in concentration on the praises and petitions: "Blessed are you, Shield of Abraham, . . . Blessed are you, Restorer of the Dead, . . . Blessed are you, who accepts repentance, . . . who heals the sick among his people Israel, . . . who rebuilds Jerusalem." Afterwards, it is recited aloud by the prayer leader. A distinctive feature of this second recitation is the expansion of the fourth benediction, called the *kedushah* (Sanctification). In the version recited privately, this benediction reads: "You are holy, and your Name is holy, and the Holy Ones each day praise you in holiness. Blessed are you, the Holy God." During the public recitation, this allusion to angelic "Holy Ones" who praise God is expanded. The worshiping community actually takes on the role of the angels, rising on tiptoe three times to the words "Holy, holy, holy is the Lord of Hosts, the whole world is full of his glory" (Isa. 6:2). At this moment of the liturgy, the barrier between mundane earthly existence and the heavenly world of God is bridged, as worshipers relocate themselves in imagination before the presence of God.

The intensity of the amidah, with its whispered silences and heavenly transports, has its parallel in the second obligation satisfied during the worship service. Strictly speaking, it is not a prayer at all. Rather, it is a moment of study that is understood, at the same time, to constitute a ceremony of rededication to the covenant and a meditation upon the unity of God. Called the *shma*, after its opening word, "Hear," it is the recitation of a series of biblical verses, culled from Deuteronomy and Numbers, that affirm the uniqueness of Israel's God and detail the history of his redemptive acts.

As worshipers recite the first verse of the shma ("Hear, O Israel! the Lord is

An Orthodox Jewish Man in Morning Worship

Strapped to his left arm and head are black leather boxes (*tefillin; phylacteries*) containing handwritten passages of the Bible. A prayer shawl (*tallit*) is common for all men of Bar Mitzvah age. In some communities, only married men wear the *tallit*. This worshiper holds a prayer book (*siddur*) in his hands. In recent years, some women in Conservative, Reconstructionist, and Reform communities have begun to wear the tefillin and tallit traditionally worn only by males. (*Source:* © Doranne Jacobson)

our God, the Lord alone" [Deut. 6:4]), they commonly shield their closed eyes with the right hand and attempt to experience as a fact the unity of God that their words celebrate. In the long history of rabbinic Judaism, the nature of this unity has been imagined with the aid of as many metaphysical theories and symbolic systems as the Jews have met in their surrounding cultures. Philosophically inclined Jews of twelfth-century Egypt might have reflected on the metaphysical uniqueness of God as the self-created and self-sufficient Cause of all reality. Jews steeped in the kabbalistic traditions of the thirteenth to the seventeenth centuries would have imagined that by unifying the letters of the divine name in concentration, they were stimulating the heavenly Sefirot to unite in world-sustaining harmony. Modernist Jews, assuming a rather different cosmos, might imagine the unity of all things in God prior to the "Big Bang" that gave birth to the universe as measured by contemporary astronomers and physicists. Jews of any period or place who were not inclined to profound reflection may have taken courage in the conviction that their God belonged to them and them alone. But for all, the same text recited in the same ritual united them across centuries and continents into a single community of memory and affirmation.

One of the verses in the shma indicates that one should recite "these instructions . . . when you lie down and when you get up" (Deut. 6:6–7). Therefore, halakhic tradition requires recitation of the shma at night and shortly after dawn. Early rabbinic communities eventually combined the morning shma and the dawn amidah into a single service and attached an evening amidah to the nighttime shma to create a new service. Because the maariv prayer has no clear precedent in Temple ritual, it is recited only in silence, without a public recitation by the prayer leader.[4]

The Cycle of Worship

The daily rhythm of worship life, geared to the rising and setting of the sun, is modulated by a set of other rhythms geared to the cycle of the lunar month and the solar year. In ways that are at turns both pronounced and subtle, Jewish liturgical life responds to these cycles. The result is that the inevitable passage of weeks, months, and years serves as a stimulus to reflect on and experience the fundamental memories of Jewish tradition.

Four times a month—every seven days—the daily pattern of worship is modified in a special liturgy that celebrates the Sabbath, the day on which the Creator of the World rested from his creativity. Since no work of any kind may be performed on the Sabbath, its worship services are leisurely and protracted. On Sabbath Eve and on the Sabbath Day, special benedictions replace the usual benedictions of the weekday amidah. Furthermore, an additional amidah, called the *musaf* (Supplemental Prayer) is added after shakharit on Sabbath morning, in commemoration of the supplemental Sabbath sacrifice once offered by the priests. Its content is a fervent prayer that the sacrifices once offered on the Sabbath will once again be brought in the messianic future, when the Temple will itself be rebuilt and Israel restored to its Land.

The Sabbath is a prime example of how Judaism extends the attitude of worship beyond the specific setting of communal prayer. Here is a day in which few acts are *not* imbued with a liturgical significance. In commemoration of God's resting from creation (Gen. 2:1–4), halakhic tradition prohibits all acts of labor on the Sabbath. These prohibitions include far more than the pursuit of one's normal livelihood or of other strenuous activity. They extend to almost any act that brings into being something that did not exist prior to the Sabbath, such as writing, or one that destroys something that had existed prior to the Sabbath, such as erasing. The parallel with divine rest is obvious; as God renounced creativity on the seventh day, so must Israel. Talmudic tradition adds another consideration. In its view, the wilderness Tent of Meeting was completed on a Sabbath. With the Tent and its successor, the Temple, gone, the Sabbath replaces both as a temporal structure in which God's presence is concentrated. When each Sabbath (as stand-in for the Temple) is "built," labor necessary to the creation of the original spatial structure is no longer permitted (Babylonian Talmud, Shabbat 49b).

How is this temporal Temple constructed? First of all, there can be no kindling of lights on the Sabbath. The day is welcomed, shortly before sunset on Friday evening, as mothers and daughters recite a Sabbath benediction over prelit candles. It is ushered out when the stars emerge on Saturday night. Sabbath time departs and everyday time is restored in a ritual known as *havdalah* (Separation). Here Jews light another candle, bless wine and sweet spices, and praise God for distinguishing "between the holy and the common, between light and darkness, between Israel and the nations, between the Seventh Day and the six days of Creation."

Since kindling is prohibited on the Sabbath, there can be no cooking on that day. Food must be cooked beforehand and kept on low heat for the twenty-five-hour period of rest. The principle of restraint from any creativity has other ramifications as well. It is appropriate, for example, to avoid using tools or other utensils that cannot be employed in service of some act necessary to the celebration of the Sabbath. Thus, a knife may held, for one can use it for the Sabbath meals; a pen, however, is off limits—*muktzah*—lest one entertain thoughts of using it in the prohibited act of writing. Without going into elaborate details, we can observe that the laws of Sabbath rest encourage only the following sorts of activities: prayer, feasting, Torah study, strolling, and sleep. Even the play of children is structured by restrictions on such common activities as, for example, drawing or outdoor climbing.

It is no surprise, therefore, that the Sabbath creates a profound sense of discontinuity with everyday life. The ritual acts and prohibitions that regulate the day impart a unique quality to time. In comparison to the rush of daily affairs, with their obsessive focus on the present and its demands, Sabbath time is experienced as a kind of timelessness in which the sacred past and the anticipated redemption infuse and transform the present. This timelessness is then interpreted in multilayered terms provided by Jewish tradition and memory. As a memorial of the act of Creation, it is a reminiscence of the peace enjoyed by the universe at the moment of its physical completion; as a reminder of the Temple, it gives all

The Mishnaic Conception of Sabbath Labor

The classic rabbinic classification of the labors forbidden on the Sabbath is found in the Mishnah's tractate Shabbat (Sabbath) 7:2:

> *The Categories of Labor are forty less one:*
>
> *One who sows, and one who ploughs, and one who reaps, and one who binds sheaves, one who threshes, and one who winnows, one who picks out chaff, one who grinds kernels, one who sifts flour, one who kneads dough, and one who bakes.*
>
> *One who shears the wool, one who whitens it, and one who combs it, and one who dyes it, and one who spins the thread, and one who sets up the longitudinal warp, and one who creates two loops around the crossbar, and one who passes two threads of the woof through the warp, and one who severs two threads to release a garment from the loom. One who ties, and one who loosens, and one who sews two stitches, one who tears in order to sew two stitches.*
>
> *One who hunts the deer, one who slaughters it, and one who skins it, one who salts the skin for tanning, and one who tans the hide, and one who scrapes it, and one who cuts it to shape or size. One who writes two letters (e.g., A, B), and one who erases in order to write two letters.*
>
> *One who builds and one who razes. One who extinguishes and one who kindles. One who strikes (the anvil) with a hammer. One who brings out from domain to domain.*
>
> *Indeed, these are the Categories of Labor, forty less one.*

The list is bewildering until you notice that the labors are organized into four major groups: acts necessary to make bread; acts necessary to make clothing; acts necessary to produce parchments for books; acts that produce tools or make the home habitable. The Mishnah seems to be saying that it is forbidden on the Sabbath to engage in actions that create the distinctively human world. If so, the point is that, in imitation of God, Jews rest from those activities in which humans are uniquely creative, just as God rested from the task of world creation.

activity within its temporal borders a liturgical flavor; as an anticipation of the messianic "day that is entirely Sabbath," it is a foretaste of the wholeness that will be restored to the universe in the era of its moral perfection.[5]

The distinctive worship services and practices of the Sabbath, which demarcate the passage of weeks, have their parallels throughout the course of the solar year. Nearly every month of the Jewish calendar has its special days and commemorations of events within the sacred memory of Israel. All of these are marked off by special changes in the daily prayers and distinctive celebrations in the home. By way of illustration, let us attend, momentarily, to the sequence of three sacred occasions called the "Pilgrimage Festivals"—the spring holiday of Pesah (Passover), the summer celebration of Shavuot (Feast of Weeks), and the autumn feast of Sukkot (Feast of Tabernacles).

Biblical laws identify these occasions as agricultural festivals of thanksgiving for harvests. Like the surrounding Canaanite culture, Israelites marked harvest seasons with sacrificial and other rituals designed to ensure a rich harvest and to

RITUAL OCCASIONS OF THE RABBINIC YEAR

In rabbinic Judaism, the yearly calendar is punctuated by festivals of various types. These may be broadly characterized as festivals of the New Year Cycle, Pilgrimage Festivals, and Commemorative Celebrations and Fasts. The following catalog will help orient you toward the way these observances carve time into Judaically meaningful units.

The New Year Cycle

1. Rosh Hashannah (New Year's Day)

   Date: 1–2 Tishrei (Sept.–Oct.)

   Biblical Source: Lev. 23:23–25

   Significance: Anniversary of Creation. Inaugurates 10 days of penitential prayer.

   Main Rituals: Blowing of the ram's horn (Shofar) during morning prayers.

2. Yom Kippur (Day of Absolution)

   Date: 10 Tishrei

   Biblical Source: Lev. 23:26–32; Lev. 16:1–34

   Significance: The day on which God formally wipes away the past year's record of sins and renews perfect relationship to Israel.

   Main Rituals: Total abstention from food, drink, luxury, and sexual activity for 25 hours.

3. Sukkot (Tabernacles) and Shemini Atzeret (Eighth Day of Assembly)/Simhat Torah (Rejoicing in the Torah)

   Date: 15–23 Tishrei

   Biblical Source: Lev. 23:33–43

   Significance: Sukkot commemorates dependence upon God's protection during 40 years of wilderness wandering. Shemini Atzeret formally concludes Sukkot. Simhat Torah is the second day of Shemini Atzeret.

   Main Rituals: During Sukkot all meals are eaten in the *sukkah* (ritual hut), and the "Four Species" of plants that grow near water are waved. Shemini Atzeret formally concludes Sukkot. Simhat Torah is the day on which the last chapter of the Torah is concluded and the first chapter is begun in a formal synagogue ritual. It is commonly celebrated by dancing with the Torah in the synagogue.

Pilgrimage Festivals

1. Pesah (Passover) (March–April)

   Date: 15–22 Nisan

   Biblical Source: Exod. 12:1–8; Lev. 23:5–8

   Significance: Commemorates liberation from Egyptian slavery.

   Main Rituals: The seder meal on the first night and the eating of unleavened bread (*matzah*) for the entire festival.

2. Shavuot (Weeks)

   Date: 6–7 Sivan (May–June)

   Biblical Source: Exod. 34:22; Lev. 23:9–22

   Significance: Anniversary of the giving of the Torah on Sinai.

   Main Rituals: All-night study of Torah on Shavuot eve.

3. Sukkot (see New Year Cycle)

   ### Commemorative Celebrations

1. Chanukkah (Dedication)

   Date: 25 Kislev-3 Tevet (Nov.–Dec.)

   Biblical Source: none

   Significance: Commemorates the Maccabean liberation of Palestine from Syrian domination in 165 BCE. When the Maccabees rededicated the Temple, a single cruse of pure oil miraculously burned for eight days.

   Main Rituals: The lighting of candles in a *menorah* (candelabra) on each night of the festival commemorates the Maccabean miracle. Gifts for children. Gambling for small stakes. Eating foods cooked in oil.

2. Purim (Raffles)

   Date: 14 Adar (Feb.–March)

   Biblical Source: Book of Esther

   Significance: Commemorates Esther's bravery and that of her adoptive father, Mordecai, in reversing a plot by a governmental official, Haman, to destroy Persian Jewry.

   Main Rituals: Reading the Book of Esther to the accompaniment of raucous celebration. A commandment of the day is to become so drunk that it is impossible to distinguish between Mordecai and Haman.

   ### Commemorative Fasts

1. Fast of 10 Tevet (Dec.–Jan.)

2. Fast of 17 Tammuz (July)

3. Fast of 9 Av (July–Aug.)

   Biblical Source: Zech. 5:19

   Significance: Each fast commemorates multiple historical catastrophes, but their main function is to recall the stages of the Babylonian and Roman sieges of Jerusalem that culminated, on 9 Av, in the destruction of both Temples.

   Main Rituals: 10 Tevet and 17 Tammuz are "daylight" fasts in which no food or drink is permitted between dawn and dusk. 9 Av is a 25-hour fast and includes all the prohibitions of Yom Kippur except that it is a workday. On each Fast day, special penitential prayers are recited in the synagogue. On 9 Av, the Book of Lamentations is read in the synagogue.

promote the land's fertility. In a ritual known from other agricultural civilizations, Israelite males were also required to make pilgrimage to the Temple on these occasions to "appear before the Lord" with sacrificial offerings (Deut. 16:16). Distinctive to Israelite culture, however, is the way the Bible imports a historical dimension into its understanding of the agricultural festivals of Pesah and Sukkot in particular. The former commemorates the liberation of Israel from Egyptian slavery; the latter commemorates the years of desert wandering prior to the entry of Israel into its Land. By rabbinic times, of course, with the Temple destroyed, the aspect of pilgrimage had long ago disappeared from the celebration of these festivals. They had been replaced by a series of elaborate, halakhically regulated commemorative procedures.

In addition to special liturgies prepared for each day and dominated by appropriate images from biblical tradition, each holiday extends its meanings well beyond the synagogue. The well-known observances connected with Pesah are the most obvious. For eight days, Jews eat thin wafers called *matzah*, a reminder of the "bread of affliction" their ancestors ate as Egyptian slaves. On the first night of Pesah, an elaborate ritual meal—the *seder*—is celebrated in the home. Modeled to some degree on ancient Hellenistic *symposia*, postdinner drinking sessions at which philosophical instruction was offered, the seder follows an elaborate script called the *haggadah*. Its pages guide diners through the consumption of symbolic foods, four cups of wine, a multicourse feast, and a series of parables and songs focused on the events surrounding the miraculous liberation from Egypt. Beginning at nightfall and lasting into the predawn hours, the seder is an elaborate reenactment of the drama of becoming the people Israel.

Shavuot, the second Pilgrimage Festival, is celebrated fifty days after the first night of Pesah. In rabbinic tradition, it commemorates the central covenant pact between Israel and God, the giving of the Torah on Sinai. Since medieval times, two customs have dominated the celebration of Shavuot. The first, a reenactment of the act of receiving the Torah, involves staying awake from the evening meal on Shavuot Eve until dawn in Torah study. In many communities, official "syllabi" have been transmitted that guide learners through a list of all the divine commandments (613 in rabbinic computation) to a series of texts drawn from the entire sacred literature of Judaism—Bible, Mishnah, Talmud, and Zohar. Torah study in this setting, as in many other contexts in rabbinic Judaism, is not simply an intellectual activity, but a ritual participation in the original moment of revelation.

A second custom concerns an apparently meaningless dietary detail. It is common to eat a dairy lunch after prayers on Shavuot morning. Normally, all Sabbaths and Festivals are celebrated with the consumption of meat, since meat was the sacrificial offering in the Temple. Why now dairy? As halakhic codifiers explain (Mishnah Berurah, Orekh Khayyim 494:3), this commemorates a Mosaic halakhic ruling made necessary by the revelation of the Torah. Among the Torah's numerous restrictions, insist the rabbis, is the prohibition of eating any meat that has not been salted and soaked sufficiently to remove all blood. Upon

**The Ritual Foods
of the Seder**

In addition to the unleavened bread (matzah) eaten at the seder, celebrants also reflect at length on the meaning of the symbolic foods arranged on the seder plate and placed prominently at the head of the table. These are: (1) a roasted egg (*betzah*), which represents the sacrifice once offered for all Festivals in the Temple; (2) the lamb bone (*zero'a*), which symbolizes the lamb slaughtered on Passover Eve prior to the liberation from Egypt; (3) chopped nuts and fruit (*haroset*), an allusion to the mortar with which the Israelites were forced to make bricks for Pharoah; (4) bitter herbs (*maror*), representing the bitterness of servitude; (5) parsley (*karpas*), eaten after a dipping in salt water, recalls the salty tears of slavery; (6) the maror and haroset are eaten together with lettuce (*hazeret*) as another representation of bitterness in servitude. (*Source:* © Doranne Jacobson)

their return from Sinai, hungry Israelites—now obligated by this new rule—had no time to engage in the lengthy procedure of leeching the blood from their meat. Instead, they ate dairy. As fanciful as this explanation might appear, it points to the core of Judaism's power to use the simplest details of home life—a holiday lunch menu—to create a sense of intimate connection with the founding events of Israel.

One final example from the autumn festival of Sukkot will conclude our discussion. The main observance of this festival, which lasts for seven days, is the construction of a small thatch-covered hut—a *sukkah*—within which all meals must be taken. According to some, it is a halakhic requirement even to sleep in the sukkah. Why? As the Bible reports (Lev. 23:42–43), these are the sorts of dwellings that Israelites endured during their trek in the wilderness of Sinai, after receiving the Torah and before entering the Land of Israel. Sukkot is a time for reexperiencing the sense of living "on the move," in fragile shelter, trusting—as did ancient Israel—solely in the sheltering presence of God.

The solar year, we have seen, is a kind of canvas upon which fundamental aspects of Jewish memory are painted. Each spring, Jews leave Egypt and gather toward Sinai where, in early summer, they receive the Torah. From there, they start off for the Land of Promise, wandering in the wilderness where, each autumn, they relive the fundamental attitude of trust in God that sustained them until the present. Combined with the weekly return to the origins of Creation and the daily regimen of the shma and amidah, halakhic tradition creates a rich setting for continued immersion in the fundamental images of Jewish memory and hope. That setting is confined neither to the synagogue nor to the home, but oscillates between them, each context confirming and responding to the experiences transmitted in its counterpart.

In premodern times, this ritual system proved so effective that it was retained throughout the rabbinic world. Where innovations were introduced, these enriched, rather than overturned, the inherited rabbinic system. The Kabbalists were particularly persistent in their creation of ritual innovations that amplified existing models. In the sixteenth century, for example, Kabbalists in the Galilean village of Safed would dress in white on Sabbath Eve and go out into the fields to "greet the Sabbath Queen" with mystical hymns as she entered with the west's setting sun. One such hymn, *lekhah dodi* ("Come, My Beloved") is sung in nearly all synagogues even today by people who would never dream of wandering into the fields dressed in white to great the Sabbath.

Similarly, the sukkah became the focus of a remarkable ritual called *ushpizin* (guests). On each evening of the seven-day Festival, the soul of either Abraham, Isaac, Jacob, Joseph, Moses, Aaron, or David is invited as a "Supernal Guest" from the divine Throne World into the sukkah to dine with the family. The custom proved particularly popular among European Jews, and instructions for the ritual are still printed in some prayer books. One can add examples from throughout the Jewish liturgical calender, but the point is simple. The basic halakhic regulations of Jewish life generated a rich variety of local amplifications that lent to Jewish culture an enormously diverse range of religious expression.[6]

MODERNITY AND THE IDEAL OF AVODAH

Judaism in Modern Culture

If you visit a local synagogue or temple in order to observe the halakhic patterns of worship we have just described, you will likely be surprised. Only the most Orthodox and Traditionalist Jewish communities, many of them rather uncompromising in their rejection of contemporary mores, remain committed to these patterns of all-embracing avodah. In any Jewish community, you will find synagogues or temples, but you will rarely find within them or in the homes of their members the comprehensive orientation toward the sacred past and redemptive future characteristic of ancient and medieval rabbinic piety. The goal of the present part of our discussion is to explain why this is so, to assess its impact on modern Judaic ritual experience, and to describe some recent attempts to retrieve a holistic avodah in a contemporary Judaic idiom.

Toward the end of Chapter 4, we allude briefly to enormous social and political changes that governed the transformation of European Jews into a modern people. These changes had important implications for the ways in which Jews thought about themselves in relation to the world around them. Among the first areas of Jewish life to confront those implications was synagogue worship. Some reflection upon the context of Jewish modernization will help to explain why.

As we shall see in detail in Chapter 19, Jews dwelling in most of the Christian territories of pre-eighteenth-century Europe were regarded as resident aliens of their host countries. Such rights of residence as they enjoyed were purchased and could be rescinded at the whim of the local ruler. Their relations with Christians were normally minimal and highly charged with mythic perceptions: Christians regarded Jews as the "Synagogue of Satan," the torturers of Christ still present among them; Jews regarded Christians as the descendants of Esau, the eternal victimizer of Jacob.

Although the eighteenth century brought about a gradual relaxation of Jewish civil rights disabilities, European attitudes toward Jews changed more slowly and not necessarily in a benign direction. This issue occupies us at length in Chapter 19. For now, it is enough to point out that medieval fear of Jews, inspired by Christian mythic memory, did not disappear with the modern weakening of Christian faith. Rather, it was transformed into anti-Semitism, a pseudo-scientific contempt for Jews as an inferior, "Oriental race of Semites." Struggling against much popular resistance, the process of enfranchising the Jews of western and central European states took nearly a century, from the emancipation of French Jews in 1791 to the granting of full citizenship to German Jews in 1870. Throughout this period—indeed, until the destruction of European Jewry under Nazi domination (1939–1945)—Jews felt great pressure to prove their worth as members of society and their loyalty to the countries of their birth.[7]

We have already seen (Chapter 4) that these pressures called forth a variety of responses among the Jews. The majority chose what we have called the Modernist path. Both Reform Jews and those of the Positive-Historical (Conservative)

movement sought to balance the claims of Jewish tradition with those of participation in modern national life. It is within the Reform party in particular that the
most far-reaching experiments in modernizing Jewish ritual patterns were conducted. Champions of Positive-Historical Judaism, for their part, sponsored less
ambitious changes in the received rabbinic worship tradition. Secularists had
abandoned religion and thus had no interest in ritual reforms, whereas the Modernist Orthodox and Traditionalists would tolerate little or no compromise on matters of halakhic ritual. It was the Modernists of Reform, therefore, who led in conceiving new forms of Judaic worship compatible with modern intellectual,
aesthetic, and religious sensibilities. Our discussion, accordingly, focuses on their
achievements.

Let us look briefly at the European sources of their inspiration. The Europeanized Jews of the early nineteenth century were deeply influenced by an
emerging pattern of religion that—in reaction against the violent religious wars
that had plagued Christian Europe since the Protestant Reformation—had become
common in liberal societies. This pattern, the source of the American Constitution's separation of church and state, held that religion was a personal expression
of conscience that the state had no power to control. The very *essence* of religion, in
this view, was the believer's personal communication with God.

This was a marked departure from medieval Catholic and earlier Calvinistic
conceptions that religion should find its ultimate expression in the institutions of
the state and society. By contrast, the new view was that the institutions of society
should be unconcerned with the private religious beliefs of its members. In particular, the civil rights of citizens of the state should not be infringed or enhanced because of their private religious beliefs. On the basis of this principle of the essential
privacy of religious belief, Christians of many persuasions could live together in a
single political system. Private faith and public duty to the body politic were in
principle separate areas of life. Religion, the teacher of moral values and the
molder of conscience, should serve society by producing good citizens. But its
public institutions should not dominate society.

European Jews, passionately committed to achieving full civil rights, gave
themselves eagerly to this liberal vision of the state as the guarantor of freedom for
private religious expressions. It shaped as well their understanding about what
was important in religion, including Judaism. If Judaism was essentially a moral
relationship with God, moral values were of far greater importance than commitment to a halakhic legal system that frequently posed many difficulties to full participation in the emerging religiously neutral society. If Judaism, like Christianity,
were a matter of private conscience, its public expressions might have to be radically reshaped to conform to emerging moral sentiments.

The greatest challenge to this point of view lay in the halakhic tradition's
perception that all of Jewish life, public and private, is a covenantal avodah, in
which strict halakhic procedures guarantee the liturgical effectiveness of the
covenant people, Israel. The halakhically inspired communal separatism of rabbinic Judaism had preserved the people for centuries. But it was now seen as a
crippling liability. It seemed to confirm anti-Semitic charges that the Jews were

essentially non-European, a parasitic people feeding on the European host. How was it possible to reconcile the all-embracing requirements of halakhic tradition with the necessity to present Judaism as a public-spirited, democratic religion of good citizenship? How to convince sceptical European Christians that Judaism was not the atavistic, primitive superstition that Christian and Secularist critics claimed it to be?

The Modernization of Worship

The history of the Reform movement suggests that many Jews could imagine no such reconciliation. As early as 1810, decades before the Reform movement declared itself a comprehensive program to transform Judaism into a modern faith, German Jews had begun to form worship groups in which they could pray in their native German language rather than in an increasingly foreign Hebrew. To a great extent, the desire to make worship a more evocative moral experience, rather than a rote performance, underlay these and later attempts to alter halakhic patterns. Moreover, the desire for change originated among common Jews, not among rabbinic leaders. Even after the Reform movement came under the leadership of such brilliant rabbinic scholars as Abraham Geiger, Reform laypeople often outraced even the most accommodating of rabbinic leaders in discarding or redefining various elements of received ritual tradition. Conscious reforms—of synagogue ritual, for example—led to unconscious changes in attitudes and sensibilities about religion. These, in return, made inherited halakhic traditions of worship and piety appear hopelessly irrational, morally questionable, or, perhaps worst of all, "Oriental" and utterly inhospitable to normative European culture.

In many ways, the most well-intended attempts to make synagogue worship more morally or aesthetically inspiring could prove problematic from a strictly halakhic perspective. An instructive case is the rapid introduction of organ music into the Sabbath worship service. Some of the most sublime compositions of European music had been written for Protestant and Catholic worship services. By the early nineteenth century, German Jews had developed a profound love of the classical music of Europe. They wanted its lofty chords to grace their own devotions to God as well. Halakhic tradition, however, had defined acts of music making as constituting forbidden Sabbath labors. In this case, the halakhic tradition was ignored in favor of the aesthetic advantage of the organ.

It is crucial to appreciate what was at stake here, for it illumines the fundamentally different conceptions of avodah at work in the classical halakhic tradition and in Reform. Halakhically speaking, restraint from music making on the Sabbath was part of the Sabbath avodah—an element in the comprehensive system of restraints that made the Sabbath time otherworldly. For proponents of Reform, however, these restraints were perceived differently. These were not an avodah that sanctified the Sabbath, but an onerous burden of minute observances that threatened the worshipers' ability to enjoy the best things of the world in which they lived. The sonorous tones of the organ, to the contrary, elicited profound aesthetic pleasure and inspired as well moving religious sentiments. There could be no compromise on this point for Reform: a detail of rabbinic Sabbath law would be violated in favor of an experience that summarized for worshipers the essence of avodah.

Thus Reform worship offered powerful moments of religious transport through music. These, however, came to be regarded as the essence of the experience of avodah. The complex observances that structured the entire day of the Sabbath in the halakhic tradition were increasingly ignored. A pattern developed in which powerful experiences in the synagogue, achieved through ritual innovations, came to replace customs that linked the experience offered by the synagogue to the world outside, including the home.

The matter of family worship is another important example. Halakhic norms, you'll recall, had since the early Middle Ages mandated the separation of men and women in prayer. But by the early nineteenth century, family prayer had become a norm in many Christian denominations. Such prayer had come to symbolize the sanctity of the family unit, standing before God in his house of worship. Reform Jews responded early to this model of family worship and viewed the halakhic separation of men and women as an outmoded custom. Accordingly, the barrier between the sexes in prayer fell. This, of course, created a whole range of opportunities for fathers, mothers, and their children to interact in the intimacy of family worship. But it also spelled the gradual disappearance of the complex set of sensibilities that had once shaped men and women in distinctive patterns of piety, both within and beyond the confines of the synagogue. We return to this issue in Chapter 13.

A final important area of worship reform concerned revisions of the actual texts of the prayers found in the medieval Siddur or prayerbook. Although the amidah and the shma were relatively accessible in form and content, many other texts were complex compositions written in various forms of ancient and medieval Hebrew and Aramaic. Most had been written by sophisticated rabbinic poets and contained esoteric allusions to talmudic legends or kabbalistic concepts. For newly modern European Jews, such prayer texts were increasingly foreign. Even in translation, they spoke of ideas that had little reality for those now reciting them.

Thus, one of the most characteristic aspects of the Reform movement was the creation of new prayerbooks. These were based on the medieval Siddur, but they made a number of crucial changes. First, the amidah was revised in relatively minor ways to reflect a more this-worldly, universalist sensibility. Along with the shma, it was rendered in elevated German. Much of the remaining liturgical texts were either omitted or thoroughly revised. Finally, new texts in German were composed as replacements for much that had been removed.

Such measures did, indeed, create prayerbooks that Reform Jews could pray from. The sentiments of the prayerbook echoed their own conceptions of the world and their own self-understanding as Modernist Jews. The material omitted from such prayerbooks was, in any case, deemed already outmoded and unworthy of survival. Nevertheless, with the loss of Hebrew as a language of prayer and with the disappearance of some of the most elegant texts of rabbinic poetry, a crucial avenue to the culture of the Bible, Talmud, and Kabbalah was lost as well.

One last, apparently meaningless change is perhaps the most illuminating: the way Reform Jews referred to themselves and their place of worship. Here, to be sure, they were followed by many other Modernists, including the Orthodox. Shunning the word "Jew," which bore negative connotations in Germany in particular, German Jews took to calling themselves Germans of "the Mosaic Faith" (*die mosäische Glaubung*). Their national identity as Germans defined them politically, and their "faith" served as the politically neutral marker of their distinctiveness from their Catholic and Protestant neighbors.

The space in which this Mosaic Faith was enacted, the synagogue, was also redefined. Jews increasingly preferred to call their house of worship a "temple," citing precedents from rabbinic literature we have mentioned. But this change was motivated not by traditionalist sentiments, but by a sense of living in a world profoundly different from that of the ancient rabbis. Many Reform Jews argued that they no longer looked forward to the restoration of Jerusalem's Temple, for the Messianic Age would unify all humanity into a single community. Indeed, for many, emancipation was the dawning of that age. The synagogue in Berlin or Hamburg that served to welcome that age was, indeed, the only temple they required. In their new homeland, it was inappropriate for their house of prayer to recall any ancient or future homeland.[8]

Let us briefly summarize. The changes in halakhic avodah fostered by the Reform movement were born of intense religious dissatisfaction with the halakhic tradition. The goal of religious Reform was not to abandon Judaism, but to recast it so that it could transmit a life of avodah to Jews in entirely novel circumstances, as citizens in a religiously neutral society. The unintended result, however, was a tendency to confine avodah to its expressions in the house of worship alone. Beyond the doors of the temple, Reform and, increasingly, other Modernist Jews lived in a world permeated not by halakhically defined opportunities for avodah, but by the simple demands of daily life in a secular society.

Worship and Ritual in Contemporary Judaism

By the middle of the twentieth century, the transformation of Judaism in accordance with European and North American models of religion had been completed. Judaism survived, except in Traditionalist circles, as a "faith" in which the synagogue or temple, as a place of public Jewish identification, served as the primary setting for religious activity of any kind. The synagogue's rituals sanctified the ethnic differences that still distinguished Jews from Christians; its afternoon or Sunday school offered remedial education in Jewish history; its social hall served as a place for Jews to come together "with their own." But, as developments in the last third of the twentieth century reveal, the synagogue—and the Judaism for which it stood—was perceived as increasingly irrelevant to the real lives of its members beyond its doors.

Against this background, North America in particular has witnessed a remarkable flowering of "alternative" Judaisms, many of them highly critical of the kinds of Judaism offered in the mainstream synagogues and temples that represented the Modernist forms of Judaism. At times taking the form of nonsynagogue groups called *havurot* (fellowships), at others retaining affiliation with the synagogue, these new Jewish forms were often characterized by efforts to selectively retrieve elements of the halakhic tradition without necessarily re-creating the classical structure of rabbinic Judaism or the formality of the official synagogue. Many of these newer forms of Judaism reflect an effort to restore to Jews a sense of religious wholeness, an engagement with Judaism that requires the commitment of the whole person. Often the chosen path is to reinstitute the abandoned home rituals of the Sabbath and the Festivals and to return to a fuller engagement with the Hebrew prayer book and halakhic synagogue custom and liturgy. This return to ritual expression has become a standard aspect of what many call the "movement of Jewish Return."[9]

One of the most important elements in this new picture is the participation of Jewish women in ways unprecedented in earlier halakhic tradition. As we have observed, the traditional rabbinic system mandated that men dominate Jewish ceremonial life. Even in Reform and Conservative synagogues until recent decades, women who prayed with men were still barred from leading the congregation in prayer or from reading from the Torah. Under the critical eye of contemporary feminism, however, many Jewish women have come to see the separation of sex roles, created and maintained by an exclusively male rabbinate, as intrinsically demeaning to women. In the search of Jewish women for religious wholeness, some have begun to ask, what, if anything, can be retrieved from halakhic tradition? Underlying this search is a quest for a comprehensive avodah, divine service, that women might wholeheartedly pursue.

Part of the answer has been to press for the admission of women to positions of religious authority. First the Reform movement (1971) and then the Conservative (1983) have begun to ordain women as rabbis and place them in roles of congregational and intellectual leadership. This move has been deplored by Orthodoxy as a violation of all acceptable halakhic tradition. Sympathetic Jews recognize that it is, at the very least, a radical innovation with only slender support in rabbinic tradition. In any case, it is now common in many non-Orthodox synagogues for women to fulfill any ritual role formerly occupied by a man, for example, as prayer leader or reader of the Torah.

In communities influenced by feminism, therefore, role distinctions between men and women are increasingly blurred or redefined, just as they are in the larger American setting. The Reconstructionist offshoot of Conservative Judaism has been particularly vigorous in creating worship environments that support new gender patterns. Challenging the halakhic judgments of Orthodox interpreters, women now engage in activities once thought to be the exclusive privilege of men. This places them in a complex relationship to halakhic tradition, retrieving it, as it were, against the grain. Recognizing both its male-oriented perspective and its power to create holistic communities, women hope to tap into the community-

The Transformation of Women's Synagogue Roles: A Woman Reads from the Torah Scroll in Public Worship

The reader's tallit is identical to those that men might wear in most synagogue settings. She is not wearing tefillin. If this photo was taken on the Sabbath, the absence of tefillin reflects the fact that they are not worn on that day. If it is a weekday photo, the absence of tefillin suggests the selectivity that many Jews exercise in their appropriation of traditional forms. (*Source:* © Beryl Goldberg)

forming power of halakhah while straining out its rigid distinctions between male and female religious obligations.

Many feminists, in fact, have argued that the full expression of women's religious lives cannot be tailored to halakhic roles fashioned exclusively by men. For them, the halakhic system is almost entirely dead as a resource for Jewish religious expression. The 1980s and 1990s gave birth to a number of self-consciously feminist Jewish communities. These men and women continue to experiment with liturgical and domestic rituals capable of expressing "nonhierarchical" or "nonsexist" spirituality. In addition to creating liturgies that celebrate God as a bigendered or even female diety, feminist communities have focused on creating rituals—for the onset of menstruation, childbirth, or menopause—that celebrate areas of women's experience invisible to the halakhic tradition. There can be no doubt that such communities respond to profound needs of many Jewish women. The question is whether, in light of their gender-oriented critique at Jewish tradition, they will be able to offer a Judaism recognizable to those pursuing more conventional religious paths. Only the future will tell if feminist transformations of Jewish ritual conventions will become part of a new normative tradition.[10]

In sum, the quest for a holistic avodah, a way of life penetrated in all its details by uniquely Jewish meanings, is richly apparent in contemporary forms of what might be called "alternative" or "post-modern" Judaism. The quest is found in all of the contemporary movements, including Orthodoxy and Traditionalists. The latter in particular have found marked success in representing devoted halakhic discipline as the cure for the alienation and fragmentation that many associate with the Modernist synagogue. Two thousand years after the destruction of the Second Temple, and two centuries after the fragmentation of the rabbinic tradition of avodah, the search for an all-embracing path of Jewish life continues.

CHAPTER 11

WORSHIP AND RITUAL
IN CHRISTIANITY

You are great, O Lord, and highly to be praised; great is your power and your wisdom beyond measure. Humans, a small part of your creation, wish to praise you; human beings, bearing their mortality, carrying with them the evidence of their sin and the proof that you resist the proud. Nevertheless, to praise you is the desire of humans, this small part of your creation. You motivate humanity to delight in praising you, because you have made us for yourself, and our heart is restless until it rests in you.[1]

Is this any way to begin an autobiography? It is, if you are Augustine of Hippo, writing your *Confessions* in the fourth century CE and your purpose is not to reveal the intimate details of your life simply for the sake of notoriety, but rather to explain through the example of your own life how God can rescue humanity from its fallen condition. Here, at the start, St. Augustine outlines the problem: our ultimate goal as humans is to return to the God who created us, but we are thwarted in fulfilling this desire by our sin and pride. As Augustine sees it, the tragedy of the human condition stems from the fact that worship is an innate drive, as essential to life as breathing, but it is a dysfunctional and unfulfillable instinct: we were destined for frustration. Had he been around to hear it, Augustine would have surely found much to like in Mick Jagger's complaint a millennium and a half later: "I can't get no satisfaction."

CONSTRUCTING A WORLD IN RITUAL

Lex orandi, lex credendi

For Augustine, as for his church, prayer and ritual were key to salvation, the means to satisfaction. Central to the faith is its ritual life, for most Christian communities have defined and identified their religion most succinctly through their worship. This comes as no great surprise to social scientists who have long analyzed ritual as "consecrated behavior," as an enactment or realization of the worldview encapsulated in any religion's myth and symbol. Ritual, it has been said, is a fusing of "the world as lived and the world as imagined."[2] Ritual does much more than encapsulate a worldview; it can actually create society for pragmatic purposes and make it intelligible.[3] Ritual is multidimensional; it is an expression and confirmation of beliefs; it is a means of transcending and redeeming mundane reality; and it is also a process of social interaction and a means of control. Many social scientists now favor the notion that ritual behavior does more than simply disclose mundane, practical realities. Ritual can be the richest expression of the collective mentality of a society, for it is not only a cultural construct: it is a form of cognition that constructs models of reality and paradigms of behavior. In other words, ritual seeks to define reality; it can be a means of imposing order on a seemingly disorderly, painful, and indifferent universe. Experts remind us that ritual is an attempt to turn the world as it is into the world as it should be, a fusing of the imagined and the real into a unified vision.[4] An ancient Latin axiom expressed this insight long before there were any anthropologists and ethnographers: *lex orandi, lex credendi* (the rule of prayer is the rule of faith).

It stands to reason, then, that when the patriarch Nikon of Moscow ordered the Russian Orthodox Church to change the number of fingers used in making the sign of the cross from three to two, he occasioned a schism in 1667, giving rise to a separate church of "Old Believers" and setting off waves of persecution. As the Old Believers saw it, the change in ritual, trivial as it might seem to outsiders, constituted a substantial change in the faith. And many willingly suffered martyrdom for the sake of their rituals.

To pray is to address the deity. One who prays is one who attempts to communicate with the divine—in praise, thanksgiving, petition, or contrition. In Christianity, prayer is ritual, and ritual is prayer. Ritual and prayer are most often called "worship" by Christians. Prayer, ritual, and worship can be either private or public, formal or informal. Christians call public acts of worship "liturgies." Through the centuries, Christians around the world have developed many different attitudes toward worship, not to mention a bewildering array of specific prayers, rituals, and liturgies. Yet, despite the diversity, some patterns of uniformity can be discerned.

Prayer

The Christian New Testament is filled with references to prayer. Jesus was constantly at prayer and urged his disciples to do the same. The gospel of Matthew

(6:5–13) tells of Jesus teaching his disciples how to pray: "Go into a room by yourself, and shut the door," Jesus advised, and "do not go babbling on like the heathen, who imagine that the more they say the more likely they are to be heard." Matthew's gospel also contains the prayer formulated by Jesus, which naturally became the single most important one in Christian life, more commonly known as the "Our Father" or the "Lord's Prayer":

> Our Father who are in heaven, hallowed be thy name; thy kingdom come; thy will be done, on earth as it is in heaven. Give us this day our daily bread; and forgive us our trespasses, as we forgive those who trespass against us. And lead us not into temptation, but deliver us from evil.

The apostle Paul also had much to say about prayer. One admonition in particular, "pray without ceasing" (1 Thess. 5:17), was taken literally by some early Christians. In the second century, Clement of Alexandria outlined a rigorous prayer schedule for Christians: part of each waking hour was to be devoted to prayer. He recommended saying the Lord's Prayer, some psalms and hymns, and some spontaneous prayer as well at least every hour. Many early Christians observed fixed times of prayer during the day. Hippolytus, for one, listed sunrise, midmorning, noon, midafternoon, sunset, and bedtime.[5] Others added midnight to the list. Cyprian of Carthage called for nothing short of continual prayer:

> There should be no hour in which Christians do not frequently and always worship God, so that we who are in Christ—that is, in the Sun and in the true Day—ought to be constant throughout the day in petitions and prayer . . . We who are in Christ—that is, always in the light—ought never to cease from prayer during the night.[6]

We cannot know with any certainty what proportion of the Christian community followed this advice, though the textual evidence points to widespread observance. By the fourth century, however, some theologians apparently feared that absorption in prayer could eclipse other significant aspects of Christian life, and they advised a broader interpretation of the devout life. Jerome, for one, saw charitable works as prayer: "Our meditation is our work," he said.[7] Theodore of Mopsuestia sounded a similar theme, saying, "A true prayer consists in good works, in love of God and diligence in the things that please him."[8]

As they were conscious of a relation between specific times and prayer, early Christians also sought to offer prayer in the correct place, under the right circumstances. The most fitting place for prayer, according to Origen, was where Christians regularly met together. Prayer at home was encouraged too, for while Christians were being persecuted, prayer in public places could be dangerous. Standing seemed to be the preferred posture for prayer (as a symbolic remembrance of the resurrection), usually with the hands extended and the eyes raised. One's tone of voice was to be subdued. Among early Christians, kneeling was uncommon, except when confessing one's sins. Tertullian condemned prayer while sitting as a sign of laziness. Augustine, in contrast, was indifferent to posture and advised, "our prayer must certainly not be put off until we have the opportunity of sitting, or standing, or falling prostrate."[9]

Different approaches to prayer would evolve in subsequent centuries, but one principle would never be abandoned: Christians were to be a prayerful people.

Fasting

Prayer and fasting were inseparable for early Christians. Jesus had fasted in the desert for forty days before beginning his public ministry (Matt 4:1; Mark 1:12; Luke 4:1) and had also advised that some demons could be expelled only through prayer *and* fasting (Matt 17:21; Mark 9:29). The *Acts of the Apostles* mentions fasting on the part of the disciples several times. Paul also counseled his flock: "Give yourselves to fasting and prayer" (I Cor. 7:5). Fasting was believed to heighten the soul's power to concentrate on prayer, since it helped to distance it from the demands of the body. Fasting was also considered an appropriate penance for sin.

Early Christians seem to have observed ritual fasting on certain days of the week. The significance of this practice could be immense, for the days of fasting could be closely linked to the identity of the community. The *Teaching of the Twelve Apostles* (*Didache*) warned: "Fast on Wednesdays and Fridays, not on Tuesdays and Thursdays, like the hypocrites."[10] Fasting on Fridays, the day of Christ's passion, remained an observance among Catholic Christians until the twentieth century.

Public Worship

In the gospels, Jesus did more than advise his disciples to pray; he also commanded them to perform certain rituals. It seems clear that within one generation, the ancient Jewish rituals of Jesus and his disciples had been abandoned or transformed, and that the autonomous identity of Christianity was most clearly expressed in its ritual life and worship.

First, Jesus commanded his disciples to baptize with water and indicated to them that this rite of purification and initiation into the community was indispensable for salvation. The ritual of baptism, thus, became the unique mark of Christian identity and the very foundation on which the church's continuity rested. One could not call oneself "Christian" if one had not been baptized. As early as 49 CE, Christian leaders agreed to supplant circumcision, the ancient Jewish rite of initiation, with this new ritual. The significance of this evolution cannot be overstressed. By ritually distinguishing itself from Judaism, the Christian community had definitively marked its break with the parent religion. At the same time, appropriately, the Christian leadership also agreed to free gentile converts from the observance of Jewish dietary laws. The Law of Moses was thus largely nullified.

Even more significant, at the celebration of Jesus' final Passover meal, he also commanded his disciples to observe a particular redefinition of this Jewish rite. Accounts of this pivotal event are found in all the synoptic gospels, but the earliest is reputedly that of Paul (I Cor. 11:23–29), who also added some theological observations.

> For I received from the Lord what I also delivered to you, that the Lord Jesus, on the night when he was betrayed took bread, and when he had given thanks, broke it, and said, "This is my body which is for you. Do this in remembrance of me." In the same way also the cup, after supper, saying, "This cup is the new covenant in my blood. Do this, as often as you drink it, in remembrance of me." For as often as you eat this bread and drink this cup, you proclaim the Lord's death until he comes.

The eclipse of the Law of Moses among Christians was sealed by this ritual. In fact, the ancient covenant between God and his people, ratified and commemorated by the Passover meal, had now been superseded by a new covenant, a new people, and a new ritual.

But Jesus' words and actions at his last Passover meal were assigned even more meaning. The symbolic significance of this ritual for Christianity proved inexhaustible, for it summed up the whole religion in infinite ways. Such is the power of key symbols and rituals: the more profound their meaning, the more open they are to interpretation and the more indispensable they are to the life of the community. Let us consider some of the more significant developments surrounding this ritual.

From early on, Christians accepted the reenactment of this "Last Supper" as a definitive ritual. Paul spoke of it as literally feeding upon the body and blood of Christ and warned the Corinthians (I Cor. 11:27–32):

> Whoever, therefore, eats the bread or drinks the cup of the Lord in an unworthy manner will be guilty of profaning the body and blood of the Lord. Let a man examine himself, and so eat of the bread and drink of the cup. For anyone who eats and drinks without discerning the body eats and drinks judgment upon himself. That is why so many of you are weak and ill, and some have died.

The apostle Paul thus expressed belief in some kind of powerful transformation or hierophany. The change effected in the bread and wine was seen as an irruption of the sacred. Paul spoke of "discerning the body," indicating that he believed the bread to actually contain the body. Belief in the *real presence* of Christ in the bread and wine made the meal a *"communion"* with Christ. The divine power that resided in the elements of the sacred meal was indeed tremendous, and it required the proper disposition. Over time, the transformation of the bread and wine and its distribution for communion became the ritual center of Christian life, so much so that the term "excommunication" came to mean expulsion from the church.

This ritual celebration, known as the "eucharist" (Greek; *eucharistia*: thanksgiving) came to be celebrated every day, but it was at first observed on a weekly basis, on Sundays, the day of the week on which Jesus was believed to have risen from the dead. The celebration of the eucharist on the first day of the week, in fact, signaled the transference of the Jewish Sabbath among Christians from Saturday to Sunday. Among the Orthodox, the eucharist was celebrated in the vernacular language; among Catholics, the ritual was preserved solely in Latin, a language most laypeople outside of parts of Italy no longer understood after the fifth century. This led to the sacralizing of Latin as a liturgical language and to the creation of yet another distinction between clergy and laity. In the Latin West, the eucharist came to be called the "mass," in reference to the final words spoken by the priest at the end of the celebration, "Go, it is finished" (Latin: *"ite, missa est"*). Evidence indicates that attendance at the weekly eucharist was high throughout Christendom. In the West, however, the reception of communion by the laity became infrequent by the medieval period. This means that in the West, the high point of the mass was the elevation of the bread and the cup by the priest, the moment at which Christ was made present. Merely being in the presence of Christ—being able to see him—was the best one could hope to do on a regular basis. Communion was reserved for special occasions, such as the Easter feast or one's deathbed.

But how did people receive communion on their deathbeds? Wasn't the eucharist celebrated in church? Yes, the mass took place in church, but the consecrated elements were routinely taken to the homes of the sick and dying. Christ's real presence in the transformed elements was believed to be permanent: once the bread and wine were changed, they never reverted back to ordinary foodstuffs. This meant, of course, that the bread and wine could be reserved and venerated outside the celebration of the mass or could even be taken outdoors in processions. By the Middle Ages in the West, one of the central holidays of the Christian calendar was that of *Corpus Christi*, the feast of the Body of Christ, when God was carried through the streets. So intense was belief in the real presence of Christ in the eucharist that witches and Jews came to be accused of stealing consecrated bread for nefarious purposes. Witches were believed to use the body of Christ for satanic rituals; the Jews were charged with torturing Christ anew, that is, piercing the bread with knives, crumbling it up, or stepping on it. Popular Christian piety was not always reverent either. We know of instances of rural folk scattering crumbs of the consecrated bread on their fields in the spring to ensure a good harvest.

The eucharist also acquired a sacrificial dimension early on, both in the East and the West. The eucharist came to be regarded as a reenactment of Christ's sacrifice on the cross, a ritual during which space and time were both transcended. Each celebration of the eucharist was believed to be Christ's continual offering of himself, not in the sense that the sacrifice was repeated, but rather as something that was made present in the here and now. Consequently, among Latin Christians, the eucharistic bread was called the "host" (Latin; *hostia*: sacrificial victim). Each eucharist was thus *the* moment of redemption, manifested time and time again; it was also the fullest manifestation of Christ's continued presence—a ritual that collapsed the boundaries of space and time. What more could one ask from a ritual?

Much more, of course. Since each mass was indeed Christ's continual sacrifice, *the* act of salvation, it did not take long in the West for the eucharist to serve other purposes, especially the reduction of penalties incurred by sin. By the end of the sixth century, the mass was already regarded as a ritual that could lessen the suffering of the dead in the afterlife. Pope Gregory I promoted this teaching, claiming that an angel had revealed to him that the soul of any individual that was undergoing purgation, or cleansing from sin, in the afterlife could be released to heaven through the celebration of thirty masses on thirty consecutive days. By 1100, the practice of offering masses for the dead had been universally embraced in the West.

Masses could be offered for an innumerable variety of purposes as well, and local "missals" (liturgical books that contained the rubrics of the eucharistic ritual) throughout Catholic Europe were replete with a great variety of votive masses. There were as many masses, it seems, as there were ills in this world: masses for blindness, masses for plague, masses for childbirth, masses for rebellious children, masses to ward off evil thoughts, masses against lust, and even masses for the recovery of stolen goods.

Differences in liturgical celebration arose gradually between East and West, and these played a significant role in creating and perpetuating the schism between Catholic and Orthodox. The East, for instance, shied away from the West's proliferation of votive masses. In the East the liturgy came to be chanted rather than recited, without the accompaniment of musical instruments. Also, because the mystery of the eucharist was considered so profound, the Eastern Christians installed a screen in their churches that separated the laity from the priests at the altar. This "inconostasis" was richly decorated with sacred icons, or images, and had three doors that opened at various times of the liturgy to provide glimpses of the sacred mysteries. In the West, the altar remained in full view, but the priests celebrated the liturgy in Latin with their backs turned to the congregation. Most often, the Latin masses were recited; these were called "low" masses. On special occasions, masses could be chanted or sung; these were "high" masses. Unlike the Orthodox, the Catholics brought musical instruments into the church, especially the pipe organ. In the East, the Orthodox to this day continue to regard standing as the only proper posture; in the West, Catholics gradually began to observe the practice of alternately standing, kneeling, and sitting. Even more significant, the communion rite itself developed along different lines. Catholics eventually came to withhold the wine from the laity, distributing only unleavened bread for communion; the Orthodox continued to dispense the wine along with leavened bread.

Differences aside, both the Catholic and the Orthodox raised the eucharistic liturgy into a grand, otherworldly spectacle, especially at the great cathedrals and basilicas (a "basilica" is a church built over a saint's grave). Pope Damasus at Rome adopted sumptuous vestments for the priests and in the fourth century was the first to hire professional musicians. At Constantinople, the eucharistic liturgy could last for several hours. In the tenth century, Vladimir, prince of Kiev, was so overawed by the liturgy at the Church of Holy Wisdom in Constantinople that he decided to accept Orthodox Christianity. "We knew not whether we were on heaven or on earth," Vladimir later reported, "for surely there is no such splendor

THE SEVEN SACRAMENTS

What the Latin Catholics call "sacraments," the Orthodox call "mysteries." Different terms, but the same meaning: sacraments or mysteries are those key rituals in Christian worship that supposedly convey God's invisible saving grace through material means. The theological formula was thus simple enough: no sacraments, no salvation. Though there was never any doubt that baptism and the eucharist were sacraments (especially because they had been instituted by Christ), it took several centuries for Christian theologians to agree on which of their many other rituals should be considered on the same plane. In the West, the number was fixed at seven by Peter Lombard in the twelfth century. In the East, the number continued to vary for five more centuries, until Latin influence fixed it at seven in the seventeenth century.

1. *Baptism.* The rite of initiation and Christian identity: washes away the stain of original sin with water. Can be received only once in a lifetime. After Christianity became a state religion in the fourth century, infant baptism became the norm. Normally, converts could be baptized as adults.

2. *Confirmation or Chrismation.* The gift of the Spirit through anointing with oil. Among the Orthodox, chrismation accompanies baptism and is normally administered to infants. Among Catholics, confirmation takes place when a child reaches the "age of reason," at age seven or eight. Received once in a lifetime.

3. *The Eucharist.* The central sacrament of the church: the celebration of Christ's redemptive sacrifice, in which he is believed to offer himself to be eaten in bread and wine. Offered repeatedly.

4. *Repentance or Confession.* Every member of the church is expected to confess all sins to a priest. This is the means of forgiveness for sins committed after baptism, through which the faithful are reconciled to the church. Offered repeatedly and considered essential for the reception of the eucharist.

5. *Holy Orders.* The rite of initiation for the clergy, performed exclusively by bishops. Numerous "orders" or clerical offices developed over the centuries, but only ordination to the priesthood granted full sacramental powers. Offered only once per individual office.

6. *Marriage.* The rite of union between man and woman. A practice, of course, that predated Christianity, but which Christian theologians sought to include among the sacraments because of the human need for grace. Offered more than once only in the case of one partner being widowed. Among Catholics, after the tenth century, marriage was forbidden to priests. Among the Orthodox, marriage was allowed to priests, but only if it took place before ordination; and only unmarried priests could rise to the rank of bishop.

7. *Anointing of the Sick, or Extreme Unction.* The *Acts of the Apostles* makes mention of Jesus' disciples anointing the sick with oil. Originally applicable in all illnesses, this ritual developed into the final rite of passage, saved for those whose lives were believed to be in grave danger. Could be offered repeatedly, as needed, but most Christians received it only once.

or beauty anywhere on earth. We cannot describe it to you: only this we know, that God dwells there among men."[11]

Holy Time: The Christian Calendar

Prayer, ritual, and sacraments have long been tied in Christian history to particular chronological rhythms, for even the earliest Christians set certain times aside for their devotional life. We have already seen several examples: prayer at specific hours, fasting and ritual celebrations on certain days, the transformation of Sunday into the sabbath. In addition to these "sacred" times, Christians also developed liturgical cycles and feast days that gave the calendar a ritual structure.

At the most basic level, Christian devotion has always been cyclical. Every week has one "Lord's Day," or sabbath, which is the liturgical high point. Every year has its high points too, and its seasons that are celebrated repeatedly. These liturgical cycles developed gradually and could vary from place to place but for the most part were in place from early on. Take Easter, the yearly springtime celebration of Christ's resurrection. In addition to commemorating each Sunday as a feast of Christ's triumph over death, early Christians also began to observe a yearly ritual celebration. This was the Christian Passover, which in some places continued for several generations to be celebrated according to the Jewish lunar calendar. In the second century, Pope Victor of Rome enforced uniformity, however, by insisting that all Christian churches celebrate the Easter feast on a Sunday, according to another lunar reckoning.

In addition to Easter, Christians developed numerous other distinctive feasts that celebrated special events in the life of Christ and the history of the church. By the fourth century, Christians were celebrating Christmas, the feast of Christ's birth, at the end of December; also by this time, the feast of Pentecost was observed fifty days after Easter to mark the descent of the Holy Spirit on the apostles. Other major feasts that assumed fixed dates were the Annunciation of Mary (nine months before Christmas), the Passion of Christ (the week before Easter), the Ascension of Christ (forty days after Easter), the Transfiguration of Christ (in August); and Epiphany (January 6). The feast of the Epiphany underwent a curious transformation: originally a celebration of Jesus' baptism among Eastern Christians, it eventually developed in the West into a commemoration of the visit of the Wise Men to the infant Jesus. In many Western Christian cultures, Christmas and Epiphany melded into one long feast.

Because the great feasts were considered sacred time, they were believed to require special preparation and purification. This attitude gave rise to the observance of liturgical seasons, or times of the year marked off by special observances and ritual gestures. Easter, the feast of feasts, required preparation by prayer and fasting. This was a period of penance, leading to the celebration of the central mystery of Christ's passion and resurrection; it was considered an especially

Early Sixteenth-Century Woodcut of a Pilgrimage to a Marian Shrine in Regensburg, Germany.

Devotion to Mary was intense in late medieval Catholicism. Here, pilgrims fall to the ground before an image of the Mother of God, pleading for her intercession. The miracles and favors granted by Mary to pilgrims at this shrine are attested by the ex-votos, or votive offerings, hanging from the church's portico. This is precisely the kind of piety that the Protestant Reformers would reject as idolatry.

This particular wooden chapel was hastily erected on the site of the Regensburg synagogue, which was destroyed in 1519 when the Jews of that city were expelled for usury and for having denied the virginity of Mary. A Christian stone mason critically injured while helping demolish the synagogue recovered miraculously, and it was believed that this miracle was a sign from Mary indicating her gratitude for the destruction of the synagogue. The stone mason's recovery instantly turned the site into a wonder-working shrine. The artist, Michael Ostendorfer, was an eye-witness to this frenzied pilgrimage in 1520. (*Source:* Foto Marburg/Art Resources, NY)

propitious time for mending one's life and becoming more seriously committed to one's faith. Originally a fast of two or three days, this observance gradually lengthened in the fourth century into a forty-day season of self-denial called "Lent" (a consciously ritualistic means of imitating Christ's forty-day fast in the desert, which was, in turn, a ritual imitation of Israel's forty-year journey out of Egypt). In the early medieval period, the fasting was rigorous: only one meal was allowed each day. By the ninth century, however, the observance began to be relaxed. Christmas, too, demanded penance, and by the sixth century, Christians were observing a season of fasting, Advent, in the weeks preceding this feast. Eventually, each season was assigned specific colors of liturgical vestments and church decorations.

Feasts and "holy days" proliferated in the Christian calendar during the first millennium. Most of these special days commemorated the memory of specific saints by marking the anniversary of their death, a practice that began among persecuted Christians who believed their martyrs entered heaven directly upon dying. Some saints' feast days could be universally celebrated: John the Baptist, Peter, Paul, and the other apostles, for instance, enjoyed wide popularity. Other saints had more localized celebrations. As Christians traveled from place to place, they would thus not only feel a sense of kinship and universality through the celebration of common feasts, but would also discover particular local rhythms of sacred time.

Holy Space: Pilgrimages

As the sacred could be encountered most intensely during particular times, so could it also be experienced more fully in particular places. The idea that some places are "holier" than others is common to many religions, but in Christianity it has long been closely related to belief in the Incarnation. If redemption was effected through the joining of heaven and earth in the person of Jesus, so reasoned early Christians, should not the structure of physical reality manifest this cosmic union? In other words, if God became fully human, taking on a particular material body, did this not mean that heaven and earth could now intersect?

The first generation of Christians believed in the localization of sacred power. In the gospels, Jesus was believed to be the focal point, or locus, of divine power: those touched by him could be miraculously cured. Similarly, in the *Acts of the Apostles,* Peter and Paul worked miracles through their physical presence. Evidence indicates that the first generation of Christians believed that the divine presence and power inherent in Jesus and the apostles was intimately related to the physical spaces they occupied, and that, in the case of the apostles and other saints, this power continued to reside in their corpses after death, as well as in objects they had touched and in places where they had stood.

By the fourth century, Christians were focusing their attention intently on places that had been consecrated by the presence of Christ, the apostles, and the martyrs. No place, of course, contained as high a concentration of this power as

Christian Expansion after the Year 1000

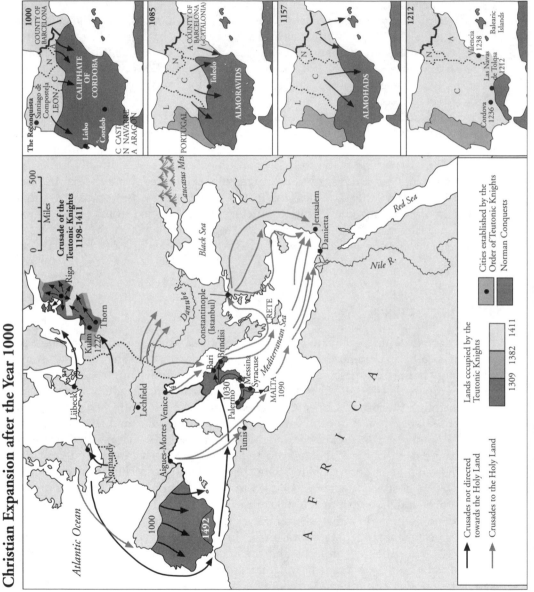

From *The Harper Atlas of World History*, rev. ed. by Librairie Hachette. Copyright © 1992 by HarperCollins Publishers, Inc. Reprinted by permission of HarperCollins Publishers, Inc.

did Palestine, "the Holy Land" where the incarnate God had walked on earth. But Palestine was not the only place worth visiting. Anywhere an apostle, or saint, or martyr was buried could be a place where heaven and earth intersected. The inscription on the tomb of St. Martin at Tours summed up this belief:

> Here lies Martin the bishop, of holy memory, whose soul is in the hand of God; but he is fully here, present and made plain in miracles of every kind.[12]

The practice of journeying to such holy places, known as making a pilgrimage, became a central feature of Christian ritual. By the late Middle Ages, the map of Christendom bristled with holy places. Among Catholic Christians, one of the most popular sites was Santiago de Compostela in northwestern Spain (where the apostle James was supposedly buried), which attracted pilgrims from all over Europe. Another was Rome, where the apostles Peter and Paul and thousands of other martyrs were entombed. Other significant international shrines were at Canterbury and Walsingham in England, Conques in France, Einsiedeln in Switzerland, and Aachen in Germany. National and local shrines abounded. If one could not journey to Rome or Santiago, one could always at least visit a nearby shrine. People undertook pilgrimages for a number of reasons, none of which were mutually exclusive: to obtain supernatural help, to gain forgiveness for sins, to offer thanksgiving, to fulfill a vow, or simply to travel and enjoy a change of scenery. Geoffrey Chaucer's *Canterbury Tales*, a fourteenth-century collection of stories told by pilgrims on their way to the most sacred shrine in England, reveals that pilgrimages could be far from pious events.

A small-scale version of the pilgrimage was the procession, a ritual parade on the local level, in which the faithful promenaded in groups, usually in the open, outside the church building as a public act of witness. Processions, like pilgrimages, could serve various functions. They could be celebratory (to mark a feast day or offer thanks), rogatory (to pray for some intention), or penitential (to beg forgiveness). Processions were an essential part of lay ritual life, even of civic life among Christians. Urban and rural communities alike depended on processions to punctuate the rhythms of the Christian calendar as well as the necessities of nature. Processions brought the community together and confirmed identities; they also affirmed beliefs and served practical purposes. Corpus Christi processions, for instance, sanctified the community by taking the consecrated host—the body of Christ—to the streets and byways. Processions in times of drought, famine, and plague sought to gain sorely needed divine favors.

In the Christian West, processional life gradually became dominated by confraternities, or brotherhoods. These lay associations were dedicated to a vast array of devotional functions, such as providing spiritual support for their members, engaging in works of charity, praying for the dying, and burying the dead, but their attention also focused on the organizing of feasts and processions. Though they depended on the sacramental ritual assistance of the clergy, these confraternities were run by lay people: they were the means whereby ritual was lived at street level, literally.

TRANSFORMATION OF RITUAL

The Ritual Revolution

In human relations, one person's ritual can be another's "idolatry," or false religion. Idolatry is a fighting word, for it presupposes a definition of what is true and what is false in religion. The ritual life of Western Christendom changed rapidly and dramatically in some places beginning in the sixteenth century, as some Christians began to argue that much of Catholic ritual was wrong or "idolatrous." Suddenly—in some places within the space of one day—prayers and liturgies were changed, the sacraments were redefined or abolished, feasts were canceled, fasts were ridiculed, pilgrimages were forbidden, processions were halted, and confraternities were disbanded.

This ritual revolution is also known as the Protestant Reformation. At bottom, the change in ritual stemmed from a change in thinking about the "sacred" and the way humans can relate to the divine. There were vast differences of opinion among the various Protestants as to what constituted "true" Christian ritual, but, on the whole, they agreed on one thing: the relationship between matter and spirit was not the same as that proposed in Catholic and Orthodox Christianity. Luther was not opposed to the idea of a sacramentally centered faith, and he even continued to believe in the real presence of Christ in the eucharist; but he reduced the sacraments to two (baptism and the eucharist) and also reoriented the liturgical life of the community toward Scripture. The Reformed, who were guided by the axiom *finitum non est capax infiniti* (the finite cannot convey the infinite), redefined the nature of worship from top to bottom. John Calvin formulated the relation between matter and spirit in worship thus:

> Whatever holds down and confines the senses to the earth is contrary to the covenant of God; in which, inviting us to Himself, He permits us to think of nothing but what is spiritual.[13]

Zwingli agreed: "They who trust in any created thing whatsoever are not truly pious."[14]

The Reformation focused on the Word of God not only as the sole authority among Christians, but also as the sole focus of ritual. As the Reformers saw it, the Word of God contained in the Bible was not only the truth itself but was the very presence of God among his people. This thinking affected ritual in two ways. First, it made the Reformers measure all forms of devotion against Scriptural norms: all "unbiblical" ritual was to be abolished. "Nothing, therefore, of ours, is to be added to the Word of God, and nothing taken from his Word by rashness of ours," said Zwingli.[15] Second, it made the reading and interpretation of Scripture the core of Christian worship. Luther would say that which is "first and foremost of all" and "on which everything else depends, is the teaching of the Word of God."[16] No matter how much they disagreed on the meaning of the sacraments and the structure of the liturgy, Protestants of every kind could agree on the ritual supremacy of the Word. The sermon, therefore, became the centerpiece of Protestant liturgical life.

The eucharist, while still celebrated, was no longer offered on a daily basis. Some Protestants continued to celebrate it each Sunday; others reduced it to a monthly celebration; others to a yearly event.

Moreover, all Protestants abandoned the use of Latin, turning their liturgies into services that could be understood by the congregation. On the whole, Protestants also encouraged congregational singing. Martin Luther firmly believed that music and singing could drive away the devil, and he composed many hymns, including the well-known "A Mighty Fortress Is Our God." Ulrich Zwingli favored the singing of the psalms without instrumental accompaniment; consequently, in Zurich and other Reformed cities, pipe organs were removed from the churches. Calvinists and Anabaptists, too, favored singing the psalms of the Old Testament but were not always opposed to instrumentation.

In the Church of England, all ritual was standardized by *The Book of Common Prayer* (1549), which aimed to steer a middle course between Catholic tradition and Protestant liturgical simplicity. Calvinists in England, however, objected to "traces of popery" such as the use of vestments, candles, and incense. Because they sought to "purify" England from all remnants of "idolatry," these dissenters came to be known as Puritans. Their struggle against the Anglican Church would result in the settlement of New England in North America (1620), the outbreak of civil war in England (1642–1649), the beheading of King Charles I (1649), and the establishment of a Puritan commonwealth (1649–1659).

The two sacraments retained by Protestants became the focus of intense disagreement. Luther and Zwingli could not agree on the interpretation of Christ's words "this is my body." The Reformed and the Radicals saw the eucharist not as a communion with Christ, but rather as a memorial service that commemorated Christ's saving work. Anglicans, as always, adopted a middle way, using language that simultaneously implied the real presence and a commemorative celebration. Baptism also gave rise to dissension. Whereas the Lutherans, the Reformed, and the Anglicans continued to baptize infants, thus including the entire civic community in the church, the Radicals called for a voluntary "believer's" baptism and for a total separation between church and state. Eventually, some English Puritans would also reach this conclusion, giving rise to the English and American Baptist churches.

At the most radical end of the Protestant spectrum, spiritualists argued that ritual was unnecessary. If the Spirit dwelt within each individual, then every person could deal with God directly. Sebastian Franck argued that God had allowed Christians to practice rituals in the past because they had not been spiritually advanced enough at the time. "God," he said, "gave the outward signs to the church in its infancy, just like a doll to a child." He continued:

> Why should God wish to restore the outworn sacraments and take them back from the Antichrist [the Pope], yea, and contrary to his nature (which is Spirit and inward), yield to weak material elements.[17]

Another spiritualist, Caspar Schwenckfeld, proposed that all Christians stop celebrating communion until they could agree upon its meaning.

But few Christians thought along the lines of Franck and Schwenckfeld in the sixteenth and seventeenth centuries. Instead of abandoning ritual, the leaders of Christendom, now divided, contended with one another over the "right" way to worship. Thus, in the process of arguing over the blood of Christ, Christians spilled rivers of their own blood in the costly ritual of war.

The Word Read, Sung, and Preached

As the wars of religion subsided, the emergent Enlightenment, with its emphasis on the capabilities of the individual, sparked reconceptualizations of the status of the laity in Christian churches. As a part of that rethinking of religious life, Christian worship and ritual were restyled to accommodate lay individuals. This development amounted to a privatization of worship across several fronts, including the emergence of reading as a spiritual exercise. As printing presses rapidly increased in number in the West, the production of Bibles—translated into many languages—made possible private Bible study. Beginning in the sixteenth century, Christians no longer had to rely largely on formal worship set in churches in order to encounter the words of scripture. Bible reading and study at home blossomed rapidly into a leading feature of Protestant religious life.

Lay Bible study was not encouraged in the Roman Catholic church because the church hierarchy feared that lay readers might not make connections between the language of the Bible and Catholic doctrines. Popes sometimes had encouraged lay reading of the Bible, but the proliferation of "unauthorized" editions (i.e., those with Protestant-flavored translation or commentary) by the early nineteenth century convinced Pope Pius VII to discourage lay Bible societies. Fifty years later, in 1864, Pius IX outrightly condemned Bible societies as part of his sweeping "Syllabus of Errors" of modernity.

The Syllabus did not explicitly prohibit Catholics from reading the Bible or from reading most other Christian religious literature (with the exception of those on the Council of Trent's *Index of Forbidden Books*). But its effect was to retard Bible study generally among Catholics. This by no means meant that Catholics did not read religious literature, however. In fact, the nineteenth century introduced a golden age of Catholic devotional reading. Encouraged by church superiors, Catholics consumed a rich fare of autobiographies, biographies, and manuals of spiritual life. Such reading communicated to the Catholic audience a sense of the mystery of religion (and so rebutted swelling modernist and Protestant claims for the leading role of reason in religion). Typical were the spiritual autobiographies of Teresa of Avila and John of the Cross, which were published in new editions in the nineteenth century. Accounts of the lives of mystics Angela of Foligno and Catherine of Genoa were among the scores of others that also attracted attention. Alongside Thomas à Kempis's enormously popular *The Imitation of Christ*, there appeared a host of manuals for the spiritual life, ranging from Andre-Marie Menard's *La Science de la Priere* (*The Science of Prayer*) to Jean Nicholas Grou's *Caracteres de la Vraie Devotion* (*Characteristics of True Devotion*). The English convert John Henry Newman authored a series of popular books including *All for Jesus* (1853) and *The Foot of the Cross* (1858). In the United States, the rapidly growing circulation of Catholic magazines, newspapers, and other periodical literature fostered by midcentury a lively culture of lay devotions. Much of this literature was well-received by Protestants. And among both Catholics and Protestants, the settings for this species of devotion were diverse: the privacy of the domestic "prayer closet," family gatherings, church libraries, and, especially in urban areas, public reading rooms supported by broad-based organizations such as the YMCA. Finally, even though it is clear that Catholic culture did not promote the sort of Bible study common among Protestants, Catholic devotional reading, by inspiring meditation on God and the spiritual life, functioned for many as a form of worship. Moreover, it served to reinforce and focus the most traditional of all forms of lay piety, prayer.

Lay reading and praying, for all their popularity, did not replace the public performance of religious ritual. By the mid-nineteenth century, however, it was clear to some Roman Catholic authorities that ritual life, left unattended since the standardization of the liturgy of the mass in 1570, was losing its gravity, its power to focus and enlarge the meanings of Christian life. One response was the Liturgical Movement. More a process than a movement, it took shape over the course of a century as a series of initiatives aimed at drawing rank-and-file Catholics more fully into ritual life and especially into participation in the mass. The movement also included the promotion of the veneration of various saints, reemphasis of the Sacred Heart of Jesus (with the physical heart of Jesus as its focus), and new devotions to Mary. Pilgrimage to the sites of miracles and visions was an important ritual aspect of these devotions. In 1858, Bernadette Subirous announced that the Virgin Mary had appeared to her in a grotto near Lourdes, France. In the half century that followed, over five million persons visited the shrine of Our Lady of Lourdes. Similar devotions and pilgrimages, encouraged by Rome, emerged elsewhere in Europe and America. As a consequence, the Liturgical Movement came to be defined as something other than a narrow reemphasis of tradition. By blending promotion of traditional church ritual with encouragement of popular forms of worship such as pilgrimage, rosary guilds, and the novena (nine days' cycle of prayer), the Catholic Church to some extent prevented a full-scale fissure of private and public worship. This process culminated in the Second Vatican Council (1962–1965), which both reformed the liturgy in a way designed to promote wider and more frequent participation and recognized the value of lay piety. Preeminent among those reforms was the replacement of the Latin mass with the vernacular (a modification that had been sought by Catholic Jansenists 250 years earlier).

For both Catholics and Protestants, musical accompaniment as a part of the overall performance of ritual emerged as a key aspect of worship. During the seventeenth century, the works of Orlando Gibbons, Henry Purcell, and Heinrich Schutz set passages of scripture to music for Protestant congregations. In Germany, Dietrich Buxtehude, Georg Telemann, and Johann Sebastian Bach transformed the Italian cantata into a hallmark of the Lutheran service. Bach and George Frederick Handel subsequently made the seventeenth century the age of the oratorio, or sacred vocal music. From their initial setting in Lutheranism, oratorios such as Handel's *Messiah*, with its well-known "Hallelujah" chorus, found their way into other churches. Protestant Psalters, or hymnbooks that set the

Sacred Heart of Jesus

Allusions to the power of the Sacred Heart of Jesus were taken
literally. During the nineteenth century, when devotion to the
Sacred Heart peaked, numerous miraculous events were
associated with the heart of Jesus, as well as the hearts of various
saints and holy men and women. In one case, a heart talked after
it had been removed from the body of a priest in Montreal,
Canada. (*Source:* Corbis-Bettmann)

Psalms to music, were published in large numbers in vernacular languages during
and after the Reformation. Often set to the melodies of folk songs, the Psalms were
sung in church and on the street. By the mid-nineteenth century, Protestants had at
hand as well numerous collections of sacred songs, again usually set to folk
melodies, that were not based exclusively on the Psalms, such as those in *The
American Vocalist* or *The Revivalist*. As a part of the Catholic Liturgical Movement,
the Latin Gregorian chant, the invention of which generally is attributed to the
sixth-century pope Gregory the Great, was restored in the early twentieth century.
But it was not until the Second Vatican Council that the singing of hymns in the
vernacular became a standard feature of Catholic worship.

Preaching, which has always played a role in Christian ritual, became more
important for both Protestants and Catholics after 1500 (as it did for New World
Jews, as well). We have seen how Protestantism placed the Word at the center of

religious life and constructed ritual performances of preaching and hearing as a part of public worship. In the eighteenth and nineteenth centuries, Protestant preaching was refined and adapted to several dramatic contexts, the most striking of which was the religious revival. Revival as a public display of religious emotions developed as a style of worship that hinged on the capability of the preacher to provoke an audience to remorse, repentance, and hope. The drama of spiritual rebirth, ritualized in the revival setting, unfolded through the agency and authority of the preacher. For the American revivalist Charles Grandison Finney, a revival was the product of the calculated and rational use of certain "means," the most important of which was good preaching. Since strong audience response certified the authority of the preacher, there was little need for a man or a woman to acquire formal ministerial credentials in order to succeed in this calling.

As Europeans explored the Americas—and later Asia and Africa—the interrelationship between strong preaching and public worship intensified. Frontier revivalism was the epitome of informal public worship. In wilderness settings, preaching, conversion, and revival served as the backbone of Protestant worship; the itinerant preacher Peter Cartwright observed in his reflections on religion on the American frontier that the barely literate "Methodist ministers actually set the world on fire" whereas the educated ministry "were lighting their matches."[18]

The expanding demands of the missionary enterprise among Roman Catholic clergy in the Americas profoundly affected Catholic ritual. Like revival, missionizing is a ritualized form of worship, both for the clergy who preach as well as for those who listen and embrace as truth the words of the preachers. Catholic clergy, in coming to terms with the enormity of their program of converting millions of American and Asian natives to Roman Catholicism, learned to preach in styles suited to their agenda. Accordingly, the seventeenth century— during which time Spanish, Portuguese, and French Jesuits, Dominicans, and Franciscans crossed the Atlantic and Pacific oceans in large numbers—has been called the golden age of Catholic preaching.

Adaptation of Ritual

The early modern encounters of Christianity with native cultures stimulated a process of reconceptualization of worship and reconfiguration of ritual. Christians, Jews, and Muslims had debated for centuries various points of religious belief and practice. The fact that they often were able to agree on what they disagreed about signaled a measure of shared roots, of common cultural background. Latin Christianity, dressed out in the culture of western Europe in which it arose, did not readily translate to American, African, or Asian contexts, however. European missionaries discovered in the various cultures of other continents certain ways of thinking about the world and styles of ritual expression that bore no likeness to Western Christianity. Frequently, Europeans were unable to adequately comprehend even *how* their own culture differed from those of the peoples they encountered. Consequently, missionaries discovered that their claims for the truth of their religion and the superiority of their ritual—claims they believed were confirmed

Edward Laning, *Camp Meeting* **(1937)**

Protestantism in America regularly has featured the highly
emotional ritual of "born-again" religion. Weeping, shouting,
barking, fainting, jumping, and rolling on the ground have often
been a part of revivals. (*Source:* Edward Laning/Wichita Art Museum)

by hundreds of years' investment in critical disputation and scores of religious
wars—were misunderstood at least as often as they were accepted.

Such misunderstandings often were centered on religious language. More
striking were confusions about ritual. Let us take sub-Saharan Africa as an example. Catholic missionaries brought with them a religious calendar organized by
four seasons: spring, summer, fall, and winter; in the tropics, however, there was a
rhythm of two seasons, the dry season and the rainy season. Some Catholic holy
days called for reddish vestments (violet, crimson, etc.), but in many traditional
African societies, red was a color with distinctively negative connotations. The eucharist was organized around the element of bread; yet millet and sorghum, not
wheat for making bread, were consumed in Africa. Protestant clergy opposed to
dancing and church music discovered that religious drumming and dancing were
fundamental to many African cultures. Christian missionaries who baptized persons by pouring water over their heads did so against the grain of African cultures
in which actual *immersion* in water was valued as symbolic action.

The Christian churches in Africa that developed against the background of such differences frequently manifested syncretism in their ritual. This was most obvious in the independent African Christian churches (i.e., in those not formally aligned with European denominations). In some cases, syncretism took the form of blending reverence for certain sites (and especially topographical features such as mountains, rivers, etc.) with Old Testament emphases on "holy places," so that a pool of water or a rock outcropping became a center of sacred power, of cosmic meaning. In other cases, dancing, drumming, ritual cleansings (ranging from anointings to vomitings), hand clapping, and the use of ritual objects such as metal or wooden "prophet rods" as well as prayer cloths manifested an accommodation between native and Christian worship.

Religious syncretism, which was most obvious in ritual, was the fruit of virtually every encounter with native peoples, whether in Africa, the Americas, Asia, or Oceania. Religious syncretism was nothing new to Christianity, however. Movements that blended primal religious rituals (drawn from "folk cultures") with Christianity had emerged regularly in Europe over the centuries as popular religious movements of various sorts. But the mixture of native and Christian ritual that was manifest in churches that grew on non-European soil represented a new dimension to Christianity. In Europe, popular religions often were forcibly dissolved by church authorities in the interest of preserving tradition. Church authorities, however, in spite of their comfortable relationship with colonialist armies, in the end were poorly equipped to enforce strict orthodoxy on distant continents. Consequently, missionaries and their directorates in Europe learned to live with a certain amount of syncretism, and they began to think seriously about how to convey ritual meanings in non-European cultures.

CHAPTER 12

WORSHIP AND RITUAL IN ISLAM

FOUNDATIONS OF WORSHIP IN ISLAM

Muslims have always been profoundly grateful for the structures and processes of formal worship that they have inherited from the past and that they consider to be a vital divine imperative in the present. Islamic worship is collected under the concept of *'ibāda*, meaning "service" (cf. the Jewish idea of avodah, which is formed with the same Semitic root and also denotes worship as well as service). The pillars of Islam are called *'ibādāt*, that is, "services" or "worships." Islamic law books generally open with worship regulations and detailed guides to performance based on the Qur'an and Sunna. All the required worship practices are commanded by the Qur'an, but fuller details are contained in the prophetic hadith. Sometimes there is variation in practice, so the law schools have taken them into account in their written commentaries.

Purification

Although the first pillar of Islam is the witnessing to the unity of God and the messengerhood of Muhammad, the legal discussions relegate the Shahada to the theological books—whose principal domain is faith, known as iman—and get down to ritual practices rather than to doctrinal discussions. And although the salat (required worship) is the second pillar, before it can be treated one must know how to approach its performance, which is done by means of ritual purification. Notice that I have already used the word "ritual" twice in this paragraph. It is important to note that Muslims are sometimes suspicious of this word as applied to their worship, because it has a somewhat analytical and calculating sense to their ears. I was once discussing "Islamic ritual" at a professional meeting and a senior Muslim scholar tactfully told me afterward that he preferred that scholars use the term 'ibada instead. He did not fault my knowledge of the details but felt uncomfortable with a clinical scholarly discussion of what to him is the means of drawing near to God and fulfilling his spiritual obligations. "Ritual" had a negative tone, I suppose, because of many people's sense that much of formal worship is "rote, empty ritual." This view is perhaps fostered by some Protestant Christian attitudes, but it could as easily be aimed at Islamic and Jewish practices as at Roman Catholic liturgy and ceremony, which extreme Protestants have often dismissed as "popery." But there can be a sturdy Islamic opposition to rote ritual, too, although most Muslims would not embrace al-Hallaj's aphorism that "once one knows (through gnosis), prayer is unbelief."

"Purity is half the faith," goes a much-quoted hadith. Before a Muslim may perform the salat, a state of ritual purity must be attained, if any impurity has been contracted. The types of impurity are generally divided into two classes, minor and major. Minor impurity is caused by such things as the evacuation of bodily wastes, sleep, bleeding, breaking wind, contact with a dog, and fainting. The removal of such impurities is done by a ritualized washing called *wuḍū'*. This consists of washing the hands, arms to the elbows, face, ears, feet, and ankles; rubbing water on the ears and over the hair; and cleansing the mouth and nostrils with water. During this process, various prayers may be offered to God. If no clean water is available, a dry process called *tayammum* may substitute for the minor ablution. Tayammum is patting clean earth or sand on a cushion or pillow to raise a little dust, which is then applied to the body as water would be. This rite is much simpler and quicker than wudu proper.

Major impurity is caused by sexual intercourse, seminal emission, menstruation, childbirth, a large flow of blood, and touching a corpse, among other things. The major ablution, called *ghusl*, is a full, ritualized bath. It is necessary to perform ghusl before entering a mosque on Friday. One should also have performed ghusl before handling a copy of the Qur'an. This does not mean that a Muslim must take a bath before picking up the Scripture. Rather, he or she should not have experienced a major impurity between the last bath and taking up the Qur'an. Most of the time, a Muslim needs only to perform the minor ablution before performing the salat. The purification requirements of Islam have contributed to a strong awareness of proper hygiene, as well as a constant consciousness of the need for sincerity and inward purity. The requirements of ablution and bath remind Muslims several times a day of their duties and responsibilities as believers. Before each prayer period—and there are five each day—the Muslim must recall what has occurred in the way of bodily discharges and contact with other forms of impurity. This discipline engrains a constant mindfulness that Muslims consider a mercy from God.

Although the Islamic way of life requires much mastery of ritual detail, the practices are not in themselves complex or strenuous. Muslims consider their religion to be a reasonable, indeed, easy religion, not requiring spiritual athleticism such as ascetic renunciation, intensive technical training, or threats explicit or implied. The following excerpts from prophetic hadith give a clear sense of this matter:

> Religion is easy, and no one exerts himself too much in religion but it overpowers him; so act aright and keep to the mean and be of good cheer and ask for (Divine) help . . . (Bukhari). Only that is binding on you which you are able to do; by Allah, Allah does not get tired but you get tired . . . (Bukhari).[1]

A certain man's practice of fasting all day and standing up in prayer all night was made known to Muhammad, who said:

> Do not do so; keep fast and break it and stand up in devotion (in the night) and have sleep, for thy body has a right over thee, and thine eye has a right over thee, and thy wife has a right over thee, and the person who pays thee a visit has a right over thee. (Bukhari)[2]

The Salat Prayer

The salat is a required worship service performed five times each day: at dawn, noon, midafternoon, just after sunset, and in the evening. The prayer may be performed alone or with others in a clean, quiet place: at home, at the workplace, outdoors, or in a mosque. The word "mosque," from the Arabic *masjid*, means "prostration place." It does not necessitate a building, although masjid does connote a permanent worship location. Some of the most magnificent buildings erected in world architectural history have been mosques. A fuller description of the mosque is given in Chapter 18.

The time of salat is announced by a chanted call to prayer in Arabic, called *adhān*. Its text is as follows:

> God is most great! (4 times)
> I bear witness that there is no god but God (twice);
> I bear witness that Muhammad is the Messenger of God (twice).
> Hasten to prayer! (twice) Hasten to success! (twice)
> God is most great! (twice)
> There is no god but God (once).

Notice that the call contains the Shahada and that it opens with the declaration of God's greatness and closes with the first Shahada, concerning his uniqueness. All utterances during the salat are in Arabic, thus linking the worshiper(s) with God, his revealed scripture, and the universal Muslim community in time and space. The word "success" is a translation of Arabic *falāḥ*, which also has the senses of "felicity," "prosperity," "good fortune," and "salvation." According to the Qur'an (2:2–5), those who are God fearing, believe in the Unseen, regularly perform the salat, spend (for others as well as oneself) from what God has provided, believe in revelation sent down (in the Qur'an) and in previous scriptures, and who have faith in the Hereafter, such are on true guidance from

The Ka'aba Shrine in Mecca; the Black and Gold-Silver
Embroidered Covering Is Known as the Kiswa

(*Source:* Abdulaziz A. Sachedina)

their Lord, and it is these who shall prosper by means of falah. So, falah as "success" is not worldly good fortune, although that may be included. Falah includes what in medieval Christianity were called the "theological virtues" of faith, hope, and charity.

When Muslims pray in a group, the congregation, no matter how small, must have a leader who stands in front and provides a pattern for the smooth, synchronized performance of the salat. This leader is called an *imām*. In the sense being discussed here, imam does not connote extraordinary or professional knowledge of Islamic doctrine and practices; it means an adult who possesses the moral and religious qualifications to lead fellow Muslims in the prayer service. Generally, a group planning to observe the salat together reaches a quick, friendly consensus about who will serve as imam. If the salat is the Friday noon observance, the imam will usually be a professional religious leader who will also deliver the sermon, which is required at the weekly congregational service at Friday noon.

In a mixed congregation, only a male may serve as imam. A woman imam serves an all-female congregation. Males and females may pray in the same mosque, but they are separated, with the males in front and the females in back, on a balcony, or even in a separate room or building. A Muslim family may pray together in the same room, because the Islamic laws requiring the social separation of the sexes do not apply within the boundaries of close blood relationships.

The congregation stands in even rows behind the imam, all facing Mecca. The direction of Mecca is called *qibla* and should be ascertained with as much certainty as circumstances allow. Hotel rooms in Muslim countries usually have an arrow or other marker showing the qibla. Some Muslim travelers carry prayer rugs with small compasses and a chart containing qibla settings for major cities around the world. In a mosque, the qibla is marked by a niche in a wall. This *miḥrāb*, as it is called, may be plain or richly decorated. The imam stands before it as he leads the worshipers.

Niyya

Before performing the salat, the worshiper stands and composes her or his mind by reflecting on what is about to take place. This preliminary rite is called *niyya*, meaning "intention," and is legally required by the Shari'a before performing any of the Pillars as well as other rites. Islamic law judges people's actions by their intentions, so having a sincere, responsible attitude is necessary. Without niyya, the salat or other rite to be performed is invalid. Niyya is similar to the Jewish practice of *kawwanah*, in which the worshiper seeks spontaneity and sincerity in prayer.

Rak'a

Each salat contains a set of prescribed cycles of standing, bowing, kneeling-sitting, and prostrating with forehead touching the carpet or other clean floor or ground surface. Throughout the performance, set phrases are uttered, beginning with "God is most great!" and closing with "Peace be with you"—"*al-Salāmu alaykum*" (cf. *shalom aleichem* of the Jews). Each cycle of postures is called a *rak'a*, and the number of postures varies with the daily prayers: two at dawn, four at noon, four in the afternoon, three at sunset, and four at night. The rak'as also vary between having their liturgical utterances performed out loud or silently: out loud at dawn, silent at noon and afternoon, the first two out loud and the third silent at sunset, and the first two out loud and the remaining two silent at night. The liturgical passages include set phrases as well as Qur'anic verses. The Fatihah, the Qur'an's opening chapter, is always recited during the salat, which takes only a few minutes to perform. Although there are minor variations in detail among legal schools, the rite is essentially uniform worldwide. This consistency is a testimony to Muslims' strong belief in the Divine Unity as reflected in the religion.

Friday Congregational Salat

Another visible reminder is the Friday noon salat, which requires a male congregation for its authentic observance. Females also must observe the Friday salat but are not required to perform it in congregation. The custom of women attending

Friday congregational salat varies from country to country, but in any case, they worship in their own group, separated from the males, as was observed earlier. The minimum legal size of a congregation ranges from three adult males besides the imam to forty, including the imam, depending on the *madhhab* (legal school) in force. As has been mentioned, a sermon is also featured on Friday, delivered by the imam from atop a *minbar,* or staired pulpit, before the actual prayer rak'as. The sermon may be expository, based on the Qur'an and/or on hadith, or inspired by some current topic. In addition to a main subject, the sermon always includes the invoking of blessings on the Prophet, his family, and the Companions.

In addition to the required daily and Friday salats are salats marking the close of Ramadan fasting, funerals, and the occurrence of solar and lunar eclipses. Muslims may perform additional, nonobligatory salats for merit.

Zakat: Almsgiving

The Qur'an frequently mentions performing the salat and paying the *zakāt* as two cardinal obligations of Islam. Zakat is a kind of tax on one's wealth, through which set proportions—for example, 2.5 percent of liquid assets and 10 percent of agricultural profits—are set aside at the end of each year for legal almsgiving as a form of worship service to God. Although zakat is sometimes characterized as charity, it is more than that. Charity is to be given throughout the year, as needs are recognized, whereas zakat is a formal duty with fixed legal requirements as well as specified classes of recipients. Further, zakat serves to make pure and honorable the wealth remaining to the giver. Certain Islamic acts, such as pilgrimage, may not be considered legal unless paid for by assets on which zakat has been paid.

Zakat is required of adult Muslims only if a minimum level of wealth is owned. Poor people are not required to pay zakat. The umma's strong ethic of mutual responsibility and support can be seen in the pillar of almsgiving. In countries with Islamic governments, such as Pakistan and Saudi Arabia, the collecting of zakat is a formal bureaucratic process. In Pakistan, for example, zakat is calculated on individual bank accounts and automatically deducted from the balance at the end of each year. In non-Muslim jurisdictions, zakat is a matter of personal choice both as to its collection and its distribution. Individuals in America, for example, calculate their legal obligation and devote it to recipients of their choosing, following principles and procedures established in Islamic law.

Fasting During Ramadan

The Muslim calendar consists of twelve months marked by the phases of the moon. Each lunar year contains 354 and a fraction days. Because this year falls some eleven days short of the solar year, it sees periodic observances occurring in different seasons, with a complete circuit through the solar year taking about thirty-three such years. Thus, fasting and the pilgrimage to Mecca, the two pillars yet to be described in this chapter, will be distributed over hot and cool seasons for most Muslims during an average lifetime.

Ramadan is the most sacred month of the Muslim year, chiefly because it was the month when the Qur'an was first revealed. As Sura 97 puts it, Ramadan contains a special night called the "Night of Power . . . better than a thousand months," when the revelation first descended. 'Ali's birth and death dates are also in Ramadan, as is Khadija's death date. The transition from one month to the next in the Islamic calendar is officially certified by viewing the appearance of the new moon in the western skies. There is a certain excitement with the approach of Ramadan. Children and their parents will search the dusk skies for a glimpse of the new moon when it appears. The Muslim day, like the Jewish day, begins at sundown. In some Muslim countries, Egypt, for example, cannon fire marks the beginning of Ramadan, when the new moon has been sighted by religious officials. Each day of fasting will also be ushered in with a cannon shot. Likewise, the fasting month ends with the sighting of the next new moon, thus ushering in the Festival of Fastbreaking (*'Eid al-Fiṭrī*), one of the two canonical feasts of the Muslim year. The beautiful sliver of crescent is called the *hilāl* and serves as the main symbol of Islam on flags, seals, mosque domes, and other objects. The international Muslim medical emergency service, known as the Red Crescent Society, has pictures of the hilal painted on its ambulances and dispensaries in Muslim countries.

The Ramadan fast is known by the technical term *ṣawm* or *ṣiyām*, meaning "abstention." The rule requires that no food or drink be taken between dawn and dark and that no sexual relations or smoking or other sensual pleasures be experienced. Only healthy persons, adults, and older children who have practiced limited fasting are required to keep the fast. Certain persons, such as pregnant women, are exempted from the fast. Travelers on a long journey are not required to fast while en route, although they must make it up later. This is also true of those who must refrain from fasting because of sickness or ill health during Ramadan.

The Ramadan fast provides a good case for the person—mentioned early in this chapter—who objected to characterizing Islamic devotional duties as "rituals." Indeed, the fast is a considerable physical as well as spiritual discipline that enables the believer to enter into a different state of mind, reflecting on her or his mortality while remembering that all people are essentially equal before God, regardless of their temporary worldly circumstances. Ramadan is a month of serious devotion, to be sure, but it is not a somber time. People feel close to God and to each other as they take this time out of ordinary time to renew themselves and submit in deeper measure to God's will. Ramadan evenings are joyful, with eating, family gatherings, visiting religious book fairs, and participating in special mosque services featuring chanted litanies known as *tārawīḥ*. During the last ten days of Ramadan, many men take up a nightly vigil at the mosque in order to experience the "Night of Power," the time when the Qur'an was first revealed. It is believed to be an annual event occurring, most likely, on the twenty-fifth, twenty-seventh, or twenty-ninth of Ramadan. This practice is known as *i'tikāf*, meaning, approximately, "spiritual retreat":

> The Night of Power is better than a thousand months.
> Therein come down the angels and the Spirit [Gabriel]

by Allah's permission on every errand: Peace, this is,
until the rising of the dawn. (97:3–5)

The end of the Ramadan fast is a time of great rejoicing, with a large, open-air festival salat service and the giving of a special alms for the poor, known as *zakāt al-fiṭrī* (alms of fastbreaking). Muslims also often feed poor people during the fasting month and may even be exempted from the fast if thirty people are fed each night of the month.

Living in a Muslim country or community during Ramadan is a special experience. Not everyone fasts each year, but many people raised in an Islamic home come round to making a decision about their Muslim commitment and often see the fast as a means of getting back on track with the spiritual side of their lives. Some countries, such as Saudi Arabia and Malaysia, enforce the fasting rules by making sure restaurants are closed during the day and scrutinizing the behavior of people. But most Muslims are not invasive of their neighbors' lives, and one can find early authority for viewing the fast as a privilege, not a penalty. As one hadith expresses the predicament of the inadvertent fast breaker:

When one forgets and eats and drinks, he should complete his fast, for Allah made him eat and drink.

Another hadith reads:

Ibn Abbas said, "There is no harm that one should taste of the food in the cooking-pot and anything else." And Hasan said, "There is no harm in rinsing the mouth with water, and getting cooled, by one who fasts."[3]

Hajj: The Pilgrimage to Mecca

The fifth pillar of Islam is also the most dramatic and emotionally thrilling, because it involves a sometimes arduous journey to the ritual center of Muslim devotion: the Ka'aba in Mecca. As the Qur'an states:

Follow the religion of Abraham, the pure monotheist (*ḥanīf*); he was not one of the idolaters. The first house of worship established for the people was at Mecca, full of blessing and guidance for all peoples. . . . Pilgrimage (*ḥajj*) thereto is a duty the people owe to God—those who can afford the journey. (3:95–97)

Mecca and its companion sacred precinct Medina are forbidden to non-Muslims. Muslims may visit Mecca at any time of the year. If the visit includes observance of some of the pilgrimage rites at and near the Ka'aba, it is called '*umra*, a "little pilgrimage." But one may perform the hajj proper only during the hajj month, according to the schedule and procedures established in Islamic worship

Boys Performing Ablutions Before Prayer at Muhammad Ali Mosque, Cairo, Egypt

(*Source:* F. M. Denny)

---

law. And the hajj includes essential elements performed outside Mecca and the Ka'aba precincts.

Medina and Mecca are known in Islam as *Al-Ḥaramayn,* "The Two Sanctuaries." Mecca was a great pilgrimage center long before the coming of Islam, whereas Medina came to be a sanctuary when the umma was established there after the Hijra in 622 CE. The hajj applies only to Mecca, but Muslims traditionally have looked forward to visiting Medina at some point during their pilgrimage journey to pay respects at the tomb of Muhammad and to tour the many historic sites. The journey to Medina is called *ziyāra,* "visit." A pious journey to any holy place in Islamic lands is called a ziyara, whereas the hajj as "pilgrimage" is uniquely associated with the required fifth pillar of that name.

The hajj rites are detailed and extend over several days. Essentially, they entail remembrance, repentance, meditation on one's own mortality, incorporation into the believing community in a deeper way, and rededication. The Qur'an often speaks of the duty of Muslims to remember God often in their prayers and meditations. The hajj provides an opportunity to remember God as such, as well as his great acts in history. Muslims on hajj become intensely conscious of the ancient tradition of faith and dedication that has preceded them. Everywhere are reminders of the sacred past, which in a sense becomes internalized in the pilgrims' lives through the rites. For example, pilgrims stand at the "Station of Abraham" (*maqām Ibrāhīm*) and offer prayers. They perform a running ceremony between the two hills of Safa and Marwa, where (according to Islamic sources) Hagar frantically searched for water for her son Ishmael after the two were sent away by Sarah (cf. Gen. 21:9–20).

Muslims see a strong identification between themselves and the tradition of Abraham on the side of his Egyptian mate Hagar and their son Ishmael. The Jews trace their descent from Abraham by way of Sarah and Isaac. Thus, in a metaphorical sense at least, Jews and Muslims are "half-brothers," having the same father but different mothers. The emphasis on Abraham and his tradition in the hajj is closely tied with the Qur'an's teaching that Abraham preceded both the Law and the gospel:

> Abraham was not a Jew nor yet a Christian; but he was true in faith and submissive (*musliman* [i.e., to God]) and not one of the polytheistic idolaters (*mush rikīn*). Without a doubt, the people closest to Abraham are those who follow him, as are also this Prophet [i.e., Muhammad] and those who believe, and Allah is the Protector of the faithful. (3:67–68)

Another point in which the pilgrims identify with Abraham's generation occurs when they drink from the well of Zamzam, located under the Ka'aba plaza. This well was opened by the foot of Ishmael, when God intervened to save him and his mother Hagar in the desert. Still another point of identification occurs when the pilgrims throw stones at three pillars representing the devil. This commemorates the time when Abraham and his son Ishmael (Isaac in the Bible version) were making their way to the place where God had commanded the father to sacrifice his son. The devil whispered to Abraham to refrain from carrying out the terrible deed, whereupon Abraham pelted him with stones on three different occasions. As it turned out, the incident was a test of Abraham's obedience and faith, with Ishmael spared and a ram provided as a substitute sacrifice. At a certain point, the pilgrims all sacrifice an animal (or, in the case of women, have this done by a male agent). Muslims share this great occasion all over the world, and it is known as "The Feast of Sacrifice" ('*Eid al-Aḍḥā*), the greater of the two canonical festivals in the Muslim year.

Before pilgrims enter Mecca, they must enter a state of ritual consecration, known as *iḥrām*. In this state, the following prohibitions pertain: sexual intercourse, hunting, uprooting plant life, wearing precious metals or scent, and cutting any hair from the head or body. Males are required to don a two-piece, seamless, white cotton garment, which is wrapped in a prescribed way around the waist and around the shoulders and torso. Women do not wear the ihram garment but cover themselves except for the face and hands with clothing of their choosing. Women's hajj clothing often shows their ethnic and cultural membership and thus symbolizes the rich variety of the umma alongside its religious unity as exhibited in the men's uniform garment.

The white ihram cloths also symbolize the grave clothes and remind the pilgrims of their mortality. Pilgrims often go on hajj with the anticipation of death, either because they are ill or old, or because the journey often entails hardships and danger. To die in Mecca, or indeed during the journey, is to be assured of paradise, for the pilgrim who falls is a martyr in the way of Islam. The Swiss pilgrim and explorer John Lewis Burckhardt, writing in the early nineteenth century, provides details of pilgrim deaths:

> Poor Hajjis, worn out by disease and hunger, are seen dragging their emaciated bodies along the columns [of the Grand Mosque in Mecca]. . . . When they feel their last moments approaching, they cover themselves with their tattered garments; and often a whole day passes before it is discovered that they are dead. . . . There are several persons in the service of the mosque employed to wash carefully the spot on which those who expire in the mosque have lain, and to bury all the poor and friendless strangers who die at Mecca.[4]

Modern times have seen a major development in accommodations for pilgrims, including medical and security services. Even so, there can still be risk, as has been seen in recent years when many have died from crowd stampedes, plane crashes, and other causes. When over a million people are gathered in a relatively small place, safety is difficult to guarantee. And although the hajj shows the unity and mutual support of Muslims worldwide, it also can be a focal point for occasional political disagreements when conflicting parties descend on the sanctuary, sometimes with specific agendas connected with their causes.

Pilgrims follow the prescribed rites as best they can. Most often, they enjoy the services of professional guides, who also see to their food, lodging, and travel needs. No one checks up on each pilgrim to make sure that all requirements have been meet. Pilgrims know that the most essential stage of the hajj is the standing ceremony some miles from Mecca near the Mount of Mercy. The pilgrims stand in the hot sun from noon until sundown, repenting their sins and asking God's forgiveness. If this ceremony is missed, and this includes performing it on the set day, then the whole pilgrimage is voided and the individual will have to attempt to fulfill this pillar another year.

Earlier, the ʿumra, or little hajj, was introduced. This takes place only in Mecca, in the Kaʿaba precincts, and can be performed anytime during the year. The hajj proper begins with the ʿumra ceremonies of circumambulating the Kaʿaba seven times, praying at the Station of Abraham, running between the two hills, drinking Zamzam water, and other rites. Then the pilgrims travel outside Mecca to Mina and the Plain of Arafat for a period of five or six days, during which the standing ceremony, the sacrifice, stoning of the devil, and a hair clipping are performed. The haircutting, which may be simply a symbolic cutting of a small lock, marks the beginning of the emergence from the state of ihram, although sexual relations are still forbidden until all the rites have been concluded. A farewell circling of the Kaʿaba is recommended, though not required, and pilgrims ending their hajj must depart from Mecca. Often, pilgrims will visit Medina after the hajj, if they have not done so before.

We have considered the commemorative aspects of the hajj and have also pointed out its death symbolism. These both serve to help the pilgrims rededicate themselves to God and to fulfill the duties of Islam the rest of their lives. As was noted earlier, Sufis say: "Die before ye die!" The hajj is the most dramatic and meaningful manner to do this for most Muslims. Finally, the hajj also reincorporates the pilgrims into the Muslim community with a new identity, that of *ḥājjī*. Although there is no hierarchy or caste system in Islam, the title hajji is borne with pride and gratitude. The returning pilgrims have an enhanced identity that serves to act as a sort of leaven in the common life of Muslims in every region of the world. In Egypt, for example, returning pilgrims often have scenes of their hajj painted on the outside walls of their homes, celebrating their experience and providing a renewal of spiritual blessings and protection for their neighbors.

Jihad: Exertion in the Way of God

Sometimes Muslims recognize a sixth pillar of Islam, known as jihad. Although this word is most often translated, especially in the non-Muslim world, as "holy war," it means, simply, "exertion." Jihad may take the form of armed resistance to aggression, especially when such aggression is considered to be anti-Islamic. And sometimes jihad has been launched as a means of conquest and subduing others in the name of Islam. But the Qur'an commands that there is to be "no compulsion" in religion (2:256), although spreading Muslim rule is not the same as forcing people to convert to Islam. However, jihad as holy war should also include the call to submit to God as Muslims. Only the religious authorities—the *'ulamā'*—can certify whether an armed response can be considered a genuine jihad. Sometimes Muslims call for jihad against fellow Muslims, although this does not appear to have legal warrant. The laws pertaining to jihad are complex and subject to considerable interpretation.

Muslims do not talk about jihad much, although it often surfaces in Western discussions as a kind of monster. The Prophet declared that "Islam is a dominant force and is not to be dominated." This means that every means must be taken to ensure that Muslims are not subjugated by non-Muslims. The Prophet also distinguished between a "lesser Jihad," holy armed combat, and a "greater Jihad," the struggle of each individual against his lower tendencies and sins. Finally, ijtihad, independent legal decision making is based on the same Arabic root as jihad and contains the sense of serious exertion toward responsible understanding and administration of God's law.

The pillars of Islam—Shahada, salat, zakat, sawm, and hajj—provide meaning and structure to Islamic life. They are more than a formal list of obligations and should be considered within the total context of Muslim individual and communal convictions and habits. One flows naturally into the others, providing a stout, interwoven texture binding Muslims with God and with each other:

> Whoever submits his whole self to God, and is a doer of good, has grasped indeed the strongest handhold (*al-'urwa al-wuthqā*); and with God rests the outcome of all affairs. (31:22)

ISLAMIC LIFE CYCLE RITES

In addition to the pillars are practices associated with the life cycle as understood and regulated according to Islamic principles. There are important rites associated with birth, naming, circumcision, reciting the Qur'an, marriage, and death.

Birth and Childhood Rites

At birth, the father of a close male relative whispers the call to prayer into the ears of the baby, thus setting the course for a life attentive to God's beckoning. The parent chews a morsel of date until soft and then puts it into the infant's mouth, marking the time when solid food will usher the person along a continuum to responsible adult life. Usually after seven days, the baby gets a name. Muslims prefer to use the names of respected Muslims from the foundational era: Muhammad, Fatima, Ali, Khad, 'Umar, Hamza, A'isha, and the like. According to the Prophet, the most worthy names include Abdullah (lit., Servant of Allah) and Abd al-Rahman (Servant of the Most Merciful). But many good names from before Islam are also fully acceptable when augmented by a Muslim name.

To this day, converts to Islam take a Muslim name, sometimes as replacement of their former name, sometimes in addition. Famous American athletes, such as Muhammad Ali (formerly Cassius Clay) and Kareem Abduljabbar (formerly Lew Alcindor), have made Islamic names both well known and acceptable in the West. The two examples just mentioned were somewhat exotic at the time. Today, many babies born in America are given Muslim names at birth, such as Rashaan Salaam, the Muslim African American who grew up to be a Heisman Trophy winner in 1994. The Muslim name of the Egyptian actor Omar Sharif has long been a part of Western consciousness. Egypt's great modern leader, Nasser, is known in his native country as Jamal Abdul Nasir. Nasser, meaning al-Nasir, "The Victorious," is one of God's "Most Beautiful Names," which number ninety-nine. Abdul Nasir means "Servant of the Victorious," something a Muslim would never fail to discern. In the strict sense, then, to call the Egyptian president "Nasser" is inappropriate, for he was Allah's servant. In actuality, Egyptian and other Muslims have never made this a problem, understanding that sometimes a name is simply a global convention, whatever else it might also signify.[5]

Often, especially in the Muslim Arab world, a sacrifice is performed after the birth of a child. The baby's hair is cut and exchanged for its weight in silver, which is given to the poor. A feast is enjoyed by the family and relatives. This optional rite is called *ʿaqīqa*.

Circumcision

Khitān is universally practiced by Muslims, although it is not mentioned in the Qur'an nor is it required by the Shariʿa. Usually, the operation is performed on boys from birth to age seven or later, with varying ceremonial forms in different regions. Sometimes, when the operation is carried out in later childhood, the one

Egyptian Prayerbead Seller in Traditional Gallabiya Robe and Religious Scholar Turban

(*Source:* F. M. Denny)

circumcised will also recite publicly a portion of the Qur'an, thus marking a significant passage to a new stage of accountability and religious awareness as an emerging adult. Adult converts to Islam may choose to be circumcised, and there are often strong motivations to do so, although it is not legally required.

So-called "circumcision" of females has no Islamic warrant but is nevertheless still practiced in certain traditional societies (e.g., Somalia, Sudan, Sumatra) as a folk custom emotionally connected with what some people regard as Islamic tradition. Such an operation entails excising the clitoris, or simply scarring it a little. Extreme forms include cutting away the labia and sewing up the vaginal opening except for a small passage. Needless to add, there is much to reflect on concerning this custom and its psychosexual meaning(s). A considerable scholarly as well as controversial literature has emerged in recent years treating all aspects of "female genital mutilation," as it is often called.

Marriage

Marriage is another important passage in a person's life. Islamic marriage requires a legal contract to be agreed to by both parties. The signing of such a contract is arranged most often by a male representative of the bride and the prospective groom. Although not required, the concluding of the contract usually includes a short homily on the privileges and responsibilities of marriage. Often an Islamic official will witness the proceedings and ensure their legality. Wedding festivities range from the simple to the extravagant and vary considerably from region to region. Generally, they include music, dancing (males with males and females with females only), special foods, and Qur'an chanting. Today, it is not uncommon to see the couple wearing Western-style wedding garb—a white gown and veil for the bride and a formal suit for the groom—while following the traditional rites and festivities.

Islamic matchmaking is still conducted most often along traditional lines. The prospective couple may meet each other, but only under strict chaperonage. They are not permitted to be alone, and dating is unacceptable in any case to observant Muslims. Most often, marriages are arranged and involve relatives as spouses. Sometimes this proves unsatisfactory, but often it works to the benefit of the couple, who discover love and harmony by living together and working on their relationship within the ideals and defining boundaries of Islam. The couple rarely exists in isolation, separated from relatives. Close family ties are maintained, with most social occasions revolving around the nuclear and extended families.

Muslim males are permitted by Islamic law to have as many as four wives at the same time, but only if they are all treated equally. This provision is considered by many to be impossible to fulfill. Polygamy exists, but it is increasingly uncommon and often disapproved of, as well, except in unusual circumstances. Muslim wives have rights to their own money and property and keep their maiden names and are principally responsible for the care of home and children, whereas the husband has the responsibility to provide shelter, food, clothing, and security for the wife and children. Increasingly, women work outside the home at jobs and professions, but the ideal continues to be a division of labor, with the wife managing the domestic matters of life and the husband earning a living in the public arena of business and occupations. But times are changing, and new ways of dividing tasks according to Islamic principles are being tried.

Death

The final passage of the life cycle is, of course, death. When a Muslim senses the approach of death, he or she will try to sit or lie facing Mecca and recite something from the Qur'an, such as Sura Yā Sīn (no. 36), which is considered to be the "heart" of the Qur'an and contains much about the Hereafter. Relatives and friends help by praying for the dying person. Someone recites the first Shahada ("There is no god but God") into the dying person's ear. If a person is about to be killed, whether by legal execution or otherwise, he or she should try to perform two rak'as of prayer before the deed is carried out.

After death, the corpse is prepared for burial, which should be on the same day if possible. Embalming is not permitted by Islamic law. Instead, the body is respectfully given a final full bath, by the spouse or a close relative of the same sex, or by a professional washer. This washing is performed according to a prescribed manner, with three washings, cloth inserted into the orifices, and scent applied. The winding is done in various ways, but the final covering of both sexes is tightly secured. A coffin is optional. A Muslim who has died a martyr's death need not be washed or wound, because the bloody body and garments are considered pure and consecrated. The martyr is rewarded with immediate entry to paradise.

The funeral features a salat in four brief parts with participants standing throughout. The salat is not usually performed in a mosque; rather, any clean and dignified site will do. The procession to the grave provides an opportunity for onlookers to note the passage and to follow, if only for a short distance. The grave should be deep enough to be secure from digging up by animals and to prevent the odors of decomposition from escaping. The body should be laid on its right side, facing Mecca, on a shelf carved out of the side of the grave wall. The last person to be with the deceased in the grave should whisper a final Shahada into the corpse's ear, to remind the soul of the core of the true religion for when the angels arrive for a postmortem questioning of the deceased's religious knowledge. Each person in attendance adds some soil to the grave, filling it in with earth.

Nothing more elaborate than a simple gravestone should mark the grave. Loud lamentation and rending of the garments are thought by the orthodox to increase the suffering in the grave, where the deceased is sufficiently stressed by the interrogation of the angels of death. Mourning should be done with dignity and restraint for varying lengths of time, according to the local custom. There are many folk practices pertaining to death as a final passage, but this summary has emphasized canonical Muslim practices acknowledged universally.

VARIATIONS AND POPULAR PRACTICES

What has been described thus far are practices regarded throughout the Muslim community as canonical. This applies particularly to the Five Pillars. We have provided a minimal description and analysis of the canonical practices. Much specific detail on myriad questions may be found in the legal sources, which are based on the Qur'an and Hadith as well as on juridical interpretation and opinion over centuries. Although there are variations in the practice of salat, for example, and although many circumstances and conditions may intervene that require improvisation and adjustment (physical handicaps, warfare, natural disasters, illness, ignorance of the proper procedures, and so forth), it is important to remember that the salat nevertheless is performed with an astonishing uniformity worldwide and to a degree unimagined in Judaism and Christianity. In my travels to extremely diverse Muslim countries, such as Egypt, Turkey, Yemen, Jordan, Bangladesh, Pakistan, Malaysia, and Indonesia, not to mention ethnically and culturally diverse Muslim communities in Canada and the United States, I have been continuously struck by the essential sameness of Muslim worship as categorized under the Pillars and regulated by the Shari'a.

Isolated regions, such as an outer Indonesian island or a remote desert tribal region, where deviation from the canonical norm occurs, may be found occasionally. A Muslim community on the Indonesian island of Lombok, for example, is said to observe only four daily salats. And on a Philippine island, called Simunul, in the Sulu Sea, cow sacrifice is performed in connection with death rites. This old local custom, combined with other folk practices pertaining to death, burial, and mourning, is expensive to observe. But even there, the orthodox Muslims—influenced by Pakistanis and natives returning from the hajj—complain, saying: "In the Holy Qur'an there is nothing about cows."[6]

A tug-of-war goes on in many Muslim regions between scripturalist, that is, orthodox-orthoprax Islam, and local traditions. Many years ago, the American anthropologist Robert Redfield characterized the two types of authority as "great tradition" and "little tradition." Although that distinction, which may be applied to many cases beyond Islam, requires considerable explication and qualification, as well as case analyses, to understand fully, it does apply heuristically to this discussion. Much of variation in ritual practices by Muslims has to do with more peripheral—with respect to the Shari'a—aspects of observances. Most of the time, Islamic law is indifferent to what people do: it is neither meritorious nor required, nor sinful and punished—it just is. An example are the extremely varied marriage festivities that go on around the world. In Java, there may be gamelan music (from a Javanese orchestra of gongs and xylophones) and a shadow puppet play (although purists consider the traditional Hindu characters inappropriate in a Muslim context). In the Arab world, there is often a display of a bloody sheet after the consummation of the marriage, proving the bride's virginity and therefore preserving the honor and good name of her family. (The old women of the family tend to this matter, sometimes with all the ingenuity that old women are known for.) Festivities may extend over a day or may last for weeks, but Islamic law is indifferent to them so long as non-Islamic practices are avoided (such as mixed dancing, drinking alcoholic beverages, serving forbidden foods such as pork, and dressing improperly).

SAINT VENERATION

One significant category of Muslim ritual practices is visiting the tombs of saints for spiritual blessings and favors. This activity is not prescribed by Islamic law, and there are some jurists—particularly in puritanical Saudi Arabia—who outlaw saint veneration as idolatry (*shirk*). The erection of saint shrines, often impressive architectural structures with staffs and endowments, is considered by many Muslims to be forbidden. But from Morocco to Egypt to Iraq, Iran, Pakistan, India, Bangladesh, and down through the Malaysian-Indonesian archipelago cultic shrines are found, usually complete with congregational mosques, where pilgrims visit on the saints' birthdays and perform special litanies and march in elaborate processions, beating drums, carrying large banners, singing odes, and in general having a joyous period of spiritual and indeed social and economic renewal.

Saint veneration often entails considerable commercial involvement in which merchants and shopkeepers profit and goods from many regions are exchanged. Business has always been viewed as a most important, honorable, and beneficial dimension of human life, in the Islamic perspective, so that Islam knows no sabbath rest (although commerce and work are supposed to cease during the time of Friday congregational salat). The hajj grew from a regional Arab observance before Muhammad's time to a worldwide ritual, exponentially compounding the wealth that entrepreneurs have been able to earn in a huge variety of ways. Similarly, local pilgrimages, although they are not required and cannot be called hajj, express Muslim values and goals concerning spiritual and, at the same time, worldly blessings. Islam does not despise *Ḥayāt al-Dunyā,* "the life of this world," so long as it does not blind the believers to the infinitely better life to come, and the discipline to work for it, in *al-Ākhira,* "the afterlife."

WORSHIP AND RITUAL

QUESTIONS FOR DISCUSSION AND REVIEW

1. Worship is an expression of the religious experiences of Jews, Christians, and Muslims, and at the same time it serves to structure that experience. What kinds of activities does worship include? How do they express and shape religious life in Judaism, Christianity, and Islam?

2. Much worship is organized as ritual, as the practice of officially set exercises. What is the relation of ritual to worship in Judaism, Christianity, and Islam? In what ways is worship ritually structured in each of the three traditions? To what extent is it left relatively unstructured?

3. The ritual life of a community is attuned to a religious calendar, as well as to the human life cycle. What are the key times in the religious calendars of Jews, Christians, and Muslims? Are there similarities in the ways in which these three traditions conceive religious seasons or specific dates of the calendar as especially important for worship? To what extent does each tradition organize ritual around the life cycle?

4. Monotheistic religions have developed alongside each other for hundreds of years. How have rituals and devotional practices of Jews, Christians, and Muslims influenced one another? To what extent is Christianity indebted to Judaism? Has Christianity in turn influenced Judaism? How are certain aspects of Islamic ritual related to Judaism and Christianity?

5. Worship sometimes takes place in public; at other times it is conducted in private. Identify public and private aspects of worship for all three

traditions. In what ways is private worship similar across all three traditions? What are some similarities in terms of public worship?

6. Jews, Christians, and Muslims have developed and adapted ritual over the course of time. Outline some of the ways in which this has happened in each tradition. How has modernity affected worship and ritual in these traditions? What themes of change are common in the development of ritual in Judaism, Christianity, and Islam?

7. Ritual frequently involves religious professionals, clergy who take key roles in the performance of ritual or in organizing religious practice. How is this visible in each of the three religious traditions? To what extent is there a distinction made between clergy and laity in each tradition? Are these distinctions of status, or role, or both?

8. Popular religious practices, as distinguished from officially sanctioned rituals and activities, constantly emerge within communities of believers. What are some examples of popular religion in these traditions? What is the relation between popular and official forms of worship in each tradition? Do popular practices endure in the life of a community?

PART V

ETHICS

Judaism, Christianity, and Islam are commonly referred to as religions of "ethical monotheism." This label, which has predominated among Christian historians of Western religious traditions, identifies a devotion to standards of justice, duty, and the pursuit of good that is characteristic of all three traditions. This term, however, also flattens the varying emphases among these religions. "Ethics" is by no means fixed as a specific body of questions and concerns. By the same token, beliefs about how to live ethically vary from tradition to tradition. And the way in which fidelity to doctrine is related to obedience to codes of behavior takes a different form in each religion as well.

Obedience is the key word in our exploration of ethics among Jews, Christians, and Muslims. In order to appreciate the importance of obedience, it is first of all important to acquire a sense of the kinds of behaviors that are encouraged and those that are forbidden in everyday life. Equally as important, however, is the matter of why members of these religions do in fact choose to obey. What is at stake in their decision to live ethically? On the positive side, to live ethically is to worship and serve God. On the negative side, we discover a range of rationales. For Jews, faithlessness to God's will as revealed in Torah is construed as disloyalty both to a community of people in the world and to Israel as a transhistorical entity. In the case of Christians, deeply rooted concerns about the consequences of behavior for the afterlife historically have played a leading role in shaping the will to live ethically. Muslims likewise are aware of a final judgment that may lead to damnation to hell; but Islam, like Judaism, also views failure to obey the law of God equally as alienation from the umma, the community.

The inculcation of ethical standards in members of these three religious traditions begins at a very early age. Indeed, it may be argued that ceremonies or prayers linked to birth are the first steps toward preparing a person to live an ethical life. Ethical training undertaken in family and community contexts ranges from the teaching of good manners to solemn encounters with the core of ethical tradition, such as, for example, the Ten Commandments. In some cases, reflection on the reasoning behind ethical commands is encouraged. Frequently, however, the difference between right and wrong is learned as an aspect of devotion, of obedience to God, and therefore is not cast as part of an investigation into the superstructure of monotheism as a religious worldview.

For Jews, Christians, and Muslims, ethical living is more than mere adherence to certain rules and regulations governing behavior. Ethics is not a discrete element of religious life, a component of the whole that can be plainly isolated and studied in itself. It is interwoven with worship, ritual, authority, community, and personal spirituality in the total composition of religious life. As we look at the "ethical" aspect of "ethical monotheism," we must bear in mind that ethics is a kind of piety, a sense of group, and an embrace of tradition as much as it is a guide to knowledge of duty, justice, and compassion.

CHAPTER 13

ETHICS

IN JUDAISM

In the Western philosophical tradition stemming from classical Greece and elaborated by Christian and Islamic philosophers, "ethics" is usually understood as the systematic philosophical study of proper objects of moral value.[1] They ask, "How do we know what is 'good,' and how do we live so that our actions conform to what we know to be good?" The Judaic tradition reflected in the Hebrew Bible and the rabbinic literature, by contrast, is almost entirely innocent of disciplined inquiries into the assumptions that should guide ethical judgment. More commonly, one finds collections of sayings authoritatively recommending certain actions as "wise" or others as "wicked" or "foolish." Thus, for example, the biblical book of Proverbs 23:19–21 provides the following advice to people of a certain disposition:

> Listen, my son, and get wisdom; lead your mind in a proper path. Do not be among those who guzzle wine, or glut themselves on meat; for guzzlers and gluttons will be impoverished, and drowsing will clothe you in tatters.

Compare the rather chastening perspective recorded many centuries later in the mishnaic tractate Avot 3:1:

> Akavya ben Mahalalel said: "Consider three things and you will not fall into the grips of transgression. Know from where you've come, where you are going, and before whom you will give an account of yourself. Where have you come from? A stinking drop. Where are you going? To a place of dust, worms and maggots. Before whom will you give an account? Before the King of Kings of Kings, the Holy One Blessed be He."

As a phrase popular among medieval Bible commentators would have it: "The one who has understanding will understand!"

Accordingly, if you could have asked Jews nourished on biblical and talmudic sources, "How do you reflect on the fundamental goods that humans should strive for?" or "On what grounds do you reach decisions about proper action?," they might have answered as follows: "It is good to obey God's will as revealed in his Torah. As for proper action, we are guided by the halakhic decisions reached by our sages." In the history of Jewish thought, therefore, ethics in the Western sense had only episodically been recognized as an intellectual domain requiring sustained attention. Almost universally, such episodes have emerged when Jews were actively engaged in intimate intellectual communication with the non-Jewish world.

The Hellenistic period is the first example. Greek-speaking Jews, you recall, were intensely aware of the need to defend the dignity of the Torah in broader cultural terms. A number of Jewish writings from this period attempted quite clearly to interpret the laws of the Torah as allegorical expressions of moral values celebrated in the Hellenistic world. Thus, the first-century CE Jewish philosopher Philo of Alexandria interpreted puzzling details of biblical law, such as prohibitions against eating certain animals, as ways of teaching such valued Greek character traits as "gentle manners" and "endurance and self-control" (e.g., his *The Special Laws*, IV). Similarly, he saw in the biblical law of retaliation ("an eye for an eye") a sublime hint regarding the role of the eye in bringing the mind to direct knowledge of God (*The Special Laws*, III).

Philo's reflections, written in Greek, had little impact on the Hebrew-Aramaic talmudic tradition that would dominate ancient and medieval rabbinic Judaism. Medieval Islamic culture, from the tenth century and onward, provided the first setting in which Jews nurtured on talmudic study actively engaged ethical questions in a philosophical idiom. Now the conversation was largely in Arabic, the language into which Muslim intellectuals had translated the ancient Greek classics. Especially in Iraq and Spain, where Jews enjoyed wide access to a sophisticated Islamic intellectual culture, some Jews actively engaged in philosophical reflection on the nature of good character and the proper goals of life. Such thinkers as Saadia ben Joseph (882–942, Iraq, *Book of Beliefs and Opinions*), the eleventh-century Bahya ibn Pakuda (Spain, *Duties of the Heart*), and the twelfth-century Moses Maimonides (Egypt, *Guide of the Perplexed*) wrote extensive treatises in which such questions were prominent. Their Arabic writings continued to be read, in Hebrew translation, long after philosophy fell into general disrepute among Jews and was replaced by Kabbalah. But such books inspired pious living, not further writings on the philosophical problem of the good life. By the fifteenth century, Jewish philosophy had reached a dead end, at least in its Islamic cultural incarnation.

With the modern entry of Jews into the general life of European culture, a concern for conceiving Judaism as a European religion of personal morality focused attention once again on questions of philosophical ethics. A tradition of German-Jewish ethical thought began with Moses Mendelssohn's *Jerusalem* (1770), which argued that the essential truths of Judaism were contained in universal categories of reason and morality. This tradition of using European ethical thought to explain

**Moses Maimonides
(1135–1204)**

Rabbi Moses b. Maimon (or Rambam, as his name
is commonly abbreviated in Jewish tradition) was
the greatest thinker to emerge from the philosophical
tradition of medieval Sephardic Judaism. Author
of works of philosophy (*The Guide of the Perplexed*),
mishnaic scholarship (*Commentary on the Mishnah*),
and a great halakhic code (*Mishneh Torah*), his
impact on Jewish thought remains apparent even
today. His ethical thought is deeply influenced by
the Aristotelian doctrine of the "Golden Mean."
(*Source:* The Granger Collection, New York)

(and defend) the content of Judaism continued until the twentieth century's destruction of European Jewry under Nazi Germany. It included such exceptional
thinkers as Hermann Cohen (1842–1918), Franz Rosenzweig (1886–1929), and Martin Buber (1878–1965), all of whom were convinced that the values crucial to the
survival of European culture were most clearly expressed in Judaism.

The task of spelling out the implicit ethical views of Jewish tradition was
taken up on the American continent in the twentieth century as well. Many

university-trained intellectuals have reflected thoughtfully on Jewish ethics, but none has achieved the international stature of Rosenzweig, Buber, or Cohen. In contemporary Jewish thought, the French philosopher Emmanuel Levinas (1905–1996) is regarded as the preeminent thinker capable of illuminating Jewish tradition from the perspective of European philosophical ethics.

This tradition of ethical thought is fascinating as a study of intellectual history. Yet we will confront it only obliquely here. The reason is that with the rare exception of such figures as Maimonides and Bahya ibn Pakuda, the philosophical works of Jewish ethicists have been little-read by Jews. Indeed, such brilliant figures as the ancient Philo and the modern Buber have been far more influential among Christian intellectuals. Until the nineteenth century, Jews sought guidance on the question of values from the classical rabbinic tradition, augmented by perspectives drawn from Kabbalah. Since modern times, as often as not, they brought their questions about Jewish values to modern interpreters of Jewish history rather than to philosophers of Judaism.

Accordingly, most of our attention in this chapter is devoted to the ways halakhic norms structure Jewish questions about ultimate values. In many cases, the halakhic path was viewed as a profound struggle to embody important traits of character (Heb.: *middot*). No less frequently, halakhic thought served to define a person's moral obligations to others. Even when, in recent centuries, most Jews left halakhic culture, its stress on personal character and social responsibility remained a crucial touchstone of Jewish identity. At the end of this chapter, therefore, we focus on the way the enormously influential modern movement, Reform Judaism, sought a nonhalakhic path to the expression of Jewish values.

HALAKHAH AND THE CULTIVATION OF CHARACTER

The Moral Completion of Male and Female

Shortly after the birth of a Jewish child, while the mother may still be confined to her bed, the halakhic tradition followed by contemporary Orthodox and Traditionalist Jews enjoins the father to engage in a minor ritual in the synagogue. Called to the lectern to read from the Torah, he makes a charitable contribution to the synagogue in return for the recitation of a brief petition for the health of the mother and new child. The words of this petition speak volumes about how the halakhic tradition conceives of the goals toward which Jews should devote themselves.

For a male child the following is recited:

> May he who blessed our ancestors, Abraham, Isaac and Jacob bless this birthing woman, (X, the daughter of Y), and her son born to her at a propitious moment, for her husband has vowed charity on her behalf. By the merit of this act, may the child's father and mother be graced to bring him into the covenant of Father Abraham, to raise him to a life of Torah, marriage and good deeds.

Compare, now, the recitation recited for a girl. Identical to the former text until the last sentence, it continues:

> Let the child's name in Israel be called (*A*, daughter of *B*). By the merit of this act, may her father and mother raise her to marriage and good deeds.

You may have noticed three differences. First, the female baby receives her name during this service, while the male receives none. Second, the male child is expected to enter "the covenant of Father Abraham," but no mention of this appears in the girl's petition. Finally, whereas both children are expected to marry and lead their lives of good deeds, only the boy is expected to pursue "a life of Torah."

It will be worth a few moments to reflect on the meanings of these differences. In the halakhic tradition, the girl receives her name and becomes a member of Israel at this ceremony because, unlike the boy, it is the only formal ceremony that will usher her into the community. The boy child, to the contrary, will formally enter Israel eight days after his birth, when he is circumcised in accordance with the custom inaugurated by Abraham (Gen. 17:9–14). At that time, he, too, will receive a name. Thus our first observation: a girl enters Israel by the simple fact of her birth, receiving a name almost immediately; the boy undergoes a waiting period. He becomes part of Israel only by virtue of a surgery that marks his sexual organ for the rest of his life.

Female Jews, one might say, are born; male Jews are made. This helps explain the third key distinction we noticed. Both children are expected to embark on marriage and a life of good deeds, lived in accordance with covenantal values. But only the boy is expected to be raised to "a life of Torah." Male and female, that is, are expected to live in accord with the halakhic system, but only males are destined to engage it intellectually in a life of sustained study.

Here again, the female Jew seems to be complete as she is at birth; the male Jew must be created after birth, physically through circumcision and morally through study of Torah. The male's life, in fact, through puberty and up to the point of marriage, is shaped as a continual process of being molded by the stamp of Torah. At puberty, when he begins to mature sexually, the male undergoes a ritual designed to consecrate his emerging sexual powers to "a life of Torah." As a *bar mitzvah* ("one obliged to perform commandments"), the thirteen-year-old boy makes his formal entrance into public Jewish life, reading from the Torah scroll in public worship and giving an extended discourse designed to demonstrate his knowledge of rabbinic learning. Just as he becomes aware of his own sexuality, he is reminded by the community that his adult identity can be fulfilled only through mastery of the Torah.

After some further years of study, the boy is then deemed marriageable. His sexual powers, prepared from infancy by circumcision and consecrated by years of immersion in the study of sacred tradition, are now released to their intended purpose, the re-creation of Israel. His bride will now join him, first, under the marriage canopy and, later, upon the marriage bed. Her powers of fertility, shaped to their purpose under the tutelage of her mother, and his, refined under the father's

THE HISTORY OF A PUBERTY RITUAL

Talmudic law holds that girls become legally responsible for their actions at the age of twelve, whereas boys do so at thirteen. Thus, puberty is taken as a biological event that signals a child's passage into legal adulthood. Part of being a legal adult is that one is now obliged to fulfill the covenant contract entered into at Sinai.

The earliest evidence that a ritual accompanied this change comes from medieval times, when reference is made to a rite in which the *bar mitzvah* (one obliged to observe commandments) is formally called to the Torah and is counted among the ten members of the prayer quorum. In medieval and early modern times, this was, of course, a male rite exclusively, since women were not called to read from the Torah in public. Practiced in all Jewish communities until the present day, its rituals are modified appropriately in light of the specific values of the Reform, Conservative, Reconstructionist, and Orthodox movements.

Since the 1920s, Reform, Conservative, and Reconstructionist congregations have invited girls to participate in a similar rite. Now the *bat mitzvah* ("the daughter obliged to observe commandments") has become as common among girls as the bar mitzvah is among boys. In recent decades, a new twist has been given to the bat mitzvah in these communities. Mature women who, in their teen years, had been given no opportunity for a formal Jewish rite of passage into adulthood, now commonly engage in a course of Jewish study prior to their own bat mitzvah. Called to the Torah on a Friday evening or Sabbath morning, they proudly announce that they, too, have, at last, "come of age in Torah."

Even among Orthodox Jews, who still adhere to the exclusion of women from public reading of the Torah, the bat mitzvah has become an important rite of passage to womanhood. In deference to halakhic restrictions on woman's public role, the Orthodox bat mitzvah celebration is usually a gathering of girls and women in which the honoree displays her mastery of Torah by delivering a learned discourse on the interpretation of the biblical passage corresponding to her birthday.

discipline of Torah, now join to replenish the world. The "natural Jew" and the "created Jew" together produce the next generation.

The perception of male and female otherness and complementarity is crucial to the entire halakhic tradition and has a profound impact on the ways in which men and women within this tradition have imagined themselves as moral beings. The difference goes beyond the division of household chores or allocation of roles in the synagogue. As "natural Jews" from birth, Jewish women have been encouraged to understand the simplest acts of child rearing and homemaking to have a covenantal significance. They perfect their moral life, therefore, through the circumstances that confine them to the cultural role of guardian of the hearth. It is in this role that they express the most praiseworthy Jewish trait, "awe of Heaven" (*yirat shamayim*).

Men, on the contrary, understand themselves to be in a constant struggle against their nature. "Awe of Heaven" cannot be expressed simply by engaging in what is "natural" to their social roles, earning a livelihood or otherwise contributing to the needs of the household. In addition to cultivating character traits of humility and restraint of the appetites (sexual in particular), "awe of Heaven" imposes upon men a daily regimen of ritual activities—prayer and study of Torah—through which they are constantly demonstrating their willing submission to the covenantal norms of the halakhah.

The social result of these perceptions of male and female are easy to observe. Although all Jews are expected to cultivate "awe of Heaven" as a constant element of their character, Jewish men have had far greater access than women to the intellectual tradition in which the content of that awe is explored and the social settings—communities of learning men—in which it is embodied in behavior. Women follow halakhic norms, but men study, interpret, and apply them. The contents of holy books, from childhood, are more firmly woven into men's conceptions of themselves and the kinds of persons they ought to become. Acknowledging that they require more discipline than women in order to become worthy Jews, they have also accorded to themselves an enhanced status as the ones who have mastered a difficult discipline. The paradox, invisible to ancient and medieval Jewish culture but increasingly obvious to many contemporary Jews, is that the "natural" Jewishness of women places them outside most definitions of what it means to be a Jew fully "completed" by mastery of the complex tradition of Torah. It is for this reason that most reflections within the halakhic tradition on ideal traits of character and the nature of the perfected human life focus on men and their challenges. The "moral struggle of the Jew" most often refers to that of the male Jew in particular. This being said, what kind of challenges does the life of Torah impose?[2]

The 613 Commandments and the Moral Life

The talmudic tradition affirmed by Orthodox and Traditionalist Jews asserts that the Torah received by Moses and elaborated by the rabbinic sages contains no fewer than 613 covenantal commandments or *mitzvot* (sing.: *mitzvah*). These mitzvot, of which the famous "Ten Commandments" (Exod. 20:1–14, Deut. 5:6–18) are only the tip of the iceberg, include 248 commandments to perform certain acts (e.g., to honor one's parents) and 365 commandments to refrain from certain acts (e.g., not to murder). Drawn from biblical and rabbinic tradition, the mitzvot include comprehensive obligations that cover all areas of life. It is not possible to be "moral" within the rabbinic system without pursuing a lifestyle devoted to fulfilling the commandments in all the details established by halakhic tradition. To be "in awe of Heaven" is nothing less than to be *shomer mitzvot* (a preserver of Commandments).

The comprehensiveness of the mitzvot is best expressed in the Babylonian Talmud's picturesque explanation (Makkot 23b). The 248 "prescriptions" (*mitzvot aseh*) correspond to the number of organs of the body, each of which must be mobilized in divine service. The 365 "proscriptions" (*mitzvot lo ta'aseh*) correspond to the days of the year, in which Creation calls out to Jews to refrain from disobeying the will of the Creator. Thus, the body finds its perfection only through the performance of the divine will, and every day of the year is an opportunity for perfectly embodying that will.

Rabbinic tradition clearly recognizes that the body's role in performing mitzvot is incomplete without the willing, engaged attention of the mind and emotions. It is impossible to have "awe of Heaven" without engaging in the halakhic discipline; but even full compliance with halakhah is not "awe of Heaven" unless such compliance stems from an inner attitude of devotion and submission to God. A frequently argued issue in talmudic literature, accordingly, is whether a commandment performed without the proper inner disposition (*kavanah*, "intention") has indeed been performed at all (e.g., Babylonian Talmud, Berakhot 13b). The ideal is to perform every commandment with full reflection upon its meaning in the larger economy of the life lived before God.

Among medieval Jewish jurists, the issue was given particularly acute attention. Maimonides, for example, saw a life lived in reflective performance of commandments as the best form of training in the moral life, the goal of which is an unhindered contemplative relationship with God. "The essence of the Torah," he wrote in an official halakhic letter to the Jewish community of Yemen, "lies in the deeper meaning of its positive and negative precepts, every one of which will aid man in his striving after perfection" (*Epistle to Yemen*). His view is amplified on one of his explicitly theoretical writings: "if you perform a commandment merely with your limbs, . . . without reflecting either upon the meaning of that action or upon Him from whom the commandment proceeds or upon the end of the action, you should not think that you have achieved the end" (*Guide of the Perplexed* 3:51).

In medieval kabbalistic theology, the role of the mind in fulfilling the body's action was interpreted in a dramatically different fashion. Some early Kabbalists believed that Maimonides' stress on the intellectual meaning of the commandments could lead to laxity in their actual performance. The Kabbalists proposed instead that the commandments were actual divine spiritual organs, stemming from the world of the Sefirot and grounded in the corresponding material organs of the human body.

Thus, the 613 commandments are linked entirely to the body, now said to consist of 248 limbs and 365 inner organs. "All the mitzvot of the Torah," asserts the Zohar, "are united with the body of the King, some with the head, some with the torso, some with the hands of the King, some with the feet. None exists beyond the body of the King" (Zohar 2:85b). When each limb and organ of the earthbound Jew is engaged with proper concentration in its divinely created mission, the supernal organs of the worlds of the divine Sefirot are brought into harmony, and blessing flows into the world as in the days of the Temple. Correspondingly, when the limbs and organs defy their created nature, "it is like one who sins against the body of the King" (ibid.), and the upper worlds are thrown into disorder: "Woe to those sinners who transgress the words of the Torah, not knowing what they cause!" (ibid.).

The life of the commandments, then, bears an enormous moral weight. Not only are the consequences of failure potentially cataclysmic for the world, as in the kabbalistic view, but success requires constant self-scrutiny and vigilance. There is the perpetual danger of being lulled into a ritualized piety devoid of the inner consciousness—*kavanah*—that transforms behavior into a sign of the "awe of Heaven." Accordingly, the history of halakhic piety is rich in efforts to reawaken awareness of life as a profound struggle with one's own inner dispositions.[3]

Disciplines of Character

In classical rabbinic writings, this struggle is imagined as a struggle between two forces that compete for dominance in the human heart. The force for good, the *yetzer hatov* (good impulse), lies at the essence of the soul and spontaneously inclines toward obedience and love of God. But it is always in competition with the *yetzer hara* (the evil impulse). Conceived at times as a neutral power necessary for the creative acts of civilization (Bereshit Rabbah, 9:7), the yetzer hara is more commonly grasped as a power of rebelliousness that, in some opinions (Babylonian Talmud, Sanhedrin 91b), enters the heart at birth. The moral life of human beings is nothing but the struggle to aid the good inclination in conquering its evil counterpart. "What is a hero?," asks the Mishnah. "He who vanquishes his yetzer!" (Avot 4:1). This hero's sword, as we should expect, is the study of Torah. "If the All-Merciful created the yetzer hara, he also created Torah as an inoculation against it" (Babylonian Talmud, Baba Batra 16a).

The history of Jewish piety is in large part the history of attempts to conquer the evil impulse so as to be perfectly obedient—inwardly as well as outwardly—in the service of God. Especially in medieval times, under the influence of Kabbalah, many Jewish men took on themselves lives of self-imposed asceticism well beyond any formal halakhic requirements. Rising long before dawn to study Torah or to recite psalms was a common way of repressing seductive appetites for food, wealth, or illicit sexual relations. Many, in addition, engaged in periodic fasts, immersions in freezing waters, and other practices designed to subdue the power of the instincts for bodily comfort and pleasure.

The one concession made to physical needs, besides the taking of food, was for sexual activity. One of the 613 commandments is "be fruitful and increase" (Gen. 1:28). Even ascetics, therefore, felt bound to marry and pursue normal marital relations. The challenge was to engage in such relations "for the sake of Heaven" rather than out of sexual appetite—to use the covenantal organ within the constraints of the Torah's guidelines. Under kabbalistic influence, the sexual relations of marriage, which could (one supposes) easily turn to recreational purposes, were placed under the transforming (and sobering) power of ritual. The Zohar set apart Sabbath Eve as a uniquely propitious time in which conjugal relations enabled the partners to participate in "the exalted mystery concerning the time when the Consort is united with the King" (Zohar II:89a).

In order to understand the nature of this "exalted mystery," one must recall our discussion of the Kabbalah's theory of gendered divine emanations or Sefirot (Chapter 4). The Consort and the King of our passage represent two Sefirot. They are symbolized in kabbalistic thought as *Shekhinah* (Presence)—a feminine aspect of divinity that is "in exile" from other aspects of God—and *Tiferet* (Glory)—a

THE STRUGGLE WITH THE YETZER

The Talmud recognizes that the struggle against the evil impulse is unrelenting and that at times a person will lose. What is to be done, therefore, when a person finds it impossible to resist? As the following passage from Tractate Hagigah 16a makes clear, one should, at the least, sin in a way that does not cause public dishonor to God.

> Said Rabbi Ilai the Elder: "If a person sees that his impulse is getting the best of him—let him go to a place where he is unknown, let him garb himself entirely in black, and let him do what his passions compel him to do. But let him not desecrate the Name of Heaven in public!"

Presumably, it is always possible to repent for one's sinful actions. But once the Torah is violated in public, the memory will linger despite any public repentance by the sinner. In this sense, the public violation of the Torah is a greater sin than is the act to which one was originally compelled.

masculine element that is in continuous longing for Shekhinah. One of the goals of the Kabbalah is to reunite Shekhinah and Tiferet, for the return of Shekhinah from her metaphysical exile will also inaugurate the return of Israel from its historical exile. The coupling of man and woman on earth at the moment of God's rest from Creation, therefore, is more than "sex." In the kabbalistic view, the human Consort and King imitate and enable a similar unification of the female and male powers in God. Common marital relations are thus transformed into a ritual act anticipating the redemption of the ultimate Sabbath. Moreover, just as human coupling yielded children, the divine coupling was believed to produce the souls that would animate them at their birth (Zohar I:257a).[4]

This kabbalistically inspired pursuit to transform the passions into opportunities of divine service continues to inform the most traditional of Jewish communities well into the present day. In addition to Hasidism, which many have seen as a movement of moral regeneration, nineteenth-century Eastern European Judaism gave birth to an important movement called Musar. Although the Hebrew term usually means "moral instruction," the proper rendering in this context should probably be "moral self-scrutiny." The Musar tradition remains alive in many contemporary Orthodox settings, in which writings from the "Musar-school" continue to be widely reprinted, studied, and interpreted.

Founded by the Lithuanian-born sage Rabbi Israel Salanter (1810–1883) as an explicit alternative to Hasidism, the institutional center of the Musar movement was its special schools (*yeshivot*; sing., *yeshivah*) for young men. In addition to conventional studies in Talmud and Kabbalah, the Musar curriculum focused on classical ethical treatises by Maimonides, Bahya ibn Pakuda, and other rabbinic authorities. Measuring their own "awe of Heaven" against extraordinary standards, students cultivated extreme suspicion of all pretensions to moral virtue.

Salanter, who was a perceptive student of the mind's secret motivations, held that self-deception was a powerful barrier to awareness of one's inner motivations. Therefore, Musar sessions, led by special teachers, were designed to foster the recognition that achievements in scholarship and piety could be transformed unconsciously into the traps of self-importance and complacency. The tools of one's struggle against the evil impulse, in other words, could be used to cultivate it. Thus *teshuvah* (penitential turning toward God), highly prized throughout the history of rabbinic Judaism, was cultivated as the goal of all study and performance of mitzvot. The life of penitential teshuvah and intense self-examination became the center of life in the Musar yeshivah and in all communities affected by the movement.[5]

HALAKHAH AND THE SOCIAL ORDER

Justice and Charity

The intense self-reflection cultivated by rabbinic conceptions of the moral struggle corresponds to an equally acute concern for the moral condition of society as a whole. This is expressed as early as the Mishnah (Yoma 8:9) by a common division of commandments into those that concern a person's relation to God (i.e., *mitzvot bain adam l'makom*) and those concerning a person's relation to others (*mitzvot bain adam l'khavero*). Transgressions of the latter are regarded as so severe that one must atone for them prior to atoning for actual sins against God. One must restore justice to one whom one has harmed before it is possible to receive mercy and forgiveness from God.

Emerging among the hierarchical societies of the ancient Middle East and flourishing under highly stratified Christian and Islamic societies, Judaism has imagined justice (*mishpat* or *tzedek*) largely in terms of social equilibrium. That is, justice is a state of affairs in which each stratum of society properly meets its obligations to its superiors and its responsibilities to its inferiors. In the Torah and the prophetic writings of the Hebrew Bible, social justice is routinely defined as a situation in which the powerful in society protect the weak, for example, the poor, the widows, and the orphans. Similarly, justice is fulfilled whenever the less-empowered (slaves, children, and wives) obey those to whom their care is entrusted (owners, parents, and husbands). Such hierarchical ideas of justice are, of course, different from the egalitarian ideals proposed by the political and social revolutions of secular modernity. We saw in Chapter 10 that most forms of Modernist Judaism have absorbed egalitarian ideals, especially those in which women are concerned. Nevertheless, they are modern innovations that should not be read back into classical expressions of Judaism.

In light of this conception of justice, it should be no surprise that the halakhic tradition views the essential task of communal leaders to be the maintenance of proper relations between unequal groups. Since Jewish communities had no state structure to administer for nearly two millennia, halakhic tradition has focused most of its attention on the administrative role of the rabbinic sage as a judge and mediator of disputes. Much of the civil law of the Mishnah and the Talmuds, accordingly, concerns outlining the proper rights and privileges of various social groups. The medieval halakhic tradition built on and systematically expanded these earlier foundations.

The area of marriage law provides an interesting set of examples. The most comprehensive treatment of marriage as a legal relationship is found in the sections on Family Law (*Even Ha-Ezer*) and Civil Law (*Khoshen Mishpat*) of Rabbi Joseph Karo's great sixteenth-century halakhic code, the *Shulkhan Arukh* (*The Set Table*). There, marriage is viewed from two perspectives. On the one hand, as we have seen, it is a means of sanctifying sexuality, of putting procreative powers to legitimate ends. On the other, it is also an economic relationship between the families of the bride and groom. Both aspects of the relationship, therefore, carry with them clear implications for the rights and obligations of man and wife.

When considering the wife as a sexual being, the *Shulkhan Arukh* regards her as the property of her husband, consecrated to him alone. His legal obligation to her, therefore, is to provide her with regular sexual satisfaction in accord with his abilities and her needs (Even Ha-Ezer 76:1–5). As a consequence of his obligation to her, it is illegal for her to engage sexually with another man. Should she do so, her husband has the unquestioned right to divorce her (ibid., 11:1), for she has violated his rights by giving to another what he owns. Once she is divorced from her husband, however, her sexuality returns to her as her own property. If she engages in sexual liaisons with another man, she may be acting lewdly, but not unjustly or illegally (Babylonian Talmud, Yevamot 61b). Her problem is with God, not with the small claims court.

Although a woman's reproductive power is her husband's property, her economic power is viewed more subtly. A husband is obliged to provide his wife's total economic support (Even Ha-Ezer 69:2). Nevertheless, property brought by a woman into marriage remains hers in the event of divorce (ibid., 66:11). Similarly, her husband's right to benefit from such property or from her earnings during the marriage is limited. He may benefit only if he continues to support her fully and to the degree that she benefits as well from any use to which he puts her earnings (ibid., 69:4). Thus, for example, he cannot use her property or earnings to defray his own personal debts (*Khoshen Mishpat* 97:26).

In sum, as a sexual being consecrated to a man, the woman becomes his possession and owes him a certain standard of justice. But as an economic being, justice entitles her to a far larger degree of autonomy from her husband. Whereas the legal system views him as the "owner" of her sexuality, she is independent as regards economic production, a partner in a common economic venture. "Justice" between husband and wife, therefore, is determined by the degree to which procreative or productive powers are at issue.[6]

The conception of society as an aggregate of different classes of people with various rights and obligations to one another governs one of the most important social institutions of the halakhic tradition. This is the institution of *tzedakah*. Normally translated as "charity," the term has a broader resonance in rabbinic

Judaism. It is derived from the word *tzedek*—"justice." Tzedekah, then, is not "charity" in the etymological sense of "gift," a noble gesture of the haves to the have-nots. Rather, it is part of a web of obligations that bind the haves and have-nots into a single community. The rich, in other words, pay for their privilege by giving justice—tzedakah—to the poor; they thereby acknowledge that inequality of wealth, precisely because it is part of the divine plan, obliges them to consider the poor as their moral responsibility. According to the *Shulkhan Arukh*'s laws regarding the pious pursuit of commandments (*Yoreh De'ah* 247:1), the failure to give tzedakah, precisely because the life of the poor may depend on it, disrupts the social order no less surely than does an act of murder.

The point is driven home by the principle that even those who receive tzedakah are obliged to give it to those in worse circumstances (ibid., 248:1). It is a community-wide obligation, each person obliged to give in accordance with his or her circumstances. Thus, every synagogue has its charity box. Further, it is common to offer tzedakah prior to holidays, weddings, anniversaries of the deaths of loved ones, and, as we have seen, at the birth of a new child. The proceeds are used to provide for the entire complex of community institutions that serve the weak: schools, hospitals, public kitchens, and even the collections of dowries for impoverished brides.

Jewish Society and Non-Jewish Society

Halakhic theories of social justice are shaped by long experience in harmonizing the conflicting claims of groups and individuals within Jewish society. It is an equally long experience with non-Jewish societies—summarized in Chapter 19—that has shaped halakhic perspectives of the larger social world within which Jews have lived. At least since the Christianization of the Roman Empire, Jews have commonly—and often with good reason—perceived themselves as the victims of that larger world. Halakhic conceptions of justice, accordingly, tend to stop at the borders of the Jewish community. You will recall that the conquering empires of Christendom and, later, those of Islam were personified respectively as the biblical anti-heroes, Esau and Ishmael. The hostility of these monotheistic traditions to Israel was interpreted mythically. They were descendants of ancient brothers whose loss of God's covenantal love to Israel's ancestors, Jacob and Isaac, caused an endless jealousy. This jealousy, however, served God's purpose—to purge exiled Israel of its own disobedience.

Accordingly, halakhic tradition developed so as to limit as far as possible all but the most essential economic and social transactions between Jews and non-Jews. What Jews owed to one another by way of justice and charity was not owed to non-Jews in principle, although as a matter of prudence—"for the sake of peace"—it might be extended on an informal basis (Babylonian Talmud, Gittin 61a). In hostile environments, Jewish communities maintained only necessary economic and social relations with surrounding societies. Yet, in times of relative toleration, as under the Cordova Caliphate of tenth- and eleventh-century Spain,

THE EIGHT LEVELS OF TZEDAKAH ACCORDING TO THE *SHULKHAN ARUKH*

Maimonides was the first jurist to develop a scale on which to evaluate specific kinds of tzedakah. From his *Mishneh Torah*, it was reproduced in Rabbi Jacob b. Asher's fourteenth-century code, the *Arba Turim* ("The Four Pillars"). Finally, it was included in Rabbi Joseph Karo's *Shulkhan Arukh* (*Yoreh De'ah* 249:6–13):

> *There are eight levels of tzedakah, one greater than the next:*
> *The greatest level, beyond which there is no other, is to strengthen the hand of a Jew who has fallen by giving him a gift, or a loan, or by entering into partnership with him, or by finding him work. By so doing one strengthens him and makes him independent of others. . . .*
> *Beneath this is one who gives tzedakah to a poor person without knowing to whom he is giving, and in such a way that the poor person does not know from whom it comes. And similar to this is a person who contributes to a tzedakah fund. . . .*
> *Beneath this is one who knows to whom he is giving, while the poor person is unaware of who has given to him. An example is provided by the great sages who would go about secretly depositing money in the doorways of the poor. . . .*
> *Beneath this is when the poor person knows who has given to him, but the donor does not know who has received what he has given. An example is provided by sages who would bundle coins in their kerchiefs and throw them behind themselves. This permitted the poor to come after them and take without embarrassment.*
> *Beneath this is one who gives to the poor person before he asks.*
> *Beneath this is one who gives to the poor person what he needs after he asks.*
> *Beneath this is one who gives him less than he needs, but does so in a respectful way.*
> *Beneath this is one who gives with a sour face.*

the halakhic norm of separation was often breached in practice, providing for rather free interactions of Jews and non-Jews at various levels of social intimacy.

In any event, in premodern times the halakhic tradition has usually regarded Jewish and non-Jewish society as essentially distinct entities. The modern situation is more complex as large sectors of Jewry live beyond the reach of rabbinic legal authority. It is clear, however, that when Jews have felt welcomed by the larger society, as in most of twentieth-century North America, Jewish custom has permitted and even encouraged the extension outward of inner-communal standards of justice. An important example is the extensive American Jewish philanthropy supporting social and cultural institutions, such as hospitals, universities, and civil rights groups, that benefit society as a whole.

In light of the difficult history of Jews among Christians and Muslims, an important fact should surprise us. What the halakhic tradition is sceptical of in the framework of human relations—justice between Jew and non-Jew—is embraced at a different level, justice between non-Jews and the God of Israel. Rabbinic thought recognizes a category of "Laws of Noah," seven commandments that were given to the pre-Israelite hero of the Flood. These include prohibitions of idolatry and murder, a requirement to establish courts of law, and other rules of basic morality. Don't look for these laws in Genesis, because you won't find any mention of them. Imagined wholly within post-biblical and rabbinic tradition (e.g., Babylonian Talmud, Sanhedrin 56a-b), they constitute the terms of a covenantal relationship between God and all non-Jews, parallel to the 613 commandments of Sinai. Any non-Jew obedient to the Laws of Noah is accounted as "righteous" and, accordingly, fully qualified to celebrate with Israel the messianic redemption of history in "the world to come" (ibid., 105a). At the end of time, the worldly barrier between Israel and the nations is overcome in a just world administered by God's Messiah.[7]

JEWISH COMMITMENTS
IN A NON-HALAKHIC FRAMEWORK

At this point in our study of Judaism, you should already anticipate that what holds true for premodern Judaism rarely describes the Judaism of modern times. The fact of the matter is that the halakhic system that for more than fifteen hundred years shaped personal morality and social vision in Judaism is today the living experience of a small minority of Jewry. If we want to understand the character of the moral life for modern Jewry, then, we cannot confine our attention to a tradition that today nourishes only a few.

It will be most helpful, therefore, to return once more to the highly influential Modernist movement, Reform Judaism. From its informal origins among German Jews in the 1810s and 1820s, it rapidly became popular throughout central and western Europe. By the 1840s and 1850s, it had spread, with the influx of German Jewish immigrants, to North America. There it dominated American Jewish religious life until well into the twentieth century. Earlier chapters described the general historical setting of Jewish Emancipation within which the Reform movement tried to present Judaism as an ethical religion of good citizenship. You'll recall as well the variety of changes in synagogue worship and home ritual inspired by Reform's concern for achieving Jewish social integration into European society. Of interest now are ways in which Reform Jews defined the ethics and social vision of Jews wishing to be both "good citizens" and "good Jews."[8]

Heir to a centuries-old tradition that viewed personal life as a profound struggle to serve God with all one's will and strength, Reform Judaism had little trouble arguing that ethics stood at the center of Judaism. Its principal challenge was to explain how Jewish morality could thrive beyond the constraints of halakhah. Reform Jews, contemplating the full entry of Jewry into the life of modern nations, perceived the halakhic system as an ancient and outmoded hindrance. But how could it be replaced without losing the ethical values it fostered? The most articulate early leaders of Reform, such as the brilliant rabbi and theologian Abraham Geiger (1810–1874), argued that the "essence" of Judaism could not be contained in ancient laws. In sermons and scholarly writings, Geiger insisted that the ritual commandments of the Written Torah and the various halakhic norms of the Oral Torah were historically conditioned "forms." They expressed Jewish spirituality at a particular historical moment, but could never define its "essence" for all time. The expression of the ethical "essence of Judaism" required continually new historical "forms."

Geiger, and the Reform movement after him, found the "essence of Judaism" in the idea of a single, universal God who united humanity in his service through a stress on universal laws of morality. The Jews, in this view, were the first people to discover such an ethical God, although Christianity and Islam later borrowed the idea and spread it beyond the Jewish community. Because the Jews' history of exile preserved them from the corruptions of worldly power, they remained the purest bearers of this "ethical monotheism" in history. Their task in the future was to continue to bear witness to it and bring it to historical fulfillment.

No earlier "form" of Judaism, however—biblical or otherwise—fully expressed for all time the "essence" of ethical monotheism. Whereas the biblical Ten Commandments and the teachings of the Hebrew prophets served as a main inspiration, the details evolved historically, emerging out of the life of the people. Rabbinic halakhah was one such historical expression of Mosaic and prophetic values. Emerging during centuries of persecution and prejudice, it preserved ethical monotheism by preserving the Jews, creating rigid barriers between Jews and a hostile environment. But now that the full emancipation of the Jews neared, the historical "form" of halakhic separatism proved a hindrance to the next evolving stage of Jewish ethical expression. A new "form" was emerging.

This was the blending of Jewish ethical monotheism with the humanistic liberalism of modern Europe. The spirit of universal human solidarity, fostered by European political liberalism, was seen as nothing less than an expression in secular terms of the original religious core of Judaism. Reform leaders believed that the time was right for the Jews to fully join humanity in the creation of a just human order and to enrich liberal visions of humanity with the monotheistic faith of the Jews. This struggle for universal justice was Reform Judaism's answer to the question of what could replace halakhic discipline as the form of Jewish moral expression. Abstention from pork at the table or from labor on the Sabbath now seemed pointless rituals, devoid of any instructive ethical message. They hid from Jews the universalist "essence" of the Torah and prevented non-Jews from seeing in Judaism the original expression of their own highest values.

Accordingly, the rabbinic leaders of the Reform movement sought to cultivate among their congregations a deep sense of mission to embody Jewish universalism in the world as a whole. Geiger, for example, in his influential lectures entitled *Judaism and Its History,* spoke of a Jewish "genius for religion" that had enabled the Jews to "discern more clearly the close relationship between the spirit of man and the Universal Spirit . . . and perceive the profound ethical quality in man with greater clarity and intensity." This was the gift that Jews could offer the world.[9]

In light of such universalism, traditional notions of justice and tzedakah were quickly shorn of the ethnocentric focus of rabbinic culture. Jews were encouraged to interpret justice in egalitarian political and social terms. Under the influence of Reform, accordingly, Jewish political activists often saw the struggle against anti-Semitism as part of a larger, more important struggle against social injustice in general. Reform Jews also began to define their notions of charity in terms of general, rather than specifically Jewish, society. Thus, Jewish philanthropists were more likely to donate large sums to general social or cultural institutions instead of supporting the particular needs of the Jewish community. If the new liberal age of Europe was to be the hoped-for Messianic Era of universal human solidarity, Reform Jews eagerly took upon themselves the role of chief bearers of the good news.

The Messianic Era, of course, did not come as expected. A century after the origins of the Reform movement, German society was swept up in the racist exclusivism of the Nazi Party. The details await us in Chapter 19. As a result, however, Jewish confidence in the universalism of European values disintegrated as millions of Jewish men, women, and children were murdered and incinerated in Nazi death camps, often with the active or passive assistance of Christian Europeans. In light of what Jewish memory records as the "Holocaust," few Reform Jews would today express too much hope that our own age is in any way redemptive. Many recognize that the security of Jews in the world remains precarious, even under the best of circumstances. Nevertheless, the fundamental conviction of Reform Judaism remains unshaken: that the essence of Judaism is the vision of a just society for all humanity. Ideally, to be a Reform Jew is to struggle with other people of moral vision toward its creation.[10]

CHAPTER 14

ETHICS
IN CHRISTIANITY

Odd things can happen on American television. For instance, a Jewish comedian once told the following joke to late-night viewers:

> A man dies and goes to face judgment in the afterlife. At the gates of heaven, St. Peter asks him, "Why do you think you belong here?" The man says, "Hey, last week I gave a bum two dollars." "Is that it?," asks St. Peter. "Is that all the good you have done?" "Come to think of it," says the man, "last month I also gave two bucks to an old lady." St. Peter leaves his post at the pearly gates to consult with God: "Wait here," he tells the man. "Should we let him in?," St. Peter asks God; and God answers: "Give the guy back his four bucks, and tell him to go to hell."

To tell such a joke and expect a laugh, of course, is to assume that most of the audience would be acquainted with one of the chief characteristics of Christianity: the fact that it is a religion interested both in "orthopraxis" (correct behavior) and in "orthodoxy" (correct belief).

THE STRUCTURE OF CHRISTIAN ETHICS

Christians of all stripes have long believed that true faith and good ethics are one and the same. When asked, "What is the greatest commandment?" in the Gospel of Matthew, Jesus replies: "You shall love the Lord your God with all your heart, and with all your soul, and with all your mind. . . . And you shall love your neighbor as yourself" (Matt. 22:36–40). Similarly, the Letter of James warned that "faith by itself, if it has no works, is dead" and added: "Religion that is pure and undefiled before God and the Father is this: to visit orphans and widows in their affliction, and to keep oneself unstained from the world" (Jas. 1:27, 2:17). The Gospel of Matthew, too, underscored this intimate relation between behavior and salvation by indicating that reward and punishment will mark the beginning of the Kingdom of Heaven:

> When the Son of man comes in his glory, and all the angels with him, then he will sit on his glorious throne. Before him will be gathered all the nations, and he will separate them one from the other as a shepherd separates the sheep from the goats, and he will place the sheep at his right hand and the goats at his left.

The kingdom is awarded only to the sheep, to those who fed the poor, clothed the naked, welcomed strangers, gave drink to the thirsty, and visited the sick and the imprisoned. Those who do not perform such deeds will hear the terrible words "depart from me, you cursed, into the eternal fire prepared for the devil and his angels . . . and they will go away into eternal punishment, but the righteous into eternal life." In other words, the unethical will be told to go to hell.

The *Oxford English Dictionary* defines "ethics" as "the science of morals; the department of study concerned with the principles of human duty." The Greek *ethike*, from which the English word is directly derived, comes from the root *ethos*, or character, which means the same in English. So "ethos" and "ethics" are related. If ethos defines the true nature of anything, so does ethics define the characteristics of human behavior. Jesus, the founder of Christianity, referred to this inseparable relation between character and behavior when he cautioned his disciples:

> Beware of false prophets, who come to you in sheep's clothing but inwardly are ravenous wolves. You will know them by their fruits. Are grapes gathered from thorns, or figs from thistles? So every sound tree bears good fruit, but the bad tree bears evil fruit. (Matt. 7:15–17)

Christian ethics, then, are much more than values or morals or behavioral guidelines; Christian ethics are the ethos of Christianity, its very character.

But, given the fact that all communities—even formally atheistic societies—have ethical codes, what is it that defines Christian ethics as "religious"? In the first place, Christians believe that their code of behavior has been revealed by God through his incarnation in Jesus Christ. Furthermore, Christian ethics are based on the twin premises that the ultimate happiness of humans resides in following God's rules for behavior and that these rules are ultimately grounded in love. Many Christian books of instruction since the time of the Fathers have asserted that all human acts should correspond to the purpose of human existence. The Baltimore Catechism used by North American Catholics began with a question at once simple and profound: "Why did God make me?" The answer was succinct: "God made me so I could know Him and love Him."

The knowledge of God promised by Christianity has usually been more than mere gnosis, for its promise of salvation hinges on adherence to specific ethics. The gospels of Matthew, Mark, and Luke tell the story of a rich young man who asked Jesus, "Rabbi, what must I do to inherit eternal life?" Jesus draws him out by giving him too basic an answer: "If you would enter life, keep the commandments." The young man then asks him "Which?," trying to discern which laws are most crucial; and Jesus replies, "You shall not kill, You shall not commit adultery, You shall not steal, You shall not bear false witness, Honor your father and mother, and You shall love your neighbor as yourself." Seeking assurance, the young man continues to probe Jesus: "All these I have observed; what do I still lack?" As a final response, Jesus offers him a tough command, "If you would be perfect, go, sell what you possess and give it to the poor, and you will have treasure in heaven; and come, follow me" (Matt. 19:16; Mark 10:17; Luke 18:18).

The rule of life prescribed here by Jesus is that of the Ten Commandments: the Law revealed to Moses by God. But in this key gospel passage, Jesus reveals another dimension to the Law, that of love and total self-renunciation. It is not enough merely to keep the Law. To be perfect, one must deny the self for the sake of God and neighbor. Elsewhere in the Gospels, this insistence on self-negation is continually asserted by Jesus:

> If any man would come after me let him deny himself and take up his cross and follow me. For whoever would save his life will lose it, and whoever loses his life for my sake will find it. For what will it profit a man, if he gains the whole world and forfeits his life? (Matt. 16:24–26)

> He who loves his life loses it, and he who hates his life in this world will keep it for eternal life. (John 12:25)

The Dialectic of Christian Ethics

Ethics, ritual, and dogma are closely interrelated in Christianity. In fact, it is somewhat misleading to deal with these three components of the religion as separate realms, for the definition of orthodoxy has always been linked to ethics. In the minds of many Christian leaders, false belief would necessarily lead to immorality. Quite often, then, those accused of heresy have been also charged with immorality. The definition of heresy, or false belief, is directly related to behavior. The English word "heresy" derives from the Greek verb *haeresin*, to choose. The "heretic," therefore, is someone blamed for obstinacy, someone who bends the will toward evil in spite of the truth. Christians have long considered heresy to be a matter of the will.

Correct behavior is the essence, even the promise, of the message of salvation: to be saved from sin and its corollary punishment, death (Rom. 6:23:

The wages of sin is death). But since everyone dies, even the "saved," what does good Christian behavior really promise? This is where the transcendent dimension of Christian ethics is brought into high relief: the reward is not to be in this life, or in this world, but rather in some life to come, in the "world to come." It is a salvation that is here, and yet not completely; it begins here, but is fulfilled only after death.

But if the reward for good behavior is promised in another world, what is the Christian to do with this world? Christian ethics have functioned in an uneasy dialectic between life here and now and life in the world to come. As if this polarity were not enough, the Christian is also poised between two societies: the company of fellow Christians and those who do not believe in Christ. How is a Christian to relate to the rest of society? Since ethics and rituals are complex sets of signs through which social groups define themselves, including members by participation and excluding others by nonparticipation, Christians throughout the past two thousand years have had to wrestle with the question, "How do we approach 'the other,' that is, those who do not behave, believe, or worship as we do?" Generally, those outside Christian society have been lumped together into the category "the world" or "this world." The word "world" appears 241 times in the New Testament. Quite often, it is used to refer to all that which is opposed to the Kingdom of God or to the life of salvation.

So what have Christians done with the world? The answer varies, according to time and place. For the sake of simplicity, it could be said that Christians have gone through four stages of development in their attitude toward the world. At first, Christians saw themselves as diametrically opposed to the world. Early Christians lived in a ruthless society that held human life as cheap. From the arena, where killing for sport was routine, to the slave market, where people were bought and sold as commodities, there seemed to be little room for the love and compassion of Christian ethics. (The word "love" appears 174 times in the New Testament.) Furthermore, since Christians were often persecuted and cruelly executed for their beliefs, it is not surprising that they did not wish to accommodate themselves to the world. After Christianity became the predominant religion of the Roman Empire and the Barbarian kingdoms of medieval Europe, Christians found, much to their surprise, that they had become the world or at least exercised some control over it. Byzantine and Medieval Christianity accommodated to the world, but never completely. The tension between accommodation and opposition remained strong and, as we see shortly, allowed for the flourishing of Christian monasticism.

When the Protestant Reformation brought a sudden end to the politico-ecclesiastical unity of Christian Europe, Christians found themselves battling one another. Suddenly, it was no longer a question of Christians against the world, but Christians against Christians. And within this battleground those who waged war had different notions of what to do with the so-called world. Finally, in the modern age, Christians have come nearly full circle. To a considerable extent, Christian ethics since the eighteenth century have been framed against the backdrop of a hostile world once again, the world of unbelief.

The Early Christians Versus the World

In the first century after the death of Jesus, his followers quickly assembled a society of like-minded believers who enforced definite rules of behavior, not only to define themselves, but also to differentiate themselves from "others." The development of Christian ethics, therefore, had a twin focus: inwardly, Christians built up defining characteristics spun from the deeds and sayings of Jesus; outwardly, Christians constructed barriers by reacting against specific limitations and pressures exerted by the so-called world. As far as the world or the other was concerned, Christians sought to steer clear of two traditions: first, they sought to distinguish themselves ethically from the mother religion, Judaism; second, they attempted to steer clear of the pagan culture and religion of late antiquity.

Inwardly, Christians followed the Jewish pattern of focusing on rules and laws, interpreted as God-given commandments, and retained most of the moral values of Judaism. Nonetheless, Christians abandoned much of Jewish ceremonial law. As early as 49 CE, Christian leaders decided to do away with circumcision and Jewish dietary restrictions. Much more important to Christians was the avoidance of behavior that the Jewish law had deemed "immoral." The Teaching of the Twelve Apostles (or *Didache*) spoke of two kinds of living: "the way of life" and "the way of death." The behaviors labeled as "death-dealing" were also proscribed in Judaism:

> murders, adulteries, lusts, fornications, thefts, idolatries, magic arts, sorceries, robberies, false witness, hypocrisies, duplicity, deceit, arrogance, audacity, haughtiness, boastfulness.[1]

Christian society was orderly. Clement of Rome compared Christians to an army in which Jesus was the emperor and the bishops his generals. Obedience was essential. Clement admonished his flock: "Brothers, we must march under the irreproachable orders of Jesus."[2] Ignatius of Antioch saw an even closer relation between the Christians' identity and their ethical norms: "You are all decked out from tip to toe in the commandments of Jesus Christ."[3] Ignatius could clearly identify, in reverse, those who were *not* Christian:

> Pay close attention to those who have wrong notions about the grace of Jesus Christ. . . . They care nothing about love; they have no concern for widows or orphans, for the oppressed, for those in prison or released, for the hungry or the thirsty.[4]

Christian life in the first and second centuries was ascetic (self-denying) and legalistically inclined. Wednesdays and Fridays were days of fasting, which were called "stations," as of soldiers of Christ on guard. Christians were also expected to pray several times a day. But in addition to all this, Christians were also expected to perform works of charity. One early document says, "Fasting is better than prayer, but almsgiving is better than both prayer and fasting."[5] Some Christians took this duty so much to heart that they sold themselves into slavery and used the proceeds to take care of the needy. From early on, Christians also developed a stringent sexual ethic: "abstain from carnal passions; do not corrupt boys"

**The Final
Judgment. German
Woodcut, Sixteenth
Century**

Christians expect Christ to return from heaven at some
unspecified time when the earth as we know it will be
destroyed; the dead will rise from their graves, and all of
humankind will be judged. Christ himself will do the judging:
Those whose lives were not good will be given over to the
devil and sent to eternal torment in Hell; those whose lives
were good will be admitted to an eternal heavenly paradise.
Christ balances justice and mercy—depicted by the sword
(justice) and the lily (mercy). (*Source:* Albrecht Durer/Art Resource)

counseled the Teaching of the Twelve Apostles.[6] Virginity and celibacy gained favor as virtues. Second marriages were discouraged, even in the case of widows
and widowers. Homosexuality, contraception, masturbation, abortion, and infan-
ticide were strongly condemned. Violence in general was shunned, although there
is evidence that soldiers could be Christians. The cruel spectacles of the arena were
forbidden, as were pagan festivals and plays. Personal excesses of any kind were

also forbidden in regard to drink, food, and attire. Women were encouraged to dress simply and to use no hair dyes, wigs, or cosmetics. Tertullian went so far as to advise Christian men not to trim their beards too much.

Martyrdom

Shunning the world came at a high price for early Christians, for they were persecuted as atheists and subversives. As early as the first century, Christians were being put to death for refusing to pay homage to the heathen gods of the Empire. Martyrdom was quickly elevated into one of the highest Christian virtues. Refusing to profane one's religion at the cost of one's life came to be regarded as a singularly holy form of behavior. In fact, to suffer as a "martyr" (Greek, *martus*: witness) was to profess the faith to the utmost; and it was also a guaranteed entrance to a blessed afterlife. Ignatius of Antioch wrote an astonishing letter shortly before his own death that summed up the Christian ethic of martyrdom:

> Let me be fodder for the wild beasts—that is how I can get to God. I am God's wheat and I am being ground by the teeth of wild beasts to make a pure loaf for Christ. I would rather that you fawn on the beasts so that they may be my tomb and no scrap of my body be left. . . . Pray Christ for me that by these means I may become God's sacrifice . . . if I suffer, I shall be emancipated by Jesus Christ; and united to him, I shall rise to freedom. What a thrill I shall have from the wild beasts that are ready for me! I hope they will make short work of me. I shall coax them on to eat me up at once and not to hold off, as sometimes happens through fear. And if they are reluctant, I shall force them to it.[7]

As Ignatius made clear through his use of eucharistic and sacrificial language, the martyr imitated Christ in the most complete way, conforming to his suffering and death. At its core, the ethic of martyrdom was an ethic of imitation: the ultimate immersion by Christian individuals in the central mystery of salvation. Martyrdom was the continuation of the saving work of Christ. Ignatius also said: "Let me imitate the passion of my God. . . . I give my life as a sacrifice." By the end of the fourth century, when martyrdom was no longer likely, one Christian writer would rhapsodize about it in extreme terms:

> Baptism in water is certainly good, but better and best of all is the baptism of the martyr. The former is forgiveness, the latter a reward. The former is the remission of sins, in the latter a crown of virtues is merited.[8]

The ethic of martyrdom could have proven self-destructive to Christianity had it been carried to an extreme. Early Christians drew a sharp distinction between genuine martyrdom and suicide. "True" martyrdom was considered a gift: those who sought out persecution or incited trouble could end up condemned rather than revered. Clement of Alexandria, for one, thought that those who provoked the Roman authorities shared in their guilt. Similarly, the Council of Elvira (fourth century) denied the title of "martyr" to anyone who had actually brought death upon himself or herself by publicly disparaging Roman religion. It was not uncommon, therefore, for Christians to flee or hide in times of persecution. Martyrdom was a special calling, something to be willingly suffered only when no escape was possible.

Official caution notwithstanding, the prospect of being martyred seems to have attracted the world weary to Christianity; paradoxically, martyrdom came to be seen as one of the reasons for the growth of the new religion. As Tertullian put it in the third century, "The blood of the Martyrs is the seed of the Church."[9] In the fourth century, Athanasius pointed to martyrdom as proof of the truth of Christianity: the fact that so many suffered so willingly—even women and children—testified to the power of Christ as nothing else could.[10]

Virginity and Celibacy

Being eaten alive by lions and tigers or being set ablaze as a human torch were not the only ways to become a martyr. By the third century, Christians were also considering abstention from sexual activity a kind of martyrdom. Some churchmen praised virginity as one of the highest Christian virtues (a "virgin" was anyone who remained committed to a celibate life, not just someone who had never been sexually active). Methodius of Olympus, for instance, maintained that virgins would be the first to enter Christ's kingdom, for

> their martyrdom did not consist in enduring things that pain the body for a short period of time; rather it consisted in steadfast endurance throughout their whole lifetime, never once shrinking from the truly Olympian contest of being battered in the practice of chastity.[11]

The close relation between martyrdom and virginity stems from the world-denying ethic of early Christianity. As Ignatius of Antioch had said before his own martyrdom, "I shall be a convincing Christian when the world sees me no more. Nothing you can see has real value."[12] This dualistic tendency in early Christianity manifested itself intensely when it came to sexual ethics, for sex is the bodily function responsible for procreation. Without sex, there would be no bodies. Since the early Christians firmly believed in the superiority of the soul over the body (the spirit over the flesh, the Kingdom to come over this world), it stood to reason that abstinence from sex should have been seen as a virtue.

Moreover, since self-control was a prime Christian concern, and since sex involved the passions, it also stood to reason that early Christians came to associate it with a loss of control and with impurity. In the fourth century, Gregory of Nyssa spoke of virginity as "divinization" and a "pure mystery" precisely because virgins tamed their passions. Gregory saw sexlessness as a participation in the uncorruptedness of God: "Virginity enjoys communion with the whole celestial nature; since it is free from passion it is always present to the powers above." Because it allowed Christians to ignore passions and bodily urges, thought Gregory, virginity allowed them to "assimilate themselves to spiritual reality."[13]

Yet, no matter how strong their praise of virginity, orthodox Christians steered clear of outright dualism. Though they distrusted sex, they could not condemn it as sinful, for that would have meant that procreation and creation it-self were evil. This was the heresy of the Gnostic dualists and the Marcionites, who saw sex as the means whereby spiritual essence was repeatedly trapped in the ma-terial world and who therefore made celibacy necessary for salvation. The Mon-tanists were not as extreme, but their distrust of human sexuality ran deep; among them, marriage was deemed not much different from fornication, and second mar-riages were strictly forbidden under all circumstances. Among orthodox Chris-tians, virginity was praised, but so was marriage. Gregory of Nazianzen honored marriage as a natural virtue and deemed it an affirmation of the goodness of God's creation:

> In carrying out this law and union of love we aid one another mutually and, since we are born of the earth, we follow the primitive law of the earth, which is also the law of God. . . . For marriage does not remove from God, but brings all the closer to him, for it is God himself who draws us to it.[14]

On the whole, however, world-denying Christians remained apprehensive about human sexuality. Their fear of uncontrollable passions and their fear of du-alism made for an uneasy dialectic. Small wonder, then, that Fathers such as Jerome could exclaim, "Marriage is only one degree less sinful than fornication."[15]

Monasticism

A virtuous life can be defined either positively, as a good life, or negatively, as a life without sin. For many early Christians, the call to virtue took on a negative char-acter, as avoidance of sin. Increasingly, sinfulness came to be associated with social interaction, and, conversely, sinlessness with social withdrawal. By the third cen-tury, we find stories such as that of Arsenius, a young Egyptian who prayed for en-lightenment: "Lord, show me the way to salvation." A voice came to him: "Arse-nius, run from men and you shall be saved." He went on to become a hermit and in his solitude kept repeating the same prayer. Again, he heard a voice: "Arsenius, be solitary, be silent, be at rest. These are the roots of a life without sin."[16]

The English word "monk" is derived from the Greek word *monos,* meaning "alone" or "solitary." Monks are people who live apart from their society—singly, as hermits, or in communities known as "monasteries." Monasticism is not peculiar to Christianity alone. Buddhism, for instance, has a rich monastic tradition. Jewish and pagan influences cannot be ruled out, but there is no denying the fact that many commands found in the Christian scriptures point naturally to the intrinsic devel-opment of a monastic ethic, such as Jesus' advice to the rich young man: "If you would be perfect, sell all you have, give it to the poor, and come follow me." Literal interpretation of this passage means nothing less than renunciation of all normal so-cial connections. Add to this advice the commands to "take up the cross," remain "unstained by the world," and "pray ceaselessly," and mix in the early Christian craving for martyrdom and virginity, and you have a formula for monastic life.

The birth of Christian monasticism cannot be pinpointed with great accu-racy, but it evidently began to take shape as early as the second century, flourished in the third, and became dominant from the fourth century on. Syria and Egypt appear to be the birthplaces of this phenomenon, where increasing numbers of men and women sought to live as hermits in the desert. From the start, these monastics had as their goal not only to renounce the world, but also to dedicate themselves wholly to prayer and fasting. The immediate goal of the monks was self-control, which was seen as the key to the perfection demanded by Jesus, "Be ye therefore perfect, as even your heavenly Father is perfect" (Matt. 5:48); their long-term goal was the undisturbed contemplation of God. The advice given by third- and fourth-century hermits, collected in the Sayings of the Desert Fathers, points to an uncompromising way of life: in order to "tame" the body and its desires and to concentrate wholly on prayer, these desert hermits sought to banish all comforts and extinguish all desire. "As the shadow goes everywhere with the body, so ought we to carry penitence and lamentation with us wherever we go," advised one old monk. Food and drink were kept to a bare minimum and so was sleep. "One hour's sleep is enough for a monk," proclaimed one hermit. "All rest of the body is an abomination to the Lord," said another. Silence was a virtue. "Our form of pilgrimage is keeping the mouth shut," declared one hermit. Sex was literally unthinkable. One story told of a monk who dared not touch his own mother. "A woman's body is fire," he explained to her, "simply to touch you would bring the memory of other women into my soul."[17] The desert hermits became spiritual athletes. In fact, the term for their way of life, "asceticism," is derived from the Greek word for athletic training, *askesis*. Some hermits locked themselves away in cells too small for standing or laying down; some wrapped themselves in chains or tethered themselves to walls and stakes; others lived in trees; others wore nothing but loincloths made from thorns. Symeon Stylites, one of the most famous Syrian hermits, had himself sealed into a cistern without food, chained to the wall, before moving up to the top of a pillar (much like twentieth-century flagpole sitters). Symeon lived atop this column in some ruins for thirty years, sixty feet from the ground, fully exposed to the elements; and he inspired many others to become stylites, or pillar dwellers.

The demands and excesses of "eremitical" (hermit) monasticism, however, were soon eclipsed by a more moderate tradition of "coenobitic" (communal) monasticism. In the fourth century, monasteries began to flourish throughout the Christian world, beyond Syria and Egypt. These communities varied tremendously in size and structure. At one end of the spectrum, monasteries could consist of a loosely organized handful of monks; at the other end, monasteries could be rigidly ordered small towns with hundreds of residents. These coenobitic monks usually elected one of their number to be their leader, or abbot (Hebrew; *Abba*: Father), and they closely followed a written rule that outlined their behavior down to minute details. Membership in such a community entailed taking three vows: poverty (no private ownership), chastity (no sex), and obedience (follow the rule and the abbot's commands). The sixth-century Rule of St. Benedict focused on obedience as the essence of the monastic ethic, for Benedict saw the taming of the human will as the goal of human existence. His rule begins with the admonition:

> Receive willingly and carry out effectively your loving father's advice, that by the labor of obedience you may return to Him from whom you had departed by the sloth

of disobedience . . . renounce your own will to do battle under the Lord Christ, the true King, and take up the strong, bright weapons of obedience.[18]

Monasticism was as much for men as for women. (The term for female monastics in English is "nun," derived from the Latin *nonna,* a respectful form of address for older women.) We know that communities of female virgins existed in Egypt as early as the mid-third century. The influence of nuns on males could be great; and vice versa. St. Basil of Caesarea, the author of the principal rule followed by Orthodox monks, was led to the monastic life by his sister Macrina. St. Benedict of Nursia, the author of the chief rule followed by Catholic monks, had an immense impact on his sister Scholastica and her community of nuns.

The monastic calling became more popular as Christians ceased to be persecuted in the fourth century and as the church became more closely identified with the Empire. In many ways, the growth of monasticism was inversely related to the increasing worldliness of the church. Monasticism acted as a counterbalance among Christians at a time when their religion was becoming increasingly more closely identified with earthly realms. On one level, then, monasticism was an interiorization of the ethic of martyrdom; on another level, it was a protest against the encroachment of the world; on yet another level, it was a safety valve of sorts, providing an outlet for those who sought perfection in an ever more imperfect church.

One cannot underestimate the effect that the sudden growth of Christianity in the fourth century had on monasticism. By one estimate, in 313, when persecution ceased, there were probably about five million Christians in the Empire. A hundred years later, the number had swelled to somewhere around thirty million! The church of the highly committed, where martyrdom was always a possibility, had been replaced by the church of the unenthusiastic masses in which baptism was performed out of social pressure and bishops increasingly dressed and lived like the Roman nobility. The worldly church, in the minds of the seriously committed, made monasticism necessary. Gregory of Nazianzen tried to live austerely when he was appointed bishop of Constantinople, but he was severely criticized. As he could not compromise, he resigned. His ironic farewell sermon gives us a glimpse of the worldliness that had invaded the church, and which the monastics were trying to flee:

> I was not aware that we bishops ought to rival consuls, governors, and famous generals . . . or that our stomachs ought to hunger for the bread of the poor, and expend their necessities on luxuries, belching forth over the altars. I did not know that we ought to ride on fine horses, or ride in magnificent carriages, with processions in front of us.[19]

Among both Catholics and Orthodox, monasticism came to be regarded as essential for the church as a whole, especially because of the ever increasing worldliness of the higher clergy. The monks and nuns served a vital function as those who prayed for the entire community: "Monks are the sinews and foundations of the Church," said St. Theodore the Studite in the ninth century. Some monastic writers went even further, claiming that the prayers and asceticism of the monks were all that kept God from destroying the world. Moreover, as we see in Chapter 17, the monks and nuns became points of contact with God for the community, as well as being witnesses of God's presence on earth. In a society that equated otherworldliness with sanctity and that valued sacredness and holiness as essential for social well-being, the monastic life was not considered a "waste," but was rather the noblest and most virtuous calling, the most perfect way to love both God and neighbor.

THE HISTORICAL DEVELOPMENT OF CHRISTIAN ETHICS

The Middle Ages

The millennium following the collapse of the Western Roman Empire was officially dominated by the monastic ethic, both among Catholics and Orthodox. But the church could not exclusively equate monasticism with salvation, for that would have turned Christianity into a dualist society, much like the Manicheans, Bogomils, and Cathars, who had two distinct types of believers: the "perfect" and the "hearers" or "learners." Once again, we see the development of a forceful dialectic in Christian thinking; the monastic life was promoted by the church as the ultimate Christian commitment, but salvation was not limited to the monks, which meant, of course, that a path of salvation had to exist for those Christians still in the world.

Salvation for the bulk of the Christian community, as for the monks, was linked to behavior. Thus, the most basic Christian instruction focused on ethics as much as, or perhaps even more than on theology. Learning the Ten Commandments and the laws of the church was considered absolutely necessary. To break any divine law upheld by the church was to commit a sin; to commit a sin was to imperil one's salvation. The list of sins was long and precise, both among Catholics and Orthodox. One event in the ninth century gives us a glimpse of the moral precision demanded of Christians. When Boris I, king of Bulgaria, converted to Christianity in the 860s, he consulted both the patriarch of Constantinople and the pope at Rome. The questions he asked focused mainly on behavior, not on doctrine; and the answers he received tell us much about Orthodox and Catholic legalism. The Orthodox wanted the Bulgarians to observe laws such as the following: no bathing on Wednesdays and Fridays; no eating of meat butchered by eunuchs; and no taking of communion without wearing a belt. The Catholics, too, deemed specific behaviors as sinful, such as working or having sex on Sundays.[20]

From early on, Christians developed a sliding scale of sinfulness: since some wrongs were weightier than others, they required stiffer penalties. In the West, "mortal" sins were those that barred one from heaven; lesser sins were known as "venial." Most commonly, Christians were taught to think in terms of broad categories as well as specific rules of behavior. The many specific acts that were deemed mortal sins all fell under the broad category of the seven "deadly" or "cardinal" sins: pride, greed, envy, anger, lust, gluttony, and sloth. Each of these

**Personification of Lust, Mid-Fourteenth-Century Sculpture
in the South Transept, Auxerre Cathedral**

Lust, one of the seven "deadly" or "cardinal" sins, was an
especially troublesome temptation for a Christian society that
valued virginity and chastity above married life. The goat in
medieval Catholic art symbolized the uncontrollable animal
instinct present in human sexuality and also pointed to the
demonic element. (*Source:* Girandom/Art Resource, NY)

categories encompassed a multitude of specific sins. Lust, for instance, included
every form of sexual misbehavior, from adultery to unchaste thoughts; sloth
covered all aspects of idleness, from paralyzing despair to negligent laziness;
and so on.

All sins had to be confessed to a priest who, as Christ's representative, was
believed to hold the power of forgiveness. This was the sacrament of penance.
Confession was a practice that evolved gradually and with some differences between East and West. The bottom line was this: Christians were required to know
their sins, examine their consciences, repent, and confess every individual sin,
from the most insignificant to the most awful. By the twelfth century, confession
had become an art of introspection that demanded much from the individual
Christian. Confessional manuals asking very specific questions were developed

CHRISTIAN VIRTUES AND VICES

Christian ethics are defined to a large extent by lists of "do's" and "don'ts." The lists can be long and detailed, but have for centuries been summarized under a succinct number of categories of behavior, known as virtues and vices. The virtues, of course, are the do's, whereas the vices are the don'ts. Both lists employ the mystical number seven.

Virtues

The first four virtues are considered discernible in natural law and are in fact derived from the writings of the Greek philosophers Plato and Aristotle. They are known as the cardinal virtues (Latin: *cardo*, "hinge"):

1. Prudence
2. Temperance
3. Fortitude
4. Justice

Though these virtues make for harmonious social relations, they cannot bring humans to salvation. Christian theologians added three theological virtues to the list, which can be obtained only with God's gift of grace:

5. Faith
6. Hope
7. Love

Vices

Also known as the Seven Deadly Sins, these vices represent tendencies toward an imbalance of the human passions, bad habits, and addictive behavior. These vices can be overcome only through the gift of grace and by the practice of virtue.

1. Pride
2. Envy
3. Greed (avarice)
4. Anger
5. Lust
6. Gluttony
7. Sloth (laziness, despair)

for both the clergy and the laity. Some examples from a fifteenth-century manual give us a glimpse of the soul searching and moral accounting required of late medieval Catholics:

> Sins against the first commandment: Have you honored temporal rulers more than God, Mary, and the sacraments? Have you loved relatives, friends, or other creatures more than God? Have you practiced or believed in magic?
> Sins against the second commandment: Have you questioned God's power and goodness when you lost a game? Have you muttered against God because of bad weather, illness, poverty, the death of a child or a friend?
> Sins against the third commandment: Have you dressed proudly on Sundays, sung and danced lustily, committed adultery [a doubly serious sin on the Lord's Day], girl-watched, or exchanged adulterous glances in church or while walking on Sundays?[21]

The distinction between mortal and venial sins was linked to the development of a nuanced understanding of the afterlife and its relation to Christian behavior. If salvation depended on behavior, would not a merciful God take into consideration the difference between venial and mortal sins? By the fourth century, Christian writers such as Augustine were speaking of the possibility of purgation, or cleansing, in the afterlife. By the end of the sixth century, it came to be commonly believed in the West that the vast majority of Christians would not enter heaven directly on dying, but rather would pass through a period of cleansing punishment after death. By the twelfth century, Catholic Christians had already developed not only a precise list of sins and their respective penalties, but also an elaborate geography of the hereafter. The formula was at once complex and simple: one's location in the afterlife and the duration of one's suffering were determined by one's behavior in this life. Only the holiest men and women—most of them monastics—were believed capable of entering heaven directly. Purgatory, a flaming place of torment located beneath the earth's crust, would have to be endured by most Christians for varying lengths of time. Hell, the fiery dwelling of Satan and his devils at the earth's core, was reserved for eternity for all the unbaptized and all unrepentant Christian sinners. Thus were the differences among Christians on earth reflected in the world beyond. Thus, too, was the perfectionist strain of monasticism at once maximized and minimized, for whereas the doctrine of purgatory restricted immediate access to heaven only to the "holy," it simultaneously offered a slow and gradual opening of the pearly gates to those throngs of the less-than-holy who made up the vast majority of the Christian community.

Ethical thinking in the medieval period, especially in the West, was marked by another development: the acceptance of "natural law." In some significant ways, natural law ethics had already been formulated by early Christians. A salient example is Clement of Alexandria; who argued that the moral law should be obeyed for its reasonableness, not simply for its divine derivation. But with the rediscovery of Aristotle in the twelfth century, natural law theory took hold of Western Christian thinking. Those who upheld this theory maintained that the correctness or incorrectness of most human behaviors could be discerned by human reason, independently of revelation. In brief, medieval Christians developed a way of thinking about their ethical code that made it seem the most reasonable and "natural" for all humans: nature itself revealed the proper end or purpose (Greek: *telos*) of all actions. All acts, therefore, were judged on the merits of whether or not they fulfilled a natural purpose. Of course, in many cases, Christians strained to find the teleology (natural purpose) behind particular church laws, but for the most part, this development had a positive effect on the development of Western thinking, for it moved the Christian West gradually away from thinking of ethical codes as derived from God's arbitrary will. The Declaration of Independence of the United States, for instance, depends on natural law theory for its intelligibility ("We hold these truths to be *self-evident*, that all men are created equal . . . ").

This is not to say that Christianity moved irrevocably toward naturalistic thinking and notions of human freedom. On the contrary, the dialectical and paradoxical nature of Christian thinking made for much controversy and disagreement. A good case in point is the issue of private property. The New Testament is replete with statements that denounce wealth and private property. Many of the early Fathers, such as Irenaeus, Ambrose, Jerome, and John Chrysostom protested against economic inequality and called upon all Christians to renounce the concept of "mine" and "thine." Chrysostom's thinking on this point relied as much on natural law as on the New Testament:

> The beginning and root of wealth must lie in injustice of some sort. And why? Because, in the beginning, God did not create one person wealthy and another to go wanting. . . . He gave one and the same earth to all alike. And, inasmuch as the earth is a common possession, how is it that you have acres and acres of land, while your neighbor has not the tiniest fraction of the earth? . . . Isn't the fact that you claim sole ownership of what belongs to the Lord, of what is common property, something evil?[22]

Not all the Fathers were so hostile to wealth. Clement of Alexandria made it clear that the wealthy had an important role to play in the Christian community, as dispensers of charity. Augustine, too, thought that rich people could be saved, and he saw economic injustice as part of God's inscrutable plan: "The Lord made the rich in order to come to the aid of the poor, and the poor in order to prove the rich."[23] Both ways of thinking coexisted uneasily among Christians throughout the Middle Ages.

Naturally, poverty was exalted among monastics. Several reform movements attacked social and ecclesiastical corruption by appealing to the monastic poverty ethic, employing both natural law arguments and appeals to revelation. Some of these movements were incorporated into the church, such as that of Francis of Assisi, who established a monastic order devoted to poverty. Others, however, such as the Waldensians (twelfth century) and the more radical followers of Francis (thirteenth to fourteenth centuries) were declared heretical. The issue remained controversial: was property-owning natural or not? Christian or un-Christian? Thomas Aquinas, a member of the Dominicans, an order committed to poverty, employed natural law arguments to defend the appropriateness of private ownership among Christians, and it was this kind of thinking that prevailed.

The Reformation

The changes brought about by the Reformation in the sixteenth century were at once sudden and profound, both in a theological and a practical sense. The most radical departure made from medieval ethical thinking was the rejection of what Luther called "works righteousness," that is, the idea that individual Christians are either saved or damned on account of their behavior. Martin Luther, Ulrich Zwingli, John Calvin, and most other Reformers denied the capacity of humans to influence God's judgment: one was saved by God's grace, freely given, not by any merit one could earn through virtuous deeds. Convinced of the total depravity of human nature, Protestants believed that it was impossible for the human will to avoid sin. Since all Christians were sinners, their salvation depended not on their actions, but rather on God's forgiveness. One could do nothing to earn or merit God's saving grace. After closely studying Paul's letters, Luther came to the following conclusion and sparked a religious revolution in the process:

Reformation and Counter-Reformation at the End of the 16th Century

Lutheran Region

Reformed region (Calvinists, Zwinglians)

Calvinist minority in France

Anglican region

★ important center of Reformation

■ important Protestant university

▨ area of mixed religion (Catholics, Protestants)

Catholic region

Catholic minority in Protestant region

☆ center of Catholic Counter-Reformation

□ principal Jesuit college at end of 16th century

area regained by Catholicism at end of 16th century

mission region dependant on the congregation for spreading the faith

> Since works justify no one . . . it is very evident that it is faith alone which, because of
> the pure mercy of God through Christ and in his Word, worthily and sufficiently jus-
> tifies the person.[24]

Ultimately, this meant that one had to be predestined or chosen by God, for if redemption was an unearned gift, then only the giver (God) had the power to decide who would be saved. Luther shied away from predestinarian theology but pressed nonetheless for an understanding of salvation as freely and mysteriously given by God. It would be John Calvin who would take this theology to its logical conclusion:

> Scripture, then, clearly shows that God once established by His eternal and un-
> changeable plan those whom He long before determined once and for all to receive
> into salvation; and those whom, on the other hand, he would devote to destruction.
> We assert that, with respect to the elect, this plan was founded upon His freely given
> mercy, without regard to human worth; but by His just and irreprehensible but in-
> comprehensible judgment, he has barred the door of life to those whom he has given
> over to damnation.[25]

This teaching had immense practical consequences. To begin with, it did away with the need for confession: forgiveness now came directly from God, not from any priest. More significantly, this teaching undermined the concept of holiness that had been so central to medieval Catholics and to the Orthodox. One could fast to excess, go without sleep, pray ceaselessly, and perform constant works of mercy, and one would still be a sinner in God's eyes. This meant, of course, that the monastic ethic was useless to Protestants, as was the distinction between the cloister and the world. Since Protestants thus thought of "holiness" and "purity" as unrealistic expectations, they could no longer consider virginity and celibacy a virtue. On the contrary, the Protestant Reformers railed against celibacy as unnatural, calling instead for an exaltation of marriage and child rearing. Furthermore, the rejection of "works righteousness" also led to the abandonment of the doctrine of purgatory and of everything connected with it, such as prayers and masses for the dead.

Saying that virtue cannot save, however, is not the same as saying that virtue is unnecessary. Protestants may have reformulated Christian ethics according to what they saw as scriptural norms, but they did not at all advocate abandoning the divine law. Paradoxically, Prostestantism aimed to revive a stricter Christian ethic. This stemmed from the fact that Protestants believed that if one received the gift of grace, one would necessarily become a good person. Works were, in fact, still required, but in the Protestant formulation, they were seen as *flowing* from salvation rather than as *causing* salvation. As Luther said:

> We do not, therefore, reject good works; on the contrary, we cherish and teach them
> as much as possible. We do not condemn them for their own sake but on account
> of . . . the perverse idea that righteousness is to be sought through them.[26]

Among Reformed Protestants, especially Calvinists, this reformulation of the relation between works and salvation led to the creation of rigidly structured societies in which good Christian behavior was strictly enforced. In Calvin's Geneva—and subsequently in most Calvinist communities—the law of the church became the law of the land, and the Christian elites policed the community's behavior through a court known as the "consistory." Attention to detail was not spared. In Geneva, for instance, anyone who used foul language or took God's name in vain could be punished. Gambling was strictly forbidden, as were "indecent" songs and dances or "lewd" forms of apparel. Every tavern in Geneva had a Bible, and for some time the authorities insisted on appointed times of Bible reading in the taverns. Innkeepers were to ensure that all their guests were in bed by nine at night and were also required to inform the consistory of any improper conduct. Even the names one could give to one's children and pets were carefully regulated. One man who named his dog Calvin found himself imprisoned on bread and water for several days. This was the kind of society that God's elect expected to have, for their covenant, or pact, with God made it necessary for the community as a whole to live righteously and avoid God's wrath. Rather than stifling human effort, the doctrine of predestination thus increased the need for good works and a godly, law-fearing society.

Among the Radicals, especially the Anabaptists, separation from the world was considered necessary, for they believed the true church should be composed only of genuine believers. Curiously, most of the Anabaptists continued to believe in the cooperation of the human will with God's grace and therefore to profess the necessity of good works for salvation. Most Anabaptists established separatist communities in which good Christian behavior was expected. One of their chief manifestos, *The Schleitheim Confession*, explained it succinctly:

> A separation shall be made from the evil and from the wickedness which the devil planted in the world; in this manner, simply that we shall not have fellowship with the wicked and not run with them in the multitude of their abominations. . . . For truly all creatures are in but two classes, good and bad, believing and unbelieving, darkness and light, the world and those who have come out of the world . . . and none can have part with the other.[27]

Separating from the world also meant abandoning all forms of violence for most Anabaptists, including using the sword in self-defense or having law courts, prisons, and executioners. Some Anabaptist communities, such as the Hutterites, sought full conformity to the New Testament church by denouncing the concept of private ownership and practicing full communal sharing of all goods and property. Since most of them did not believe in coercion, they policed behavior through excommunication. Anabaptist communities expected more or less the same kind of puritanical behavior as Calvin's Geneva but enforced it differently. Whereas in Geneva one would be imprisoned, fined, or executed, among the Anabaptists one would be merely shunned or expelled.

Some Anabaptists, however, took to violent revolution, as at Münster (1534–1536), where they freely used the sword for warfare and the enforcement of Christian law. The extremists at Münster saw themselves as the chief players in an apocalyptic drama and were convinced that God was beginning his Kingdom on earth through them. Thinking they were the New Jerusalem prophesied in the *Book of Revelation,* the Münster Anabaptists established what they considered a fully biblical ethic that included the communal sharing of all property and the practice of polygamy (having more than one wife). Somehow, the elders of this New Jerusalem found biblical justification for the beheading of all women who refused their offers of marriage. As the city lay under siege and its food supply began to dwindle, rumors began to circulate that the Münsterites were eating human flesh, presumably from the corpses of those they had routinely beheaded. "This must be what they mean by 'right baptism'," observed one unsympathetic chronicler of these events.

The New Jerusalem at Münster was wiped out in 1536 through the combined efforts of Lutheran and Catholic armies. Nonetheless, although they could agree that communities such as Münster Anabaptist were dangerous, the fractured churches of Christian Europe could not agree on much else. When their quarrel turned violent in the second half of the sixteenth century, the ethics of Western Christians became a scandal to some, especially among the educated elite. In the seventeenth century, it became increasingly difficult for an unbeliever to speak as Tertullian says that pagans spoke in the third century: "See how those Christians love one another." Once again, the relation between Christianity and the world entered a period of redefinition.

Virtue and Conscience

In the view of the second-century Christian writer Clement of Alexandria, a Christian does good not because of the promise of reward or the prospect of eternal damnation in hell, but solely "so as to pass life after the image and likeness of the Lord." We have seen, however, how the rank and file have been acutely concerned with the relationship between their thoughts and actions and their fate in an afterlife. Christian meditation on punishment for evil deeds and faithlessness was widely represented in literary and pictorial images of eternal torment, and in early modern Europe, the fear of hell was fundamental to Christian consciousness. The figure of God as a judge who sentenced human souls to unquenchable fire found expression in a wide range of genres, not the least of which was John Milton's *Paradise Lost* (1667), which depicted

> a region dolorous,
> O'er many a frozen, many a fiery alp,
> Rocks, caves, lakes, fens, bogs, dens, and shades of death,
> A universe of death, which God by curse
> Created evil, for evil only good,
> Where all life dies, death lives, and nature breeds,
> Perverse, all monstrous, all prodigious things,
> Abominable, unutterable, and worse
> Than fables yet have feigned, or fear conceived,
> Gorgons and hydras, and chimeras dire. (II, 619–628)

In the eighteenth century, the figure of God the angry judge gave ground to a merciful God who offered heavenly rewards to the faithful. The reconception of

God as a forgiving comforter attenuated the fear of hell and jibed with the emerging notion of ethics as the science of the cultivation of virtue. In other words, the context for ethical reflection began to shift from nervousness about punishment for failure to hopefulness about success in living morally. The Enlightenment contributed the key elements to this translation: the postulation of cosmic uniformity and regularity and trust in the human capability to detect that cosmic order through science. Previous Christian emphases on inherent human sinfulness, ongoing cosmic battles between good and evil, and uncompromising law as revealed in the Bible were progressively softened, so that by the late eighteenth century, a few Christians came to reject the notion of hell entirely and embraced "universalism," or universal salvation.

The desire of Christians to lead a moral life by no means evaporated, however, as fear of hell became less dominant in Christian psychology. In fact, the Enlightenment brought with it an unprecedented interest in what came to be called "moral philosophy." Beginning in the eighteenth century, Protestant theologians tended to translate questions about good and evil into philosophical inquiries about ways in which persons could cultivate virtue. Visions of hell still loomed in the background of Protestant reflection on personal conduct, but the emphasis had decisively shifted to defining and promoting virtue as the pathway to knowing God. It is clear that the eighteenth century did not invent the notion that the practice of virtue brought one close to God. But Protestant thinking about the nature of Christian life increasingly took on a tone of confidence in reason to identify the virtuous course and to embrace it. Moral philosophy thus emerged as a vaguely scientific and optimistic program aimed at developing models for human good by studying the order in creation as a whole.

Some models for the moral life were constructed out of critical philosophical and theological arguments. (Precedents for this included traditional Roman Catholic "Thomism," or focus on the systematic theology of St. Thomas Aquinas.) Writing at length about the nature of God, the capabilities of humans, and the proper ends of life, theologians across a spectrum ranging from Jonathan Edwards in New England to Immanuel Kant in Germany sought to articulate religious ethics within the framework of the methods and questions that characterized the Age of Reason. In a few cases—as with Kant—moral philosophers all but reduced Christian doctrine solely to ethics, rejecting miracles, mysterious rituals, and prayer as superstition. Edwards sought to demonstrate that morality was logically grounded in piety, in consciousness of the beauty and majesty of God, and that virtue grew alongside piety. In general, the swing to moral philosophy affected Prostestantism through its conceptualization of virtue as simultaneously the worship of God and a rational program to achieving personal happiness. From this thinking arose the nineteenth-century emphasis on "conscience" and the fullblown emergence of "moral religion."

Conscience had been around for a while. The popular "morality play" of the fourteenth and fifteenth centuries, which was produced in the church or churchyard and pitted vice against virtue was a harbinger of the interest in conscience in later centuries. Premodern Christian views of conscience consist essentially in a confidence that Christians would act morally even though they sometimes were unable to explain the precise nature of their belief. Conscience was a kind of guide to spiritual growth. As trust grew that humans were capable to know order in creation, conscience acquired a more detailed meaning as a human faculty, alongside reason, that made sense of the world. Most important, it came to be associated (like reason) with "scientific" processes of gathering and interpreting data about the cosmos, and in the case of conscience, especially the information that a person needed in order to choose between good and evil. Such was the picture of conscience that took shape in treatises devoted to it. One of these was the English Puritan William Perkins's *Discourse on Conscience,* which at the beginning of the seventeenth century was already achieving popularity that would last for a century and a half. Various other writers—Joseph Butler, Catherine Beecher, and Thomas Brown, among others—spun theories accenting different aspects of the workings of conscience. Indeed, the Protestant confidence in the faculty of conscience was a significant contribution to the modern development of Western notions about the self.

Reason and conscience were fundamental to the new moral philosophy and thus were fundamental to the cultivation of virtue. Naturally, then, Christians sought practical outlets for the awakened conscience in a spectrum of movements for personal and moral reform. Roman Catholicism had long emphasized the role of conscience in moral life, but for Catholics, the exercise of conscience was heavily conditioned by church precepts (and Catholic "moral theology" had its distinctive elements, as we see momentarily). But this does not not seem to have mattered in the organization of myriad conscientious projects of reform after 1800. Undertaken by both Catholics and Protestants, such reform movements were in many cases led by laity and often were organized around a rallying cry of duty and responsibility. Emblematic of the rush to embrace Christian duty were the missionary societies that were organized and flourished in the nineteenth century. Other kinds of moral reform movements targeted literally every aspect of life from personal diet, to sexual relations, to transactions with the state, to childrearing and to economic order. In each case, reformers characterized their activities as the Christian response to conscience. In the mid-twentieth century, the Reverend Martin Luther King Jr. articulated this view of Christianity in a series of sermons, "The Trumpet of Conscience" (1967), in which he called for conscientious objection to war, racism, and social injustice.

Justice

The Social Gospel and Liberation Theology clearly illustrate the theme of social justice that has become prominent in post-Enlightenment Christianity. The Social Gospel refers to an assortment of movements in Europe and North America that began to take shape in the mid-nineteenth century. Both Christians and Jews, influenced by nascent socialist ideologies, sought more aggressively to articulate the relationship between religious faith and moral responsibility. In the case of Christians, this endeavor unfolded as an attempt to chart a course of reform that would realize a Kingdom of God on earth; for Jews, it developed in connection with the nativity of modern Zionism. In both cases, fresh articulations of social justice set the terms for theological revision.

The Anglican clergyman Frederick Denison Maurice, the son of a Unitarian minister, was concerned above all with fostering actual unity among Christians. He criticized the fragmentation of Christianity into competing groups, condemned the churches' dereliction of their duty to tend to the lower classes, and offered an alternative vision of *The Kingdom of Christ* (1837) that he claimed was characterized by unity, equality, and justice. His vision was refined in England by Charles Kingsley, in Germany by Adolf Stöcker and Hermann Kutter, in Canada by Salem G. Bland, and in America by Washington Gladden and Walter Rauschenbusch. The last of these penned a manifesto entitled *Christianity and the Social Crisis* (1907) in order to "discharge a debt" to the working people in his New York congregation. In his work, he emphasized the social message of the Old Testament prophets and argued for the inseparableness of religion and ethics. The Roman Catholic seminary professor John A. Ryan similarly endeavored in *The Living Wage* (1906) and other writings to articulate principles of social justice and to explain their relevance to remedying unequal distribution of wealth.

In spite of the similarity of purpose in Rauschenbusch's and Ryan's advocacy of social reform, Roman Catholic approaches to questions of right and wrong and of duty and virtue developed in a context of theological reflection that differs in certain ways from the general framework of Protestant ethics. "Moral theology" designates the Roman Catholic counterpart of Protestant "religious ethics." Both have to do with the identification and embrace of good and the avoidance of evil. But Catholic moral theology developed in connection with the sacrament of penance, as a system to orient the priest in his role in that ritual. Like a Jewish rabbi whose juridical role is grounded in his familiarity of halakhah, a priest operates as a teacher and as a judge or evaluator within the range of his expertise in a body of canon law (i.e., official church teaching). Roman Catholic moral theology in general differs from Protestant ethics by virtue of its specificity, comprehensiveness, and unflinching deductive argumentation.

So, for example, Ryan's call for reform of the socioeconomic order was grounded in "natural philosophy," in a clear appeal to the "natural right" to know and love God. Ryan systematically deduced from that principle the specific proposal of $2.10 per day as a minimum living wage. Rauschenbusch, on the other hand, pointed out that Scripture taught that the leading theme in the teachings of Jesus and the prophets was social justice and that Christians should endeavor to devise ways to apply that lesson to their immediate circumstances.

In short, the language of Protestant ethics tends to be biblical, shaped by lessons about right and wrong revealed in Scripture. Moreover, it is a responsive ethic in the sense that it adjusts its approach to ethical argument in order to answer specific ethical problems as they surface in a culture. Catholic moral theology, on the other hand, stresses what are believed to be universal philosophical truths and represents a drive for absolute moral specificity and certitude, applicable across time and place. Both of these currents of ethical thinking have been reinforced by the culture of the Enlightenment: Protestant religious ethics have emphasized the experiences of the individual within changing historical contexts, whereas Catholic moral theology has displayed the Enlightenment's promotion of natural order, uniformity, and law.

In the second half of the twentieth century, some measure of common ground has opened between Protestant ethics and Catholic moral theology. As might be expected, this has been displayed most prominently in theological reflection on social reform and above all in the rise of liberation theology in Latin America in the 1960s. Liberation theology, which coalesced around the ideas of Roman Catholic writers such as Gustavo Gutierrez, is based on the belief that a rational unity of theory and practice (or praxis) must precede actual theologizing. That is, Christians must be dedicated to justice for the poor and oppressed as a precondition to forming a theological ethic. Explicit in this view is the claim that social and economic problems are not a fault of nature (including human nature), but rather are a consequence of structural inequalities native to capitalist institutions. By thus stressing the conditioning nature of the particular historical context, inequalities rooted in modern capitalism, Roman Catholic liberation theologians detoured around traditional Catholic emphases on undifferentiated, universal natural order. They said, as it were, "Sensitivity to the specific, real problems of the poor and oppressed in Latin America, not uncritical embrace of the abstract arguments and principles of natural law theology, form the starting point for thinking about morality." In so doing, they joined forces with Protestant theologians whose ethics took shape as a response to their perceptions of the dynamics of power in specific cultures. For Catholic writers, like some Protestants before them, this has opened up the possibility of acknowledging moral pluralism.

The theme of justice in religious ethics that has been increasingly visible in two centuries of reform movements now characterizes the writing of Protestant and Roman Catholic feminist theologians. The notion of justice present in movements such as the Social Gospel has been significantly reworked by some feminist ethicists, however. In order to appreciate how this has happened, we must recognize that Enlightenment trust in reason and laws of nature has been undermined in recent decades by postmodern theories claiming the impossibility of objectivity in thinking about existence. The emphasis on wholeness, on coherent interrelatedness, remains essential to Christian writings about morality, however. Feminist writers have been particularly vocal in stressing this ecological aspect of ethics. Ecology does not here refer specifically to the natural environment (water, atmosphere, trees, etc.), but rather more broadly to an intuition of oneness and interconnectedness in all life. The seventeenth-century writer Spinoza's outright identification of God with nature (monism) opened the door to theorizing about ethics as protectiveness and care toward all life. The rise of quantum mechanics in twentieth-century physics, which has led to popularized arguments for the universe as an integrated system in which matter and force are relative, also has contributed to recent ethical theory. Ecological ethics as envisioned by Christian

A Worldwide Roman Catholic Church

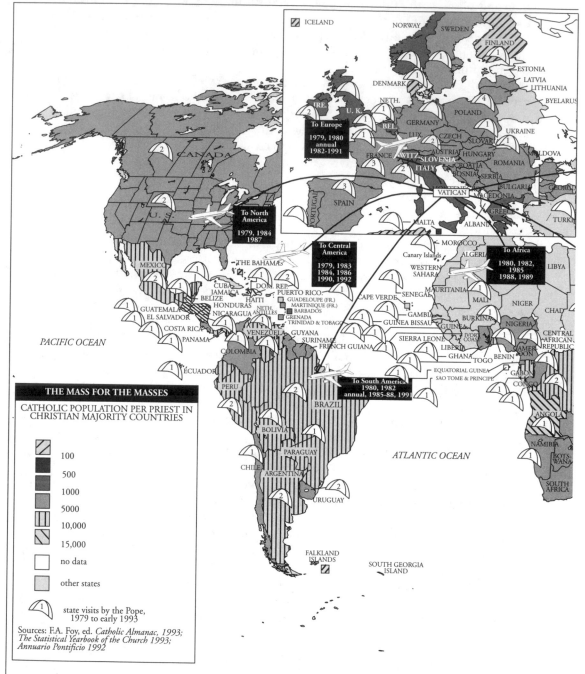

THE MASS FOR THE MASSES

CATHOLIC POPULATION PER PRIEST IN CHRISTIAN MAJORITY COUNTRIES

- 100
- 500
- 1000
- 5000
- 10,000
- 15,000
- no data
- other states
- state visits by the Pope, 1979 to early 1993

Sources: F.A. Foy, ed. *Catholic Almanac, 1993;*
The Statistical Yearbook of the Church 1993;
Annuario Pontificio 1992

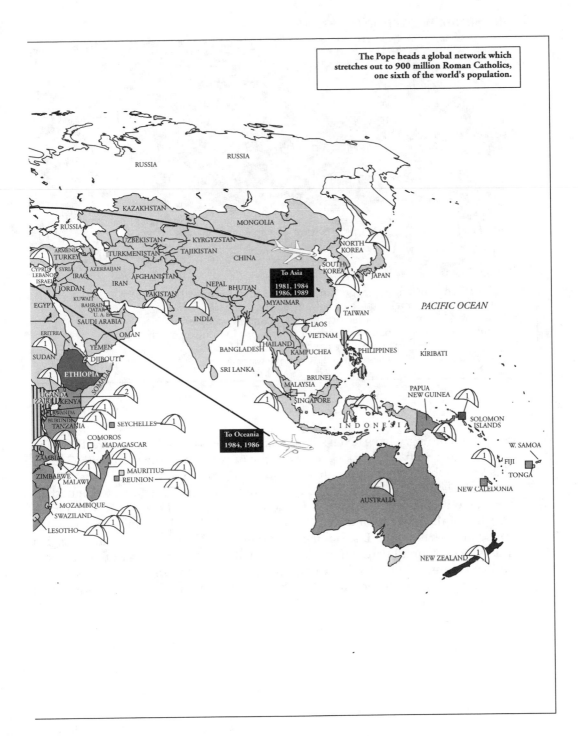

The Pope heads a global network which
stretches out to 900 million Roman Catholics,
one sixth of the world's population.

RUSSIA

RUSSIA

KAZAKHSTAN

MONGOLIA

UZBEKISTAN   KYRGYZSTAN   NORTH
RUSSIA   KOREA
ARMENIA TURKMENISTAN TAJIKISTAN
TURKEY   CHINA   SOUTH
CYPRUS SYRIA AZERBAIJAN   KOREA   JAPAN
LEBANON IRAQ   To Asia
ISRAEL   AFGHANISTAN   1981, 1984
JORDAN   IRAN   NEPAL BHUTAN 1986, 1989
EGYPT   KUWAIT PAKISTAN   MYANMAR   TAIWAN
BAHRAIN   PACIFIC OCEAN
QATAR
U. A. E.
SAUDI ARABIA   OMAN   INDIA   LAOS
ERITREA   VIETNAM
YEMEN   BANGLADESH THAILAND
SUDAN   DJIBOUTI   SRI LANKA   KAMPUCHEA   PHILIPPINES   KIRIBATI
1
ETHIOPIA SOMALIA   BRUNEI
UGANDA   MALAYSIA   PAPUA
ZAIRE KENYA   2   SINGAPORE   NEW GUINEA   SOLOMON
RWANDA   ISLANDS
BURUNDI 1   SEYCHELLES   1   INDONESIA   W. SAMOA
TANZANIA   1
COMOROS   To Oceania   FIJI
ZAMBIA   MADAGASCAR   1984, 1986   TONGA
1   NEW CALEDONIA
ZIMBABWE MAURITIUS
MALAWI REUNION   1
1
MOZAMBIQUE   AUSTRALIA
SWAZILAND   1
LESOTHO

NEW ZEALAND 1

321

Ben Shahn, *WCTU Parade* (1933–1934)

Christian reform movements ran the gamut from organizations for the improvement of the morals of children to societies that agitated for the rights of factory laborers. Women occupied important roles in many such organizations, but in none as much as in the campaign against the consumption of alcoholic beverages. (*Source:* © Museum of the City of New York)

writers accordingly have taken shape as an emphasis on calls for a transition from self-love to a realization of oneness with the universe and therefore with God. In this view, which is sometimes referred to as "deep ecology" for its emphasis on ways of seeing and valuing that emerge from a sense of cosmic interconnectedness, an ethics of duty is naturally replaced by an ethics of care. That is, duty as a sacrifice of the interests of the ego in favor of the "other" is no longer relevant because there is no other. Instead, the self progressively unfolds outward in such a way that care for all nature (including persons) is experienced as care for the self. Justice is thus reinterpreted as care. Not surprisingly, theorists who work in this area have drawn upon nondualistic religions such as Buddhism as reinforcement for a Christian ecological ethics.

CHAPTER 15

ETHICS

IN ISLAM

ENJOINING THE GOOD AND FORBIDDING THE EVIL

A corollary to the belief in only one God is the affirmation that this God is the source of all values and norms. Islam, like its older siblings Judaism and Christianity, can be characterized as "ethical monotheism." We described Islam as a monotheistic creed in Chapter 6, and it was apparent that humans are called not only to obey God but also to reflect his goodness and justice in the structures and processes of individual and communal life in the umma. In this chapter, we discover the principal ways by which Muslims discern what is right, just, and good and how they seek to live in accordance with these ways.

The Islamic term for ethics is *akhlāq*. Muslim thinkers have contributed much to the history of ethical discourse as a branch of philosophy. But the Muslim community as a whole has not so much raised the question of "What is the good and how shall I realize it?" as to assert that "God is the source of all value and he has commanded me to live the good life by obeying his commands." Thus, ethics in Islam is much more a matter of living by the Shari'a than of reflecting on moral questions. Islamic ethics are enacted more than they are thought about. Nevertheless, such a strong institutionalization of moral precepts and prescribed attitudes and acts assumes a general theory of value, a "metaphysic of morals," as it were, holding it up and sustaining it. This ultimate structure of meaning and purpose is rarely, if ever, questioned by Muslims, for whom it is as familiar and self-evidently reliable as is the air they breathe.

The classical place for approaching the Islamic idea of good and evil is not in the abstract, philosophical realm but in behavior. The Qur'an several times commands the believers to "enjoin the good and forbid the evil." It is interesting to examine the two Arabic terms that are here rendered as "good" and "evil." The first is *ma'rūf* and the second *munkar*. Ma'ruf derives from a root meaning "to know," "be aware," "discover," "approve." A potent religious term derived from the same root is *ma'rifa*, "gnosis," that is, the saving knowledge that the Sufi mystic seeks through spiritual disciplines. Ma'rifa is a kind of enlightenment. Ma'ruf, on the other hand, is what is "known" in the sense of what is acceptable, standard moral behavior; it is what is "approved," as well. It does not take a genius, Islam seems to hold, to know what is right and acceptable behavior. Nor does it require literacy, as if direct access to scripture or moral tracts provided otherwise unavailable insight into matters of right and wrong. The Qur'an is necessary, of course, but it is written in a "clear Arabic speech," as it describes itself, and was not originally available to Muhammad and his hearers as a written text. Rather, it was principally a recited message, preserved in the minds and hearts of the Muslims. Munkar, the wrong, derives from an Arabic root that means "not to know," "to deny," and "to renege." Munkar may also mean "denied," "disowned," "shocking," and "abominable."

Notice that neither ma'ruf nor munkar means, in itself, "good" or "evil" in an abstract or essential sense. The terms signify acts, states, and things that are either acceptable or unacceptable, owned or disowned, the knowledge of which is derived from both revelation and human reason. The Mu'tazilite rationalist theologians, introduced in Chapter 6, were intensely concerned with matters of right and wrong. Their general position was that human reason can discern universal right and wrong and judge people's acts accordingly. They acknowledged God as one who always wills and acts justly according to a universal standard, which is perfectly reasonable and intelligible. An act is not right because God declares it such; rather an act is right according to universal justice, which God upholds and follows. The old German hymn "Whate'er my God ordains is right" would be true for the Mu'tazilites, only in the sense that God always chooses the true, the good, and the just before he ordains anything.

The Mu'tazilite position that acknowledges humankind's rational ability to distinguish good from evil carried with it the imperative to believe and act in the strictest ethical manner, examining motives and carefully deliberating which actions to perform or avoid. Humans, according to this view, possess free will and with it an awful responsibility in acting as God's "caliphs" on earth. Liberal Western scholars have sometimes admired the Mu'tazilite position as just described, but they have not always considered the human cost. This theological movement pursued moral, theological, and political correctness in a relentless manner. At one point in its history, when it was accepted as the official court theological system in Baghdad, a harsh inquisition (*miḥna*) was instituted to ferret out deviants among the religious and legal scholars and force them to comply with the Mu'tazilite vision of the good. One of the victims of Mu'tazilite hegemony was the legal scholar Ahmad ibn Hanbal (d. 855), who refused to assent to the dominant group's position that the Qur'an was created in time rather than being eternal. Many religious scholars submitted to the official view of the court theology. Although Ibn Hanbal

The Traditional Lands of Islamic Civilization

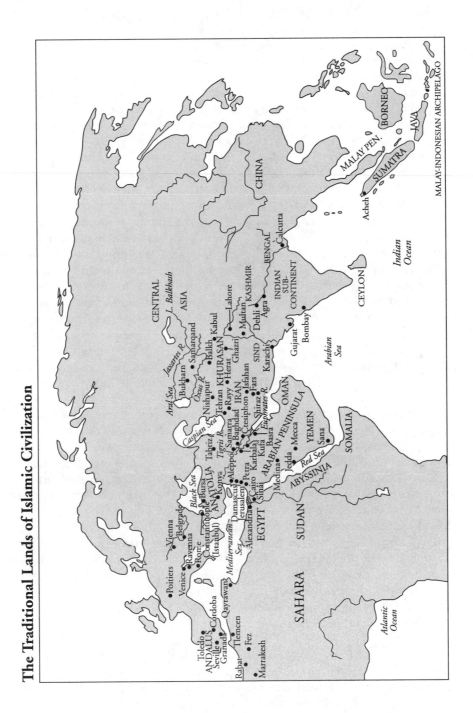

was imprisoned and whipped, he did not change his beliefs. He was later exonerated by the succeeding caliph, and his views came to be accepted, as a groundswell of contrary theological and moral sentiment met the Mu'tazilite challenge and ultimately overthrew it in the name of a populist Islam that has dominated until the present in Sunni regions.

The phrase "Whate'er my God ordains is right" would mean, for the pious opposition to Mu'tazilism, "Whatever is good and true and just is so because God has willed it, not because of an independent, universal criterion of abstract good and evil." The highest good is God's eternal, inscrutable decree. God does not act according to an external standard of right and wrong; his actions are good and just because he performs them. He is the criterion of all value in the universe. If rational contradictions arise when humans attempt to answer difficult moral questions—such as Job's asking why evildoers prosper and good folk suffer—then Muslims must seek only God's pleasure and patiently endure all misfortune and calamity without questioning God's motives or acts. "God is with those who patiently endure," the Qur'an teaches (2:153), while they maintain regular worship, as well. That is, patient endurance uninformed by a relationship with God is not enough; dumb suffering is surrendering to evil rather than resisting it by means of the sacred combat of jihad, which requires above all prayer and patience.

A practical example of how Muslims view acceptable and unacceptable conduct is in the dietary law prohibiting pork. Although people do sometimes become ill from eating improperly prepared pork dishes, most people have been safely consuming pork since prehistory. An informed Muslim, when asked about the prohibition of pork, will say that Muslims avoid it altogether because God has forbidden it. The important thing for such a person is obeying God, without seeking subsidiary reasons for so doing. However, there is often speculation of a "medical materialist" kind, arguing that God knows what is good for us and prevents us from dangerous substances in the natural world. The consumption of pork is, for Muslims, munkar, that is "not recognized," "disowned," and "abominable."

An important consequence of Islam's dietary and purification laws is the setting apart of Muslims as a special community. The abstention from pork, for Muslims as for Jews, is a powerful boundary marker. This marking is not so evident in an all-Muslim society, such as Saudi Arabia or Iran. But in Malaysia, where Malay Muslims number about 55 percent and Chinese (who are mostly non-Muslim) 34 percent, the dietary prohibitions of both pork and alcohol have visible social and political consequences. Many Chinese enjoy both pork and alcoholic beverages. Simply to be brushed up against by a (non-Muslim) Chinese person, for example in the market, may cause a pious Malay Muslim to recoil in disgust. The pork-handling, whiskey-drinking outsider has brought pollution up close. It matters not whether a particular Chinese drinks alcohol or eats pork; he or she represents a *class* of human beings for whom those substances are lawful. Similar thoughts fill Muslims' minds when dealing with Westerners, and migration from a Muslim society to England, Germany, or America raises mixed feelings. Freedom of religion, in the West, is also freedom from religion if a person chooses it. So the dietary prohibitions take on added meaning when Muslims struggle to maintain their Islamic identity as a minority in a context of secularism and religious pluralism.

The "Five Categories" or "Principles" of Actions

Islam, as an orthoprax religion emphasizing laws and behavior, is not simply formalistic, overlooking interior aspects of motives, habits, drives, weaknesses, wickedness, and the like. Most things are neutral with respect to the Shari'a. And the moral as well as the legal status of any act is considered only with respect to the actor's intention. That is, a technically illegal or even immoral act may be rendered lawful if the agent's intention is sincere according to Islamic principles. An example follows.

Islamic law maintains five principles by which acts are to be categorized in light of divine authority. They are briefly described as follows, although it should be understood that a considerable commentarial literature accompanies them.

1. *Wājib* or *farḍ*: "obligatory," "absolutely required." Examples: the "Five Pillars," purification. Performance of such a duty is rewarded by God whereas nonperformance is punished. Usually, the punishment is understood to be in God's hands, but in strict Muslim societies—Malaysia and Iran, for example—breaking the Ramadan fast improperly, socializing with a nonfamily member of the opposite sex, and other acts may also be punished by an Islamic court.

2. *Mandūb*: "recommended." An example is extra prayers beyond the required salat. Performance is rewarded, but nonperformance is not punished. Acts in this category are also called sunna, but not in the sense that they derive from the custom of the Prophet Muhammad.

3. *Mubāh*: "permissible." A very wide category, by no means uniform with respect to qualities. Something may be permissible in that it does not entail disobeying God. It is a matter of indifference to God whether a person prefers chocolate over nougat, silk over wool, or red over blue. But it is another matter when one is forced to commit an otherwise forbidden act in order to survive, for example, eating pork when no other food is available and when starvation threatens otherwise. What is ordinarily not permitted becomes permitted in such a situation. Concerning the eating of pork and other forbidden meat, the Qur'an says, in mitigation of an extreme situation:

> But if one is forced by extreme necessity, without willful disobedience, nor transgressing due limits—then he is guiltless. For Allah is Oft-Forgiving, Most Merciful. (2:173)

Mubah prescribes neither reward nor punishment.

4. *Makrūh*: "reprehensible." This category does not prohibit certain acts or substances, although it abominates them. Not to perform a mandub (recommended) action does not bring censure or punishment. Similarly, performing a mubah act does not bring either (although one legal school holds that certain makruh acts invoke moral blame but are not punished[1]). Interestingly, not performing what is recommended is makruh, abominable, even though what is simply recommended and meritorious is not obligatory. The hearts and minds of morally discerning Muslims are frequently agitated by questions of whether they

Camel Boy at Wadi Rum

(*Source:* F. M. Denny)

are following the right path in a variety of behaviors. That is one reason why practical manuals of Qur'anic and Sunna behavior are so popular. The Prophet once said that "The most abominable of permitted things is divorce." Makruh is the "lowest degree of prohibition."[2] Sometimes it comes close to the fifth and final principle, *ḥarām*, "forbidden" acts. An example of an act that is very close to haram is the wearing of gold or silk by men. Such behavior is not forbidden, but its avoidance is rewarded by God.

Ḥalāl: Before considering the fifth principle, mention should be made of the concept of *ḥalāl*, that which is permissible to Muslims. Most moral decision making by Muslims is occupied with questions of permission and prohibition. The five principles themselves occupy a spectrum of permitted and prohibited things. So, a Muslim seeks always to secure halal foods and to perform halal acts. The category makruh, considers the many things that seem to fall somewhere between halal and haram, and thus cause uneasiness and doubt.

5. *Ḥarām*: "forbidden." This term is a particularly rich one for students of religion, because it perfectly embodies the ambiguity of the sacred. The Arabic root *ḥ-r-m* produces several important words: *ḥaram*, "sanctuary"; *ḥarīm*, the female members of a household, the "harem"; *iḥrām*, the state of ritual consecration during the pilgrimage to Mecca (the pilgrim is also known as a *muḥrim*, "ritually consecrated"); *ḥurma*, "sacred, inviolate, holy," but it can also mean "woman," who must be respected and kept inviolate. The Grand Mosque in Mecca, surrounding the Kaʿaba, is known in Arabic as *al-masjid al-ḥarām*, "the Inviolable Worship Site."

Haram may signify prohibition of something that is impure, abominable, sinful, and the like, such as pork, alcohol, murder, adultery, and irreverence. But haram also may refer to something that is not to be violated, that is taboo because it is sacred and pure, such as the Kaʿaba. As the fifth legal category, haram means that which has been definitively forbidden by God, whether as understood from the divine word itself or in the agreement of qualified legal opinions. The technical legal literature treats this category at great length because of its occasionally ambiguous character. God may punish the commission of haram acts and reward their avoidance.

RIGHTEOUSNESS AS TRUE PIETY

The five principles do not sum up all of Islamic ethics, but they do provide clear guidance as to the legal status of most acts, as law and ethics are tightly intertwined. There is a broader sense of what informs Muslims' sense of good and right and thus animates such legalistic categories as the five principles. That is, Muslims do not look to the five principles for inspiration toward right behavior so much as for correct guidance. Goodness is not reducible to legalism. The Qur'an defines righteousness—known in Arabic as *birr*—as true piety and true piety as righteousness in the following much quoted passage:

> It is not righteousness (birr) that ye turn your faces toward east or west; but it is righteousness to believe in God and the Last Day, and the Angels, and the Book, and the Messengers; to spend of your substance, out of love for Him, for your kin, for orphans, for the needy, for the wayfarer, for those who ask, and for the ransom of slaves; to be steadfast in worship (salat) and regular in almsgiving (zakat), to fulfill the promises you have made; and to be firm and patient in pain and adversity and throughout all periods of panic. Such are the people of truth, the God-fearing. (2:177)

This passage nearly sums up the whole of Islam. Note the opening line about East and West; it refers to outward formalism in worship, making a public show of piety, like the hypocrites, as Jesus observed. Or, to seek a comparison with Judaism, it reflects an attitude similar to Amos's outburst when Yahweh roars: "I hate, I despise your feasts, and I take no delight in your solemn assemblies. . . . Take away from me the noise of your songs. . . . But let justice roll down like waters, and righteousness like an everflowing stream (Amos 5:21–24, Revised Standard Version). Neither Judaism nor Islam abandons worship—far from it—but each directs a severe criticism toward empty formalism and any hint that piety is a kind of bribe offered to God.

The relationship between the Muslim and God is moral only if it has an outcome in the sharing of one's resources with other people, as described in the previously quoted Qur'anic passage. But these good deeds are not primarily for others' benefit, although they should include consideration for the recipients' feelings and needs. The righteousness passage says that the believers should spend of their substance "out of love for him." Love of God entails loving acts toward our neighbors. And moral behavior resides foremost in acting out of duty, with devotion to and love of God. An act is truly moral, then, if it is done for God's sake first. This ethical position resembles the deontological (duty-based) ethics of the great German Enlightenment philosopher Immanuel Kant, who argued that an act is moral only if it is performed out of pure duty, and not principally for the pleasure or benefit of the recipient, which may produce corrupting feelings of self-satisfaction or confusion about motives.

God is the source of all good. He has created the cosmos for just ends and appointed humankind as his stewards on earth, as was noted in Chapter 6. Muslims approach God through worship in a purified state, because God is holy and just and good. Worship is a privilege and a duty. It renders the worshiper morally alert and endows him or her with the capacity to act righteously in the world, out of love of God and also out of reverential fear of God. If a Muslim fears only God, then nothing in the created order can truly harm that person, although it might snuff out his or her individual existence. The martyr in the way of God realizes paradise with God and an eternal life in company with the Lord.

FEAR AND FRIENDSHIP

The goodness at the core of God's being, expressed in mercy and compassion, is the basis of Islam as ethical monotheism. The profound ethical quality of God is based in his desire to be in mutual relationships with thinking, willing, loving beings. The Sufis love the divine saying, quoted earlier, that depicts God as a "Hidden Treasure" who wanted to be known and so created the universe for community. God is "friend" of the believer, and the believer is privileged with the invitation to be God's friend, too. But friendship with God is not easy amiability. It goes much deeper and entails accountability. God sees and knows all, yet permits his human creatures to pursue their lives in freedom.

The Central Islamic Lands

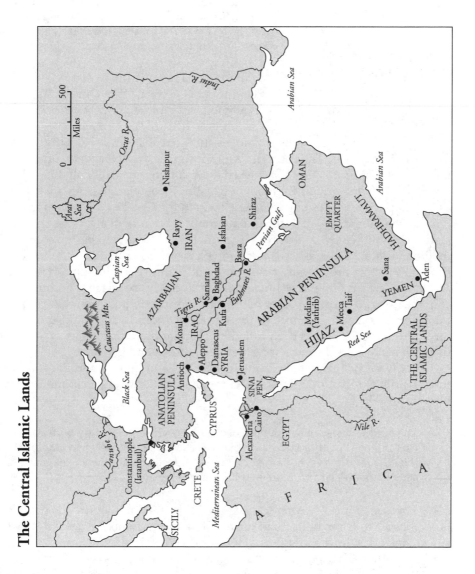

In whatever business you may be, and whatever portion you may be reciting from the Qur'an, and whatever deed you [humans] may be doing—We are Witnesses thereof when you are deeply engrossed therein. Nor is there hidden from your Lord so much as an atom's weight on earth or in heaven. And not the least and not the greatest of these things but are recorded in a clear Record. Truly, on the friends of God there is no fear, nor shall they grieve. Those who believe and are constantly on guard [against evil]—for them are glad tidings, in the life of the present and in the Hereafter. There can be no change in the words of God. That is a mighty success. (10:61–64)

Friendship and fear are odd companions in any human interrelationship, but notice the line "on the friends of God there is no fear." The Qur'an, like the Bible, recognizes two major kinds of fear: religious and nonreligious. The latter is the kind of fear mentioned in the passage just quoted. It is ordinary creaturely fear of danger and harm. The former—religious fear—involves respect, awe, moral awareness, and devotion to God. The passage about those who are "constantly on guard" contains a root that produces *taqwā*, a word that is often translated into English as "reverential fear." One prominent modern Muslim theologian has characterized taqwa as "perhaps the most important single term in the Qur'an."[3] Taqwa is the reverential fear that guards against evil and immorality because of awareness of the divine justice that ultimately shall prevail over all. But, as there is to be "no compulsion in religion" (Sura 2:256), justice is not a forced issue either but flows from conditions in which people are morally discerning and courageous in support of the truth. Taqwa is God's moral gift to humankind. It includes conscience and renders worship meaningful because prayer becomes sincere and vital through it. Taqwa is the main form of moral guidance in the world. Without it, rules and principles lack force and direction. It has been called "that inner torch that can enable one to distinguish between right and wrong, between justice and injustice."[4]

Taqwa is not always the same in strength and quality, for like conscience, it must be developed throughout a lifetime of devotion and discipline. Fazlur Rahman wrote:

> The kind of being "made public" of the inner self so poignantly portrayed as occurring on the Day of Judgment is what the Qur'an really desires to take place here in this life; for a man who can X-ray himself effectively and hence diagnose his inner state has nothing to be afraid of if his inner being goes public.[5]

The contemporary American saying "Friends don't let friends drive drunk" is applicable to Islam in its main thrust. God and humankind are not pals but are sincere friends who are in a mutual moral relationship that includes honest regard for each other. The Qur'anic Arabic term *walī*, which is sometimes translated "saint" as well as "friend," can, in addition, mean protector, guardian, and kin. Muslims are friends of God, and God is the friend of the believers. But Muslims also are called to be friends to each other, and sometimes that means exerting influence for the other's well-being. Muslim friends do not let their fellows engage in destructive, unjust behavior.

MUSLIMS "THINK GLOBALLY, ACT LOCALLY"

The "enjoining of the good and the prohibiting of evil" with which this chapter opens must be carried out at the individual-personal as well as the societal-governmental level, or it will not be realized at all in the ways envisioned by the Qur'an. "Think globally, act locally" is a popular modern saying that has meaning in the moral community of the umma. Although the umma is the worldwide community of Muslims in the most general and inclusive sense, the idea of umma also applies to regional Muslim populations that are capable of acting for their common good in the specific contexts—political, economic, social, moral—they inhabit. The Muslims in an American prison, for example, constitute an umma, with particular parameters and conditions that need to be met with a moral vision that is both creative and adaptive. The Muslims of Bosnia-Herzegovina comprise a regional umma, too, as do the Muslim minorities in other European countries.

Muslims in North America speak of establishing an umma in Canada and the United States, by which they mean a self-conscious, mutually supportive moral and spiritual community that "enjoins the good and forbids the evil." Although Islamic traditions of political unity between religion and government are not operable in European and North American countries, all of the worship and many of the personal status laws of the Shari'a can freely be observed. In Canada, where much debate has been going on in recent years about framing a new constitution, some Muslims are requesting that it recognize Shari'a laws regarding marriage, inheritance, and other matters pertaining to personal status, an area that, characteristically, combines both the legal and ethical dimensions of the Islamic view of things.

THE DEVIL IN THE DETAILS

So far in our discussion of ethics and morality in Islam, we have focused on divine commands and human responsibility. But there is more to the Islamic moral vision than these. There is also an acknowledgment of perverse evil that defies rational and responsible awareness. We were introduced to Iblis in Chapter 6. He was the angel who refused to bow down to Adam when God had commanded it of the angels. Sometimes Iblis is identified with Satan, or satans, but not always. The devil was of the jinn, those creatures made of fire that parallel humankind and have a moral nature to discern and choose the good over evil. According to the Qur'an, Satan or the devil, who preexisted humankind, is nevertheless a rival and enemy of humanity. Satan tries to insinuate himself into human affairs and win people away from loyalty to God.

Satan is extremely persuasive although not actually strong. He seeks always to beguile and deter and cajole, sometimes by appearing as a friend of humans. Human moral awareness must be alert to the wiles of Satan at all times. That is what "guarding" against evil is all about. Taqwa enables people to put up a stout defense against Satan, recognizing that evil—although it may be faceless and

Istanbul at the Waterfront

(*Source:* F. M. Denny)

impersonal—must be met personally with courage, discernment, and decision. Just when people feel secure and at rest with their Lord is the time when Satan springs traps and seduces weak, forgetful people. Often Satan appears as good, offering opportunities to achieve seemingly noble ends. But he is at base a deceiver and a killer.

Muslims believe in the actual existence of Satan, just as many Christians do. It is not acceptable to blame Satan for one's sins and failings, for humans have been created on a sound framework, a *fiṭra* that enables them to distinguish between right and wrong, justice and injustice. And the Qur'an greatly augments the innate moral compass that humans are endowed with at birth. But humans are not inevitably good and just. Rather, their fitra is the moral equipment necessary to make judgments. Revelation is absolutely necessary in order to know the right way and follow it, using the moral nature that comes with existence.

Whether most Muslims hold Satan to be a literal personality with an independent existence is not possible to determine. At the least, Satan is a personification of evil and is closely entwined in the human condition. Satan seems to stand for the evil that people do regardless of their attempts to avoid it. Sometimes Satan appears to be identified with Iblis in the Qur'an but other passages speak of "satans," impersonal evil forces that affect humans.

Although Islam does not recognize original sin, it does admit that there is mysterious wickedness in the world and that humans are the greatest purveyors of it. When a Muslim reads the Qur'an or engages in other religious activity, he or she recites the formula of "refuge-taking," namely "I take refuge with God from the accursed Satan." That formula is remarkably potent as a charm against evil and its accompanying terror. Even Muhammad was vulnerable to the wiles of Satan when he believed that God had revealed permission for the pre-Hijra Meccans to worship the "Daughters of Allah" alongside Allah at the Ka'aba sanctuary, as a compromise with the powerful, polytheistic Qurayshi oligarchs. God later admonished Muhammad for listening to those "Satanic verses" while imagining he was hearing the words of God. Henceforth, all readers of the Qur'an have had to preface their recitation with the formula of refuge taking lest Satan intervene and cause the reader to stray.

In addition to Satan is another strong notion of evil known as *ṭāghūt*. This concept is not a personification of evil, as Satan and the devil are. Rather, taghut is a principle of evil in the world:

> Let there be no compulsion in religion: sound conduct is clearly distinguished from transgression. Whoever rejects evil (*ṭāghūt*) and believes in God has grasped the strongest handhold that never breaks. (2:256)

Taghut sometimes means an idol or a false god that tempts humans to stray. But in the passage just quoted, it stands for all that is opposed to God and the Straight Path of Islam. It is interesting to note that Satan and Iblis occur mostly in the Meccan revelations of the Qur'an, before the Hijra to Medina. Taghut becomes prominent in the Medinan period, when the umma was being established and a more comprehensive system of Islamic faith and action was achieved. In a sense, taghut can be used to signify the tendencies toward *shirk*—taking something other than God as one's ultimate concern. Satan and the devil are dramatic personifications of evil, but taghut may show the face of evil and corruption to be mirror images of ourselves. Through enslavement to God, the Muslim becomes freed from the dominion of evil, although the struggle against taghut continues until death because the created order is dually divided between good and evil.

Etiquette and Morality in Islam

An important topic for treatment under the general subject of Islamic ethics is etiquette, known in Arabic as *adab*. This term means several related things, including "good manners," "refinement," "proper breeding," and "courtesy." Although the Qur'an does not contain the word adab, it provides, along with the Hadith, most of its content. Muhammad declared that "good breeding (adab) is a part of faith," and that it is a "mark of those God loves." The kinds of things that come under adab may be suggested by the following examples from a still widely used collection of Hadith dating from classical times:

Good conduct: Muhammad said: "I have been sent to complete good manners."

Actions: "There is no wisdom like efforts, no piety like self-denial, and no goodness like good conduct."

Show: "I fear for this people every hypocrite who will speak with wisdom but act unjustly."

Monkery: "Do not be excessively pious."

Patience: "Patience is half of faith."

Control of tongue: "Whoso can stand security to me for what is between his jaws and what is between his two legs, I can assure him Paradise."

Anger: "The strong man is he who can control himself at the time of anger."

Gratefulness: "Whoever is not grateful to man is not grateful to Allah."

Gifts: "Give presents to one another; for a present removes hatred."

Company and friendship: "There is no good in friendship with one who does not see for you what he sees for himself."

Pondering: "Pondering for an hour is better than divine service for a year."

Greeting: "He who greets first is free from vanity." (This applies between Muslims. Traditionally, a Muslim does not greet a non-Muslim first, but may return a greeting.)

Beard and moustache and hairs: "Natural habits are five: circumcision, shaving hairs of private parts, clipping the moustache, pairing the nails, and shaving the hairs of the armpit."

Sports and games: "He who plays backgammon has indeed disobeyed Allah and his Messenger." (Islam favors games and sports that enhance the community's fighting abilities, such as archery and horse racing. Backgammon and chess have been thought to be pastimes of effete, unmanly people; moreover they may involve gambling. Not all Muslims follow this admonition, as can abundantly be seen in such places as Cairo coffee houses at night, where the banter of men playing "tric-trac," as backgammon is known there, can be heard until very late.)[6]

ON THE BOUNDARY OF LAW AND MORALITY:
SOME CONTEMPORARY ISSUES

Earlier, we spoke of Muslims living in North America and striving to establish an Islamic environment there. We mentioned Canadian Muslims requesting that Islamic marriage laws be incorporated into a new national constitution for application to Muslim citizens, potentially an extremely vexing matter. Should a secular nation pass laws that apply only to religious minorities in their population? If members of a religious minority with special laws applying to them were to opt out of abiding by them, for example, Muslims who might not want to be regulated by Islamic marriage law, would they be subject to prosecution? Is it the state's duty to enforce the religious laws of its minorities? In Canada, an arrangement might be worked out along that line, although it is doubtful that such a situation could occur.

An especially difficult issue is the Islamic law of apostasy, which regards conversion from Islam as a capital offense, at least for males who do not recant. Muslims deeply resent other religions' attempts at proselytization of their members, but in Western countries people have the freedom to choose their own religion, change it if they wish, or have no religion at all. Yet in Islamic countries that are governed by the Shari'a, only Muslims are permitted to engage in activities aimed at converting others to their religion. Minorities are permitted to conduct their own affairs among themselves, but they may not preach their messages to Muslims. Other restrictions apply, also, such as limiting the religious buildings that can be constructed or even repaired. But in Western countries, Muslims benefit from the liberal, pluralistic laws that prevail. In France, especially, frequent angry discussions are occurring aimed at Muslim immigrants who are establishing Islamic norms of conduct there, though it would not be possible at the present time for French citizens to pursue their own religious freedom, as they know it in France, in a Muslim country such as Iran.

In the United States, the First Amendment to the Constitution recognizes a strict separation of church and state. Yet American legal jurisdictions, principally the states, do govern personal status in all kinds of ways, particularly marriage, divorce, and inheritance. It is illegal anywhere in America to have more than one spouse, and this applies to either sex. Yet Islamic law provides for up to four concurrent wives for a Muslim male, provided they are equally provided for, both financially and emotionally. As we observed in Chapter 12, much Muslim opinion has, through the centuries, considered such treatment to be an impossible condition, thus suggesting that polygamy should be practiced only in the most unusual circumstances. Nevertheless, there are many Muslims who resist anything that might infringe on their rights in this regard. If the Qur'an permits polygamy, then who can challenge the ordinance of Allah?

According to a lecture that an American Muslim leader gave to a marriage-and-family retreat sponsored by his progressive mosque in California, polygamy does occur among Muslims in America, but it is kept hidden, for obvious reasons. The people who engage in the practice believe that they are free to do so as Muslims and that, in any case, God's authority is greater than that of the secular government in the United States. This Muslim lecturer, a physician originally from Egypt, deplored the practice of polygamy in the American context and went so far as to opine that it contradicts the Shari'a under the circumstances. Why? Because it requires concealing the condition(s) of one or more of the wives, thus depriving her (them) of the full rights that marriage, as a contract, provides. In a Muslim legal environment, a polygamous household is legal and everyone has clearly defined rights as well as duties under the Shari'a. There is no scandal about a legally constituted polygamous household in an Islamic country (although many contemporary Muslims actually disapprove of polygamy—but that is another matter). However, a polygamous household in America requires deceit and furtiveness, which go against the ethics of Islam. Muslims who live in the United States, the speaker said, are subject to the laws of that country. To break a law, in this case concerning marriage, makes the agent an outlaw twice over: with respect to U.S. law and with respect to the Shari'a.

A Fiqh (jurisprudence) Council of North America is engaged in meeting the challenges posed to Muslims by life in the region. In the case of marriage, although Muslim men are permitted to have more than one wife at a time, there is no requirement that they do. Therefore, being restricted to one wife may be seen as not really interfering with the performance of the *required* duties of Islam. This discussion makes no attempt to bring this matter to a final conclusion; that will have to be done by Muslims themselves in their engagement with life in new contexts, outside the protections and requirements of life under the Shari'a. But most Muslims in the world do not live under Shari'a rule, except in voluntary ways—for example, observing the Five Pillars, avoiding haram behavior and habits, and many other behaviors that are matters of personal choice in any case—as they seek to order their lives according to Allah's Straight Path of Islam.

ETHICS

QUESTIONS FOR DISCUSSION AND REVIEW

1. A deep concern for ethics characterizes monotheism. Describe the place of ethics in each tradition. How are ethics related to revelation? To what extent are ethics embedded in scripture? How do ideas about God in each of the three traditions represent the importance of ethics to monotheism? In what ways does worship overlap the area of ethics in Judaism, Christianity, and Islam?

2. Ethics map relations between a person and God, a person and nature, and a person and other persons. How is this visible in Judaism, Christianity, and Islam? Are there differences in the manner in which ethics in these three traditions set forth understandings about these relationships? What similarities do you detect in the three ethical systems? What are the common themes? Do these traditions view the role of ethics in a similar manner? Do they articulate the ethical "problem" in the same way?

3. Religions articulate and enforce ethics in various ways. How are ethics enforced in each tradition? Why do persons act ethically? What have they to gain or lose? How are church officials involved in the articulation and implementation of ethics?

4. Ethics are constructed against specific cultural backgrounds and are adapted as those backgrounds change. What background factors influenced the development of ethics in each of the three traditions? How have Jews, Christians, and Muslims revised, supplemented, and modified ethics within various cultural settings?

5. Faith, worship, and ethics are woven together in all three traditions. How is the piety of the individual seen as a component of ethics? How has conscience represented the capabilities of the individual as a practitioner of religious ethics? How is the character of the individual related to the ethical life? In what ways has virtue been defined to reflect the responsibilities of the individual? How has each tradition combined emphases on the person and the group in ethical systems?

6. Ethics and law are closely related. How is that relationship conceived in each tradition? Are there similarities across the three traditions? What are the differences?

7. The ethical systems of Judaism, Christianity, and Islam all contain ideas about justice and charity. What are some of the ways in which these ideas appear in each tradition? In what ways do ideas about justice differ from one tradition to another? In what ways are they similar?

8. To what extent does each tradition take into account the difference between believers and nonbelievers in articulating religious ethics?

PART VI

MATERIAL CULTURE

The buildings, dress, food, paintings, musical instruments, ritual objects, and the many other material products of Judaism, Christianity, and Islam are exceptionally revealing of the world views of these religions. A picture is, indeed, sometimes worth more than a thousand words. When we look carefully at what we suppose to be even the simplest material objects associated with a tradition, we frequently discover that those objects reveal a complexity of meaning well beyond what we had expected to find.

Moreover, material culture frequently speaks for those whose voices have been only faintly present in these three traditions. The ideas and arguments contained in tomes of theology or religious law tell us much about a tradition. So also do accounts of the lives of great religious leaders and chronicles of landmark events.

Literary artifacts, however, frequently reflect the experiences of a cultural elite and the emphases of "official" religion. And whereas the rank and file membership of Judaism, Christianity, and Islam share in certain aspects of that official religion (as, for example, in universal embrace of ethical monotheism), they nevertheless often experience religious life in ways that differ from elites. Specifically, popular forms of religion include emphases that are not present in the official religion. How do we retrieve the experiences of such people? For those who have not left a trail of writings or other easily recoverable traces of their belief, material culture provides a way of entering their world. It helps us in identifying their religious interests and aspirations and in analyzing their relationship to official religion.

Material culture comes in all shapes and sizes and can be functional, decorative, built to last, or fashioned for limited use. It is always grounded in the experience of community, either reflecting dominant views among a group of persons or challenging them. We must remember, however, that Judaism, Christianity, and Islam have been in contact with one another for centuries. Accordingly, we find that the cultural idioms of one religion sometimes find their way into the material culture of another. By the same token, we see borrowing of styles on a more general plane, as regional communities of Jews, Christians, and Muslims integrate features of neighboring cultures or host cultures into the designs of their material products. By studying material culture, we thus are able to chart influences on a religious tradition that often are not apparent in other aspects of religious life.

When we read the "language" of material culture, we are reading an open-ended text. The possibilities for discovery of meanings in religious architecture, statuary, candelabra, relics, furniture, and every other of the categories of material culture are unlimited. As we examine some aspects of the material culture of Judaism, Christianity, and Islam, we should be especially attentive to the ways in which they more fully inform our understanding of authority, community, ritual, myth, ethics, and religious thought in each of these three traditions.

CHAPTER 16

MATERIAL CULTURE IN JUDAISM

JUDAIC MATERIAL CULTURE: THE PROBLEM OF CONTEXT

A distinctively "Jewish" material culture is difficult to identify. Archeologists of ancient pre-Exilic Palestine, for example, cannot easily point to patterns of building or pottery designs that decisively distinguish Israelite remains from those of non-Israelite "Canaanites." Similarly, whereas the Palestinian Jews of the Second Temple era certainly produced their own unique religious civilization, the archeological remains of their homes, public buildings, and crafts reveal close communication with the architectural and artistic styles of the Hellenistic culture thriving around and in the midst of that of the Jews. A similar situation pertains to the Diaspora Jewish communities that took firm root in North Africa, Asia Minor, Europe, and the Middle East. Wherever we cast our eyes, what is "Jewish" in the remains of architectural structures, domestic articles, and so forth is in fact a Judaic expression of cultural themes shared with non-Jewish neighbors.[1]

Discussion of Jewish material culture, therefore, must view Judaic material culture *contextually* as a Jewish modification of conventions common to the environment in which the Jews lived. It is nearly impossible, therefore, to point to any *particular* patterns of material culture that are either exclusive to Jews or that were transmitted intact by them across broad geographical, cultural, or chronological borders. A synagogue building or a costume style that might appear quintessentially "Jewish" to Christians of tenth-century France would hardly appear "Jewish" even to the *Jews* of sixteenth-century Persia, not to mention their Muslim neighbors. It would simply be "foreign."

That Jewish material culture is deeply embedded in the surrounding cultural forms should by now strike a familiar note. As we have seen in Chapter 4, even the core theological symbols of Judaism have been continuously restated and re-thought in the various cultural idioms that Jews have adopted and adapted to their own needs. Material culture, no less than religious or intellectual, is a kind of "language"; and Jews, in their long history of dispersion, have become most adept at using a variety of such languages.

In order to highlight the fluid borders between "Judaic" and "non-Judaic" expressions of material culture, our discussion routinely makes reference to one or more of five cultural languages or styles that have proven particularly influential among Jews. We will see how these languages have been employed in the construction of the sanctified space of synagogues, the crafting of ritual objects and holy texts, and even in the choices of male and female costuming. By noting the way several cultural styles have served Judaic material creativity, we add some nuance to our claim that the "Jewishness" of material culture is discerned primarily in the *context* of distinct non-Jewish cultural settings rather than in an *essential* trait transmitted, like a gene, throughout any and all cultural environments.

You are by now familiar with the earliest of the five cultural languages that shape our study. This is the Hellenistic and later Byzantine culture of the ancient Mediterranean (ca. 300 BCE–650 CE). Extending from the entire Mediterranean basin eastward all the way to the borders of India, this culture shaped nearly all ancient Jewries. It also had an immense impact on the cultures of Christians and Muslims that succeeded it in Europe, North Africa, and the Middle East. These cultures, in turn, provided the comprehensive environment within which, from roughly the eighth through the seventeenth centuries, Jews of three continents—Europe, Africa, and Western Asia—explored the possibilities of Judaic material culture.

The "Christian" culture of medieval Europe, in reality a complex of local pre-Christian cultures infused by Latin Christian symbolic imagination, provided the background for a distinctive Northern European Jewish civilization that came to call itself "Ashkenazic." An obscure kingdom mentioned in the Bible (Jer. 51:27–28), "Ashkenaz" was identified by the tenth century with the German-speaking countries of North Central Europe. After the various expulsions of Jews from western Europe in the late thirteenth century and thereafter, Ashkenazic culture spread eastward into the Christian Slavic lands, where it reached its cultural zenith by the sixteenth and seventeenth centuries. Most North American Jews, and perhaps half of all Israeli Jews, are of Ashkenazic descent and continue to express themselves as Jews, to a greater or lesser degree, in forms derived from Ashkenazic culture.

In contrast to Ashkenazic Jewry, Jews of eighth- to thirteenth-century Spain and Portugal ("Sepharad" in a biblical allusion [Obad. 1:20] as vague as "Ashkenaz") were profoundly integrated into the Iberian and North African versions of Islamic culture. With the Catholic Church's expulsion of Muslims and Jews from the Iberian Peninsula, completed in 1497, the culture of "Sephardic" Jewry spread to the North African, Balkan, and Middle Eastern regions in which the exiles found refuge. There it blended in a variety of ways with the indigenous traditions of native Jews. Iberian Sephardic culture reached its classical period as early as the twelfth and thirteenth centuries, whereas various North African and Middle Eastern outgrowths of it continue to nourish the cultural expression of broad sectors of Jewry. The State of Israel is today a major center of Sephardic cultural life, yet there remain important Sephardic communities in such North American cities as Seattle, New York, and Montreal.

The fourth culture important for our discussion is also by now familiar. This is the complex mixture of national cultures we may term the "Modernist" or "Secular" culture of Europe and North America. With twin roots in the Protestant Reformation and the political restructuring of the European territories into national entities, this culture formed the matrix of the political emancipation of European Jewry in the nineteenth century. It also set the terms for the various reformations and transformations of Judaism since emancipation. The European context of secularism explains, of course, why its primary impact was on Jews of Ashkenazic descent. But with the present century's spread of European and American cultural influence throughout the Islamic lands, secularism has made itself felt among Sephardic and Middle Eastern Jewries as well.

Nowhere is this more clear than in our final cultural language, the "multilingual" Jewish culture that is the modern State of Israel. Created by and, at times, in conflict with the Zionist project of Jewish national independence (see Chapters 4 and 19), Israeli culture is the most dynamic and diverse within contemporary Jewry. Absorbing the cultural styles of Ashkenazic, Sephardic, and many other traditional Jewish communities, Israeli culture nevertheless remains deeply affected by its origins in a secular movement committed to the political and social ideals of European modernity. The creativity of Israeli culture is largely a result of the tensions between Jewish secularism and diverse premodern Judaic traditions built into its cultural life.[2]

In this chapter, of course, our main task is to track the diversity of Judaic cultures through the evidence of such material objects as synagogue buildings, ritual implements, and clothing. We will see, along the way, that modern Jews inherit a remarkably complex combination of cultural languages. It is conceivable, at least in theory, for a contemporary North American or Israeli Jew to inherit elements of *both* Sephardic and Ashkenazic culture, as modulated by the cultural languages of secular North America *and* contemporary Israel. Toward the end of this chapter, we illustrate this complexity through some pertinent observations about ways in which an aspect of material culture, such as clothing, composes a rich code by which Jews communicate to each other and to non-Jews.

THE SYNAGOGUE AS A CULTURAL PUZZLE

Contemporary Forms: North America and Israel

Contemporary synagogues are as diverse as the communities of Jews who use them.[3] A tour of a North American metropolitan area with a large Jewish population would turn up a surprising range of examples.

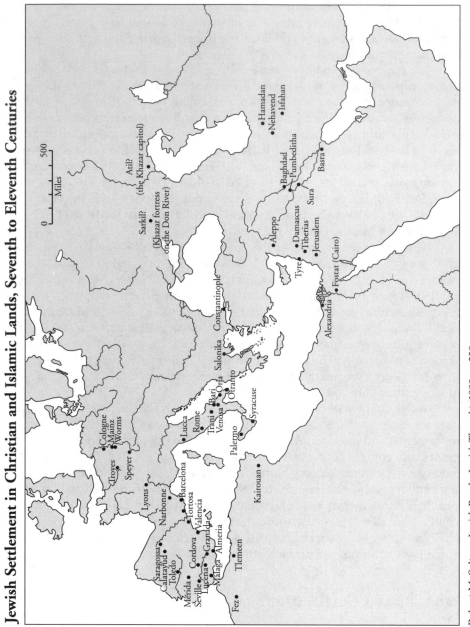

Jewish Settlement in Christian and Islamic Lands, Seventh to Eleventh Centuries

Robert M. Seltzer, *Jewish People, Jewish Thought*, 1980, p. 338.
Reprinted by permission of Prentice Hall, Upper Saddle River, NJ.

European Jewish Settlement in High Middle Ages

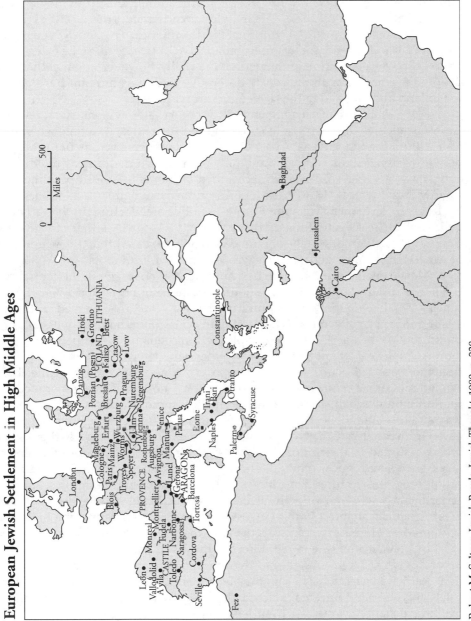

Robert M. Seltzer, *Jewish People, Jewish Thought*, 1980, p. 338.
Reprinted by permission of Prentice Hall, Upper Saddle River, NJ.

In older neighborhoods of the Atlantic seaboard's cities of original Jewish immigrant settlement, for example, there might remain some old synagogue buildings built by Dutch and English Sephardic immigrants from the eighteenth and early nineteenth centuries. Their styles already reflect these settlers' adaptation to the emerging material culture of North America. The Touro Synagogue of Newport, Rhode Island, for example, built in 1763, appears from the exterior to be a typical colonial structure of the period. Internally, however, colonial themes are deeply intermeshed with the ornate decorative traditions brought by Sephardim to Holland and England in the sixteenth century.

Midwestern urban synagogues built a century later by Ashkenazic Jews from German lands, to the contrary, tend to be grand structures. At a time when American culture beyond the East Coast was still widely perceived as unformed, German Jews signaled the venerable antiquity of their own tradition by building synagogues in a variety of "classic" styles then fashionable in Europe. Cincinnati's Isaac M. Wise Temple (1866) is the first American synagogue to exploit the "Moorish Revival" style then sweeping European public architecture. In the early twentieth century, massively domed "Byzantine" styles—such as that of Cleveland's Congregation Tifereth Israel—announced to all who cared that a new generation of American-born Ashkenazic Jews was laying down firm roots.

Most contemporary synagogues, however, are no longer in the central cities, but in the suburbs, reflecting the "suburbanization" of post–World War II American Jewry. Here one is likely to find impressive structures, framed in the most avant-garde of architectural styles, containing classrooms and banquet halls in addition to a "sanctuary" capable of holding hundreds of worshipers. Such enormous complexes, often referred to as "Synagogue-Jewish Centers," perfectly reflect the extended character of contemporary American communal life. Unlike synagogues of the central city, there is commonly no "Jewish neighborhood" surrounding these synagogues. Rather, serving a community dependent on the freeway and the automobile, they constitute a Jewish cultural "hub" drawing a population from throughout a given metropolitan area. The social services they offer are broad, reflected in their impressive physical plants. In addition to worship services, such synagogues commonly host religious schools for children, adult education programs, lectures by visiting scholars or Israeli cultural figures, and so on. A particularly well-known example in Elkins Park, Pennsylvania, designed by the great American architect Frank Lloyd Wright in 1959, is breathtaking in its use of contemporary forms and materials to evoke the majesty of Sinai.

In Israel, matters are rather different. In a land until recently unfamiliar with urban sprawl and freeways, the North American Synagogue-Center has little function. Rather, synagogues are almost always neighborhood structures, designed solely for prayer or informal study, patronized by people who live within close walking distance. A city such as Jerusalem contains innumerable such synagogues, mostly aligned with one or another Orthodox tradition, with some neighborhoods boasting more than one per block. The architectural style of such synagogues is often fortuitous, determined by the style of building common when the neighborhood was planned (anywhere from the fifteenth century in Jerusalem's Old City to the 1990s in the newer neighborhoods). The facades of buildings

The Diversity of Modern Synagogue Design

The Touro Synagogue of Newport, Rhode Island, is a well-known example of colonial style in the construction of public buildings. The main entrance is on the right. The doorway on the left leads to the women's gallery. (*Source:* John T. Hopf)

Cincinnati's Isaac M. Wise Temple, Congregation B'nai Yeshurun, was the first American synagogue to exploit Europe's Moorish Revival style. The three entrances lead into a main sanctuary where families worshiped together in pews. (*Source:* Archives of the Isaac M. Wise Temple)

The Diversity of Modern Synagogue Design

The domes and rounded arches of the Byzantine style are richly apparent in Cleveland's Congregation Tifereth Israel, which was built in 1924. (*Source:* The Temple-Tifereth Israel)

Evoking the crags of Mt. Sinai, this enormous metal and translucent plastic pyramid of Congregation Beth Shalom (Elkins Park, Pennsylvania), designed by Frank Lloyd Wright, provides a canopy over the main sanctuary and the Ark. A member of the congregation interprets Wright's design as "the victory of time over space that is the architectonic incarnation of Jewish thought, all the more significant because it has been realized by a non-Jew." (*Source:* Paul Rocheleau/Photographer)

designed explicitly for synagogue use are often drawn eclectically from a variety of design traditions brought to Israel by its Jewish immigrant populations, as modified by the aesthetics of Jerusalem's largely Ottoman architectural traditions. The relatively few synagogues built for the "general public" or for other kinds of ceremonial purposes tend to employ explicit modernist architectural principles that suit the Israeli physical and cultural landscape. The synagogue that serves the Jewish students of Jerusalem's Hebrew University is a representative example.

What all these synagogues have in common are a few basic furnishings, found entirely within the building. Upon entering a contemporary synagogue, from the simplest to the most stylish, the eye's attention is drawn immediately to the eastern wall (or, in Israel, whichever wall faces Jerusalem's Temple Mount), the site of a rather impressively fashioned closet, "The Holy Ark" (*aron hakodesh*). Behind the embroidered curtain that covers the doors of this Ark stand the most treasured objects in the room, one or more elaborately clothed scrolls of the Torah. The structure of curtain, Ark, and Torah scroll explicitly recalls the desert Tabernacle described in Exodus 25–26, in which an embroidered screen veiled the Ark, which contained the tablets of the covenant received on Sinai. The point of this arrangement is obvious: the synagogue orients the worshiper to the Torah, which represents the Mosaic covenant, and to the Jerusalem Temple, where the ancient Tabernacle rested until the Destruction of 587 BCE. In American congregations, it is not unusual to find, flanking the Ark at a respectable distance to the right and the left, American and Israeli flags. Framing the Torah, these symbols represent the community's American national identity and simultaneous commitment to the international Jewish security represented by the Jewish state (see Chapter 19).

The other key furnishings reinforce the basic orientation provided by the Ark. A raised platform (*bimah*), either in the center of the floor plan (as in medieval Ashkenazic and Sephardic practice) or close to the Ark (as in later Ashkenazic practice), serves as the place from which the Torah is read in public during Sabbath and weekday worship. All seats are arranged to afford a clear view of the Ark and to provide good aural access to the Bimah, from which the Torah is read. In most contemporary traditions, prayers are led and sermons are delivered from either the Bimah or from a podium convenient to it. In synagogues following Orthodox halakhic norms, the seating plan is divided in a variety of ways to provide for the separation of the sexes during worship (Chapter 10).

Most contemporary synagogues in Israel or North America are spare in visual ornamentation. Biblical quotations usually surround the Ark, and the six-pointed "Shield (or Star) of David" often serves as a multipurpose design motif. Although this symbol appears on the flag of the State of Israel, it is not in origin a Zionist symbol. Neither is it particularly ancient in its association with Judaism or synagogues. Like the related sign, the pentagram, this hexagram seems to originate in ancient magical traditions. The symbol entered Jewish culture through the medieval Kabbalah, at which time it acquired its association with David. Its first use in the synagogue seems to be in sixteenth-century Prague, where it appears in the Altneushul (the "Old-New Synagogue"), that city's oldest surviving

Open Ark Containing Torah Scrolls

This contemporary Ark is opened to reveal five Torah scrolls. Every synagogue needs at least one, which would be read on most Sabbaths or on Monday and Thursday Torah readings. Some occasions require readings from two or three sections of the Torah. A synagogue with only one scroll would have to roll from one section to the next. In the synagogue pictured here, a separate scroll would be used for each reading. The donation of a Torah scroll to a synagogue is a major act of charity in Jewish life. These scrolls are typical in being dressed with fine velvet sheaths and silver ornamentation in the form of breastplates and covers for the wooden rollers of the scroll. (*Source:* © Doranne Jacobson)

THE SHIELD OR STAR OF DAVID

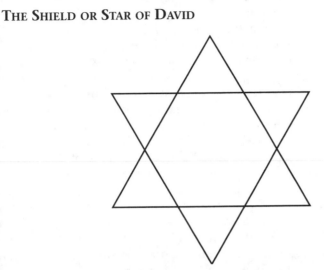

As a yellow badge imposed by the Nazis upon the Jews, or as a blue emblem emblazoned upon the white flag of the State of Israel, this form has come to symbolize Judaism in the modern world. Its history as a Jewish symbol, however, begins in synagogue decoration, but only in early modern times.

synagogue. From there, it seems to have rapidly become a fundamental symbol of Jewish identification in Europe.[4]

The geometric form of the Shield of David is normally supplemented by other stylized representations of such items as the Temple's seven-branched candelabra *(menorah)*, the Mosaic Tablets of the Covenant, or an ancient symbol of the Davidic dynasty, the Lion of Judah. Contemporary menorahs are usually freestanding metal furnishings. Images of the Tablets or of Lions are usually confined to the decoration of the embroidered cloth coverings designed for the Ark and the Bimah. In some cases, especially in synagogues built since the nineteenth century by more wealthy communities, one might even find decorative, nonrepresentational windows of stained glass. The lack of representational art is usually understood as an expression of compliance with the biblical commandment against creating "graven images" that might lead to a confusion of God with his creation.

The Synagogues of the Ancient World

It is impossible in our limited space to expand on the remarkable diversity of contemporary architectural and artistic styles employed for synagogues. The point is that even this degree of unanimity in the synagogue's basic furnishings and symbols blends ancient and relatively recent elements. The menorah and the lion, for example, are present in the most ancient of known synagogues, whereas the Shield of David, as we have seen, makes its earliest appearance only a few centuries ago.

Prior to the late Middle Ages, a variety of forms existed that have, in many instances, passed out of the contemporary language of synagogue design and decoration. Let us now survey some illustrative examples.

In Chapter 7, we noted that the term *synagogue* was used very early in the Hellenistic period to describe Jewish communal gatherings. There is, however, no firm consensus among archeologists regarding when Jews first began to employ or design special buildings for their own communal or liturgical functions.[5] Most archeologists agree, however, that by the second century CE, remains of buildings indisputably built to serve as official Jewish gathering places can be identified from Rome in the West to Syria-Palestine in the East, with important examples in Asia Minor as well. Despite much stylistic diversity, many of these remains suggest a common idea of the synagogue as a multipurpose place in which prayer was perhaps one among many other activities. They are not modeled on ancient Hellenistic Temples at which rites were offered. Rather, their architectural inspiration is the repertoire of ground plans and facades commonly found on all manner of public meeting halls in the Roman world. All create enough room for comfortable seating and contain a relatively open central space, presumably for teaching or for the recitation of prayers. Larger examples have many rooms, presumably for non-liturgical functions. In some Diaspora and Palestinian synagogues, a richly carved stone chair, identified in some inscriptions as the "Seat of Moses," may have served as an honored seat for a community patron or, perhaps, a teacher.

How do we know that these structures are synagogues? In many cases, writing provides the clue. In dedicatory inscriptions, a leader of the community or a simple member announces that he or she has donated the funds for this or that part of the building, as in this inscription from Bet Guvrin in southern Judea (fourth to seventh centuries): "May . . . Shimay . . . be remembered for good, for he bought this column for the honor of the synagogue. Shalom." Other inscriptions are found in the name of the main architect, stone carver, or mosaic artist—a kind of "signature." A pair of mosaic artists, Marianos and his son, Haninah, have left their signatures on at least two Galilean synagogues. In one remarkable find of another sort, at a seventh-century synagogue in Israel's Bet Shean valley, a floor mosaic inscribes an extended quotation from the Palestinian Talmud, the earliest material evidence of rabbinic literature.

The inscriptions of stone carvers and artists are often supplemented by examples of their work. Most synagogues of this period have impressively carved doorways or other masonry that incorporates into the design Temple symbols such as the menorah, the ram's horn, and other ritual objects. Many others are distinguished by sophisticated mosaic tile floors depicting these same objects in addition to illustrations of biblical scenes and, quite commonly, representations of signs of the zodiac. The floor mosaic of the Galilean synagogue of Bet Alpha (ca. fifth century)—signed, incidentally, by Marianos and Haninah—is a superb example.

Upon entry into this synagogue, the eye first falls on an illustration of Abraham's near sacrifice of Isaac (Gen. 22). The next panel, occupying the center of the room, contains a representation of the Sun-Chariot moving through the sky surrounded by zodiacal signs and symbols of the four seasons. Beyond it, at the opposite end of the floor, is depicted a parted curtain behind which lies a series of images depicting the Temple's Ark, its menorahs, ram's horns, the Lion of Judah, and other cultic objects. Presumably, if this synagogue housed a Torah scroll, it would have been stored in some sort of movable Ark beyond the mosaic describing the Temple implements. But there is no evidence of this in the present remains. Nor does the present ruin contain any indication of where the Torah reader or prayer leader might have stood.

In at least one remarkable case, the third-century synagogue unearthed in the Syrian town of Dura-Europos, illustrations were found not on the floors, but in a series of richly conceived wall paintings that surround an elaborate wall niche designed to hold the Torah scroll. These paintings seem to have been intended as a pictorial commentary on various biblical stories, a kind of visual "midrash" anticipating, in its didactic function, the famous stained-glass art of Latin Christianity and the iconography of Byzantine churches. Incidentally, these paintings provide a fascinating glimpse of such mundane matters as male and female hairstyle and fashions in clothing.

Many archeologists have noted, we may add, that neither these nor other synagogues of the Hellenistic period give any certain indication of the separation of the sexes that became the norm in the medieval synagogues of Ashkenazic and Sephardic Jewry. Perhaps seating was demarcated by movable furniture that has left no trace. But synagogues preserve no permanent structures that might have segregated worshipers by sex. Furthermore, numerous grave inscriptions from throughout the Greek-speaking Jewish world testify that women were frequently major donors to synagogues and, in some cases, bore prestigious titles of office, such as "Archisynogogus" (Chief of the Synagogue) or "Presbyteros" (Elder). On balance, then, the separation of men and women in prayer may be a post-Byzantine development.

In the Dura and Bet Alpha synagogues, as well as in other equally interesting sites, the artistic styles of the pictorial material have much in common with those employed in non-Jewish settings. What makes the art "Jewish" is not its style, but its location—a place of Jewish worship—and subject—biblical episodes or symbols of the Temple. Here, to be sure, there are also some surprises. Until the discovery of these synagogues, most modern Jews, from Orthodoxy to Reform, would have rejected as "un-Jewish star worship" (*avodah zarah*) any artistic personifications of the sun or renderings of zodiacal forces, such as those at Bet Alpha and elsewhere. Similarly, Dura's representation (just to the right of the Torah niche) of a naked woman (probably Pharoah's daughter) descending to bathe in a river would be regarded as scandalously immodest in Sephardic and Ashkenazic synagogues of later times. Clearly, later scruples against representing the planets or female nudity did not trouble the builders of these synagogues or those who offered prayers within them.

The Synagogues of Sepharad and Ashkenaz

In medieval times, the increasing influence of rabbinic halakhic tradition, which frowned on representation of the human form in the synagogue, contributed to important changes in the nature of synagogue art. In most cases, especially in

Islamic lands, interior decorations became ornamental rather than representational. In Ashkenazic areas, representational art was usually confined to "natural" objects, such as animals or imagined scenes of Jerusalem, to the exclusion of human beings. More than the issue of representational art, however, what distinguishes Ashkenazic and Sephardic synagogues from each other are the artistic traditions that artisans employ in their work.[6]

Relatively few medieval synagogues have survived in their original form; therefore, we must be careful in making generalizations. Yet the stark internal simplicity of medieval Spanish and North African synagogues, relieved only by intricate Hebrew calligraphic decorations and geometric patterning along walls and the Torah niche, seems a clear Judaic expression of the nonrepresentational ornamentation lavished by Muslim artisans on their mosques. There are also innovations in furnishings that seem inspired by the Muslim environment. Typical is the elevated reading desk, the *al memor,* corresponding to the modern Bimah, which has its Islamic parallel in the mosque's pulpit *(al minbar).* Indeed, so closely did synagogal architecture and decoration in these areas align with Islamic standards of simplicity that it was not uncommon in Spain in particular for Jewish communities to acquire former mosques for their own prayer use. Three such mosques are mentioned in the thirteenth-century declaration of the Catholic King Alfonso X, by which he transferred all of Seville's mosques, including those "which are now synagogues of the Jews," to the property of the Church.

After the expulsion of Iberian Jews and Muslims was completed in 1492, such appropriation was common. A famous surviving example of a synagogue transformed into a place of Christian worship is the fourteenth-century synagogue of Toledo, Spain. After the expulsion of the Jewish community, it was dedicated as the El Transito Church. In some cases, "Jewish" and "Islamic" material culture and aesthetics come to have an important influence in the expression of Spanish Catholicism as well.

Although the history of the Ashkenazic synagogue building is difficult to trace prior to the fourteenth or fifteenth century, it is quite clear that its forms were thoroughly European in character. The case of Polish synagogues is illustrative. Synagogues commissioned by Jews living in royal towns in the fifteenth and sixteenth centuries betray many influences of Baroque styling emanating from Italy. But this has little to do with Jewish artisans adapting local tradition to their own needs. To the contrary, during these centuries, when Jews in larger towns received permission from civil and Church leaders to build a synagogue, they needed to commission a Christian architect and Christian artisans for this purpose. In Cracow, Poland, for example, the renowned Christian architect Mateo Gucci was hired in 1570 to entirely remodel that community's Stara synagogue after it was ruined by fire. The synagogues thus produced—no less than their modern parallels designed by a host of professional American architects—are remarkable instances in which "Jewish" material culture is the product of non-Jews adapting their craft to the specifics of Jewish tradition and ritual.

Where Polish Jews lived in privately owned townships, under the direct rule of a landowner, restrictions on the location and style of synagogues were often less severe. Some of the most characteristic examples of Polish synagogues were elaborate wooden structures built from the seventeenth through nineteenth centuries in a host of small villages. Many of these were multitiered structures, replete with ornately carved decorations within and without.

Our concluding observation should by now be clear. The holiest site of post-Temple Judaism, the house of prayer, is from the perspective of its external and internal form a playground of cultures. Since the medieval period, its stock of required furnishings are few: a reading desk, a housing for the Torah, seats for worshipers, and a teaching area. Symbolic images are equally meager: perhaps the menorah and the lion persist from antiquity to the present as common symbols. The synagogue's "Jewishness" is indisputable in each specific contextual setting; but the *form* of that Jewishness is always an expression of complex negotiations (conscious or unconscious) with the surrounding constraints and opportunities of local material culture.

MARKING THE JEWISHNESS OF THE HOME

We observed in an earlier chapter that until relatively recent times, the home has served as an important setting for the ritual life of Judaism. Indeed, if there is anything historically "Judaic" about the material objects of Jewish homes, it lies solely in the various ritual objects that have been found within them. These include artfully designed candelabras for the Sabbath and Festival lights, including the unique eight-branched menorah for the Hanukkah festival. Much attention has been lavished as well on cups for holding the wine that is blessed at the beginning and end of Sabbaths and Festivals, as well as the spice container that lends its fragrance to the *Havdalah* ceremony that concludes the Sabbath.

As you would expect, such ritual objects employ in their construction every conceivable material and style available to Jewish artisans throughout the lands of Jewish settlement. In modern times, such objects are commonly found even in the homes of Jews who do not perform the rituals associated with them. Often they are lovingly collected as "art objects," material reminders of ancient attachments strongly affirmed, if imperfectly understood. In some cases, collectors of such objects prefer "traditional" examples made in the vanished cultures of pre-Holocaust Ashkenazic Jewry or in the Sephardic communities of Islamic lands. Other collectors might prefer contemporary designs emanating from professional designers and artisans in North America or Israel.[7]

No discussion of the ritual objects of the Jewish home, however, can be complete without an emphasis on the way written texts are used to mark the home as a place of Jewishness. From front door to interior, Jewish homes have commonly been distinguished by the prominent display of the written word associated with the Torah. Of particular significance in this regard is the *mezuzah,* an amulet affixed to the righthand entrance of the front door and of all other rooms of the house.

The word mezuzah means "doorpost," as in the following passage from

A Contemporary Havdalah Set

The Sabbath is ritually concluded by the ceremony of *Havdalah* ("Separation") that demarcates the Sabbath's holy time from the common time of the week. At this ceremony, Jews pour wine, inhale fragrant spices (representing the sweetness of the departing day), and light a candle to signify the renewal of light. This illustration shows a contemporary set of Havdalah objects—the spice box, candleholder, and wine goblet. (*Source:* © Doranne Jacobson)

Deuteronomy 6:9: "Inscribe [the words of the Torah] on the doorposts of your house and upon your gates." The Bible is not clear which words in particular are to be posted in fulfillment of this commandment. Halakhic tradition since the time of Maimonides prescribes extracts from the series of biblical passages that now constitute the text of the *shma* (Deut. 6:4–9, 11:13–21; see Chapter 10). These are written by a trained scribe on a carefully prepared parchment that is then tightly rolled and placed in a protective case. This object—the scroll in its case—now bears the name mezuzah, which originally designated the place it was to mark.

How have Jews understood the significance of this common object that so clearly marks off their homes as Jewish dwellings? As early as the first century CE, the Jewish historian Josephus took pains to explain that the mezuzah is not a crude good-luck charm, but an expression of gratitude for all the benefits received from God (Antiquities 4:213). That he had to address this issue suggests that, in fact, many Jews did regard the mezuzah as a charm. The Palestinian Talmud, for its part, records an interesting story about Rabbi Judah the Patriarch. In gratitude for the gift of a pearl, the third-century compiler of Mishnah sent a mezuzah. Rebuked that his gift was hardly equivalent in value to the precious pearl, Rabbi is said to have replied: "What you sent me I must guard, what I sent you will guard you!" (Peah 1:1, 15d).[8]

Indeed, over the course of centuries, the mezuzah became the focus of a minor ritual that became widespread among Jews. It is still commonly observed among many observant Jews today, even though its original meaning is unclear. Upon entering and leaving the home, inhabitants or guests touch the mezuzah with the right hand and place the hand to their lips, thus invoking a descent of the protective powers represented by the holy words from their heavenly palaces on behalf of the earthly faithful. The family doorpost, guarded by the mezuzah, constitutes not only a barrier between public and domestic space, but also a clear border between the sanctified environment of the home and the dangers lurking in the profane space beyond.

Like so many other aspects of ancient Jewish custom, the meaning of the mezuzah has undergone dramatic change in modern times. During the religious innovations and secularizing movements of the nineteenth and twentieth centuries, many Jews abandoned the practice entirely. Some did so out of simple lack of conviction in its effectiveness. Others because—in times when the real or implied threat of anti-Semitic violence led Europeanized Jews to minimize their visibility—the mezuzah called unwelcome attention to their origins. Nevertheless, in the latter half of the twentieth century, the mezuzah is making a comeback. In both North America and Israel, where signs of Jewish distinctiveness are eagerly cherished, the mezuzah is often found on the homes even of Jews who are marginally observant or are entirely nonobservant of halakhic norms. Crafted in a self-consciously "traditional" style, or designed of synthetic materials in the most contemporary of visual forms, the mezuzah rarely represents a conduit of blessing from the heavenly realm. More commonly, it constitutes for such Jews a proud symbol of national or ethnic survival after the near annihilation of Jewish life in the twentieth century.

THE BOOK IN JUDAIC CULTURES

The importance of texts in Judaic cultures, you have probably realized, extends well beyond the door jamb's mezuzah. Indeed, the mezuzah, which is, after all, a citation from the Torah, simply serves as a reminder that the book of Torah has perhaps been the central material object in any Judaic culture. As handwritten scrolls or codexes, and as printed volumes, books of Scripture and rabbinic literature have been venerated as the tangible traces of the Sinaitic words that brought Israel into covenantal relationship with the Creator of Heaven and earth. For this reason, the book of Torah is always something more than a source of information. As a medium for the preservation of holy words, it invokes a presence beyond itself.

Despite its otherworldly significance, however, the physical form of the book of Torah has always been intertwined with the cultural patterns of its producers. The archaic scroll, from which Jews of all contemporary movements still read in public worship, was once the dominant form for all books throughout the ancient Mediterranean and Middle East. Made of sewn animal hides or sheets of papyrus glued together end to end, these sturdy rolls protected the words inscribed upon them in inks compounded of ash and other vividly toned substances.

As an information storage system, the scroll had its disadvantages. For one thing, it was hard to look up passages, since the desired words might be anywhere in a scroll that could be well over twenty feet long. By the early centuries CE, under the impact of Roman culture, a far more convenient book form, the codex, rapidly gained in popularity. The material basis of the codex was also leather or papyrus and ink. But instead of sewing the leaves end to end, individual surfaces were cut into squares, laid on top of each other, sewn at one end, and placed between durable covers. This is essentially the form of any modern book.

The advantage of the codex is that it is easier to find information within it, as pages can be identified and flipped through. Christian communities pioneered in transferring their scriptural books to the codex.[9] Perhaps as a result of the Christian preference for the codex, this type of book penetrated Judaic culture much more slowly. Scrolls remained for centuries the preferred form for preserving scriptural works. But by early medieval times, Jews as well used the codex for preserving copies of Scripture and, eventually, the rabbinic literature. But halakhic norms continued nevertheless to insist that for purposes of public worship, the Torah must be read from a scroll inscribed in halakhically regulated scripts without any adornment—a stark black-and-white image that recalls the rabbinic tradition with which the Sinaitic Torah was written "with black fire on white fire."

As in medieval Christian and Islamic cultures, the artisans who actually made Jewish scriptural codexes lavished all their skills on them, producing an object that was not only holy, but beautiful as well. Similarly, prayerbooks, Passover *haggadot* (plural of *haggadah*, the book used on Passover to relate the Israelites' exodus from Egypt), and manuscripts of halakhic codes were all objects of exquisite artistic attention. Ashkenazic and Sephardic scribes copied them in an elegant hand derived from regional scribal custom, and artists gave their best efforts to designing beautiful illustrations to accompany the texts. Ashkenazic illustrations tend, under the influence of surrounding Christian taste, to be figurative; Sephardic decorations, guided by Islamic custom, are usually nonrepresentational, making broad use of elaborate calligraphy. Such books were expensive to produce and could normally be owned only by the rich. Alternatively, a donor could commission such a text as a gift to the community. It was kept in the synagogue and treasured as a prestigious public possession.

Sephardic and Ashkenazic Bible Illustration

This title page of the biblical Book of Joshua was made in Lisbon, Portugal, in 1482. It is a good example of the Sephardic tendency to limit biblical illustrations to geometric patterns and calligraphic detail. (*Source:* By permission of The British Library, Ms. 2627, Title page of the *Book of Joshua,* Lisbon, Portugal, 1482)

Compare, by contrast, this title page from Rashi's commentary on the Book of Daniel, copied in Germany and dated by the scribe Solomon b. Samuel of Wuerzburg to 1233. The illustration depicts scenes from the biblical book. (*Source:* Bayer Staatsbibliothek)

When European communications were transformed by the invention of the printing press in the fifteenth century, both Sephardic and Ashkenazic Jews took eagerly to the new technology. Rabbinic scholars proclaimed the press as a divinely sent opportunity to make texts of Torah available cheaply over wide stretches of territory. Major Jewish communities of Spain and Italy were soon dotted with presses yielding printed versions of biblical books, talmudic tractates, and other medieval rabbinic compilations of theology and law.

The remarkable cultural paradox of Jewish printing is the degree to which the physical form of Jewish books was profoundly indebted to the influence of medieval and Renaissance Christian book culture. One of the most influential sixteenth-century Venetian publishers of Jewish books, Daniel Bomberg, was a Christian who accurately predicted the economic implications of the growing interest of Christian Hebraicists in Hebrew writings. Among other achievements, his publishing house made available between 1519 and 1524 the first complete editions of the Babylonian and Palestinian Talmuds.

Jewish publishers, such as the Soncino family of Milan (whose press still publishes works of classical Judaica), were also fearless pioneers in adapting conventions of Christian book culture to their own needs. When designing the layouts of Talmud pages in the 1480s and 1490s, Soncino adapted important design features common in the creation of medieval manuscripts of canon law. Thus, they placed the actual text of the Talmud in the center of the page, surrounding it with commentaries by the tenth-century scholar Rashi and with supplementary commentaries (Heb.: *Tosafot*) composed by his grandsons. The format was continued by Bomberg a generation later and by nearly all successive printers. It culminated in the most famous talmudic edition of all, published in Vilna, Poland, by the Widow Romm and her sons (1880–1886). The twenty volumes of the Romm Talmud include, in addition to the talmudic text and the main commentaries, a wealth of appendices, halakhic treatises, and marginal notes representing roughly eight hundred years of rabbinic study of the Talmud in Ashkenaz and Sepharad.

Economic necessity also played a crucial role in the aesthetic production of the printed Jewish book. Under the influence of the medieval traditions of manuscript illumination, Christian publishers eagerly commissioned elaborately designed etchings with which to frame the texts of their books. Working with smaller financial resources, Jewish printers often found themselves purchasing worn-out decorative blocks from Christian publishers for their own use. This could have ironic results. For example, we find tractates of the Talmud in which the text is surrounded by nude Renaissance Cupids. Few purchasers of such volumes seem to have complained.

Since its emergence, printing has played a crucial role in Judaic cultural movements. The ability of the *Shulkhan Arukh,* for example, to establish itself as the most authoritative code of halakhah is at least partially due to the fact that it was written just as print became available. Similarly, the controversial publication of the Zohar in Italy between 1558 and 1560 played a crucial role in the spread of kabbalistic ideas throughout the Jewish world, as the opponents of its publication feared. A century later, the Shabbatean messianic movement, deeply dependent on kabbalistic concepts, spread rapidly from Palestine and Turkey to Holland, England, and Eastern Europe. As with the Protestant Reformation, these radical ideas were spread from country to country largely through the medium of the cheaply reproduced propaganda broadsheet. The eighteenth-century controversy over Hasidism was also brought to a head by the publication of otherwise unknown teachings by the founding authorities of the movement. Finally, all the Modernist, Secularist, and Traditionalist movements of the nineteenth century routinely used print as the vehicle for their polemics over the nature of Judaism in modernity.[10]

THE SYMBOLIC VOCABULARY OF COSTUME

Travelers to Israel or to some of the larger North American centers of Jewish life, such as New York City or Montreal, are often astounded to discover Hasidic or other Traditionalist Jewish communities comprised of people whose way of dress marks them off entirely from their surroundings. Women wear long dresses and cover their arms and legs with elbow-length sleeves and thick stockings. Their heads are covered by tightly wound cloths or, in some cases, wigs. Men are dressed in knee-length black coats and elaborate fur or black-felt hats. White twines of thread hang from the ends of four-cornered vests. As a kind of tonsorial complement, the face is festooned with an untrimmed beard and long curls (Heb.: *pe'ot*; Yid.: *peyis*) hanging from the temples. Both those who dress this way and the tourists who stare at them share a common perception: that this way of dress is the "traditional" Jewish way.

It depends, of course, on what you mean by traditional. The people we have described are in fact dressed in the Eastern European Ashkenazic styles of the seventeenth and eighteenth centuries, updated in small ways by modern methods of production. To preserve these styles in the late twentieth century has little to do with nostalgia or isolation from modern tastes. Rather, people so attired intend to make a point. Expressed negatively, the point is that Jewish identity constitutes a negation of all that is represented by the Secularist culture of Europe and North America. Positively stated, the point is that to be a Jew is to be "holy," set apart from the "ways of the nations" by a total commitment to the entirety of premodern halakhic tradition. A basic social expression of this commitment is to visibly mark one's body as "separate," sanctified by the cut of one's garments. No halakhic code specifies that a Jewish male must wear a long dark coat and a fur hat. Nevertheless, the preservation of premodern costume has become for these Jews a fundamental expression of their *Yiddishkayt*, their "Jewishness" (see Chapter 4).

For most of their history, however, Jews did not seem to have been particularly concerned to mark themselves off so dramatically from non-Jews by their dress. Indeed, in both Christian and Islamic lands, distinctive Jewish dress (such as badges or clothes of unusual color) was most often imposed upon the Jews by governmental mandate. Moreover, as we shall see, contemporary Traditionalists have no monopoly on distinctively "Jewish" dress even in recent times. But their example is a useful place to begin our necessarily brief survey of how the specifics of Jewish tradition have interacted with the constraints of surrounding cultures to produce distinctively Jewish fashions.

As far back as evidence exists, the main distinction in male dress concerned a biblical requirement (Num. 15:38 ff.) to wear fringes of twine (Heb.: *tzitzit*) on the corners of one's garment as a reminder of the encompassing nature of divine commandments. Indeed, representations of such fringes are common in the Dura-Europos synagogue, dangling routinely from the cloaks of males. In the rabbinic literature of late Antiquity, tzitzit are mentioned as a requirement for any garment with four edges. Later, a special garment, the *arba kanfot* ("four-corners"), was in fact designed for this purpose. Worn under the shirt, the arba kanfot is the first garment donned in the morning and is the subject of an appropriate blessing ("Blessed are You . . . who commanded us regarding the tzitzit"). This is the vest displayed in contemporary traditionalist communities, the fringes hanging clearly at the sides as an explicit statement of Traditionalist commitment. Aside from this apparently universal item, male dress, as reflected in a host of illustrations, from third-century Dura-Europos to sixteenth-century manuscript illuminations, appears to be largely determined by prevailing local styles.

Biblical law prescribes no particular garments for women. But halakhic tradition, echoed by illustrations of Jewish women from throughout the ancient and medieval world, insists that married women in particular cover their hair as a sign of modesty. Even at Dura-Europos, where the depiction of female frontal nudity is deemed appropriate in the case of a non-Jewish woman, illustrations of Jewish women clothe them very modestly and portray them with covered hair. The nature of the covering has varied dramatically: from veils that might cover the entire face in Islamic lands, to loosely pinned cloths draped down the back at Dura-Europos and medieval Germany, to elaborate turbans in Italy. Along with covered hair, modesty for all women past puberty entailed keeping most of the body covered. Nearly all illustrations from premodern times portray women in long dresses or cloaks except where, as in certain Islamic lands, billowy pantaloons were commonly worn by Muslim and Jewish women alike.

The transformation of Jewish women into women of modernity has wrought dramatic changes in sensibility regarding the nature and meaning of "modesty." In North American and Israeli cultures, even among Jews labeling themselves as Orthodox, women have largely abandoned covering their hair. Where the undressed female body has become a marketing staple even in family newspapers, uncovered hair seems hardly a sensual provocation. Women who continue to cover their hair normally select stylish wigs. Paradoxically, the modesty intended by the halakhic requirement can be subverted by wigs far more attractive than the wearer's natural endowment.

Similarly, the vast majority of Jewish women—except for the more scrupulous of the Orthodox—can be found wearing the whole array of contemporary women's fashions, even though these may display lengths of leg or depths of bosom deemed inappropriate by rabbinic norms of modesty. A daring fashion choice for many a North American Orthodox woman, to the contrary, might be a choice to wear jeans or slacks rather than a skirt in a public place. Israeli women of an Orthodox bent would, perhaps, feel more constrained by social conservatism to remain skirted. But in the general Israeli culture, women's fashion is dictated by the tastes of New York or Paris rather than by those of the Chief Rabbinate.

A word is appropriate at this point about one visible item of female costume of particular popularity in North America. Since the 1950s, a common article of Jewish jewelry is the mezuzah. Reduced to the size of a small charm and stylized in intricate gold or silver ornamentation, it can be found hanging not on doorposts but around many necks, a kind of Jewish counterpart to the equally popular crucifix worn by many Christian women. There is, of course, no halakhic requirement for *wearing* a mezuzah. Nor is a mezuzah so worn "kosher," since it does not contain the appropriate parchment produced by a trained scribe. Nevertheless, a woman choosing to wear such an article to work in her office at a Minneapolis law firm marks herself off from her surroundings just as clearly as does her contemporary in a sequestered Jerusalem neighborhood, covered from head to toe from prying male eyes.[11]

Perhaps the most familiar item of male Jewish garb is the skullcap (*yarmulke* in Yiddish; *kipah* in Hebrew). In contemporary Judaism, it is the single most highly charged symbol of Jewish identification. How it is worn, when it is worn, by whom it is worn, its fabric and design—all of these convey meanings and implications within the highly diverse cultures of North American and Israeli Judaism. Here we can only hint at some of the ways in which this simple piece of headgear communicates complex cultural meanings.

Among Israeli men of Traditionalist and Modernist Orthodox leanings alike, the skullcap is worn at all times except during bathing or sleep. Traditionalists—such as Hasidim or others with an oppositional stance to the secularist Zionism that dominates modern Israeli culture—normally prefer a rather large black cap of velvet or cloth, which sits tightly on most of the head from the crown to close to the base of the skull. Orthodox men, to the contrary, normally more sympathetic to the achievements of the secular Israeli state and its Zionist ethos, usually sport kipot knitted in a variety of fashionable designs and colors. Some might feature the wearer's name embroidered around the border (a kind of Israeli version of American personalized license plates). These kipot cover less of the head than the Traditionalist yarmulke—some are no more than a few inches in diameter—and usually require fastening to the hair with clips or, in a recent innovation, Velcro.

In Israel, therefore, the covered head is a political as well as a religious statement. A man's decision to cover his head in public or leave it uncovered immediately locates him on one side of the Israeli cultural divide between the "religious" and the "secular." The *kind* of head covering he chooses locates him at some point in the complex spectrum of pro-Zionist, non-Zionist, and anti-Zionist "religious" communities. Highly nationalist Israeli settlers on the disputed territories of the West Bank, for example, convinced that their Jewish presence will hasten messianic redemption, are often distinguished in their headgear from equally messianic anti-Zionists, who regard the Jewish State as the primary impediment to the restoration of the Exiles.

This does not, however, address all the possibilities. More than a few North American Orthodox, Conservative, or Reform Jews who cover their heads in

A Fifteenth-Century Italian Wedding with a Bareheaded Groom

This depiction of a Jewish wedding ceremony is found in an illustrated biblical manuscript containing the books of Psalms, Job, and Proverbs. The bride's hair is braided and covered, and the officiant (whether a rabbi or not is unclear) wears a formal head covering. But note that the men are clean shaven and that the groom's head is bare. Numerous other medieval illustrations of religious activities, for example, of Passover, seders, study sessions, and so forth, suggest that the male head covering was not mandatory prior to the sixteenth century and that beards were often worn only by rabbinic scholars. (*Source:* Biblioteca Palatina, Parma, Italy, Ms. Parm. 3596 fol. 275 recto)

public in Israel would do so in their native cities only when engaged in a religious ritual at home or in the synagogue. Here the Zionist context is most salient. Covering the head in the Israeli street becomes an expression of Jewish freedom of self-expression, a freedom less easily exercised outside the Jewish state, where a Jewish head covering might provoke unpleasant comment.

The phenomenon of the covered Jewish head in North America has its own interesting set of meanings. By the 1960s, the skullcap was purely a ritual object for most American Jewish men. In Reform circles, it had been widely abandoned by the beginning of the twentieth century, worn neither in the synagogue nor in public. The Conservative movement, coming to full expression in North America by the 1930s and 1940s, distinguished itself from Reform in part through the preservation of the head covering for men engaged in synagogue prayer or home rituals. Until the past few decades, even most Orthodox men would function in the public domain with a bare head, their unwillingness to appear "too Jewish" a concession to the subtle dynamics of anti-Jewish social prejudice in North American society.

Matters have changed rather dramatically in the past few decades. As part of a more widespread interest in traditional Jewish forms, the pendulum is swinging back to the covered head, even in Reform congregations that once regarded it with hostility. Orthodox and, to some degree, even Conservative Jews are increasingly likely to wear a kipah as part of their daily attire, at least in areas of dense Jewish settlement. Moreover, among Jewish women interested in exploring dimensions of Jewish observance previously reserved for males (see Chapter 10), it is not uncommon to see artfully made caps modeled on the traditional yarmulke. These are worn only at prayer, as would be the custom among most men in Conservative congregations.

A comparison of the skullcap in the Israeli and North American settings yields important differences. In Israel, it necessarily implicates the wearer in the complex debates over the nature of an independent Jewish state that, as we see in Chapter 19, have characterized Zionism since the late nineteenth century. In the American context, however, the Zionist implications of the skullcap are quite muted. Rather, it more commonly represents a decision to "come out" in one's Jewishness, to display one's ethnic pride. Like a mezuzah on the door, it signals freedom from the old discomforts of being Jewish in a dominantly Christian society.

In view of all the symbolic meaning attached to this simple head covering among contemporary Jews, you should be prepared for a surprise: the kipah, like the Shield of David, is a relatively recent addition to "traditional" Judaism. Although the covered head originated, perhaps, as a symbol of rabbinic authority during talmudic times, it is mentioned even in late medieval halakhic writings only as a venerable custom and not a halakhic obligation. Illustrations of Jewish men from ancient and medieval sources, for example, routinely portray them even in synagogue and ritual settings with uncovered as well as covered heads. But the recent origin of the custom is insignificant in relation to its powerful meaning as a sign of Jewish identity. Once a symbolic touchstone in the modern controversy over religious reform, the kipah remains a principal way in which men—and, to a degree, women—locate themselves within the political and religious framework of contemporary Judaic culture in Israel and North America.[12]

CHAPTER 17

MATERIAL CULTURE
IN CHRISTIANITY

Christianity is a paradoxical religion that thrives on dialectical tensions. Of its many dense unresolved tensions, none perhaps has been more pronounced than that between matter and spirit. Once again, fiction can provide us with an entry into a dense subject; and once again, the author is Flannery O'Connor, a woman who understands the essence of Christianity better than many theologians.

In the short story "Parker's Back," O'Connor deals with the paradox of the incarnation and the conflicting ways in which it can be approached. O. E. Parker, a hard-drinking, no-good, tattooed low-life, has somehow married a stern Christian woman who is out to save him. Parker's wife is a good Calvinist who does not smoke, drink, or cuss. Parker loves tattoos so much he has covered his entire body with them, except for his back. As could be expected, unrelenting hostility and frustration dominate the lives of both partners. Looking for ways to improve his marriage without actually becoming religious, Parker stumbles on the bad idea of having a picture of God tattooed on his back and of surprising his wife with it. At the tattoo parlor, he picks out from a book "the haloed head of a flat stern Byzantine Christ with all demanding eyes." Much to his surprise, the first time he looks upon the image on his back in the mirror, he feels transformed, thinking that "the eyes that were now forever on his back were eyes to be obeyed." Parker feels saved. When he comes home filled with fervor, he is in for a rude surprise. His wife, good Calvinist that she is, will not even look at his back. "Another picture," she growls.

> "I might have known you was . . . putting some more trash on yourself." Parker's knees went hollow under him. He wheeled around and cried, "Look at it! Don't just say that! Look at it!"

"I done looked," she said.

"Don't you know who it is?" he cried in anguish.

"No, who is it?" Sarah Ruth said. "It ain't nobody I know."

"It's him," Parker said.

"Him who?"

"God!" Parker cried

"God? God don't look like that!"

"What do you know how he looks?" Parker moaned. "You ain't seen him."

"He don't *look*," Sarah Ruth said, "He's a spirit. No man shall see his face."

"Aw, listen," Parker groaned, "this is just a picture of him."

"Idolatry!" Sarah Ruth screamed. "Idolatry! Enflaming yourself with idols under every green tree! . . . I don't want no idolator in this house!" and she grabbed up the broom and began to thrash him across the shoulders with it.

Parker was too stunned to resist. He sat there and let her beat him until she had nearly knocked him senseless and large welts had formed on the face of the tattooed Christ. Then he staggered up and made for the door.[1]

Christianity promises the redemption of the material world through the incarnation of God, that is, through the materialization of the ultimate spiritual essence. Paradox is heaped upon mystery and enigma; Christ is professed to be a God-man who saves humanity from its fallenness by spilling his blood and dying on two mean pieces of wood, and who seals his promise of an eternal embodied life to come by rising from the dead and taking his resurrected body back to Heaven. As if this were not perplexing enough, this savior instructs his followers to perform a cleansing ritual with water and to celebrate a ritual meal in which bread and wine are consumed as his body and blood.

From the start, Christians eagerly embraced the idea of a redeemed material world and the promise of a bodily resurrection, but they nonetheless found the reconciliation of matter and spirit a vexing dialectic. The same Jesus who said "Take, eat; this is my body" (Matt. 26:26) and "he who eats my flesh and drinks my blood has eternal life, and I will raise him up at the last day" (John 7:54) is also recorded as saying "It is the spirit that gives life, the flesh is of no avail" (John 7:63). In the Acts of the Apostles, Jesus' followers are dumbfounded when he ascends bodily into Heaven; having grown accustomed to his resurrected presence, they now watch him quickly disappear into the clouds. Angels appear and say to the crestfallen disciples:

> Men of Galilee, why do you stand looking into heaven? This Jesus, who was taken up from you into heaven will come in the same way as you saw him go into heaven. (Acts 1:11)

One way of phrasing the paradox of Christ's ascension would be to say, Now you see him, now you don't, or, you need that divine-human body, take and eat it, but do not expect to see or touch it as you see and touch all other material things; you are saved by its being here and not-here simultaneously. No wonder, then, that Christians have produced a rich material culture over two millennia. No wonder, also, that like Parker and his wife in O'Connor's story, they have also often disagreed about how best to reconcile matter and spirit in their theology and ritual.

RELICS

The gospels tell us that Jesus was a miracle worker, that is, someone who literally embodied supernatural power and could physically alter the natural course of events. Almost every page of the gospels narrates a miracle story: Jesus healing the sick, raising the dead, controlling the weather, walking on water, changing water into wine, feeding thousands with a handful of loaves and fishes. Though these accounts would prove an embarrassment to Thomas Jefferson and other Deists in the eighteenth century—we have seen how Jefferson took it upon himself to expunge all such stories from his own reasonable edition of the New Testament—there is no denying the fact that belief in miracles was central to the early Christian message. In one gospel story, a woman is healed merely by touching the hem of Jesus' robe. "If I touch even his garments, I shall be made well," says the woman. In the Acts of the Apostles, Jesus' disciples continue to work all sorts of miracles, and those around them expect it, even to the point of carrying the sick out into the streets so that "as Peter came by at least his shadow might fall on some of them" (Acts 5:15). This belief in miracles was founded on the conviction that divine power could indeed be encountered through matter and that heaven and earth could intersect.

As a persecuted minority drawn largely from the lower social classes, early Christians were not able to produce much in the way of a long-lasting material culture. But there is plenty of evidence indicating that they firmly believed in the propriety—even the necessity—of seeking spiritual benefits through the material world. Persecution defined the material culture of early Christians more intensely than anything else, for it not only prevented them from assembling in large or conspicuous buildings, but also furnished them with their most cherished treasure, the remains of the martyrs. Ritually, the rise of the cult of the martyrs among Christians stemmed from the natural instinct of humans to treat their beloved dead with reverence and affection. If in secular twentieth-century America commonplace objects once owned by Elvis Presley can fetch thousands of dollars—and even attract pilgrims, imagine how much more ritual devotion early Christians would have shown for their martyrs. The cult of the martyrs made sense to early Christians. Theologically, the veneration of the martyrs stemmed from belief in their imitation of Christ and in their participation in his redemptive suffering. As *The Martyrdom of Polycarp* explained it (ca. 156 CE), Christians loved the martyrs "as disciples and imitators of the Lord."

The material remains of saints and the objects associated with their bodily existence came to be revered as relics by Christians from early on. *The Martyrdom of Polycarp* spoke of the martyr's bones as "more precious than costly stones, and more valuable than gold" and reported that while Polycarp was alive he seldom got a chance to take off his own shoes, "because the faithful always vied with one

**Purse of St. Stephen
Kunsthistorisches Museum,
Vienna**

The relics of Christian martyrs and saints were lavished with attention as vessels of divine power and were venerated in ritual settings. This jewel-encrusted reliquary from the court of Emperor Charlemagne (early ninth century) contained blood-soaked soil recovered from the site of the martyrdom of St. Stephen in Jerusalem. This purse of St. Stephen is typical of the types of relics most highly prized by Catholic and Orthodox Christians: those associated with New Testament events and personages. Beginning in the fourth century, Christians ransacked Palestine in search of such objects. Palestine itself became a giant relic of sorts—the "Holy Land"—an awesome place radiating sacred power, a magnet for pilgrimages, and a nexus between Heaven and earth. (*Source:* Erich Lessing/Art Resource, NY)

another as to which of them would be first to touch his body." This remarkable document also tells how the Jews of Smyrna tried to prevent the Christians from gaining access to Polycarp's remains immediately after the saint was burnt to death, arguing before the Roman authorities that this could start yet another troublesome sect: "They will abandon the crucified and begin worshiping this one."

Apparently, the Christian love of relics was well known, but misunderstood. The Christians said they wished "to have fellowship with his holy flesh" because Polycarp was now one with Christ, and they succeeded in gaining access to Polycarp's charred remains. Having gathered his bones, they laid them away in a place where they could become the focal point of ritual veneration:

> There the Lord will permit us, so far as possible, to gather together in joy and gladness to celebrate the day of his martyrdom as a birthday, in memory of those athletes who have gone before, and to train and make ready those who are to come hereafter.[2]

The cult of relics spread quickly among Eastern and Western Christians. These relics were not only revered and made an integral part of eucharistic celebrations, but were also sought out for their miraculous powers. Much like Christ's body in the gospels, relics were seen as connecting points between matter and spirit, Heaven and earth. Since the soul of the martyr was believed to be in Heaven, with God, the martyr's remains on earth were believed to somehow share in the glory and power of Heaven. Relics, thus, were also tokens of the promised resurrection of the body. They were believed to manifest obvious physical signs of sacredness, most notably a wonderful smell. When Polycarp was martyred, for instance, his followers immediately detected a sweet aroma. This odor of sanctity became a distinguishing characteristic of holiness, sometimes believed present in living saints, but most often associated with their relics. In the sixth century, Gregory of Tours described it as similar to the fragrance of flowers. And the odor could heal, as reportedly happened in fourth-century Jerusalem at the discovery of the body of St. Stephen (who, incidentally, was the first Christian martyr):

> At that instant the earth trembled and a smell of sweet perfume came from the place such as no man had ever known of, so much that we thought that we were standing in the sweet garden of Paradise. And at that very hour, from the smell of that perfume, seventy-three persons were healed.[3]

Healing powers "proved" the sacredness of the relic and the truth of the faith. Healing was also an immensely practical aspect of Christianity, perhaps the most practical and popular. Salvation was surely important, but in an age of crude and ineffective medicine, the promise of release from immediate pain and illness might indeed have been one of Christianity's strongest selling points. This was a religion that offered immediate as well as long-term redemption. Whereas the bulk of the Christian community probably had trouble understanding doctrines such as the incarnation and the trinity and rituals such as the eucharist, they certainly could appreciate an immediate release from bodily suffering.

From the earliest days of the Christian faith, it was commonly believed that the divine power inherent in holy people radiated from their bodies and could be transferred to objects touched by them. Although distinctions were made in nomenclature between noncorporeal "real" relics (items touched by the saints during their life on earth), and the so-called "representative" or "contact" relics (items touched by the saints' presence after their death), no practical discrimination was exercised in their veneration. Gregory the Great argued that the saints and martyrs were as fully present in church through their contact relics as through their bodies.

To touch a saint's body, or anything that had come in contact with it, was to knock on Heaven's door. Through their death, the martyrs had entered the realm of God and could serve as advocates before him. Furthermore, relics transcended space and time. Space was transcended through relics in two ways: by the joining of Heaven and earth and by the scattering of the saints' presence beyond the grave through the wide distribution of small portions of their remains (which happened frequently after the sixth century). Time collapsed before the relics, as the boundaries were erased between past, present, and future. Saints' relics could work miracles because of what they had accomplished in the *past*, where they were located at *present*, and how they already enjoyed the promised resurrection *to come*. It was precisely this connection with the resurrection that had made St. Augustine marvel when he contemplated the miracles wrought by the flesh of the saints. As another Church Father put it, the great wonder of it all was the way in which each and every fragment of a saint's body was "linked by a bond to the whole stretch of eternity."[4] The relics of the saints, then, did more than cure when they worked miracles; they served as a negation of death itself and as evidence of the resurrection to come.

In the millennium between the fifth and fifteenth centuries, the cult of relics continued to enjoy enormous popularity among both Eastern and Western Christians. As soon as Christianity became legal in the Empire, the cult of relics expanded by leaps and bounds. The relics of the martyrs no longer had to be revered in obscure places: instead, they could fill the churches that Christians were constructing everywhere. Churches were built over the graves of well-known saints; in time they would come to be known as "basilicas," or places of power (Greek, *basileus*: king). Suddenly, Christians began to search for the best possible relics, which of necessity had been hidden for three centuries: the bodies of the apostles and physical objects associated with Jesus and Mary. The mother of Emperor Constantine, Helena, traveled to the Holy Land and found one of the most precious of all relics, the cross and nails through which Jesus had effected the salvation of humanity.

Many other similar relics were found in the first fifty years after the end of persecution: the pillar on which Jesus was scourged, the chair of St. James, the head of John the Baptist, the chains of St. Paul. Others were found throughout the medieval period, including the Holy Grail and the Holy Chalice used at the Last Supper; the so-called Veil of Veronica, which was believed to contain a miraculous imprint of the face of Jesus; and the Shroud of Turin, which many still believe to contain a full image of Jesus' body. Belief in Christ's bodily ascent to Heaven did not deter some from searching for—and finding—corporeal relics of Jesus, such as the foreskin removed at his circumcision, baby teeth, hair and nail clippings, and even milk from Mary's breast that had been spilled by the infant Jesus. Christians could explain how these items had survived: they had been prudently saved by angels for the express purpose of veneration by later Christians. Angels were also believed responsible for the miraculous relocation from the Holy Land of relics that seemed incongruously out of place, such as the entire Holy Staircase on which

CREATION AS GOOD

Despite pronounced dualistic tendencies, Orthodox Christians have always affirmed the goodness of God's material creation. This Christian affection for the material world has expressed itself not only in art, music, and poetry, but also in prayer. St. Francis of Assisi (1181–1226) saw all of creation as interconnected and refused to consider "matter" and "spirit" as opposed to each other. Francis's mystical love of nature, expressed in the following prayer, has been adopted by many in the twentieth century as the foundation for theological environmental ethics.

The Canticle of Brother Sun

Most high, all-powerful, all good, Lord!
    All praise is yours, all glory, all honor,
    And all blessing.
To you alone, Most High, do they belong.
    No mortal lips are worthy
    To pronounce your name.
All praise be yours, my Lord through all that you have made,
    And first my lord Brother Sun,
    Who brings the day; and light you give to us through him.
How beautiful is he, how radiant in all his splendor!
    Of you, Most High, he bears the likeness.
All praise be yours, my Lord, through Sister Moon and Stars;
    In the heavens you have made them, bright,
    And precious and fair.
All praise be yours, my Lord, through Brothers Wind and Air,
    And fair and stormy, and all the weather's moods,
    By which you cherish all that you have made.
All praise be yours, my Lord, through Sister Water,
    So useful, lowly, precious and pure.
All praise be yours, my Lord, through Brother Fire,
    Through whom you brighten up the night.
    How beautiful is he, how gay! Full of power and strength.
All praise be yours, my Lord, through Sister Earth, our mother.
    Who feeds us in her sovereignty and produces
    Various fruits with colored flowers and herbs.
All praise be yours, my Lord, through those who grant pardon
    For love of you; through those who endure
    Sickness and trial.
Happy those who endure in peace,
    By you, Most High, they will be crowned.
All praise be yours, my Lord, through Sister Death,
    From whose embrace no mortal can escape.
Woe to those who die in mortal sin!
    Happy those She finds doing your will!
    The second death can do no harm to them.
Praise and bless my Lord, and give him thanks,
    And serve him with great humility.

Jesus had been questioned by Pilate, brought from Jerusalem to Rome; and the body of the Apostle James at Compostela, in the most remote corner of Spain.

Given time and sufficient demand, some relics could multiply. By the fifteenth century, for instance, there were at least seven "genuine" heads of John the Baptist; three Holy Prepuces, or foreskins of Christ; hundreds of fragments from the crown of thorns; and thousands of pieces of the "true" cross. Tiny slivers and large chunks of the cross could be found nearly everywhere. The pious were not necessarily troubled or offended when they learned of these duplications; some theologians argued that these relics were so necessary for humans that God, out of his infinite mercy and power, had decided to reproduce them many times over. If Jesus had multiplied a few fish and some loaves of bread by the thousands, so reasoned the theologians, should not he also be able to do the same with relics? By the sixteenth century, well-educated Western skeptics could scoff at the credulity of the masses. Erasmus of Rotterdam joked: "Though one man alone carried the cross, now a whole ship could be built from it." John Calvin would steal Erasmus' joke and never give him credit for it.

The ritual significance of relics for Catholics and the Orthodox cannot be underestimated, and not just because they ostensibly worked miracles and warded off evil. Relics played a key part in the Christianization of the Germanic and Slavic peoples, for their supposed power gave missionaries something concrete on which to base their authority. Eventually, no church or altar could be properly consecrated without a relic. For the newly Christianized who had no saints of their own, relics were wondrous gifts from the older community that tied them not only to Heaven, but also to Rome and Constantinople. Relics also became the focal points of pilgrimages, that quintessential medieval ritual. Even civil justice sometimes relied on relics, for they could be sworn upon in much the same way modern Protestant Christians swear upon Bibles. The authority of kings could be strengthened and sanctified by the relics they owned, as well as by the saints' bodies near which they were buried. Relics became such prized commodities that they could fetch vast sums of money or even be stolen. As early as the fifth century, the Emperor Thedosius enacted a law against trafficking in relics, but to little avail. In fact, the practice of pious relic stealing, known as "sacred theft," was endemic during the Middle Ages.

ART AND ARCHITECTURE

Because persecution made it difficult to sacralize any single building or site, Christian ritual spaces were not firmly fixed until the fourth century, and the development of ritual art was circumscribed by this situation. This is why so few traces survive of early Christian material culture, aside from texts and relics. As soon as persecution ceased, however, Christian art and architecture blossomed. From the start, the cult of relics was intimately related to the development of this material culture.

Ample evidence has survived linking relics to sacred art and architecture. In Rome, where large numbers of martyrs could be found, Christians began

Stone Testaments to an Age of Faith: Most Significant Medieval Christian Church Buildings

10 5 0 5 15

North Sea

KINGDOM OF
NORWAY AND
SWEDEN

Oslo

Glasgow

St. Andrews

Roskilde

Lund

Baltic Sea

BRITISH ISLES

York

Lübeck

Krakow

Lichfield
Peterborough
Ely

Bremen

Ghent

GERMANY

Wells
London
Canterbury
Salisbury

Bruges
Utrecht
Cologne
Aachen

Mainz
Worms
Speyer

Bamberg
Nürmberg
Ratisbon

Atlantic Ocean

Mont Saint-
Michel
Rouen
Coutances

Amiens
Rheims

Strasbourg

Ulm
Augsburg

Prague

Quimper

Paris
Chartres
Tours

Langres

Freiburg

Munich

Vienna

Nantes

Vezelay

Poitiers
Bourges

Bay of Biscay

Autun
Clairvaux
Basel

Santiago
de Compostela

León

Angouleme
FRANCE

Geneva
Lyons

Zurich

Bordeaux

Le Puy
Conques

Vienne

Milan

Verona

Salamanca
Valladolid

Burgos

Pamplona
Jaca

Albi
Toulouse

Avignon

Venice

Genoa

Dubrovnik

Coimbra

Avila

Saragossa
Lérida

Bayonne

Narbonne
Huesca
Montserrat

Arles

Aix

Pisa

Florence

Assisi

Adriatic Sea

Alcobaça
Lisbon

Gerona

Siena
Orvieto

Barcelona

CORSICA

Rome

ITALY

Guadalupe

Toledo
SPAIN

Monte Cassino

Córdoba

Valencia

Balearic
Sea

Palma
MAJORCA

SARDINIA

Naples
Amalfi
Salerno

Seville

Tyrrhenian Sea

Mediterranean Sea

Palermo

Ionian
Sea

Alboran Sea

Monreale
SICILY

Messina

MALTA
(Br.)

**View of the Stained-Glass
Windows from the Interior
of the Sainte Chapelle, Paris
(1246–1248)**

A prime example of the gothic predilection for light and of the
perfection of stained glass technology, this chapel housed a
relic from the Crown of Thorns. (*Source:* Girandon/Art Resource,
NY)

assembling and worshiping in the underground burial chambers, or catacombs,
which stretched for hundreds of miles in the suburbs, along the major roads leading to the city. Similar rites were celebrated elsewhere throughout the empire, as
we know from documents such as *The Martyrdom of Polycarp*; but physical evidence of these gatherings has not survived. The Roman catacombs are unique because of their vastness, location, and legal standing in the empire. Since Roman
law regarded all burial places as sacred, Christians could not be legally persecuted
in the catacombs. The Roman catacombs consisted of underground labyrinths of

galleries and connecting rooms, two to four stories deep; the dead were buried in niches carved out of the walls. The catacombs were gradually filled with decorated stone coffins (sarcophagi), and their walls were covered with stucco paintings. These are the first surviving examples of Christian art. When the persecutions ceased in the fourth century, Christians gradually abandoned these worship sites, transferring the more significant relics to churches above ground. During the Middle Ages, the Roman catacombs were forgotten; but since their rediscovery in the sixteenth century, many of them have been excavated and restored. Their treasures, humble as they are, reveal nearly as much about early Christianity as all surviving texts.

Moving the relics out of hiding and into public worship sites gave rise to a new Christian understanding of sacred space and sacred art. This shift also changed the topography of cities and towns as "the world" was gradually Christianized in a fully spatial, physical sense. The buildings in which Christians gathered to worship came to be called "churches," bringing into full association the macrocosm and the microcosm: the church was at once the entire Christian community and each individual place of worship, the universal institution and every single ritual space. (The English word "church" is derived from the Germanic *kirika*, which in turn comes from the Greek *kuriakos*: of the Lord; the church, then, is literally the "house of the Lord.") Christian churches served multiple purposes, but their sacred character was determined by two key ritual functions: (1) they were the places where the eucharist was celebrated, that is, where Christ made himself physically present; and (2) they were sites where the martyrs and saints were also present, through their relics.

Sacred buildings are not unique to Christianity, of course. Early Christians knew all about sacred buildings, for the whole world was filled with temples dedicated to "false" gods. Christians were fully aware that their new legal worship spaces served the same function as pagan temples: they were sacred spaces, houses of the holy. But whereas most pagans were willing to grant that all temples were truly sacred, Christians were convinced that only their houses of worship were *genuine* places of linkage between Heaven and earth. The church buildings might have physically looked very much like the pagan temples, but they were different for Christians, who viewed them as microcosms of the heavenly kingdom. As one writer put it, the church was "a place of perfection, the heavenly Jerusalem, its walls and buildings made in heaven, transferred to this spot." One inscription at the shrine of St. Martin of Tours said it all: "How awesome is this place! This is none other than the house of God, and this is the gate of heaven."[5]

The architecture of Christian churches evolved directly from that of pagan temples. In many cases, as the empire grew officially hostile to paganism, Christians took over pagan temples and reconsecrated them. Often, too, Christians would raze pagan temples and build a church over the same spot. The purpose was clear: Christians were physically sacralizing the world. But the space within the buildings remained much the same: a transitional space at the entrance, a long open assembly space inside (usually divided into a central nave and two narrower side aisles), and the "sanctuary" containing the altar or sacred table at the far end

Christ Pantocrator and the Virgin and Child with Angels, Apostles and Saints. Twelfth–Thirteenth Century Mosaic in the Central Apse of the Cathedral, Monreale (Sicily)

Christ, ruler of all, dominated most Byzantine churches. The other icons in this church are typical of church decoration among the Orthodox: Mary, angels, and saints. (*Source:* Alinari/Art Resource)

(Latin, *sanctus*: sacred). Within the sacred precincts of this space, the altar was the holiest spot, for it was the place where Christ was made present in the eucharist. The altar was also situated directly over a relic or even a saint's tomb. Eventually, most churches were built with the sanctuary facing eastward, toward the rising sun, a vivid symbol of the resurrection.

In the medieval West, the practice arose of installing other altars within the church building, creating a hierarchy of sacred spaces within. These side altars or chapels proliferated in the larger churches; most often, they were erected by confraternities, guilds, families, or wealthy individuals who sought to simultaneously express their devotion and claim a measure of ownership over sacred space. Nobles and wealthy merchants routinely built burial chapels for themselves and their families inside the churches. The vast majority of Christians were buried in consecrated ground, usually adjacent to the church, but customs varied from place to place. In some Spanish towns, for instance, most burials took place inside the churches, in vaults beneath the worship space. The belief was that the closer one was to an altar and a relic, the better one's chances would be in the afterlife.

The Christian emperors of Rome lavished much attention on church building, but after the collapse of the Western Empire, bishops and kings largely assumed the responsibility. Among the Orthodox, who lived mainly in the surviving Byzantine Empire, church building remained an imperial concern. Constantinople came to have the largest and most sumptuous churches in all of Christendom. Constantine built the Church of the Apostles in the fourth century so he could be buried alongside the apostles Andrew, Luke, and Timothy. In the 530s, the Emperor Justinian constructed a new church of the Holy Wisdom (*Hagia Sophia*) that dwarfed all others in size and splendor. Capped by a vast dome that seemed suspended from Heaven and filled with light, this church strained to physically embody the cosmic truth of the Christian faith. This was the church of the Patriarch of Constantinople and the site of all imperial coronations. The dome of Hagia Sophia, which sought to represent the cosmos, was one of the dominant architectural features of Orthodox churches. When Constantinople was captured by the Moslem Turks in 1453, Hagia Sophia was converted into a mosque and minarets were added to it. Today, it is a museum.

Church architecture in the medieval West came to be dominated first by the Romanesque style, which featured rounded arches and small windows. Romanesque churches tended to be dark, solemn places. They were also cruciform, that is, built in the shape of a cross. Beginning in the twelfth century, the Gothic style began to spread from northern France; by the fifteenth century, it could be found nearly everywhere in the West. It was a style well suited for large imposing churches, such as cathedrals. Gothic churches retained the cruciform plan, but featured pointed arches and large windows. Thanks to the engineering innovation of flying buttresses—masonry supports that carried the weight of the building's stone to the exterior and lessened the load on the church walls—Gothic churches could have extraordinarily large windows. In some cases, practically the entire wall space could be made of glass. Since the manufacture of stained glass had been perfected by the twelfth century, Gothic churches made full use of this material, suffusing the worship space with many colors. The intended effect inside the building was the same as at Hagia Sophia: to raise the worshiper's mind to the Divine Light through the sense of sight. Engineering, art, and theology came together in Gothic architecture to produce a sublime physical statement of faith. Abbot Suger, who directed the construction of the first Gothic church at the Abbey of St. Denis outside Paris, explained it thus:

> When the enchanting beauty of the house of God has overwhelmed me, when the charm of the multicolored gems has led me to transpose material things to immaterial

things and reflect on the diversity of the sacred virtues, then it seems to me that I can see myself, as if in reality, residing in some strange region of the universe which had no previous existence either in the clay of this earth or in the purity of the heavens, and that, by the grace of God, I can be transported mystically from life on this earth to the higher realm.[6]

The vast majority of Christians may have had very few possessions, but many of these splendid churches, especially the shrines, basilicas, and cathedrals, were places open to all and in a way "owned" by all. The opulence of these sacred buildings was shared by all Christians collectively and offered to God. In one sense, this was shared wealth, but in another very real sense, of course, it was not. Some monastics were not at all pleased by the resources lavished on churches. Bernard of Clairvaux, for instance, railed against Abbot Suger and his Gothic innovation at St. Denis:

> Oh vanity! vanity! and folly even greater than the vanity! The church sparkles and gleams on all sides, while its poor huddle in need; its stones are gilded, while its children go unclad; in it the artlovers find enough to satisfy their curiosity, while the poor find nothing there to relieve their misery.[7]

But critics such as St. Bernard were a small minority. Most of the Christian elite agreed that churches should overwhelm the human senses and manifest the redemption of the material world. Priests dressed in colorful vestments and used liturgical vessels made of gold and silver and studded with precious stones; even the ceilings could be decorated in gold leaf. Baptismal fonts were carved from marble. The walls could be festooned with dazzling hangings made from the finest textiles. Silver canopies could cover the altar. Candles could blaze everywhere, sometimes by the hundreds or thousands. Great clouds of sweet-smelling incense could fill the sacred space and the worshipers' nostrils, reminding them of the odor of sanctity (in an age without deodorants this may have been doubly welcomed in crowded churches). At Santiago de Compostela, a place routinely filled with dirty, reeking pilgrims, the smoky incense was spread by means of a silver censer so immense that it took several men to swing it from the ceiling with ropes.

There was also sound. Bells called the faithful to worship, marked special hours and feasts, tolled for the dead, or even warned of impending danger. City streets as well as the countryside could resound with the tolling of church bells on Sundays and feast days. In the West, the use of bells evolved into greater complexity than in the East. Medieval Catholic churches began to use bells of various sizes that produced different tones. Bell towers became one of the most prominent features of Western churches, soaring toward Heaven, visually and audibly punctuating the skyline of every town like exclamation points. Bells were used inside as well, to call attention to special moments during the liturgy.

There was music, as well. So much music, and so sublime, that in some places the worshipers could say they felt transported to Heaven. We know that the early Christians sang hymns and that some of their pagan critics envied the music's beauty. Unfortunately, only a few of these hymns survive. In the fourth century, Arians used hymns to spread their "heretical" teachings. The Orthodox countered by intensifying the use of music in ritual. The hymns of St. Ambrose of Milan, composed to fight the Arian heresy, played a key role in the conversion of St. Augustine:

> The tears flowed from me when I heard your hymns and canticles, for the sweet singing of your church moved me deeply. The music surged in my ears, truth seeped into my heart, and my feelings of devotion overflowed, so that tears streamed down. But they were tears of gladness.[8]

Antiphonal singing, which required two choirs singing verses in response to each other, spread from the Near East and came to dominate Christian liturgical music by the fifth century. Among the Orthodox, elaborate chanting without instrumental accompaniment became the norm: Byzantine and Russian chants aimed to stir the soul and raise the mind to ethereal heights. Catholics had the same goal, but among them chanting developed along different lines. One type of antiphonal choral singing used in Rome became dominant in the West after the sixth century. Known as Gregorian chant because it was (incorrectly) attributed to Pope Gregory I, this sacred music summed up the ethos of Medieval Catholicism as much as did Gothic architecture and stained glass windows. By the ninth century, the pipe organ was introduced in the West to accompany the choirs and gradually became dominant. Medieval churches were constructed with a fine ear for acoustics, and their interiors were designed as much for the sound of the choir and organ as for sheer visual delight.

Finally, because it was a text-centered religion, Christianity also produced thousands of manuscripts. Before the invention of the printing press in the mid-fifteenth century, all texts had to be copied by hand. This was difficult labor, especially in an age when only a few men and even fewer women could read and write. The Bible had to be endlessly copied, as did the writings of the Fathers and, later, of other theologians. Liturgical books and hymnals, too, were constantly being copied. Especially in the earlier medieval period, most of this work was accomplished by monks, for whom it was a sacred task akin to prayer. Most monasteries had one room dedicated to the copying of manuscripts, the scriptorium, and it was in these rooms that the culture of Christendom was preserved and passed on from one generation to the next. But the monks did not simply crank out their manuscripts without inspiration. As monks lavished attention on their buildings and images, so did they pour their soul into the art of copying, turning out illuminated manuscripts that continue to inspire awe. For the medieval and Byzantine copyists, God was in the details.

IMAGES

From the second century on, Christians began to employ painted images in worship. The Roman catacombs alone offer sufficient evidence that the early Christians arrived at a liberal interpretation of the Second Commandment ("Thou shalt not make any graven images," Exod. 20:4–6; Lev. 5:8–10). But widespread use of

St. Matthew's Gospel

Monks lavished love and attention on their sacred manuscripts, producing texts that were works of art. This eighth-century Irish manuscript page from the Lindisfarne Gospels is the beginning of Matthew's Gospel, an excellent example of monastic attention to detail and love of the Word. In this painstaking manner, monks transmitted Christian culture and faith from one generation to the next, until the invention of the printing press in the fifteenth century. (*Source:* Bridgeman/Art Resource, NY)

images did not begin until the fourth and fifth centuries, as church building increased.

This development was rapid but did not go unopposed. Individual voices were raised against the cult of relics and images. We know that in the fourth century, Vigilantius denounced both relics and images as "idolatrous" and that Epiphanius of Salamis destroyed an image of Christ in Palestine. Also, the Council of Elvira (ca. 312) had pronounced that images were "not to be painted on walls to be revered and worshiped." But this resistance was drowned out by a chorus of popular and elite approval. Paintings and statues of Jesus, Mary, and the saints proliferated in the newly built churches and also in Christian homes. Christians prostrated themselves, prayed, lit candles, and used incense in the images' presence. As they gained ritual prominence, much like relics, these religious images gained favor as points of contact with a higher spiritual reality. Images, too, began to work miracles and to attract pilgrims. Some images appeared miraculously, suddenly materializing or dropping from Heaven as angel-borne gifts. Then there were also ancient images supposedly dating back to the time of Jesus. Edessa, a Christian city beyond the eastern border of the Empire, claimed to have a "portrait" of Jesus that the savior himself had sent before his crucifixion to the King of Edessa. Constantinople boasted of its portrait of Mary painted by the apostle Luke.

But the ever expanding cult of images was not universally accepted in the East. Conflict over the ritual use of images erupted in the Byzantine Empire suddenly, much like a summer thunderstorm, in the eighth century, and continued for more than a hundred years in two distinct phases (725–780, 815–843). The first outbreak of image-smashing began when Byzantine Emperor Leo III ordered the removal and destruction of all religious images in 725. This policy was continued by his son Emperor Constantine V. What is most odd about the Byzantine iconoclastic controversy (Greek, *eikon*: image + *klastes*: breaker) is the fact that it was initiated by the emperor, for disputes within Christianity had almost always been provoked by bishops and theologians. In this case, other motives besides the wiping out of "idolatry" can be discerned in the imperial mandates against icons, for the emperor also opposed monasticism, pilgrimages, and special devotion to shrines. Some have interpreted this controversy as an attempt by the emperor to gain greater control of the church, pointing to the fact that he had religious images replaced by portraits of himself.

No matter what the emperor's motives might have been or what was the source of his distrust of images (iconophobia), his policy proved unpopular. Though the army did a thorough job of destroying images, a groundswell of support among the laity and especially the monks kept the spirit of image veneration alive. Emperor Constantine V assembled a council at Constantinople in 753 to place a theological seal of approval on iconoclasm. To no one's surprise, the gathered bishops—supporters of the emperor—pronounced image veneration heretical and declared that the only lawful representation of Christ was the eucharist. The emperor's men ruthlessly hunted down image supporters and imprisoned, exiled, and even martyred them. They closed down many monasteries, confiscating them and turning them into army barracks and public baths.

After the death of Constantine V, imperial policy was suddenly reversed in 780 by Empress Irene, who was devoted to images. Where Leo III and Constantine V had failed to gain theological legitimacy, Irene succeeded. In 787, she convened another council at Nicaea. This council resoundly accepted the veneration of images and, instead, denounced iconoclasm as heretical. A distinction was made by this council between two types of worship: *latria* (adoration), which can be offered to God alone, and *dulia* (veneration), which can be offered to saints and their images. At bottom, the council affirmed the inherent goodness of matter and its capacity to act as a link with the divine. This council was guided in its thinking by the theology of John of Damascus (675–749), who had argued against iconoclasm on Christological terms. As John of Damascus saw it, the incarnation of Christ had sanctified all matter and had thus canceled out the biblical command against images:

> In former times God, who is without form or body, could never be depicted. But now when God is seen in the flesh conversing with men, I make an image of the God whom I see. I do not worship matter; I worship the creator of matter who became matter for my sake, who willed to take his abode in matter; who worked out my salvation through matter. Never will I cease honoring the matter which wrought my salvation![9]

Despite the pronouncements of the Council of Nicaea, the emperors continued to favor iconoclasm. In 815, Emperor Leo V began once again to persecute icons and their defenders. For an entire generation, iconoclasm continued to trouble the Eastern church; because the emperor favored iconoclasm, many among the faithful bravely endured exile and death because of their devotion to images. But Christian belief and piety have always been difficult to legislate or impose from above. Leo's policies met with defeat after his death, when Empress Theodora once again reinstated image veneration in 843. The centrality of images in Orthodox piety was finally confirmed. The significance of this victory for the supporters of images can be seen not only in the wholehearted acceptance of icons after 843, but also in the custom of celebrating Empress Theodora's decrees as "The Triumph of Orthodoxy," a feast that continues to be observed as Orthodoxy Sunday each year at the beginning of Lent.

The legacy of iconoclasm on Orthodox art was nonetheless profound. Fear of idolatry turned Orthodox icons into a highly stylized art form. Three-dimensional images were forbidden. The only acceptable icons were flat pictures with a golden background. Since icons were believed to be windows into heaven, prototypes of celestial realities, the gold depicts the divine light. Icon painting among the Orthodox assumed an impersonal quality: icons were not to be the products of individual artists who stamped their own creative imagination on them, but rather were to be anonymous works of art produced under nearly liturgical circumstances. Icon painting thus became a sacred craft, practiced mainly in monasteries, along with prayer and fasting, according to precise guidelines with specially consecrated materials. This has given Orthodox icons a certain sameness and timeless quality; even experts find it difficult to determine where and when some icons were painted.

Orthodox icons are not mere works of art; they are instruments of prayer. Every icon has to be properly consecrated in a special liturgy. Orthodox churches are filled with sacred icons that are reverently kissed by the faithful, who also light candles and offer incense before them. The interior of every Orthodox church is visually dominated by the *iconostasis*, or icon screen, that separates the sanctuary from the nave. Among the Orthodox, the sacred liturgy of the eucharist came to be regarded as such a great holy mystery that it should not be witnessed in its entirety by the faithful. The image screen is considered the appropriate demarcation line; the three doors on it open at key points in the liturgy to reveal some part of the great mystery behind it. Icons are also venerated in Orthodox homes and are usually assigned a prominent place of honor on eastern walls. Upon entering an Orthodox home, it is customary for visitors to first greet the icons by bowing and making the sign of the cross; only afterwards do guests greet their host. Because they consider all icons as sacred, many Orthodox still consider it blasphemous to exhibit them in museums.

THE REFORMATION

In the West, the iconoclastic controversy produced hardly a ripple. Already in the sixth century, Pope Gregory I had defended the use of images as the *libri pauperum,* or "books of the poor," arguing that they taught the faith to the illiterate. In 731, as Byzantine iconoclasm was raging, a Roman synod denounced image breaking and excommunicated the iconoclasts. In the Middle Ages, Western theologians continued to defend and promote the use of images, elaborating on the latria/dulia distinction. Unlike the Orthodox, however, the Catholics were not restricted to flat painted images. Consequently, their art could be as lifelike as possible, even three dimensional. Though images never achieved the same kind of exalted sacred status among Catholics as they did among the Orthodox, they were fully integrated into devotional life. In the fifteenth century, one theologian even proposed that the laity could be led to piety more effectively through a picture than through a sermon.

Until the fourteenth century, Western criticism of images was sporadic and limited. The early Cistercians, for instance, showed contempt for lavish ornamentation. As we have already seen, St. Bernard of Clairvaux advised it would be better to clothe the poor, whom he called "living images of Christ," than to fill images with religious art. More often than not, hostility to images was a "heretical" trait in the West. The Albigensians (Cathars) despised images because they were material objects; some Albigensians, it is said, would spit on the ground any time they saw a cross or an infant. The Waldensians, who exalted poverty, saw religious art as an impediment to true love of neighbor. The Lollards in England (fourteenth century) and the Hussites in Bohemia (fifteenth century) not only attacked images on paper, but actually destroyed them whenever they could, citing the Second Commandment.

These were limited attacks on Catholic cultic life. It would take the Protestant Reformation of the sixteenth century to effect changes on a large scale. The Reformation was a ritual revolution. The rejection of much of Catholic cultic life as idolatrous was an integral part of the expansion of the Reformation (1520–1648) in northern Switzerland, southwest Germany, France, the Netherlands, Scotland, and England. Images were not the only sacred objects to be vilified and destroyed. Relics, altars, consecrated hosts, chalices, vestments, missals, lamps, organs, windows, and holy water fonts also fell victim to iconoclastic ruin.

The Protestant war against idolatry began with Andreas Bodenstein von Karlstadt (ca. 1480–1541), a colleague of Martin Luther at the University of Wittenberg. Well versed in the Scriptures, Karlstadt was also an avid reader of Desiderius Erasmus, a humanist who had popularized in learned circles a negative attitude toward much of medieval Catholic piety, especially the cult of saints, images, and relics. In 1518, Karlstadt began to condemn the use of holy water; by 1521, he was attacking the veneration of images and denying the sacrificial dimension of the eucharist. In December 1521, during Luther's absence from Wittenberg, Karlstadt spearheaded the first iconoclastic riots of the Reformation. At the same time, Karlstadt published a treatise entitled "On the Abolition of Images, and That There Should Be No Beggars Among Christians." In this influential manifesto, Karlstadt argued that the veneration of images polluted the Christian community and angered God. Two central points of "The Abolition" became the foundation of all subsequent iconoclastic theology: (1) the commandment against images in the Decalogue should be observed by all Christians; and (2) the spiritual realm cannot be approached through the mediation of the material world, as assumed in Catholic sacramental theology and piety, for infinity cannot be conveyed by anything finite (*finitum non est capax infiniti*).

When Karlstadt incited yet another iconoclastic riot in February 1522, Luther hurried home to Wittenberg and preached against Karlstadt's tactics, forcing him to leave. Undaunted, Karlstadt continued developing a revolutionary iconoclastic theology. In another pamphlet, "Whether One Ought to Behave Peacefully and Spare the Feelings of the Simple" (1524), Karlstadt proposed a revolutionary policy against Catholic ritual: if "idolatry" would not be abolished by the civil authorities, he argued, then all true Christians were to destroy the "idols" by force.

Luther's disagreement with Karlstadt marks the first major parting of the ways in the Reformation. Since he was not concerned with the metaphysical issue of matter versus spirit, but rather with the soteriological question of law versus gospel, Luther saw Karlstadt's iconoclastic theology as a legalistic return to "works-righteousness," that is, belief in the power of one's own actions to bring about salvation. Luther and his followers remained indifferent to images, arguing that it was better to remove them from the hearts of Christians than from the walls of churches. Consequently, the Lutheran church developed a cautious, rather than a hostile attitude to religious imagery and generally shied away from iconoclasm. Luther's illustrated Bible, in fact, is one of the most enduring monuments of German Christian culture.

The seeds planted by Karlstadt germinated and bore fruit in Switzerland among those who came to be known as Reformed Protestants and also among the Anabaptists. As early as 1519, Ulrich Zwingli began preaching against the cult of saints and images in Zurich. Sporadic attacks on religious images began to take place in and around Zurich in 1523, as Zwingli and other pastors intensified their attack against images and the Mass from the pulpit. A series of public disputations on the worship question held at Zurich in 1523–1524 resulted in a victory for the iconophobes. On June 15, 1524, the Zurich magistracy called for the abolition of the Mass and the orderly removal of all religious imagery. Swiftly, during a two-week period, each of Zurich's churches was carefully "cleansed" of its religious images by teams of craftsmen behind closed doors.

Zurich established a pattern. Image destruction spread in waves to smaller towns under its jurisdiction and, in turn, to other Swiss cities and their territories, where it was often employed as a means of challenging the status quo and of ushering in the Reformation. Some Lutheran cities in the Baltic region also turned iconoclastic. The Anabaptists, too, became vehement iconophobes, but their pacifism and their separatist beliefs prevented the majority from actually smashing cultic objects. Only those radicals who advocated revolutionary violence actually engaged in iconoclasm, particularly during the Peasant's War (1524–1525) and in the uprising at Münster (1534–1535).

After 1536, the intellectual and moral leadership of iconoclasm shifted to Geneva and its Reformer, John Calvin (1509–1564). Though he never engaged in image destruction and always publicly condemned illegal acts, Calvin further intensified Reformed Protestant animosity toward idolatry in his magisterial *Institutes* (four editions, 1536–1559) and in numerous treatises, letters, and sermons. In Calvin's native France, sporadic acts of image destruction and desecration had been occurring since the early 1520s, but it was not until 1560 that the French Calvinists, known as Huguenots, dared to launch a full-scale attack on idolatry, sparking iconoclastic riots throughout the kingdom. This violence led to the French Wars of Religion (1562–1598), during which iconoclasm would become the external earmark of the Calvinist Huguenot movement. Other waves of Calvinist iconoclasm would alter the material culture of Christianity in Scotland (1559), the Low Countries (1566–1609), Germany (1570–1618), and Poland-Lithuania (early 1600s).

English iconoclasm has a complex and protracted history. King Henry VIII (1491–1547) had decreed the abolition of "abused" images, giving rise to unsystematic and relatively moderate attacks on idolatry. This equivocal policy was followed by all of Henry's Protestant successors and became a focus of discontent among the growing number of Calvinist Puritans in the late sixteenth and early seventeenth centuries. In fact, the name "Puritan" is derived from the animosity these Calvinists felt toward the material culture of the established Anglican church, which they very much wanted to see "purified" of all material traces of idolatry and popery. When these Puritans finally came to power in 1640, England and Ireland would be ravaged by intense iconoclasm.

Animosity toward the symbolic structure of medieval Catholicism was an inevitable effect of the Reformation, for the rejection of external forms and the creation of an inner/outer dialectic are necessary components of all attempts at religious reform. Moreover, the prohibition of religious imagery found in Exodus 20:4–6; Leviticus 5:8–10, and in numerous other biblical texts made it difficult for scripturally centered Protestants to skirt the issue of idolatry.

Since iconoclasm was an expression of discontent and was most often carried out by the laity, it was not only the most visible change brought about by the religious crisis of the early modern age, but was also one of the most radical and democratic, advancing the Reformation tangibly at street level and allowing for popular participation in the political process. Though it is possible to identify social, political, and economic grievances that contributed to the development of iconoclasm, it would be wrong to isolate them or, even worse, to distinguish them over and against religion as more pressing motives. If symbols function on multiple levels of meaning, so do the actions taken against them.

On an intellectual and spiritual level, iconoclasm was a means of proving the falsehood of Roman Catholicism and of desacralizing its symbolic structure. Often, it was not enough to destroy the images; public acts of defilement ensured they would be discredited as well as destroyed and that the community would know it had been ritually cleansed from its "idolatrous" pollution. Sacred objects were routinely put to the test by Protestants. For instance, at Wesen, Switzerland, in the late 1520s, the images were piled up in a public place, ritually mocked, and asked to protect themselves from the flames as they were set afire; in St.-Jacques, France, in 1566, a Christ figure was scourged with tree branches and taunted: "If you are God, speak!" Similarly, soldiers at LeMans, France, in 1562, and at Saffron Walden, England, in 1640, proved images powerless by using them to cook their meals. Images were thrown into rivers and lakes, stuck with pikes and shot at, buried in mass graves, and thrown into charnel houses. Debasement and destruction could go hand in hand. Images were thrown into latrines, ditches, and sewers; used as construction materials for town walls and barricades; and given as toys to children. Consecrated hosts were routinely fed to animals, trod underfoot, or defiled in some other way. Total destruction was not necessary; disfigurement and ridicule served the same purpose. In Perth, Scotland, a St. Francis statue was desecrated in 1544 by having a ram's horns nailed to its head and a cow's tail to its rear before it was hung from the gallows. In Poland, near Lublin, in 1628, a young man fashioned a carnival mask for himself by slicing off Mary's face from a painting and cutting out its eyes and mouth. On many occasions, hurried iconoclasts saved time by merely lopping off heads and limbs or, more frequently, by gouging out the eyes from images.

Iconoclasm was often also linked to social and economic issues. The wealth lavished on church decorations in medieval times seemed a waste to iconoclasts, who saw it as a squandering of resources that could have been spent on the poor and needy. As Martin Bucer summarized it in one of his sermons, idolatry was "both against faith and love." Throughout Switzerland in the late 1520s, ravaged wooden images were routinely given to the poor as firewood, and precious metals were redeemed for charitable or civic purposes. Since images, altars, and other devotional objects could be donated only by those who had sufficient wealth—nobles, successful artisans and merchants, guilds, and confraternities—iconoclasm could also be an expression of class hostility; many eyewitnesses later blamed the destruction on the lowest elements in society. In addition, one cannot discount youthful unrest, for adolescents and children were often blamed for the violence. Nonetheless, it should not be assumed that all iconoclasts were poor or young. There are also numerous examples of mature, wealthy, and powerful iconoclasts throughout the entire Reformation period. In France, particularly, the nobility often cooperated with the poorer folk in the sacking of churches.

Protestant iconoclasm derived mainly from the Jewish biblical condemnation of idolatry, and it aimed not only to destroy the physical idols and their ritual objects, but to abolish a complex symbolic system and to remove the clerics who sustained it. Images, relics, and sacramental objects were a crucial part of the restricted code of medieval Christian society, the embodiment of the social myth that gave shape and form to accepted values and enabled them to be transmitted and enforced. Reformation iconoclasm was revolutionary on two fronts. First, it was a theological upheaval, a redefining of the sacred. Forsaking much of medieval Christian metaphysics and epistemology, Reformation iconoclasts denied certain correlations between body and soul, or Heaven and earth, and transfigured the meaning of prayer and sacrament. Iconoclasm was also revolutionary in a practical sense, for it was an act of violence against the accepted symbolic code and its guardians, a fact that may have given rise to the rare cooperation of rich and poor in some places and that may have been inchoately grasped by those young iconoclasts in Geneva who burst forth from the Cathedral in May 1536, carrying fragments of the images they had just shattered, roaring, "Here we have the gods the priests; would you like some?"

Catholics responded to Protestant iconoclasm by intensifying their commitment to religious art. The creed of the Council of Trent (1564) summed it up:

> We hold that the saints reigning together with Christ should be honored and invoked . . . and that their relics should be venerated. We firmly assert that images of Christ, of the Mother of God ever Virgin, and of the other saints should be owned and kept, and that due honor and veneration should be given to them.

Sacred music met with a varied response among Protestants. Martin Luther was enormously fond of music. He not only made congregational singing a central part of his liturgical reform, but actually wrote several psalm hymns in German, including the well-known "A Mighty Fortress Is Our God." This was a substantial change. Previously, most of the singing in the churches was in Latin and was performed by cantors and choirs. Zwingli, in contrast, rejected all sacred music as a distraction from true spiritual worship and would not allow the singing even of psalms. Calvin took a more moderate position and reintroduced congregational singing into the Reformed tradition, especially through the publication of the Genevan psalter. The Radicals as a whole favored singing. The Anglicans retained a rich choral tradition but also favored congregational singing. Roman Catholicism continued to stress the importance of music in the early modern age. In fact, the composition of music for an entire mass became one of the high points of the musical arts in this period, attracting the creative genius of the greatest musicians. Unlike the Protestants, however, Catholics did not as a rule favor singing by the congregation and also continued using Latin lyrics.

At the dawn of the modern age, then, there began to develop a new kind of Christian material culture in Western Europe and its nascent overseas colonies. The rich heritage of Orthodoxy and Catholicism continues to be embraced by many, to the present day. In the case of Catholicism, the Reformation was followed by the Age of the Baroque, a period of unparalleled artistic exuberance. Among Protestants, whose material culture was centered on the Word of God, all art became subordinate to the Bible. For a Calvinist, a "beautiful" church could never be one filled with artwork; on the contrary, "beauty," being one with truth, demanded utter material simplicity. The starker the material setting, the more "beautiful" and the more true to the supremacy of the Word.

CHRISTIANITY AND PRINT CULTURE

The supremacy of the Word made Christians "people of the book." But what is the meaning of the expression "people of the book" that is sometimes used by Christians (as well as by Jews) to describe themselves? In order to understand this designation, we must first recognize that the allusion to a book—which, of course, is to the "good book," or Bible—identifies an actual book, a bound collection of writings. The ideas expressed in writing inside the covers of the book are essential to Christian religious belief. But so, too, is the book's physical existence as paper, ink, and glue. The good book is an object of reverence, an icon displayed in the church, in the home, and in the hands of the religious professional standing before a congregation.

The rise of a print culture about the time of the Reformation transformed Christianity. When Johannes Gutenberg began printing with movable metal type about 1540, he opened the gates for a flood of books. Rising literacy (as many as 400,000 persons in Germany alone by 1500) created demand, technological advance brought down the price of paper, and profit-chasing investors poured money and energy into the business of publishing and distribution. The power of the book to shape thought was recognized by all, and not least by the Roman Catholic Church, which by the mid-sixteenth century had enlarged its Index of Forbidden Books to include a wide range of theological and political works that it considered subversive of Catholicism. In fact, in Bohemia, two hundred years later, illiteracy could be offered as proof of one's Catholic orthodoxy.

The proliferation of inexpensive vernacular Bibles (rather than Latin versions) was essential to the religious upheavals of the sixteenth century. Subsequent Enlightenment emphases on the capability of the individual, democratic government, and the dissemination of knowledge through print reinforced Protestant opinion that it was the right of every person to own and read the Bible and that reading the Bible was essential for salvation. Thus, the Enlightenment provided ideas that, as they were selectively appropriated by Christians, served to sharpen Christian focus upon the Bible at the same time that it developed a current of thought that eventually would undermine the authority of the Bible. The act of purchasing a Bible, even touching a Bible, remained representative of devotion to the invisible, transcendent, and mysterious in Christianity. The book came to be valued as if it were the bone of a saint, a scrap of the Blessed Virgin's clothing, or a sliver of the true cross. The Bible was a book like any other book, a book to hold in one's hands and read, but it was inexpressibly more than a book as well.

For example, a Bible had power to shelter persons from harm, and a Bible in hand was a first line of defense against Satan. Indeed, so pervasive was recourse to the Bible for protection against perceived evil that church authorities in early modern Europe were provoked to legislate against wearing the Bible or excerpts from it as amulets for fear that faith would turn to superstition (a distinction not always shared by the rank and file). Christians nevertheless continued to deploy the power of the Bible in settings ranging from the barnyard to the bedroom. A seventeenth-century English farmer who believed that he had lost a pig to witchcraft placed a Bible over the door of the sty after he had bought a new animal. At the end of the eighteenth century, a Sussex newspaper reported that two women

Belgian Engraving, ca. 1740

Holding a Bible in one's hands, turning the pages, and reading the words were acts of religious devotion. In fact, the act of reading the printed word, even if it were not a part of Scripture, was itself an activity rich with religious meaning. Here, the printing press, accompanied by Minerva and Mercury, descends from the heavens, a gift from God. (*Source:* Prosper Marchand, *Histoire d'origine et des premiers progrès de l'imprimeric.* The Hague: Pierre Paupie, 1740.)

accused of witchcraft were acquitted of the charge after "the Clerk was dispatched for the Church Bible which the two were weighed against, and which they out-weighed, *a sure proof they were not witches.*"[10] (The weight of truth in the form of the Bible proved, indeed, a formidable challenge for evil.) And in the twentieth century, we witness belief in the protective capabilities of the Bible—now fused with routine strategies of personal security—in the soldierly practice of entering battle with a small steel-jacketed Bible buttoned into the left breast pocket, over the heart.

Popular Christianity has exploited fascination with the actual "good book" most effectively. New religious movements frequently issue new translations of the Bible, but just as important are the garments in which those translations are clothed. Even a recycled King James version becomes something new and distinctive when it is bound in rawhide, leopard skin, pink angora, gold and leather, or denim with a "good news" patch on the front. The Bible effectively represents various religious identities in its incarnations as a "study Bible," a "micro-Bible," a "picture Bible," or the "Living Word Pendant Bible" (1984),[11] which consists of microfiche text implanted in a fourteen-carat gold cross and worn around the neck in a manner reminiscent of the practice of demon-fearing Christians centuries earlier.

Prayerbooks, psalters (booklets of Old Testament Psalms), and devotional publications also are an important part of Christian print culture. Though they do not command awe and wonder to the same degree as the Bible does, prayerbooks and liturgical guides such as the Anglican *Book of Common Prayer* or the New England *Bay Psalm Book,* or the Lutheran *Service Book and Hymnal,* or the American Jewish prayerbook *Minhag America* all benefit in standing from the cultural valuation of printed religious documents. The distribution of tracts, or small pieces of paper on which excerpts from the Bible are printed, became an important religious industry in the nineteenth and twentieth centuries on the strength of popular association of spiritual power with the printed word. The explosion of religious presses dedicated to denominational newspapers and magazines has followed the same path. Religious diaries, autobiographies, and other inspirational and devotional works are consumed in ever-increasing numbers by Christian readers. The rapid growth of Christian bookstores suggests that religious literature is essential to the life of Christianity in a print culture. Christians are, finally, people of the book and people of the books, a reality that was not lost on Joseph Smith in 1830 when he decided to call his collection of decoded divine revelations *The Book of Mormon.*

MODERNITY AND RELIGIOUS IDENTITY

Christianity since the Enlightenment has been characterized, like other western religions, by two seemingly opposite trends. On the one hand, the sweeping social changes and intense intercultural encounters of recent centuries have faded the contrasts among Christian denominations and have engendered cooperation among groups previously at odds. In the eighteenth century, one could not mistake a Congregationalist house of worship in Massachusetts for a new Catholic church in an Italian town. But by the mid-twentieth century, the Modern

Movement in church architecture had softened the distinctive features of denominational architecture. By conceiving the church structure essentially as a room for shared experience and religious community, rather than as a platform for professing pure doctrine and ritual, modernist architecture downplayed the expression of differences among Christian denominations. On the other hand, the West continues to witness the survival of movements that assert traditional doctrines and distinct styles of religious life. Such movements find expression not only in church architecture, but across a broad spectrum of material culture. Religious identity is expressed in various ways, including doctrines, rituals, moral codes, and the organization of community. Material culture, which includes among other things architecture, art, dress, food, furniture, landscape design, and personal decoration, communicates and confirms religious identity in an active and forceful manner. In the modern context, it has proven effective in identifying religious difference.

For example, the Old Order Amish who are concentrated in Pennsylvania, Ohio, Iowa, and Indiana (with others in Ontario, Canada), are descended from Swiss Anabaptists who desired to restore the church of the earliest Christians. In the view of the Old Order Amish that means, among other things, simplicity, nonconformity, pacifism, and religious community that is separate from the world. These elements of Amish religion are vividly manifest in Amish communities, where men and women live as ecologically minded farmers, carpenters, and craftspersons. Their first "protest" to the world is apparent in their personal appearance. At the age of two, a boy begins wearing trousers and a stiff black hat with a minimum of three inches of brim. As he grows older, he is expected to wear a full beard, suspenders, and dark pants with no pockets. In his first years of married life, he wears a special style of hat; on Sundays, he wears a black vest and coat, both of which close with hook-and-eye fasteners (buttons and zippers are not allowed); on ceremonial occasions such as a Sunday preaching service, he will wear the *mutze,* or a longer, split-tailed coat. A girl learns to avoid garments that show her form and is certain that her dresses are no more than eight inches from the floor. She does not cut her hair, and at the age of twelve, she begins to wear a small black or white brimless *kapp* over it; after she marries, she wears a white kapp. As a woman, she wears plain dresses, aprons, and shawls tied around her or fastened with straight pins.

Amish do not electrify their homes, though occasionally they may use a generator to provide electricity in a factory. They travel by horse and buggy rather than by car and farm without mechanized equipment. Reputed as skilled carpenters, Amish raise barns, build silos, and fashion furniture. Women are proficient quilters, and quilting, like much of Amish activity, is conceived as a religious endeavor. Women also cook, bake, preserve foods, and organize the family meals, at which a specific seating pattern and rules governing conversation are in effect. Amish children do not attend public school but are educated in the community, where they learn how to live in accordance with the advice of the Dutch Anabaptist leader Menno Simons: "Rent a farm, milk cows, learn a trade if possible, do manual labor as did Paul, and all that which you then fall short of will doubtlessly be given and provided you by pious brethren."[12] There is little ritual or formal ceremony among the Amish. Instead, their material culture serves as the principal expression of the distinctiveness of their faith.

Let us look at another modern example of how material culture represents religion, in this case, Italian Catholicism. One way of distinguishing Catholicism from Protestantism is to recognize that the former regularly has featured firsthand personal contact with the divine in the form of apparitions to believers, and the latter has not. In Italy, those apparitions have been of many sorts, but especially of the Virgin Mary. In fact, in comparison to other parts of Europe, the number of Marian apparitions in Italy is historically quite large. There are hundreds of Marian sanctuaries (usually churches) in Italy, and many are believed to mark the spot of an appearance of the Virgin to one or more persons. Some apparitions have been authenticated by Catholic authorities; a great many others, while not officially approved, have influenced the religious life of Catholic communities because of the sheer drama and persuasive force of their accounts.

Popular veneration of Mary, even in cases in which an apparition has not been formally legitimated by the church, coexists with official Catholic religion in Italy. The attractiveness of Marian devotions is suggested by the names of her sanctuaries there; frequently they stress the willingness of Mary to grant requests for miraculous intervention in the affairs of the community. Accordingly, we discover numerous sanctuaries for *Madonna delle Grazie* (favors) and *dei Miracoli* (miracles) and *del Soccorso* (help). Moreover, specific incidents involving the favor of the local madonna are always publicly acknowledged. Indeed, essential to the cult of Mary in Italy is the understanding that persons who are favored by a madonna (e.g., delivered from hurt or harm of some sort) must evidence a vow of devotion to Mary through their presentation to the church of an *ex voto*.

An ex voto ("from the vow") can be any sort of object brought to the church and displayed there. In many cases, the ex voto is a wax model of a body part that has been healed by the madonna—a wax arm, or leg, or eye, or an internal organ. It is installed on the wall of a side chapel alongside other ex voto, which taken together sometimes cover all of the walls. Other devotees bring to the sanctuary a representation of a heart, sometimes of pressed metal, usually not meant to identify a healed body part, but to represent a broad offering of oneself to the madonna. Common as well are small paintings of persons experiencing an infirmity or injury. These pictures depict the nature of the ailment, so that the setting may be the bed, an operating room, an automobile accident, or a person falling from a tree, or shot by an arrow, or in a storm at sea. Pictures, wax models, and metal hearts are hung together in the sanctuary, where they are visible in the glow of another ex voto, the wax candle or "votive candle."

The material culture of Marian devotions illustrates an important aspect of the practice of Catholicism in Italy. For centuries, it has vividly expressed local concerns and sentiments in material form, and in so doing, has contributed to the formation and reinforcement of local religious identity. And like the material culture of the Amish, it reveals a depth and complexity to everyday religious life that is not always apparent in surveys of standard church ritual or statements of doctrine.

The Last Supper

A bas relief in red wood in a church in Ruzo. Notice the detail of the Last Supper. The table is set in the courtyard of the royal house. Christ's necklace is that of a crescent moon of a grant Tutsi. The pitchers, baskets, and gourds are all traditional. The bread is a concession. (*Source:* Maryknoll Photo Library)

As in the case of Italian devotion to Mary, the examination of material culture reveals much about other forms of popular or quasi-popular Christianity. The culture of Latin American Catholics is accessible through a rich material culture that features devotions to madonnas and saints alongside art, architecture, statuary, and ritual objects that reflect the influence of pre-Columbian inhabitants. The drums, sacred staffs, carved wooden figures, colorful dress, and various objects associated with death and burial among African Christian groups are keys to the ways in which primal and Christian traditions have blended. Popular forms of Protestantism in twentieth-century America feature prayer towels, the plastic dashboard Jesus, T-shirts, drive-in churches, bumper stickers, Christian recipes for food, and, increasingly, the radio, television, and videotape player. Sometimes these items represent continuity with the past, sometimes they do not. In all cases, these material products of the imagination signal the complex meanings of religious life in remarkably effective ways.

CHAPTER 18

MATERIAL CULTURE IN ISLAM

We have seen that Islam is an act and not a thing. It is submission to God and the commitment to live according to the doctrines and laws that have been revealed in the Qur'an and set forth in the life and teachings of the Prophet Muhammad. Thus far, we have proceeded with an emphasis on the beliefs and practices of Islam as a religious way of thinking and doing. But Islam is very much an embodied phenomenon, with a material culture that is both distinctive and richly varied. One of the wonders of the system is that even with wide cultural, ethnic, geographic, linguistic, and social diversity, there is nevertheless a persistent core "culture" that unites Muslims around the world and endows them with a distinctive quality that sets them apart from other peoples, even in countries where a common language and public life as well as many regional customs are shared.

Muslims have long celebrated the colorful diversity of their community's cultures and peoples, even as they have agreed that their umma is essentially one and to be preserved as far as possible from compromise and assimilation to non-Islamic attitudes and ways. This is one of the greatest challenges facing Muslims who have moved, for example, to the West and are surrounded by non-Muslim majorities. Although in the present many conflicts are being engaged in by Muslims in the name of their religion—more often intramurally than with non-Muslim opponents—the long history of the tradition has most often been one of civilizational stability, tolerance toward others, and peaceful coexistence.

In the interests of clarity and balance, it is helpful to distinguish between Islam's authoritative doctrines and practices, on the one hand, and Muslims' diverse opinions, customs, and preferences, on the other. Viewed in this manner, we may see that although there is one Islamic religion, there are differing ways in which Muslims experience, appropriate, understand, interpret, and transmit it. Often, when I am conversing with Muslims about matters of faith and conduct, when issues of diversity and even disagreement arise—as in the split between Sunnis and Shiʿites—someone or other usually observes that, regardless of differences, "the *dīn* is one." To be sure, Muslims assert that there is no distinction between religious and secular in Islam and that Islam is a "complete way of life." But the core doctrines and duties, known collectively as the din, are distinguishable from the multiple details, tasks, and disagreements of everyday existence. To live life Islamically requires adherence to the din that, as a "system of symbols," sustains what the contemporary American anthropologist and Islam specialist Clifford Geertz calls "powerful, pervasive and long-lasting moods and motivations."[1] The great success of Islam, and indeed of any world religion, is due to the effective translation into ordinary life of what the eighteenth-century American preacher and theologian Jonathan Edwards called the "religious affections," involving fully both heart and mind.

Marshall G. S. Hodgson (d. 1968), an American historian of Islam, carefully distinguished between the notions of "Islamic" and what he called by his invented term "Islamicate."[2] The former refers to what is authentically Islamic in the religious and legal senses, based on the Qurʾan, Sunna, and their interpretation and application by means of the Shariʿa. The latter refers to thinking and practices and indeed material culture that have been influenced by Islam but are not essentially Islamic. Examples of Islamicate phenomena are the use of the arabesque—a design based on Arabic calligraphy—for decoration in nonreligious contexts, as on flatware, hollowware, jewelry, and textile products. Another is the adaptation of mosque architecture for movie palaces (Denver, Colorado), shrine temples (Pittsburgh, Pennsylvania), and railroad stations (Kuala Lumpur, Malaysia). This type of Islamicate expression is often characterized as "Moorish," not Islamic. Both arabesque and moorish design styles have their originating contexts in Islam, but their uses have strayed far from it and have become standard elements of global material culture.

Another way to distinguish between first-, second-, and even third-order realities is to refer to the din proper as Islamic and to the social and cultural constructions of believers by means of the adjective Muslim. This requires making a distinction between a Muslim as an individual submitter and something that a Muslim or Muslims believe and do. Put another way, all things pertaining to the adjective "Islamic" are included in the notion Muslim, at least ideally, but the reverse is not the case. That is, Muslims believe and do many things that may not be considered as necessarily Islamic. A Muslim may sin; but according to the consensus of tradition, a sin does not invalidate the individual believer's faith. Likewise, some things that Muslims believe and practice may be judged to be, if not sinful, then not essential to Islam. Marriage festivities are not required by the Shariʿa, although it seems impossible to imagine a Muslim wedding, which strictly speaking is the signing of a contract, without some kind of celebration afterwards. The great

Minbar (Pulpit), to the
Right, and Mihrab (Niche
Showing Direction of
Mecca), to the Left; Mosque
of Abraham's Tomb, Hebron,
West Bank of Palestine

(*Source:* F. M. Denny)

variety of Muslim wedding festivities shows their Muslim as distinguished from
their Islamic character.

A more difficult example is following the interpretations and procedures of
a particular school of Islamic law as if that were the only permissible way. Although the sources of Islamic jurisprudence are beyond question, the specific
structures and processes of the law are products of human effort. So, jurisprudence concerning Islam could be referred to as Muslim because of its origins and
nature as a product of human intelligence. The revelation is immutable and final,
but its human interpretation and legal application are subject to serious ongoing

attention and, when necessary, correction and revision. A problem for advanced scholarship, at this point, is the relationship between prescription and actual practice in the early development of legal decision making. But in general, the principle applies that there is a fundamental difference between what Muslims accept as God's revelation and what must be considered as human construction, however piously motivated and carefully formulated according to the Qur'an and Sunna.

THE MOSQUE AS BOTH ISLAMIC AND MUSLIM ASPECTS OF MATERIAL CULTURE

The material culture of Islam is largely a product of Muslims applying their Islamic convictions to a certain vision of the world. The mosque is Islamic in conception, although it is clear from the Qur'an that the word sometimes also applies to places of worship in other religions. However, *masjid* as "place of prostration" soon became distinctively Islamic in the early practice of the umma. There is no question that Muslims are required, in Islamic terms, to utilize a mosque, even if it is interpreted literally as a place of prostration.

The mosque is, in the first place, a liturgical and not an architectural concept, because it denotes the climactic posture of worship: abject prostration before Almighty God. A sound hadith from Muhammad declares that "for me the earth has been made a mosque and a means of purification; therefore, if prayer overtakes any person of my community, he should say his prayers [wherever he is]."[3] As the English scholar Kenneth Cragg has observed,[4] the mosque in its most elementary form is the human body itself, for it is the postures of prayer, along with the words uttered, that comprise the salat service. Salat derives from an Aramaic word meaning "to bow, bend, incline toward."

The first Muslims in Mecca performed the salat in a side street and in houses and even at the Ka'aba, alongside the idolaters who worshiped the many deities represented there. After the hijra, Muhammad had a large plaza, with sun-dried brick walls surrounding it, laid out in front of his home. This was the main mosque of the new umma until Mecca was conquered and the Ka'aba was purified of idols and rededicated as the House of Allah, as it had been believed to be in Abraham's time. Other early mosques were known; and before long, with the spread of the religion among various Arabian tribes, there were mosques established far and wide. The setting aside of land for a mosque came to be a major symbol of the arrival of Islam in a region. It was a sort of sacralizing of the place, although no sacred objects have ever been venerated in mosques, at least according to orthodox Islamic teaching. Later times would witness the rise of saint cults, in which people journeyed to mosque tombs to venerate the dead and seek intercession. This continuing practice has caused great controversies and is, in any case, not part of the ritual requirements of Islam.[5] The sacralization is in the recognition that the people of a locale are publicly worshiping God there and fostering an Islamic environment.

The Design and Furnishings of Mosques

Mosques were soon laid out and constructed in the form of architecturally enclosed space. Sometimes the worship area remained open to the sky, but most often a roof with a dome was constructed. The dome, or *qubba,* as it is known in Arabic, although long used for Christian churches in the Near East, became a symbol of Islamic worship space, along with an accompanying tower, known in English as minaret (from the Arabic *manāra,* "lighthouse"). The direction of Mecca, toward which the worshipers face when praying, is the main axis of any mosque. This direction, or *qibla,* is marked by a niche in the mosque wall, known as the *miḥrāb.* Although there is no requirement of decoration, mihrabs are often beautifully ornamented with calligraphic and abstract geometric designs. No human or animal representation is permitted in a mosque or in the decoration of a Qur'an.

Next to the mihrab is a pulpit, usually of traditional design in which a stairway leads up to a platform where the Friday preacher sits during the weekly congregational worship service. This *minbār,* as it is known, is often topped by a little dome with a new-moon figure on top. In Southeast Asia, the minbar is sometimes a low structure, like a litter on which royalty is transported by bearers. In America, the pulpit may be a simple podium with lectern; there is no religious requirement that this minbar be in a particular style. There will also usually be a clock, folding or stationary Qur'an stands, some bookshelves, and in modern times, a loudspeaker system. All mosques observe a separation between males and females, with the latter occupying a balcony overlooking the male congregation or the back section of the main floor or sometimes a separate room or building for women alone. The floor is invariably covered by carpeting or clean mats of some kind. Worshipers take off their shoes before entering the mosque and keep the interior as clean as possible of dirt from the street. The anterooms of mosques usually have shelves for shoe storage and a clearly marked point beyond which shoes must not be worn.

In addition to the spatial arrangement and appurtenances of the mosque proper, there are also ablution areas for males and females. It is unlawful to perform the salat except in a state of ritual purity. Although it is not essential for a mosque to have a minaret, Muslims very much like to see minarets marking the landscape of their towns and cities, much as Christians are reassured by the sight of steeples and spires. The minaret, as the Arabic origin denotes, is a "lighthouse" or "watchtower" guiding people to Islam. It is also the place from which the call to prayer has traditionally been given; and so in some Muslim lands, for example, Egypt and Syria, the tower is called *ma'dhana,* "place for performing the *adhān,*" or "call to prayer."

There is a wide variety of types, styles, and sizes of mosques, from the great Friday worship mosque, known as *masjid jāmi'* ("congregational mosque"), to small prayer rooms where individuals or a small congregation worships. The Friday mosque is at the center of the traditional Muslim town or city and is surrounded by markets and businesses. Mosques have often been used as community centers, as in Medina during the Prophet's time. People attend religion and Qur'an recitation classes in mosques. Sometimes people use a mosque as a place to sleep and be safe during a journey. It is common for mosques also to be used as places of brief rest and physical as well as spiritual refreshment during the workday or at other times.

The support and maintenance of mosques may be realized in a variety of ways. Often mosques are maintained and their staffs paid by a governmental ministry. Some mosques are supported by pious endowments. Others, as in the West, are built and financed by congregations incorporated as religious bodies according to whatever laws apply. For example, in the United States, mosques are sometimes built with the help of a loan from a Muslim foundation—the North American Islamic Trust is one such organization—and the funds are paid back on a prearranged schedule, without interest (because charging or accepting interest on loans is forbidden by Islamic law). Old, established Muslim countries—Saudi Arabia, the United Arab Emirates, and Pakistan, for example—sometimes provide the funds to build mosques in Western countries where Muslim communities are in the process of forming.

Some of the world's most imposing and beautiful buildings are mosques, such as the Suleymaniye Mosque in Istanbul, Turkey (sixteenth century), designed by the great Ottoman architect Sinan; the open-court style mosque of Ahmad ibn Tulun in Cairo, Egypt (ninth century); the Masjid-i Shah in Isfahan, Iran (seventeenth century); and the modern Masjid Negara in Kuala Lumpur, Malaysia (1970s). Other notable Muslim buildings are the fourteenth-century Alhambra Palace in Granada, Spain; the seventeenth-century Taj Mahal mausoleum in Agra, India; and the seventh-century Dome of the Rock monument on the ancient Temple Mount in Jerusalem, from whence Muhammad ascended to heaven in his miraculous "Night Journey."[6]

Recent times have seen a rebirth of interest in designing mosques, university campuses, governmental complexes, and other public buildings according to Islamic principles. A productive debate has been sustained about what constitutes Islamic design for the present era, with some voices urging continuation of traditional styles and others seeking new expressions without abandoning core spiritual and aesthetic values.

In Indonesia, for example, modern times have seen widespread adaptation of Mughal-style mosque design, with obligatory domes, even if constructed of cheap materials such as sheet metal. There has been a tacit assumption that a mosque should "look like a mosque," that is, like a Middle Eastern or South Asian domed edifice. The early style of mosque in Java was a three-roofed structure resembling a pagoda, with design details and furnishings—such as lotus patterns, large call-to-prayer drums, and sky-chariot pulpits—influenced by Hinduism, Buddhism, and traditional Javanese customs and symbols. A few of the old "stacked-roof" or "Mt. Meru" (after the Buddhist cosmic mountain) mosques survive, including magnificent monumental examples in Kudus, Gresik, and Yogyakarta in Java. Moreover, at least one large industrial complex has erected a modern adaptation for its workforce (in Gresik, East Java), but there is sharp difference of opinion over whether such a regional design should be encouraged today. In any event, mosque architecture is highly varied in contemporary Indonesia, with new ideas finding expression following neither the domed prototypes of classical Islam nor the indigenous stacked-roof styles.

PUBLIC SPACE IN MUSLIM PERSPECTIVE

From its origins, Islam has been a religion that emphasizes people living together in mutually supportive, responsible communities. There has always been a strong town and urban bias to the religion, and migration to a city or otherwise secure and stable settlement with a Friday mosque, adequate defenses, a vital and diversified commercial life, and dignified domestic dwellings has been meritorious. Modern scholars have noted a bias in favor of nomadism and against agriculture. Ironically, it was people of pastoral-nomadic ways that mounted the great conquests in which cities were taken and new cities established. Farmers are tied to the land they cultivate, and so agricultural life went on in traditional ways. The bedouin, although invaluable for their military and long-distance travel abilities, were no more than tools for the expansion of Islam.[7] The five daily prayers, Friday congregational worship, modest dress for women, segregation of the sexes, and availability for bath facilities for ablutions work in favor of town and city life.[8]

In the traditional Muslim town and city, the Friday congregational mosque and surrounding central marketplace—known as the *sūq* in Arab regions, as bazaar in Persia and South Asia, and by other names in other places (e.g., *pasar*, from bazaar, in Southeast Asia)—compose the core of urban life. Otherwise, the layout is often one of apparent randomness and confusion, with labyrinthine streets and alleys proceeding every which way with no obvious order or logical connections. But the traditional Muslim urban environment radiates outward in concentric circles, with the Friday mosque, public baths (for ablutions), and teeming marketplace, through industrial and craft neighborhoods, on to residential neighborhoods, and finally to the boundaries of the city, sometimes marked by a defensive wall. There has traditionally been little in the way of municipal government and institutions, beyond overseeing the weights and standards of commerce and policing the marketplace. Muslims have enjoyed almost total freedom in locating, building, and furnishing their dwellings, with security and privacy of the greatest importance. Houses have most often been low, inward-focused structures, often with atria and always with quarters for women and children safe from the eyes of outsiders. Ostentatious construction materials and multiple stories have usually been avoided in order to turn away envy and the attention of the powerful.

Larger cities—such as the classic centers of Cairo, Damascus, Fez, Istanbul, Aleppo, San'a, and Baghdad—have been comprised of numbers of quarters rather than a single municipal center. The great number and excellence of crafts, industries, educational and religious establishments; recognized and secure quarters for Jews, Christians, and other minorities; and other civilized ventures are what has made such cities great, distinctive, and enduring. Furthermore, great Muslim cities have invariably enjoyed advantageous locations with respect to trade routes, as

**National Mosque of Malaysia, Kuala Lumpur,
with Modern Dome and Minaret**

(*Source:* F. M. Denny)

well as abundant fresh water. Craft and trade guilds, as well as various religious brotherhoods (Sufi orders), have typically flourished in great Muslim cities, as well as in larger towns. This listing of elements in Muslim city life is selective and simplified. In reality, the complex diversity of economic, industrial, social, religious, political, and agricultural details and interconnections is overwhelming.[9] No two Muslim cities of classical type are the same, for there was no paradigm for urban life (as is found in ancient Greek city planning, for example) beyond the provision of the aforementioned congregational mosque (which often requires at least forty male worshipers for its valid functioning) and the presence of a market (Islam has always placed great emphasis on trade and commerce), as well as adequate bathing facilities, which for economies of scale obviously require a large number of patrons.

The traditional street in a Muslim town or city belongs to everyone and may be used accordingly for buying, selling, hauling goods, and sometimes even dumping refuse (although towns and cities usually have had designated refuse dumps). Squatters have generally been tolerated, until public thoroughfares have sometimes become impassable. It seems, when reading travelers' accounts of Cairo, Damascus, and other Muslim cities in premodern times, that streets were always crowded and confusing places. The Moroccan traveler Ibn Batutah (d. 1378), a contemporary of the English poet Geoffrey Chaucer, wrote of Cairo:

Cairo is the metropolis of the country, master of widespread regions and rich areas; it has attained the ultimate possible limits in the size of its population and is proud of its beauty and brilliance. It is the meeting place for travelers, a station for the weak and the poor. All kinds of men are found there, scholarly or ignorant, diligent or trivial, noble or plebian, unknown or famous. The number of inhabitants is so great that they seem to move in waves making the city look like a choppy sea. The city is almost too small to hold them in spite of its large area and capacity.[10]

In modern Cairo, with a population of more than fifteen million, traditional uses of space are intermixed with modern urban planning. Sidewalks are often used for parking motor vehicles and other conveyances, while the streets are teeming with vehicles and pedestrians. But this crowding is not unique to places where Muslims live; rather, it is a condition of contemporary life the world over with excessive population growth and preference for city living and its increased employment opportunities and services.

Although regional differences exist in the lands of Islam with respect to urban life, the general pattern described here has long been dominant from Morocco to Indonesia. Modern times, however, have seen more rationally planned settlements being located next to medieval ones. Cairo began seeing the laying out of wide streets and boulevards after its opening to the West by Napoleon. Jerusalem has both the old walled city, with its beloved shrines and monuments belonging to the three Abrahamic religions, and its new city alongside the ancient and medieval quarters.

Islamabad, the capital of Pakistan, is an example of a pioneering effort toward Muslim city planning. The new city was designed from scratch (interestingly, by the Greek design firm of Constantine Doxiadis Associates) on a grid plan as a rationally ordered Muslim environment subdivided into eight zones for government buildings, educational institutions, an industrial area, and so forth. Construction began in 1961, and the first inhabitants moved in two years later. Thirty years later, the spacious city is a beautiful, orderly urban environment of wide, tree-lined avenues and boulevards, well-apportioned shopping and residential districts, and public parks. So far, Islamabad lacks the intimate, friendly, pleasantly funky qualities of traditional Muslim urban street life. But those can still be found in abundance in the old city of Rawalpindi, just a few miles away.

Surabaya, the vast and teeming East Java seaport, with old quarters and new residential and industrial suburbs, still has an old "Kota," the market and mosque center, where perfume sellers, book vendors and publishers, leather workers, batik merchants, and other traditional products and occupations thrive in the shadow of the great Friday mosque of Sunan Ampel, named for a Chinese Muslim trader-missionary who planted Islam there centuries ago. Although Javanese is spoken by most inhabitants of Surabaya, and although Indonesian is the universal language of the Republic, one can still often hear Arabic being spoken in the old marketplace, where traders descended from Arab families dwell and work and where Qur'an teachers drill their students—young and old—in Arabic grammar and scriptural recitation in the vicinity of the mosque. Strangely, Old Surabaya, although densely populated, is now a rather peaceful island of tranquility surrounded by a bustling modern metropolis with roaring traffic, glitzy air-conditioned shopping malls, and entertainment centers featuring provocative movie posters. Many neighborhoods have their own Friday mosques to serve the needs of more than four million inhabitants.

MUSLIM DOMESTIC SPACE

As important as public space is in Islamic perspective, the market, mosque, and streets are largely the domain of males in traditional Muslim societies. One cannot get a balanced idea of the totality of Muslim life without venturing into the homes of Muslims, those essentially private domains where women and children complement the public life of the adult males. The Muslim family consists first of the husband and wife—or husband and up to four wives, by Qur'anic permission and if they are equally provided for—plus the children of the union(s) and often grandparents, grandchildren, and other members of the extended family.

From the time of the Qur'an, Muslims have been aware of the importance of the idea of "house." The Qur'an speaks of the House of God, the Ka'aba in Mecca, as a sanctuary. Interestingly, the word that is most often used for the Ka'aba is *bayt*, "house," a domestic term. God is the householder of the Ka'aba, and he wants to ensure that it is managed and regarded properly. The Qur'an also speaks of people's houses, their homes, and establishes regulations concerning their social use:

> O ye who believe! Enter not houses other than your own, until ye have asked permission and saluted those in them: that is best for you, in order that ye may heed (what is seemly). If ye find no one in the house, enter not until permission is given to you: if ye are asked to go back, go back: that makes for greater purity for yourselves: and Allah knows well all that ye do. (Sura 24:27–28)

This passage establishes the religious right to domestic privacy, a cardinal precept of Islam. The following verses define the bounds of legal consanguinity and thus the circle of people who may dwell together and be set apart from the rest of society. The technical term for the circle within which males and females may socialize freely is *maḥram*, literally "taboo" in the sense that members within the circle are forbidden to marry each other. Believing women are to guard their modesty and not display either their physical beauty (their bodies) or ornaments, except what would ordinarily appear by one's modest deportment. Although a woman's nakedness should not be seen by anyone except her husband, her unveiled and partially clothed figure may be seen by members of the household: her husband, her near relatives, her female servants, her slaves (in earlier times), old and infirm male servants, and infants and children who do not yet have sexual awareness.[11] Another passage (24:61) specifies that lame, ill, and blind people may be invited to share food in one's house (against pagan superstition); that members of an extended family as well as sincere friends may eat together in their houses; and that when entering a house, people should greet each other with a godly blessing.

Many other references to houses and proper deportment concerning them—particularly the household of the Prophet in Medina—provide knowledge of their religious character.[12] The types and styles of Muslim houses have varied widely over time and in the many differing geographic and cultural regions where Muslims have lived. But certain prevailing practices are discernible, practices I have witnessed in visiting Muslim homes in such diverse places as Egypt, Jordan, Pakistan, Bangladesh, Malaysia, Indonesia, and the United States. First is a sense that the Muslim home is a private place, where decorum, physical cleanliness, order, and separation between spaces for guests and family members are maintained. Muslims normally deposit their shoes at the door and treat the interior floor space as if it were a mosque. Some room or other—often the living room—does indeed serve as the family mosque, although children and others may also pray in their bedrooms. Because prayers are performed in the home, the inhabitants are careful to avoid displaying pictures or statues representing human or animal shapes. It is common, however, to see framed paintings or photos or tapestries depicting the Ka'aba in Mecca and the Prophet's mosque in Medina. Calligraphic displays of Qur'anic verses are also often displayed on walls.

So far as the rest of the house is concerned, personal preference largely determines the material objects therein. It is rare to find any facilities for storing or serving alcoholic beverages because of the strict prohibition of them in the Qur'an. Children may play with toys shaped like humans and animals, and girls may have dolls, as the Prophet approved the practice in various hadiths. Muslims should refrain from keeping any kinds of statues that keep the angels away from a home. Statues are believed to bring the danger of idolatry. Some have argued, because of a hadith that permitted a statue by a door if the head were removed, that it is acceptable to keep statues that have been defaced or otherwise rendered incomplete. This view has little support among Muslims, who sometimes believe that to display a bust of a famous person is even more objectionable than to display a full statue because of the emphasis on avoiding excessive glorification of people.

Paintings, drawings, photographs, and other types of representational art in two dimensions are permissible. But owners of such items must follow Islamic principles so as to avoid idolatry (thus no divinities or holy persons, such as Jesus, Moses, and Muhammad should be represented). Abstract sculpture and other forms of artistic constructions are permissible so long as they do not represent humans or animals. Erotic and pornographic pictures are forbidden. Also, symbols of religions other than Islam (e.g., crosses) should not be displayed in the Muslim home. Finally, Muslims of both sexes are forbidden to keep utensils made of gold or silver, as well as pure silk spreads, cloths, cushions, and the like. Such materials are associated with extravagant living and ostentation. Islamic economic

**Faisal Masjid, Pakistan's National Mosque, Islamabad;
One of the World's Largest**

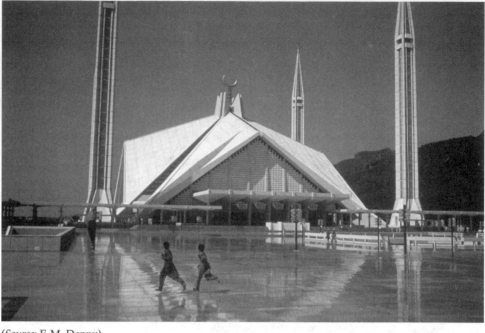

(*Source:* F. M. Denny)

principles discourage hoarding precious metals; they should circulate freely as money. Women, however, may possess and wear gold and silver jewelry (and precious stones) as well as pure silk clothing. Men are forbidden to own or wear any of these materials, although they may abundantly enjoy their beauty when used as adornment for their wives, which is the point of the ruling.

Muslims are repelled by the keeping of dogs in the home, although it is permissible to own and use work dogs outside. Dog saliva is particularly polluting, according to Islamic law, and dogs like to lick things and people, which would render the home impure. Moreover, dogs track in impurity with their feet, but that is a small matter compared to the saliva problem. Cats are considered ritually clean and are often kept in Muslim homes. Cats may often be seen walking their beat in mosques. Black cats, however, are not liked by Muslims because they are associated with Satan. Indeed, one of the Prophet's Companions was accorded the name Abu Hurayra, "Father of the Kitten," because of his constantly having a cat in his lap. Muslims also may keep birds in cages.

The core of a Muslim home is a kind of sanctuary where the honor and safety of the family members, particularly the women and children, are safeguarded. Guests do not enter the private quarters, known traditionally as the *ḥarīm* (harem). When a family hosts nonrelated friends for meals, the males and females are usually strictly separated. Although modernized (and westernized) Muslim families sometimes sit together with their male and female guests for food and conversation, this is the exception rather than the rule in Muslim societies. Muslim homes are open to outsiders for purposes of hospitality other than simple social meal sharing, namely during times of rejoicing (weddings) and mourning (a death in the family).

The actual dwellings that Muslims have designed and utilized have varied enormously, from the tents of Arabia to the stone structures of the wealthy in Cairo and Damascus, to mud houses in West Africa, to bamboo and thatched stilt houses in Southeast Asia. Local conditions influence the choice of materials, while regional customs also determine location, interior arrangement, and other details.

Private and public morality should be in harmony with each other, whether in a Muslim's home or in the street. In East Java, for example, a proper house should observe the Islamic teachings about domestic space mentioned earlier. And although privacy is essential inside, the entrance to a house must not be screened from the public in the street. Once some Western neighbors of ours had arranged plantings and screening materials to conceal their front porch and entrance area from public view from the street. Other neighbors were upset and considered the screening to be a breach of public morality, because any sort of people would be able to enter and exit the house in secrecy (there was a private driveway behind a gate). A private home is indeed private, but it is expected to look from the outside like what it is supposed to be on the inside: a moral space. The preceding description pertains to Java, but in the Arab Middle East, entrances to homes may be quite private. This is partly what has led to such a disordered appearance of traditional Middle Eastern residential neighborhoods. Of course, the sanctity and privacy of the *interiors* of homes—whether in Syria or Indonesia—is a matter of equal importance.

THE MUSLIM BODY: CLOTHING, ADORNMENT, COSMETICS, GROOMING

The Islamic laws concerning ritual purity have also strongly influenced habits of personal hygiene. Furthermore, the hadith specify many details about dress and grooming, which has done much to develop an Islamic style of the presentation of the self in public, as well as the proper cultivation of one's physical nature at all times. Strict Islamic practice requires the covering of women, with only the face and hands visible. The rest of the body is known as *ʿawra,* and it must not be seen by anyone outside the mahram circle of close family (as explained earlier in the discussion of the Muslim home). Some legal experts also include the female voice in this category, requiring a male representative to convey vocal messages when males are present.

Although debate is ongoing as to whether women must cover their hair in public (a practice known as *ḥijāb*), most agree that it is not necessary to cover the face. The main principle in women's dress is modesty and not drawing attention to a woman's sexual characteristics, which are reserved for her husband. Islamic female dress protects the modesty and honor of women when they venture into public places. Such dress signifies respectability and the observing of the proper boundaries. It also tends to make contact, when necessary, between non-mahrams straightforward and businesslike, for example, in the market, at the workplace (Muslim women often must help support their families in these times), at banks and government offices, in educational institutions, and in other settings where the strict Islamic rules are usually eased. The extent to which Muslim women's dress may be stylish and elegant depends on where one is and what the occasion may require. We have already seen how women may wear fine jewelry and silks to provide pleasure for herself and her husband. But opinions vary as to whether high-style dress should be seen outside the mahram circle of the home.

Once, in Saudi Arabia, I took a Thai Airways flight to Bangkok. Saudi couples boarded the flight, the men mostly in good-quality leisure suits or flowing white robes, but the women in extremely modest, shapeless clothing covering their whole bodies, including the faces of some. But once the plane had been prepared for takeoff, with the doors sealed, some of the women repaired to the rest rooms where they changed into stylish, in some cases low-necked, Western clothing in preparation for the enjoyable journey with cocktails (for some), a delicious Thai dinner, a movie, and lots of animated conversation and laughter. Such public dress and behavior would be impossible in Saudi Arabia. In any event, what strict rules may stipulate and what ordinary people actually do can sometimes be far apart. In my many travels through the Muslim world, I have never before or since witnessed a spectacle as unexpected as well as entertaining as that Bangkok flight. I hasten to add that the passengers—even though in a festive mood—conformed fully with civilized, international standards of proper public behavior. Muslim men and women in public places generally dress and behave modestly and with sensitive regard for their Muslim dignity as well as the rights and feelings of others, whether Muslim or not.

Men's 'awra extends from the navel to the knees. Male clothing should be modest and not made of silk. Styles of clothing vary as much for men as for women across the Muslim world. In Cairo and other Arab locales, it is still common to see men dressed in flowing robes, known as *gallabiya*, with a vest and loose-fitting underdrawers. Often one also sees men in striped pajamas going for a loaf of bread at the bakery, having a cup of Turkish coffee and a cigarette at a neighborhood cafe, or playing backgammon with cronies late at night. Egyptian men still wear turbans in different styles and sizes. Graduates of the Islamic University of Al-Azhar wear a distinctive turban with a red cap in the center. Saudi and Gulf men like to wear white robes with white headdresses wrapped with a black or a gold cord. Often, Arab men will wear a red-and-white checked headdress, with the tails causally thrown over the shoulder. In South Asia, it is common still to see men in jodhpurs and "Nehru" jackets, as well as the Muslim world's nearly ubiquitous variations on the leisure suit. In Malaysia and Indonesia, one sees men in sarongs cinched at the waist, topped with a batik shirt, and on dress occasions such as Friday prayers, wearing a fezlike songkok cap. The leisure suit is also worn by many Indonesian and Malaysian men. It is a comfortable style of dress, with short sleeves and open neck suited to hot climates. Muslim men with international experience are usually accustomed to wearing the Western business suit, at least occasionally.

Islamic practices extend to the grooming of the body as well as to what kinds of clothing to wear and are covered in many hadiths. There is not necessarily universal agreement among Muslims concerning some practices, but a few indications of preferred Muslim practice are interesting. Women should normally not remove their facial hair, although the plucking of the eyebrows in order to thin them is not an offense. On the other hand, bodily hair should be removed, as on the legs and in the pubic region. Wigs and hairpieces are forbidden, as they falsify what the true nature of an individual's body is. Dyeing the hair, however, is recommended, because it was *not* practiced by the Jews and Christians of the Prophet's time. Here we have a case of community boundary marking. Muslim males should grow both mustaches and beards, but at least the former. As to their beards, strict opinion holds that they should never be shaved off, although they may occasionally be trimmed for neatness (but not for stylish appeal). Ibn Taimiya, the great Hanbali jurist and theologian (d. 1328), wrote:

> The Qur'an, the *Sunnah,* and the consensus of Muslim scholars all teach Muslims to be distinct from nonbelievers and in general to avoid resembling them. . . . The imitation of the appearance [e.g., trimmed beards, not dyeing gray hair] of the nonbelievers [i.e., Jews, Christians, Zoroastrians] will lead to imitation of their immoral behavior and evil qualities—indeed, even of their beliefs. Such influences can neither be brought under control nor easily detected, and consequently it becomes difficult or even impossible to eradicate them. Accordingly, whatever is a cause of corruption has been prohibited by the Law-Giver [i.e., Allah].[13]

Once I attended a Qur'an recitation tournament on the island of Borneo. On the night of the grand opening, the president of Indonesia was in attendance with his ministers and the diplomatic corps as were many Muslim dignitaries from abroad. I did not see any of the men wearing anything except dark Western business suits with white shirts and sober neckties because of some protocol dictated by the state occasion. I felt men's eyes regarding me with mixed amusement and envy in the torrid tropical evening, because I alone had on a comfortable, light cotton batik shirt with slacks and sandals. Was Ibn Taimiya turning over in his grave as the strains of the recited Qur'an mixed with the light of a full moon in that California of the umma—light years from Damascus—where the sartorial order of the day came from Brooks Brothers rather than from the Law Giver?

MUSLIM EXPRESSIONS OF THE BEAUTIFUL: PAINTING, THE DECORATIVE ARTS, AND MUSIC

The ancient Arabs expressed themselves artistically mostly in their poetry, as we saw in Chapter 3. Muslim peoples came to develop noble and beautiful architectural traditions, as we have seen in this chapter. In addition, Muslims have achieved high distinction in painting, textiles, metalwork, ceramics, woodworking, leathercraft, bookmaking, and music. Further, Muslims made notable scientific, technological, and production advances and innovations in the techniques and weapons of warfare, astronomical and navigational instruments, maps and almanacs, surgical and other medical procedures, time-keeping instruments (e.g., waterclocks), and pharmacology.

Although there is great variety in the arts of Muslim peoples, there has also traditionally been an underlying unity of aspiration and "coding." This unity is the commitment of Muslims to tawhid, the belief that God is one and that the religion should be one in its essentials, not cultural or artistic uniformity, but an overall devotion to Islam as a way of life that provides coherence and meaning to all levels of existence: personal, social, economic, environmental, and aesthetic. The arts of Islam cannot be universally characterized as two-dimensional and flat, nor can they be assumed to be devoid of animal and human figural representations outside liturgical settings. The great modern historian of Islamic art, Richard Ettinghausen, says:

> Islamic art has a general harmony, balance of parts, and perfection of the whole composition. This is, indeed, ubiquitously found and should, therefore, be regarded as the most important Islamic element.[14]

Ettinghausen observes that Muslim art—whether painting or decoration or writing—may be comprehended at varying levels of understanding and Islamic awareness. It may be enjoyed as beautiful in itself or as a vision of higher reality. Thus, Islamic art satisfies both aesthetic and psychological needs. The former is the reason for producing the art, whereas the latter involves the manner in which this is done (design, shape, proportion, colors, etc.). Further, there is a moral need that is satisfied by art. As the mystical theologian al-Ghazali (d. 1111) wrote:

> The beautiful painting of a painter or the building of an architect reveals the inner beauty of these men.[15]

Ettinghausen concludes that the most advanced level of comprehension is the metaphysical, particularly as expressed in Sufi mystical theosophy. At this level, art becomes symbolic of "higher verities."

Painting in the Muslim world goes back to early times and was deeply influenced by the peoples who came under the rule of the Caliphs, from Spain to India. In early Islamic history, mosaics were also of importance. The representation of humans and animals was practiced, but depiction of God, prophets, and other religiously important people was generally forbidden. In Central Asia, however, there were artistic depictions of Muhammad and angels, as in the representation of the Prophet's miraculous Night Journey to Jerusalem and up into the heavens. Usually such depictions showed the body but veiled the face. Persian and Mughal miniature paintings abundantly included scenes of everyday domestic life, hunting and warfare, and royal personages, both in profile and in their various court activities. Although forbidden by Islamic teachings, a tradition of painting featuring erotic subject matter also flourished. This genre is paralleled in contemporary Hindu, as well as in Taoist painting. It is possible to believe that artists who

The Dome of the Rock, Jerusalem

(*Source:* F. M. Denny)

produced such pictures were acting in accordance with the established belief that conjugal lovemaking is indeed an important dimension of Islamic devotion and that the highest joys of paradise will include sexual pleasure as an aspect of union. Tantric practices (using sexual intercourse as a meditative ritual) have chiefly been associated with Hinduism and Buddhism, but parallels exist in mystical Islam.

At the heart of much Islamic artistic expression is the written Qur'an, with its beautiful Arabic cursive script. Muslims consider the chanted Qur'an to be the most beautiful way to use sound, whereas calligraphy is the most noble visual expression possible. The ownership of such an aesthetic resource as the Qur'an is shared by everyone in Muslim societies. Although Arabic letter styles vary—from the early, block-letter Kufic script to the elegantly flowing Naskhi—the principle of beautifying the Arabic Qur'an by means of calligraphy runs through them all. And although the major scripts developed at different times and in different places, by the fourteenth century they composed a repertory used across the Muslim world. Qur'anic passages have long been used in the decoration of mosques, as well as being adapted to coins, textile designs, wooden panels, ceramicware, metal goods, and other media.

The greatest calligraphy was achieved in copies of the Qur'an. From the earliest period, the Qur'an was written down on sheets of parchment or papyrus and bound in codex (i.e., "tablet" or "book") form. This is in contrast to the Jewish use

Minbar and Mihrab in Shrine-Mosque of Sunan Ampel, East Java, Indonesia. The pulpit is modeled after a Hindu chariot for a god.

(*Source:* F. M. Denny)

of scrolls, at least in preserving copies of the Torah. Typically, a Qur'anic codex (known as *muṣḥaf*) is bound with leather or cardboard covers, with the bottom board having a flap that wraps around the loose page edges. The cover may be plain or attractively tooled, whereas the leaves exhibit the best quality of writing possible. Of the greatest concern is that the text be scrupulously preserved from error of any kind. Illuminated Qur'ans have survived from early Islamic times, and to own an illuminated Qur'an is a joy and honor. Although the most magnificent illuminated Qur'ans have been commissioned by royalty and the wealthy, even more modest Qur'ans may have at least the opening sura decorated with designs and rich colors. Of course, illuminations must refrain from representations of animal or human forms. Vegetal and floral patterns may be used, as well as abstract geometric designs. One modern example of an illuminated Qur'an has letters in the shape of palm trunks and fronds, with a background of lilies floating in a pool. Art exhibits in Muslim locales today often feature Qur'anic illumination and calligraphy.

Music and the Muslim Acoustic Sense

The question of musical expression and enjoyment has sometimes been a source of controversy in Islam. In actuality, Muslim peoples have cultivated and enjoyed a wide variety of musical expression, from what developed into flamenco music in Muslim Spain to the perfection of the 'oud (which was further transformed into various lute types in Renaissance Europe) to the plangent sounds of the Persian *santur*, the thrilling Turkish military brass band (one of the variations on the main theme of the last movement of Beethoven's *Ninth Symphony*—"The Ode to Joy"— was inspired by the Turkish military-band style of orchestration and rhythm), and the subtly elegant tones and beats of the Javanese gamelan. Love poetry, as well as stirring poems of heroic persons, were traditionally performed with melodies, and art song (*ghinā'*) has been widespread in the vernaculars of the Middle East, South, and Southeast Asia.

Qur'an recitation occupies the highest place in the valuation of rhythmic and melodic sound in Islam. But Qur'anic chanting is not considered to be music, strictly speaking, although it obviously relates to it. Muslim legal and theological specialists have sometimes expressed strong disapproval of music that seduces the senses and glorifies worldly pleasures. Sufis have traditionally approved of music in the cultivation of spirituality, to the extent of making dance a central form of meditation, as in the Mevlevi Order of "Whirling Dervishes" founded by the Persian mystic Jalal al-Din al-Rumi in the thirteenth century. Sufi seances, known as *samā'*, use both vocal and instrumental music to bring on ecstasy. Popular Muslim bardic performances reciting epics and hymns about the Prophet Muhammad or any number of Muslim saints may be heard during saints' birthday celebrations in many parts of the Muslim world.

The Islamic Republic of Iran, as well as other strict Muslim jurisdictions, severely condemns popular music, both traditional and Western, but especially the latter. And the abjuration of popular music is often a behavioral feature of contemporary revivalist Muslims around the world. But to generalize from such attitudes and behavior to Muslims as a worldwide religious community would be a mistake. Wherever I have traveled in the Muslim world, I have been pleasurably aware of beautiful music in many idioms. Although most of the music I have heard is secular in essence, it also often carries the stamp of centuries of particular cultural and aesthetic traditions of sound and rhythm fully harmonic with a Muslim ethos. Qur'anic recitation, which admits of several styles, stands alone among the sounds of Muslims as essentially uniform throughout the umma. The stirring sounds of Qur'an chanting define an acoustic space that is unmistakably Islamic as well as Muslim, in the senses defined at the opening of this chapter.

MATERIAL CULTURE

QUESTIONS FOR DISCUSSION AND REVIEW

1. Material culture discloses much about religious communities. What sorts of things constitute the material culture of Judaism, Christianity, and Islam? What does material culture make visible about religion? How does it add to our understanding of religion in ways that go beyond what ritual and doctrine can tell us?

2. Material culture serves both as a link with that which traditionally has been held important by religion and as an expression of the changing cultural settings in which a religion thrives. In what ways has this been true for Judaism, Christianity, and Islam? What are some examples of material culture that represent the conservation of tradition? How has material culture represented the incorporation of new ideas, peoples, and places into each of the three traditions?

3. Material culture frequently shows multiple influences in its manufacture. In what ways has material culture illustrated the manner in which Judaism, Christianity, and Islam have influenced one another over the course of centuries?

4. Jews, Christians, and Muslims conceive of the place of worship in terms of what activities take place there and who attends, as well as in terms of what does not take place there and who is absent. How do synagogues, churches, and mosques represent these understandings in their architecture and decoration? In what ways does the house of worship differ from other public space? Are there similarities between the two? How is the home viewed?

5. Decoration, architecture, dress, and other aspects of material culture can serve as a means to bind persons together in community, or they can accentuate differences among believers within a tradition, and across traditions. How has this been the case with Judaism, Christianity, and Islam? In what ways have groups identified their distinctiveness and represented their differences with others through material culture? How have certain attitudes about material culture affected the process of community building or differentiation?

6. If material culture is a "text," how does one read it? Is it possible to read it at several different levels? To what extent does context—geographical, cultural, linguistic, ethnic, gender, and so forth—affect the manner in which material culture expresses religious meanings? How has the circulation of these three religions around the globe influenced the manufacture of material culture within each?

PART VII

RELIGION AND THE POLITICAL ORDER

The organization of people and space as political community can challenge, support, or simply coexist with religion. The experiences of Jews, Christians, and Muslims in relation to the political order have varied widely from one place and time to another. And those experiences are likely to continue to develop in ways that we cannot foresee. Accordingly, we cannot speak of a standard form of relationship between any of these three religious traditions and the political order. However, as we observe the range of relationships between religious and political community in each of these religions, we can identify certain "types" of relationships, certain models for the intersection of religious and political interests that have recurred in Judaism, Christianity, and Islam.

In our study of religion and the state, we see how this particular area of investigation brings into focus certain other themes we have already explored. For example, we see how the nature and extent of religious authority is brought into relief against the claims to authority made by the state. And we see how public religious life, such as participation in public worship or ceremony, can be a badge of belonging or a mark of exclusion from the state. We should be aware, as well, that "ethical monotheism" not only predates the emergence of the modern state in the West, but that it has been the bearer of certain elements such as the notion of civic virtue that over time have been incorporated into the state as its own.

Periodically in the West, and especially in the last hundred years, Jews, Christians, and Muslims have lived together within the borders of a single state. But religious pluralism remains an experiment in the West. It is not at all clear that the bits of cultural background that are shared by these three traditions will translate into a permanent basis for coexistence within the political order. The distinctive emphases of Judaism, Christianity, and Islam show no signs of dissolving into a single tradition. Moreover, the ancient and constant imperative of each tradition to draw every aspect of personal and public life into the framework of tradition ensures competition among all three communities for influence and power in state matters.

Finally, we should exercise caution in speaking about "religious community" in relation to "political community." Such terms are useful as tools to explore specific aspects of Western religious traditions. They do not, however, identify two entirely separate objects of study. Community is always first of all human community, and human community is complex, made up of ambiguities, contradictions, overlapping systems of meanings, and the flux of ideas and attitudes. Religion and politics are two aspects of human community, each highlighting a particular set of questions, problems, and expectations. As we begin this final part, we should bear in mind that we will understand Western religious traditions only as well as we are able to remain aware of the complexity of our own experience as individuals living simultaneously in an assortment of communities.

CHAPTER 19

RELIGION AND THE POLITICAL ORDER IN JUDAISM

THE JEWISH STATE BETWEEN MESSIAHS

"Freedom from the domination of the Empire." With that clipped phrase, Moses Maimonides—a refugee from persecution at the hands of Almohad Muslim revolutionaries in his native Spain and a physician in the Fatimid Muslim court of Salah a-Din in his adopted country of Egypt—summed up the principal difference between the exilic era and the Days of the Messiah (*Mishneh Torah, Hilkhot Melakhim* 12:2). Actually, he had much more in mind. Summarizing his entire *Mishneh Torah,* Maimonides devoted his final pages to the "Halakhah of Kings" and concluded with the laws by which a future Jewish king—descended from David, restored by God to the Jerusalem throne, and anointed to sacred office—would rule humanity according to the principles of the Torah.

The messianic theocracy for which Maimonides legislated has, of course, yet to arrive. And its Davidic archetype, we noted in Chapter 4, is unlikely to have existed as Maimonides imagined it. Indeed, in all the centuries since the cessation of the Davidic monarchy in 587 BCE, there has been only a brief period, the Hasmonean dynasty (152–163 BCE), when Jews in the Land of Israel governed their own affairs under laws enforced by an independent Jewish king. But the Hasmoneans claimed no Davidic descent; and, to judge from the anti-Hasmonean references in some of the Dead Sea Scrolls, at least some Jews believed that the laws of the Hasmonean state were hardly identical to those of Moses.

Until quite recently, then, the relationship of religion and the state in Judaism applied primarily to the ways in which Jews understood the relation of halakhic norms to the laws of the *non-Jewish* states in which Jews lived.[1] This understanding has its roots in the rabbinic community of Greco-Roman antiquity, which rapidly accustomed itself to life as a legally tolerated ethnic subculture. That status continued, with appropriate modifications, in the Christian and Islamic successor civilizations of Europe and the Middle East. Accordingly, part of this chapter's task is to trace the origins of exilic Jewish institutions of self-government and to describe how these institutions fared or were transformed in the territories of medieval Christianity and Islam. To the extent that the emancipation of Western Jewry required radical rethinking of these medieval traditions, we revisit this moment in modern Jewish history as well.

The question of religion and the state in Judaism, however, grew more complicated in 1948. In that year, three generations of intensely disciplined Zionist activity in Palestine, as well as in European and American capitals, culminated in the United Nations' recognition of the right of Jewish national self-determination in the sovereign State of Israel. But this Jewish state, even though the seat of its government in Jerusalem lies within view of Mt. Zion, is hardly the messianic Torah state of Maimonidean legislation. Its laws, for example, are not formulated by an anointed Torah scholar of Davidic ancestry. To the contrary, legislative authority is vested in a popularly elected parliament (Knesset) in which a minority of halakhically observant Jews shares power with Jewish secularists as well as with Arabs of Israel's Christian and Muslim communities. The principles informing the Knesset's legislation, moreover, normally have stronger relations to Ottoman and British legal traditions than to those of the halakhah. Clearly, from the beginning of the rabbinic reconstruction of Judaism until the advent of Zionism, such a Jewish state was literally unimaginable.

But the formerly unthinkable is now mundane reality and has been for half a century. Precisely because the state created by Zionism is a secular democracy, it has raised profound questions for Jews. For example: since the law of the state is not established by halakhic masters, in what sense is the state itself "Jewish"? Which *version* of Judaism provides the standard of values against which the "Jewishness" of the Jewish State is to be evaluated? Finally: what is the meaning of the Jewish political self-determination in the context of the Jews' historical dependence on non-Jewish powers? These questions have profound implications not only for Israeli Jews whose political and religious identities are deeply intermeshed, but they also reverberate within North American Jewry, for whom the path of Jewish national self-determination remains the road often praised and defended, but rarely taken.[2]

JEWISH SELF-GOVERNMENT UNDER PATRIARCH AND EXILARCH

The fundamental patterns of rabbinic Judaism's self-government were sketched within the first centuries after the Roman obliteration of Palestinian Jewish political resistance in the war of 66–73 and the Bar Kokhba rebellion of 132–135.[3] By the late second century, Palestinian Jewry was organized politically under the authority of a Patriarch (Greek, "Leader of the Fatherland"; Heb., *nasi*: "Prince"). Rome's policy was to permit the Jews throughout the Roman Empire to preserve their ancestral customs as long as these were compatible with Roman law and did not lead to social unrest. The role of the Patriarch, therefore, was complex. For Jews outside Palestine—in Egypt, Asia Minor, or Italy—he was an important symbol of Jewish ethnic solidarity within the polyglot environment of the empire's diverse peoples. In the homeland, he administered a delicate balance of political submission and cultural autonomy, ensuring at the same time that the taxes were paid.

The Patriarchal office seems to have been a hereditary one, passed on to the sons of a prominent rabbinic family cleaning Davidic ancestry through the first-century sage Gamaliel. It remains unclear why Rome chose a rabbinic family for this powerful position. Nevertheless, the results are obvious. Wherever, in or beyond Palestine, Patriarchal influence extended, rabbinic halakhah came effectively to enjoy the status of Jewish civil as well as ritual law. The principal architect of this transformation of rabbinic halakhah from the tradition of a community to the law of the entire Jewish people was the most famous Patriarch, Judah b. Shimon b. Gamaliel, who ruled in the late second and early third centuries. You will remember him from Chapter 1 as Rabbi Judah the Patriarch, the principal compiler of the Mishnah. Rabbi (as he is known in rabbinic literature) ensured that rabbinic legal tradition would become the main source of law in Jewish courts under Patriarchal jurisdiction. It was under his reign, and those of his successors, that the Mishnah became the central nourishment of rabbinic intellectual life, spawning the tradition that would eventually issue into the vast talmudic literature.

The Palestinian Patriarch, as the sole legal representation of the Jewish polity in the Roman Empire, enjoyed enormous influence and prestige. But with the Emperor Constantine's Edict of Milan (313), which established Christianity as one of the tolerated religions of the Roman state, the institution of the Patriarchate became problematic. After Constantine, with the exception of the brief reign of Julian (361–363), the emperor was a Christian. It was one thing for Imperial Rome, the persecutor of the Church, to acknowledge the political and cultural integrity of a subdued Jewish ethnic minority; it was quite another for Christian Rome to tolerate expressions of Jewish royal nostalgia among the people who had rejected the kingship of Christ. The Patriarchate survived the transition of the Roman Empire to Christianity for about a century. By 425, with the death of the incumbent, Gamaliel VI, the Emperor Theodosius allowed the office to lapse. An unseemly expression of pride among a people who were privileged to survive in Christendom only in conditions of subordination, the Patriarchate was an office whose time had passed.

During the centuries of the Patriarchate, a parallel institution, the Exilarchate, was developing in Mesopotamia under the Parthian and, from 226, the Sasanian Empires. Called in Aramaic the *resh galuta* (Head of the Exiles), the Exilarchate had its roots in the mid-second century under the Parthians. It appears to have been born from that empire's calculations regarding the possible role of the Jews as tools of its foreign policy relating to Rome, its chief rival for control of the

Middle East. The Parthians carefully cultivated the loyalties of the substantial ancient Jewish communities within its borders. These communities had grown, by the mid-century, through significant migrations of Jews from war-ravaged Palestine, among whom were numbered many rabbinic disciples. Such refugees were hardly supporters of Rome. The appointment of a prominent figure, Huna, as Exilarch in 170 was at least in part an effort to demonstrate to Palestinian Jews the sympathies of Persia for their plight. If anti-Roman Jewish unrest could be fomented in Rome's Palestinian eastern frontier, this might serve as a pretext for a Persian invasion and a restoration of Palestine (with its fertile fields, rich Hellenistic cities, and valuable coastal ports) to its ancestral Persian political constellation.

The Parthian goals ultimately went unfulfilled, and even the Sasanian successors to the Parthian territories were frustrated in their own designs against Rome. Nevertheless, the Exilarchate proved to be an institution of crucial importance for Mesopotamian Jewry. Shapur I, the great Sasanian emperor, significantly enhanced the authority and standing of the Exilarchate after 242. Although never, like its Palestinian counterpart, the familial perquisite of a prominent rabbinic house, the Exilarchal families nevertheless claimed Davidic descent. A series of Exilarchs, relatively poor in rabbinic learning but rich in power conferred by the Sasanian state, tried to work with the increasingly influential rabbinic masters then establishing centers of learning in the empire. Requiring rabbinic legal expertise for their own operations and seeking rabbinic approval for their legitimacy, the Exilarchs were crucial in establishing rabbinic legal and ritual custom as the binding traditions in Mesopotamia's Jewish courts and schools.

As long as the Palestinian Patriarchate remained in existence, the Exilarch cultivated a posture of submission to the prestigious institution emanating from the Land of Israel. Patriarchal prerogatives in such crucial matters as establishing the religious calendar and ordaining rabbinic disciples as teachers were readily acknowledged. After 425, however, the vacuum in Palestinian leadership enabled the Exilarch to emerge for a time as the premier political figure in the Jewish world. In the late fifth century, however, the existence of the Exilarchate was threatened by governmental policies against Judaism and Christianity. The Exilarch Huna V was executed in 470, and the office lapsed for a time, until it was restored early in the sixth century. Thereafter, it remained tightly controlled by imperial policies.

Rabbinic attitudes toward the Exilarch, recorded in the talmudic literature, were complex. During the existence of the Patriarchate, which was usually headed by a figure who joined advanced rabbinic learning with Davidic lineage, Mesopotamian sages owed their primary allegiance to the Patriarch. Yet in order to pursue rabbinic religious goals in Mesopotamia, it was necessary to work with the Exilarch. Thus, while rabbinic sages lampooned the Exilarch's relative ignorance of halakhic tradition or otherwise questioned his competence to rule, they were bound to him in a marriage of political convenience. The heads of the great rabbinic academies (Heb., *yeshivot*) of the cities of Sura and Pumbedita were cultivated by the Exilarch, and they in turn enhanced their prestige by their relationship to him.

Under Roman and Sasanian imperial systems, then, the Jews exercised through their official leadership a significant degree of political, social, and cultural autonomy. At the same time, these leaders were officials of "foreign" (non-Jewish) governments, political appointees whose service was always subject to imperial review and approval. Jewish political life in late Middle Eastern antiquity, therefore, was at its best an exercise of significant freedom within the context of official subordination.

A crucial expression of this reality in the halakhic terms of legal jurisdiction emerged among Babylonian sages early in the third century. Attributed to one of the founders of Babylonian rabbinic culture, Samuel, the principle holds that "the law of the Empire is legitimate law" (Aramaic, *dina d'malkhuta dina*, Babylonian Talmud Nedarim, 28a). As understood in rabbinic and later Jewish cultures, the point of the principle is that the laws of the state legitimately bind Jews as long as such laws do not violate essential halakhic norms.

Thus, for example, the state's sole prerogative to exact capital punishment for certain crimes effectively and legitimately prevented rabbinic courts from executing sentence for those and other crimes that, in halakhic tradition, may be punishable by death. Halakhically mandated legal administration, that is, conceded certain of its jurisdictional prerogatives to the state. This extended even to relatively minor matters, such as the power to prescribe indemnification for personal and property damage. However, were a gentile government to place the study of Torah or the practice of circumcision under a ban, Jews would be obliged to resist. In some cases, as in forced participation in idolatrous worship, that resistance might include the requirement of enduring torture and death. Effectively speaking, then, the principle of "the law of the Empire is the law" created a distinction between the communal exercise of Jewish devotion to God, on the one hand, and public acts of Jewish legal-political sovereignty on the other. The former are inviolable, the latter negotiable on terms set by the powers under which Jews live and upon whose tolerance they depend.

JEWISH AUTONOMY UNDER ISLAMIC AND CHRISTIAN EMPIRES

The theory of Judaism and the non-Jewish state expressed in this principle proved immensely fruitful as the ancient Roman and Sasanian Empires yielded to new political and religious constellations of the Middle Ages. The Jewries of European Christendom and Middle Eastern Islamic civilization depended on it in forging their own relationships with the powers that controlled their destinies.[4]

Let us look first at a crucial development within the Islamic world. Here, the continuation of the Exilarchate as the political head of the Jews was complemented by the rapid rise of rabbinic religious leadership under an institution known as the Gaonate. When Arab armies conquered Mesopotamia for Islam in the mid-seventh century, they inherited, with the remains of the Byzantine and Sasanian empires, a large Jewish community. It was headed by a struggling Exilarchate still dependent on the legitimacy offered by the heads of the Suran and Pumbeditan rabbinic academies. By the mid-eighth century, with the establishment of Baghdad as the center of a vast Islamic empire under the Abbasids, a new arrangement had been worked out. The Exilarch and the academy heads (Hebrew, *gaon*; plural, *gaonim*) were constituted as mutually enhancing powers, the holders of one office having consultation privileges in the appointment of the other.

Both institutions survived into the thirteenth century, their destinies tied to those of the Abbasid Caliphate. The Exilarch and the Gaonim of Sura and Pumbedita jointly constituted the official leadership of the Jews of Islam. But it was the Gaonate that in time exerted the primary influence over the historical development of Jewish religious culture. The Hebrew word gaon means "pride" and stems from the biblical phrase "The Pride of Jacob" (Ps. 47:4). The official and his trappings of office matched the title, often imitating in pomp the Abbasid Caliphate itself, whose holder styled himself "The Shadow of God on Earth." Many of the Gaonim proved, like their Exilarchal colleagues, to be mediocre leaders. Nevertheless, some of the most brilliant figures in the history of rabbinic scholarship under Islam occupied the Gaonates of Sura and Pumbedita. Masters of the complex heritage of ancient rabbinism such as Yehudai ben Nahman (reigned in Sura, 757–761), Amram ben Sheshna (Sura, 858–871), Saadyah ben Joseph (Sura, 928–942), Sherira ben Hanina (Pumbedita, 968–998) and Hai ben Sherira (Pumbedita, 998–1038) molded the diverse traditions of the past into a coherent, universalizable system. Gaonic figures played crucial roles in turning the Babylonian Talmud into an effective tool of rabbinic education, compiled the first versions of the Jewish prayerbook, and resolved thousands of halakhic questions left open in the Talmud. They were crucial in inner-Jewish politics as well, serving, from the days of Yehudai, as the principal rabbinic controversialists in the attempted suppression of Karaism (see Chapter 1).

The influence of the Gaonim was made possible by two complementary factors: (1) the rabbinic perspective on the legitimacy of the non-Jewish state (*dina d'malkhuta dina*) and (2) the authority granted the Gaonate under Islamic principles for governing monotheistic religious minorities. As *ahl al-kitab* (Arabic, "People of the Revealed Book"), the Jews (as well as Christians and certain other religious-ethnic communities) were regarded as bearers of an early and somewhat corrupted form of true religion. As we observed briefly in Chapter 4, they thus enjoyed Islamic protection as *dhimmi* (Arabic, "protected minorities"). By law, they could pursue their own affairs under Islamic rule in exchange for the payment of a special protection tax and a promise to conduct themselves with due respect for the political dominance of Islam and the personal honor due to Muslims. With this system, the Exilarchate and the Gaonate under the Abbasids administered the Jewish community's internal affairs, coordinated its financial responsibilities to the government, and otherwise filled the combined duties of prime minister and chief justice of the Jews.

By the thirteenth century, the waning of Abbasid power brought an end to the Exilarchate and Gaonate as formal institutions. But the influence of this model continued throughout the Islamic world. In twelfth-century Egypt, for example, where Maimonides found refuge, the emergence of an independent Fatimid Caliphate resulted in the creation of an Egyptian version of the Exilarchate-Gaonate, the *ra'is al-yahud* (Arabic, "Head of the Jews"). Elsewhere in the domains of Islam, similar models were applied. In each Islamic domain, direct political authority resided in an appointed Jewish official. Ultimately responsible to the Muslim ruler, he could also depend on the ruler for aid in enforcing his policies among the Jews. As in ancient Rome and Sasania, Jewish self-government under Islam depended on and worked closely with the ruling powers, viewing the stability of the state as the primary guarantor of the Jewish autonomy and safety.

Whereas the halakhic rulings of the Gaonate were taken with utmost seriousness even among the Jewries of Christian Europe, its political authority was, of course, confined to Islamic lands. European Jews worked out their own arrangements of self-government with Christian rulers. Reflecting the fragmented character of political authority in Christian European feudal society, no central Jewish political institution comparable to the Gaonate emerged in Europe. Rather, Jews of diverse Christian territories juggled the overarching framework of the Church's laws regarding Jewry with the self-interests of secular rulers to negotiate for themselves a large measure of local autonomy. If Islamic Jewry under the Exilarchate and Gaonate looks like a Jewish empire under Islamic supervision, medieval Jewry under Christendom looks like a collection of rabbinic fiefdoms presided over by a series of local Christian kings, princes, and bishops. Only in the rarest of instances, as in the Polish Council of the Four Lands of the sixteenth to eighteenth centuries, do we find extensive Christian territories unified politically under a specific Jewish political authority.

The official terms of Jewish residence in Christian Europe were rather bleak. In the pre-Christian Roman Empire, Jews had received full citizenship as of Emperor Caracalla's edict of 212. They continued to enjoy this status, at least in legal theory, into the eighth century in some areas. Nevertheless, as we observed earlier, the Church viewed Judaism as a false faith and the Jews as a rebellious nation refusing to acknowledge God's redemptive revelation in Christ. Under the influence of the brilliant fourth- to fifth-century theologian and bishop Augustine of Hippo, the Church had come to see itself as the preserver of Israel in exile. The contrast between a humbled Israel and the imperial Church would serve as visible instruction in the truth of Christian faith. When Gregory the Great ascended to the Roman papacy in 590, he established Augustine's views as Church policy.

In the Christian Roman Empire, this became the state's view as well. The sixth-century promulgation by the Emperor Justinian of the *Corpus Iuris Civilis* (Latin, "Code of Civil Law") preserved the Jews by legally protecting their lives and property. It also ensured their humility by placing limitations on Jewish social, economic, and even religious freedom. Technically free to pursue their own traditions, Jews were commonly forced to listen to anti-Jewish sermons. Indeed, from 634 to 638, seeking to solidify his power in response to the Islamic invasions of the Middle East, the Emperor Heraclius outlawed Judaism and demanded forced conversions. Whereas Roman law was unhindered by countervailing factors, the theological punishment of exile was often expressed in concrete political and economic terms. In most areas, Jews could own land only in certain instances and might reside in a given territory only as a privilege dependent on royal pleasure.

In actual practice, however, Jews were often able to circumvent or ameliorate such legal strictures, particularly as the central power of the Roman state weakened.

Precisely because they were denied land ownership and access to many professions, Jews concentrated their economic activity in trade and other occupations that permitted the accumulation of significant capital. In an agricultural bartering economy, transportable wealth in the form of metals and gems was of great utility, especially to kings and princes presiding over military projects, public works, and the creation of new settlements in their territories. Accordingly, in many instances, Jews were courted by local rulers and granted generous charters of residence that provided, as part of the arrangement, nearly total cultural and religious autonomy under rabbinic leadership.

From at least the thirteenth century on, Jewish communities in central and western Europe were accorded a special status as *servi camerae* (Latin, "Servants of the Royal Chamber"), special property of the ruler. It remains unclear whether this status implied a limitation of earlier freedom or a kind of protective privilege. At any rate, this arrangement freed Jewish communities from certain forms of taxation and it provided them with far more freedom of movement and economic life than, for example, Christian serfs, who were bound to the land for generations as the human property of landholders. Of course, such protection could be rescinded at the ruler's whim, a fact making for great insecurity. Yet in many instances, royal forces protected Jews from vicious anti-Jewish uprisings among the townspeople and lesser nobility. Not infrequently as well, it neutralized the threats of regional bishops concerned about Jewish prominence in local economies. When such protection failed or was overcome, as in the anti-Jewish massacres associated with the Crusades of 1096 and thereafter, the loss of Jewish life and property could be catastrophic. Jewish prayerbooks still contain hymns first composed as eulogies for the martyrs of Rhineland Jewry in 1096.

The dependence of the Jews on special royal privileges helps to explain what emerged as a common pattern of Jewish leadership in Europe. Wealthy Jewish families, because of their usefulness to Christian authorities as sources of loans and other financial services, served as intermediaries between such authorities and the Jewish community. In order to broaden their status within the Jewish community beyond their financial function, such *parnasim* (Heb., "providers") might arrange marriages with prominent rabbinic families. Thus, political leadership of the Jews, grounded in wealth, was often linked to religious leadership, grounded in learning. The joining of two sorts of authority served as the foundation for the great achievements of rabbinic scholarship in Christian Europe.

From tenth-century France to sixteenth-century Poland, talented scholars enjoyed great opportunity to explore the intricacies of rabbinic intellectual tradition and to apply the results to their own communities. Building on the achievements of the Gaonim and their Islamic heirs, these Ashkenazic scholars created encyclopedic works of exegesis and synthesis parallel, in their way, to those of the monastic and university communities supported in Christendom by the wealth of Church and king. The Abelards and Aquinases of medieval Christian theology have their Jewish counterparts in such luminous figures as Rabbi Gershom ben Judah ("Rabbenu Gershom," Germany, tenth century), Rabbi Solomon ben Isaac ("Rashi," France, eleventh century), Rabbi Jacob ben Meir Tam ("Rabbeno Tam,"

The Jewish "Desecration of the Host"

In 1478, the German town of Passau witnessed a trial in which local Jews were accused of stealing sanctified Hosts from Christian churches and torturing the sanctified body of Christ until it bled. The Jews were sentenced and executed. This woodcut memorializes this procedure. In the upper row, from left to right, a Christian opportunist steals the Hosts and brings them into the synagogue, where they are pierced. In the second row, the plot is discovered and a ringleader, having converted to Christianity, is executed humanely by being beheaded. In the third row, coconspirators are tortured and burned. (*Source:* Robert H. Seltzer, *Jewish People, Jewish Thought*, 1980, p. 365. Reproduced by permission of Prentice Hall, Upper Saddle River, NJ)

Germany, twelfth century), Rabbi Meir ben Baruch of Rothenburg (Germany, thirteenth century), and Rabbi Moses Isserles ("Rama," Poland, sixteenth century), men whose works of halakhic scholarship remain staples of rabbinic learning at the end of the twentieth century. In Ashkenazic culture, therefore, as in the Jewish cultures of Islam, the dependence of the Jews on the powers of the state often carried with it its humiliations. But it also enabled remarkable developments in the articulation of the halakhic tradition, which had become the essence of medieval Jewry's religious and political culture.[5]

JUDAISM AND THE MODERN EUROPEAN STATE

The political and economic transition of medieval feudal Christendom into the international system of modern nations, about which you have read a good deal in these pages, is crucial for understanding the modern relations of Jews to the state. Indeed, in many cases, the Jewish experience of exile became more chaotic than ever.

From the sixteenth century onward, some Church and royal leaders dealt with the political challenges to Christianity by imposing profound limitations on Jewish life. This period saw the origins of the ghetto in Italy, an official confinement of Jewish residence to sectors of cities that, isolated from the normal life of the city, became increasingly squalid. Such ghettoization of Jews, a kind of residential imprisonment, proceeded in other areas of central Europe as well. By the end of the eighteenth century, Jews in the Russian Empire were confined to a Pale of Settlement in the western provinces. Although few Russians, outside the nobility, enjoyed full freedom of residence or movement, the Jews were subjected to a deliberate imperial policy of economic exploitation and legal harassment. At the same time, by contrast, Jews in Holland and England had begun, since the seventeenth century, to enjoy unprecedented freedoms of economic activity and social mobility.

This is the complex background—from deliberate impoverishment to unprecedented freedoms in different parts of Europe—against which we must interpret the radical political transformation of European Jewry from the late eighteenth through the nineteenth centuries. We have seen in Chapters 10 and 13 that eighteenth-century European political ideas of national self-determination, within the context of a constitutional state composed of citizens equal before the law, had immense, if originally unintended, consequences for the Jews. For a millennium and more, the Jews of Christendom had enjoyed revocable *privileges.* Now constitutional bodies had to ask: was it conceivable for them to exercise, on equal terms with Christians, the *rights* of citizenship? And if conceivable, was it practical?

Such puzzles are, in a nutshell, the essence of the Jewish Question that plagued European political discourse throughout the nineteenth and early twentieth centuries.[6] As you will recall from Chapters 4 and 10, the Jewish Question was debated hotly among Jews and non-Jews from the moment of French Emancipation in 1791 to the unification of Germany in 1870. Jews, constantly appealing to the egalitarian models of the state fostered by the French Revolution, lobbied for and eventually won full rights of citizenship in the European states west of the Russian Empire. By the end of the Russian Revolution of 1917, Jewish citizenship was a fact in all of Europe. The Jews of modern Europe, not unlike their medieval ancestors, were now justified in viewing the constitutionally legitimate political regime as their legal ally and social protector. But the constitutional state, subject to popular approval, was not the same as a local prince's self-interest. Thus, the legal resolution of the Jewish Question did not resolve its cultural dimensions.

As we have observed earlier, a principal condition of Jewish citizenship rights was the definition of Judaism as a private "religious confession" without national significance. That is, French or German Jews regarded themselves as Jewish in religious faith but French or German by national loyalty. Their Jewish identity, in other words, was to be irrelevant to their political identity. Catholics and Protestants, of course, accepted the same ground rules. Even though the state might have a national church—the Anglican Church in England, Roman Catholicism in Italy, the Evangelical Church in Germany—Christian religious minorities expected that their religious preference would be respected as long as their loyalty to the state was complete. In the case of Christian minorities, of course, this expectation was fulfilled rather more routinely than in the case of the Jews.

The reasons are complex. To a certain degree, rapid Jewish penetration of the free professions and the middle economic classes, from which they had earlier been excluded, aroused alarm and resentment among non-Jews. Other more subtle factors, however, are probably more important. Whereas German Catholics and Protestants, for example, might be embittered by memories of Reformation battles, they nevertheless shared a host of pre-Reformation and even pre-Christian ethnic memories and folk traditions. Differing in faith, they nevertheless recognized each other as belonging to the same folk or nation. In such a cultural setting, Jews—the perennial "guests" of Christian Europe—could hardly make a convincing claim to German ethnic identity, however long their residence in Germany or however loyal they might be to the German state itself. The rights they enjoyed as citizens were frequently viewed as unearned, benevolent privileges of the nation to outsiders. And privileges, as those recalling the Middle Ages well knew, might at any time be revoked.

The anti-Semitic political movements of the late nineteenth century brought these cultural perceptions to the level of explicit ideologies. Especially powerful in France, Germany, and the Austro-Hungarian Empire, anti-Semitic political parties called for the cultural isolation of the Jews, restrictions on their rights of citizenship, and in some cases, their expulsion from the state. Prior to the First World War, such parties were vocal, but remained politically marginal. State constitutions remained the protectors of Jewish legal equality. Matters changed dramatically thereafter. Particularly, in postwar Germany, which had suffered a disastrous defeat, signed a humiliating peace treaty, and endured a decade of social chaos, anti-Semitism enjoyed unparalleled success. Its ideologists were able to link Germany's misfortunes and the chaotic nature of the modern world as a whole to the machinations of International Jewry.

Anti-Semites such as Adolf Hitler asserted that the Jews had never entered into an honest pact with constitutional states, nor had they ever submerged their Jewish loyalties. To the contrary, they had designed the entire structure of modern constitutional liberalism as a means of controlling European destinies. The social integration they now enjoyed had been engineered by them as part of a larger plot to pollute Europe's "Aryan ethnic purity" with "Semitic blood." As soon as Hitler's National Socialist (Nazi) Party gained control in the German elections of April 1933, it began to use the powers of the state to implement laws that would reduce German Jewry to a level of political impotence unknown even in medieval times.

The European Art of Caricaturing the Jews

In Nazi Germany, Jews were commonly portrayed as obese, wealthy capitalists hoarding the world's wealth. The caption of the above cartoon reads: "The God of the Jews is money. And in the service of money he commits the greatest crimes. He cannot rest until he sits upon a huge sack of money, until he has become king of money." (*Source:* The Granger Collection, New York)

With the advent of the Second World War and the German conquest of vast European territories in 1939, Nazi attention turned to a "Final Solution to the Jewish Question" in Europe. Jews in all lands occupied by Germany were deprived of citizenship. As stateless persons, they had no legal rights whatever in their countries and no foreign power obliged to protest on their behalf. They were powerless to oppose policies that herded them into ghettos or forced labor camps. By the early 1940s, the nature of the Final Solution was clear. Germany would rescue the world from the Jews by mass executions in ghettos and forests, and by starvation and gassing in specially designed slave-labor extermination camps. But Germany

The Destruction of European Jewry: 1939-1945

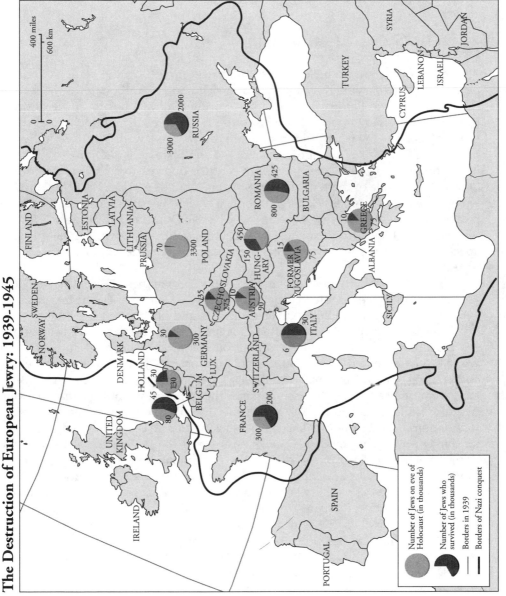

Source: Ninian Smart, *Religions of the West,* 1994, p. 87. Reproduced by permission of Prentice Hall, Upper Sadd:e River, NJ.

lost the war, upon which the success of its policies against the Jews depended, to the Allied Powers. European Jewry, for its part, lost nearly two thirds of its prewar population, a cultural infrastructure built over fifteen hundred years of European experience, and, in many cases, any confidence that Jewish legal rights could be negotiated with Christian states on European soil.

JUDAISM AND THE SECULAR JEWISH STATE

The State of Israel owes the legal basis of its existence to United Nations declarations of 1947–1948, which established a Jewish and an Arab state in the former British Mandate of Palestine. Indeed, but for international horror at the destruction of European Jewry and the presence on European soil of hundreds of thousands of stateless Jewish survivors of death camps, the Jewish State would hardly have come into being. The political roots of the State of Israel, however, strike much more deeply into the nineteenth-century debates over an earlier Jewish Question—the role of the Jews as European citizens. As early as the 1880s and the emergence of political anti-Semitism, some Jews had begun to argue that emancipation was a failure. The real solution to the Jewish Question in Europe was for the Jews to create their own national state. Only as a politically sovereign people on a specific territory might the Jews enter the modern age in true equality with the European nations.

By 1897, such perceptions were forged by the Viennese journalist Theodore Herzl into a movement for Jewish national renewal—Zionism. The history of Zionism, which includes numerous diverse currents and philosophies, is well beyond our scope here. The point for us is that Zionism in all its forms shared a single crucial perception, namely, that the cultural foundations of European anti-Semitism were intimately linked to the nonterritorial character of Jewish society. Therefore, any political or legal solutions to the Jewish Question that ignored Jewish landlessness were doomed to failure. For Zionists, the implications of this analysis were twofold: (1) Jews had to organize to create the cultural, economic, and political foundations of an autonomous territorial society; and (2) they had to engage in extensive efforts to convince European powers (and the Jews themselves) that the Zionist solution to anti-Semitism was the correct solution. By 1904, the Zionist movement as a whole, attracting masses of Jews in Eastern Europe and vocal supporters in the West as well, had resolved that the most likely site for such a Jewish society was Palestine, then an administrative district within the Ottoman Empire.[7]

For most Zionists, the return to Palestine did not imply a rejection of European culture. Rather, the point of their movement was to enable the Jews to contribute their unique gifts to the larger human community, in which Europe was clearly seen as the standard of progress. From this perspective, Zionism's retreat from Europe was a strategic withdrawal until the Jews could reenter the larger life of European culture from a vantage point of genuine legal and political equality. By creating their own state, Zionists believed that Jews would deprive anti-Semitism of the reasons for its existence. Jews would no longer be viewed as perpetual aliens, living parasitically off the labor of host societies. As a free nation, they could then encounter other free nations on terms of self-respect. Jewish rights, at last, would be recognized both legally and culturally as genuine rights rather than as privileges.

Zionists believed that anti-Semitism, despite its irrational hatred and fear of the Jews, was grounded in social and political realities. This accounts for their general optimism that anti-Semitism could be eradicated by eliminating its social causes. Accordingly, Zionists rejected the traditional rabbinic view that hatred of the Jews was an unchangeable fact of history, mandated by God as a punishment for Israel's disobedience. The Zionist task was not to labor in Torah and prayer until God brought the Messiah; rather, it was to labor in the fields and factories of Palestine until the Jewish people achieved the means to sustain their political independence. As we observed in Chapter 13, rabbinic and medieval Judaism could normally imagine a community of Jews and non-Jews only in terms of messianic times. For Zionism, that ideal community was wholly realizable in history by means of political energy and legal structures. Esau and Ishmael had ceased to be mythic brothers in perpetual competition for divine love with Jacob or Isaac. Instead, they were Christian and Arab nations that could, in principle, be reasoned with. Community with them was achievable in this world by the Jews' own efforts.

Over the next decades, hundreds of thousands of Jews, mostly from Eastern Europe, flooded Palestine. Founding numerous agricultural communities and, in the case of Tel Aviv and others, entire cities, these Zionist settlers created the social structures, economic institutions, and political leadership that would serve as the basis for the later Israeli policy. Despite vigorous Palestinian Arab opposition to Zionism, Jewish migration to Palestine increased in the wake of the First World War: when Palestine passed from Ottoman to British administration. With the mounting victories of Nazism in Europe in the 1930s and 1940s and the closing of the North American continent to Jewish immigration, Palestine became a desperate refuge even for Jews who had no particular ideological commitment to Jewish national independence. After the Allied victory in 1945, with hundreds of thousands of Jewish survivors of Hitler languishing in refugee camps throughout Europe, Palestinian Jews found themselves in a position to provide a solution. Their Jewish society was ready to become a formal Jewish state and to absorb Europe's remaining Jews. Zionism's original thesis about the hopelessness of Jewry in Christian Europe appeared to have been borne out by the historical process. As corroboration, in 1948, the State of Israel was granted international recognition.

With statehood, Israel inaugurated a unique historical experiment in establishing the boundary between religious and state law in the context of a secular Jewish democracy.[8] Although Zionist polemics had often represented the movement as a continuation of millennial Jewish messianic aspirations, relatively few Zionists saw much of a future in the modern world for Judaism. From Herzl to most of the actual founders of the state, such as David Ben-Gurion and Chaim Weizmann, Zionism's principal leaders imagined that the Jewish state would be governed by a wholly secular code of law, reflective of the Jewish cultural revival. Judaism would have an honored role as the ancestral faith and its rights, along with those of other religious minorities within the state, would be protected, as in other constitutional states of Europe. But the "Jewish state" was to be Jewish in terms of its cultural and national identity, not through the sources of its laws.

Political realities, however, made this vision untenable. Some Orthodox Jews had, for example, developed their own Zionist theory that saw Jewish secular statehood as the first step in the creation of a state grounded in halakhic norms. In order to gain the support of such Jews for the state's cause, therefore, it was necessary to compromise on the absolute separation of religious and state law. Drawing on Ottoman and European precedents, Ben-Gurion's government established that the religious communities of the state would be governed by a single law in all areas but those regarding personal status, for example, family law, conversion rituals, and so forth. In these areas, the norms of the religious community, as administered by its religious leaders, would be the state's law. In the case of Judaism, the norms held to constitute "Jewish law" were those of Orthodoxy, as determined by an official Chief Rabbinate appointed jointly from the Ashkenazic and Sephardic communities. Thus was created a situation that continues to cause much friction in Israeli society as well as in the Jewish Diaspora, particularly among the majority of Jews who regard themselves as nonreligious or religious in an unorthodox way.

There is in Israel, for example, no civil marriage or divorce. All such occasions must be managed through the religious institutions of Judaism, Christianity, or Islam. Let us look at a common hardship this can create for Jewish citizens in particular. Halakhic regulations prevent a man of priestly lineage from marrying a divorcee. But what happens when Yaakov Kohen, a descendant of priests who for four generations have never entered a synagogue, falls in love with Sarah Mizrahi, who was divorced three years ago from Mark Goodman, an American immigrant who "returned to Judaism," bought a black suit, and disappeared into a yeshivah in Jerusalem? As a secular state, Israel is bound to recognize the legality of marriages contracted beyond its borders. Yet within the state, only religious law can solemnify the marital relationship. The routine solution is that the couple flies to the Mediterranean island of Rhodes and contracts a civil marriage. At best, Yaakov and Sarah have spent more than necessary on their wedding. At worst, they feel their personal freedom infringed upon by a religious law that they do not recognize.

The case of conversion is equally difficult and draws in its wake a profound debate regarding the standards by which Jewish identity can be legally defined. The Law of Return was established in 1950 to ensure that any Jew seeking refuge in Israel might be granted immediate citizenship. That law makes no stipulations that Jewishness must be defined by adherence to religious beliefs or halakhic practices. On its terms, "Jewish identity" is an ethnic fact claimed by its holder as self-evident. There is, however, an interesting sticking point. Converts to Judaism must be covered by the law, since conversion in Judaism incorporates one into Jewish ethnic identity as well as into a community of belief. The question is: what standards ensure that a conversion is in fact a legal conversion?

The Chief Rabbinate—the state's sole official definer of Judaism—upholds the Orthodox consensus that the halakhic procedures governing conversion are valid for all Jews as long as they are administered by an Orthodox rabbi. This has two implications. First, conversions designed by the Conservative, Reconstructionist, or Reform communities, which may deviate from Orthodox procedures, are deemed nonhalakhic and, thus, invalid. Second, even if the procedure conforms to Orthodox halakhic guidelines, it is invalid if presided over by a Conservative or Reform rabbi. In practice, the solution has usually been similar to that applied to halakhically troublesome marriages: to accept all international converts under the Law of Return without question, but to ensure that people converted in Israel do so under Orthodox auspices. The principle, however, remains under dispute, and many an Israeli government has had to explain to its Orthodox constituents how and why the Law of Return cannot be emended to specify halakhic conversions. Similarly, one of the most divisive issues in Israel's relations with Diaspora Jewish communities, highlighted by this aspect of the Law of Return, is the fact that the law of the Jewish state defines dominant forms of Diaspora Judaism as deviant.

In sum, although Israel has radically transformed Jewish political life in modernity, it has not as yet solved the problems of Jewish political independence. Some problems, such as those we have just discussed, are essential to the structure of Israel as a secular Jewish democracy in which halakhah is not and can not be the law of the state. In other ways, Israel has replicated at a different level the original conditions that Zionism hoped to change. For example, Zionist optimism about the capacity of Jews to become part of the world community was, in retrospect, not without its glaring blind spots. Nowhere is this more clear than in the way Zionists imagined the relationship of the Jewish nation in Palestine to the Palestinian Arabs. Until the 1920s and 1930s, the leading Zionists were convinced that Palestinian Arabs would see the benefits of a Jewish state and welcome it. They failed to grasp that Arab national claims in Palestine were in essential conflict with those of the Jews. Since the establishment of the State of Israel, the conflict of Zionism and Palestinian Arab nationalism has remained bitter, bloody, and unresolved. Only in the last decade of the twentieth century has it been possible to establish even preliminary discussions toward a resolution of the national conflict.[9]

The irony of Zionism's history, therefore, is inescapable. Zionism created the conditions for Jewish membership in the community of modern states. It has redeemed and infused with profound meaning millions of Jewish lives, both within and beyond the Jewish state. But its solution to the Jewish Question did not transform the Jews into an uncontroversial people. To the contrary, Zionism's political conflict with Arab nations has often served as a pretext—not only among European and American Christians, but also in the Islamic world—for the reemergence of the anti-Semitic ideologies that Zionism sought to overcome. The unbridgeable chasm between Israel and the nations, a staple of biblical and rabbinic historical thought, is eerily confirmed in the eyes of many contemporary Jews by the political marginalization of the Jewish State in the international community. As the earliest Jews of European modernity had discovered, neither pacts with powerful allies nor legal assurances can in themselves overcome the cultural resistance to the Jewish presence. At the end of the twentieth century, as at the beginning of the nineteenth, Jewish political rights are in some quarters still seen as illegitimate privileges.

Anti-Semitic Traditions in Anti-Zionist Propaganda

Political conflict with Israel has at times expressed itself, especially in the Arab and Islamic worlds, through anti-Semitic images borrowed from Europe. This cartoon, from an Egyptian newspaper *Al-Massa* (April 19, 1964) is captioned: "A great festival is approaching." The allusion is to the extinction of Israel, here represented as a goat about to be slaughtered by an Egyptian celebrant. (*Source: Encyclopedia Judaica*, Jerusalem, 1972, vol. 5, p. 178)

JEWISH CIVIL RELIGION IN ISRAEL AND AMERICA

The close proximity of the destruction of Europe's Jews to the emergence of the State of Israel and the continued precariousness of Israel's international standing have thrust the Jewish state into a profoundly symbolic role. The generation that endured the Nazi slaughter is in its very old age. Yet most Jews alive at the end of the twentieth century regard themselves as in some sense survivors of the European catastrophe and, therefore, at least vicarious participants in the Israeli triumph. The catastrophic loss of life and culture in Jewish Europe has come to be grasped symbolically in the image of a fiery "Holocaust," wholly consuming Jews trapped in its path. The emergence of Jewish political independence came almost inevitably to constitute a "rebirth" of the Jewry consumed in the Holocaust. Israel symbolized a Jewish "Yes" to the "No" of the Holocaust.[10]

We may conclude our discussion of religion and politics in Judaism, therefore, by reflecting briefly on a final dimension of its expression. This is the way the twin symbols of European Holocaust and Israeli Redemption have come to serve Jewish expressions of common citizenship in an international Jewish polity that transcends divisions of citizenship and religious persuasion. As the "civil religion" of contemporary Jewry, these expressions are most complex. Exploiting to some degree sentiments of Jewish solidarity rooted in ancient traditions, this civil religion is nevertheless fervently affirmed by Jews who regard themselves as entirely beyond the bounds of religious belief. At the same time, many Jews deeply entrenched in the timeless rhythms of halakhic life respond emotionally to themes of the civil religion drawn from the wholly secular image of the State of Israel as an international defender of the Jews from anti-Semitism. Thus, Jews on either side of the divide between "secular" and "religious" can respond to the major themes of "Holocaust and Redemption."

In Canada and the United States, where Diaspora Jews now enjoy unprecedented political security, the symbols of Holocaust and Redemption serve to mobilize Jews of all persuasions to political and charitable work on behalf of the State of Israel. Jews of both countries have their own network of Jewish Federations that absorb the energies of countless people, both professionals and volunteers, in fund-raising campaigns involving hundreds of millions of dollars. For religiously unaffiliated Jews, these Federations often serve both the volunteer workers and those who write checks as their sole expression of Jewish affiliation. The fund-raising season is the primary public act of communal participation. The act of giving takes on the character of a vote "against Hitler" and for "Jewish survival." Jews of the various religious streams of contemporary Judaism find in the fund drive one of the few opportunities of the year to rub elbows with Jews from competing streams.

A large portion of the funds collected supports national networks of Jewish schools, charitable work, and, of course, Holocaust education. Indeed, the opening in 1993 of the National Holocaust Memorial Museum in Washington, DC, is unimaginable without Jewish efforts to place reflection on the Holocaust at the center of the American moral conscience. The prominence of Holocaust awareness explains as well why, in recent decades, perhaps one half of American Jewish fund-raising dollars have gone to the State of Israel in the form of direct contributions to its continued efforts to absorb Jewish immigrants. In recent years, the absorption of Jews from Ethiopia and the former Soviet Union has been a particularly important project. As fund-raising campaigns for these efforts commonly assert, every successfully relocated refugee from a hostile regime constitutes one more Yes to the Holocaust's No. In the Federation fund drive, even Diaspora Jews can share in that Israeli victory.

In North America, where Jews have blended into a larger non-Jewish culture, they are distinguished from their neighbors largely by the prominence of the symbols of the Holocaust and Israel in their personal lives. In Israel, by contrast, the symbols of Holocaust and Redemption pervade the entire fabric of society.

Whereas North American Jews might attend special observances on the Day of Holocaust and Heroism or on Israel Independence Day, in Israel these are state holidays. On those days in particular, the print and electronic media provide endless reflections on the nature of Jewish history, the meaning of the Holocaust in that history, and the role that Israel must play in redeeming that history for the future. Similarly, every Sabbath and religious holiday of the year calls forth its own set of meanings in light of the modern Israeli experience, with competing interpretations coming from the airwaves and the newsstands.

Inevitably, the Holocaust is often figured in such reflections as the ultimate explanation for the centrality of Israel in the cultural life of world Jewry. Israel, correspondingly, comes to symbolically enjoy among large sectors of Israeli society a kind of secularized messianic meaning. As the one state in which the government can *never* regard Jewish rights as revocable privileges, Israel is more than a Jewish refuge. It is seen as a radical transformation of historical Jewish dependency, a final transformation of the Jewish condition among the nations. In such a frame of reference, of course, the specter of the the Holocaust often serves as well to justify whatever measures the state and its Jewish citizens must take against those who appear to threaten Israel's survival. Where Arab enemies are viewed mythically as embodiments of Hitlerian principles, no extreme of resistance can be regarded as excessive. Similarly, the divisive political atmosphere that contributed to the assassination of Israeli Prime Minister Yitzhak Rabin in November 1995 was fostered by months of bitter accusations among opponents to Rabin's policies that his government was planning to make peace with people committed to the extermination of the Jewish people.

Accordingly, one of the principal challenges of Israeli political thought in the 1990s has been to distinguish the symbolic images of the Holocaust and Redemption, which compellingly express the sentiments of broad sectors of the Jewish community, from the pragmatic need to reach a political solution to the issue of Palestinian national autonomy. This question bitterly divides Jews both in North America and Israel. To reject the symbolic language of Holocaust and Redemption, on the one hand, challenges a fundamental Jewish consensus that the fate of Jews should not depend on the goodwill of people who have hated them. To embrace it, on the other hand, is to risk the political isolation of Israel within the community of nations and the perpetuation in Israel of a society deeply divided by religious and ethnic fissures. These themselves, many Jews fear, may compromise the state's security and threaten its survival. Whatever choice is taken, the Jews of Israel and North America will be feeling their way along a path that neither their religious traditions nor their modern political experience among the nations has prepared them to travel.

CHAPTER 20

RELIGION AND THE POLITICAL ORDER

IN CHRISTIANITY

As we have seen, Christians have always lived in an uneasy dialectic with "the world." This tension has surfaced in myriad ways throughout Christian history, beginning with Christ himself. In fact, the crucifixion—the central mystery of the Christian faith—is in essence but a manifestation of the conflicting power claims we now call "the church/state conflict": Jesus, the Son of God, the ultimate spiritual power, is arrested, tried, and executed as a common criminal by the Roman authorities in Palestine. According to Jewish prophecies, the Messiah would be a king. In the gospels, Jesus continually speaks of "the Kingdom of God." At his trial, Christ is asked by the Roman procurator, Pilate: "Are you the King of the Jews?" Jesus says "yes," but in a most peculiar way:

> My kingship is not of this world; if my kingship were of this world, my servants would fight, that I might not be handed over . . . but my kingship is not of this world (John 19:36).

This passage, more than any other, lays bare the dialectical nature of Christian thinking on politics: Christ is to rule the world, but only in a very "other-worldly" way; the church is the visible manifestation of Christ's kingdom on earth, but its rule is not to be determined by the world itself. The tension that has always existed in Christianity between secular and spiritual rulership is the clearest and most forceful expression of the unresolved and unresolvable dialectic between the two spheres of existence accepted by Christians. By the twelfth century, Western Christians had adopted the term "secular" to denote anything related to the world, anything that was not spiritual, sacred, or religious. This term had an eschatological dimension, for it referred to the period of history before the promised second coming of Christ as "this age" (Latin, *saeculum*: age or period), to distinguish it from "that age" to come when the kingdom of God would be fully realized on earth. In its simplest form, the distinction between "secular" and "spiritual" came to be understood in Christianity as follows: the secular or worldly power was invested in civil rulers, in emperors, kings, nobles, magistrates, and executioners; the spiritual power was invested in the church and its elites, in popes, patriarchs, bishops, and priests. This distinction was not purely abstract, though it relied on a certain metaphysical framework. In practical terms, there has always been a visible difference between the two powers in Christianity, for sheer brute force has been the prerogative of the "secular" realm. Unlike the secular powers, the church has never had a standing army or police; its weapons have been excommunication, interdict, intrigue, and persuasion.

FROM PERSECUTION TO RULERSHIP

Early Christians did not have to fret over the integration of secular and spiritual power, for the relation between church and state in the first three centuries of Christian history was brutally simple. Christianity was an illegal religion in the Roman Empire, and the state was thus the enemy of the church. Christians were found guilty of "atheism" and "anarchy" for refusing to worship the official state gods of the empire and also for denying the divinity of the emperors who proclaimed themselves gods. Persecution was a government affair, but in many cases it began on a popular level. Christian disrespect of the traditional gods was apparently feared in pagan society: would not the gods grow angry at being ignored or offended?, reasoned some pagans. Christians, thus, could be blamed for pestilence, famine, and other natural disasters. Persecution of Christians was cruel and intense, but not as unrelenting as many imagine. Until the third century, persecutions were sporadic and localized. As Christians grew in number, the emperors began to direct widespread persecutions, beginning with Decius (250) and continuing in waves under Valerian (257) and Diocletian (284–305). Even then, the severity of the persecutions could vary from place to place.

Christian thinking about "secular" power changed overnight when Emperor Constantine issued the Edict of Milan in 313, granting full toleration to the church. The change seemed shocking, even apocalyptic to some. Eusebius, the first church historian, was awestruck by the sight of the emperor sitting at the same table with Christian bishops at the Council of Nicaea: "One might easily have thought it a picture of the kingdom of Christ, the whole a dream rather than a reality."[1] Constantine's motives have been the subject of much debate. At one end of the spectrum of opinion, some have viewed Constantine's turnabout as a genuine conversion; at the other end, others have seen Constantine's moves as sheer political expediency. The truth is probably somewhere in between. But no matter what his motives might have been in tolerating—and favoring—Christianity, one thing is clear: Constantine sought to make Christianity as much a part of his rulership as pagan religion had been for his predecessors. Though he remained unbaptized until he was on his deathbed, Constantine began to meddle in church affairs almost immediately after granting toleration. It seems Constantine favored the idea of a priest/king, a Christian version of the office of Pontifex Maximus (supreme pontiff) that the pagan god-emperors had held in the Roman state religion. He once told a group of bishops: "You are bishops whose jurisdiction is within the church. But I am also a bishop, ordained by God to oversee those outside the church."[2] As Constantine apparently saw it, Christianity was the completion of a process of unification that had long been in process. The empire had one emperor, one law, and one citizenship. Why not one religion that professed one God and one church as well, instead of the multitude of gods and sects of paganism?

Constantine set a pattern for future emperors. He embarked on an ambitious program of church building throughout the empire. His new capital city, Constantinople (named after himself), was to be a wholly Christian city, dominated as much by his presence as by the churches and relics within it. Constantine also began to enact laws that favored the Christian church (such as exempting the clergy from public obligations) and even forced Christian observances on all of society (such as forbidding work on Sundays). Moreover, Constantine began to employ the power of the state to enforce uniformity within Christendom. In 325, Constantine took it on himself to settle the Arian controversy by convening the Council of Nicaea, the first truly ecumenical, or worldwide assembly of Christian bishops. The sociopolitical legacy of Nicaea would prove as profound as its theological one. When Arius and his followers were condemned, it was the state that stepped in to ensure that they did not continue to hold office or exert influence over other Christians. Whereas the state had previously persecuted all Christians, now it selectively used its power against Christian heretics. Within the brief span of a dozen years, then, the state transformed itself from the church's worst enemy into its best friend, and Christians mutated from martyrs to inquisitors. From this point forward, all those who were denounced as heretics in a state-supported council would find themselves ostracized, imprisoned, or even killed. In 333, Constantine made Arianism a capital crime:

> If any treatise composed by Arius is discovered, let it be consigned to the flames . . . and if anyone shall be caught concealing a book by Arius, and does not instantly bring it out and burn it, the penalty shall be death.

By the year 380, the empire had made freedom of conscience a legal impossibility for Christians. One had to be orthodox, or else. Sanctions were issued against "those who contend about religion . . . as authors of sedition and disturbers of the peace of the church." This same imperial statute commanded: "There shall be no opportunity for any man to go out to the public and to argue about religion, or to discuss it, or to give any counsel."[3]

Heresy, once identified as such, could vanish more quickly and thoroughly, at least within the empire. Beyond the empire's borders, the situation remained more fluid. Imperial persecution of "forbidden" sects eventually led to the extinction of many Christian communities. And one should never forget that

PERSECUTION AND HOLY WAR

Persecutions of Christians by Non-Christian States

64–67	Emperor Nero accuses Christians of "hatred for the human race" and holds them responsible for a great fire at Rome. Many Christians are killed in the arena for sport, or are burned alive. According to ancient tradition, the apostles Peter and Paul were martyred during this persecution.
110–210	Christianity is branded as a crime in the empire; executions increase.
249–251	Emperor Decius orders an empire-wide drive to wipe out Christianity.
257–260	Emperor Valerian steps up imperial attempts to crush Christianity by concentrating on the persecution of bishops.
303–311	Emperor Diocletian brings on "The Great Persecution," which creates thousands of martyrs and continues after his abdication in 305.
313	Emperor Constantine grants toleration to Christians with the Edict of Milan. End of imperial persecutions.
8th–9th c.	Sporadic persecutions in the Middle East, North Africa, and Iberia under various Muslim rulers.
1614–1639	Persecution and extermination of all Christians in Japan.
18th–19th c.	Sporadic persecutions of Christians in China.
20th c.	Sporadic persecutions of Christians under various totalitarian regimes: the Spanish Republic, the Third Reich, and the Soviet Union, China, and other Communist nations.

Persecutions of Christians by Christians

325–381	Arians and Orthodox persecute one another, depending on which party gains imperial favor. After the Council of Constantinople (381), the Emperor Theodosius drives Arians out of the empire.
4th–5th c.	Imperial persecution of the Donatist Christians of North Africa.
5th c.	Nestorian Christians driven out of the empire and into Persia and points East.
6th–7th c.	Imperial persecution of Monophysite Christians in North Africa and Middle East.
8th–9th c.	Persecution of image venerators in the Byzantine Empire.
12th–13th c.	Persecution of the Bogomils in the Balkans; the Cathars and Waldensians in Western Europe.
14th c.	Persecution of the Free Spirit Heretics in Western Europe.
14th–15th c.	Persecution of the Lollards in England, and the Hussites in Bohemia.
16th–17th c.	Widespread persecutions erupt as the Reformation tears Catholicism asunder.
	Protestants are sporadically persecuted by Catholics.
	Catholics are sporadically persecuted by Protestants.
	Anabaptists are systematically persecuted by both Protestants and Catholics.

Protestants sporadically persecute their own heretics.

18th c.	Russian Czar orders the persecution of "Old Believers" in his empire.

Christian Persecutions and Holy Wars Against "The Other"

7th c.	The Visigothic kings of Iberia place ultimatums on the Jews, ordering them to convert or be expelled.
711	Conquest of Christian Iberia by Muslim invaders.
8th–15th c.	*Reconquista,* or Christian reconquest of Iberia from its Muslim rulers.
1096–1396	The Crusades, a series of military expeditions against Islam, repeatedly conquer and lose control of the Holy Land and surrounding regions in Syria. Those who engage in this warfare are promised full forgiveness of their sins; those who die in battle are considered martyrs.
1096	First major popular uprising against Jews in Western Europe accompanies the beginning of the Crusades, especially France and Germany. Thousands of Jews are killed or forcibly converted by angry mobs, often with the support of local authorities. Many bishops object, however, and come to the aid of the Jews.
1182	Jews temporarily expelled from the Kingdom of France.
1215	Fourth Lateran Council calls upon Jews and Muslims living among Catholic Christians to wear distinctive dress.
1290	Jews are expelled from England; not readmitted until the 17th century.
1348–1350	As the bubonic plague, or Black Death, sweeps through Western Europe, Jews are once again set upon by mobs who blame them for all the suffering. Pope Clement VI condemns the violence, but is unable to stop it.
1391–1392	Mob violence against Spanish Jews results in thousands of deaths, forced conversions, and exiles.
1394	Jews are once again expelled from France; not readmitted until the 17th century.
1492	Spanish Jews are ordered to convert or leave the Kingdoms of Castille and Aragon by King Ferdinand and Queen Isabella. Thousands flee, but thousands also convert under duress.
1497	Portuguese Jews are given the same ultimatum as their Spanish brethren.
1502	Remaining Muslims in Spain are given the same choice as Jews: conversion or exile.
16th c.	The Spanish and Portuguese Inquisitions persecute thousands of Jewish converts and their descendants (*Conversos* or *Marranos*) who are accused of continuing to practice Judaism in secret.
16th–17th c.	The remains of ancient pagan religion among Christians, feared as "witchcraft," are systematically persecuted by Protestant and Catholic alike, in both Europe and America. Thousands of "witches," most of them women, are hunted down and executed.
1609–1614	Expulsion of the *Moriscos,* or descendants of the Muslim Moors, from Spain.
1648–1658	Massacres and expulsions of the Jews in Poland.
18th–19th c.	Sporadic persecution of Jews in Russian empire.

fourth-century Christianity was a complex mosaic of churches. In one single Phrygian town, for instance, there were at once Christian churches composed of Montanists, Novatianists, Encratites, and Apoctatites. Toward the end of the fourth century, one Italian bishop drew up a list of all existing heresies, coming up with a total number of 156! The fact that no one remembers much, if anything, about these heresies stems in large measure from the empire's efficient persecution of false Christian beliefs.

Not all heresies slipped quietly into oblivion, however. Arianism proved an intractable problem for many emperors, and it survived for centuries; Nestorianism and Monophysitism successfully resisted all imperial attempts to wipe them out. Arriving at orthodoxy through an imperially convened council, following the pattern set by Constantine at Nicaea, became the accepted method. But, as we have seen in earlier chapters, not all councils prevailed (witness the so-called Robber Council of Ephesus, 439, and the iconoclastic Council of Constantinople, 753), and not all emperors had their way.

As much as Christians were beset by internal disagreement, however, they presented a united front against paganism; and on this battlefront, the power of the emperors did prevail. Between the fourth and sixth centuries, the old pagan religion was dismantled and, if not crushed, at least driven underground. The legal assault on paganism began with Constantine, who stripped many temples of their precious stones and metals or even demolished them to make way for Christian basilicas. Emperor Constantius II passed the first antipagan law in 341. Temples were allowed to stand only outside the city walls, and they were to be used only for plays, the circus, contests, and other long-established amusements of pagan Roman culture. By mid-fourth century, it was becoming increasingly difficult to find the old rituals still being performed in pagan temples. The Christian elite, now nearly identical with the ruling elite, pressed for the total suppression of the old religion. One such plea demanded that pagan rituals be completely suspended and destroyed. By the end of the fourth century, many cities throughout the empire were plagued by popular riots against paganism, in which mobs stormed temples and brought them to ruin. Even monks played an active role in some of these riots. In the eastern half of the empire, where the ruling elite of society had become largely Christian by the late fourth century, relatively little resistance seems to have been offered by paganism. In the West, it was a different story. The elites of the Western Empire seem to have clung more tenaciously to their ancient customs than their Eastern counterparts. The Roman aristocracy in particular made an attempt in the late fourth century to uphold the religion of their forebears along with the classical culture that went along with it. By the 430s, however, the children and grandchildren of these aristocrats joined the church. Although many in the church decried these conversions as hypocritical, in the long run sincerity was not what mattered.

By the fifth century, the Roman Empire was a Christian state. This would be the norm for Christianity for over one thousand years; membership in the church would be a given, required of all who resided within certain geopolitical boundaries. The law code of Emperor Justinian in the sixth century set in stone what had already been observed for generations: baptism was required of all who dwelt in the empire. Since baptism was made compulsory—a rite performed at infancy, much like circumcision among the Jews—Christianity became identical with nationality. And this would prove true outside the empire as well, for in the late antique and early medieval world, the religion professed by any ruler was also required of his subjects. For example, the kingdoms of Ethiopia and Armenia, which were outside the empire, also required baptism. The same was also true of the "barbarian" kingdoms beyond the empire's borders. As soon as a king converted, so did his people. This is the way the Germans, Scandinavians, Slavs, and many other European peoples were Christianized. By the year 1000, long after the collapse of the Western Empire, Christianity had spread far beyond the former empire's borders and the key to expansion was the conversion of entire nations or states. National, ethnic, and religious identities became fused, and the Christian religion became an integral component of every aspect of life and also of civil "secular" law. Christianity became an obligation rather than a choice; and within this religiopolitical reality, orthodoxy was also required. The notion of a "Christendom" as a geopolitical reality was no abstraction. Moreover, the state came to depend on Christian ritual and theology for its claims to authority. In this manner, then, the church and the state achieved a symbiotic relationship that lasted for well over a millennium (and in some societies until the twentieth century).

After the fifth century, the Christianization of the "other" became as much a concern of the state as of the church. Cyril and Methodius, missionaries to the Slavs in the ninth century, were supported by the Byzantine emperor and even found themselves caught in a power struggle when the king of the Franks began to compete for their services. Conversions of entire nations often occurred en masse, such as that of Bulgaria (865), Poland (966), or Russia (988). What this meant, of course, was that Christianity would be imposed from above on millions of people who had little or no say in the matter. Consequently, one must be careful about speaking of the "Christianization" of Europe, for the Christian religion could not replace the native religions of so many people overnight. The process was slow, gradual, and in many cases painful. In the sixteenth century, many Protestant Reformers argued that Roman Catholicism was nothing more than a monstrous hybrid: pagan idolatry and superstition covered by a thin Christian veneer. Some contemporary scholars have indeed argued that Europe was not fully "Christianized" until the sixteenth and seventeenth centuries, when the persecution of witches finally put the old pagan religion to rest.

This pattern was not universal. One notable exception were the Jewish people, who were the only non-Christians allowed to retain their faith within Christendom. Jewish communities could be found in most cities of the empire and even beyond, especially after the collapse of the West. Christians had always found it difficult to come to terms with the continued existence of Judaism and often related to the Jews as a "problem." Theologically, the Jews were an embarrassment and a puzzlement: if Christianity fulfilled Judaism, why were there still Jews to be found? Were they still the "chosen people," and if so, why did God allow them to remain so "blind" to the truth? Even more disturbing to some Christians was the practical question of how to deal with the Jews legally. If Christianity was to be the state religion, should Judaism be tolerated? Should any exception be made in their case? On the whole, the church Fathers agreed that the continued existence of the Jews was a mystery and that Christians should not interfere in God's plans by wiping out the Jews. Nonetheless, some church Fathers favored making life as difficult as possible for the Jews. Fathers whose writings are otherwise filled with talk of love poured out the strongest venom against Judaism. Gregory of Nyssa revealed much about Christian attitudes when he described the Jews as

> slayers of the Lord, murderers of the prophets, enemies of God, haters of God, adversaries of grace, enemies of their fathers' faith, advocates of the devil, brood of vipers, slanderers, scoffers, men of darkened minds, leaven of the Pharisees, congregation of demons, sinners, wicked men, stoners, and haters of goodness.[4]

John Chrysostom labeled the Jews "the most miserable of all men" and accused them of being "lustful, rapacious, greedy, perfidious bandits." Even worse, the Jews were reviled as "God killers" because they had crucified Christ. Many Christians believed the Jews would never be forgiven by God: Their punishment would be survival without a homeland, or temple, or the same legal protection as other people. As Chrysostom saw it, this punishment came directly from God, not from the church.[5] St. Augustine summed up the attitude adopted in the Christian West: the Jews still had some mysterious providential role to play and were at once witnesses of evil and witnesses of Christian truth. They were allowed to exist "for the salvation of the gentiles, but not for their own." Their dispersion and their suffering witnessed at once to their election, their betrayal of God, and the superiority of Christianity. Like Cain (Gen. 4:15), they carried a sign, but were not to be killed.[6]

The law of the empire came to reflect this intense Christian distrust of the Jews. The *Codex Theodosianus* (438) granted toleration and protection to Jews but severely circumscribed their rights. Jews could not convert others to their faith, were not allowed to own Christian slaves, and were barred from holding civic office or from joining the army. Jewish-Christian marriages were forbidden under penalty of death (unless the Jewish party became Christian). Even the building and decorating of synagogues were restricted and carefully controlled by Roman legislation. As Christianity grew ever more closely identified with the sociopolitical and cultural identity of Europe during the Middle Ages, this animosity toward Jews would intensify and the list of restrictions would grow even longer.

SECULAR AND SACRED IN CONFLICT

Constantine's political legacy came to be known as Caesaropapism, that is, a form of rulership that is at once secular (Caesar) and sacred (papal). But Caesaropapism has never been fully realized in the person of any single emperor or monarch: it has been a tendency rather than a political reality. For as soon as the emperors began to meddle in church affairs, the bishops began to oppose them. Once again, a dialectic was set in motion. As much as the bishops enjoyed the benefits of imperial support, they also carefully protected the integrity and independence of the church and their own office.

The conflict between secular and sacred spheres of power began almost as soon as Christianity became the imperial religion. St. Ambrose, bishop of Milan in the fourth century, was among the first of the church elites to delimit the boundaries of secular authority. Ambrose came from the ruling class, his father had been Praetorian Prefect of Gaul. He had grown up with power and knew how to exercise it. As bishop, he could stand up to the pagan senators; when these aristocrats tried to restore the pagan Altar of Victory in the senate house, Ambrose prevented it. Ambrose could also stand up to the emperor and humble him; when the Emperor Theodosius slaughtered thousands of people in Thessalonica as a mass reprisal (something Roman emperors had routinely done for generations), Ambrose excommunicated Theodosius and required him to do public penance before readmitting him into the church.

Another altercation between Ambrose and the Emperor Theodosius reveals even more clearly how the church made claims to a "higher" spiritual power that could override civil law. As mentioned earlier, Jews stood on a precarious legal footing in the late empire. During the reign of Theodosius, mob attacks on synagogues and Jewish communities became common. Civil law required that Jews be protected from hostile attacks and that they be compensated for any loss of property suffered during these riots. In 388, a synagogue was burnt to the ground by a mob in Callinicum, on the eastern fringe of the empire, at the instigation of the local Christian bishop. When Theodosius upheld the law and ordered the bishop of Callinicum to build the Jews a new synagogue, Ambrose reprimanded the emperor. What business did Theodosius have ordering a bishop about? To humiliate a bishop and his community in such a way would be to damage the church's prestige. "Which is more important," asked Ambrose, "the parade of discipline or the cause of religion?" Ambrose's final argument against Theodosius summed up what became the dominant church policy toward the state for over a thousand years: "The maintenance of civil law is secondary to religious interest."[7] Fearing excommunication, Theodosius withdrew his orders and denied the Jews of Callinicum the compensation that was legally theirs.

In Constantinople, where Christian emperors continued to rule until 1453, the position of the "secular" ruler assumed markedly spiritual characteristics. The Byzantine emperor was not a priest but had sacred powers. It was the emperor alone who could convene councils of bishops to decide doctrinal questions; he could also depose bishops and patriarchs. The emperor was the only layman allowed to attend the eucharistic liturgy inside the sanctuary, behind the iconostasis; he could preach sermons, wear sacred vestments, and cense the altar. Moreover, the emperor was considered God's representative on earth; in a religious culture where icons were dominant, the emperor was conceived as a living image of God. As they prostrated themselves before icons of Christ in church, so did the Byzantine Christians prostrate themselves before the emperor.

But the Byzantine emperors received their sacred rulership from the hands of the patriarch of Constantinople. The coronation ceremony was itself a ritual that confirmed the symbiosis of church and state. By the seventh century, the power

The Crowning of David

This Byzantine depiction of the crowning of David shows how ancient Jewish history and Hellenistic political philosophy merged to produce a uniquely Christian notion of government. (*Source:* Corbis-Bettmann)

relation between emperor and patriarch had been set into the imperial law code as a careful balance of "secular" and "sacred" spheres. On paper, at least, the emperor and patriarch were to work together in a *symphonia,* or harmony, that aimed to maintain peace, justice, and orthodoxy; the emperor had control over the bodies of his subjects, but the patriarch cared for their souls. Emperor and patriarch could at times oppose and correct each other. In practice, the harmony was not constant. Witness, for instance, the prolonged iconoclastic controversy when the emperors tried to force their views on the whole church over the opposition of the patriarchs. After the collapse of the Byzantine Empire in 1453, the Byzantine system survived in Russia, where the czar (Russian for Caesar) and the patriarch of Moscow maintained a similar balance of powers.

In the medieval Catholic West, relations between secular and ecclesiastical rulers were not as clearly defined. In the five centuries following the collapse of Rome, the "barbarian" rulers of Europe ruled in close cooperation with the pope and the bishops. Though Pope Leo III tried to make it clear that the ultimate secular power derived from his office when he took it upon himself to crown the king of the Franks, Charlemagne, as "Roman" emperor in 800, the emperors and kings of the West controlled their regional churches directly. Westerners thought of their monarchs as sacred also, though not in as thorough a way as did the Byzantines. Tensions between the secular and ecclesiastical elite began to intensify in the eleventh century, however, as the popes increased their claims to supremacy over all Christians.

In addition to affecting East-West relations, papal claims to supremacy also affected the way in which church and state interacted in the West. If the pope was the supreme ruler of the church, and the church was coextensive with the civil realm, how did the pope's authority relate to that of emperors, kings, and princes? As could be expected, civil rulers were not willing to grant the pope absolute authority. In the eleventh century, a controversy arose between Pope Gregory VII and Emperor Henry IV over the appointment and installation of bishops. According to ancient custom, secular rulers throughout Europe routinely appointed bishops and "invested" them with symbols of authority in public ceremonies. Pope Gregory wanted to assume control of all episcopal appointments and to halt this custom of lay investiture of bishops; Emperor Henry refused to give in. Gregory did more than excommunicate the emperor: he declared Henry a rebel, stripped him of his authority, and released all his subjects from obedience to him. In the bitter dispute that followed, Emperor Henry prevailed through violence, proving that his authority rested on brute force. After his German bishops deposed Gregory and elected a new pope, Henry invaded Rome, laid siege to the city for three years, and in 1084 installed his "anti-pope," Clement III, in the papal throne. Pope Gregory fled and died in exile in southern Italy.

Instead of chastening the papacy, the sad spectacle of Gregory VII made subsequent popes even more vocal about their claims to supremacy. Beginning in 1198, Pope Innocent III made claims that, if accepted, would have made the pope the supreme ruler of all Christendom. Innocent described himself as "lower than God, but higher than man." He asserted that Peter was given "not only the universal church but the whole world to govern." Even further, he argued that all secular power was derived from papal authority: "just as the moon derives its light from the sun." The pope, he maintained, "judges all and is judged by no one."[8]

This line of reasoning could only bring popes into further conflict with civil rulers, for such claims undermined the authority of emperors and kings. Of course, to claim such power is not always to actually have it. Another controversy in the early fourteenth century between a pope and a monarch brought to light the real weakness of the papal claims. Seeking to affirm his sovereignty, Pope Boniface VIII tried to prevent the French King Philip IV from taxing his clergy. Philip IV refused to obey. Pope Boniface replied with a pronouncement (*Unam Sanctam,* 1302) that did not address the controversy directly but raised the theological arguments for papal supremacy to new heights. "We declare, state, define, and pronounce," roared Pope Boniface, "that it is altogether necessary to salvation for every human creature to be subject to the Roman pontiff."[9] Brute force finally ended this dispute, proving again that authority is not an abstraction. As Boniface was preparing to excommunicate King Philip IV, soldiers working for the French king attacked the pope and seized him. Pope Boniface died in their custody, possibly from injuries inflicted upon him. The king's triumph was complete, for he also quickly engineered the election of a French bishop as pope, Clement V, who then moved from Rome to Avignon in southern France. For the next seventy years (1308–1378) the bishops of Rome would rule timidly from Avignon, under the thumb of the French monarchs.

Numerous other conflicts between popes, emperors, kings, and bishops took place in the medieval West. At bottom, these various disputes stemmed from the unresolved tension between "the world" and "the spirit" that was so much a part of the Christian mentality. All papal claims to supremacy were based on the assumption that as the spirit was superior to the flesh, so was the power of the church superior to that of secular rulers. The papacy also favored a descending view of rulership, in which all authority on earth was seen as derived from above, from the supreme power that God had given directly to the pope. By the fourteenth and fifteenth centuries, many elites began to press for the acceptance of different schemes. Some, like John of Paris (d. 1306), proposed a view known as "parallelism" in which authority was divided between the secular and the ecclesiastical spheres. Others, such as Marsilius of Padua (1320s), pressed for an ascending scheme, in which authority was seen as derived from below, from the people. Though Marsilius of Padua was condemned in 1327, his way of thinking could not be extinguished. The Lollard and Hussite movements were to a large extent founded on political assumptions similar to that of Marsilius. Whereas Marsilius, Wycliffe, and Hus failed to successfully challenge the status quo, the Protestant Reformation succeeded.

THE REFORMATION

The Reformation of the sixteenth century was as much a political as a religious revolution, and much of its political thinking was derived from ascending views of rulership. If all authority resided in the Word of God and all Christians were equally priests, as Luther claimed, then the relation between church and state had to change. Gone were the pope and his claim to supremacy; gone was any conception of the clerical office as an especially privileged estate; gone was the notion of the church as something superior to the world. But this is not to say that the Reformation made the church subservient to the state. On the contrary, the Reformation ended up blurring the boundaries between secular and sacred to such an extent as to actually increase the power of the church in many places.

Without a doubt, the single most profound political change brought about by the Reformation was the abolition of the priestly office, its claims, and its privileges. Protestant clergy were considered citizens of the secular realm who were no different from anyone else. Unlike the Catholic priests, who did not pay taxes and could not be tried by "secular" courts, the Protestant clergy were fully incorporated into the sociopolitical fabric of the community. This is because they were viewed as "ministers" rather than as priests; that is, they were representatives of the community, who ministered to its needs, rather than divinely ordained intercessors who had special powers. (See Chapter 8). The only special power the Protestant clergy had was the call of the community to serve; their office was not derived from above, then, but rather from below. In Luther's words:

> There is no true, basic difference between laymen and priests, princes and bishops, between religious and secular, except for the sake of office and work, but not for the sake of status. They are all of the spiritual estate, all are truly priests, bishops, and popes. But they do not have the same work to do.[10]

Despite their many differences, the various Protestant traditions shared this vision of the clerical state. But if the clergy were not superior to "secular" rulers, how was the church to relate to the state? Answers to this question varied tremendously.

Among the Lutherans, the state was seen as responsible for actually ensuring that the Word was correctly preached and the sacraments purely administered. Luther laid out his thinking on this issue as early as 1520 in his *Address to the Nobility of the German Nation*, in which he argued that the princes had a duty to reform the church when the ecclesiastics refused to do it. Luther's thinking was to a large extent determined by his own precarious situation and on his dependence on the Saxon princes to effect the changes he proposed. Consequently, in the Lutheran territorial churches, it would be the princes who had the ultimate responsibility for maintaining the church. The Lutheran clergy, now considered representatives of the community rather than spiritual superiors, would serve in territorial churches run by the princes. Luther realized that this was a fragile arrangement, for he observed:

> A wise prince is a rare bird, and an upright prince even rarer. They are generally the biggest fools or the worst scoundrels on earth; therefore, one must constantly expect the worst from them and look for little good, especially in divine matters which concern the salvation of souls. . . . If a prince should happen to be wise, upright, or a Christian, that is one of the great miracles, the most precious token of divine grace upon that land.[11]

Lutheran churches as a whole maintained a healthy skepticism about the princes but nonetheless depended on them for survival.

Among the Reformed, as we have seen, there was a pronounced tendency toward the establishment of theocracies in which the church and the state worked closely together to create and maintain Christian commonwealths. In Zwingli's Zurich, Calvin's Geneva, and Cromwell's England, there was to be no friction between "secular" and ecclesiastic: the clergy and the secular rulers performed different functions but worked toward a common goal. Martin Bucer, the Reformer of Strasbourg, summed up the theocratic mentality in a treatise with a title that says it all, *The Kingdom of Christ*:

> The first concern of every Christian magistrate ought to be directed to this: that the citizens be faithfully taught and eagerly learn pure religion. Therefore, it is necessary for the magistrates themselves to excel others both in knowledge of and zeal for the Christian religion.[12]

And this was no mild-mannered collusion between church and state. Ultimately, it was the executioner's sword that enforced Christian living. What Bucer said in *The Kingdom of Christ* would have an enormous influence on John Calvin and all his followers:

> In every state sanctified to God capital punishment must be ordered for all who have dared to injure religion, either by introducing a false and impious doctrine about the worship of God or by calling people away from the true worship of God.[13]

Among the Radicals, separation from the world made each of their communities a political entity unto itself. The Radicals shunned contact with all things secular simply by not taking part in civic life at large and by making their churches self-enclosed spiritual enclaves. This does not mean that the Radicals were apolitical; on the contrary, their separation from the world was an intensely political conclusion. Internally, their communities tended to be even more theocratic than those of the Reformed. Of course, what was most "radical" about the Radicals was the fact that they called for an end to compulsory Christianity. In saying that only believers should be baptized (as adults), the Radicals were denying the validity of the church/state relation that had dominated Christianity since the fourth century. In essence, the Radicals were self-consciously seeking a return to the world/church dialectic of early Christianity. Tragically, the same fate befell them as it did the early Christians. Persecuted by civic authorities, Protestant as well as Catholic, the Radical communities endured martyrdom and exile.

It could be argued that it is among the Radicals, rather than among the Lutherans and Reformed (who are sometimes called "magisterial reformers" because of their support for the magistracy or secular powers), that the dawn of the modern age among Christians can be seen most clearly. What made the Radicals seem so dangerous in the sixteenth century was the fact that they sundered completely the relation between church and state, Christianity and society. Belief was a matter of private conscience and not something to be enforced or maintained by violence. Unlike the Catholics, or Bucer and Calvin, who favored societies "sanctified to God" in which heretics would be executed, the Radicals preferred for "the world" to remain un-Christian and for heretics and unbelievers to be left to their own devices.

But in the early modern age, the Radicals were pushed aside, literally. The more liberal voices among them, the spiritualists who denied even the need for an organized church, would be true harbingers of things to come. The thousand-year-old paradigm of church-state relations was difficult for Christians to abandon, however, and the end result would be bloodshed. One man who saw this as a tragedy was Sebastian Castellio, a contemporary of Calvin. It is in Castellio's *Advice to a Desolate France* that we can hear the voice of "modernity" speaking:

> I see a difficulty that must, if possible, be overcome, namely that there are some who teach and have taught . . . that it is the function of princes and lords of the judiciary to put heretics to death, and that they are acting against God, and will be punished, if they do not do this. This teaching is the principal cause of the carnages and butcheries which are taking place for the sake of religion today, and as long as the princes believe in it, I see no remedy for the situation. . . . But the crowning misfortune in this matter is the fact that those very ones who conceived and published this doctrine, are themselves regarded as heretics by all other sects, and for that reason persecuted and massacred.[14]

PLURALISM: CHURCHES AND THE STATE

In 1648, the terrible carnage of the European wars of religion came to an end. In its aftermath, the policy of allowing the secular rulers to determine the religion of their subjects (*cujus regio, ejus religio*) proved unworkable. Consequently, Christians were obliged to accept the futility of the traditional correlation of political entity with a specific religious confession of faith and to come to terms with the fact of pluralism. The thorough transformation of social and mental structures necessitated by pluralism did not take place immediately, however. Indeed, in the late twentieth century it is still not clear that it has occurred. But in fits and starts, European nations developed legal instruments to facilitate the transition to religiously plural societies. And by degrees, the mentality that identified citizenship with specific religious beliefs gave way to a broader understanding of the relation of church to state.

The transition to pluralism was to a certain extent hindered by nostalgia for the old order. Accordingly, change was gradual and often took the form of alternating advances and retreats. So, for example, the Edict of Nantes (1598) gave religious and political autonomy to Huguenots in about a hundred towns within Catholic France. In 1685, King Louis XIV, believing that religious diversity undermined the security of the state, revoked the Edict and chased several hundred thousand Huguenots from his Catholic domain. Or witness the case in England, where the Act of Toleration (1689) broadened religious freedom for Protestants but allowed Catholics, Jews, and Unitarians to suffer exclusion from the full rights of citizenship. Subsequent acts of toleration in Norway (1845), Denmark (1849), Austria (1861), and other European nations formally articulated the ideal of religious freedom, but minority religions remained under suspicion and frequently were hounded and abused. Spain, Portugal, and Italy remained staunchly Catholic; but even in those countries, infighting among Catholics led to frequent purges of religious orders and bouts of anticlerical activism, as rival groups competed for power and influence.

Formal separation of church and state was a decisive step in Western struggles to come to terms with religiously plural societies. From the fourth century, when Christianity became the official religion of the deteriorating Roman Empire, Christians had believed that the state was obliged to sponsor religion. Moreover, many feared that without state enforcement of religious life morals would degenerate and social cohesion would be lost. Against this background, we should understand that the constitutional separation of church and state, which first took place in the United States in the late eighteenth century, was a daring act, a break with fourteen hundred years of tradition. It is also an experiment still in progress.

The first amendment to the Constitution of the United States, which took effect in 1791, stipulates that "Congress shall make no law respecting an establishment of religion, or prohibiting the free exercise thereof." Over the course of two centuries, there have been diverse interpretations of the meaning of these words, and even when meaning is agreed upon, there has not always been enforcement of the law. So, for example, although the amendment prohibits the state from taxing its citizens for the support of religion (in other words, religion is "disestablished" in the United States), some New England states continued to do so well into the nineteenth century. Other states denied slaves the freedom to practice the non-Christian religions that they brought from Africa. The state has at times officially condemned the Mormon practice of polygamy, various Native American religious rituals, snake-handling services among evangelical Protestants, and a host of other activities claimed by religious groups as protected under the First Amendment. And Protestantism, though not the state religion, generally wielded such power that it functioned as the informal established religion well into the twentieth century. In spite of ongoing debate about the application of the First Amendment to specific cases and the issue of Protestant influence, it nevertheless is clear that the separation of church and state in the United States has occasioned an environment in which a wide variety of religious groups flourish. In some cases, this has led to active cooperation and association among different religious groups; at other times, it has been visible as vigorous attempts to preserve tradition, to safeguard religious distinctiveness.

How, then, did an intolerant Christianity that fueled the Thirty Years' War in the seventeenth century participate in the separation of church and state in the eighteenth? Why did Christians who had been accustomed to centuries of state religion decide to disconnect religion from the state? To begin with, although a state church historically claimed the membership of Christians within its borders, the diversity and vitality of popular religions (either tolerated or discouraged by the state church) indicates that frequently there was not uniformity of belief among Christians who lived under the canopy of an official state religion. The host of religious movements during the Reformation of the sixteenth century represent the flowering of religious impulses that long had been percolating beneath the surface of official religion. As religious diversity among Christians increased, minority religious groups began to seek protected status from the state (as in the Edict of Nantes).

The Enlightenment contributed other kinds of arguments to the separation of church and state. Not the least of these was its emphasis on the capability of an individual to reason to an understanding of moral good. Such a notion helped to alleviate fear in some circles that state withdrawal from its role as enforcer of religion would lead to immorality and social disarray. Anticlericalism, vividly apparent in France but present as well in Spain, Italy, Switzerland, and other places, also contributed to shaping public disenchantment with state religion. And European encounters with the cultures of the Americas and Asia led to the construction of a new image of the non-Christian, against which the similarities among various Christian groups appeared more positively in relief. In short, a combination of historical events and forces fostered a reevaluation of church and state. And even though Christianity remains established in certain places (e.g., the Church of England), and there is by no means complete religious freedom even in those countries where freedom is formally professed, the separation of church and state has dramatically changed not only relations among Christian churches, but also between Christians and non-Christians.

NATIONAL DESTINIES

Religious pluralism and formal reorganizations of church-state relations make up only one part of the modern story of church and state in nations with predominantly Christian populations. Alongside these developments, and in contrast to them, the West continues to witness the integration of national or regional histories with Judeo-Christian myths.

The models for Christian understanding of national purpose or destiny derive from the Bible, and especially from the Old Testament. Stories about Yahweh's promise to multiply and protect Jews in the Promised Land in exchange for their obedience to his law sometimes are blended with ideas about a coming "millennium," or thousand-year period of Christian peace and prosperity (especially as suggested in the New Testament book "The Revelation to John"). Different nations or groups have articulated the religious dimension to national goals in different ways, but some vision of a "promised land" and the expectation of national progress toward realizing the millennium remain at the core of Christian conceptualizations of national destiny.

Let us take the example of the United States. At the same time that Americans were ratifying the First Amendment, with its explicit separation of church from state—a "wall of separation" as Jefferson noted and later courts approvingly cited—they were vigorously enlarging the argument that America was destined to become the "Kingdom of God." Such was the viewpoint of the Princeton Commencement poem of 1771, entitled "The Rising Glory of America."[15] Flushed with

Diego Rivera, Mural, Twentieth Century

The mixing of political and religious themes in Latin American Christianity takes many forms. Here Emilio Zapata, revered as a revolutionary leader and advocate of radical agrarian reform in Mexico, is pictured with a halo (his white hat) surrounded by the twentieth-century equivalent of the evangelists Matthew, Mark, Luke, and John, the musicians who tells stories in songs. (*Source:* Diego Rivera/Art Resource)

confidence following the successes of the revolt against England, the ratification of the Constitution, and the early stages of the revolution in France (which Americans believed to be modeled on their example), American writers detailed the promise of that glory. The *Columbian,* a magazine published in Philadelphia, sounded the popular theme that the mission of America was to export globally the democratic institutions and benevolent social philosophy of postrevolutionary

Christian America. Americans openly proclaimed their Christian destiny to lead the world to the embrace of religious truth; or as one contributor versified in 1791, "That voice, which by the western world was heard,/By the whole world shall be shortly rever'd."[16] Samuel Hopkins, in *A Treatise on the Millennium* (1793), pictured the Kingdom of God on earth as a homogenous world of Christianity and predicted that "In that day, men will not only be united in peace and love, as brethren; but will agree in sentiments, respecting the doctrines and truth contained in the Bible, and the religious institutions and practice, which are there prescribed."[17] In short, even while the nation moved to disjoin church and state in the Constitution, Americans fervently embraced a view of national destiny grounded in a sense of Christian mission to the world.

Another example of Christian national self-understanding is modern Germany.[18] Even as Germany experimented during the nineteenth century with various programs for loosening state control of churches, the notion of a special German Christianity grew more popular. That growth was grounded in the notion of a nation, or *Volk*, as it was articulated by Friedrich Schleiermacher: "Each Volk was designated to illustrate a special aspect of the image of God, in its own peculiar setting and by its own specially determined position in the world." From this understanding grew a German religious patriotism that linked Germany, the Bible, Martin Luther, and the duty to bring a particular brand of Christian piety to the rest of the world. During the First World War, German pastors compared their congregations to the "chosen people" of the Old Testament and referred to the nation as "the Israel of the New Covenant." Johann Kessler, a Lutheran pastor in Dresden, accordingly explained:

> We believe in a world calling for our nation. A nation that God has equipped with such gifts of the Spirit and such depths of mind, that he called to be a bearer of the gospel in the days of the Reformation. . . . God has great things in store for such a nation. . . . We are the tools with which God will construct his Kingdom today. We are the soldiers with which he will win his victory.

In short, the early twentieth century witnessed the outright identification of national aspirations with Christianity in Germany, or, as pastor Reinhold Dietrich put the matter, "the Christianizing of Germanness and the Germanizing of Christianity."

A third example of the blending of nationalism with Christianity is the somewhat different case of Roman Catholicism in twentieth-century Latin America. As we have seen in Chapter 14 the liberation theology that took root in Latin American Christianity in the latter half of the twentieth century initially articulated resistance to economic oppression. (Historically, resistance to the state has been intertwined with Christian beliefs on many occasions.) In time, liberation theology coalesced around calls for the implementation of socialist governments and in so doing came to function as a scaffolding for organizing and directing the power of the state, with important consequences for church-state relations. So, for example, the influential Uruguayan Jesuit Juan Luis Segundo envisioned a socialist state in which church institutions ranging from universities to newspapers worked hand

The Christian Mission

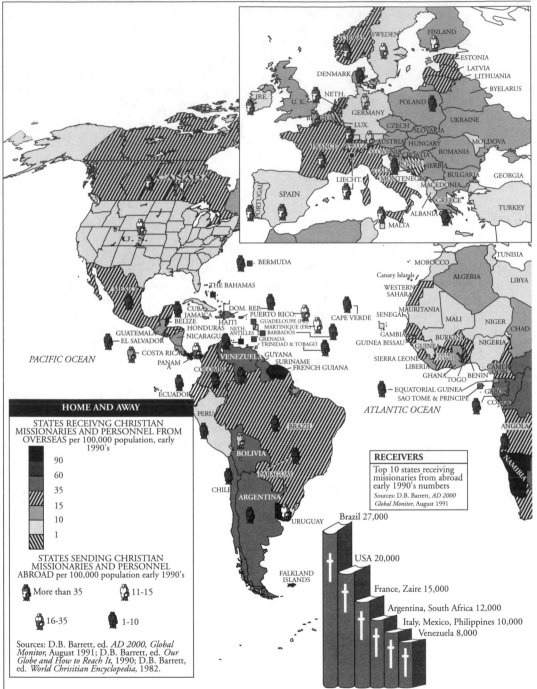

HOME AND AWAY

STATES RECEIVING CHRISTIAN MISSIONARIES AND PERSONNEL FROM OVERSEAS per 100,000 population, early 1990's

- 90
- 60
- 35
- 15
- 10
- 1

STATES SENDING CHRISTIAN MISSIONARIES AND PERSONNEL ABROAD per 100,000 population early 1990's

- More than 35
- 11-15
- 16-35
- 1-10

Sources: D.B. Barrett, ed. *AD 2000, Global Monitor*, August 1991; D.B. Barrett, ed. *Our Globe and How to Reach It*, 1990; D.B. Barrett, ed. *World Christian Encyclopedia*, 1982.

RECEIVERS

Top 10 states receiving missionaries from abroad early 1990's numbers

Sources: D.B. Barrett, *AD 2000 Global Monitor*, August 1991

Brazil 27,000
USA 20,000
France, Zaire 15,000
Argentina, South Africa 12,000
Italy, Mexico, Philippines 10,000
Venezuela 8,000

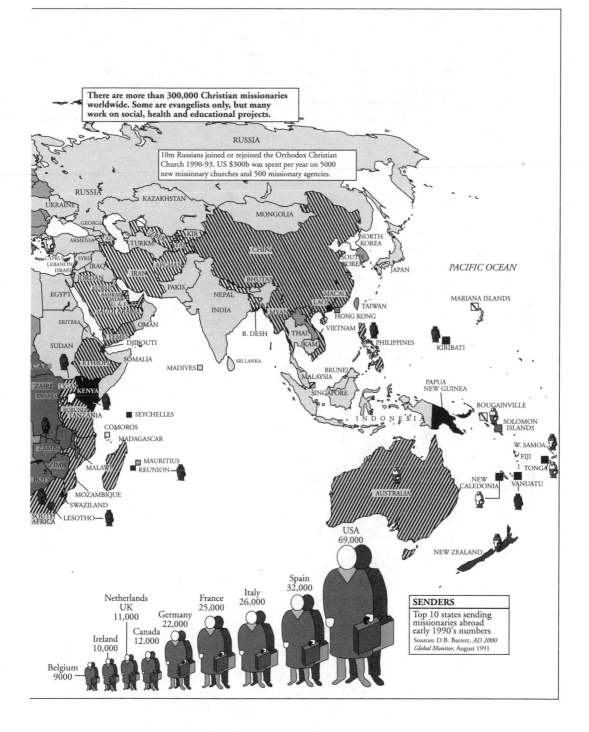

There are more than 300,000 Christian missionaries worldwide. Some are evangelists only, but many work on social, health and educational projects.

RUSSIA

10m Russians joined or rejoined the Orthodox Christian Church 1990-93. US $300b was spent per year on 5000 new missionary churches and 500 missionary agencies.

RUSSIA
UKRAINE
KAZAKHSTAN
GEORGIA
ARMENIA
TURKM
KIR
MONGOLIA
NORTH KOREA
CYPRUS
LEBANON
SYRI
ISRAEL
IRAQ
AFGHAN
CHINA
SOUTH KOREA
JAPAN
PACIFIC OCEAN
JORDAN
IRAN
BHUTAN
KUWAIT
BAHRAIN
PAKIS
NEPAL
MACAO
LAOS
TAIWAN
MARIANA ISLANDS
EGYPT
SAUDI ARABIA
QATAR
U.A.E.
INDIA
MYAN
HONG KONG
ERITREA
OMAN
B. DESH
THAI
VIETNAM
YEMEN
KAM
PHILIPPINES
KIRIBATI
SUDAN
DJIBOUTI
SOMALIA
MADIVES
SRI LANKA
ETHIOPI
BRUNEI
MALAYSIA
C.A.R.
PAPUA NEW GUINEA
ZAIRE
UGA
KENYA
SINGAPORE
BOUGAINVILLE
RWANDA
BURUNDI
SEYCHELLES
SOLOMON ISLANDS
TANZANIA
COMOROS
INDONESIA
ZAMBIA
MADAGASCAR
W. SAMOA
ZIMB
MAURITIUS
FIJI
BOTS
MALAWI
REUNION
TONGA
MOZAMBIQUE
SWAZILAND
NEW CALEDONIA
VANUATU
SOUTH AFRICA
LESOTHO
AUSTRALIA

USA
69,000

NEW ZEALAND

Spain
32,000

Netherlands
UK
11,000

France
25,000

Italy
26,000

Germany
22,000

Ireland
10,000

Canada
12,000

Belgium
9000

SENDERS

Top 10 states sending missionaries abroad early 1990's numbers

Sources: D.B. Barrett, *AD 2000 Global Monitor*, August 1991

in hand to develop new structures for human community.[19] For Segundo, and for other liberationist theologians such as Gustavo Gutierrez, the manifestation of compassion, unselfishness, and justice in authentic Christian community was the key to overcoming the suffering and evils embedded in Latin American society. In several Latin American nations, and especially in El Salvador and Nicaragua, reformers experimented in the 1970s and 1980s with programs for organizing the state on principles derived from Christian theology. In the context of extreme political and military struggle, these experiments have been limited in their effectiveness.

CHAPTER 21

RELIGION AND THE POLITICAL ORDER

IN ISLAM

Islamic civilization was, for several centuries, in a position of prominence on the stage of world history. From the time of the great Arab Muslim conquests in the first century of the Hijra until the Mongol invasions of the Middle East, the Islamic Empire extended from India and Central Asia to the Atlantic coasts of Spain, Portugal, and Morocco. And after the Mongol sack of Baghdad, the capital of the Abbasid Caliphate, in 1258, those distant Asian conquerors themselves became Muslim and produced subsequent empires, including the Mughal dynasty of India. In the Anatolian peninsula, a Turkish-dominated tradition of rule developed, culminating in the Ottoman dynasty that lasted from the fourteenth to the twentieth centuries. The Ottomans ruled much of the Mediterranean world and the Balkans and even threatened Vienna in the seventeenth century. In the year 1453, a great symbolic date of Ottoman Muslim control in eastern Europe, the Eastern Orthodox Christian capital Constantinople was conquered. The Muslim subjugation of Constantinople had been a primary goal of the Muslim caliphs since Umayyad times in Damascus during Islam's first century. In Persia, a great tradition of Shi'ite Muslim rule under the Safavid dynasty dominated from around 1500 until the 1730s. Indeed, the centuries following the classical or "golden" age of the Islamic civilization of the Abbasids (750–1258) saw a greater extent of Muslim power than had been achieved during those early centuries when the major institutions of Islamic religion, law, learning, and society had reached their mature forms.

The period beginning with the Renaissance and Protestant Reformation in western Europe—the fifteenth through the seventeenth centuries—was marked especially by the European discovery, exploration, and exploitation of the Western Hemisphere, as well as the development of new sea routes to South, East, and Southeast Asia. This great complex of achievements ushered in a new era in world power relations. Although the Muslim lands, dominated by the dynasties of the Ottomans in eastern Europe and the eastern and southern Mediterranean and the Safavids and Mughals in Persia and India, continued to be powerful for centuries, they stagnated in comparison with western Europe. During the centuries of exploration, world sea trade, and colonialist imperialism that reached their climax in the nineteenth century, the British, Dutch, French, Portuguese, and Spanish exercised hegemony in the Americas, Africa, the Middle East, India, and Southeast Asia. Meanwhile, imperial Russia extended its power to the Caucasus, Central Asia, and Siberia. The list of places dominated indicates that the majority of the world's Muslims were subjugated during the long period of Western colonialism and imperialism.

Muslim peoples in many places experienced the impact of Western domination, from which they have emerged only in the present century. Any nation that experiences foreign domination suffers great harm and humiliation. Muslims, however, have had a particularly bitter experience because of Islam's long rivalry with Christendom and Muslim peoples' ancient triumphalist temperament and sense of destiny as "the best umma" brought forth in human history, committed to "enjoining the good and forbidding the evil" in human affairs, as the Qur'an commands. As one scholarly specialist put it, "The fundamental malaise of modern Islam is a sense that something has gone wrong with Islamic history."[1]

Muslims have long been stereotyped by Westerners as medieval, backward, violent, fanatical, sexually licentious, and abusive of women. It was not until Vatican Council II in the early 1960s that the Roman Catholic Church, whose numbers are comparable to the global Muslim community of approximately one billion, officially ended its long negative stance toward Islam in its historic declaration on the world religions. Islam was warmly acknowledged as a related monotheistic tradition with high moral ideals and a prophetic tradition of scripture-based doctrine, conscience, and behavior:

> Although in the course of centuries many quarrels and hostilities have arisen between Christians and Moslems, this most sacred Synod urges all to forget the past and to strive sincerely for mutual understanding. On behalf of all mankind, let them make common cause of safeguarding and fostering social justice, moral values, peace, and freedom.[2]

Other Christian bodies, in addition to Roman Catholics, have entered into dialogue with Muslims in increasing contexts during the second half of the twentieth century. Moreover, Jews and Muslims have done so in a number of contexts, including the National Conference of Christians and Jews, which welcomes Muslim representatives. In addition, there is an academically oriented Center for Islamic-Judaic Studies at the University of Denver that sponsors conferences and publishes books on topics of mutual interest to Jews and Muslims. A recent meeting brought together Muslim and Jewish as well as other scholars to present and discuss papers on women and family life in the two religions.

Although Muslims have long resented Western hegemony and regarded it as a continuation of the crusader mentality of the Middle Ages, recent decades have witnessed a most significant migration of Muslims from traditionally Islamic societies in the Middle East, Africa, and South Asia to Western countries in both Europe and the Americas. The dissolution of the British and other European colonialist empires after the Second World War did not mean the end of social, political, cultural, and economic relations between the great powers and their former colonies. Many former British Empire subjects, from such countries as India, Pakistan, Bangladesh, and Malaysia, migrated to Britain, where they represent a sizable Muslim minority today. Similarly, former subjects of French colonialism in North Africa and other former African colonies now live in France. Indonesians have long traveled between the archipelago and Holland, and there is a sizable Indonesian minority permanently dwelling in the Netherlands. Although Muslim residents in Germany are not former colonial subjects—at least to the extent that others just mentioned are—nevertheless, large numbers of Turks, for example, have contributed to the post–Second World War German labor market as "guest workers," often commuting seasonally between the two countries. Significant numbers of such workers, as well as other Muslim migrants (including asylum seekers from troubled Muslim regions such as Iran, Iraq, and Afghanistan), have settled in Germany, particularly in its major industrial centers. Italy hosts many Muslim guests and migrants from its former Libyan, Eritrean, and Somali colonies, as well as from other places, such as Albania and Bosnia.

Although Muslims started emigrating to the United States from countries such as Lebanon and Syria in the latter part of the nineteenth century, it was not until the 1960s that large numbers of Muslims started arriving in the United States from the Middle East and Asia. Canada has also received many Muslim immigrants in recent decades as have Latin American countries such as Argentina, Brazil, Chile, and Mexico. With the sizable Muslim minorities now in the West, the umma has a global sweep for the first time in history.

Meanwhile, the major concerns of Muslims occupy them in their traditional countries of residence, where they often comprise majorities from North Africa through the Middle East, Central, South, and Southeast Asia. Indonesia, for example, contains the world's largest Muslim national population, some 88 percent of nearly two hundred million people. When the similar cultural regions of nearby Malaysia, southern Thailand, and the Philippines are added, the numbers approach 20 percent of the world Muslim population of about one billion. The combined Muslim population of the Indian subcontinent (Afghanistan, Bangladesh, India, Pakistan) is around 330 million, or a third of the world total. The former Central Asian republics (including Azerbaijan) of the Soviet Union have a combined total of at least 50 million Muslims. So, it can be seen that more than half the world's Muslims live outside the Middle East and Africa, a significant fact in light of the usual Western perception of Islam as principally a religion of Arabs, Turks, and Persians.

The twentieth century has witnessed the rise of modern nation states in many parts of the world, including the areas just mentioned, that have large Muslim populations. The end of colonialist imperialism, however, did not signal the end of the colonialist powers' economic and military domination in what became known as the Third World of mostly poorer and developing nations in Latin America, the Afro-Eurasian land masses, and the Southeast Asian archipelago. Muslims began in the nineteenth century to be aware of their plight as weak and backward compared to the West. Reform and revivalist movements arose in countries such as Egypt, India, Iran, Sudan, and Libya, calling Muslims back to the principles and processes of Islamic belief, law, and community loyalty that had made the umma strong in earlier periods. The twentieth century has seen a great increase in Islamic revivalism, so much so that by the 1970s, Muslims had taken their destiny into their own hands and, instead of pondering so much what had gone wrong with their history, proceeded to rescue it in decisive ways. A worldwide Islamic revival has resulted, with a wide range of expressions.

ROOTS OF ISLAMIC REVIVAL

Every major religion possesses an indwelling capacity to adapt, assimilate, renew, and reform itself. It has been said about the Christian tradition that "the church is always reforming itself." Similarly, Muslims have maintained an alert regard for authenticity of the faith and order of Islam, continuously returning to the Qur'an, the hadith, and the authoritative legal and theological expositions of its trusted teachers. Although the contents of the Qur'an and hadith are unchanging, their interpretation and application are not. Moreover, the legal and theological discourses of Muslims, although they often have an enduring quality, are nonetheless open discourses in certain respects. That is, Muslims do not imagine that they have exhausted the possible meanings and applications of God's revelations and the Prophet's Sunna.

There have been numerous efforts at renewal and reform in the history of Islam. There came early to be a tradition, based on an actual prophetic hadith, that God would appoint a renewer of the religion every century. This *mujaddid*, as he is known, would restore the authentic teachings of Islam and inspire the Muslims to return to the Straight Path. Among the renewers of early times were the great jurisconsult al-Shafi'i (d. 820) and the omnicompetent al-Ghazali (d. 1111) who synthesized philosophical-theology, jurisprudence, and mysticism into a vision of the complete Muslim life. His greatest work is the multivolumed "Revivification of the Sciences of Religion."

ISLAM AND REFORM IN MODERN INDONESIA

The great Egyptian religious scholar and educational administrator Muhammad 'Abduh (d. 1905) was thought by many to be a mujaddid-renewer, not only in the Middle East but also in far-off Indonesia, where his influence was spread through the establishment of the Muhammadiyah movement by Haji Ahmad Dahlan in 1912. Dahlan had studied in Mecca for several years and, upon returning to Java, imported the Islamic modernist ideas he had learned in the Middle East. His movement literally means the followers of Muhammad. It is one of the first voluntary religious associations in Southeast Asia and from the beginning was dedicated to improving Islamic education, keeping pace with modernity in Islamic ways, and providing social services. Although Muhammadiyah's origins are in Yogyakarta, the cultural capital of Java, its ideas have spread to other parts of Indonesia. Its membership includes rural Muslims of a somewhat rigorist bent and urban elites with a more tolerant and intellectual temperament. A female branch was founded by Dahlan's wife in 1917 under the name 'A'isyiyah (from 'A'isha, Muhammad's wife).[3] This active organization has done much in the areas of family welfare, health-hygiene services, nutrition, and education. There are mosques, schools, and associations throughout Indonesian that have strong Muhammadiyah programs.

In the Islamically strict Minangkabau region of the huge Indonesian island of Sumatra, Muhammadiyah took on a strongly puritanical cast, seeking to cleanse the society of regional, non-Islamic cultural forms and practices, such as the matrilineal social system there. In this system, women own the property and work the land, while men tend to enter international business ventures and travel widely overseas. Aging men and boys remain at home helping with crops and enjoying the quiet life of the beautiful coastal and mountainous province, while many of the men in their prime live overseas, returning home only for religious festivals and to help with harvests. Boys must sleep in the mosque or a bachelors' hostel after age eight. And although husbands may visit their wives in their apartments in the traditional long-houses, they may not spend the whole night there, but must depart before dawn, to avoid taboo encounters with male blood members of the matriliny on their property at a forbidden time of day. This—to Islamic sensibilities—strange behavioral pattern is part of Minangkabau *adat*, "customary law," as Indonesian traditional regional practices are known.

An interesting twist is that men often have their main family in the Minangkabau region, whereas their popular Padang-style spicy-hot cuisine restaurants or other businesses in, say, Jakarta or Surabaya require their presence most of the time. Islamic law permits males to have up to four spouses at a time, so long as they are equally provided for. Therefore, Minangkabau men sometimes have a second family where their overseas business is. In these cases, we can understand why the old matrilineal system has survived as long as it has in coexistence with the traditionally patriarchal Islamic religion. Partly as a result of this flexible arrangement, Minangkabau men and women are famous for their business acumen and wealth. But the matriliny is gradually disappearing, both because of increased Islamic reforming awareness and the growing numbers of non-Minangkabau people transmigrating under government auspices to relatively uncrowded Sumatra to relieve the intense population pressure of Java.

Puritanical Islam—known generally in Indonesia as *santri* Islam— exists also in Java, the political, economic, and cultural center of that country's life. Java has many religious and cultural forms, as well as religious minorities. Its population of nearly one hundred million is crowded into a land area about the size of North

Carolina. As is occurring elsewhere in heavily populated Muslim (as well as non-Muslim) countries, urbanism is spreading to former rural areas, connecting them in a continuous network.

There are several dimensions of Javanese society, but social scientists have classified them roughly under three headings.[4] The first is the *priyayi,* the old, urban elite bureaucratic class of people who adhere to Islam but also value their high Javanese cultural roots as well as aspects of the Hindu-Buddhist past and see no conflict among the elements. The second is the *abangan,* the large, mostly rural peasant class for whom Islam and culture comprise one interlaced meaning and action system with worship, magic, local spirit propitiation, and Hindu-Buddhist elements all coexisting syncretistically. The third group, numerically fairly small but ideologically potent, is the *santri* component of pious Sunni Muslims, who identify with like-thinking Muslims in the worldwide umma and emphasize Qur'an and Sunna as their authority. The Muhammadiyah is essentially comprised of santri Muslims. It would be a mistake to equate santri Islam in Indonesia with fundamentalism, although there are fundamentalist santris who would like to see Shariʻa rule (for Muslims) in their country, as well as more liberal santris.

Indonesia, as mentioned earlier in this chapter, has the world's largest Muslim population. What happens Islamically in Indonesia may have important consequences for other Muslim regions. Generally speaking, Indonesian Muslims are moderate, tolerant human beings who value spirituality and high moral character, whether of Muslims or of people of other faiths. The nation's constitution recognizes five official religions: Islam, Roman Catholicism, Protestantism, Hinduism, and Buddhism. It is essential that every Indonesian belong to one of those faith traditions, and in any case all Indonesians are expected to believe in one God. Unlike most other Muslim majority national populations, Indonesians may freely choose their religion. Conversion out of as well as into Islam occurs, although the former is extremely hateful to most Muslims. Santris, especially, preach that Shariʻa rule would put a stop to it, due to its dictum that apostasy is a capital offense (if not recanted). The Shariʻa, through religious courts, today does regulate the life of Muslims in such areas as marriage and family law and inheritance. In Dutch colonial times, it was possible for non-Muslim males to marry Muslim females in Indonesia, but that is now a long discontinued practice.

POLITICAL ISLAM

A common feature of Islamic reform movements around the world is the call for ijtihad (independent legal decision making), which, although it continued to be practiced by some jurisconsults, was discouraged by the end of the third century after the Hijra. In a way, the reform of Islam in modern times is an exercise in memory, a strong sense of an ideal past when Muhammad and his generation, followed by subsequent visionary and courageous Muslim leaders, established history's first justly balanced community, the umma. Many think that if Muslims of today could return to the old days of common life under the holy Shariʻa, the umma would regain its rightful place in the center of human affairs, instead of struggling in a weakened, marginalized state, threatened from without by a hostile, immoral, and godless West and betrayed within by corrupt, cruel, and hypocritical leaders.

There is, in fact, great deprivation and suffering in many Muslim countries that, since nationhood, have often been ruled by military regimes lacking commitment to democratic, not to mention Islamic principles and values. Western observers have often dismissed Muslim countries as medieval, backward places, lacking in the dispositions, habits, and institutions needed for success in the modern world. Oil-rich Muslim nations—such as Iran, Iraq, Saudi Arabia, Kuwait, the United Arab Emirates, and Libya—have reached impressive levels of economic, educational, and technological development. But war, revolution, and other persistent problems have kept some of them from enjoying the wealth that their natural resources have brought. Poor Muslim countries—such as densely populated Egypt (where the largely desert terrain forces most to live in the Nile Valley and Delta) and Bangladesh (which has few natural resources for its more than two thousand people per square mile)—have populations doomed to joblessness, little or no education, poor health, and very limited horizons for mind or spirit.

Egypt has long been the principal center of Islamic education and publishing, as well as being a producer of seminal ideas in Islamic thought. Muslims from all over the world have traveled to Cairo to study at its great Azhar University, which has been operating continuously since the tenth century. Nineteenth-century Islamic reform found a welcome in Egypt, especially in the work of the great theological and educational thinker Muhammad 'Abduh who was introduced earlier. 'Abduh became the rector of the Azhar University and sought to bring it out of its medieval ways and into the modern world in both curriculum and pedagogy (even recently, Islamic studies students have had to memorize classical texts before receiving certification as experts). 'Abduh argued that Islam and science were in no way opposed to each other, that Muslims had made some important contributions to the sciences in earlier centuries, and that if their educational institutions were reformed in the modern age, they could return to the kinds of creative intellectual leadership they had excelled in earlier. 'Abduh recognized that the Western countries were far advanced over the East. He thought that it was not at all required that in order to benefit from and contribute to modern life Muslims had to forsake their own religious and ethical values. 'Abduh's views were controversial, rejected by old-fashioned minds but eagerly embraced by those seeking a way out of the stagnation of Muslim thought and institutions.

'Abduh did not endear himself to many in the area of social relations in Islam, for he held that polygamy and easy divorce (for males) were injurious to Muslim society and interests. Polygamy had its place as a recourse in emergency situations—war, for example, when the number of males decreases or during times when there is a surplus of unprotected women—but it is unacceptable most of the time, because of the suffering it brings to women and family circles.

'Abduh's theological thought was influenced by rational method in the service of the Qur'an and prophetic Sunna. Although his influence has been great, it has waned in recent decades as Muslims have turned more to political forms of

Egyptian Woman in Hijab Head Covering

(*Source:* F. M. Denny)

Islam and less to the modernist solutions of 'Abduh, which the more extreme reformers consider to be too accommodating to modern life and thought. Translated, this means that moderates such as 'Abduh were not assertive enough in the pursuit of Islamic goals, however well intentioned and sincere. The past three decades have witnessed an increasing emphasis on Islam as a complete way of life that can be fully realized only in an Islamized environment. To many proponents of this way of thinking, nothing short of an Islamic state will satisfy their desire to have an environment for obeying God's command to "enjoin what is good and forbid what is evil."

In 1928, the Egyptian Muslim activist Hasan al-Banna' founded the Muslim Brotherhood that attracted many members from among both the poor and middle class in towns and cities throughout the country and beyond. The Brotherhood was the first modern attempt to translate Islamic ideals into social and economic action. It has a strongly antimaterialistic and anti-Western perspective. The Brotherhood's strict discipline and closely guarded internal life—resembling a labor union—came to threaten the Egyptian government in the 1940s and after, even though the movement claimed not to be political. The founder was murdered in 1949, after a stormy period when a Brother had assassinated the Egyptian prime minister. The Brotherhood was suppressed and then outlawed for a long period, but in recent years has been tolerated to the point that members now serve in the

Egyptian National Assembly. Although it has moderated its extremist views and activism, the Brotherhood is still a symbol of militant Islamic reform.

Sayyid Qutb

The Muslim Brotherhood's most influential member after al-Banna' was Sayyid Qutb, a radical activist whose writings, including a brilliant modern commentary on the Qur'an, have done much to define and direct recent Muslim extremism in Egypt and far beyond. Sayyid Qutb's last book, *Milestones*, written in prison during the Nasser period, characterizes much of Muslim as well as all of non-Muslim society as *Jahiliyya*, the Age of Ignorance that reigned in pagan Arabia before the Islamic dispensation arrived. Qutb called for a return to the ideal practices and institutions of the Prophet's period in Medina, thus invoking memory as a means of correcting the wrongs of the present. Muslims must first rid themselves of false Muslims in their own midst, especially leaders and governments, before they can move out to provide Islamic witness and inspiration to the vast world of unbelievers in need of right guidance. Sayyid Qutb's views were extreme and, especially in their proneness to violence, have not been universally endorsed in their entirety even by militant Muslims. Qutb was executed in 1966 for participating in a plot to bring down the Egyptian government led by Gamal Abdel Nasser. Qutb's final resting place remains unknown to the public. That has not prevented his being widely considered as a matyr for Islam. His teachings have provided perhaps the most influential impetus for the more radical Islamic revivals of recent decades, such as the Islamic Group, which will be introduced shortly.

For about the past twenty years, beginning symbolically, at least, with the oil crisis of the 1970s, the world has become increasingly aware of Muslim unrest and dissatisfaction. Dramatic events have made certain stereotypes of Islam and Muslims omnipresent in the media. Cartoon caricatures often depict fat, hook-nosed men in robes and headcloths carrying swords against a background of camels and oil derricks. Or bearded, dark-eyed young men glare from crowds marching with banners declaring "Death to America! Death to Israel!" Hollywood movies revel in terrorist plots with Arab or Iranian zealots raging against Western targets with high-tech weapons, only to be defeated by Western heroes safeguarding democracy and human rights. Muslim women are often depicted in subordinate, even abused roles. Headlines speak of "Muslim terrorists," "extremist Muslim fundamentalists," and so forth. Books bear titles such as *The Dagger of Islam, Roots of Muslim Rage*, and *The Islamic Threat: Myth or Reality?*[5]

The Rushdie Affair and Muslim Attitudes Toward Freedom of Expression

The uproar that greeted the publication of Salman Rushdie's novel *The Satanic Verses* in 1988 was a case study in the different ways in which Muslims and others view the world. Rushdie, a Cambridge University–educated British citizen and member of London's literary elite, was born in India to a Muslim family and grew up culturally, at least, Muslim. He wrote in his book about uprooted people from South Asia. Immigration has become one of the major realities of modern life, with multitudes moving from poorer, Third World countries to wealthy Western nations. Rushdie's characters are Muslim and move in a world comprised of realistic and fantastic elements. Some of the fictional characters closely resemble the Prophet Muhammad, his Companions, and members of his family. The episodes contain outlandish situations, including sexual ones, not to mention passages considered blasphemous by faithful Muslims.

Although Rushdie and the majority of global literary opinion consider the book purely a product of the literary imagination, reaction in Muslim countries and communities around the world was vehement. Iran's leader, the Ayatollah Khomeini, issued a *fatwā* (legal opinion) declaring Rushdie a blasphemer and giving permission to kill him wherever he could be found. Many Muslims are in complete agreement with Khomeini's fatwa, although probably many more deplore both Rushdie's novel and the fatwa equally. In any case, the saga, which continues with Rushdie still in hiding, has shown how varied people can be in their thinking about the limits of free expression.

Many Christians were greatly disturbed by the release of the movie *The Last Temptation of Christ* in the 1980s for its fictional treatment of Jesus of Nazareth that strayed far from the gospel narratives. Many Muslims in the West objected to *The Last Temptation* because, even though their christology differs from Christianity's, they also revere Jesus and place him among the greatest prophets. Generally speaking, Muslims believe that visual media depiction of holy personages—and this means biblical and Qur'anic figures such as Abraham, Moses, Elijah, Mary, and Jesus, as well as Muhammad and his family—should be forbidden. In the 1970s, a film about Muhammad, *The Message,* was produced in Tunisia by a Muslim firm. Starring Anthony Quinn as the Prophet's formidable uncle, Hamza, the movie proceeds to view events through his eyes without physically depicting Muhammad except by a spoken part. The movie is as sensitive and historically accurate as could be imagined, with due reverence for characters and events depicted. Nevertheless, the movie was banned in virtually every Muslim country because it violated the taboo regarding visual depiction. Once, while visiting London, I noticed long lines of apparent Middle Easterners (some were speaking Arabic among themselves) waiting to view *The Message* at a downtown cinema. When I once scheduled the movie for my introductory Islam class, several Muslim students politely informed me that because of religious scruples they would not be able to view it.

Muslims often cannot understand or condone the freedoms of the West, especially when religion and traditional values are viewed as being challenged and even tarnished with impunity. The Rushdie affair continues to symbolize the vast gap between Muslims and especially secularized Westerners concerning basic ideas of belief, value, public expression, and religious authority. Muslims who move to liberal, secularized, Western democracies often feel tension between their Islamic beliefs and customs and the civil liberties they enjoy. Nevertheless, the perceived godlessness of the West is a threat and something Muslims want to safe-guard themselves and their children against, while enjoying the varied benefits of life there.

MUSLIM EXTREMISM

The stereotyping of Muslims is deplorable, but Muslims are also aware that the views and activities of some of their coreligionists are unacceptable. Muslim extremism occurs in various regions and sometimes seeks to draw attention to its cause, as well as to effect change, through violence. Militant Muslims belonging to a semi-clandestine organization known as "Holy War" (*Al-Jihad*) assassinated Egyptian president Anwar Sadat in 1981 in the name of Islam. Egypt has continued to be disturbed by Muslim extremists who want to overthrow the government and establish an Islamic state governed by the Sharīʿa. A major player in this activity is an organization known as The Islamic Group, comprised of a cross-section of Egyptian Muslims. Although the Group plays a positive role by providing badly needed social and medical services to poor Egyptians, it also has sponsored violent activities against Coptic Christians in the Upper Egyptian city of Asyut, mounted attacks against government officials and police, and warned foreign tourists to avoid visiting Egypt on threat of death (several tourists have been killed), thus depriving that chronically impoverished country of needed revenues. The Islamic Group wants to bring down the current Egyptian government, but has suffered setbacks through severe police repression and the imprisonment of large numbers of its members. The outcome of the struggle between this extremist group and the Egyptian government is impossible to predict. But it appears that the more such groups are repressed by the government, the more rank-and-file Egyptian Muslims sympathize with their aims.

Although most Egyptian Muslims deplore extremism and violence, there is such great deprivation, suffering, and hopelessness among the masses that a clear religious solution appears attractive to many. There is something about being part of an uncompromising, disciplined religious movement that brings self-respect and courage to people, even though the movement's policies, methods, and goals may be simplistic in the extreme. Some observers compare certain types of Islamic radicalism as a kind of liberation theology parallel to Christian forms in Latin America.

Fundamentalism

The Western media frequently characterize Islamic extremism as "fundamentalism." That term originated in early twentieth-century America as the label applied by extremely conservative Protestant Christians to what they held to be the fundamentals of the Christian faith. The closest parallel between Muslims and Christians in this regard is that both regard their scriptures as the actual Word of God, which should be interpreted literally and be second to no other authority for all of life. Muslims prefer not to use the term fundamentalism in describing Islamic movements, although they agree with scholars who do that there are resemblances in religious and ideological movements across traditions. To apply the term to all militant Muslim revivalist movements, however, runs the risk of missing what is unique and different about individual movements in various places.

The Influence of Wahhabism in Contemporary Saudi Arabia

Militant Muslim revivalism did not begin with the oil crisis. Its modern roots can be traced to the puritanical Wahhabi movement in Arabia in the eighteenth century. This movement, inspired in part by the uncompromising Shar'ia-centered theology of the medieval Syrian scholar Ibn Taymiya (d. 1328), harked back to what it conceived to be the straightforward monotheistic program of the early Muslims. Wahhabis, named for the movement's founder, Muhammad ibn 'Abd al-Wahhab (1703–1792), destroyed mausoleums and shrines as idolatrous, cleansed the sacred places of Mecca and Medina of corruption, promulgated the strict Hanbali legal code, and called for the renewal of ijtihad. The Wahhabis joined in an alliance with the powerful tribe of Ibn Sa'ud and succeeded in uniting much of the Arabian Peninsula under their program. Wahhabism and the Saudi dynasty continue today to rule the Kingdom of Saudi Arabia as a potent religio-political combination that tolerates neither criticism nor dissent.

In the Kingdom, as Saudi Arabia is widely known, women are forbidden to drive, coeducation is nonexistent, and theft is punished by amputating the right hand, adultery by stoning, and the drinking of alcohol by public flogging. No movie theaters exist (viewing of media may be done only at home), and unrelated women and men are forbidden to mix socially. Moreover, religious minorities—mostly foreign nationals in the country for official or business reasons—are forbidden to conduct worship services (although they do often meet informally for "lectures").

The presence of hundreds of thousands of non-Muslim military personnel in Saudi Arabia during the Gulf War to liberate Kuwait (1990–1991) was culturally and religiously very stressful for all concerned. Muslim critics of Western intervention—and there were many—deeply resented the presence of "infidels" in the country that is charged with protecting the inviolable sanctuaries of Mecca and Medina. In fact, it was humiliating to be protected from fellow Muslims—the Iraqis—by non-Muslims in the Muslim's own "house," as it were. The intensely felt need to protect Saudi Arabia's and the Gulf's oil resources for the Western markets brought about the strange alliance against Iraq's Saddam Hussein. But many Muslims, while deploring that tyrant's invasion of Kuwait and his blood-thirsty and rapacious rule at home, nevertheless took some satisfaction in his being an "in your face" Muslim warrior against the West. And Saddam Hussein himself attempted, rather unsuccessfully, to clothe his actions in Islamic symbolism, declaring a jihad against the West. In the event, such diverse Muslim countries as

Egypt, Syria, Morocco, and Pakistan rallied, however reluctantly in some cases, to the cause of liberating Kuwait alongside American and British troops. The fact that a fair number of American military personnel are said to have converted to Islam during their tours of duty somewhat appeased Muslim opinion about the presence of infidels in Arabia.

Iran

The Shiʿite nation of Iran underwent a major revolution in the late 1970s when the pro-Western, modernizing regime of Shah Reza Pahlavi was overthrown and an Islamic republic was established under the leadership of the prominent religious scholar, the Ayatollah (a title meaning "Sign of God") Ruhollah Khomeini (d. 1989). The thoroughgoing transformation of Iran's political, social, educational, and cultural institutions according to strict Islamic principles since the revolution has had profound impacts across the Islamic world. Iran is one of the few nations attempting to rule itself by the principles of Islam as set forth in scripture and legal tradition. There continue to be vigorous efforts to export the Iranian idea of Islamic revolution and reform to other countries, for example, through financial support of Islamist movements, as with the Hizbullah (Party of God) in Lebanon. The Islamic Republic of Iran has until the present been staunchly antagonistic toward Israel and the United States, in particular, and toward the West, in general.

Political Islam in Algeria

Other countries with strong political Islam movements are Sudan and Algeria. In Sudan, Islamic law is the supreme law of the land, and dissidence of any kind is forbidden. In Algeria, the situation is more complex. Colonized by France since 1830, Algeria won its independence in 1962 after a lengthy struggle for independence.[6] The new government pursued socialist policies, and the country prospered from oil and natural gas revenues. Although Algeria became modern and technologically capable in many ways, the majority of its citizens remained true to Islamic beliefs and norms. When the country experienced a downturn in revenues in the 1980s, followed by a deterioration in political, educational, economic, and social conditions, discontent mounted among the population. Wide unemployment, answered by inadequate measures and reforms, led to increased alienation between the rather authoritarian government and the citizens. By the end of the 1980s, political parties were permitted and a new approach to government was inaugurated thereby. A powerful Islamic movement—the Islamic Salvation Front, or FIS—emerged. The FIS won a great victory in the parliamentary elections of 1991. A runoff election was scheduled for early 1992, and the assumption was that FIS would gain control of the parliament. Viewing this with extreme alarm, the Algerian military intervened by persuading the president to step down and by annulling the elections. The FIS was outlawed. As of this writing, civil conflict between the Algerian military rulers and the supporters of Islamic rule, with the FIS in the lead, has caused the death of more than sixty thousand people, at the hands of both the government and Islamic militants. The most extreme Islamists have warned Westerners to leave the country on pain of death and have carried out their threats in a number of incidents, including the hijacking of an Air France passenger jet during December 1994, when three passengers were executed and an apparent plan to explode the airplane over Paris was foiled by French commandos while the plane was being detained in Marseilles en route from Algiers to the French capital. Many Algerians—writers, intellectuals, and secularists—have left their country for safety overseas.

Algeria is a tragic case. Most think that the violent conflict could have been avoided if the Islamic majority had been allowed to reap the rewards of their election victory. A difficult question is whether the FIS, which won its votes in a fair contest, would then honor democratic practices once in power. Many Algerians, for example, secularists and women, feared that a FIS-dominated government would have imposed conservative Islamic standards of dress and deportment on women and restraints on the free expression of political and religious ideas. Other observers think that, although establishing participatory democracy in Algeria as well as in other Middle Eastern countries is a risky prospect in the best of times, it would have been far better to chance a FIS-led government than end up where Algeria is at present. But, as the old Muslim saying goes: *Allāhu aʿlam*—"Allah knows best."

MUSLIM VIEWS OF SEX AND GENDER

Why has so much space in this final chapter been devoted to political and social issues, while relatively little attention has been given to matters usually considered religious in the West? Islam is a way of life that includes all aspects of human belief and behavior. To be a Muslim is to hold that everything is under the sovereignty of God, that there is no proper secular realm separated from religious concerns. One of the most frequently, and often passionately, discussed areas of Muslim life is the nature, roles, relations, and responsibilities of the sexes.

The Qur'an teaches equality of the sexes with respect to human worth and duties to God. But equality of worth does not mean identity of roles. Women's and men's different natural makeups have been ordained by God for the benefit of humankind. Both sexes are meant to complement each other. Generally speaking, the woman's proper place is in the home, bearing and caring for children and managing domestic affairs. Men occupy the public sphere, earning the family's living, defending the honor of the home, and contributing generally to the welfare of the larger Muslim society outside the family circle. Muslims consider the family to be the basic foundation of Muslim personal and communal life, without which the larger Muslim community cannot survive.

Modern times have brought radical departures from this ideal situation. Women have left the domestic sphere to pursue occupations traditionally held by men. Public education has grown to include females and to offer them avenues to the public regions of business, the professions, industry, and government. In fact, most Muslims agree that contemporary economic, technological, and social conditions often make it necessary for both husband and wife to share in earning the family's livelihood. And many Muslim fathers and mothers have embraced a practice of providing educational and career opportunities for both daughters and sons, realizing that times have changed and Muslims need to be competitive and progressive in today's global village.

Nevertheless, Muslims are aware of many difficulties concerning sex and gender roles and responsibilities. Recent analysis among Muslim feminists has focused on the difference between what the Qur'anic revelation sets forth as the proper doctrine of sex roles and responsibilities and what Muslim law and custom came to uphold. The Qur'an, in general, propounds an ethic that provides for much greater equality between the sexes than does developed Islamic law. The latter draws from the Qur'an, to be sure, but also from the hadith and from the cumulative assumptions, precedents, and procedures of the male-dominated Muslim legal system.

All three Abrahamic monotheistic traditions have in modern times been undergoing critiques and revisions of their traditional views and practices concerning women and gender issues. Judaism and Christianity have broad spectrums of ideas and practices that differ from one another considerably. For example, Orthodox Judaism maintains a highly traditional and conservative separation of the sexes in synagogue worship, seeing the proper place of women to be in the home. It is unacceptable for women to be ordained or to serve as rabbis or cantors in Orthodox Judaism. Indeed, although women may attend synagogue services, their main place for religious worship and reflection is in the home, or among other women. A passage in a recent book about women and the synagogue closely parallels the Islamic situation:

> The architects of Judaism were, by and large, male. Consequently, Jewish law and tradition reflect male experience and were developed—in general—to meet male needs. By excluding women from serving as religious or political officials of the community, men retained the sources of power and influence.[7]

Similarly, Christianity has traditionally been a male-dominated religion. And although recent decades have witnessed a trend in some denominations toward sexual equality and the empowerment of women through ordination, education, and high leadership positions, Roman Catholicism and Eastern Orthodoxy still steadfastly deny ordination to women, as do many Protestant bodies. Reform Judaism now has many ordained women rabbis, and Conservative Judaism has also permitted the ordination of women. Roman Catholicism, with a worldwide community about as numerous as the Muslim umma, has empowered its laywomen with new roles of leadership in public worship, education, and social services. Women actually run some parishes in localities where priests are in short supply; they conduct the worship, preach the sermons, lead the prayers, and serve communion. However, they still may not consecrate the elements of communion—bread and wine—in the sacrament of the Mass; that is reserved for ordained male priests.

Western forms of feminism have had some influence in Muslim societies, but most Muslims prefer to realize sexual equality and liberation from oppressive traditional practices and institutions by Islamic means. Muslim women and men sincerely want to discern unjust attitudes and behaviors in their midst and correct them. They realize that it is difficult, perhaps in some cases impossible, to reverse the customs and views of centuries, but significant progress is being made to improve conditions for women and thus for all Muslims along Islamic lines. Westerners often wonder why Muslim women "put up" with their treatment. It must be understood that an outsider's view is different from an insider's. Emancipated Western women have differing agendas for their and other women's lives than do Muslim women. Added to this difference is the fact that Western feminism is widely considered by Muslims—indeed also by traditional religious Christians and Jews—to be secular, godless, relativistic, and selfish.

In a university class on Islam in today's world, the students discussed the widely held scholarly idea that sex and gender representations and roles are social constructions and not in any way derived from a transcendent, revealed authority such as the Qur'an or the Bible, as their communities consider them to be. Indeed, scripture is often itself viewed as a historically conditioned, sociocultural reinforcement of traditional sex and gender views and institutions. Several in the class agreed with the "social construction" thesis. Some of the Muslim students, however, believed that the idea that sex and gender roles and representations depended on nothing more than human invention was totally in error because it ignored revelation and the general consensus of the faithful (the latter of which, legally, is considered by Sunni Muslims to be infallible in itself). Here, in general, is the great difference between relying on traditional religious authority and the "religion" of the Enlightenment, which holds reason to be autonomous; this is the great divide that separates most Muslims from the prevailing Western view of reality and values.

Fundamentalisms, whether Muslim, Jewish, or Christian, share a distrust and even a fear of modernity and seek ways to restore what are thought to be the pristine and proper ways of old. To suggest radical changes in sex and gender roles and representations is, therefore, a particularly threatening thing for tradition-minded people. As Fatima Mernissi, the controversial Moroccan Muslim feminist sociologist writes:

> It is not true that our mothers were happy with our fathers, wrapped in their own certitudes. My uncle Hajj Muhammad would overturn the table and threaten to pronounce the formula of repudiation [divorce] every time Aunt Kanza put a little too much salt or pepper in the couscous on Fridays. She wept on the day of his death, and keeps his memory alive and nurses it, but did she love him? Can you love a man who is always right because the law binds the wife to marital obedience? . . . What is certain is that women have decided to listen no longer to *khutaba* (sermons) they have

not had a hand in writing. They are ready for takeoff. They have always known that the future rests on the abolition of boundaries, that the individual is born to be respected, that difference is enriching. For them, the San Francisco charter [i.e., The Universal Declaration of Human Rights] is neither a novelty nor a breakthrough. It is just the formulation of a dream that losers have always cherished, like a talisman that protects them.[8]

Mernissi, like other feminists, sees much of the conflict about the emancipation of Muslim women to be discourses of male power and dominance more than what Islam genuinely teaches about sex and gender roles and rights. In a radio interview, she said that her mother, who was herself confined to a traditional harem in her Moroccan home, instilled in her daughter a yearning for freedom. During Mernissi's mother's youth the time was not right for radical change. But Fatima Mernissi was born during the great changes of the Second World War, after which North African and Muslim peoples in general entered "brave new worlds" of nationhood, independence, migration to the West, universal education, technology, and global rather than merely regional ways of thinking and doing.

Most of the Muslim world remains quite traditional with respect to sex and gender roles and attitudes. But it is significant that women have risen to be heads of state in the major Muslim countries—Turkey, Pakistan, and Bangladesh—in recent years. And Muslim women are prominent in universities and scientific organizations from Morocco to Indonesia. The fact that dress conventions—for example veiling and modest covering of the body generally, and social codes, especially separation of the sexes in many regions, are Muslim rather than Western does not mean that Muslim women are failing to make progress, because advancement is regarded differently for different peoples. This is a large subject that cannot be treated adequately in a brief space. We conclude by observing that women and gender questions and problems in Muslim contexts are in a state of intense discussion and flux, with universal generalizations one way or the other both erroneous and misleading. To declare categorically that Islam mistreats women is as wrong as to imagine that women are content with their status in the umma. The realities are far more complex than can be fairly included in sweeping judgments. That generalization applies equally to the Jewish and Christian communities, which, in their own ways, continue to face problems and challenges in the discourse on sex and gender.

RELIGION AND THE POLITICAL ORDER

QUESTIONS FOR DISCUSSION AND REVIEW

1. Alongside religious community is community as defined by the political order. In what ways do religious communities—Jewish, Christian, and Muslim—overlap with the political order? How do these two kinds of community remain distinct in each tradition? To what extent can a political order comprehend more than one religious community?

2. Religious communities sometimes are persecuted by the state. How has this been the case in Judaism? When, where, and how have Christians been persecuted? To what extent has there been friction between Muslims and the state? Why are religious groups persecuted?

3. Religion frequently furnishes a standpoint for criticism of the political order. How is this visible in Judaism, Christianity, and Islam? In what contexts do we find an increase in such activity?

4. The nature of the relationship between monotheistic communities and the state periodically undergoes sweeping change. When has this occurred in Judaism, Christianity, and Islam? How does such change come about? What are the roles of religious authorities in such cases? To what extent are laypersons involved?

5. Political orders sometimes embody religious views of the world. What is civil religion? When and where do we find civil religion in Judaism? What are some examples of civil religion in Christianity and Islam?

6. Thinking about national destiny sometimes is influenced by religious beliefs. How have Jews thought about themselves as a people and how have they framed their thinking about national destiny in religious terms? What are some examples of ways in which Christian beliefs have been joined to national self-understanding? What has been the case with Muslims? In what manner has Islam been a determining force in nationalistic thinking?

7. There are historical instances in which different religious groups within the same tradition compete for control of the political order. Outline several ways in which this has taken place in Judaism, Christianity, and Islam.

8. Explain some relationships between religion and the political order—for Judaism, Christianity, and Islam—in terms of the sacred and the secular. What is meant by secular? Are sacred and secular mutually exclusive categories in relation to the political order? Can a religious view of community exist alongside an understanding of community as secular? Can there be religious freedom for all in a religious state? Can religion flourish within a secular state?

9. Describe some of the ways in which Judaism, Christianity, and Islam exist in relation to the modern state. In what ways are those relationships similar across traditions? How do they differ?

Notes

CHAPTER 1

1. Wilfred Cantwell Smith, *What Is Scripture? A Comparative Approach* (Minneapolis: Fortress, 1993).
2. John Bright, *A History of Israel*, 3rd ed. (Philadelphia: Westminster, 1981); Philip R. Davies, *In Search of "Ancient Israel"* (Sheffield: Sheffield Academic Press, 1992); and John Van Seters, *Abraham in History and Tradition* (New Haven and London: Yale, 1975).
3. James A. Sanders, *Torah and Canon* (Philadelphia: Fortress, 1972); and Richard Elliott Friedman, *Who Wrote the Bible?* (New York: Harper & Row, 1987).
4. W. Lee Humphreys, *Crisis and Story: Introduction to the Old Testament*, 2nd ed. (Mountain View, CA, London, Toronto: Mayfield, 1990); Christian E. Hauer and William A. Young, *An Introduction to the Bible: A Journey into Three Worlds*, 3rd ed. (Englewood Cliffs, NJ: Prentice Hall, 1994); and Rolf Rendtorff, *The Old Testament: An Introduction* (Philadelphia: Fortress, 1991).
5. Jacob Neusner, *From Politics to Piety: The Emergence of Pharisaic Judaism*, 2nd ed. (New York: KTAV, 1979); and Shaye J. D. Cohen, *From the Maccabees to the Mishnah* (Philadelphia: Westminster, 1987).
6. James A. Kugel and Rowan A. Greer, *Early Biblical Interpretation* (Philadelphia: Westminster, 1986), pp. 13–106; and Jacob Neusner, *The Oral Torah: The Sacred Books of Judaism* (San Francisco: Harper & Row, 1986).
7. *Karaite Anthology: Excerpts from the Early Literature*, ed., Leon Nemoy (New Haven and London: Yale, 1952, 1980).
8. Gershom Scholem, "Revelation and Tradition as Religious Categories in Judaism," in *The Messianic Idea in Judaism and Other Essays on Jewish Spirituality* (New York: Schocken, 1971), pp. 282–303.

CHAPTER 2

1. Eusebius, *History of the Church*, 39. I. Tr. by G. A. Williamson (New York: Penguin Books, 1965), p. 150.
2. *Letters written by Paul*: Galatians, Romans, 1 and 2 Thessalonians, 1 and 2 Corinthians, Philemon,

Philippians; *Letters attributed to Paul, but probably not written by him:* Colossians, Ephesians, Timothy, Titus, Hebrews.

3. As quoted by Eusebius, *History of the Church,* 6:14; 7.

4. "The Letter of the Church of Rome to the Church of Corinth," commonly known as "Clement's First Letter," 42:1–5. *Early Christian Fathers,* tr., Cyril C. Richardson, Library of Christian Classics, vol. 1 (Philadelphia: Westminster Press, 1955), p. 62.

5. "Letter of Ignatius to the Ephesians," 3:2; 6:1. *Early Christian Fathers,* pp. 88–89.

6. Origen, "On First Principles," 4:7. *Origen,* tr., Rowan Greer, *Classics of Western Spirituality* (New York: Paulist Press, 1979), pp. 176–77.

7. Cited by Robert M. Grant, *A Short History of the Interpretation of the Bible* (New York: Macmillan, 1963), p. 119.

8. Philip Jacob Spener, *Pia Desideria,* tr. and ed., T. G. Tapert (Philadelphia: Fortress Press, 1964), p. 117.

9. Quoted in Edwin Scott Gaustad, *A Religious History of America,* rev. ed. (San Francisco: Harper & Row, 1990), p. 190.

10. *The Writings of Thomas Jefferson,* ed., Albert Ellery Bergh, vol. 14 of 20 vols. (Washington, DC: The Thomas Jefferson Memorial Association of the United States, 1907), p. 385.

CHAPTER 3

1. Seyyed Hossein Nasr, *Ideals and Realities of Islam* (Boston: Beacon Press, 1975), p. 65.

2. Maulana Muhammad Ali, *A Manual of Hadith* (New York: Olive Branch Press, 1988), pp. 10–11.

3. The Qur'an translation used in this book is *The Holy Qur'ān: Text, Translation and Commentary,* Abdullah Yusuf 'Ali, rev. ed. (Brentwood, MD: Amana Corporation, 1989), with some minor alterations based on the author's reading of the Arabic text.

CHAPTER 4

1. Jon D. Levenson, *Creation and the Persistence of Evil: The Jewish Drama of Divine Omnipotence* (San Francisco: Harper & Row, 1985), pp. 3–50.

2. *Essential Papers on Messianic Movements and Personalities in Jewish History,* ed., Marc Saperstein (New York: New York University, 1992), pp. 1–31; and *Judaisms and Their Messiahs at the Turn of the Christian Era,* ed., Jacob Neusner, et al., (Cambridge: Cambridge University, 1987).

3. John J. Collins, *Between Athens and Jerusalem: Jewish Identity in the Hellenistic Diaspora* (New York: Crossroad, 1983); *Jews in the Hellenistic World: Josephus, Aristeas, The Sibylline Oracles, Eupolemus,* ed., John R. Bartlett (Cambridge: Cambridge University, 1985); and *Jews in the Hellenistic World: Philo,* ed., R. Williamson (Cambridge: Cambridge University, 1985).

4. David Stern, *Parables in Midrash: Narrative and Exegesis in Rabbinic Literature* (Cambridge, MA: Harvard, 1991), pp. 178–79.

5. Gershom Scholem, *Major Trends in Jewish Mysticism* (New York: Schocken, 1961), pp. 40–79; and Peter Schafer, *The Hidden and Manifest God: Some Major Themes in Early Jewish Mysticism* (Albany, NY: SUNY Press, 1992).

6. Saperstein, *Essential Papers,* pp. 113–249.

7. Scholem, *Major Trends,* pp. 157–243; David S. Ariel, *The Mystic Quest: An Introduction to Jewish Mysticism* (New York: Schocken, 1988), pp. 51–119; and *Zohar: The Book of Enlightenment,* ed., Daniel C. Matt (New York: Paulist, 1983).

8. Gershom Scholem, *Sabbatai Sevi: The Mystical Messiah* (Princeton: Princeton University, 1973); and Scholem, *Major Trends,* pp. 287–324.

9. Joseph L. Blau, *Modern Varieties of Judaism* (New York: Columbia University, 1966); and Jacob Neusner, *Death and Birth of Judaism: The Impact of Christianity, Secularism, and the Holocaust on Jewish Faith* (New York: Basic Books, 1987), pp. 75–253.

10. Samuel Heilman, *Defenders of the Faith: Inside Ultra-Orthodox Jewry* (New York: Schocken, 1992); and Janet Aviad, "The Messianism of Gush Emunim," *Jews and Messianism in the Modern Era:*

Metaphor and Meaning, ed., Jonathan Frankel (New York and Oxford: Oxford University, 1991), pp. 197–213.

11. *Forward*, "Orthodox Rabbis Score Lubavitch," June 21, 1996, p. 3, col. 1.

CHAPTER 5

1. Dionysius the Areopagite, *The Divine Names*, XIII.3. Tr. C. E. Rolt (London: SPCK, 1979), p. 188.

2. Augustine, *Sermons*, 53.11.12.

3. Irenaeus of Lyons, *Against the Heretics*, 3.24.1. In *The Writings of Irenaeus*, Vol. IX (Edinburgh: Ante-Nicene Christian Library, 1868–1869).

4. Athanasius, *Against the Pagans*, ch. 46. Tr. E. P. Meijering (Leiden: E. J. Brill, 1984).

5. Gregory of Nyssa, "Oration on the Deity of the Son and the Holy Spirit." In J. P. Migne, ed., *Patrologia Graeca*, vol. 46 (Paris: Garnier Fratres, 1863), p. 558.

6. John H. Leith, ed., *Creeds of the Churches* (Richmond: John Knox Press, 1973), p. 33.

7. Gregory of Nazianzus, "An Examination of Apollinarianism." In Henry Bettenson, ed. and tr., *Documents of the Christian Church* (Oxford: Oxford University Press, 1963), p. 45.

8. Apollinaris, "Ep. ad episc. Diocaes," ch. 2. Cited by H. Lietzman, *Apollinarius von Laodicea und seine Schule* (Tübingen, 1904/Hildesheim, 1970), p. 256; and tr. Boniface Ramsey, O.P., *Beginning to Read the Fathers* (New York: Paulist Press, 1985), p. 75.

9. E. R. Hardy, ed., *Christology of the Later Fathers* (Philadelphia: Westminster Press, 1954), p. 373.

10. Sebastian Franck, "A Letter to John Campanus." In George H. Williams, ed., *Spiritual and Anabaptist Writers* (Philadelphia: Westminster Press, 1967), p. 156.

11. Sidney L. Lee, *The Autobiography of Edward, Lord Herbert of Cherbury* (New York: Scribner and Welford, 1886), pp. 248–249.

12. Quoted in Kerry S. Walters, *The American Deists: Voices of Reason and Dissent in the Early Republic* (Lawrence: University of Kansas Press, 1992), p. 184.

CHAPTER 6

1. Ali, *Manual of Hadith* (New York: Olive Branch Press, 1977), pp. 7, 17.

2. Ibid., p. 22.

3. A. J. Wensinck, *The Muslim Creed: Its Genesis and Historical Development* (London: Frank Cass, 1965), p. 112. The quotations from Fiqh Akbar I are also taken from this source, p. 103.

4. Ibid., p. 188.

5. Harry Austryn Wolfson, *The Philosophy of the Kalām* (Cambridge, MA: Harvard University Press, 1976), pp. 244–63.

6. Wensinck, *Muslim Creed*, p. 189.

7. Ibid., p. 190.

8. *Rūmī: Poet and Mystic (1207–1273): Selections from His Writings*, tr. and ed., Reynold A. Nicholson (London: Allen & Unwin, 1950), p. 181.

9. Cyril Glassé, *The Concise Encyclopedia of Islam* (San Francisco: HarperSanFrancisco, 1991), p. 328.

10. A. J. Arberry, *Sufism: An Account of the Mystics of Islam* (New York: Harper Torchbooks, 1970), p. 42.

11. I am indebted, for this group of attributes, and the manner in which God shares them with humans, to Seyyed Hossein Nasr, *Ideals and Realities of Islam* (Boston: Beacon Press, 1972), pp. 18–20.

CHAPTER 7

1. Delbert R. Hillers, *Covenant: The History of a Biblical Idea* (Baltimore and London: Johns Hopkins University Press, 1977).

2. *Ideal Figures in Ancient Judaism*, eds., George W. E. Nickelsburg and John J. Collins (Chico, CA: Scholars, 1980).

3. *The Dead Sea Scrolls In English*, ed., Geza Vermes, 4th ed. (New York and London: Penguin, 1994).

4. Jacob Neusner, *There We Sat Down: Talmudic Judaism in the Making* (New York: KTAV, 1978), pp. 44–128; and Steven D. Fraade, "The Early Rabbinic Sage," *The Sage in Israel and the Ancient Near East*, eds., John G. Gammie and Leo G. Purdue (Winona Lake, IN: Eisenbraun's, 1990), pp. 417–36.

5. Emanuel Etkes, "Hasidism as a Movement—The First Stage" and Yaacov Hasdai, "The Origins of the Conflict Between the Hasidim and the Mitnagdim," *Hasidism: Continuity or Innovation?* ed., Bezalel Safran (Cambridge, MA: Harvard University, 1988), pp. 1–26, 27–46.

6. Arthur Green, "Typologies of Leadership and the Hasidic Zaddiq," *Jewish Spirituality from the Sixteenth Century Revival to the Present*, ed., Arthur Green (New York: Crossroad, 1987), pp. 127–56.

7. Naftali Loewenthal, *Communicating the Infinite: The Emergence of the Habad School* (Chicago: University of Chicago, 1990).

CHAPTER 8

1. Ignatius of Antioch, "Epistle to the Smyrneans," ch. 8, tr., Cyril Richardson, in *Early Christian Fathers, Library of Christian Classics*, vol. 1 (New York: Macmillan, 1970), p. 115.

2. Tertullian, *De praescriptione haereticorum*, chs. 20, 21. Tr. in *Documents of the Christian Church*, 2nd ed. ed., Henry Bettenson (New York and Oxford: Oxford University Press, 1963), pp. 70–71.

3. Cyprian of Carthage, *Epistle* 33.1. Tr. in Bettenson, *Documents*, p. 74.

4. St. Jerome, *Epistle* xv, I, 2, tr. in Bettenson, *Documents*, pp. 80–81.

5. Martin Luther, "The Babylonian Captivity of the Church," tr. in John Dillenberger, ed., *Martin Luther, Selections from His Writings* (New York: Doubleday Anchor, 1961), p. 345.

6. Quoted in Edwin Scott Gaustad, *A Religious History of America* (San Francisco: Harper & Row, 1990), p. 15.

CHAPTER 9

1. *Ṣaḥīḥ al-Bukhārī*, vol. I (Cairo: Dār wa Maṭabi' al Sha'b, n.d.), p. 157. Tr. adapted from Maulānā Muḥammad 'Alí, *A Manual of Hadith* (New York: Olive Branch Press, 1977), pp. 90–91.

2. 'Ali, *A Manual of Hadith*, pp. 14–15.

3. Ibid., p. 30.

4. Ibid., p. 42.

5. Ibid., p. 284.

6. Ibid., p. 309.

7. Ibid., pp. 352–53.

8. Ibid., p. 398.

9. Annemarie Schimmel, *And Muhammad Is His Messenger: The Veneration of the Prophet in Islamic Piety* (Chapel Hill, NC: University of North Carolina Press, 1985), pp. 105–22, 257–59.

10. A. J. Wensinck, *The Muslim Creed* (London: Frank Cass, 1965; orig. pub. 1932), p. 104, with commentary on p. 113.

11. Sir Hamilton Gibb, *Mohammedanism* (New York: Oxford University Press, 1962), pp. 100–101.

12. Fazlur Rahman's expression, in *Islam*, 2nd ed. (Chicago: University of Chicago Press, 1979), p. 100.

13. *Forty Ḥadīth Qudsī*, ed. and tr., Ezzeddin Ibrahim and Denys Johnson-Davies (Beirut and Damascus: Dar al-Koran al-Kareem [The Holy Koran Publishing House], 1400 A.H./1980 A.D.), p. 78.

14. William A. Graham, *Divine Word and Prophetic Word in Early Islam* (The Hague: Mouton, 1977), p. 184.

CHAPTER 10

1. Elias J. Bickerman, *The Jews in the Greek Age* (Cambridge, MA & London: Harvard University, 1988), pp. 133–160; and E. P. Sanders, *Judaism: Practice and Belief 63 BCE–66 CE* (Philadelphia: Trinity Press International, 1992), pp. 47–169.
2. *Ancient Synagogues Revealed*, ed., Lee I. Levine (Detroit: Wayne State University, 1982), pp. 1–10.
3. Richard S. Sarason, "Religion and Worship: The Case of Judaism," *Take Judaism, for Example*, ed., Jacob Neusner (Chicago: University of Chicago, 1983), pp. 49–65.
4. Joseph Heinemann, *Prayer in the Talmud* (Berlin: Mouton de Gruyter, 1977); Ismar Elbogen, *Jewish Liturgy: A Comprehensive History* (Philadelphia and New York: Jewish Publication Society and the Jewish Theological Seminary of America, 1993); and Stefan C. Reif, *Judaism and Hebrew Prayer: New Perspectives on Jewish Liturgical History* (Cambridge: Cambridge University, 1993).
5. Abraham Joshua Heschel, *The Sabbath: Its Meaning for Modern Man* (New York: Farrar, Straus, 1952).
6. Jacob Neusner, *The Enchantments of Judaism: Rites of Transformation from Birth Through Death* (New York: Basic, 1987), pp. 69–113; and Monford Harris, *Exodus and Exile: The Structure of the Jewish Holidays* (Minneapolis: Augsburg/Fortress, 1992).
7. Michael A. Meyer, *Jewish Identity in the Modern World* (Seattle and London: University of Washington, 1990).
8. Elbogen, *Jewish Liturgy*, pp. 297–333; and Michael A. Meyer, *Response to Modernity: A History of the Reform Movement in Judaism* (New York and Oxford: Oxford University, 1988).
9. Marshall Sklare and Joseph Greenblum, *Jewish Identity on the Suburban Frontier: A Study of Group Survival in the Open Society* (Chicago: University of Chicago, 1979), pp. 97–178; Riv-Ellen Prell, *Prayer and Community: The Havurah in American Judaism* (Detroit: Wayne State University, 1989); and Janet Aviad, *Returning to Judaism* (Chicago: University of Chicago, 1982).
10. *Daughters of the King: Women and the Synagogue*, eds., Susan Grossman and Rivka Haut (Philadelphia: Jewish Publication Society, 1992); and Elizabeth Resnick Levine, *A Ceremonies Sampler: New Rites, Celebrations, and Observances of Jewish Women* (San Diego, CA: Women's Institute for Continuing Jewish Education, 1991).

CHAPTER 11

1. Augustine of Hippo, *Confessions*, I.1., tr. John K. Ryan (New York: Image Doubleday, 1960), p. 43.
2. Clifford Geertz, "Religion as a Cultural System" in *Anthropological Approaches to the Study of Religion*, ed., Michael Banton (London and New York: F. A. Praeger, 1966), pp. 3, 28–29.
3. Victor Turner, *Dramas, Fields, and Metaphors: Symbolic Action in Human Society* (Ithaca, NY and London: Cornell University Press, 1974), pp. 55–56.
4. Victor Turner, *From Ritual to Theatre* (New York: Performing Arts Journal Publications, 1982), pp. 82 ff.
5. Hippolytus, *Apostolic Tradition*, ch. 41, tr. in Boniface Ramsey, O.P., *Beginning to Read the Fathers* (New York: Paulist Press, 1985), pp. 165–66.
6. Cyprian of Carthage, *On the Lord's Prayer*, chs. 35–36, in Ramsey, *Fathers*, p. 167.
7. St. Jerome, *Tract. de Psalm*. 1, in Ramsey, *Fathers*, p. 168.
8. Theodore of Mopsuestia, *Ad baptizandos*. 1, in Ramsey, *Fathers*, p. 169.
9. Augustine, *De div. quaest. ad Simplic*. 2:4, in Ramsey, *Fathers*, p. 174.
10. "The Teaching of the Twelve Apostles, Commonly Called the Didache," tr. Cyril C. Richardson, *Early Christian Fathers* (New York: Macmillan, 1970), p. 174.
11. Kallistos (Timothy) Ware, *The Orthodox Church* (New York: Pelican, 1980), p. 269.
12. Cited by Peter Brown, *The Cult of the Saints* (Chicago: University of Chicago Press, 1981), p. 4.
13. John Calvin, *Commentary on the Last Four Books of Moses, Opera Calvini*, ed. W. Baum et al. (Brunswick: C. A. Schwetske & M. Bruhn, 1863–1880), vol. 24, p. 387.
14. Ulrich Zwingli, "Commentary on the True and False Religion," in *The Latin Works and the Correspondence of Huldrych Zwingli*, ed. S. M. Jackson (Philadelphia: G. P. Putnam's Sons, 1929), vol. 2, p. 92.

15. Ibid.

16. Martin Luther, "Concerning the Ministry," in *Luther's Works,* ed. J. Pelikan et al. (St. Louis and Philadelphia: Fortress Press, 1958), vol. 40, p. 21.

17. Sebastian Franck, "Letter to John Campanus" in *Spiritual and Anabaptist Writers,* ed. G. H. Williams (Philadelphia: Westminster Press, 1957), pp. 154–155.

18. *Autobiography of Peter Cartwright, The Backwood Preacher,* ed. W. P. Strickland (New York: Carlton & Porter, 1856), p. 79.

CHAPTER 12

1. Maulana Muhammad Ali, *A Manual of Hadith* (New York: Olive Branch Press, 1988), pp. 18–19.

2. Ibid., p. 20.

3. Ibid., p. 230.

4. As quoted in F. E. Peters, *The Hajj: The Muslim Pilgrimage to Mecca and the Holy Places* (Princeton: Princeton University Press, 1994), pp. 256–57.

5. For a full discussion of naming, see Annemarie Schimmel, *Islamic Names* (Edinburgh: University of Edinburgh Press, 1989).

6. Patricia Horvatich, "Mosques, Misunderstandings, and the True Islam: Muslim Discourses in Tawi-Tawi, Philippines," unpublished doctoral dissertation in Anthropology, Stanford University, 1992, p. 168.

CHAPTER 13

1. *Contemporary Jewish Ethics* (Brooklyn, NY: HPC, 1988), pp. 3–18; and Robert M. Seltzer, *Jewish People, Jewish Thought: The Jewish Experience in History* (New York and London: Macmillan, 1980), pp. 373–418, 547–79, 684–764.

2. Rachel Biale, *Women in Jewish Law: An Exploration of Women's Issues in Halakhic Sources* (New York: Schocken, 1984); Blu Greenberg, *On Women and Judaism: A View from Tradition* (Philadelphia: Jewish Publication Society, 1981); and Judith Plaskow, *Standing Again at Sinai: Judaism from a Feminist Perspective* (San Francisco: Harper & Row, 1990).

3. Daniel C. Matt, "The Mystic and the *Mizwot,*" *Jewish Spirituality from the Bible Through the Middle Ages,* ed., Arthur Green (New York: Crossroad, 1986), pp. 367–404; and Joseph Dan, *Jewish Mysticism and Jewish Ethics* (Seattle and London: University of Washington, 1986).

4. Biale, *Women in Jewish Law,* pp. 121–46; and Daniel Boyarin, *Carnal Israel: Reading Sex in the Talmud* (Berkeley: University of California Press, 1993).

5. Immanuel Etkes, *Rabbi Israel Salanter and the Mussar Movement* (Philadelphia: Jewish Publication Society, 1993); and Pinchas H. Peli, *On Repentence in the Thought and Oral Discourses of Rabbi Joseph B. Soloveitchik* (Jerusalem: Orot, 1980).

6. Biale, *Women,* pp. 44–101; Elliot N. Dorff and Arthur Rosett, *A Living Tree: The Roots and Growth of Jewish Law* (Albany: SUNY, 1988); and Judith Romney Wegner, *Chattel or Person? The Status of Women in the Mishnah* (New York and Oxford: Oxford University Press, 1988).

7. David Novak, *Jewish-Christian Dialogue: A Jewish Justification* (Oxford and New York: Oxford University Press, 1989), pp. 26–41.

8. Michael A. Meyer, *Response to Modernity: A History of the Reform Movement in Judaism* (New York and Oxford: Oxford University Press, 1988).

9. *Abraham Geiger and Liberal Judaism: The Challenge of the Nineteenth Century,* ed., Max Wiener (Philadelphia: Jewish Publication Society, 1962).

10. Eugene B. Borowitz, *Liberal Judaism* (New York: Union of American Hebrew Congregations, 1984).

CHAPTER 14

1. "Didache" tr. Cyril C. Richardson, in *Early Christian Fathers* (New York: Macmillan, 1970), p. 173.

2. Ibid., p. 60.

3. Ignatius of Antioch, "Letter to the Ephesians," in ibid., p. 90.

4. Ignatius of Antioch, "Letter to the Smyrneans," in ibid., p. 114.

5. "Second Letter of Clement," in ibid., p. 200.

6. "Didache," in ibid., p. 173.

7. Ibid., p. 119.

8. Chromatius of Aquilea, *ep.* 14.2, cited by Boniface Ramsey, *Beginning to Read the Fathers* (New York: Paulist Press, 1985), p. 132.

9. Tertullian, *Apol.* 50, cited in ibid., p. 126.

10. Athanasius, *"On the Incarnation,"* ch. 27, tr. E. R. Hardy, *Christology of the Later Fathers* (Philadelphia: Westminster Press, 1954), pp. 81–82.

11. Methodico of Olympus, *Symposium* 7:3, cited in Ramsey, *Beginning to Read the Fathers*, p. 136.

12. Ignatius of Antioch, "Letter to the Romans," in Richardson, *Early Christian Fathers*, pp. 104–105.

13. Gregory of Nyssa, *On Virginity* 5: 1–2, in Ramsey, *Beginning to Read the Fathers*, p. 142.

14. Gregory Nazianzen, *Carm in laudem virg.*, in ibid., pp. 138–39.

15. Cited in Paul Johnson, *A History of Christianity* (New York: Atheneum, 1979), p. 110.

16. "The Sayings of the Desert Fathers," tr., Owen Chadwick, *Western Asceticism* (Philadelphia: Westminster Press, 1958), p. 40.

17. Ibid., pp. 53–59.

18. *St. Benedict's Rule for Monasteries*, tr., L. J. Doyle (Collegeville, MN: Liturgical Press, 1948), p. 1.

19. Cited in Johnson, *A History of Christianity*, p. 100.

20. Ibid., pp. 181–82.

21. Cited by Steven Ozment. *The Reformation in the Cities* (New Haven: Yale University Press, 1975), p. 24.

22. Cited in Ramsey, *Beginning to Read the Fathers*, pp. 188–89.

23. Ibid., p. 184.

24. Martin Luther, *Treatise on Christian Liberty*, tr., W. A. Lambert (Philadelphia: Fortress Press, 1957), p. 24.

25. John Calvin, *Institutes of the Christian Religion*, III, 21.7, tr., Ford Lewis Battles (Philadelphia: Westminster Press, 1960), vol. II, p. 931.

26. Luther, *Treatise on Chrisitian Liberty*, p. 26.

27. In Lowell Zuck, ed., *Chrisitanity and Revolution: Radical Christian Testimonies, 1520–1650* (Philadelphia: Temple University Press, 1975), p. 73.

CHAPTER 15

1. Mohammad Hashim Kamali, *Principles of Islamic Jurisprudence* (Petaling Jaya, Malaysia: Pelanduk Publications, 1989), p. 419.

2. Ibid., p. 420.

3. Fazlur Rahman, *Major Themes of the Qur'an* (Minneapolis: Bibliotheca Islamica, 1980), p. 28.

4. Ibid., p. 120.

5. Ibid.

6. All the examples are from *Al-Hadis* [i.e., al-hadīth], *An English Translation and Commentary of Mishkāt-ul-Maṣābīh*, vol. I, tr. and ed., Fazlul Karim (Lahore: The Book House, n.d. [ca. 1938]), pp. 389, 405, 423, 434, 442, 452, 478, 519, 527, 552, 559, 576, 606, 655. I have slightly altered some of the translations in light of the original Arabic text provided in the work. The *Mishkāt al-Masābīh* ("Niche for Lights") dates from the fifth to sixth Islamic centuries.

CHAPTER 16

1. Robert B. Coote and Keith W. Whitelam, *The Emergence of Early Israel in Historical Perspective* (Sheffield: Almond, 1987), pp. 117–38; and Eric M. Meyers and A. Thomas Kraabel, "Archeology, Iconography and Nonliterary Written Remains," *Early Judaism and Its Modern Interpreters*, eds., Robert A. Kraft and George W. E. Nickelsburg (Atlanta: Scholars, 1986), pp. 175–210.

2. Gertrude Hirschler, *Ashkenaz: The German Jewish Heritage* (New York: Yeshiva University Museum, 1988); Paloma Diaz-Mass, *Sephardim: The Jews from Spain* (Chicago and London: University of Chicago, 1992); and Daniel J. Elazar, *Israel: Building a New Society* (Bloomington: University of Indiana, 1986).

3. "Synagogue," *Encyclopaedia Judaica* (Jerusalem: Keter, 1972), vol. 15, pp. 620–27; and Brian de Bréffny, *The Synagogue* (New York: Macmillan, 1978), pp. 130–202.

4. Gershom Scholem, *The Messianic Idea in Judaism and Other Essays on Jewish Spirituality* (New York: Schocken, 1974), pp. 257–81.

5. *Ancient Synagogues Revealed,* ed., Lee I. Levine (Detroit: Wayne State University, 1982).

6. *The Synagogue,* de Bréffny, pp. 52–128; Carol Herselle Krinsky, *Synagogues of Europe: Architecture, History, Meaning* (Cambridge, MA, and London: MIT, 1985); and Maria and Kazimierz Piechotka, *Wooden Synagogues* (Warsaw: Arkady, 1959).

7. Abram Kanof, *Jewish Ceremonial Art and Religious Observance* (New York: Harry N. Abrams, n.d.); and Samuel Heilman, "Jews and Judaica: Who Owns and Who Buys What?" *Persistance and Flexibility: Anthropological Perspectives on the American Jewish Experience,* ed., Walter P. Zenner (Albany: SUNY, 1988), pp. 260–79.

8. "Mezuzah," *Encyclopaedia Judaica,* vol. 11, pp. 1474–77.

9. Harry Y. Gamble, *Books and Readers in the Early Church* (New Haven, CT: Yale University Press, 1995), pp. 49–66.

10. *The Hebrew Book: An Historical Survey,* eds., Raphael Posner and Israel Ta-Shma (New York and Paris: Leon Amiel, 1975); and Marvin J. Heller, *Printing the Talmud: A History of the Earliest Printed Editions of the Talmud* (Brooklyn, NY: Im Hasefer, 1992).

11. Therese and Mendel Metzger, *Jewish Life in the Middle Ages* (New York: Alpine, 1982), pp. 111–150; and Riv-Ellen Prell, "Why Jewish Princesses Don't Sweat: Desire and Consumption in Postwar American Jewish Culture," *People of the Body: Jews and Judaism from an Embodied Perspective,* ed., Howard Eilberg-Schwartz (Albany: SUNY, 1992), pp. 329–59.

12. Tamar Hermann and David Newman, "The Dove and the Skullcap: Secular and Religious Divergencies in the Israeli Peace Camp," *Conflict and Accommodation Between Jews in Israel: Religious and Secular,* ed., Charles Liebman (Jerusalem: Keter, 1990), pp. 151–72; Samuel Krauss, "The Jewish Rite of Covering the Head," *Beauty in Holiness: Studies in Jewish Customs and Ceremonial Art,* ed., Joseph Guttman (New York: KTAV, 1970), pp. 420–67; and "Head, Covering of the," *Encyclopaedia Judaica,* vol. 8, pp. 1–6.

CHAPTER 17

1. Flannery O'Connor, *The Complete Stories* (New York: Farrar, Straus, and Giroux, 1971), p. 529.

2. "The Martyrdom of Polycarp," tr., Cyril Richardson, *Early Christian Fathers* (New York: Westminster Press, 1970), pp. 154–56.

3. Peter Brown, *The Cult of the Saints* (Chicago: University of Chicago Press, 1981), p. 92.

4. Brown, *Cult,* p. 77 citing St. Augustine, *City of God* 22.9, and Victritious of Rouen, *De laude sanctorum* 11.

5. Cited by Robert Markus, *The Oxford Illustrated History of Christianity* (New York: Oxford University Press, 1992), p. 80.

6. Cited by Georges Duby, *The Age of Cathedrals: Art and Society, 980–1420* (Chicago: University of Chicago Press, 1981), p. 102.

7. Cited in ibid., p. 123.

8. Augustine, *Confessions,* IX.6–7, tr. J. K. Ryan (New York: Image Doubleday, 1960), pp. 214–16.

9. St. John of Damascus, *On the Divine Images,* tr., David Anderson (New York: St. Vladimir's Seminary Press, 1980), p. 23.

10. Montague Summers, *A Popular History of Witchcraft* (New York: Causeway Books/Gale Research Co., 1973), p. 72.

11. Wayne Elzey, "Popular Culture," *Encyclopedia of the American Religious Experience,* eds., Charles

H. Lippy and Peter W. Williams, vol. 3 of 3 volumes (New York: Charles Scribner's Sons, 1988), pp. 1730–31.

12. Quoted in John A. Hostetler, *Amish Society*, 4th ed. (Baltimore: Johns Hopkins University Press, 1993), pp. 114–15.

CHAPTER 18

1. Clifford Geertz, "Religion as a Cultural System," In *Anthropological Approaches to the Study of Religion*, ed. Michael Banton, A.S.A. Monographs 3 (London: Tavistock Publications, 1966), p. 4.

2. Marshall G. S. Hodgson, *The Venture of Islam: Conscience and History in a World Civilization*, vol. 1 (Chicago: University of Chicago Press, 1974), pp. 56–60.

3. Maulana Muhammad Ali, *A Manual of Hadith* (New York: Olive Branch Press, 1988), pp. 70–71.

4. Kenneth Cragg, "Muslim Worship," in *Encyclopedia of Religion*, vol. 15, ed., Mircea Eliade et al. (New York: Macmillan-Free Press, 1987), pp. 455–56, 462.

5. Frederick M. Denny, "God's Friends: The Sanctity of Persons in Islam," in George D. Bond and Richard Kieckheffer, eds., *Sainthood: Its Manifestations in World Religions* (Berkeley and Los Angeles: University of California Press, 1988), pp. 69–97.

6. Oleg Grabar, "The Umayyad Dome of the Rock in Jerusalem," *Ars Orientalis*, iii (1959), pp. 32–62.

7. According to the French geographer Xavier de Planhol, "The Geographical Setting," in Bernard Lewis et al., *The Cambridge History of Islam*, II (Cambridge: Cambridge University Press, 1970), p. 447.

8. Ibid.

9. Carleton Coon, *Caravan: The Story of the Middle East*, rev. ed., ch. 14: "Town and City" (New York: Holt, Rinehart and Winston, 1966), pp. 226–59; and Gustave E. Von Grunebaum, "The Structure of the Muslim Town," in *Islam: Essays in the Nature and Growth of a Cultural Tradition*, in *The American Anthropologist*, vol. 57, no. 2, part 2, Memoir no. 81 (April 1955), pp. 141–58.

10. Gaston Wiet, *Cairo: City of Art and Commerce* (Norman: University of Oklahoma Press, 1964), p. 73.

11. Based on Sura 24:31 and the summarizing note no. 2985 in the A. Y. Ali translation, *The Holy Qur'an: Text, Translation and Commentary* (Brentwood, MD: Amana Corporation, 1409 A.H./1989 A.C.), p. 872.

12. Juan Eduardo Campo, *The Other Sides of Paradise: Explorations into the Religious Meanings of Domestic Space in Islam* (Columbia: University of South Carolina Press, 1991).

13. Yusaf Al-Qaradawi, *The Lawful and the Prohibited in Islam* (Indianapolis: American Trust Publications, n.d. [first published in Arabic in 1960]}, p. 95.

14. Richard Ettinghausen, "Decorative Arts and Painting: Their Character and Scope," in *The Legacy of Islam*, 2nd ed., eds., Joseph Schacht and C. E. Bosworth (Oxford: Oxford University Press, 1974), p. 284.

15. Ibid., p. 287.

CHAPTER 19

1. David Biale, *Power and Powerlessness in Jewish History* (New York: Schocken, 1986).

2. Charles S. Liebman and Eliezer Don-Yehiya, *Civil Religion in Israel: Traditional Judaism and Political Culture in the Jewish State* (Berkeley: University of California Press, 1983); and Charles S. Liebman, *The Ambivalent American Jew: Politics, Religion, and Family in American Jewish Life* (Philadelphia: Jewish Publication Society, 1976).

3. Lee I. Levine, *The Rabbinic Class of Roman Palestine in Late Antiquity* (Jerusalem and New York: Yad Izhak Ben-Zvi and Jewish Theological Seminary of America, 1989), pp. 134–91; Michael Avi-Yonah, *The Jews of Palestine: A Political History from the Bar Kochba War to the Arab Conquest* (Ox-

ford: Basil Blackwell, 1976), pp. 208–31; and Jacob Neusner, *Israel's Politics in Sasanian Iran: Jewish Self-Government in Talmudic Times* (Lanham, MD: University Press of America, 1986).

4. Norman A. Stillman, *The Jews of Arab Lands: A History and Source Book* (Philadelphia: Jewish Publication Society, 1979), pp. 22–63; and Kenneth R. Stow, *Alienated Minority: The Jews in Medieval Latin Europe* (Cambridge, MA and London: Harvard University Press, 1992), pp. 1–120.

5. Stow, *Alienated Minority*, pp. 89–101; and Jacob Katz, *Tradition and Crisis: Jewish Society at the End of the Middle Ages*, tr., Bernard Dov Cooperman (New York: Schocken, 1993), pp. 72–75.

6. Jacob Katz, *From Prejudice to Destruction: Anti-Semitism, 1700–1933* (Cambridge, MA: Harvard University Press, 1980).

7. Arthur Hertzberg, *The Zionist Idea: A Historical Analysis and Reader* (New York: Atheneum, 1977).

8. Charles S. Liebman and Eliezer Don-Yehiya, *Religion and Politics in Israel* (Bloomington: Indiana University Press, 1984), pp. 15–56.

9. Baruch Kimmerling and Joel Migdal, *Palestinians: The Making of a People* (New York: Free Press, 1993).

10. Jacob Neusner, *Death and Birth of Judaism: The Impact of Christianity, Secularism, and the Holocaust on Jewish Faith* (New York: Basic, 1987), pp. 254–84; and Menachem Friedman, "The State of Israel as a Theological Dilemma," *The Israeli State and Society: Boundaries and Frontiers*, ed., Baruch Kimmerling (Albany: SUNY, 1989), pp. 165–215.

CHAPTER 20

1. Cited by Ernst Benz, *The Eastern Orthodox Church, Its Thought and Life* (New York: Doubleday, 1963), p. 165.

2. Paul Johnson, *A History of Christianity* (New York: Atheneum, 1979), p. 69.

3. Ibid., p. 87.

4. Gregory of Nyssa, *Homilies on the Resurrection*, 5; in J. P. Migne, ed., *Patrologia Graeca*, 46:685 (Paris: Garnier, 1912).

5. John Chrysostom, *Homilies Against the Jews*, in Migne, *Patrologia Graeca*, 48:843–942. Homily 4:1; 1:4; 6:1–4.

6. Augustine, cited in E. H. Flannery, *The Anguish of the Jews* (New York: Macmillan, 1965), p. 50.

7. Cited in Johnson, *History of Christianity*, p. 105.

8. Quoted in Brian Tierney, *The Crisis of Church and State, 1050–1300* (Englewood Cliffs, NJ: Prentice-Hall, 1964), pp. 128, 132.

9. Ibid., p. 189.

10. Martin Luther, "Address to the Nobility of the German Nation," in J. M. Porter, ed., *Luther: Selected Political Writings* (Philadelphia: Fortress Press, 1974), p. 41.

11. Martin Luther, "Temporal Authority: To What Extent It Should Be Obeyed," in Porter, *Political Writings*, pp. 62–63.

12. Martin Bucer, "De Regno Christi," tr., Wilhelm Pauck, in *Melanchton and Bucer* (Philadelphia: Westminister Press, 1969), p. 362.

13. Ibid., p. 378.

14. Sebastian Castellio, *Advice to a Desolate France*, tr., Marius Valkhoff (Shepardtown, WV: Patmos Press, 1975), p. 30.

15. *The Rising Glory of America, 1760–1820*, rev. ed., ed. with Intro. and notes, Gordon S. Wood (Boston: Northeastern University Press, 1990), p. 341.

16. *Columbian Magazine*, March 1791. Quoted in Lawrence J. Friedman, *Inventors of the Promised Land* (New York: Knopf, 1975), p. 7.

17. Samuel Hopkins, *A Treatise on the Millennium* (Boston: Isaiah Thomas and Ebenezer T. Andrews, 1973), quoted in Wood, *Rising Glory*, p. 48.

18. A. J. Hoover, *God, Germany, and Britain in the Great War: A Study in Clerical Nationalism* (New York: Praeger, 1989), pp. 63, 85–102.

19. Juan Luis Segundo, *The Hidden Motives of Pastoral Action* (Maryknoll, NY: Orbis, 1978).

CHAPTER 21

1. Wilfred Cantwell Smith, *Islam in Modern History* (New York: Mentor Books, 1959), p. 47.

2. "Declaration of the Relationship of the Church to Non-Christian Religions" *(Nostra Aetate),* in *The Documents of Vatican II,* Walter M. Abbott, S.J., gen. ed. (New York: Guild Press, 1966), p. 633.

3. Transliteration into the Roman alphabet of Arabic names and terms varies around the Muslim world. Usually, the Prophet's wife's name would be transliterated as `A'isha, but in Indonesia the "sh" (for the Arabic consonant *shin*) is rendered "sy."

4. Clifford Geertz, *The Religion of Java* (Glencoe, IL: The Free Press, 1960); and Koentjaraningrat, *Javanese Culture* (Singapore: Oxford University Press, 1989), pp. 196–98 and *passim.*

5. The last title mentioned, John L. Esposito, *The Islamic Threat: Myth or Reality?* (New York: Oxford University Press, 1992).

6. Lawrence G. Potter, "Islam and Politics: Egypt, Algeria and Tunisia," in *Great Decisions: 1994 Edition* (New York: Foreign Policy Association, 1994), pp. 71–80 (Algerian situation on pp. 76–77).

7. Susan Grossman and Rivka Haut, "Introduction: Women and the Synagogue," in *Daughters of the King: Women and the Synagogue—A Survey of History, Halakhah, and Contemporary Realities* (Philadelphia: The Jewish Publication Society, 5752/1992), p. 7.

8. Fatima Mernissi, *Islam and Democracy: Fear of the Modern World* (Reading, MA: Addison-Wesley, 1992), p. 152.

GLOSSARY

Abangan: The majority of Javanese Muslims, mostly rural and traditional, mixing folk customs with standard Islamic beliefs and practices.

Abbasids: An Islamic dynasty founded in Baghdad in the mid-seventh century. Abbasid caliphs played a major role in the preservation of Hellenistic culture within Islam. Their cultivation of the rabbinic Gaonim enabled the latter to play a crucial role in the spread of rabbinic Judaism throughout Islamic lands.

Abbot: The superior of a monastery (Heb, *abba:* father). (*See also* Monasticism.)

Abd: A "slave" or "servant" of God. Often part of a Muslim name, e.g., Abd Allah.

Adab: Refinement, good manners, etiquette; belles lettres.

Adat: Traditional folklore in the Malaysian-Indonesian archipelago.

Adhan: The Muslim call to prayer, traditionally recited from a minaret or other prominent place.

Adoptionism: Second-century Christian belief, also known as dynamic monarchianism, which proclaimed that Jesus of Nazareth was not the eternal Son of God, but had been made divine by adoption; condemned as a heresy. (*See also* Monarchianism.)

Aggadah: Hebrew for "lore." In rabbinic usage, it designates the nonhalakhic portion of Oral Torah concerned with theological, ethical, and historical themes. (*See also* Halakhah.)

Ahl al-Kitab: "People of the Book," meaning the Jews and Christians from an Islamic perspective.

Ahl al-Sunna wa 'I-Jama a: "People of the [Prophet's] Sunna and the [main] Community". More often known as "Sunnis." The majority of Muslims, ca. 85.

A'ishiyyah: Indonesian women's Islamic educational and service organization. Connected with Muhammadiyah, a similar Muslim men's organization.

Akhlaq: Islamic "ethics."

Albigensians: Also known as Cathars, these twelfth-thirteenth-century dualistic Christians, akin to the gnostics and Manicheans, were prevalent in and around southern France, with a stronghold in the town of Albi. Condemned as heretics, they were systematically wiped out. (*See also* Gnosticism, Manicheanism.)

Allah: The Arabic term for "God," used by Muslims everywhere, as well as by Arabic-speaking Christians. Allah was also used by Jews in the medieval Arab world.

Allegory: An interpretive method by which Hellenistic readers found philosophical truths and moral values in the classical myths of Greece, in particular the poetry of Homer. Allegory became very popular among Greek-speaking Jews in antiquity.

Amidah: Hebrew for "standing." In rabbinic Judaism, it refers to the main prayer, recited in a standing posture thrice daily. Its forms vary from weekdays to sabbaths and festivals, depending upon the occasion. (*See also* Tefillah.)

Amish: Christian religious group that originated in Switzerland in the seventeenth century whose members aspire to live as they believed early Christians lived, by emphasizing simplicity, pacifism, and religious community separate from the world.

Anabaptists: Broad spectrum of various radical Protestants who thought that the church should be composed solely of genuine believers and who rejected the baptism of infants and instead baptized only those adults who professed a desire to join the church (Greek, *ana:* again + *baptizein:* to baptize).

Anathema: Curse, malediction, or excommunication pronounced by a church on those who challenge or deny its definition of the truth.

Anglican: Pertaining to the Church of England and those churches in other nations that are derived from it and maintain communion with the Archbishop of Canterbury.

Anticlericalism: Popular rejection of the authority of the clergy, sometimes leading to violent actions against them.

Anti-Semitism: A European racist ideology coming to prominence in the 1880s. Its principal idea is that the emancipation of the Jews and their consequent assimilation to European culture had diluted the authentic culture of Europe and threatened Europeans with the loss of their culture and power. Anti-Semitism was a principal element of the Nazi ideology that dominated Germany from 1933 to 1945. (*See also* Holocaust.)

Apollinarianism: The followers of Apollinaris (fourth c.) taught that the *Logos,* or Word of God, took the place of the human soul in Jesus Christ. This belief was condemned as heretical.

Aqiqa: Haircutting ceremony shortly after the birth of a Muslim child.

Aramaic: Semitic language, closely related to Hebrew, that was widely used in the Fertile Crescent in ancient times until the spread of Islam in the region.

Arianism: The followers of Arius (fourth c.) believed that the Son of God was not eternal or of the same essence as the Father. Condemned at the Council of Nicaea (325), this belief nonetheless survived among Christians for several centuries.

Ashkenazic: Designation for Jews of Central and Eastern European origin. (*See also* Sephardic.)

Avodah: Hebrew for "work" or "service." Originally a biblical reference to the offering of animal sacrifice to God, the term was extended in rabbinic Judaism to include all forms of divine service, especially prayer, Torah study, and the performance of commandments.

Awra: The parts of the body that should be covered. For females, everything except the face, hands, and feet; for males, from the navel to the knees.

Aya: "Sign"; also "verse" of the Qur'an.

Ayatollah: "Sign of God," a Shiʿite title of honor for the foremost religious scholars in contemporary Iran. A twentieth-century innovation.

Banu Hashim: "Sons of Hashim," the clan to which Muhammad belonged.

Baptism: A Christian sacrament, symbolic of spiritual regeneration; a rite of initiation, performed with water, through which the individual is cleansed from sin and admitted into the church.

Bar Mitzvah: A puberty ceremony, medieval in origin, signifying a boy's acceptance of full responsibility for observance of the Torah's commandments. (*See also* Bat Mitzvah.)

Bat Mitzvah: A modern puberty ceremony signifying a girl's coming of age as a Jew responsible for observance of the Torah's commandments. (*See also* Bar Mitzvah.)

Bid'a: "Innovation" in religious doctrines or practices, usually regarded as heresy.

Birr: "Piety, reverence, righteousness," as in Sura 2:177.

Bishop: Clerical official who supervises a diocese, or administrative region of the church. It is bishops who have the power within the church to ordain the clergy. The title is derived from the Greek for "overseer" (*Episkopos*).

Bundism: Yiddish for "unionism." An Eastern European secularist movement of the late nineteenth and early twentieth century that sought to organize the Jewish proletariat as a force for international socialist revolution.

Caliph: From Arabic *khalifa*, "successor, deputy." The title applied to the political leaders who succeeded the Prophet Muhammad. Caliphate is the office, from *khilafa*.

Calvinists: Followers of John Calvin (d. 1564).

Canon: This term has several meanings. 1. The books of the Bible officially recognized by the church. 2. The calendar of saints accepted by the Roman Catholic Church. 3. A church law or code of laws. 4. A priest serving in the bishop's church.

Canonization: In the Roman Catholic Church, the process whereby individuals are proclaimed worthy of veneration after their deaths by being added to the list (or "canon") of known saints.

Cardinal: A member of the College of Cardinals in the Roman Catholic Church, a body of clerical officials appointed by the pope who serve as his advisers and administrators and who assemble at his death to elect a successor.

Cathars: (*See* Albigensians.)

Cathedral: The principal church of a bishop, which contains his official throne (Lat., *cathedra:* seat).

Catholic: 1. Literal meaning, "universal." 2. Pertaining to the church led by the pope at Rome, also known as the Roman Catholic Church.

Charism: A divinely inspired gift or power, which Christians usually attribute to the Holy Spirit.

Christology: That part of Christian theology that seeks to explain the person of Jesus Christ.

Church: 1. An association of Christians. 2. A building used for worship by Christians.

Codex: A Latin term designating a book composed of leaves bound together on one side. This form of the book emerged in the first century CE and rapidly replaced the scroll as the way of recording knowledge. Rabbinic Judaism retained the scroll as the preferred form for copying books of the Torah.

Communion: (*See* Eucharist.)

Companions: The close associates of Muhammad.

Conscience: Human capacity to judge right from wrong and to determine morality.

Council: An assembly of church officials and theologians convened for the purpose of regulating matters of doctrine, discipline, and piety.

Covenant: In Judaism, an intimate and exclusive relationship between God and Israel in which the Torah defines the rights and obligations of each partner.

Creed: Christian confession of faith in a prayer that begins by saying "I believe" (Lat., *credo*) and enumerates and affirms the central beliefs of the Christian religion.

Crusade: Holy war undertaken with papal sanction (eleventh-fourteenth c., against the Muslims in the Holy Land or the Albigensians in Europe).

Cujus regio, ejus religio: Phrase coined in the sixteenth century to describe the policy of designating the official religion of a state to be identical to the religion of the ruler, whether the ruler was Protestant or Catholic.

Deacon: Clerical office. Among early Christians, deacons ministered to the poor, sick, and needy. In the Catholic, Orthodox, and Anglican churches, deacons rank just below priests; in other denominations they serve various functions.

Deism: Eighteenth-nineteenth-century expression of belief in a creator God, the human capability to do good, the power of reason to discover religious truth, and reward or punishment in the afterlife.

Demons: (*See* Devils.)

Devils: Fallen angels, evil spirits, foes of God. Led by Satan, devils tempt humans to sin on earth and eternally torment the damned in hell.

Devotional literature: Inspiring stories and accounts that generally do not address specific doctrinal questions.

Diaspora: Greek for "dispersion." The primary reference is to Jewish communities that, since the Babylonian Exile, have made their homes outside the Land of Israel.

Dīn: "Religion," meaning the beliefs and devotional practices of Islam, or any religion, taken as a whole. Islam is known as *Al-din al-islami*, "The Islamic Religion."

Docetism: Early Christian belief that Jesus Christ did not have a genuine human body, but only seemed to have one (Greek, *dokeo:* "to seem"). Rejected as a heresy, it remained popular among Gnostic Christians. (*See also* Gnosticism.)

Dominicans: Order of preachers, founded by Dominic de Guzman in 1206.

Donatistis: Schismatic North African Christians (fourth-sixth c.) who believed that sacraments administered by sinful clerics were not valid.

Ecclesiastical: Anything pertaining to the church, especially as an institution. In other words, anything "churchly."

Ecological Ethics: Founded on belief in the interconnectedness of God, human life, and the natural world, it replaces emphasis on duty in ethics with an emphasis on care.

Ecumenism: Used to describe the aspiration for a worldwide church, it identifies a willingness to discover common ground among different religious groups.

Eid: "Festival," namely the two annual observances: '*Eid al-adha*, "feast of sacrifice," and '*Eid al-fitri*, "feast of fast-breaking," at the end of Ramadan.

Emancipation: The modern movement to grant to the Jews full civil and political rights in emerging nation states. First receiving formal expression in the American and French constitutions of the late eighteenth century, emancipation was completed in all Western and Central European states by 1870. (*See also* Anti-Semitism.)

Enlightenment: Intellectual movement that stressed the role of a human faculty of reason and the capability of an individual to cultivate reason as a means to the discovery of truth. Also known as "the Age of Reason."

En Sof: Hebrew for "infinite." In Kabbalistic terms, En Sof refers to that aspect of the divine reality that is totally unknowable and remote. (*See also* Sefirot.)

Episcopal: 1. Anything pertaining to a bishop or bishops. 2. A church led by bishops.

Epistemology: Study of the grounds of knowledge, its limits, validity, and the manner in which it is acquired.

Eschatology: That part of Christian theology that deals with the ultimate or last things, such as death, the end of the world, judgment, heaven, purgatory, and hell (Greek, *eskhatos:* last).

Eucharist: 1. Christian ritual focused on the consumption of bread and wine, commemorating the Last Passover Supper of Jesus with his apostles, richly packed with symbolic meaning (varying among the various denominations). 2. More specifically, the sacrament of Communion in which the faithful associate the bread and wine that they eat with the body and blood of Christ (again, the interpretation of this correlation varies immensely according to the denomination).

Evangelical: 1. Anything referring to the Christian gospels (Greek, *evangelion:* "good news"; Old Eng., *Godspell:* "good news"). 2. Name employed by various Protestant churches that claim strict adherence to the gospels. (*See also* Gospel.)

Evangelical Christianity: A style of Christianity that emerged from the Protestant Reformation that seeks ongoing renewal of individual and collective Christian life through appeal to the authority of scripture, and, in some cases, through the experience of conversion.

Evangelist: 1. Any of the four authors of the Christian gospels. (*See also* Gospel.) 2. Title employed by various Protestant preachers and missionaries.

Evangelization: The spread of religious ideas by church agents, especially missionaries.

Excommunication: Formal exclusion from fellowship in a Christian church.

Exegesis: The interpretation of scriptural texts (Greek, *exegeisthai:* to show the way).

Exilarch: Greek for "Leader of the Exiles." The title was applied specifically to the leaders of Babylonian Jewry, appointed by Parthian and Sassanian emperors from the late second to the seventh centuries CE. (*See also* Patriarch.)

Exile: Among Jews, this can refer geographically to areas of the Jewish Diaspora or metaphysically to a state of estrangement between God and Israel.

Falah: "Success, felicity," the key term characterizing the Muslim's religious goal. It is sometimes translated as "salvation," but that is too colored by Christian meanings to express adequately the Islamic notion.

Faqr: "Spiritual poverty," as of the Sufi mystics. A person who renounces wealth and comfort for the Sufi way is known as a *faqir.*

Fard: "Obligatory," in the Islamic legal sense.

Fatwa: An Islamic legal opinion, rendered by a mufti, one expert in Islamic jurisprudence.

Filioque: Latin for "and from the Son," added to the Niceno-Constantinopolan Creed by the Roman Catholic Church (ninth c.), in reference to the Holy Spirit's full divinity who was believed to proceed not just from God the Father (as stated in the earlier creed), but also from God the Son. Disagreement over the insertion of "Filioque" into the creed contributed substantially to the Orthodox-Catholic schism.

Final Judgment: Christian belief that at some point in historical time the world will come to an end and every human being will be judged by Christ and either rewarded with eternal bliss or everlasting torment.

Fiqh: Lit. "understanding," but has come to mean Islamic jurisprudence in the technical sense.

Fitra: Humankind's original, sound state, as taught by the Qur'an.

Franciscans: Order of mendicant (begging) friars founded by Francis of Assisi (1208).

Gaon: Hebrew for "eminence." The title was given to a succession of rabbinic scholarly leaders under the Abbasid dynasty from the mid-seventh to the twelfth centuries. The Gaonim were influential in transforming the heritage of rabbinic literature into a coherent, international system of Judaism.

Ghusl: The greater ablution before prayers and other ritual acts.

Gnosticism: Broad term applied to a wide variety of dualistic sects, principally in late antiquity, that conceived of existence in terms of a dialectic between good and evil, in which the spiritual was associated with goodness and the material with evil, and that promised redemption through knowledge of the hidden, secret structures of the cosmos (Greek, *gnosis:* "knowledge").

Gospels: The four books of the Christian Scriptures that narrate the story of the life and work of Jesus: Matthew, Mark, Luke, and John (Old Eng., *Godspell:* "good news.")

Habad: A Hasidic movement founded in the late eighteenth century and later centered in the Russian town, Lubavitch. Since the 1950s, Habad has been an influential minority presence in North American, European, and Israeli Jewry. Its messianic expectations surrounding the late rebbe, Menachem Mendel Schneerson, have aroused great controversy.

Hadith: "Report" of something the Prophet Muhammad did or said.

Hafiz: One who has memorized the entire Qur'an by heart.

Haggadah: Hebrew for "telling." Specifically, it refers to the book that provides the script for the Passover seder.

Hajj: The Muslim pilgrimage to Mecca. One of the Pillars of Islam.

Halakhah: Hebrew for "procedure," specifically, the rabbinic procedure for performing a biblical commandment. The halakhah is the legal part of the rabbinic Oral Torah. (*See also* Aggadah, Mitzvah.)

Halal: "Legally permitted" according to Islamic law.

Hanafi: One of the four Sunni schools of jurisprudence, named after its founder Abu Hanafi.

Hanbali: One of the four Sunni schools of jurisprudence, named after Ahmad Ibn Hanbal.

Haram: "Legally forbidden" according to Islamic law.

Haramayn: "The Two Sanctuaries" of Mecca and Medina.

Harim: The private quarters of a Muslim home, where the women and children are safe and out of sight of strangers.

Hasidism: A traditionalist movement of Eastern European Jewish mystical piety that originated in the eighteenth century and continues as a small, but influential, minority movement among contemporary Jews. The distinguishing trait of Hasidism is the presence of highly charismatic holy men as spiritual leaders. (*See also* Mitnagdism, Rebbe.)

Hasmoneans: A dynastic family of priests whose heirs governed Palestine as an independent Jewish theocracy from 152 to 63 BCE. The Hasmoneans seized power after a protracted war against Hellenized Jerusalem priests and their Seleucid allies.

Havurah: Hebrew for "fellowship." In contemporary North American Judaism, intimate groups of like-minded people often gather into such fellowships as alternatives to the larger, more institutionalized synagogue movements.

Heaven: The abode of God, variously conceived among and also within the three monotheistic religions.

Hell: In Christian theology, the abode of Satan and his devils, and also the place where all the damned will be punished for eternity.

Hellenism: The graecized culture that spread throughout the Mediterranean and Middle Eastern world in the wake of the conquests of Alexander the Great in the late fourth century BCE.

Heresy: The willful profession of or adherence to theological falsehood.

Hermeneutics: The science and methodology of interpretation, especially of Scriptural texts.

Heterodoxy: Any position that differs from accepted doctrine or dogma; the opposite of "orthodoxy."

Hijab: The "covering" or "veiling" of the hair, and sometimes the face, by Muslim women outside the home.

Hijaz: West-central Arabia, where Islam arose in the seventh century.

Hijra: The "emigration" of Muhammad and his followers from Mecca to Medina in 622. Marks the beginning of the Muslim calendar.

Hilal: The crescent moon, which marks the beginning of each month in the Muslim year. A main visual symbol of Islam.

Historical Criticism: Approach to interpreting the Bible that views biblical writings through the historical circumstances surrounding their origins.

Holocaust: Greek for "burnt offering." In contemporary usage, it refers to the Nazi destruction of European Jewry from 1933 to 1945. As a symbol of the precariousness of Jewish existence, the Holocaust has played a central role in the shaping of Jewish identity in North America and the State of Israel.

Homoousios: Greek term meaning "of the same essence" in reference to the relation between God the Father and God the Son in Christian trinitarian theology; proclaimed at the Council of Nicaea (325) against Arianism. (*See also* Arianism.)

Host: The consecrated bread or wafer of the eucharist (Latin, *hostia:* "sacrifice," "victim"). (*See also* Communion, Eucharist.)

Hussites: Followers of John Hus (d. 1415).

Hypostatic Union: The union of the two natures (divine and human) in the person of Jesus Christ, proclaimed at the Councils of Ephesus (431) and Chalcedon (451). (Greek, *hypostasis:* "substance," "nature.")

Ibada: "Service," in the sense of worship of God. The five Pillars of Islam are the main forms of *ibada* (pl. '*ibadat*).

Iconoclasm: Lit. "the destroying of images." Broadly speaking, any attack—verbal or physical—upon paintings, statues, and other ritual objects such as lamps, vessels, vestments, altars, relics, etc.

Ihram: The state of ritual consecration of pilgrims to Mecca.

Ijma': "Consensus" of the Muslim community in legal matters. One of the four sources of Sunni jurisprudence.

Ijtihad: Independent legal decision making by a *mujtahid*.

Ilham: Inspiration experienced by Muslims, but not equal to revelation. (*See also* Wahy.)

Ilm: "Science, knowledge," particularly of Islamic religion and law.

Imam: "Leader," as in the salat-prayer service. Shi'ites revere their Imams as exalted leaders.

Imami: The main Shi'ite sect, which recognizes 12 Imams, the last of which is living in a mysterious state of occultation. Also known as the "Twelver" sect of Shi'ism.

Iman: "Faith." One who has faith is called a *mu'min*, "believer." Iman is also the doctrinal dimension of Islam, as distinguished from ritual practices, which are known as *islam*.

Incarnation: Central Christian belief that God became a flesh-and-blood human being, Jesus of Nazareth.

Islam: "Submission" to God. One who submits is a *muslim*. Islam is the name of the religion revealed by God in the Qur'an.

Isnad: The chain of transmitters supporting a *hadith*.

Israel: A people represented in the Hebrew Bible as the descendants of Abraham; Jews regard themselves as being biologically continuous with Israel. (*See also* State of Israel.)

Jahiliyya: The "Age of Ignorance" in pre-Islamic Arabia, according to Islamic opinion.

Jesuits: Members of the Society of Jesus, a religious order founded by Ignatius Loyola in 1540.

Jihad: "Exertion" in the way of God. Sometimes translated as "holy warfare," but that is only one meaning.

Justification: Christian theological term that refers to salvation as the condition or fact of someone being justified before God, that is, being found guiltless.

Ka'aba: The cubicle structure at the center of the Grand Mosque in Mecca, believed to have been built by Abraham as the first sanctuary for the monotheistic worship of God. Muslims around the world pray facing toward the Ka'aba.

Kabbalah: Hebrew for "tradition." Specifically, it refers to the Medieval Spanish tradition of Jewish mysticism that reached classical expression in the thirteenth century Zohar and other writings. (*See also* Zohar.)

Kalam: "Discussion" about theological matters; thus, "dogmatic theology" in Islam. One who pursues *kalam* is a *mutakallim.*

Kavanah: Hebrew for "intention." In rabbinic Judaism, it refers to an attitude of attention to one's words cultivated in prayer. In Kabbalah, the term has the broader sense of meditation on certain configurations of the Sefirot.

Ketuvim: Hebrew for "writings." Jews use it to designate the third section of the Hebrew Bible, beginning with the Book of Psalms and ending with the Book of II Chronicles. (*See also* Torah, Nevi'im.)

Khalifa: (*See* Caliph.)

Khitan: Circumcision.

Land of Israel: Biblical term for the territory of Israelite settlement. This is the dominant term by which Jews designate their ancient homeland. (*See also* Israel, Palestine.)

Liberation Theology: Twentieth-century Christian theological and social movement originating in Latin America that stressed commitment to social justice for the poor and oppressed.

Logos: Greek term meaning "thought," "reason," or "word," applied by Christians to Jesus Christ, the Word of God made flesh, as proclaimed in the Gospel of John.

Lollards: Followers of John Wycliffe in England, condemned as heretics (fourteenth-fifteenth c.).

Lutheran Church: Any church that proclaims to follow the teachings of Martin Luther or to be derived from those European churches reformed under his leadership in the sixteenth century.

Maariv: In rabbinic Judaism, the evening prayer service. (*See also* Shakharit, Minkhah.)

Madhhab: An Islamic legal school or rite.

Mahram: A close relative whom it would be illegal to marry.

Makruh: In Islamic law, something that is technically permitted but detested, such as divorce.

Maliki: The Sunni legal school named after Anas Ibn Malik.

Manara: "Lighthouse," giving English the term "minaret," a tower associated with a mosque.

Mandub: In Islamic law, something "recommended."

Manichaeans: Dualistic sect akin to gnosticism founded in Persia by Manes (third c. CE); flourished in Late Antiquity.

Ma'rifa: "Gnosis," the esoteric spiritual knowledge and illumination that Sufis attain in their meditations.

Masjid: "Place of prostration," i.e., "mosque."

Mass: Term used for the celebration of the eucharist by Roman Catholics and some Anglicans, derived from the Latin *missa,* in the phrase spoken by the priest at the end of the liturgy: *"ite missa est,"* "go, it is the dismissal."

Material Culture: The art, architecture, dress, foods, furniture, personal decoration, and other artifacts of everyday life that confirm and communicate religious identity.

Matn: The "meaning" or main story of a *hadith.*

Messiah: Hebrew for "anointed one." In the Hebrew Bible, it normally refers to a priest, king, or Prophet anointed for his holy office. In most forms of Judaism, it refers to a descendant of David who, at the end of time, will preside as God's representative over the end of the Exile and the Resurrection of the Dead. In Christianity, the term refers to Jesus of Nazareth.

Mezuzah: Hebrew for "doorpost." In common usage, it designates an amulet containing verses of the Torah that is placed on the right-hand entrance to the home.

Midrash: Hebrew for "inquiry." In rabbinic usage, it refers specifically to inquiry into the meaning of the Written Torah guided by the interpretive traditions of the Oral Torah; that is, biblical interpretation. Legal interpretation is called "midrash halakhah," while nonlegal interpretation is called "midrash aggadah."

Mihrab: The niche in a mosque wall indicating the direction of Mecca—the *qibla*.

Minaret: (*See* Manara.)

Minbar: The pulpit in a mosque, from which the imam delivers the prayer during the Friday congregational salat.

Minkhah: In Rabbinic Judaism, the late-afternoon prayer service. (*See also* Shakharit, Maariv.)

Mishnah: Hebrew for "repeated tradition." Usually, it refers specifically to a collection of legal traditions compiled by Rabbi Judah the Patriarch in third-century CE Palestine. This is the foundation of rabbinic law. The term can also refer to a paragraph of the Mishnah rather than to the document as a whole.

Mishneh Torah: Twelfth-century halakhic code composed in Egypt by Moses Maimonides.

Mitnagdism: An eighteenth-century anti-Hasidic movement among traditionalist Eastern European Jews. Mitnagdic Jews rejected the charismatic leaders of Hasidism, regarding them as charlatans who revived the dangers of the false-messianism associated with Shabbatai Zvi. In the contemporary period, the passions surrounding the Hasidic-Mitnagdic controversies are subdued, traditionalists of both camps seeing themselves as confronting together the threats of secularist and modernist forms of Judaic identity. (*See also* Hasidism.)

Mitzvah: Hebrew for "commandment." Specifically, a reference to the commandments found in the Torah. (*See also* Halakhah.)

Modalism: Also known as modalistic monarchianism, this theology affirmed the oneness of God and did not see the Father, Son, and Holy Spirit as distinctions within the divine being, but rather as different manifestations—or modes—of God's dealings with his creation. Revived in the sixteenth and eighteenth centuries. (*See also* Unitarianism, Monarchianism.)

Modernism: The nineteenth-century challenge to religious traditionalism, particularly visible as a conflict within the Roman Catholic church.

Monarchianism: Term applied to two types of theology (second-third c.) that sought to defend the oneness of God but were branded heretical; dynamic monarchianism (*see* Adoptionism) and modalistic monarchianism (*see* Modalism).

Monastery: Community of Christians who take vows of poverty, chastity, and obedience, live apart from society at large, and follow a common rule concerning prayer, ritual, and ethics. (Greek, *monos:* single, solitary.)

Monastic: Pertaining to or characteristic of monks and monasteries.

Monism: The identification of God with nature.

Monk: A man committed to the monastic life. (*See also* Monastery.)

Monophysitism: Belief that Jesus Christ has a single nature (divine/human) rather than two distinct natures (divine and human); condemned at the Council of Chalcedon in 451, but not extinguished.

Monothelitism: Belief that Jesus Christ has a single will (divine/human) rather than two distinct wills (divine and human); an outgrowth of monophysitism, condemned at the Third Council of Constantinople in 680.

Muezzin: From *mu'adhdhin*, crier who calls Muslims to prayer by means of the *adhan*.

Muhammadiyah: Twentieth-century Indonesian Muslim educational and service organization.

Mujaddid: "Renewer" of Islam, believed to be appointed by God in each century.

Mujtahid: (*See* ijtihad.)

Mu'min: (*See* iman.)

Musaf: Hebrew for "addition." It normally refers to a supplementary worship service offered after Shakharit on sabbaths and festivals.

Musar: Hebrew for "instruction." The name was applied in mid-nineteenth-century eastern Europe to a Mitnagdic movement of ethical self-scrutiny founded by Israel Salanter.

Mushaf: A copy of the Qur'an.

Muslim: (*See* Islam.)

Mutakallim: (*See* kalam.)

Mu'tazila: The "rationalist" school of Muslim theologians in Abbasid times.

Nabi: Prophet.

Natural Religion: Religion based upon the acquisition of knowledge about religious truth through its manifestation in the natural world.

Nestorianism: Nestorius (fifth c.) and his followers stressed the distinction between the divine and the human in Christ so much that they objected to using the title "Mother of God" for Mary. They were accused of turning Christ into two different persons and were condemned by three councils (431, 451, 553). Nestorians survived independently as "The Church of the East."

Nevi'im: Hebrew for "Prophets." Jews use it to designate that section of the Hebrew Bible that begins with the Book of Joshua and ends with the Book of Malakhi. (*See also* Ketuvim, Torah.)

Niyya: Right "intention" required before performing the salat and other rites.

Nun: A woman who takes up the monastic life. (*See also* Monasticism.)

Oral Torah: In Judaism, this term designates the rabbinic tradition of amplifying and applying the scriptures of the Hebrew Bible (Written Torah). Oral Torah is conceived to have originated in the same revelation to Moses that produced the Written Torah.

Orders: 1. Roman Catholic sacrament in which men are invested with clerical offices, the highest of which is the priesthood. 2. Clerical and monastic organizations or communities approved by the pope and bound by a common authority, rule, and sense of mission.

Original Sin: Doctrine widely accepted in Western Christianity that holds that all humans have an inborn tendency to sin as a result of Adam and Eve's first act of disobedience to God.

Orthodox Judaism: A modernist movement of Jewish religious identity founded in Germany in the mid-nineteenth century. Orthodoxy has insisted that conformity with halakhic norms does not prevent Jews from participating in modern society. On the defensive for most of the twentieth century, Orthodoxy is making a comeback in North America and has been the dominant form of Judaism in the State of Israel. (*See also* Positive-Historical Judaism, Reform Judaism.)

Orthodoxy: 1. True teaching—as opposed to falsehood (Greek, *orthodoxos:* "having the right opinion"). 2. The common tradition of the Eastern Christian churches.

Orthopraxis: Correct practice in a religion (e.g., correct ritual, moral conduct, worship).

Palestine: A Latin term coined by the Romans to describe the region that Jews called the Land of Israel. The name was retained as a provincial title under various Islamic empires and during the British Mandate period of 1917–1948. Since the establishment of the State of Israel in part of Palestine in 1948, Jews have tended to avoid the term. Among Arabs, Palestine continues to be the common designation for the territory. As of 1994, the term is used specifically of the expanding areas of Arab sovereignty from Israel on the West Bank of the Jordan River. (*See also* Land of Israel.)

Patriarch: 1. Greek for "Leader of the Homeland." The title was granted by Rome to a succession of rabbinic leaders in Palestine from the late first to the early fifth centuries CE. (*See also* Exilarch.) 2. Title used in the Catholic, Orthodox, Nestorian, and Monophysite churches by the bishops of principal cities.

Pelagianism: Belief in the power of the human will to freely choose between good and evil, with little or no assistance from God's grace; condemned as heresy in the fifth and sixth centuries. Named after its first proponent, Pelagius (fourth c.).

Penance: 1. The sacrament that conveys forgiveness, consisting of the confessing of one's sins to a priest (Catholic Church). 2. A specific act of prayer or charity imposed on the repentant sinner after the act of confession as penitence for his or her sins.

Pentecostal: 1. Pertaining to the Christian feast of Pentecost, which marks the descent of the Holy Spirit upon Jesus' apostles. 2. Title used by various churches or groups that profess inspiration by the Holy Spirit.

Pentecostalism: Christian religion focused on the gifts of the Holy Spirit (e.g., healing, prophecy, speaking in tongues, etc.) that were given to the followers of Jesus on the day of Pentecost.

Pietism: The emphasis on religion of the heart, or the emotional aspect of religion. It is especially important in identifying Protestant groups in the sixteenth-nineteenth centuries.

Pilgrimage: A journey to a sacred place or shrine.

Pillars of Islam: The required devotional duties of Muslims: Shahada ("witnessing" to the unity of God and the messengerhood of Muhammad), Salat ("prayer"), Zakat ("almsgiving"), Sawm ("fasting" during the holy month of Ramadan), Hajj ("pilgrimage" to Mecca).

Pope: The bishop of Rome and head of the Roman Catholic Church.

Popular Religion: Religion of the "populus," or people, so-called because it embodies ideas and rituals that have grown up outside of the official forms of religious life sanctioned and overseen by church officials.

Positive-Historical Judaism: The mid-nineteenth-century German ancestor of modernist Conservative Judaism. Proponents of this form of Judaism sought to carve out a middle path between Reform Judaism's general rejection of Halakhic tradition and Orthodoxy's insistance on the absolutely binding character of the medieval form of that tradition. North America has hosted the most vigorous forms of Conservative Judaism. (*See also* Orthodox Judaism, Reform Judaism.)

Preaching: The oral presentation of religious ideas and doctrines, including the reading or recitation of Scripture, to an audience.

Predestination: Belief that God foreordains the course of history, and more specifically, chooses only certain people for redemption.

Presbyter: Clerical title, meaning "elder" (Greek, *presbyteros*); used in the early church; revived in the Calvinist churches of the Reformation.

Presbyterian: 1. Pertaining to a church run by presbyters. 2. Any of various Protestant churches governed by elders, typically Calvinist, and derived from the Reformed Church of Scotland.

Priyayi: The Javanese Muslim bureaucratic class.

Proseuche: Greek for "prayer place." An early name for the institution of the synagogue as a place of worship.

Protestantism: Term applied to that broad spectrum of Christian churches that broke away from Roman Catholicism in the sixteenth century, professing to follow the Bible as the ultimate authority.

Ptolemies: An Egyptian Hellenistic dynasty that governed Palestine from the late fourth to the late third centuries BCE. (*See also* Seleucids.)

Purgatory: In Catholic theology, a place of torment where souls are purged or cleansed of their sinfulness before being admitted into Heaven.

Qadi: An Islamic judge.

Qibla: The direction of Mecca toward which Muslims face during the salat-prayer; marked in mosques by the *mihrab*.

Qiyas: "Analogical reasoning" in Islamic jurisprudence.

Quakers (Society of Friends): Christian religious group that emerged in England in the 1650s, rejecting sacraments, creeds, and the priesthood and emphasizing simplicity and religious feeling.

Qur'an: "Recitation," God's oral revelations gathered in the book known as the Qur'an.

Rabbi: Hebrew for "my Master." In historical Jewish usage, the term refers to a qualified master of the Oral Torah in general and halakhic tradition in particular. In modernist forms of Judaism, rabbis commonly fill pastoral and organizational roles in addition to providing formal religious instruction.

Rak'a: A cycle of postures during the salat-prayer: standing, bowing, prostrating, sitting.

Ramadan: The month in which the Qur'an was first revealed and during which Muslims observe an obligatory fast during daylight hours.

Rasul: "Apostle, messenger" of God, entrusted with a scriptural revelation.

Ra'y: Personal "opinion" as a source of Islamic legal reasoning.

Rebbe: Usually refers to the charismatic leader of a Hasidic community. (*See also* Tzaddik.)

Redemption: (*See* Soteriology.)

Reformed Protestantism: That family of churches that claim some adherence to the theology and piety professed by the Swiss Reformer Ulrich Zwingli and his French follower John Calvin (sixteenth c.).

Reform Judaism: A modernist movement of Jewish religious identity founded in Germany in the 1820s and highly influential throughout the twentieth century, especially in North America. Reform Judaism stresses the ethical content of Judaic tradition and encourages an attitude of autonomy in relation to rabbinic halakhic norms. (*See also* Orthodox Judaism, Positive-Historical Judaism.)

Relics: The remains of holy men and women and other physical objects associated with their bodies that are venerated and sought out as points of contact with the sacred.

Revelation: The manifestation of the divine will and truth.

Sabellianism: A form of modalistic monarchianism professed by Sabellius (fourth c.); condemned as a heresy by both the Arians and the Orthodox. (*See also* Modalism.)

Sacraments: Rituals of the church that are taken to be visible signs of invisible grace. The number of sacraments varies according to denomination.

Saint: 1. In Christian tradition, broadly speaking, any person who is redeemed. 2. In the Orthodox and Catholic churches, a person who has died and gone to Heaven and is officially recognized as worthy of veneration and as being capable of interceding with God for the faithful on earth.

Salam: Arabic "peace," similar to Hebrew *shalom*.

Salat: The Islamic prayer service, observed five times daily. One of Islam's five Pillars.

Santri: Strictly observant Muslims in Java.

Satan: The chief fallen angel, ruler of hell and master of all the devils. (*See also* Devil.)

Sawm: The obligatory Islamic fast during the month of Ramadan; one of Islam's five Pillars.

Schism: A split into factions, or more specifically, a formal breach of union within a Christian church.

Scholasticism: A style of theology indebted to philosophy and centered on a dialectical question-and-answer method; developed in the monastic schools and universities of the Middle Ages and predominant from the twelfth to the sixteenth centuries, with some later revivals.

Second Vatican Council: Gathering of Roman Catholic religious leaders in Rome (1962–1965) for the purpose of studying church doctrine, ritual, and structure, and for framing specific reforms.

Sefirot: Kabbalistic term for the ten divine emanations. By tracing the impact of these emanations in the empirical world, Kabbalists believe it possible to direct the power in the Sefirot toward redemptive ends. (*See also* Kabbalah, Zohar.)

Seleucids: A Syrian Hellenistic dynasty that controlled Palestine from the beginning of the second century BCE until the Hasmonean revolt of 175–152 BCE

Sephardic: Designation for Jews of Spanish origin living throughout southern Europe, North Africa, and the Middle East. (*See also* Ashkenazic.)

Septuagint: Greek for "seventy." It refers to the third-century-BCE translation of the Torah into Greek.

Servi Camarae: Latin for "servants of the chamber." This was a legal institution by which Jews in medieval Christian Europe were classified as the property of the local secular ruler. This status often served as an occasion for exploitation of the Jews, but it also protected them from anti-Jewish policies of the Catholic Church.

Shafi'i: One of the Sunni legal schools.

Shakers: Christian communal society that emerged in the eighteenth century, practiced sexual abstinence, and stressed the female element in divinity alongside the male.

Shakharit: In rabbinic Judaism, the early-morning prayer service. (*See also* Maariv, Minkhah.)

Shari'a: The whole structure of divinely revealed Islamic legislation, based on the Qur'an and Sunna.

Shekhinah: Hebrew for "presence." In rabbinic Judaism, it refers to that dimension of God's being that is intimately available to human experience. In Kabbalah, it is the last of the Ten Sefirot.

Shi'a: "Party," meaning the followers of Ali who became the main minority community of Islam. The Shi'ites believe that the leadership of the Muslims should come from descendants of the Prophet Muhammad through the line of Ali and Fatima.

Shirk: "Associating" anything with God; considered idolatry and Islam's one unforgivable sin.

Shma: Hebrew for "hear." In Judaism, it refers to the three passages from Deuteronomy and Numbers that are recited as a twice-daily expression of submission to the norms of the covenant with the God of Israel.

Shulkhan Arukh: Sixteenth-century halakhic code composed in Palestine by Joseph Karo.

Sin: An act of disobedience to God, worthy of punishment.

Social Gospel: An assortment of movements in Europe and America in the nineteenth and twentieth centuries that focused Christian moral responsibility upon social justice.

Soteriology: That branch of Christian theology that deals with how humanity is saved from sin and death by Jesus Christ. (Greek, *soter:* savior.)

State of Israel: Established in 1948 as a sovereign Jewish state in part of Palestine. (*See also* Palestine, Zionism.)

Stigmata: Mystical phenomenon in which the crucifixion wounds of Jesus are made manifest on the bodies of holy men and women.

Sufism: Islam's mystical path.

Sukkah: A temporary thatched dwelling in which rabbinic Jews eat during the autumn festival of Sukkot.

Sunna: The "custom" of the Prophet Muhammad, known through the literary form of *hadith*, "report" of something Muhammad said or did.

Sunni: (*See* Ahl al-Sunna wa 'I-Jama a.)

Sura: Chapter of the Qur'an.

Synagogue: Greek for "community." It came to designate the organized Jewish communities of the Hellenistic world and, eventually, their places of gathering. Synagogues became primary locations of prayer and Torah study. (*See also* Proseuche.)

Syncretism: A process of religious innovation characterized by the blending of elements drawn from two or more different religious traditions, and frequently including entirely new ideas and rituals as well.

Synod: A gathering or assembly of churches or church officials; an ecclesiastical council.

Tafsir: Qur'anic exegesis.

Tajwid: The art of reciting the Qur'an.

Talmud: Hebrew for "learning." It refers to the scholarly traditions of the rabbinic sages of late antiquity. These were compiled into the Palestinian Talmud (ca. 425 CE) and the Babylonian Talmud (ca. 525 CE). The Babylonian Talmud remains the single most authoritative document of rabbinic Judaism.

TaNaKH: An acrostic standing for Torah, Nevi'im, and Ketuvim. It is commonly used by Jews to refer to the Hebrew Bible.

Taqlid: Blind imitation in Islamic jurisprudence; opposite of *ijtihad.*

Taqwa: Reverential fear of God.

Tariqa: Sufi brotherhood; also means a specific Sufi method of discipline and meditation.

Tawhid: The Divine Unity.

Tefillah: Hebrew for "prayer." Usually used in reference to the Amidah.

Theologia ("theology"): A form of reasoning about the divine; the science of the study of God.

Theotokos: "God-bearer" (Greek), or "Mother of God," a reverent name for Mary, mother of Jesus.

Torah: Hebrew for "teaching." Jews use it narrowly to designate the first five books of the Hebrew Bible; more broadly, it refers to "authoritative teaching" in Judaism, of whatever source. (*See also* Ketuvim, Nevi'im.)

Transsubstantiation: In Catholic theology, this doctrine proclaims that in the eucharist the substances of bread and wine actually transform, or change into the body and blood of Christ, even if their external appearances remain the same.

Trinity: Christian doctrine that proclaims that while there is only one God, he has revealed himself as triune; one God in three persons, the Father, the Son, and the Holy Spirit.

Tzaddik: Hebrew for "righteous person." In Hasidism, the term is usually applied to a rebbe or other charismatic leader. (*See also* Rebbe.)

Tzedakah: Hebrew for "righteousness." In rabbinic Judaism, it designates each person's obligation to give charity to the poor.

Ulama: The "learned" in religion and law.

Umayyads: The first Muslim dynasty, ruling from Damascus from 661 to 750.

Umma: The Muslim community. Any religious community.

Umra: The "Little Pilgrimage" to Mecca, with observance of the Hajj rites that take place only in Mecca proper in the vicinity of the Ka'aba.

Unitarianism: Religion that emerged from Christianity, in which Jesus is viewed not as a part of the Godhead, but as an emissary, or mediator, between humanity and God.

Universalism: In Christian tradition, the belief that all persons will be granted eternal reward in the afterlife.

Usul al-fiqh: The sources of Muslim jurisprudence.

Vodou: A syncretistic religion originating in Haiti that combines Roman Catholic and non-Christian African religious traditions.

Vow: In Christianity, a solemn or earnest promise made to God that binds one to perform a specified act or to live in a certain manner.

Wahy: Divine revelation of scripture.

Wajib: Legally required.

Written Torah: In rabbinic Judaism, this term designates the scriptural collection of revelations to Moses and later Prophets found in the Hebrew Bible. (*See also* Torah, Oral Torah.)

Wudu': The lesser ablution.

Yehud: An Aramaic form of the Hebrew, Yehudah. Consisting of a small settlement in and around Jerusalem, Yehud was repopulated by exiled Jews as a result of the Edict of Cyrus in 539 BCE.

Yeshivah: Hebrew for "sitting." In rabbinic usage, it refers to a formal academy of Torah scholarship directed by a sage.

Yetzer Hara: Hebrew for "rebellious urge." In rabbinic Judaism, this refers to an innate human desire to deviate from the Torah's commandments. (*See also* Yetzer Hatov.)

Yetzer Hatov: Hebrew for "good urge." In rabbinic Judaism, this refers to an innate human desire to be an obedient servant of God. (*See also* Yetzer Hara.)

Yirat Shamayim: Hebrew for "awe of Heaven." In rabbinic Judaism, the term designates an attitude of mind cultivated by a person who feels that the smallest details of one's life are lived in the intimate presence of God.

Zakat: Legal almsgiving; one of Islam's Pillars.

Zionism: Modern secularist movement of Jewish national self-determination, founded by European Jews in the last decades of the nineteenth century. The success of Zionism resulted in the establishment of the State of Israel in 1948. (*See also* State of Israel.)

Ziyara: Visiting Muslim holy places, such as Medina.

Zohar: Hebrew for "splendor." The title of a late thirteenth-century Kabbalistic work pseudepigraphically written by Rabbi Moses de Leon of Guadalajara, Spain. The Zohar, regarded as the authentic tradition of an ancient rabbinic sage, Rabbi Shimon bar Yohai, became the major source of mystical theology in medieval and early-modern Judaism. (*See also* Kabbalah.)

SUGGESTIONS FOR FURTHER READING

PART I

Judaism

Martin Jan Mulder, *Mikra: Text, Transmission, Reading and Interpretation of the Hebrew Bible in Ancient Judaism and Early Christianity* (Assen and Philadelphia: Van Gorcum & Fortress, 1988).

Gershom Scholem, *On the Quaballah and Its Symbolism* (New York: Schocken, 1969).

Gunther Stemberger, *Introduction to Talmud and Midrash*, 2nd ed. (Edinburgh: T & T Clark, 1996).

Christianity

George Aichele et al., *The Postmodern Bible* (New Haven: Yale University Press, 1995).

Robert Morgan, *Biblical Interpretation* (Oxford: Oxford University Press, 1988).

Beryl Smalley, *The Study of the Bible in the Middle Ages* (Oxford: Blackwell, 1983).

Frederick C. Tiffany, *Biblical Interpretation: A Roadmap* (Nashville: Abingdon, 1996).

Islam

A. J. Arberry, *The Seven Odes: The First Chapter in Arabic Literature* (New York: Macmillan, 1957).

Karen Armstrong, *Muhammad: A Biography of the Prophet* (San Francisco: Harper San Francisco, 1992).

The Meaning of the Glorious Koran, an explanatory translation by Mohammed Marmaduke Pickthall (New York: Mentor Books, n.d. [frequently reprinted]).

PART II

Judaism

Eugene B. Borowitz, *Choices in Modern Jewish Thought: A Partisan Guide,* 2nd ed. (West Orange, NJ: Behrman House, 1995).

Jacob Neusner, *Judaism's Theological Voice: The Melody of the Talmud* (Chicago & London: University of Chicago Press, 1995).

Aviezer Ravitsky, *Messianism, Zionism, and Jewish Religious Radicalism* (Chicago & London: University of Chicago, 1996).

Christianity

John Bossy, *Christianity in the West, 1400–1700* (Oxford: Oxford University Press, 1985).

Edmund J. Fortman, *The Triune God: A History of the Doctrine of the Trinity* (Philadelphia: Westminster Press, 1992).

Robert M. Grant, *Gods and the One God* (Philadelphia: Westminster Press, 1986).

Islam

Fazlur Rahman, *Islam,* 2nd ed. (Chicago: University of Chicago Press, 1979).

W. Montgomery Watt, *The Formative Period of Islamic Thought* (Edinburgh: Edinburgh University Press, 1973).

Arendt Jan Wensinck, *The Muslim Creed: Its Genesis and Historical Development* (Cambridge: Cambridge University Press, 1932).

PART III

Judaism

Moshe Idel, *Hasidism: Between Ecstasy and Magic* (Albany: SUNY, 1995).

Lawrence H. Schiffman, *The Eschatological Community of the Dead Sea Scrolls* (Atlanta: Scholars Press, 1989).

Sacha Stern, *Jewish Identity in Early Rabbinic Writings* (Leiden, New York, and Keoln: E. J. Brill, 1994).

Christianity

David Christie-Murray, *A History of Heresy* (Oxford: Oxford University Press, 1990).

Edward H. Davidson, *Paine, Scripture, and Authority: The Age of Reason as Religious and Political Ideal* (London and Cranbury, NJ: Associated University Presses, 1994).

Scott Hendrix, *Tradition and Authority in the Reformation* (Brookfield, VT: Variorum, 1996).

Aristides Papadakis, *The Christian East and the Rise of the Papacy* (Crestwood, NY: St. Vladimir's Seminary Press, 1994).

Islam

Husayn al-Baghawi and Wali al-Din al-Khatib al-Tibrizi, *Mishkat al-Masabih* ("The Niche for Lamps"), trans. James Robson, 4 vols. (Lahore: Sh. Muhammad Ashraf, 1964–1966).

Marshall G. S. Hobson, *The Venture of Islam: Conscience and History in a World Civilization*, 3 vols. (Chicago: University of Chicago Press, 1974).

Mohammad Hasim Kamali, *Principles of Islamic Jurisprudence* (Petaling Jaya, Malaysia: Pelanduk, 1989).

PART IV

Judaism

Lawrence A. Hoffman, *Beyond the Text: A Holistic Approach to Liturgy* (Bloomington and Indianapolis: Indiana University Press, 1987).

Jacob Neusner, *Contemporary Judaic Fellowship in Theory and in Practice* (New York: KTAV, 1972).

T. Zahavy, *Studies in Jewish Prayer* (Lanham, New York, and London: University Press of America, 1990).

Christianity

Peter Brown, *The Cult of the Saints* (Chicago: University of Chicago Press, 1981).

Carlos M. N. Eire, *War Against the Idols* (Cambridge: Cambridge University Press, 1986).

Miri Rubin, *Corpus Christi: The Eucharist in Late Medieval Culture* (Cambridge: Cambridge University Press, 1991).

Islam

Hammudah Abdalati, *Islam in Focus* (Indianapolis: Islamic Trust Publications, 1977).

Constance E. Padwick, *Islamic Devotions* (London: S.P.C.K. Press, 1961).

PART V

Judaism

Gersion Appel, *A Philosophy of Mizvot: The Religious-Ethical Concepts of Judaism, Their Roots in Biblical Law and the Oral Tradition* (New York: KTAV, 1975).

Elliot N. Dorff and Louis E. Newman, eds., *Contemporary Jewish Ethics and Morality: A Reader* (Oxford and New York: Oxford University Press, 1995).

Emanuel Levinas, *Beyond the Verse: Talmudic Readings and Lectures* (Bloomington and Indianapolis: Indiana University Press, 1994).

Christianity

Ian S. Markham, *Plurality and Christian Ethics* (Cambridge and New York: Cambridge University Press, 1994).

R.E.O. White, *Christian Ethics* (Macon: Mercer University Press, 1994).

J. Philip Wogaman, *Christian Ethics: A Historical Introduction* (Louisville, KY: Westminster and John Knox Press, 1993).

Islam

Dwight M. Donaldson, *Studies in Muslim Ethics* (London: S.P.C.K., 1953).

Richard G. Hovannisian, ed., *Ethics in Islam* (Malibu, CA: Undena Publications, 1985).

Fazlur Rahman, *Major Themes of the Qur'an* (Minneapolis and Chicago: Bibliotheca Islamica, 1980).

PART VI

Judaism

Lee I. Levine, *Ancient Synagogues Revealed* (Detroit: Wayne State University, 1982).

Theresa Metzger and Mendel Metzger, *Jewish Life in the Middle Ages* (New York: Alpine, 1982).

Ralph Posner and Israel Ta-Shema, eds., *The Hebrew Book: An Historical Survey* (New York and Paris: Leon Amiel, 1975).

Christianity

Georges Duby, *The Age of Cathedrals* (Chicago: University of Chicago Press, 1981).

Colleen McDannell, *Material Christianity: Religion and Popular Culture in America* (New Haven and London: Yale University Press, 1995).

R.L.P. Milburn, *Early Christian Art and Architecture* (Aldershot, UK: Scholar Press, 1988).

Islam

Donna Lee Bowen and Evelyn A. Early, eds., *Everyday Life in the Muslim Middle East* (Bloomington and Indianapolis: Indiana University Press, 1993).

Barbara Brend, *Islamic Art* (Cambridge, MA: Harvard University Press, 1991).

Carleton Coon, *Caravan: The Story of the Middle East*, rev. ed. (New York: Holt, Rinehart and Winston, 1966).

PART VII

Judaism

Mark R. Cohen, *Under Crescent and Cross: The Jews in the Middle Ages* (Princeton: Princeton University Press, 1994).

Arthur Hertzberg, ed., *The Zionist Idea: A Historical Analysis and Reader* (New York: Atheneum, 1977).

Christianity

J. F. Maclear, ed., *Church and State in the Modern Age: A Documentary History* (New York: Oxford University Press, 1995).

Steve Ozment, *Protestants: Birth of a Revolution* (New York: Doubleday, 1992).

Brian Tierney, *The Crisis of Church and State* (Englewood Cliffs, NJ: Prentice Hall, 1964).

Islam

Akbar S. Ahmed, *Living Islam: From Samarkand to Stornoway* (New York: Facts on File, 1994).

John L. Esposito, editor-in-chief, *The Oxford Encyclopedia of the Modern Islamic World*, 4 vols. (New York and Oxford: Oxford University Press, 1995).

Gilles Kepel, *Muslim Extremism: The Prophet and the Pharaoh* (Berkeley and Los Angeles: University of California Press, 1993).

TIMELINE

ca. 1000 BCE: Founding of Davidic Dynasty in Jerusalem, Judah

ca. 1000–587 BCE: Dynastic Period

960 BCE: Division into Northern (Israel) and Southern (Judah) Kingdoms

722 BCE: Assyrian Empire conquers and destroys Israel (Northern)

597–87 BCE: Babylonian Empire deports main economic, intellectual, and religious leadership of Judah to Babylonia

587 BCE: Refugees from Judah, including Prophet Jeremiah, establish Israelite colonies in Egypt

ca. 560 BCE: Ezekiel serves as Prophetic Teacher of Babylonian exiles

539 BCE: Babylonia conquered by Persian Emperor Cyrus

538 BCE: Cyrus issues edict that repatriates exiled Judeans

538–530 BCE: Persian Period

520–515 BCE: Jerusalem Temple restored in Jerusalem, capital of Persian province of Yehud (Judah)

ca. 450–398 BCE: Religious and social reforms of Ezra and Nehemiah; likely period for editing of the Torah of Moses and other literary traditions of pre-Exilic Israelite culture

331 BCE: Alexander of Macedonia conquers Persian Empire

330–200 BCE: Egyptian Jews develop rich Greek culture in Alexandria; Greek-speaking Jewish communities thrive in the growing western Diaspora

330–63 BCE: Hellenistic Period

ca. 200 BCE: Palestine passes from Egyptian (Ptolemaic) to Syrian (Seleucid) control

168–165 BCE: Hasmonean priests revolt against high priestly administration of Judah; the revolt becomes a war of liberation against Syria

152 BCE: Hasmonean Dynasty formally established under Jonathan

63 BCE: Roman army occupies Palestine and brings end to Hasmonean state

63 BCE–340 CE: Roman Period

37–4 BCE: Reign of Herod the Great under Roman protection

20 BCE: Herod begins expansion of Jerusalem Temple

ca. 4 BCE: Birth of Jesus

ca 27–30 CE: Public ministry of Jesus

ca. 30 CE: Execution of Jesus of Nazareth

30–70 CE: Jesus communities begin to win non-Jewish converts

ca. 46 CE: Paul begins his missionary journeys in the Eastern Mediterranean

ca. 49 CE: Council of Jerusalem proclaims Gentile converts do not have to observe Jewish law and ritual

64 CE: Emperor Nero persecutes Christians in Rome; traditional date for the martyrdom of Peter and Paul

67–73 CE: Jewish rebellion against Roman occupation ends with the destruction of the Temple in Jerusalem; Jewish Christians dispersed

70 CE: Herodian Temple destroyed

ca. 75–80 CE: Gospel of Mark is written

ca. 80–95 CE: Gospels of Matthew and Luke are written

ca. 95–110 CE: Gospel of John is written

115–117 CE: Anti-Roman rebellions in Jewish Diaspora suppressed by Emperor Trajan

132–135 CE: Emperor Hadrian suppresses Palestinian rebellion of Shimon bar Kosiba

135 CE: Second Jewish revolt ends with the razing of Jerusalem; final dispersion of the Jewish Christian church

ca. 135 CE: Valentinus begins to spread his gnostic teachings in Rome

ca. 144 CE: Marcionites are condemned by the church of Rome

ca. 150–340 CE: Synagogues begin to become centers of study and ritual life in both Diaspora and Palestinian Jewry

ca. 160 CE: Montanists are condemned by the bishops of Asia Minor

170–210 CE: Consolidation of Galilean rabbinic movement under Rabbi Judah the Patriarch

176 CE: Persecution by Emperor Marcus Aurelius

ca. 190 CE: Dynamic monarchianism (adoptionism) and modalistic monarchianism begin to gain favor

ca. 200 CE: Compilation of the Mishnah

202 CE: Persecution by Emperor Septimus Severus

211–217 CE: Persecution by Emperor Caracalla

212 CE: Emperor Caracalla grants Roman citizenship to Jews

ca. 220–330 CE: Emergence of Babylonian academies of rabbinic learning

226 CE: Sassanian Dynasty of Babylonia inherits rule of Babylonian Jewry

242 CE: Sassanian Emperor Shapur I enhances powers of Jewish exilarch; exilarchate begins to compete with Palestinian patriarchate for international prestige

250–59 CE: Persecutions by Emperors Decius and Valerian

ca. 270 CE: Christian hermits begin to proliferate in Egypt and Syria

303 CE: Persecution by Emperor Diocletian

313 CE: Emperor Constantine issues the Edict of Milan, granting toleration to Christianity

315 CE: Pachomius establishes the first coenobitic monastery in Egypt

ca. 320 CE: Arianism begins to spread

325 CE: Emperor Constantine summons bishops to the Council of Nicaea; Arianism is condemned

337 CE: Emperor Constantine is baptized on his deathbed by an Arian bishop; rival sons compete for emperorship

340 CE: Roman Empire divided among Constantine's heirs into Western (Roman) and Eastern (Byzantine) Empires

340–650 CE: Byzantine Period

361–63 CE: Emperor Julian "the Apostate" renounces Christianity and attempts to revive paganism

ca. 370 CE: Visigoths convert to Arian Christianity

381 CE: Council of Constantinople reaffirms the full divinity of Christ

385 CE: Jerome begins his translation of the Bible into Latin (the "Vulgate" Bible)

392 CE: Emperor Theodosius forbids pagan worship

395 CE: Augustine becomes Bishop of Hippo in North Africa, begins to struggle against Donatist schismatics

ca. 400 CE: Palestinian Talmud compiled in Rabbinic Academies of Galilee

410 CE: The Visigoths sack Rome

ca. 412 CE: Pelagian controversy begins

ca. 420 CE: Augustine writes *The City of God*

425 CE: Palestinian patriarchate ceases under Emperor Theodosius

428 CE: Nestorius becomes Patriarch of Constantinople, begins to preach against the title of "Theotokos" for Mary ("Mother of God")

431 CE: Council of Ephesus condemns Nestorius; Nestorian churches go their own way as the "Church of the East"

432 CE: Patrick begins his missionary work in Ireland

447 CE: Monophysite controversy begun by Eutyches

451 CE: Council of Chalcedon proclaims Christ as one person with two natures—fully divine and fully human; Monophysite churches go their own way

452 CE: Attila the Hun ravages Italy

455 CE: The Vandals sack Rome

ca. 500 CE: Neoplatonic writings of a Syrian monk claiming to be "Dionysius the Areopaqite" begin to gain wide acceptance

ca. 500–600 CE: Babylonian Talmud compiled in Rabbinic Academies of Babylonia

527 CE: Emperor Justinian closes the last remaining pagan philosophical schools of Athens and compiles Christian law code for the Empire

ca. 529 CE: Benedict of Nursia writes his rule for the monastery of Monte Casino

ca. 570 CE: Birth of Muhammad

ca. 585 CE: Irish monks begin their missionary work in Europe

590 CE: Gregory I ("the Great") is first monk to be elected Pope

ca. 595 CE: Marriage of Muhammad and Khadija

ca. 610 CE: Muhammad receives first Qur'anic revelations

ca. 615 CE: Some Muslims emigrate to Abyssinia

ca. 619 CE: Death of Khadija

ca. 622 CE: Hijra of Muslims from Mecca to Yathrib (Medina); founding of the umma and beginning of the Muslim calendar

622 CE: Islam begins its expansion from the Arabian peninsula

ca. 624 CE: Muhammad's victory over the Meccans at Badr

ca. 625 CE: Defeat of Muslims at Uhud

625 CE: Emperor Justinian's "Code of Civil Law" defines terms of Jewish life as a minority in Christendom

ca. 627 CE: Defeat of the Meccans by the Muslims at the Battle of Trench

ca. 628 CE: Peace treaty between Muslims and Meccans at Hudaybiya

ca. 630 CE: Pilgrimage of Muslims to Mecca and peaceful conquest of Mecca

ca. 632 CE: Death of Muhammad (June 8)

ca. 632–656 CE: Period of the "Rightly Guided Caliphs": Abu Bakr (632–634) 'Umar (634–644), 'Uthman (644–656), 'Ali (656–661)

ca. 633 CE: Death of Fatima; end of Wars of Apostasy (ridda)

634 CE: Sassanian Empire—first Middle Eastern empire to fall to Islamic invasions

ca. 635 CE: Muslim occupation of Damascus

ca. 635 CE: Expansion of Islam begins: leads to collapse of Christianity in the Near East and North Africa

ca. 636 CE: Defeat of Sassanians (Persian dynasty) at Qadisiya; defeat of Byzantines at Yarmuk

ca. 638 CE: Muslim conquest of Jerusalem

ca. 640 CE: Nestorian Christian missions under way in India and China

ca. 640 CE: Muslim general 'Amr ibn al-As enters Egypt; establishment of Kufa and Basra as Muslim garrison cities in occupied Iraq

ca. 641 CE: Capture of Egyptian capital of Babylon; establishment of Muslim garrison city of Fustat on the site (later to be enveloped by Cairo)

ca. 642 CE: Fall of Persia at Nihawand

ca. 650 CE: Pact of Umar defines terms of Christian and Jewish life in Islamic lands of North Africa and the Middle East

ca. 650–1096 CE: Jews, migrating from Italian Peninsula, establish loose network of communities in Christian lands of central and eastern Europe, including Spain and England; no central administration of Jewish life in central Europe

ca. 650–1650 CE: Medieval Judaism

ca. 658 CE: Battle of Siffrin between 'Ali and Mu 'awiya

661–750 CE: Umayyad dynasty rules Muslims from Damascus

ca. 661–750 CE: Umayyad dynasty rules Muslims from Damascus

ca. 661–1250 CE: Succession of Gaonim organizes the Talmudic tradition into coherent system of law, custom, theology, and worship; Gaonic achievements adopted and modified by Christendom's Jewry as well

ca. 680 CE: Martyrdom of Shi'ite Imam Husayn at Karbala

ca. 691 CE: Dome of the Rock monument erected in Jerusalem

ca. 711 CE: Muslim invasion of Spain under Tariq

711 CE: Conquest of Iberia by Muslim armies from North Africa

ca. 711–713 CE: Muslim conquests of Sind and Transoxania

716 CE: Boniface begins his missionary work among the Germans

ca. 717 CE: First Muslim expedition north of the Pyrenees

725 CE: Iconoclastic controversy begins in the Byzantine empire when Emperor Leo III orders the destruction of religious images

ca. 732 CE: Defeat of advancing Muslim forces under Charles Martel at Battle of Tours/Poitiers

ca. 750–1258 CE: Abbasid dynasty rules from Baghdad and the "Golden Age" of Islamic civilization

754 CE: Iconoclasm intensified under Emperor Constantine V

ca. 755–1031 CE: Independent Umayyad dynasty in Spain

ca. 762 CE: Founding of Baghdad as Abbasid capital

ca. 767 CE: Death of jurisconsult Abu Hanifa

787 CE: Second Council of Nicaea condemns iconoclasm, reaffirms the place of images in Christian ritual

ca. 796 CE: Death of Jurisconsult Malik ibn Anas

800 CE: Pope Leo III crowns Charlemagne Emperor of the Romans, creating a western Latin empire

809 CE: Synod at Aachen approves the addition of the "Filioque" clause to the Latin creed; East/West church conflict intensifies

ca. 820 CE: Body of the Apostle St. James "discovered" in Northern Spain at Compostela; shrine begins to attract pilgrims

ca. 820 CE: Death of jurisconsult al-Shafi'i

ca. 827 CE: Caliph al-Ma'mum promulgates Mu'utazilite theology as official doctrine of the state

ca. 855 CE: Death of jurisconsult Ahmad ibn Hanbal

865 CE: Kingdom of Bulgaria converts to Orthodox Christianity

867 CE: East/West schism develops when Patriarch Photius of Constantinople and Pope Nicholas I excommunicate one another and their respective churches

ca. 870 CE: Death of Hadith scholar al-Bukhari

ca. 873 CE: Disappearance of Twelfth Shi'ite Iman, the "Hidden Imam" who will return as a messianic deliverer at the end of time

ca. 875 CE: Death of Hadith scholar Muslim ibn al-Hajjaj

ca. 901 CE: Death of female Sufi leader Rabi 'a al-'Adawija

ca. 909–1171 CE: Fatimid Shi'ite dynasty in Egypt

910 CE: Monastic reform movement begins at Abbey of Cluny

ca. 922 CE: Execution of Sufi mystic al-Hallaj in Baghdad

ca. 923 CE: Death of historian and Qur'an commentator al-Tabari

ca. 935 CE: Death of theologian al-Ash'ari, founder of orthodox Sunni kalam

ca. 950 CE: Death of philosopher al-Farabi

966 CE: Poland converts to Catholic Christianity

ca. 969 CE: Founding of Cairo as capital of Fatimid Egypt

ca. 973 CE: Al-Azhar University founded in Cairo

988 CE: Russia converts to Orthodox Christianity

1001 CE: Expected end of the world does not occur

ca. 1020 CE: Norway becomes Christian; Christianization of Sweden, Denmark, and Finland underway

1049 CE: Pope Leo IX undertakes reform of the Catholic Church

1054 CE: Mutual excommunication of Pope Leo IX and Patriarch Michael Cerularius permanently seals the Catholic/Orthodox schism

ca. 1095 CE: Pope Urban calls for first crusade to liberate the Holy Land from Islam

1096 CE: First Crusade launched against Moslems in the Holy Land; preceded by persecution of French and German Jews

1096–1350 CE: First Crusade inaugurates centuries of anti-Jewish persecution in Christendom

1098 CE: Monastic reform movement begins at Abbey of Citeaux

ca. 1099 CE: Jerusalem conquered by Christian crusaders

ca. 1100 CE: Scholastic theology begins to develop in the West ca. 1111 CE: Death of theologian, philosopher, and Sufi master al-Ghazali

1144 CE: Abbey church of St. Denis completed; beginning of "Gothic" architecture in the West

1146 CE: Second Crusade is launched

1150 CE: Albigensian heresy (Catharism) begins to spread

1169–1193 CE: Saladin (Salah al-Din) rules Egypt

1180 CE: Spanish Rabbi Moses Maimonides publishes his revolutionary Law Code, "Mishneh Torah," in Egypt

1183 CE: Inquisition founded at the Council of Verona

1184 CE: Waldensian heresy begins to spread

ca. 1187 CE: Saladin, victorious over crusaders at Battle of Hattin, retakes Jerusalem

1190 CE: Third Crusade is joined by the Holy Roman Emperor, the king of France, and the king of England

1198 CE: Innocent III elected pope; pinnacle of papal power in the West

1198 CE: Death of philosopher Ibn Rushd (the Latin Averroes)

1204 CE: Fourth Crusade captures and sacks Constantinople; East/West schism deepens

1206 CE: Order of Preachers is founded by Dominic de Guzman

1208 CE: Franciscan Order founded by Francis of Assisi; Pope Innocent III launches crusade against Albigensian heretics

1231 CE: Order of Teutonic Knights begins the forced conversion of the Baltic lands to Catholic Christianity

ca. 1240 CE: Death of Sufi philosophical theologian Ibn 'Arabi

ca. 1250 CE: Kingdom of Castile achieves reconquest of Muslim states in the South of Spain, except for Granada

ca. 1258 CE: Mongol leader Hulagu razes Baghdad and ends Abbasid dynasty

ca. 1271 CE: Marco Polo departs for China, later notes existence of small Muslim states in Sumatra

ca. 1273 CE: Death of Persian Sufi poet Jalah al-Din Rumi

1274 CE: Deaths of theologians Thomas Aquinas and Bonaventure; Western Scholasticism at its peak

ca. 1280–1300 CE: Spanish "Book of Splendor" (Zohar) defines the nature of Kabbalistic mysticism

1290 CE: Jews expelled from England

1290–1350 CE: Jews expelled from western and central European Christendom

1302 CE: Pope Boniface VIII claims absolute papal supremacy in his bull Unam Sanctam

1305 CE: Pope Clement V moves papal court to Avignon; beginning of "Babylonian Captivity" of the papacy

1311 CE: Council of Vienne condemns "Free Spirit" heresy

ca. 1328 CE: Death of Ibn Taymiya, Syrian jurist and theologian who greatly influenced Wahhabism and more recent Muslim reform and contemporary "fundamentalist" movements

ca. 1338 CE: Hesychast controversy among Orthodox Christians

1348–1349 CE: Bubonic plague (Black Death) sweeps Western Europe; 25 percent to 30 percent of the population dies; persecution of the Jews increases

1350 CE: Migration of European Jews into Poland and other eastern European countries, leads to flowering of Jewish culture in eastern Europe by sixteenth century

ca. 1370 CE: Lollard heresy led by John Wycliffe begins to flourish in England

1378 CE: Great Schism begins in the West: two rival claimants to the papal office, one in Rome, one in Avignon

ca. 1406 CE: Death of historian and cultural scholar Ibn Khaldun

1409 CE: Council of Pisa fails to heal Great Schism, creates a third claimant to the papal office

ca. 1410 CE: John Hus leads heretical movement (Hussites) in Bohemia

1415 CE: Council of Constance ends Great Schism, restores Roman papacy, and executes John Hus

1439 CE: Council of Ferrara-Florence establishes papal supremacy over councils, proclaims union with Orthodox church

ca. 1450 CE: Movable-type press and innovation in paper technology make possible the publication of the Bible and religious writings on a large scale

ca. 1453 CE: Ottoman conquest of Constantinople and, symbolically, of eastern Christendom, after centuries of attempts

1466 CE: Birth of the Dutch humanist Erasmus

1480–1530 CE: Pioneering printings of the Talmud in Spain and Italy

1492 CE: Muslim kingdom of Granada conquered by Spanish monarchs Ferdinand and Isabella; expulsion of the Jews from Spain; Columbus stumbles upon America, claims it for Spain

1492–1496 CE: Expulsion of Jews from Iberian peninsula

1493 CE: *Padroado.* Spain and Portugal divide responsibility of converting inhabitants of newly discovered lands to Christianity

ca. 1500–1800 CE: Major Muslim empires flourish: the Ottomans in the west, the Safavids in Iran, and the Mughals in India; Islam gradually becomes strongly established in peninsular and islands in southeast Asia and in regions of Africa

1516 CE: First Jewish ghetto established in Venice; the pattern of residential exclusion spreads within a century throughout Italy and into central Europe

1516 CE: Erasmus publishes Greek text of the New Testament

1517 CE: Martin Luther begins the Protestant Reformation in Saxony

1519 CE: Ulrich Zwingli begins the Protestant Reformation in Switzerland

1521 CE: Hernan Cortez conquers Aztec Empire for Spain; Christianization of Central America begins

1525 CE: Peasant's Revolt in Germany; Anabaptist movement begins in Switzerland

1532 CE: Francisco Pizarro conquers Inca Empire for Spain; Christianization of South America begins

1534 CE: King Henry VIII breaks with Rome, establishes Anglican Church with monarch as head

1536 CE: John Calvin publishes *The Institutes* and moves to Geneva, begins to assume leadership of Reformed Protestantism

1540 CE: Ignatius Loyola founds the Society of Jesus (Jesuits)

1543 CE: Copernicus denies that the earth is the center of the cosmos

1545 CE: Council of Trent convened; reform of the Catholic Church begins in earnest

1549 CE: Francis Xavier establishes Jesuit mission in Japan

1559 CE: John Knox leads reform in Scotland along Calvinist lines

1560–1575 CE: Flowering of Kabbalah in Safed, Palestine; origins of the mystical teachings of Rabbi Isaac Luria

1562 CE: Wars of Religion begin in France; Heidelberg catechism is accepted by German and Swiss Reformed Protestants

1567 CE: Publication of Rabbi Joseph Karo's Comprehensive Legal Code, the "Shulkhan Arukh"

1577 CE: Formula of Concord accepted by most Lutheran Protestants

ca. 1580s CE: Rise of Puritanism in England

1587 CE: Jesuits establish missions in China; persecution of Japanese Christians begins

1598 CE: Edict of Nantes grants limited toleration to French Protestants

1607 CE: English colony is established in Virginia; Christianization of North America begins

1618–1648 CE: Thirty Years' War begins in central Europe: Protestant/Catholic conflict at its peak

1620 CE: English Puritan Separatists establish colony at Plymouth, Massachusetts

1624 CE: *De veritate* by Lord Herbert of Cherbury emphasizes role of reason in Christianity

1633 CE: Roman Inquisition forces Galileo to deny his heliocentric theory

1637 CE: Rene Descartes publishes his *Discourse on Method*, challenging faith with reason

1648 CE: Cossack rebellions lead to massacres of Jews in Poland and Ukraine

1649 CE: Calvinist Puritans gain control of England and execute King Charles I; Ireland conquered by Puritan army of Oliver Cromwell

1650 CE-Present: Modern Judaism

1654 CE: Jewish community organized in Dutch Colony of New Amsterdam

1655 CE: Jews readmitted to England

1665 CE: Messianic movement begins in the name of Shabtai Zvi

1677 CE: Philip Jacob Spener publishes his *Pia Desideria*, leads Pietist reform movement among German Lutherans

1678 CE: *Pilgrim's Progress*, Christian devotional classic by John Bunyan

1682 CE: William Penn founds Pennsylvania on principle of religious toleration

1692 CE: Christian worship allowed in China

1694–1778 CE: French Enlightenment thinker and Deist Voltaire

ca. 1700–1800 CE: The Age of Reason; the Enlightenment; Wahhabi reform movement in Arabia; combining with the royal house of Sa'ud

1722 CE: Count von Zinzendorf establishes Pietist community Herrnhut

ca. 1725–1750 CE: Johann Sebastian Bach composes Christian musical works

1740–1741 CE: "Great Awakening" religious revival in America peaks

1742 CE: First performance of *Messiah* by George Frederick Handel

1760 CE: Death of Israel Baal Shem Tov, the founder of eastern European Hasidism

1772 CE: Large parts of Polish Jewry incorporated into Russian Empire and confined to "Pale of Jewish Settlement"

1773 CE: Pope Clement XIV suppresses the Society of Jesus (Jesuits)

1774 CE: First English Unitarian congregation founded in London

1781 CE: Rabbi Jacob Joseph of Polnoye publishes first Hasidic book, "Toledot Yaakov Yosef"

1781 CE: Rabbi Eli-ah, Gaon of Vilna, declares Hasidism a heretical movement; eastern European Jewish communities often divide themselves into Hasidic and Opposition (Misnagdish) communities

1783 CE: Moses Mendelssohn, of Berlin, publishes "Jerusalem," a theory of Judaism as a rational religion; he becomes celebrated as proof that the Jews can join humanity on equal terms

ca. 1787 CE: Death of Muhammad ibn 'Abd al-Wahhab, founder of ultra-puritanical Wahhabi movement in Arabia

1789 CE: The Constitution of the United States of America and the Bill of Rights implicity recognize full Jewish citizenship

1789 CE: French Revolution begins and leads to violent anticlericalism

1791 CE: French Constitution extends full citizenship to Jews in France; "Emancipation" extends to all territories later conquered by Napoleon

1791 CE: Constitutional separation of church and state in the United States

1792 CE: Baptist Missionary Society founded in London

ca. 1798 CE: Napoleon Bonaparte conquers Egypt at Battle of the Pyramids; French fleet sunk by Admiral Nelson off Abu Kir

1800s CE: Increasing opening of Muslim countries to Western influence in the colonial period; rise of Muslim reform movements

ca. 1803 CE: Wahhabis capture Mecca and Medina

ca. 1804 CE: The Albanian Muhammad 'Ali becomes viceroy of Egypt, ushering in modern ideas and technologies

1815 CE: Congress of Vienna repeals Emancipation in all countries formerly occupied by France

1819 CE: William Ellery Channing argues Christ's inferiority to God

1820 CE: Rise of Reform Movement in central and western Europe

1820s–1830s CE: Suppression of Roman Catholic religious orders in Latin America

ca. 1830 CE: French occupation of Algeria

1830 CE: *Book of Mormon*

1835 CE: *Life of Jesus* by David Freidrich Strauss

1848 CE: Pope flees revolution in Rome

1850s CE: Emergence of "higher criticism" in biblical interpretation

1850–1870 CE: Orthodox and Positive-Historical Judaism define their positions vis-à-vis reform; eastern European communities reject all three Western movements as assimilationist errors

ca. 1858 CE: End of the Moghul dynasty in India

1859 CE: *The Origin of Species* by Charles Darwin

1864 CE: Anti-Enlightenment *Syllabus of Errors* issued by Vatican

ca. 1869 CE: Suez Canal opened

1869–1870 CE: First Vatican Council decrees papal infallibility

1870 CE: Germany is last western or central European state to grant full citizenship to Jews

1873 CE: Hebrew Union College founded in Cincinatti to train rabbis for Reform rabbinate

1880–1905 CE: Political anti-Semitism emerges as a popular European ideology; anti-Semitic riots spur Jewish emigration from eastern Europe to western Europe, North America, and Ottoman Palestine

ca. 1881 CE: French occupation of Tunisia and British occupation of Egypt

1882 CE: First European Jewish colonies established in Palestine

1886 CE: Jewish Theological Seminary founded in New York to train rabbis for Conservative rabbinate

1890s CE: Roman Catholic modernism

1897 CE: Zionism officially founded in Basel by T. Herzl

1990s CE: Modernization and reform continue in the Muslim world; rise of Muslim nation states in the Middle East and Asia

ca. 1905 CE: Death of modernizing Egyptian reformer and educator Muhammad 'Abduh

1907 CE: *Christianity and the Social Crisis,* Social Gospel manifesto by Walter Rauschenbusch

1907 CE: Roman Catholic encyclical *Pascendi* condemns modernism

1910–1915 CE: Publication of conservative Christian *The Fundamentals*

1917 CE: Balfour Declaration favors founding of a Jewish homeland in Palestine, to be arranged at conclusion of the Great War

ca. 1917 CE: Aisyiyah, the women's branch of Muhammadiyyah, founded by Nyai (Mrs.) Ahmad Dahlan in Indonesia

ca. 1928 CE: Hasan al-Bana' founds the Muslim Brotherhood

1933–1945 CE: Destruction of European Jewish life by Nazis; Second World War, marking a watershed between the period of Western colonialism in much of the Muslim world and its emergence into independent nation states in the Middle East, Africa, South and Southeast Asia

ca. 1947 CE: Establishment of Pakistan as an independent Muslim nation in South Asia

1948 CE: Partition of Palestine; creation of State of Israel

1948–1955 CE: Most Jews of Islamic countries emigrate to Israel

ca. 1960s CE: Rise of liberation theology

1962–1965 CE: Second Vatican Council

ca. 1965 CE: Pentecostal and charismatic movements influence Roman Catholic and Protestant churches

1965 CE: Assassination of Malcolm X

1966 CE: Sayyid Qutb, Egyptian reformer, is executed

1967 CE: Six Day War results in unification of Jerusalem and acquisition of "West Bank" under Israeli jurisdiction

1967–1980 CE: Inspired by Six Day War, North American Jewry experiences a cultural flowering; the "Holocaust" becomes a powerful symbol of Jewish identity; "Jewish Renewal" movements and Jewish feminism become important alternatives to the official synagogue movements

1972 CE: Reform Movement extends rabbinic ordination to women

1973 CE: Yom Kippur War; although technically a "victory," it sets in motion political forces resulting in the fall of the left-wing Labor Party and the rise of the right-wing Likud Party to political dominance in Israel

1975 CE: The Honorable Elijah Muhammad, leader of the African American oriented Nation of Islam, dies; his son and designated successor, W. D. Muhammad, begins the transition of the organization to mainstream global Islam

ca. 1979 CE: Establishment of the Islamic Republic of Iran under Ayatollah Ruholla Khomeini (d. 1989)

1981 CE: Egyptian president Anwar Sadat assassinated by Muslim extremists

1984 CE: Conservative movement extends rabbinic ordination to women

1988 CE: Election of a woman bishop in Episcopal Church in the United States

1988 CE: Salman Rushdie publishes *The Satanic Verses* and kindles a global Muslim reaction that views it as blasphemous with respect to Islam

1990s CE: Islamic (sometimes called "fundamentalist") movement seeks an islamic ordering of life in the face of secularism, materialism, and western hegemony; growth of Islam and Muslim communities in Europe and the Americas

1990–1991 CE: The Persian Gulf War results in the ousting of Iraqi forces from their forceful occupation of Kuwait; Muslim and Western non-Muslim troops fight side by side against fellow Muslims in a venture that caused strongly mixed emotions among Muslims worldwide

1991 CE: Dissolution of the Soviet Union and establishment of independent states with significant Muslim populations in Central Asia

1991 CE: Demise of the Soviet Union inaugurates period of cultural renewal among eastern European Jewry

1993 CE: Israel and PLO establish formal negotiations toward mutual co-existence in Israel/Palestine

1994 CE: Death of the Lubavitcher Rebbe spurs messianic hopes among his followers

1995 CE: Assassination of Israel's Prime Minister Yitzhak Rabin by an Orthodox Jew causes many to reassess the role of religion and politics in Israel

INDEX